For Reference

Not to be taken from this room

Novels
for Students

Novels for Students

Presenting Analysis, Context and Criticism on Commonly Studied Novels

Volume 8

*Marie Rose Napierkowski
and Deborah A. Stanley, Editors*

Carol Jago, Santa Monica High School, Advisor
Kathleen Pasquantonio, Novi High School, Advisor

Foreword by Anne Devereaux Jordan, Teaching and Learning Literature

GALE GROUP

Detroit
New York
San Francisco
London
Boston
Woodbridge, CT

National Advisory Board

Novels for Students

Staff

Series Editor: Deborah A. Stanley.

Contributing Editors: Peg Bessette, Sara L. Constantakis, Catherine L. Goldstein, Dwayne D. Hayes, Motoko Fujishiro Huthwaite, Arlene M. Johnson, Angela Yvonne Jones, James E. Person, Jr., Polly Rapp, Erin White.

Editorial Technical Specialist: Tim White.

Managing Editor: Joyce Nakamura.

Research: Victoria B. Cariappa, *Research Team Manager.* Andy Malonis, *Research Specialist.* Tamara C. Nott, Tracie A. Richardson, and Cheryl L. Warnock, *Research Associates.* Jeffrey Daniels, *Research Assistant.*

Permissions: Susan M. Trosky, *Permissions Manager.* Maria L. Franklin, *Permissions Specialist.* Sarah Tomacek, *Permissions Associate.*

Production: Mary Beth Trimper, *Production Director.* Evi Seoud, *Assistant Production Manager.* Cindy Range, *Production Assistant.*

Graphic Services: Randy Bassett, *Image Database Supervisor.* Robert Duncan and Michael Logusz, *Imaging Specialists.* Pamela A. Reed, *Photography Coordinator.* Gary Leach, *Macintosh Artist.*

Product Design: Cynthia Baldwin, *Product Design Manager.* Cover Design: Michelle DiMercurio, *Art Director.* Page Design: Pamela A. E. Galbreath, *Senior Art Director.*

ISBN 0-7876-3827-7
ISSN 1094-3552
Printed in the United States of America.

10 9 8 7 6 5 4 3 2 1

Table of Contents

The Informed Dialogue:
Interacting with Literature

When we pick up a book, we usually do so with the anticipation of pleasure. We hope that by entering the time and place of the novel and sharing the thoughts and actions of the characters, we will find enjoyment. Unfortunately, this is often not the case; we are disappointed. But we should ask, has the author failed us, or have we failed the author?

We establish a dialogue with the author, the book, and with ourselves when we read. Consciously and unconsciously, we ask questions: "Why did the author write this book?" "Why did the author choose that time, place, or character?" "How did the author achieve that effect?" "Why did the character act that way?" "Would I act in the same way?" The answers we receive depend upon how much information about literature in general and about that book specifically we ourselves bring to our reading.

Young children have limited life and literary experiences. Being young, children frequently do not know how to go about exploring a book, nor sometimes, even know the questions to ask of a book. The books they read help them answer questions, the author often coming right out and *telling* young readers the things they are learning or are expected to learn. The perennial classic, *The Little Engine That Could, tells* its readers that, among other things, it is good to help others and bring happiness:

> "Hurray, hurray," cried the funny little clown and all the dolls and toys. "The good little boys and girls in the city will be happy because you helped us, kind, Little Blue Engine."

In picture books, messages are often blatant and simple, the dialogue between the author and reader one-sided. Young children are concerned with the end result of a book—the enjoyment gained, the lesson learned—rather than with how that result was obtained. As we grow older and read further, however, we question more. We come to expect that the world within the book will closely mirror the concerns of our world, and that the author will *show* these through the events, descriptions, and conversations within the story, rather than *telling* of them. We are now expected to do the interpreting, carry on our share of the dialogue with the book and author, and glean not only the author's message, but comprehend how that message and the overall affect of the book were achieved. Sometimes, however, we need help to do these things. *Novels for Students* provides that help.

A novel is made up of many parts interacting to create a coherent whole. In reading a novel, the more obvious features can be easily spotted—theme, characters, plot—but we may overlook the more subtle elements that greatly influence how the novel is perceived by the reader: viewpoint, mood and tone, symbolism, or the use of humor. By focusing on both the obvious and more subtle literary elements within a novel, *Novels for Students* aids readers in both analyzing for message and in determining how and why that message is communicated. In the discussion on Harper Lee's *To*

Kill a Mockingbird (Vol. 2), for example, the mockingbird as a symbol of innocence is dealt with, among other things, as is the importance of Lee's use of humor which "enlivens a serious plot, adds depth to the characterization, and creates a sense of familiarity and universality." The reader comes to understand the internal elements of each novel discussed—as well as the external influences that help shape it.

"The desire to write greatly," Harold Bloom of Yale University says, "is the desire to be elsewhere, in a time and place of one's own, in an originality that must compound with inheritance, with an anxiety of influence." A writer seeks to create a unique world within a story, but although it is unique, it is not disconnected from our own world. It speaks to us *because* of what the writer brings to the writing from our world: how he or she was raised and educated; his or her likes and dislikes; the events occurring in the real world at the time of the writing, and while the author was growing up. When we know what an author has brought to his or her work, we gain a greater insight into both the "originality" (the world of the book), and the things that "compound" it. This insight enables us to question that created world and find answers more readily. By informing ourselves, we are able to establish a more effective dialogue with both book and author.

Novels for Students, in addition to providing a plot summary and descriptive list of characters—to remind readers of what they have read—also explores the external influences that shaped each book. Each entry includes a discussion of the author's background, and the historical context in which the novel was written. It is vital to know, for instance, that when Ray Bradbury was writing *Fahrenheit 451* (Vol. 1), the threat of Nazi domination had recently ended in Europe, and the McCarthy hearings were taking place in Washington, D.C. This information goes far in answering the question, "Why did he write a story of oppressive government control and book burning?" Similarly, it is important to know that Harper Lee, author of *To Kill a Mockingbird,* was born and raised in Mon-

roeville, Alabama, and that her father was a lawyer. Readers can now see why she chose the south as a setting for her novel—it is the place with which she was most familiar—and start to comprehend her characters and their actions.

Novels for Students helps readers find the answers they seek when they establish a dialogue with a particular novel. It also aids in the posing of questions by providing the opinions and interpretations of various critics and reviewers, broadening that dialogue. Some reviewers of *To Kill A Mockingbird,* for example, "faulted the novel's climax as melodramatic." This statement leads readers to ask, "Is it, indeed, melodramatic?" "If not, why did some reviewers see it as such?" "If it is, why did Lee choose to make it melodramatic?" "Is melodrama ever justified?" By being spurred to ask these questions, readers not only learn more about the book and its writer, but about the nature of writing itself.

The literature included for discussion in the *Novels for Students* series has been chosen because it has something vital to say to us. *Of Mice and Men, Catch-22, The Joy Luck Club, My Antonia, A Separate Peace* and the other novels here speak of life and modern sensibility. In addition to their individual, specific messages of prejudice, power, love or hate, living and dying, however, they and all great literature also share a common intent. They force us to *think*—about life, literature, and about others, not just about ourselves. They pry us from the narrow confines of our minds and thrust us outward to confront the world of books and the larger, real world we all share. *Novels for Students* helps us in this confrontation by providing the means of enriching our conversation with literature and the world, by creating an *informed* dialogue, one that brings true pleasure to the personal act of reading.

Sources

Harold Bloom, *The Western Canon, The Books and School of the Ages,* Riverhead Books, 1994.

Watty Piper, *The Little Engine That Could,* Platt & Munk, 1930.

Anne Devereaux Jordan
Senior Editor, *TALL*
(*Teaching and Learning Literature*)

Introduction

Purpose of the Book

The purpose of *Novels for Students* (*NfS*) is to provide readers with a guide to understanding, enjoying, and studying novels by giving them easy access to information about the work. Part of Gale's "For Students" Literature line, *NfS* is specifically designed to meet the curricular needs of high school and undergraduate college students and their teachers, as well as the interests of general readers and researchers considering specific novels. While each volume contains entries on "classic" novels frequently studied in classrooms, there are also entries containing hard-to-find information on contemporary novels, including works by multicultural, international, and women novelists.

The information covered in each entry includes an introduction to the novel and the novel's author; a plot summary, to help readers unravel and understand the events in a novel; descriptions of important characters, including explanation of a given character's role in the novel as well as discussion about that character's relationship to other characters in the novel; analysis of important themes in the novel; and an explanation of important literary techniques and movements as they are demonstrated in the novel.

In addition to this material, which helps the readers analyze the novel itself, students are also provided with important information on the literary and historical background informing each work. This includes a historical context essay, a box comparing the time or place the novel was written to modern Western culture, a critical overview essay, and excerpts from critical essays on the novel. A unique feature of *NfS* is a specially commissioned overview essay on each novel by an academic expert, targeted toward the student reader.

To further aid the student in studying and enjoying each novel, information on media adaptations is provided, as well as reading suggestions for works of fiction and nonfiction on similar themes and topics. Classroom aids include ideas for research papers and lists of critical sources that provide additional material on the novel.

Selection Criteria

The titles for each volume of *NfS* were selected by surveying numerous sources on teaching literature and analyzing course curricula for various school districts. Some of the sources surveyed included: literature anthologies; *Reading Lists for College-Bound Students: The Books Most Recommended by America's Top Colleges;* textbooks on teaching the novel; a College Board survey of novels commonly studied in high schools; a National Council of Teachers of English (NCTE) survey of novels commonly studied in high schools; the NCTE's *Teaching Literature in High School: The Novel;* and the Young Adult Library Services Association (YALSA) list of best books for young adults of the past twenty-five years.

Input was also solicited from our expert advisory board, as well as educators from various areas. From these discussions, it was determined that each volume should have a mix of "classic" novels (those works commonly taught in literature classes) and contemporary novels for which information is often hard to find. Because of the interest in expanding the canon of literature, an emphasis was also placed on including works by international, multicultural, and women authors. Our advisory board members—current high school teachers—helped pare down the list for each volume. If a work was not selected for the present volume, it was often noted as a possibility for a future volume. As always, the editor welcomes suggestions for titles to be included in future volumes.

How Each Entry Is Organized

Each entry, or chapter, in *NfS* focuses on one novel. Each entry heading lists the full name of the novel, the author's name, and the date of the novel's publication. The following elements are contained in each entry:

• Introduction: a brief overview of the novel which provides information about its first appearance, its literary standing, any controversies surrounding the work, and major conflicts or themes within the work.

• Author Biography: this section includes basic facts about the author's life, and focuses on events and times in the author's life that inspired the novel in question.

• Plot Summary: a description of the major events in the novel, with interpretation of how these events help articulate the novel's themes. Lengthy summaries are broken down with subheads.

• Characters: an alphabetical listing of major characters in the novel. Each character name is followed by a brief to an extensive description of the character's role in the novel, as well as discussion of the character's actions, relationships, and possible motivation.

Characters are listed alphabetically by last name. If a character is unnamed—for instance, the narrator in *Invisible Man* the character is listed as "The Narrator" and alphabetized as "Narrator." If a character's first name is the only one given, the name will appear alphabetically by the name. Variant names are also included for each character. Thus, the full name "Jean Louise Finch" would head the listing for the narrator of *To Kill a Mockingbird,* but listed in a separate cross-reference would be the nickname "Scout Finch."

• Themes: a thorough overview of how the major topics, themes, and issues are addressed within the novel. Each theme discussed appears in a separate subhead, and is easily accessed through the boldface entries in the Subject/Theme Index.

• Style: this section addresses important style elements of the novel, such as setting, point of view, and narration; important literary devices used, such as imagery, foreshadowing, symbolism; and, if applicable, genres to which the work might have belonged, such as Gothicism or Romanticism. Literary terms are explained within the entry, but can also be found in the Glossary.

• Historical and Cultural Context: This section outlines the social, political, and cultural climate *in which the author lived and the novel was created.* This section may include descriptions of related historical events, pertinent aspects of daily life in the culture, and the artistic and literary sensibilities of the time in which the work was written. If the novel is a historical work, information regarding the time in which the novel is set is also included. Each section is broken down with helpful subheads.

• Critical Overview: this section provides background on the critical reputation of the novel, including bannings or any other public controversies surrounding the work. For older works, this section includes a history of how novel was first received and how perceptions of it may have changed over the years; for more recent novels, direct quotes from early reviews may also be included.

• Sources: an alphabetical list of critical material quoted in the entry, with full bibliographical information.

• For Further Study: an alphabetical list of other critical sources which may prove useful for the student. Includes full bibliographical information and a brief annotation.

• Criticism: an essay commissioned by *NfS* which specifically deals with the novel and is written specifically for the student audience, as well as excerpts from previously published criticism on the work.

In addition, each entry contains the following highlighted sections, set apart from the main text as sidebars:

• Media Adaptations: a list of important film and television adaptations of the novel, including source information. The list also includes stage adaptations, audio recordings, musical adaptations, etc.

• Compare and Contrast Box: an "at-a-glance" comparison of the cultural and historical differences between the author's time and culture and late twentieth-century Western culture. This box includes pertinent parallels between the major scientific, political, and cultural movements of the time or place the novel was written, the time or place the novel was set (if a historical work), and modern Western culture. Works written after the mid-1970s may not have this box.

• What Do I Read Next?: a list of works that might complement the featured novel or serve as a contrast to it. This includes works by the same author and others, works of fiction and nonfiction, and works from various genres, cultures, and eras.

• Study Questions: a list of potential study questions or research topics dealing with the novel. This section includes questions related to other disciplines the student may be studying, such as American history, world history, science, math, government, business, geography, economics, psychology, etc.

Other Features

NfS includes "The Informed Dialogue: Interacting with Literature," a foreword by Anne Devereaux Jordan, Senior Editor for *Teaching and Learning Literature* (*TALL*), and a founder of the Children's Literature Association. This essay provides an enlightening look at how readers interact with literature and how *Novels for Students* can help teachers show students how to enrich their own reading experiences.

A Cumulative Author/Title Index lists the authors and titles covered in each volume of the *NfS* series.

A Cumulative Nationality/Ethnicity Index breaks down the authors and titles covered in each volume of the *NfS* series by nationality and ethnicity.

A Subject/Theme Index, specific to each volume, provides easy reference for users who may be studying a particular subject or theme rather than a single work. Significant subjects from events to broad themes are included, and the entries pointing to the specific theme discussions in each entry are indicated in **boldface.**

Each entry has several illustrations, including photos of the author, stills from film adaptations (when available), maps, and/or photos of key historical events.

Citing Novels for Students

When writing papers, students who quote directly from any volume of *Novels for Students* may use the following general forms. These examples are based on MLA style; teachers may request that students adhere to a different style, so the following examples may be adapted as needed.

When citing text from *NfS* that is not attributed to a particular author (i.e., the Themes, Style,

Historical Context sections, etc.), the following format should be used in the bibliography section:

"Night." *Novels for Students*. Eds. Sheryl Ciccarelli and Marie Rose Napierkowski. Vol. 5. Detroit: Gale, 1998. 34–5.

When quoting the specially commissioned essay from *NfS* (usually the first piece under the "Criticism" subhead), the following format should be used:

Miller, Tyrus. Essay on "Winesburg, Ohio." *Novels for Students*. Eds. Sheryl Ciccarelli and Marie Rose Napierkowski. Vol. 5. Detroit: Gale, 1997. 218–9.

When quoting a journal or newspaper essay that is reprinted in a volume of *NfS,* the following form may be used:

Malak, Amin. "Margaret Atwood's The Handmaid's Tale' and the Dystopian Tradition," in *Canadian Literature* , No. 112, Spring, 1987, 9–16; excerpted and reprinted in *Novels for Students,* Vol. 5, eds. Sheryl Ciccarelli and Marie Rose Napierkowski (Detroit: Gale, 1998), pp. 61–64.

When quoting material reprinted from a book that appears in a volume of *NfS,* the following form may be used:

Adams, Timothy Dow. "Richard Wright: Wearing the Mask," in *Telling Lies in Modern American Autobiography* (University of North Carolina Press, 1990), 69–83; excerpted and reprinted in *Novels for Students,* Vol. 5, eds. Sheryl Ciccarelli and Marie Napierkowski (Detroit: Gale, 1999), pp. 59–61.

We Welcome Your Suggestions

The editor of *Novels for Students* welcomes your comments and ideas. Readers who wish to suggest novels to appear in future volumes, or who have other suggestions, are cordially invited to contact the editor. You may contact the editor via e-mail at: **CYA@gale.com@galesmtp.** Or write to the editor at:

Editor, *Novels for Students*
The Gale Group
27500 Drake Rd.
Farmington Hills, MI 48331–3535

Literary Chronology

1547: Miguel de Cervantes Saavedra is born on September 19, 1547, in Alcalé de Henares.

1605: Miguel de Cervantes Saavedra's *Don Quixote* is published.

1616: Miguel de Cervantes Saavedra dies in April of 1616.

1821: Fedor Mikhailovich Dostoevsky is born on October 30, 1821, in Moscow.

1871: Theodore Dreiser is born in Terre Haute, Indiana, on August 27, 1871.

1876: Jack London is born in San Francisco, California.

1881: Fedor Mikhailovich Dostoyevsky's *Brothers Karamazov* is published.

1881: Fedor Mikhailovich Dostoevsky dies of a throat hemorrhage on January 28, 1881.

1882: Virginia Woolf is born in London, England.

1890: Agatha Christie is born on September 15, 1890, in Torquay, England.

1891: Mikhail Bulgakov is born in Kiev on May 3, 1891.

1892: J. R. R. Tolkien is born on January 3, 1892, in Bloemfontein, South Africa.

1897: William Faulkner is born.

1900: Theodore Dreiser's *Sister Carrie* is published.

1903: Jack London's *Call of the Wild* is published.

1916: Jack London dies of uremia.

1922: Jack Kerouac is born on March 22, 1922, in Lowell, Massachusetts.

1927: Virginia Woolf's *To the Lighthouse* is published.

1928: Virginia Woolf is awarded the Prix Femina for *To the Lighthouse*.

1928: Carlos Fuentes is born in Panama City, Panama.

1930: J. G. Ballard is born on November 15, 1930, in Shanghai.

1930: William Faulkner's *As I Lay Dying* is published.

1931: Toni Morrison is born in Lorain, Ohio.

1937: J. R. R. Tolkien's *Hobbit* is published.

1938: Joyce Carol Oates is born.

1939: Agatha Christie's *Ten Little Indians* is published.

1940: Mikhail Bulgakov dies.

1941: Virginia Woolf commits suicide.

1945: Theodore Dreiser dies in Los Angeles, California.

1947: Octavia Butler is born in Pasadena, California.

1949: William Faulkner is awarded the Nobel Prize for Literature.

1957: Jack Kerouac's *On the Road* is published.

1962: William Faulkner dies of a heart attack on July 6, 1962.

1968: Mikhail Bulgakov's *Master and Margarita* is published.

1969: Joyce Carol Oates's *them* is published.

1969: Jack Kerouac dies in St. Petersburg, Florida, on October 21, 1969.

1970: Joyce Carol Oates is awarded the National Book Award for *them*.

1973: J. R. R. Tolkien dies in Bournemouth, England, on September 2, 1973.

1976: Agatha Christie dies on January 12, 1976, in Wallingford, Oxfordshire, England.

1977: Toni Morrison's *Song of Solomon* is published.

1979: Octavia Butler's *Kindred* is published.

1984: J. G. Ballard's *Empire of the Sun* is published.

1984: J. G. Ballard receives the Guardian Fiction Prize and a nomination for the Booker Prize for *Empire of the Sun*.

1985: J. G. Ballard is awarded the James Tait Black Memorial Prize for *Empire of the Sun*.

1985: Carlos Fuentes's *Old Gringo* is published.

1993: Toni Morrison becomes the first African-American woman to win the Nobel Prize for Literature.

Acknowledgments

The editors wish to thank the copyright holders of the excerpted criticism included in this volume and the permissions managers of many book and magazine publishing companies for assisting us in securing reproduction rights. We are also grateful to the staffs of the Detroit Public Library, the Library of Congress, the University of Detroit Mercy Library, Wayne State University Purdy/Kresge Library Complex, and the University of Michigan Libraries for making their resources available to us. Following is a list of the copyright holders who have granted us permission to reproduce material in this volume of *NfS*. Every effort has been made to trace copyright, but if omissions have been made, please let us know.

COPYRIGHTED EXCERPTS IN *NFS*, VOLUME 8, WERE REPRODUCED FROM THE FOLLOWING PERIODICALS:

Arizona Quarterly, v. 32, Autumn, 1976, for 'Suffering, Transcendence, and Artistic 'Form': Joyce Carol Oates's *them*,' by James R. Giles. Copyright © 1976 by the Regents of the University of Arizona. Reproduced by permission of the publisher and the author.—*The Armchair Detective,* v. 16, Winter, 1983. Copyright © 1983 by The Armchair Detective. Reproduced by permission.—*Extrapolation,* v. 23, Spring, 1982. Copyright © 1982 by The Kent State University Press. Reproduced by permission.—*International Fiction Review,* v. 6, Summer, 1979; v. 16, Winter, 1989. © copyright 1979, 1989 International Fiction Association. Both reproduced by permission.—*The*

Markham Review, v. 8, Fall, 1978. Reproduced by permission.—*MELUS,* v. 7, Fall, 1980. Copyright, MELUS: The Society for the Study of Multi-Ethnic Literature of the United States, 1980. Reproduced by permission.—*Midwest Quarterly,* v. XIV, Summer, 1973. Copyright © 1973 by The Midwest Quarterly, Pittsburgh State University. Reproduced by permission.—*The Nation,* January 22, 1968. © 1968 The Nation Magazine/The Nation Company, Inc. Reproduced by permission.—*The New York Times Book Review,* October 13, 1984; November 11, 1984. Copyright © 1984 by The New York Times Company. Reproduced by permission.—*Twentieth Century Literature,* v. 31, Winter, 1985. Copyright 1985, Hofstra University Press. Reproduced by permission.—*University of Dayton Review,* v. 23, Spring, 1985. Reproduced by permission.

COPYRIGHTED EXCERPTS IN *NFS*, VOLUME 8, WERE REPRODUCED FROM THE FOLLOWING BOOKS:

Ashley, Leonard R. N. From *Reference Guide to American Literature, 3rd Edition.* Edited by Jim Kamp. St. James Press, 1994. Reproduced by permission.—Bleikasten, Andre. From an introduction in *Faulkner's As I Lay Dying,* translated by Roger Little. Indiana University Press, 1973. Copyright © 1973 by Indiana University Press. Reproduced by permission.—Bucco, Martin. From *Reference Guide to American Literature, 3rd Edition.* Edited by Jim Kamp. St. James Press, 1994. Reproduced by permission.—Crossley, Robert.

From an introduction to **Kindred.** Beacon Press, 1988. Copyright © 1979 by Octavia E. Butler. Introduction Copright © 1988 by Beacon Press. Reproduced by permission of Beacon Press, Boston.—Howe, Irving. From **William Faulkner: A Critical Study.** Random House, 1951. Copyright, 1951, 1952, by Irving Howe. Reproduced by permission of the estate of Irving Howe.—Matthews, Dorothy. From **A Tolkien Compass.** Edited by Jared Lobdell. Open Court, 1975. Reproduced by permission of Open Court Publishing Company, a division of Carus Publishing Company, Peru, IL.—Matus, Jill. From **Toni Morrison.** Manchester University Press, 1998. Copyright © Jill Matus 1998. Reproduced by permission.—McMillin, Arnold. From **Reference Guide to World Literature, 2nd Edition.** Edited by Lesley Henderson. St. James Press, 1995. Reproduced by permission.—McNichol, Stella. From **Reference Guide to English Literature, 2nd Edition.** Edited by D. L. Kirkpatrick. St. James Press, 1991. Reproduced by permission.—Sullivan, C. W., III. From **Touchstones: Reflections on the Best in Children's Literature.** Children's Literature Association, 1985. © 1985 ChLA Publishers. Reproduced by permission.—Unamuno, Miguel de. From **Selected Works of Miguel de Unamuno: Our Lord Don Quixote, Volume 3.** Edited by Anthony Kerrigan and Martin Nozick. Translated by Anthony Kerrigan. Princeton University Press, 1967. Copyright © 1967 by Princeton University Press. Reproduced by permission.—Wright, A. Colin. From **Reference Guide to World Literature, 2nd Edition.** Edited by Lesley Henderson. St. James Press, 1995. Reproduced by permission.

PHOTOGRAPHS AND ILLUSTRATIONS APPEARING IN *NFS*, VOLUME 8, WERE RECEIVED FROM THE FOLLOWING SOURCES:

African American soldiers during World War I, France, ca. 1918, photograph. Corbis. Reproduced by permission.—Bale, Christian (standing on truck, pointing), in the film 'Empire of the Sun,' 1987, photograph. The Kobal Collection. Reproduced by permission.—Ballard, J. G., Los Angeles, California, 1987, photograph. Corbis/Bettmann. Reproduced by permission.—Beatniks at coffeehouse, Greenwich Village, Manhattan, New York, 1959, photograph. Corbis/Bettmann. Reproduced by permission.—Beowulf, manuscript page.—Bierce, Ambrose, photograph. Corbis-Bettmann. Reproduced by permission.—Biss, J. L., Dorothy Kiefer, Washington D. C., 1931, photograph. Corbis/Bettmann. Reproduced by permission.—Bond,

Marshall and Louis for Jack London's *The Call of the Wild*, photograph. Huntington Library.—Bulgakov, Mikhail, photograph. Ardis Publishers. Reproduced by permission.—Butler, Octavia E., photograph by O.M. Butler. Reproduced by permission.—Cassady, Neal, San Francisco, California, 1966, photograph by Ted Streshinsky. Corbis/Ted Streshinsky. Reproduced by permission.—Cervantes, From the title page of Don Quixote. 1605. Corbis-Bettmann. Reproduced by permission.—Cherkason, Nikolai, Yuci Tulubeyer, in the film 'Don Quixote,' 1957, photograph. The Kobal Collection. Reproduced by permission.—Christie, Agatha, photograph. The Library of Congress.—Church of the Resurrection, St. Petersburg, Russia, 1993, photograph by Steve Raymer. Corbis/Steve Raymer. Reproduced by permission.—Cobb, Lee J., Yul Brynner, William Shatner, Richard Basehart, in the film 'The Brothers Karamazov,' 1958, photograph. The Kobal Collection. Reproduced by permission.—Communist Storming Heaven, two-dimensional painting. Corbis/Hulton-Deutsch Collection. Reproduced by permission.—Couple looking at wine glasses, in the film 'The Master and Margarita,' photograph. The Kobal Collection. Reproduced by permission.—de Cervantes, Miguel, photograph.—Dostoevski, Fyodor Mikhailovich, photograph. The Library of Congress.—Dreiser, Theodore, photograph. International Portrait Gallery.—Family tree before and after Civil War, 1880, photograph. Corbis. Reproduced by permission.—Faulkner, William, photograph by Neil Boenzi/New York Times. Archive Photos. Reproduced by permission.—Fitzgerald, Barry, Walter Huston, Louis Hayward, Roland Young, June Duprez, in the film 'And Then There Were None,' 1945, photograph. The Kobal Collection. Reproduced by permission.—Fuentes, Carlos, photograph by Hugh Peralta. Archive Photos, Inc./Reuters. Reproduced by permission.—Heston, Charlton, in the film 'Call of the Wild,' 1972, photograph. The Kobal Collection. Reproduced by permission.—Kerouac, Jack, photograph. Archive Photos, Inc. Reproduced by permission.—Kidnapping, drawing. The Library of Congress.—London, Jack, 1906, photograph. Corbis/ Bettmann. Reproduced by permission.—Members of the Cooperative Association, picking cotton, Lake Dick, Arkansas, 1938, photograph by Russell Lee. Corbis. Reproduced by permission.—Missionaries in camp on way to the Klondike, c. 1897, Alaska Territory, photograph by LaRoche. Corbis. Reproduced by permission.—Muckle Flugga lighthouse, Shetland, Scotland, 1981, photograph. Corbis/Roger

Tidman. Reproduced by permission.—Oates, Joyce Carol, 1991, photograph. AP/Wide World Photos. Reproduced by permission.—Old woman and her granddaughter being carried in a rickshaw after bomb raid, China, 1937, photograph. Corbis/Hulton-Deutsch Collection. Reproduced by permission.—Reed, Oliver, Elke Sommer, in the film 'Ten Little Indians,' 1974, photograph. Archive Photos. Reproduced by permission.—Riots, Detroit, Michigan, 1967, photograph. AP/Wide World Photos. Reproduced by permission.—Rooftops of houses, Cornwall, England, 1978, photograph by Adam Woolfitt. CORBIS/Adam Woolfitt. Reproduced by permission.—Schell, Maria, Yul Brynner, in the film 'The Brothers Karamazov,' 1958, photograph. The Kobal Collection. Reproduced by permission.—Slavery handbill offering cash for slaves, illustration. The Library of Congress.—Smits, Jimmy, Gregory Peck, in the film 'Old Gringo,' 1989, photograph. The Kobal Collection. Reproduced by permission.— 'The Hobbit,' in the film 'The Hobbit,' 1978, photograph. The Kobal Collection. Reproduced by permission.—Tolkien, J.R.R., photograph. The Library of Congress.— Traffic traveling along Broadway as seen from Dey Street, New York City, 1900, photograph. CORBIS. Reproduced by permission.—Two black men in front of Black Panther meeting place, photograph. The Library of Congress.—Villa, Francisco 'Pancho' photograph.—Waldorf-Astoria, New York City, 1897, photograph. Archive Photos. Reproduced by permission.—Woman walking across city street, Detroit, Michigan, 1930-1960, photograph. Archive Photos. Reproduced by permission.— Woolf, Virginia, photograph. AP/Wide World Photos. Reproduced by permission.—Morrison, Toni, Photograph. AP/Wide World Photos. Reproduced by permission.

Contributors

Don Akers: Freelance writer; original essays and entries on *The Hobbit* and *On the Road*.

Chloe Bolan: College professor and freelance writer. Original essay on *Call of the Wild*.

Anne Boyd: Doctoral candidate in American Studies, Purdue University. Entry on *Call of the Wild*.

Jane Elizabeth Dougherty: Freelance writer, Medford, MA. Original essays on *Song of Solomon* and *To the Lighthouse*, and entry on *Song of Solomon*.

Logan Esdale: Doctoral candidate, State University of New York at Buffalo. Original essay on *The Brothers Karamazov*.

Darren Felty: Visiting instructor, College of Charleston (SC); Ph.D. in Literature, University of Georgia. Entry on *As I Lay Dying*.

Diane Andrews Henningfeld: Professor of English, Adrian College (MI). Original essays on *Don Quixote* and *Sister Carrie*.

Jeremy Hubbell: Freelance writer; M.Litt., University of Aberdeen. Entries on *The Brothers Karamazov* and *Don Quixote*.

David J. Kelly: Professor of English, College of Lake County (IL). Entries on *Master and Marguerita, The Old Gringo,* and *them*.

Jeffrey M. Lilburn: Writer and translator specializing in twentieth-century American and Canadian literature; M.A., University of Western Ontario. Original essay on *As I Lay Dying*.

Nancy C. McClure: Educational consultant and freelance writer, Clarksburg, WV; Ed.D, West Virginia University. Entry on *Sister Carrie*.

Tabitha McIntosh-Byrd: Freelance writer; M.Litt., University of Aberdeen. Original essays on *Kindred, The Master and Margarita, The Old Gringo,* and *them,* and entry on *To the Lighthouse*.

Wendy Perkins: Assistant Professor of English, Prince George's Community College, Maryland; Ph.D. in English, University of Delaware. Original essays and entries on *Empire of the Sun* and *Ten Little Indians*.

Diane Telgen: Freelance writer; entry on *Kindred*.

As I Lay Dying

William Faulkner
1930

Although it achieved little commercial success at the time of its publication, *As I Lay Dying* has become one of William Faulkner's most popular novels. At first put off by its controversial subject matter and confusing style, commentators and readers have come to appreciate the novel's vivid characters, elusive tone, and complex narrative techniques.

As I Lay Dying chronicles the death of Addie Bundren and the subsequent journey to bury her corpse in her family's cemetery several miles away. This disastrous and darkly comic tale is enriched by Faulkner's innovative narrative technique, which features narration by fifteen characters, including a confused child and the dead woman, Addie. In addition, Faulkner mixes vernacular speech with "stream-of-consciousness" passages to enhance this unique narrative style.

Through his characters, Faulkner addresses subjects that challenge stereotypical perceptions of poor Southerners. For instance, characters contemplate issues of love, death, identity, and the limitations of language. Their actions and adventures draw attention to rural life, class conflicts, and the repercussions of desire and selfishness. Significantly, Faulkner explores the potent, complex workings of the human mind. Difficult to categorize, *As I Lay Dying* has provided a rewarding, illuminating, and, at times, unsettling experience for generations of readers.

William Faulkner

Author Biography

William Cuthbert Faulkner (changed from the original spelling, Falkner) was born on September 25, 1897, in New Albany, Mississippi. He was the first of four sons born to Maud and Murry, a prominent local businessman. The Faulkners moved to Oxford, Mississippi, when William was five; for the rest of his life, Oxford remained his primary home.

Though an avid reader, Faulkner did not like school. In 1914 he quit high school and worked in his grandfather's bank. During this time, he was devastated as a result of a broken marital engagement with Estelle Oldham, who married another man under familial pressure. In 1918 he was refused admission into the armed forces because of his size. Determined to fight in World War I, he falsified his credentials to enter the Royal Air Force in Canada, but the war ended before he completed his military training. He attended the University of Mississippi for two years as a special student, from 1919 to 1921.

After his tenure at the University of Mississippi, he worked briefly in a New York bookstore. He returned to Oxford and became postmaster at the university until 1924, when he was fired for writing and socializing while on duty. In 1924, he published his first book, a collection of poems entitled *The Marble Faun.*

In 1925, he lived for a few months in New Orleans. During that short time he socialized with Sherwood Anderson. It was Anderson's wife, Elizabeth Prall, who encouraged Faulkner to abandon poetry for fiction. He subsequently left New Orleans and traveled to Paris, toured Europe, and began to write his first novel.

His first three novels, *Soldiers' Pay* (1926), *Mosquitoes* (1927), and *Sartoris* (1929) (a shortened version of *Flags in the Dust,* published in 1973) garnered little attention. In 1929, Faulkner married Estelle Oldham, who had recently divorced her husband. She already had two children, and the couple had two daughters, one of whom died in infancy. Early on, Estelle attempted suicide; this event signaled the beginning of an unhappy union for the couple.

In 1929 Faulkner published his most ambitious work to date, *The Sound and the Fury.* It garnered much critical praise but was not commercially successful. While working the night shift as a power plant stoker, he wrote and revised *As I Lay Dying* in under three months. Published in 1930, the novel was praised by critics but attracted little commercial attention.

For the rest of his life, Faulkner made his living as a writer of fiction and Hollywood screenplays. His most accomplished works during the 1930s and 1940s include *Light in August, Absalom, Absalom!, The Hamlet,* and *Go Down, Moses.* In 1946 Malcolm Cowley's editing and publication of *The Portable Faulkner* helped to cement Faulkner's literary reputation and commercial viability.

Faulkner received the 1949 Nobel Prize for Literature and the 1954 Pulitzer Prize for his novel *The Fable.* During the last ten years of his life, he traveled, lectured, and became an outspoken critic of segregation. From 1957 until his death, he was writer-in-residence at the University of Virginia, near his daughter Jill and her children. In 1962, after years of drinking and a succession of physical problems, he died of a heart attack on July 6 in Oxford.

Plot Summary

Addie's Death

As I Lay Dying chronicles the dark, comic story of a Mississippi family's long and arduous journey to bury Addie, the family matriarch. Respecting Addie's request to be buried in her family's burial ground in Jefferson, Anse Bundren and his five children disregard the advice of friends and neighbors and embark on a forty-mile, nine-day trek in the wake of a devastating storm.

The story of the journey is presented by a variety of narrators: family members, friends, acquaintances, and objective onlookers. Each narrator provides a different perspective on individuals and events.

When the novel begins, Addie is on her deathbed. Outside her bedroom window, Cash slowly and meticulously builds her coffin. On the front porch, Jewel and Darl confer with their father about taking a last-minute job to make a bit of money. Anse reminds his sons of his promise to their mother but agrees to let them go, even though he knows that Addie may die before they return.

When Peabody, the local doctor, is finally summoned to the Bundren home, he predicts that it will be too late to do anything for Addie. Sure enough, she dies shortly after Peabody's arrival at the Bundren farm. After sending Dewey Dell away to prepare supper, Anse stands over his dead wife, listens to the sound of Cash's saw as he works on the coffin, and says: "God's will be done. Now I can get them teeth."

The Journey Begins

Cash finishes the coffin later that night in the pouring rain. Addie is kept in the coffin for three days before Darl and Jewel return home with the wagon. On the first day, the family wakes to find that Vardaman has bored the top of the coffin full of holes—two of which bored straight through Addie's face.

By the time the family finally gets the coffin on the wagon, the bridge to town has been washed away by heavy rains, adding several days to their journey. Jewel, refusing to travel with the family, follows some distance behind on his beloved horse.

Just before sundown they complete the first eight miles of their journey. They spend the night in a neighbor's barn and start off again early the next morning, trying to find a bridge that hasn't been completely destroyed by a recent storm. They finally find one near Vernon Tull's farm.

After consideration, it is decided that Anse, Dewey Dell, Vardaman, and Vernon Tull will walk across the remains of the bridge and that Cash and Darl will lead the wagon across the river at the ford. Jewel crosses ahead of them on his horse. Halfway

across the bridge, the wagon is hit by a floating log and is dragged off by the current. The wagon and Addie's coffin are recovered, but the mules drown and Cash breaks his leg.

The narrative action pauses as Addie narrates a section in the novel. She describes her youth, her miserable life as a schoolteacher, and her decision to marry Anse. Unfortunately, her marriage is an unhappy one.

After giving birth to Cash, she suffered from depression; after giving birth to her second son, Darl, she makes Anse promise to bury her in Jefferson when she dies. Her revenge, she says, would be that Anse would never know that she was taking revenge. Addie also reveals her secret affair with Reverend Whitfield—a union that produced Addie's favorite child, Jewel.

From Bad to Worse

After the disastrous river crossing, the Bundrens spend the night at Armstid's farm. In the morning, Anse rides off on Jewel's horse to purchase a team of mules. During his absence, the heat intensifies the already putrid stench of Addie's corpse. Outraged, Lula Armstid thinks Anse "should be lawed for treating [Addie] so."

When Anse finally returns, he announces that he has traded Jewel's horse for a team of mules. The family's journey resumes the next morning with Cash lying on a pallet placed atop Addie's coffin.

Like Anse, Dewey Dell has personal reasons for wanting to go to town. She is pregnant and her boyfriend, Lafe, has told her that she would be able to "get something at the drugstore" to induce an abortion. When the procession passes through the town of Mottson, Dewey Dell speaks to the druggist but is told that she will not get what she wants in his store.

Meanwhile, Darl buys cement for Cash's leg at a hardware store. Anse, waiting outside in the wagon, is told by the town marshal that he will have to leave town. After eight days in the stifling heat, Addie's body is endangering the public health.

The family leaves town, stopping briefly to apply fresh cement on Cash's broken leg. Jewel, who disappeared after Anse traded his horse, reappears and rejoins the family.

They spend the last night of their journey on a farm belonging to Mr. Gillespie. During the night, Darl sets fire to the barn and Jewel's back is burned rescuing the coffin from the flames.

A demonstration of a "psychoanalyzing machine." During the early 1900s, interest in psychology was growing and works such Faulkner's As I Lay Dying, *with its interior monologues and psychological elements, were gaining interest.*

When Gillespie discovers that it was Darl who set the fire, he threatens to sue unless Darl is committed to the mental institution in Jackson. Cash thinks that Darl "done right in a way," trying to get Addie "outen our hands," but decides that it does not excuse setting fire to a man's barn and endangering his property.

Journey's End–and a New Beginning

As they arrive in Jefferson the next day, Anse finally concedes that they will have to find a doctor for Cash's infected leg. But first, they bury Addie. Anse borrows a couple of spades on the way to the cemetery and—nine days after Addie's death—finally lays his wife to rest in her family plot. As they leave the cemetery, Darl is jumped by Dewey Dell and Jewel and handed over to the men waiting to take him to the mental institution in Jackson.

When Cash finally gets to the doctor, Peabody cannot believe that Anse treated his son's broken leg with raw cement. Shocked at the damage they have done to him, the doctor wonders why Anse

simply didn't bring Cash to the nearest sawmill and stick his leg in the saw.

Meanwhile, Dewey Dell finds another drugstore. After requesting something that will terminate her pregnancy, she is given a box of useless capsules by the drugstore clerk. The deceitful clerk proceeds to seduce her. The next morning, Anse disappears only to reappear with a new set of teeth and a new Mrs. Bundren—a local woman who loaned him the tools to bury Addie.

Characters

Armstid

A local farmer, Armstid provides shelter for the Bundren family after their disastrous river crossing. He makes cryptic comments on the treatment of Cash's injury, Anse's trade for a mule team, and the rotting smell coming from the casket.

Addie Bundren

The family matriarch, Addie is Anse's wife and the mother of the Bundren children. She dies early in the book from a lingering illness, and the action of the novel revolves around transporting her body to her family's burial ground. As a young woman, Addie was a schoolteacher in Jefferson. To escape this life, she married Anse, a local farmer. She was happy when she gave birth to her eldest son Cash; but with her next child, Darl, she began to resent her situation.

Years into her marriage, she had a passionate affair with the Reverend Whitfield. During the affair, she became pregnant with Jewel, her favorite child. She had two more children—Dewey Dell and Vardaman—more out of obligation than anything else. Considering Darl, Dewey Dell, and Vardaman products of an unhappy time, she does not feel affection for them; instead, she favors Cash and Jewel.

Anse Bundren

Anse is the patriarch of the Bundren family. A selfish and lazy man, he claims sweat will kill him, and therefore refuses to work. Instead, he connives to get others to work for him. Physically, he is hunchbacked, and his hands are gnarled.

Though his wife is dying, he allows Darl and Jewel to leave her deathbed to work. He considers himself to be a right-thinking, hard-working man who is victimized by God. In what first seems to be a selfless move, he pushes for the journey to bury Addie at her family cemetery. Later his true motive is revealed: to buy a set of false teeth in Jefferson.

When the family's mules die in the flooded river, he steals Cash's money and barters away Jewel's beloved horse to obtain new mules. During the trip, he scrimps on money wherever possible, even borrowing shovels to bury his wife. While in Jefferson, he takes Dewey Dell's money, buys false teeth, and secretly woos a local woman. He ends the novel with his new teeth, introducing his new wife to his surprised children.

Cash Bundren

The oldest son of Anse and Addie, Cash is a carpenter of extraordinary precision and skill. As his mother is dying, he carefully builds her coffin, holding up each board for her inspection. He even decides to bevel the edges of the coffin, despite the extra work it requires.

When the Bundrens try to cross the flooded river, Cash is knocked out of the wagon and suffers a severely broken leg. After the bone is reset, he rides for three days on top of the coffin before the family buys cement to cover the leg. Unfortunately, they apply the cement directly to his skin, which causes a horrible infection. Despite intense pain, Cash remains stoical. When the doctor removes the concrete from his leg, Cash loses over sixty inches of skin along with it.

While in Jefferson, Cash is torn by the decision to commit Darl to an insane asylum. On one hand, he feels empathy for his brother; on the other hand, he recognizes that a man cannot simply burn down another man's hard-earned property. He eventually agrees with the decision to commit him.

Darl Bundren

The second of the Bundren children, Darl is a veteran of World War I. He narrates more sections of the book than any other character. He is profoundly jealous of Addie's obvious preference for Jewel, and throughout the book, he scrutinizes and often goads his brother. He even connives to separate Jewel from Addie when she is dying by volunteering both himself and Jewel to haul lumber. While on this trip, a wagon wheel breaks. As Jewel tries to fix the wheel, Darl narrates his mother's death for the reader and informs Jewel of her death. This form of "second sight," or telepathy, also manifests itself in his knowledge of Dewey Dell's pregnancy.

Media Adaptations

- Initially *As I Lay Dying* was adapted for the stage by Jean-Louis Barrault. The 1935 production was performed in Paris and featured extensive pantomime, surrealistic settings and costumes, and only Addie's monologues.

- Peter Gill adapted the novel for a 1985 production at London's National Theatre. Gill also directed the play, employing sparse staging and effects.

- Frank Galati adapted and directed the work for Chicago's Steppenwolf Theatre Company in 1995. Galati previously had adapted John Steinbeck's *The Grapes of Wrath.*

- The Threshold Theatre Company of Kingston, Ontario performed the work in Toronto in August, 1995. Mark Cassidy adapted and directed the play. The company performed the play outside, and the audience walked with the actors on their funeral journey.

- Edward Kemp adapted the play in 1998 for London's Young Vic theatre company. The play was directed by Tim Supple.

Darl participates in the journey to Jefferson, but he is never committed to it. Embarrassed by his family and the experience of dragging his mother's corpse all over the county, he burns down Gillespie's barn with Addie's coffin inside. For this act, he is committed to the insane asylum in Jackson. He ends the novel on a train, laughing and talking about himself in the third person.

Dewey Dell Bundren

Seventeen years old, Dewey Dell is the only daughter of the Bundren family. Like Darl and Vardaman, she feels rejected by her mother, Addie. Because Darl knows about her pregnancy, she resents and fears him. She desperately wants to go to Jefferson so she can obtain "medicine" that will illegally abort the pregnancy. Her first fumbling attempt to acquire the medicine fails when the druggist Mosely refuses to give it to her.

While she is in Jefferson, Anse steals her money. To make matters worse, a sleazy drugstore clerk, Skeet Macgowan, gives her worthless pills filled with talcum powder. He then seduces her. After Addie's burial, Dewey Dell is strongly in favor of committing Darl to the mental institution.

Jewel Bundren

Jewel, in his late teens, is Addie's third son and her favorite child. The product of her affair with Reverend Whitfield, Jewel does not know his true paternity. After a lifetime of being his mother's favorite, he loves his mother fiercely and feels a strong devotion to her.

Described as tall and wooden in appearance, Jewel is a reticent young man. When he does talk, he usually curses, exhibiting a persistent rage. His favorite possession is his horse, which he bought by working nights for several months. The horse is as fierce as Jewel, and they engage in battles that exhibit both Jewel's violence and intense love. He loses the horse on the third day of the journey when Anse trades it for a new team of mules. Giving up his horse is one indication that Jewel is the family member most committed to fulfilling Addie's wish to be buried in Jefferson.

In addition to this sacrifice, he helps retrieve his mother's coffin when it gets thrown from the wagon during the river crossing. He also saves the coffin single-handedly from Gillespie's burning barn, suffering many burns as a result. Like Dewey Dell, he is in favor of committing Darl to the mental institution.

Mrs. Bundren

Mrs. Bundren is Anse's second wife. A "duck-shaped" woman with "hardlooking pop eyes," she marries Anse after he woos her in Jefferson.

Vardaman Bundren

Vardaman is the youngest Bundren child. He cannot fully comprehend the reality of his mother's death. At first, he blames Dr. Peabody for taking her away and releases Peabody's horse team for revenge. Then, he believes that Addie is not dead but has mutated into a fish. He bores holes in her coffin to give her air, mutilating her face. Later in the novel, his belief that Addie has become a fish causes his excited fear when Addie's coffin falls into the river. He runs along the bank, yelling for Darl to catch her so she will not escape, a thought he cannot bear.

Vardaman grows closer to Darl during the trip. At the end of novel, he sees his brother set fire to Gillespie's barn, which disappoints him. He struggles to understand Darl's insanity and feels the loss when his brother is taken away to the mental institution in Jackson.

Gillespie

Gillespie is a farmer who allows the Bundrens to stay on his farm during their journey. Darl burns down his barn to destroy Addie's coffin and end the humiliating journey.

Skeet Macgowan

Macgowan is a drugstore clerk in Jefferson. He cons Dewey Dell, giving her fake abortion pills. He seduces her in the cellar of the store.

Moseley

Moseley is a drugstore owner in Mottson. A religious man, he refuses to sell abortion drugs to Dewey Dell and condemns her for trying to purchase them.

Dr. Peabody

Dr. Peabody tends to Addie on her deathbed. His help is limited, however, because Anse sends for him too late. He comments on the family's behavior from an objective perspective. He views the family as proud, but slovenly and ignorant. In Jefferson, Peabody tries to fix the damage done to Cash's leg.

Samson

Samson is a farmer who offers shelter for the Bundren family before they try to cross the river. He unfavorably comments on their refusal to accept his hospitality.

Rachel Samson

Rachel Samson is Samson's wife. She expresses outrage at the handling of Addie's body and relates it to the treatment of all women.

Cora Tull

Cora is Vernon Tull's wife. She narrates many of the early chapters in the book, offering her perspective on the Bundrens. Throughout the chapters she narrates, her judgments are almost always self-serving and wrong, often comically so.

Vernon Tull

Tull is the farmer who lives closest to the Bundrens. A thrifty, hardworking man, he is very successful as a farmer. He helps Cash build the coffin, tries to guide the family across the flooded river, and retrieves Cash's tools from the water. He feels especially drawn to Vardaman, and his interest in the boy may result from his own lack of a son.

Reverend Whitfield

A local preacher, Reverend Whitfield had an affair with Addie in their youth; in fact, he is Jewel's father. He has never admitted the affair to anyone. He visits Addie on the night she dies, supposedly to reveal the affair to the Bundren family. When Addie dies, he believes that he has been absolved of his sin by God and remains silent.

Themes

Alienation and Loneliness

Faulkner's use of multiple narrators under-scores one of his primary themes: every character is essentially isolated from the others. Moreover, the characters in the novel do not communicate effectively with one another. Although the reader is privy to the characters' thoughts and emotional responses, none of the characters adequately express their dilemmas or desires to others. Outside of Darl, who knows Addie's and Dewey Dell's secrets through intuition, the characters can only guess at the motivations, beliefs, and feelings of others. When these guesses turn out to be wrong, misunderstandings ensue.

As a result of their communication problems, members of the Bundren family live alienated from each other—whether willfully (like Addie or Jewel), unknowingly (like Anse, Cash, Dewey Dell, or Vardaman), or painfully (like Darl). This alienation extends to neighbors, who misinterpret or simply cannot fathom the family's actions.

The more sensitive characters, especially Addie and Darl, recognize their alienation from others. In particular, Addie is a striking example of someone who both longs to transcend this isolation and stubbornly works to maintain an impenetrable individuality. As a schoolteacher, she would whip her students in order to overcome the barriers between her and others: "I would think with each blow of the switch: Now you are aware of me! Now I am something in your secret and selfish life, who have marked your blood with my own for ever and ever." One can see her selfishness here, however, as she violently imposes herself onto others without opening herself to them. Similarly, she holds back from her children, except for Cash and her favorite, Jewel. Her contradictions highlight the fundamental compulsion to maintain one's private self while yearning to connect with others.

Death

In a novel that features a disastrous journey to bury a decomposing corpse, one would expect death to be a central concern. Indeed, the outraged reactions of other characters to the journey of the Bundren family reveal both social expectations about the treatment of the dead and underlying anxieties over the basic truths of human mortality. Moreover, Vardaman's chapters revolve primarily around defining the nature of death, and his confusion proves both moving and unsettling.

The theme of death also takes other forms in the novel. Through Addie's narrative, Faulkner investigates the possibility of living in a deadened state. On the one hand, Faulkner has her "speak" from the dead. On the other hand, however, is Addie's thwarted desire to *live* life; the antithesis of her desire is Anse, who, to Addie, is dead and "did not know he was dead." To her, Anse symbolizes restriction, blindness, and emptiness. Faulkner explores the implications of such an existence by exploring its potential in all of his characters, particularly those who use platitudes to avoid genuine feeling and self-examination.

Identity

Questions about the nature and strength of self-identity recur throughout the novel. Some characters, like Anse, Cash, Jewel, and the Tulls, possess a defined senses of self. Yet it is through the characters of Darl and Vardaman that Faulkner explores the fragile nature of identity. Vardaman almost compulsively defines his relationships with others, repeating "Darl is my brother" and, more famously, "My mother is a fish." Through these repetitions, Faulkner articulates the development of identity as Vardaman relates to others.

For Vardaman, the process is incomplete but progressing. For Darl, the process will never reach completion. The absence of his mother's love leads Darl to isolation not only from others but also from himself. He expresses the differences between himself and Jewel when he says, "I don't know what I am. I don't know if I am or not. Jewel knows he is, because he does not know that he does not know whether he is or not." In such passages, Darl's insights prove both compelling and disturbing since it calls into question the very essence of human consciousness.

Topics For Further Study

- Examine and discuss the possible meanings of Faulkner's title. How do you interpret it?

- Research economic conditions for Southern farmers during the early decades of the twentieth century. How did these conditions impact class relations? Provide examples from Faulkner's novel.

- Compare and contrast the lives of Southern farmers and unskilled laborers in the early twentieth century with the lives of farmers and laborers today. Offer statistical information from reference sources to illustrate how the situation has changed.

- Explore the lives of women in Southern society at the time of Faulkner's novel. How have women's activities, opportunities, and expectations changed?

- Research Sigmund Freud's theories on the Oedipal complex and relate what you've learned to Addie Bundren's relationships with her children, using examples from the novel.

- Compare the journey of the Bundren family to famous journeys in myth, religion, or famous epics. What are the defining characteristics of these journeys?

- Construct a contemporary version of the Bundrens' journey, factoring in modern social conditions. How are Faulkner's version and your version similar? In what ways do they differ, and what does that say about how society has changed?

Language and Meaning

One of Faulkner's central themes in the novel is the limitation of language. From the inability of the characters to communicate with one another, to Addie's singular distrust of words, to the unlikely vocabulary the characters employ in their narration, Faulkner explores the inadequacy of language to express thought and emotion. Many characters communicate only through platitudes. As a result, they create misunderstanding rather than understanding between people. These instances of ineffective communication are not as comprehensive as Addie's rejection of language, however. For Addie, words cannot express human experience because they are so distant from human experience. Only action matters for her (and for the inarticulate Jewel).

Faulkner also reveals the limitations of language by contrasting the thoughts of his characters with their actual words. In their narratives, the characters often employ vocabulary far beyond their educational level or speech customs. These passages underscore Faulkner's attempts to verbalize his characters' groping for meaning and adequate expression, In this way, Faulkner comments on the tenuousness of language itself.

Love and Passion

Love and passion are major themes of the novel. The relationships and destinies of the characters rely heavily on love and intense emotions. In particular, Addie is defined by passion. Her affair with Whitfield results from genuine feeling, and the rejection of her husband and three of her children is equally intense. Her commitment to Cash and Jewel is fierce and loving. This love helps them to nurture a strong self-identity, which Darl, Dewey Dell, and Vardaman often lack.

Sanity and Insanity

By chronicling both the Bundrens' journey and Darl's descent into madness, Faulkner explores the themes of sanity and insanity. The fact that the Bundrens would undertake such an arduous journey strikes both the reader and other characters as deranged folly. For most of the Bundrens, however, the trip is perfectly sensible considering their ultimate goals: Anse's new teeth, Dewey Dell's abortion, and Jewel's loyalty to his beloved mother. They may be selfish and blind to social convention, but their desires are understandable, even if they seem misplaced in the current context. Since all of the narrators hold views that others may consider senseless, evaluations of people's sanity prove arbitrary in the novel.

Darl's case is different, however. He exhibits signs of telepathy, burns Gillespie's barn, is eventually committed to an insane asylum, and ends his final narration in a rant. Yet Darl is reacting to circumstances beyond his control. He cannot help feeling the lack of his mother's love, nor can he contain his hypersensitivity to the world. The other characters may remain "sane" simply because they work to maintain their isolation from the world. Because Darl cannot, or will not, be blind, he may be overwhelmed by *knowledge.* Perhaps, as André Bleikasten suggests in *Faulkner's As I Lay Dying,* "From the depths of his own madness, Darl discovers—and makes us discover—the madness of the universe."

Style

Setting

As I Lay Dying takes place in the northern part of Mississippi in 1928. The Bundrens must travel forty miles to bury Addie in Jefferson, the primary town in Faulkner's fictional Yoknapatawpha County. The Bundrens live in a time of economic hardship for cotton farmers, who have had to suffer through a depressed cotton market and disastrously heavy rains. They also lack modern farming equipment, instead employing farm animals and their own labor.

The modern world exists in Jefferson, however, and the Bundrens often comment on the distinctions between country people and town people. The social environment of the time features a code of ethics that obligates farm families to house and feed travelers, although the Bundrens refuse such assistance. Faulkner also depicts a natural environment that is at best indifferent and at worst actively hostile, bringing floods, heat, and intrusive buzzards.

Point of View

As I Lay Dying consists of fifty-nine chapters narrated by fifteen different characters. Darl is the most frequent voice, narrating nineteen chapters; some characters, like Addie Bundren, Jewel Bundren, and various townspeople, narrate only one chapter. Many chapters appear to unfold as events take place, particularly those narrated by the Bundrens; others relate events that occurred in the past. At times, Faulkner extends beyond the realm of credible narration, such as when Darl narrates Addie's death when he is not present and when the deceased Addie recollects her life.

Through these varying perspectives, the reader witnesses both the events that take place and the character's individual perceptions of them. Indeed, at times the reader can only discern events by comparing information from various narrators. The reader learns about the assumptions and peculiarities of the different narrators, as well as their social and religious environment. As a result, Faulkner constructs not only a rendition of events but also a series of interconnected psychological studies.

Stream of Consciousness

"Stream of consciousness" is a literary technique that reproduces the thought processes of certain characters. These thoughts appear as if they are immediate, unedited responses. Faulkner does not use this technique in all of his chapters, restricting it primarily to the Bundrens, especially Darl and Vardaman.

The stream-of-consciousness passages reveal character and allow for complicated philosophical questioning. They also imply a character's confusion or distress. A key example occurs when Addie's coffin falls into the river and Vardaman reacts hysterically: "I ran down into the water to help and I couldn't stop hollering because Darl was strong and steady holding her under the water even if she did fight he would not let her go he was seeing me and he would hold her and it was all right now it was all right now it was all right."

Although Faulkner employs paragraph breaks and, in one paragraph, italics, he does not use punctuation until Vardaman speaks to Darl at the end of the chapter. This moment and others in the novel involve the reader in the sometimes perplexing but always engaging world of the characters.

Humor

One of the most obvious features of the novel is its humor. One might expect a bleak tone from a story featuring death, a burial procession, abortion, and familial hardship, but Faulkner defies expectation by utilizing comedy, albeit dark comedy.

Faulkner employs a variety of means to achieve this effect. The family journey to bury Addie is absurd in itself, and the dogged determination of the Bundrens often evokes a humorous reaction. Faulkner also uses the characters' perceptions and faults to generate humor, such as when Anse slithers out of his responsibility for Cash's broken leg: "'It's a trial,' he says. 'But I don't begrudge her [Addie] it.'" Cash's own understatement can create humor, as well, whether it is his stoic refrain on his leg, "It don't bother me none," or his recollection of the distance he fell off of a roof: "'Twenty-eight foot, four and half inches, about.'"

Perhaps the most glaring and outrageous comic moment is the ending. After all the family has endured and the losses they have suffered, the selfish, resilient Anse appears with a set of new teeth and a "duckshaped" woman as his new wife. Such episodes make the novel difficult to categorize and greatly enrich its texture and effects.

Modernism

Critics often associate Faulkner with literary modernism, a movement that began before World War I and gained prominence during the 1920s. In fact, Faulkner was greatly influenced by two of the most celebrated modernists, T. S. Eliot and James Joyce. Eliot's poem *The Waste Land* explored, in both form and content, the dehumanizing effects of industrialization. Joyce's landmark novel *Ulysses* featured the use of "stream of consciousness," which Faulkner employs in *As I Lay Dying.*

Modernist writers experimented with language and literary form and were concerned with the limits of expression. Most modernist authors depicted characters grappling with the loss of traditional beliefs after the destructiveness of World War I. These characters are alienated from their past and from others characters, and often suffer from an inability to communicate. Faulkner's interest in these practices and themes is obvious, especially in his experiments with narrative perspective, his focus on language and its failures, and his themes of alienation and the destruction of community, including families.

Historical Context

Farm Life in the South

Despite efforts to improve technology and farming methods, a farmer's life during the 1920s involved a constant struggle for survival. The farming life was restrictive and demanding on both men and women. In fact, farmers often lived on an income of little over one hundred dollars a year. Therefore, even families who owned their land relied almost exclusively on themselves to supply both farm labor and basic necessities. Some would

hire additional help during harvesting season, yet this expense could prove burdensome as well.

One can see, then, that Darl and Jewel earning three dollars to haul wood was a good job, and the purchases of luxuries like false teeth and bananas were a big deal. In essence, a farm family's land, labor, livestock, and equipment were its only assets. To lose any of them could prove disastrous, a fact which underscores the impact of Darl's decision to burn Gillespie's barn.

According to many scholars of Southern culture, two belief systems provided many Southerners with pride and a sense of purpose: religious conviction and racism. Religion in this community was a potent emotional and psychological force, and a person's relationship with God provided one with a set of values, activities, and friends. Many critics contend that poor whites used religious beliefs as a means of coping with economic deprivation, social inferiority, and political weakness.

White supremacist beliefs also served these ends for some white citizens, providing poor white laborers with a sense of personal worth and group solidarity against a perceived menace. The economic conditions, religious beliefs, and racial views of white farmers became important factors in Southern politics in the early twentieth century.

Economics and Politics in the Rural South

On October 24, 1929, the day before Faulkner began writing *As I Lay Dying,* the American stock market crashed. This financial disaster ended a period of post-World War I economic expansion and marked the beginning of the Great Depression of the 1930s.

In the rural South, however, economic hardship had been a way of life for years, especially for poor farmers. Three factors, in particular, affected Mississippi cotton farmers. One, farmers operated under a lien system, whereby they pledged future crops to merchants in return for necessary supplies. Thus, they were in continuous debt. Second, a long-standing depression in the cotton market forced farmers to go further into debt until they could barely manage to sustain their farms or their families. Third, heavy rains and floods in the late 1920s nearly ruined production. These elements combined with outdated farming methods to make already difficult conditions even worse.

Such tensions were a staple element of Southern life in the early decades of the century. The exploitation of the working class generated populist

Farmers at the time in which As I Lay Dying *is set, such as these people picking cotton in 1928, performed backbreaking labor and generally earned barely enough to survive.*

movements that impacted Mississippi politics in the early 1900s. Sometimes termed "the revolt of the rednecks," these reforms ushered in a new breed of politician.

One of the most prominent of these men, James K. Vardaman, serves as a representative example (especially since Faulkner's family supported him and Faulkner named the youngest Bundren son after him). As Mississippi governor from 1904 to 1908 and a United States Senator from 1912 to 1918, Vardaman was a flamboyant orator and advocate of white laborers. Coming from a poor background, he called for greater regulation of corporations and supported such progressive causes as a graduated income tax, child labor laws, and women's suffrage.

One of his most potent appeals, however, was his strident racism. His views and manner earned him both the nickname "The White Chief" and a reputation as a demagogue who used racial hatred to further his own ambitions. By 1918, Vardaman had lost his once-formidable influence because he opposed American involvement in World War I. "Vardamanism," as his brand of politics was termed, had faded by the late 1920s, but populist loyalties still existed among farmers, as did the

white supremacist ideals that provided poor whites with a false sense of superiority and power.

Critical Overview

After its publication in 1930, *As I Lay Dying* garnered several positive critical reviews in America and Britain. The American reviews were generally more favorable than the British, but this early critical commentary touched on issues that were to become pronounced in later, more substantial critiques of the book.

In those early reviews, critics recognized Faulkner's talent but remained suspicious of *As I Lay Dying*. Many commentators questioned the novel's controversial subject matter—such as abortion—and its emphasis on the grotesque and violent. Some critics derided *As I Lay Dying* as tasteless and immoral. Faulkner's style and narrative method, of course, received much critical attention. In general, his use of the vernacular was praised, but his more complicated and elusive passages were deemed confusing. Social-minded critics condemned Faulkner for his lack of overt social commentary.

Compare
&
Contrast

- **1920s:** The Democratic party dominates Southern politics. Women are granted voting rights in 1920, but African Americans are disenfranchised and discouraged from participating in the democratic process.

  Today: Since the 1960s, the Republican party has gained power and influence in the South. African American citizens are more politically active, usually providing support for the Democratic party.

- **1920s:** Cotton is the dominant crop in Mississippi. Outdated farming methods, a lack of technology, the lien system, and a depressed cotton market keep most small farmers in debt.

  Today: Cotton is still a major crop in the South, but it is no longer the dominant source of agricultural income. Production is dependent on technology and corporate ownership. Industrial employment now exceeds agricultural employment in the state.

- **1920s:** African Americans are the majority population in Mississippi, followed by whites, Native Americans (primarily Choctaw), and Chinese immigrants who lived in the Delta region.

  Today: Because of migrations out of state after 1940, African Americans comprise about a third of the population with whites in the majority. Native American and Asian-American residents still remain in minority status.

- **1920s:** Laws prohibiting abortion exist in most states since the late 1800s. Drugs that supposedly induced abortion had been on the market since the mid-nineteenth century. Abortion is considered a medical, moral, and religious issue.

  Today: With its 1973 decision in the *Roe v. Wade* case, the Supreme Court legalized abortion during the first six months of pregnancy. Age restrictions apply in many areas. Abortion is considered a medical, moral, and religious issue.

Most of the early reviewers questioned both Faulkner's tone toward his characters and the genre of the work, issues that recur in later critical commentary. French critics provided Faulkner with his most enthusiastic early notices, although the novel was not translated and published in France until 1934.

After 1940, more substantive critiques of the novel began to appear. A major reason for the renewed interest in *As I Lay Dying* was the publication of *The Portable Faulkner* in 1946. The editor of the volume, Malcolm Cowley, was a seasoned literary editor who contended that Faulkner had successfully developed a distinctive Southern mythology based on his fiction set in and around Yoknapatawpha County. In his influential introduction to the book, Cowley advocated reading all of Faulkner's works as a collective project or, in his words, "part of the same living pattern." Cowley's opinions influenced Faulkner criticism in the following decades.

Critics began to take a more universalistic approach to Faulkner's fiction, viewing his Southern world as representative of the modern world and as a means of exploring timeless human dilemmas. Many commentators began to read *As I Lay Dying* as affirmative and even moral.

Irving Howe, in his 1952 work *William Faulkner: A Critical Study,* clearly articulates this stance: "Of all Faulkner's novels, *As I Lay Dying* is the warmest, the kindliest and most affectionate.... In no other work is he so receptive to people, so ready to take and love them, to hear them out and record their turns of idiom, their melodies of speech."

Other prominent critics, such as Robert Penn Warren and Cleanth Brooks, focused on the family's heroism in the face of many obstacles. Brooks's *William Faulkner: The Yoknapatawpha Country* (1963) was, in fact, the most influential critical work on Faulkner for many years. It still holds a prominent place in Faulkner studies today.

These favorable views of the Bundrens did not go unchallenged, however. In her chapter "The Dimensions of Consciousness: As I Lay Dying," from *The Novels of William Faulkner: A Critical Interpretation* (1959), Olga Vickery contends that the Bundren family's journey is not heroic. She focuses attention on the character of Addie and her relationship with her children. For Vickery, Cash becomes the most ethically reliable character since he matures during the journey.

Vickery's views proved highly influential. Other critics followed her lead and continued to debate the tone of the novel. Many rejected the notions that Faulkner is sympathetic to his characters, the Bundrens heroic, and the novel essentially moral. These commentators focused attention on Faulkner's comedic elements and satiric stance. Even the critics who explored Faulkner's journey motif and its connections to myth, Christian symbolism, or existential philosophy disputed the tone of Faulkner's treatment of these issues.

Questions surrounding Faulkner's technique, style, form, and use of genre continued to garner comment. Many commentators discussed his relationship to modernist writing and experimental painting, particularly cubism. In a 1967 essay, "Narrative Management in *As I Lay Dying*," R. W. Franklin criticized Faulkner's stylistic technique for its inconsistencies in tense and strategy. Franklin's reading has since been effectively challenged by more careful treatments, such as Catherine Patten's "The Narrative Design of *As I Lay Dying*." Various critics have viewed the novel as epic, tragic, comedic, farcical, or absurd.

André Bleikasten investigates these issues in the first book-length study of the novel, *Faulkner's As I Lay Dying* (1973). Like some critics before him and many after, Bleikasten contends that *As I Lay Dying* defies genre distinctions because it fuses multiple approaches to its subject. In summary, Bleikasten asserts, "*As I Lay Dying* offers us at once a comedy and the reverse of comedy, a tragedy and the derision of tragedy, an epic and the parody of an epic."

Recent critics have expanded on earlier treatments by integrating new theories in psychology, linguistics, gender relations, and cultural studies. Some scholars, for instance, examine the novel in light of Freud's psychological concepts, such as the Oedipal theory. Scholarship in gender construction has placed important emphasis on the female characters in the book. A few critics investigate Faulkner's linguistic constructs, such as Stephen

M. Ross in *Fiction's Inexhaustible Voice: Speech and Writing in Faulkner* (1989). In addition, sociological critiques have recently been revived in more complex forms.

Critics have detailed the effects of economics, politics, religion, and technology in the novel. Warwick Wadlington's 1992 book *As I Lay Dying: Stories out of Stories* is the most comprehensive of these studies. Almost all of the recent treatments view the work favorably, appreciating, if not always celebrating, Faulkner's ability to make the misadventures of the haggard, unfortunate Bundrens such a potent subject for critical scrutiny.

Criticism

Jeffrey M. Lilburn

Jeffrey M. Lilburn is a graduate student at McGill University and the author of a study guide on Margaret Atwood's The Edible Woman *as well as numerous educational essays. In the following essay, he explores the comic and tragic aspects of William Faulkner's* As I Lay Dying.

As I Lay Dying, Faulkner's first published novel after *The Sound and the Fury,* is comprised of fifty-nine sections or monologues told from the perspective of fifteen different speakers. Every member of the Bundren family narrates at least one section, in addition to various members of the community and onlookers who witness the journey from a more objective position. Because there is no central, omniscient narrator to make easy transitions from section to section, the variety of narrative voices provide the reader with multiple, sometimes conflicting perspectives. The result is a novel that can, at times, leave the reader a bit confused.

The novel is outrageously funny, yet contains certain scenes that evoke feelings of disgust, sadness, and sympathy. This unsettling combination of humorous and tragic elements has been the focus of much of the criticism of the novel, with some critics arguing that Faulkner's tale is a tragedy, others perceiving it as a comedy. However, this debate just shows how the novel has defied and resisted any attempt to impose reductive explanations or categorizations.

The basic plot of the novel is, without question, tragic. A dying mother, lying on her deathbed, watches as her eldest son builds her coffin just outside her bedroom window. After she dies, her husband and five children load her corpse onto a mule-driven wagon. They travel in the summer heat for nine days, hoping to bury her in her family's burial ground. Along the way, the mules drown, one son breaks a leg, one goes mad, the daughter is taken advantage of by a lecherous drugstore clerk, and the widowed husband—having stolen his children's money and traded his son's horse—buys himself a new set of teeth, remarries, and obtains a record player. Despite these tragic elements, the story exhibits traces of humor as well as pathos.

One critic to downplay the humorous elements of the novel is Robert Merrill. He asserts that to read *As I Lay Dying* as tragic is "to experience the novel as Faulkner conceived and wrote it." The comic moments in the book are, Merrill concedes, "genuinely amusing," but they almost always "merge with events of a truly compelling terribleness." In short, he describes *As I Lay Dying* as "Faulknerian tragedy in its most radical and original form."

On the other hand, Patricia R. Schroeder emphasizes the novel's humorous elements, contending that Faulkner's grotesque and black humor contribute to a comic framework that celebrates "the indefatigable in man." Schroeder views the novel as comedy that is the "inverse of tragedy: it celebrates community survival, applauds the status quo and affirms life in the face of death."

Schroeder also discusses the novel in relation to the "frustrated funeral," a type of Southwestern story that used humor to reduce death to comic and manageable proportions. The end of the novel is a modern example of the comic vision: "a vision capable of presenting the necessary darkness of human travail and then celebrating man's ability to overcome it." When the Bundrens begin their journey home, they do so with a new team of mules, a new set of teeth for Anse, a new wife and mother, and Dewey Dell's yet unborn child—evidence, Schroeder suggests, that "even when confronted with the death of an individual, life will prevail."

Although Merrill underscores the novel's tragic aspects, he does acknowledge that *As I Lay Dying* contains many memorable comic moments. He also observes that many of these humorous moments result from the removed position of the "non-Bundren narrators who think the Bundren odyssey a bizarre joke or a tawdry sacrilege."

Indeed, many of the novel's funniest moments are found within the sections told by Samson, Moseley and Peabody. When Moseley describes the arrival of the family in Mottson, for example,

his "version" of the journey reveals what the Bundrens themselves refuse to admit: "It had been dead eight days," he says. "It must have been like a piece of rotten cheese coming into an ant-hill."

Peabody's opinions of Anse are equally amusing. Examining Cash's broken and badly infected leg, he says: "I be damned if the man that'd let Anse Bundren treat him with raw cement ain't got more spare legs than I have." "God Almighty," he continues, "why didn't Anse carry you to the nearest sawmill and stick your leg in the saw? That would have cured it. Then you all could have stuck his head into the saw and cured a whole family."

However, considered from the perspective of the individuals undergoing the long and trying journey, putting up with intense heat and discomfort as well as with the scorn of passersby as they travel, the humorous scenes are suddenly less amusing. Moreover, while the scenes cited above intend to undermine the suffering of the family, other passages suggest that humor and laughter are not appropriate responses given the less than festive events that befall the Bundren family.

Just prior to the beginning of Whitfield's funeral service, for example, Tull, Armstid, Quick, Uncle Billy, and Peabody discuss the bridge that was washed away by the heavy rains. When Peabody makes a joke, the men "laugh, suddenly loud, then suddenly quiet again. [They then] look a little aside one another," realizing their slip. Suddenly, it seems as if the men realize the inappropriateness of their behavior.

Darl provides another example of a scene of inappropriate laughter. Moments after Addie is buried, Darl is ambushed by his sister and Jewel and handed over to two officials waiting to take him to a mental institution in Jackson. Initially surprised and hurt that Cash did not warn him about the ambush, Darl begins to laugh uncontrollably. To Cash, there is nothing funny about the scene: "I be durn if I could see anything to laugh at." Darl, on the other hand, sees plenty of humor in the situation. Of the Bundren children, only Darl sees the sheer absurdity of their journey; only he attempts to rescue his mother from the outrageous and disrespectful spectacles along the way. For this, he is considered mad by the rest of the family.

Darl has a privileged position among the novel's narrators: he has more sections than any other narrator and at times appears to possess an inexplicable gift of knowing things that he should not know. For instance, he knows that his mother has died even though he and Jewel are miles away in the wagon; in addition, he also seems to know, or at least suspect, that Anse is not Jewel's father.

Moreover, Darl's narrative role is special because he is the frequent subject of other people's narratives. Other characters notice that there is something different about Darl. As André Bleikasten has noted, there is little evidence in the early sections to suggest insanity and in the later sections his actions appear "rather more reasonable than those of the rest of the family." Even Cora and Vernon Tull agree that Darl simply needs a wife "to straighten him out"—evidence that not all who know him and watch him and talk about him agree that he is mad.

Consequently, Darl's capture and subsequent incarceration raise questions of the reliability of the novel's narrative. To Bleikasten, Darl's laughter at the novel's end makes it "hard to tell on which side lies sanity and on which side madness." To Cash, who for a moment thinks his brother did the right thing by trying to burn their mother's coffin, there "ain't none of us pure crazy and ain't none of us pure sane until the balance of us talks him that-a-way." He questions the right of one man to call another man crazy and concludes: "It's like it ain't so much what a fellow does, but it's the way the majority of folks is looking at him when he does it."

Darl is sent away to Jackson because a majority of people think him queer and because his family does not want to risk being sued by Gillespie. His feelings are never considered. Darl's disturbing laughter thus adds to the novel's unsettling ambiguity because it conflates further the comic and the tragic and makes us question the appropriateness of our own laughter.

By the end of the novel, however, laughter seems to be the only response. After nine days spent defying all kinds of adversities in order to bring Addie's corpse to its final resting place, the funeral procession climaxes in a scene that is described in less than two lines. All we hear of the actual burial is: "we got it filled and covered ...." The same sentence then describes how Darl is betrayed by his family and sent away to Jackson. The few remaining sections focus not the family's loss or on their sadness on burying the family matriarch, but on the individual motives that were the real driving force behind the journey.

The final section in particular—when Anse introduces the new Mrs. Bundren to his children—utilizes humor to underscore the outrageous nature of the situation. Underlying this humor is the pain and unsettling knowledge of what occurred in the sections leading up to this absurd ending: the brutal betrayal of Darl, news of Cash's serious injury, Dewey Dell's physical abuse, and Addie's final, humiliating journey. The introduction of the new Mrs. Bundren provides one of the biggest laughs in the novel—yet somehow such an ending hardly seems like a celebration of life's victory over death. Instead, this scene, like almost all of the novel's funny moments, produces an awkward laughter that is tinged with anguish and remorse.

Source: Jeffrey M. Lilburn, in an essay for *Novels for Students,* Gale, 2000.

André Bleikasten

In the following essay, Bleikasten discusses the complexities he has identified within As I Lay Dying.

Addie Bundren, a farmer's wife from the backwoods hills of Mississippi, has just died, and in order to respect her last wish her family undertakes a long and perilous journey to carry her coffin to a distant graveyard at Jefferson. That is the story of *As I Lay Dying.* It appears simple. But such a summary of the tale leaves everything to be said about the novel. For what strikes us immediately is less the story itself than the way it is told, or rather the contrast between the tale and the telling, between the simplicity of the anecdote and the sophistication of the narrative method. To make something of the pathetic, macabre, or comic potential of his subject, Faulkner could simply have relied on the proven recipes of traditional narrative. He chose, however, a more adventurous and more difficult path, experimenting again—as he had already done in *The Sound and the Fury* and, more timidly, in his early novels—with new techniques. If, by its subject matter, *As I Lay Dying* belongs to the oral and literary tradition of folktales and tall stories, the novelist's approach to his art is definitely modern. As in *The Sound and the Fury,* Faulkner uses here James Joyce's "stream-of-consciousness" method: *As I Lay Dying* is presented as a series of interior monologues, and each one of these, as well as relating a moment in the action, shows us its refraction through an individual consciousness.

But instead of arranging the monologues in large, compact sections as he had done in his previous novel, Faulkner fragments them with seeming arbitrariness. *As I Lay Dying* surprises one straightaway by its utterly disjointed composition. In fact, only in the epistolary novel could one find precedents for such extreme segmentation, and the

What Do I Read Next?

- *The Sound and the Fury* (1929) is Faulkner's first extended attempt at the stream-of-consciousness narrative techniques that he successfully employs in *As I Lay Dying*. Both novels also concern familial relationships and include penetrating psychological portraits. Many critics note similarities between Quentin Compson and Darl as well as the idiot Benjy Compson and young Vardaman.

- Faulkner's *The Hamlet* (1940) is the first in a trilogy of novels that chronicle the rise of the "poor white" Snopes family.

- *Tobacco Road* (1932), a novel by Erskine Caldwell, depicts a poor family that overcomes extreme hardship in order to survive. Caldwell's characters are noted for their ignorance and often primitive reactions to situations.

- George Washington Harris's Sut Lovingood stories, published in periodicals from 1843 until 1869 and collected in *Sut Lovingood's Yarns* (1966), are comedies in the tall tale tradition, featuring an incorrigible narrator and outlandish escapades. Faulkner professed to be a fan of these stories.

- *The Nigger of the "Narcissus"* (1897), a novel by Joseph Conrad, depicts a ship journey that is fraught with peril. The story revolves around James Wait, a dying, black sailor who becomes the center of the crew's attention. Many critics have noted the similarities of this novel to *As I Lay Dying*.

- C. Vann Woodward's influential historical study, *Origins of the New South: 1877-1913* (1951), offers a detailed account of Southern life and politics.

- *The Mind of the South* (1941), a book written by W. J. Cash, is a controversial study of Southern race relations, class systems, religion, and philosophies. The book has elicited both praise and condemnation.

---

brevity of the sections calls to mind the scenes of a play rather than the chapters of a work of fiction. Hence an impression of discontinuity, which is increased on reading by the almost kaleidoscopic rotation of the viewpoints. In each section the perspective shifts, the lighting changes, so that each time the reader is caught off balance and forced to make constant readjustments if he wants to follow the narrative through all its twists and turns.

To these breaks in the storytelling are added the equally puzzling switches in tone and style. They also derive to a large extent from the mobility of the point of view, since whenever that changes, the story assumes the voice of a different narrator. Almost all the characters of the novel, it is true, speak the same rural idiom, and their monologues often have the familiar ring of a straightforward oral tale. But Faulkner is not content simply to exploit the stylistic resources of this vernacular for humorous effects, by playing on the naive vigor of its diction and on the drollery of its unorthodox grammar. Nor does he merely vary its use according to the personality and mood of the speaker. On the earthy base of this rustic colloquial prose, he continually traces the startling arabesques of his own rhetoric. The author's presence is particularly obvious in the lyrical outbursts and metaphysical reveries of Darl, whose style is virtually indistinguishable from the writer's own. It is also to be felt in Addie Bundren's terse, impassioned eloquence in section 40. Yet this richer, denser, more freely inventive style is not restricted to any one character: even in those whose linguistic capacities seem severely limited—in Vardaman, for example, or Dewey Dell—language sometimes takes flight, and from the most halting prose suddenly springs, by virtue of an unexpected metaphor, a poetic vision which transfigures it.

Small wonder, then, that *As I Lay Dying* embarrasses critics who are hard put to define its genre. In its style as well as in its structure and significance, this will-o'-the-wisp novel seems to elude all attempts at classification.

Is it to be considered as a naturalistic novel, as a commentary on the economic deprivation and cultural illiteracy of poor whites? Faulkner's Mississippi hill-country farmers have been compared to Caldwell's Georgia sharecroppers; the odyssey of the Bundrens has been likened to the exodus of the Joads in *The Grapes of Wrath.* Yet even though Faulkner gives realism its due, nothing was further from his intentions than offering his readers an objective portrait of a family of poor whites: "it does sort of amuse me when I hear 'em talking about the sociological picture that I present in something like *As I Lay Dying,* for instance." Is it more relevant, then, to define the book as a philosophical novel? There is no doubt that moral and metaphysical concerns occupy—as in most of Faulkner's novels—a central place, but such a label, apart from recalling the lengthy arguments of the novel of ideas, tends to overlook the fact that the language of *As I Lay Dying* is the language of fiction, and it tells us nothing of the specific nature of the work.

If one tries to classify it according to mood rather than content, the same difficulties arise, and only at the cost of oversimplification can one manage to fit it into a recognized category. While allowing provisos, some have emphasized its comic elements, others its tragic aspects, and still others would make an epic of it. Does *As I Lay Dying* express Faulkner's "comic vision"? None would disagree that the novel lacks the sustained tension of *The Sound and the Fury:* there is humor in abundance, from the most innocent to the most macabre, and in all sorts of ways—in the grotesqueness of several characters as well as the extravagance of many an episode—it could be taken for a country farce. But there is too much grimness in the farce for the book to be considered as essentially comic, and the features relating it to tragedy are surely as significant: the story of the Bundrens, like that of the Compsons or the Sutpens, is the story of a family adrift, with all its tensions and conflicts; it begins with the account of a last agony, ends with scenes of hatred, violence, and madness, and the two most remarkable characters in the novel—Addie and Darl—are both, because of their tortured awareness of their destiny, purely tragic figures. Lastly, *As I Lay Dying* also has unmistakable affinities with the epic: the terrible ordeals undergone by the Bundrens in the course of their journey and their valiant struggle against the unbridled elements in-

evitably bring to mind the heroic exploits of myth and legend. And the very idea which, according to Faulkner, gave rise to the novel appears, in its sheer simplicity, as an epic idea: "I took this family and subjected them to the two greatest catastrophes which man can suffer—flood and fire, that's all."

Epic, tragedy, comedy? This is obviously not the right question to ask. To force the novel into the genres of traditional poetics is to ignore the dissonances from which it derives its originality. The distinctive aesthetic quality of *As I Lay Dying* is precisely that it is not an epic or a tragedy or a comedy, but, as it were, a gamble on being all three at once. It would perhaps be more worthwhile, therefore, to try another approach and see the novel through its narrative. What Faulkner is telling is the story of a journey. Now the journey is one of the narrative archetypes: from Homer's *Odyssey* to Joyce's, from the adventurous navigators of mythology and folklore to the restless wandering heroes of the modern novel and cinema, it has held its place through countless variations as one of the basic patterns of narration. On reading *As I Lay Dying,* one might almost think that the novelist sought to bring into play the different forms that travelers' tales have taken over the centuries, or at least to make echoes of them reverberate throughout. In the humble state of its protagonists, in the pithy vigor of its realism and the earthy tang of its humor, the novel—a story about people on the road—recalls the picaresque tradition (Anse would easily qualify for the role of the rogue). In the weirdness of its atmosphere and the often wildly implausible nature of the reported events, it makes one think of the marvelous or fantastic journeys of folktale, epic, and myth. Behind this polarity of the real and the imaginary, the distinction between "novel" and "romance" established by Simms and Hawthorne, and taken up by Richard Chase, will be easily recognized. On the face of it, *As I Lay Dying* may be taken for a rustic novel, but it is primarily a "romance" in the great symbolist tradition of American literature. If only in the motif of the strenuous journey, with all its wealth of connotations, it continues the exploration and illustration of a theme which, from the novels of James Fenimore Cooper through *Moby Dick* and *Huckleberry Finn,* has been central to American fiction.

The baffling diversity of tones and moods which characterizes the novel goes some way towards explaining the variety of interpretations it has provoked. *As I Lay Dying* offers us at once a comedy and the reverse of comedy, a tragedy and the derision of tragedy, an epic and the parody of epic. Is this simply the wry dialectic of humor, or is it not rather that the ruling force is irony? By thus forcing different genres to swallow each other, does one not end by clearing the way for absurdity? Judging by the closing pages, one might indeed think that absurdity wins the day. When Darl bursts out laughing at the monkeylike spectacle of his banana-munching family, it is hard to tell on which side lies reason and on which side madness. And in the final scene—which rings like a mocking echo of the recognition scenes one finds in the sentimental novels of the eighteenth century—when Anse, "kind of hangdog and proud too," introduces the new, duck-shaped and popeyed Mrs. Bundren to his perplexed children, the whole novel seems to tumble into sheer grotesqueness. As for the journey itself, it may seem quite as preposterous as this farcical ending. The stubbornness of the Bundrens in pursuing their funeral task reminds one at times of the blind obstinacy of burying beetles, and the result of their undertaking is perhaps less a victory of willpower than the triumph of inertia.

Are we then to conclude that all the values traditionally associated with the perilous journey are here reversed for the purpose of travesty, and that the epic overtones of the tale are only intended to point up the utter incongruity of this funeral steeplechase? Or is the burlesque not aimed rather at masking the praise of that eminently Faulknerian virtue, endurance? That irony informs the whole design of *As I Lay Dying* is beyond dispute. The point is that it may be read in more than one way. There is little justification therefore in singling out one pattern of meaning and imposing it on the novel as the only valid interpretation. As a matter of fact, all attempts to date at explaining its metaphysics or codifying its ethics have been more or less arbitrary oversimplifications. As one critic very rightly notes: "The novel has a wonderful immunity to schematization; it is innocent of both a moral and a morality, and it seems to breathe out rather than posit a world view."

Faulkner here describes a world both absurd and living. He does not tell us whether we should reject the living as absurd, or accept the absurd as living. *As I Lay Dying* leaves its readers in a state of enthralled perplexity very similar to the stupor of the novel's characters in the face of what happens to them. This is not to say that the book cannot be discussed. To be satisfied with a single meaning, however, would be to misunderstand the subtle interplay of its ambiguities.

When Faulkner was questioned on *As I Lay Dying,* he invariably replied that it was a *tour de force.* As much by the speed with which it was written as by the audacity of its technique and the superb virtuosity of its art, the novel is precisely that. It charms like a brilliant impromptu, dazzles like a perfectly executed trapeze exercise. Of all Faulkner's novels, it is perhaps the most agile, the most adroit, the one in which the writer's mastery of his craft and the versatility of his gifts reveal themselves in the most spectacular way. It is also, beneath its guise of an improvisation, one of his most complex and most intriguing works. Faulkner no doubt wrote more ambitious and more deeply moving books: *As I Lay Dying* does not achieve the grandeur of *The Sound and the Fury,* the novelist's most "splendid failure"; it does not hold us under the same dark spell as *Absalom, Absalom!* nor does if offer the imaginative scope of *Go Down, Moses.* But only slightly below these peaks, it holds its place as a masterpiece.

Source: André Bleikasten, Introduction to *Faulkner's As I Lay Dying,* Indiana University Press, 1973, pp. 3-9.

Irving Howe

In the following essay, Howe praises Faulkner for his ability to "blend extreme and incongruous effects—the sublime and the trivial, anguish and absurdity, a wretched journey through the sun and a pathetic journey toward kinship" in As I Lay Dying.

A story of a journey, an account of adventures on the road—this may be the outward form of the novel, but the journey proves exceedingly curious and the adventures disconcert. Having died while a son sawed her coffin beneath her window, Addie Bundren is carted away in the family wagon through the back roads of Yoknapatawpha. The family thereby honors her reiterated wish that she be buried in the Jefferson cemetery. Unwilling adventurers, the Bundrens can do nothing well; their journey, like their spiritual life, is erratic and confused. Prompted by awe for the dead, and by a cluster of private motives, they plod through mishaps both comic and terrible—fire and flood, suffering and stupidity—until, at last, they reach the town. The putrescent corpse is buried, the daughter fails in her effort to get an abortion, one son is badly injured, another has gone mad, and at the very end, the father suddenly remarries.

Crossing farce with anguish, *As I Lay Dying* is a story of misfortune: the father Anse is certainly right, though hardly for the reasons he supposes, when he declares himself a "misfortunate man."

There is a kind of story, like Leskov's "The En-chanted Wanderer," which heaps so many troubles on the back of its hero that the final effect is perversely comic; to this family of fiction *As I Lay Dying* is distantly related. Recalling the Dostoevskian novel in its coarse mixture of emotions, the book stumbles from catastrophe to catastrophe—a bewildering marathon of troubles. Suspense is maintained by the likelihood that still greater troubles are to come, while the ability of some characters to survive with equanimity becomes a wry celebration of mankind.

That *As I Lay Dying* is something more than a record of peregrine disaster we soon discover. As it circles over a journey in space, the novel also plunges into the secret life of the journeyers. Each of them conducts the action a little way while reciting the burden of his mind; the novel resembles a cantata in which a theme is developed and varied through a succession of voices. In *As I Lay Dying* the theme is death, death as it shapes life. The outer action, never to be neglected and always fearsomely spectacular, is a journey in a wagon; the inner action is the attempt of the Bundrens to define themselves as members of a family at the moment the family is perishing.

Neither fire nor flood is the crux of the novel, nor any physical action at all; it is Addie Bundren's soliloquy, her thoughts as she lay dying. Until that moment in the book, Faulkner lightly traces the tangled relationships among the Bundrens—the father, the daughter Dewey Dell, the sons Cash, Darl, Jewel, and Vardaman. It seems at first that Darl, the most introspective of the sons, is the cause and catalyst of family tensions. He guesses Dewey Dell's pregnancy and silently taunts her with his knowledge; he hovers over Jewel with eager attentiveness and broods upon the rivalry between them. But Addie's soliloquy makes clear that the conflicts among the children are rooted in the lives of their parents, in the failure of a marriage. It is Addie who dominates the book, thrusting her sons against each other as if they were warring elements of her own character. From her soliloquy until the end of the novel, the action is a physical resolution of the Bundrens' emotional troubles, a resolution which must be achieved if the body is to be buried in peace.

Dying, Addie remembers her youth. Always she had searched for a relation with people by which to impress her will; her energy had never found full release. As a schoolteacher she "would look forward to the times when they faulted, so I could whip them. When the switch fell I could feel it upon my flesh; when it welted and ridged it was my blood that ran, and I would think with each blow of the switch: Now you are aware of me! Now I am something in your secret and selfish life." But when she married Anse she learned that, for all her fierce willfulness, she would never penetrate to his secret and selfish life.

First came Cash and then "I knew that living was terrible. That was when I learned that words are no good; that words don't ever fit even what they are trying to say at … Love, [Anse] called it. But I had been used to words for a long time. I knew that word was like the others: a shape to fill a lack." Cash she cherished, for through his birth she reached understanding, both of Anse and herself. But when Darl came, "At first I would not believe it. Then I believed I would kill Anse. It was as though he had tricked me, hidden within a word like within a paper screen and struck me in the back through it." After Darl's birth, Anse seemed to die for her, though "He did not know he was dead, then. Sometimes I would lie by him in the dark, hearing the land that was now of my blood and flesh, and I would think: Anse. Why Anse. Why are you Anse." And then her moment of ecstasy: "I believed I had found it—that the reason was the duty to be alive, to the terrible blood." Sinning with preacher Whitfield, she bore Jewel. What came after that seemed unimportant: "I gave Anse Dewey Dell to negative Jewel—Vardaman to replace the child I had robbed him of. And now he had three children that are his and not mine. And then I could get ready to die."

The way in which the Bundren children are born, remarks Olga Vickery in a suggestive study of *As I Lay Dying,* establishes the "level of their awareness of [Addie] and the mode of their participation in her burial." Cash, the earnest and admirable carpenter, is the moral head of the family; reflecting Addie's strength and self-possession at the moment she first realizes that "living was terrible," he is free of the furies that torment his brothers. Too free, perhaps; his imagination limps behind his conscience, and he is so absorbed in the coffin that he does not notice a family crisis darkening about him.

Unlike Cash, Darl is capable of projecting himself into the feelings of his brothers; but he cannot establish a firm and distinct personality, one with which they can come to secure terms. Curious though the comparison may seem, this poor-white farm boy resembles one of those characters who prowl through Henry James's late novels, all pry-ing awareness and no core of self. His eyes con-tinually lighting on the family wounds, Darl speaks more frequently and in many more scenes than the other Bundrens. He senses that Jewel is the truly beloved son despite the fact that he, Darl, proffers and receives the gestures of love; and he knows, too, that the horse on which Jewel bestows such fierce care is a surrogate for Addie. Darl even hints that he has discovered the reason for Addie's vio-lent love of Jewel:

> She would fix him special things to eat and hide them for him. And that may have been when I first found it out, that Addie Bundren should be hiding anything she did, who had tried to teach us that deceit was such that, in a world where it was, nothing else could be very bad or very important, not even poverty. And at times when I went in to go to bed she would be sitting in the dark by Jewel where he was asleep. And I knew that she was hating herself for that deceit and hating Jewel because she had to love him so that she had to act the deceit.

It now becomes clear what Darl meant when he said, somewhat earlier, "I cannot love my mother because I have no mother. Jewel's mother is a horse." The motherless Darl must acknowl-edge, "I don't know what I am."

Jewel speaks only once, and then in a fantasy which aligns mother and himself against the Bun-drens: "It would just be me and her on a high hill and me rolling the rocks down the hill at their faces … by God until she was quiet." Dewey Dell and Vardaman, both the issue of Addie's indifference, are vegetable and idiot, the one concerned only with her ease and the other pure in feeling but un-able to distinguish between dead mother and the fish he carries in his hand. The ineffectual Anse de-claims in self-pity: "It's a trial. But I don't begrudge her it. No man can say I begrudge her it." Addie is right; in some deep sense her husband is dead.

Softened and dulled, Addie's emotional yearn-ings reappear among her children, as indeed they suffuse the entire novel. In their struggle for self-definition, her sons discover that to answer the question, *Who am I?* they must first consider, *What was my mother and how did she shape me?* The ri-valry between Darl and Jewel, which recurs through the book like an underground tremor, is a rivalry in sonship, and it is Darl's sense of being unwanted which drives him to his obsessive ques-tioning and finally his fall into madness. As the children try, each in his fumbling or inarticulate way, to discover the meaning of being a son or brother, Addie's authority persists and increases. And in this search for identity they demonstrate

their mother's conviction that language is vanity which action is the test of life: "I would think how words go straight up in a thin line, quick and harm-less, and how terribly doing goes along the earth, clinging to it." This sentence prefigures the Bun-dren history and announces the theme of the book.

Tyrannical in its edict of love and rejection, the will of the mother triumphs through the fate of her children. Cash, the accepted son, endures a pre-posterous excess of pain largely because of his own inattention and the stupidity of the others. Thereby he learns the meaning of kinship, his brothers im-pinging on him through the torment they cause him; and at the end he takes his place as the mature wit-ness of the wreckage of the family. Jewel, by break-ing from his violent obsession, fulfills his mother's prophecy: "He is my cross and he will be my sal-vation. He will save me from the water and the fire." Literally, that is what Jewel does, and when he parts from his horse in order to speed Addie's burial he achieves a direct expression of filial love. Dewey Dell, munching her banana, continues to move in an orbit of egoism; Vardaman, pathetic and troubled, is locked in his idiocy; and Anse gets himself another wife, "duck-shaped" and with "hard-looking pop eyes."

Darl is the family sacrifice. An unwanted son, he seeks continually to find a place in the family. The pressures of his secret knowledge, the pain of observing the journey, the realization that he can never act upon what he knows—these drive Darl to madness. Now he dares taunt Jewel: "Whose son are you? Your mother was a horse; but who was your father, Jewel?" From the sobriety of Cash he moves to the derangement of Vardaman; in a bril-liant passage he and Vardaman "listen" to their mother in the coffin:

> She was under the apple tree and Darl and I go across the moon and the cat jumps down and runs and we can hear her inside the wood. "Hear?" Darl says. "Put your ear close."
>
> I put my ear close and I can hear her. Only I can't tell what she is saying.
>
> "What is she saying, Darl?" I say. "Who is she talk-ing to?"
>
> "She's talking to God," Darl says. "She is calling on Him to help her."
>
> "What does she want Him to do?" I say.
>
> "She wants Him to hide her away from the sight of man," Darl says.
>
> "Why does she want to hide her away from the sight of man, Darl?"
>
> "So she can lay down her life," Darl says.

Betrayed by Dewey Dell and assaulted by Jewel, Darl is taken away to the asylum. Only Cash understands him; only Cash and Vardaman pity him. Referring to himself in the third person, a sign of extreme self-estrangement, Darl says: "Darl is our brother, our brother Darl. Our brother Darl is in a cage in Jackson where, his grimed hands lying light in the quiet interstices, looking out he foams. 'Yes yes yes yes yes yes yes yes'." To the end it is a search for kinship that obsesses Darl, and his cryptic row of affirmatives may signify a last, pathetic effort to proclaim his brotherhood.

Upon this investigation of a family's inner history, Faulkner has lavished a dazzling virtuosity. Like *The Sound and the Fury, As I Lay Dying* stakes everything on the awareness of its characters. There is neither omniscient narrator nor disinterested observer at the rim of the story; nothing being told, all must be shown. But where *The Sound and the Fury* is divided into four long sections, of which three convey distinct and sustained points of view, *As I Lay Dying* is broken into sixty fragments in which fifteen characters speak or reflect at various turns of the action and on numerous levels of consciousness. The prolonged surrender to a few memories in *The Sound and the Fury* permits a full dramatic recall; the nervous transitions in *As I Lay Dying* encourage a sensitive recording of character change. It would be difficult to exaggerate the complexity of *As I Lay Dying,* or the skill with which Faulkner manipulates its diverse points of view. So remarkable is this skill, the critic runs a danger of regarding the novel merely as a fascinating exercise in dexterity.

Once it is agreed that in a final estimate the critical emphasis belongs elsewhere, this dexterity is a thing to enjoy and admire—particularly the way each Bundren, speaking in his own behalf, comes to illuminate the others. The first word of the book, uttered by Darl, is "Jewel," and it announces a major theme: Darl's fitful preoccupation with his brother. On the same page Darl quickly sketches Jewel: "Still staring straight ahead, his pale eyes like wood set into his wooden face, he crosses the floor in four strides with the rigid gravity of a cigar-store Indian dressed in patched overalls and endued with life from the hips down." Several pages later Darl speaks again, describing Jewel as the latter caresses his horse with obscene ferocity. After these introductory glimpses, Jewel comes forward for one page, a page of fantasy concerning his frozen love for his mother. The perspective shifts to Cora Tull, a comically righteous neighbor who sees

much yet not enough, and from her we learn that Jewel has been favored by years of Addie's "self-denial and downright perversity." Speaking for the first time, Dewey Dell remarks that "Jewel don't care about anything he is not kin to us in caring, not carekin." When Darl learns his mother is dead, he thinks immediately of Jewel: *"I say, she is dead, Jewel, Addie Bundren is dead."*

Jewel has now been seen from several points of view, each different yet complementary to the other, and he has spoken once; but he is to be fully understood only when we reach the Addie section and discover the condition of his birth. "With Jewel—I lay by the lamp, holding up my own head, watching him cap and suture it before he breathed—the wild blood boiled away and the sound of it ceased." We can now surmise why it is he, and none of his brothers, who saves Addie from water and fire, why he consents to sell his horse, why he pummels Darl when they reach Jefferson. From a multitude of slanted impressions and remarks, an image of Jewel is slowly composed; but any final interpretation must be our own for there is no detached observer who speaks for Faulkner, not even to the extent that Dilsey does in *The Sound and the Fury.* The secondary characters surrounding the Bundrens as a chorus of comment and comedy never achieve more than a partial understanding. Faulkner presents; the reader must conclude.

The method of *As I Lay Dying* brings with it the danger that the frequent breaks in point of view will interfere with the flow of narrative. In a few scenes this does happen, particularly in those of Darl's reflections which become so densely "poetic" they claim more attention than they warrant. But once Addie's soliloquy is reached, the physical journey in the wagon and the psychological journey through the family closely parallel each other; and the first gains dramatic relevance and lucidity from the second.

Each character provides a line of action and impression, but not, of course, with the same sureness and plausibility. Picturesque as they may be, Dewey Dell and Vardaman are hardly bold originals; they serve well enough as foils and accessories, but they seem to have been borrowed from the common store of Southern fiction rather than created in their own right. One minds less their being measured from a ready-made pattern than the neatness and predictability of the measure—their very idiosyncrasies prove neat and predictable. Still, a distinction is to be made even among stereotypes; Vardaman has a kind of stock vividness, while Dewey Dell is the one Bundren who fails to emerge clearly.

Similar strictures might be made against the father but not, I think, with equal justice. Faulkner's critics have been very hard on Anse, cracking the whips of morality over his frail back. Poor Anse, he is hardly the man to support judgment; he is merely a figure to be watched, resourceful in exploiting his laziness, gifted at proclaiming the proper generalities at not quite the proper time, and in his shuffling sort of way, diffident and almost humble. In drawing Anse, Faulkner may have had in mind one or another important moral lesson; more probably, he had struck upon a universal comic type, the tyrannically inept *schlemiehl* whose bumbling is so unrelieved and sloth so unalloyed that he ends by evoking only an impatient, irritated sympathy.

But Darl raises problems. Because we quickly identify with him, and eagerly respond to his restless search for self-knowledge, Darl's sudden breakdown comes as a jolt; and while Faulkner's motives for introducing it may easily be inferred, I doubt that he has sufficiently prepared for it in the immediately preceding text. Darl's part of the novel is an instance of the "misplaced middle"; the introductory presentation bulks so large that there remains little space in which to prepare and justify the denouement. Given the large demands made on his vision, Darl's later collapse could be accepted only if Faulkner devoted more attention than he does to showing the boy's movement from sanity to madness. There are hints, of course: for the first time Darl dares taunt Jewel openly and Vardaman alludes to his knowledge that it is Darl who has fired the barn. But these intimations span a gap that needs to be filled. Darl's madness does not follow "inevitably" from what has preceded it; and, if only because our identification with him has been too sharply punctured, we are left with a surplus of unused sympathy.

Quite as excessive as Darl's fate is the burden of language Faulkner thrusts upon him. Between author and character there seems to be an unfortunate personal entanglement, certainly a lack of ironic distance—and in a way that recalls Faulkner's relation to Quentin Compson in *The Sound and the Fury*. When Darl is used merely to observe the other Bundrens, as in the splendid scene in which he remembers Jewel's sacrifice to buy his horse, the closeness between author and protagonist does not disturb, for then Darl is largely

removed from our vision. But when he turns in upon himself, exploring his muddled consciousness, he is assigned reflections violently out of character. That he occasionally abandons Southern idiom for poetic reverie is in itself unexceptionable, a heightened style being as good a way as any to simulate the life of the inner mind. Nor is the difficulty merely that these reflections do not seem cognate to Darl; they would be as dubious from a philosopher as from a farm boy:

> The river itself is not a hundred yards across, and pa and Vernon and Vardaman and Dewey Dell are the only things in sight not of that single monotony of desolation leaning with that terrific quality a little from right to left, as though we had reached the place where the motion of the wasted world accelerates just before the final precipice. Yet they appear dwarfed. It is as though the space between us were time: an irrevocable quality. It is as though time, no longer running straight before us in a diminishing line, now runs parallel between us like a looping string, the distance being the doubling accretion of the thread and not the interval between.

About the remaining Bundrens there can be no qualms. Jewel is done with harsh, rapid strokes, seldom brushed as delicately as in the portrait of Darl; but for a figure whose behavior forms a ballet of turbulence the harshness and rapidity are exactly right. Addie Bundren is a remarkable image of a passionate woman who, except for an illicit interval, has known only barrenness. Driven dark into herself, unable to express her love for her favorite son, and ending with a realism of attitude more stringent than her husband can imagine, Addie spends her years in loneliness and can bequeath her sons nothing but unfulfilled passion. In her desperation to preserve her family and to raise her children properly, she seems classically American. This harassed, angular and fervent woman—have we not met her in Willa Cather's novels of pioneer life and Sherwood Anderson's memoirs of his childhood? Long before we reach Addie's soliloquy we see her overbearing effect upon the children; and when she does speak, it comes as an explosion of ecstasy—a piece of writing that for emotional intensity may justly be compared with the great forest scenes of *The Scarlet Letter*.

It is on Cash, however, that Faulkner bestows his most admirable touches. Lacking the intensity of Jewel or the moody restlessness of Darl, he comes through with greater resonance and richness than the other Bundrens; he alone among the brothers is neither delusional nor obsessed; and he is one of the few Faulkner characters who are not merely revealed but also grow as a consequence of their experience. At the beginning he is lightly sketched into the story, with an affectionate mockery that hardly suggests his later importance. How far did you fall, Cash, that time you slipped off the church roof? "Twenty eight foot, four and a half inches, about," he solemnly replies. And when he speaks directly for the first time, it is to explain in thirteen marvelously adduced reasons why "I made [the coffin] on the bevel. 1. There is more surface for the nails to grip … 13. It makes a neater job."

Throughout the journey Cash says very little and suffers in quiet; but he is now watching the drama within his family, almost as if he were seeing it for the first time. Thereby he gains an understanding of the journey, implicitly taking it as a test of character and integrity. He matures in his feelings and in his power to express them. Sometimes, he says about Darl,

> … I ain't so sho who's got ere a right to say when a man is crazy and when he ain't. Sometimes I think it ain't none of us pure crazy and ain't none of us pure sane until the balance of us talks him that-a-way. It's like it ain't so much what a fellow does, but it's the way the majority of folks is looking at him when he does it.

This growth from unimaginative self-containment to humane concern appears again in Cash's musings over a phonograph:

> I reckon it's a good thing we ain't got ere a one of them. I reckon I wouldn't never get no work done a-tall for listening to it. I don't know if a little music ain't the nicest thing a fellow can have. Seems like when he comes in tired of a night, it ain't nothing could rest him like having a little music played and him resting.

But surely the final emphasis belongs not to the novel's matter or technique; its claim to our affection rests on more than its study of family relations or its brilliance in handling points of view. Such things matter only insofar as they bring us closer to the book's essential insight or vision, its moral tone. Of all Faulkner's novels, *As I Lay Dying* is the warmest, the kindliest and most affectionate. The notion that Faulkner is a misanthrope wallowing in horrors is possible only to those who have not read the book or have read it with willful obtuseness. In no other work is he so receptive to people, so ready to take and love them, to hear them out and record their turns of idiom, their melodies of speech. Smaller in scope than Faulkner's other important novels, *As I Lay Dying* lacks the tragic consistency of *The Sound and the Fury,* the grandeur of *Absalom, Absalom!,* the power of *Light in August.* But it shines with virtues distinctly its own: a superb sympathy for the lowly and inco-

herent, an implicit belief that the spiritual life of a Darl Bundren can be as important as the spiritual life of a Lambert Strether, a readiness on Faulkner's part to immerse himself in people radically unlike himself. Look—he seems to be saying—look at the capacity for suffering and dignity which human beings have, even the most absurdly wretched of them! The book is a triumph of fraternal feeling, and because it is that, a triumph, as well, in the use of idiom. No finer example of American lyricism, that indigenous style stemming from *Huckleberry Finn,* could be found in twentieth-century writing than this passage in which Darl remembers….

> When I was a boy I first learned how much better water tastes when it has set a while in a cedar bucket. Warmish-cool, with a faint taste like the hot July wind in cedar trees smells. It has to set at least six hours, and be drunk from a gourd. Water should never be drunk from metal.
>
> And at night it is better still. I used to lie on the pallet in the hall, waiting until I could hear them all asleep, so I could get up and go back to the bucket. It would be black, the shelf black, the still surface of the water a round orifice in nothingness, where before I stirred it awake with the dipper I could see maybe a star or two in the bucket, and maybe in the dipper a star or two before I drank. After that I was bigger, older. Then I would wait until they all went to sleep so I could lie with my shirt-tail up, hearing them asleep, feeling myself without touching myself, feeling the cool silence blowing upon my parts and wondering if Cash was yonder in the darkness doing it too, had been doing it perhaps for the last two years before I could have wanted to or could have.

Or consider this passage in which Darl describes Addie's coffin being carried into the house:

> It is light, yet they move slowly; empty, yet they carry it carefully; lifeless, yet they move with hushed precautionary words to one another, speaking of it as though, complete, it now slumbered lightly alive, waiting to come awake. On the dark floor their feet clump awkwardly, as though for a long time they have not walked on floors.

Almost as vivid is Jewel thinking of his mother as she dies:

> … her hands laying on the quilt like two of them roots dug up and tried to wash and you couldn't get them clean. I can see the fan and Dewey Dell's arm. I said if you'd just let her alone. Sawing and knocking, and keeping the air always moving so fast on her face that when you're tired you can't breathe it, and that goddamn adze going One lick less. One lick less …

Because he writes of the Bundrens with a comely and tactful gravity, a deep underlying respect, Faulkner is able to blend extreme and incongruous effects—the sublime and the trivial, anguish and absurdity, a wretched journey through the sun and a pathetic journey toward kinship. An American epic, *As I Lay Dying* is country farce and human tragedy. The marvel is that to be one it had to be the other.

Source: Irving Howe, "*As I Lay Dying,*" in *William Faulker: A Critical Study,* Random House, 1951, pp. 127-42.

Sources

André Bleikasten, *Faulkner's As I Lay Dying,* translated by Roger Little, Indiana University Press, 1973, pp. 7, 73.

Cleanth Brooks, *William Faulkner: The Yoknapatawpha Country,* Yale University Press, 1963.

Malcolm Cowley, "Introduction to *The Portable Faulkner,*" in *Faulkner: A Collection of Critical Essays,* edited by Robert Penn Warren, Prentice-Hall, Inc., 1966, p. 36.

Irving Howe, "*As I Lay Dying,*" in *William Faulkner: A Critical Study,* The University of Chicago Press, 1951, 1975, p. 189.

Olga Vickery, *The Novels of William Faulkner: A Critical Interpretation,* Louisiana State University Press, 1959.

Warwick Wadlington, *As I Lay Dying: Stories out of Stories,* Twayne Publishers, 1992.

Floyd C. Watkins, "*As I Lay Dying:* The Dignity of Earth," in *In Time and Place: Some Origins of American Fiction,* The University of Georgia Press, p. 180.

For Further Study

Carvel Collins, "The Pairing of *The Sound and the Fury* and *As I Lay Dying,*" *Princeton University Library Chronicle,* Vol. 18, 1957, pp. 114-23.
    Carvel's influential early study details myth patterns in the book, particularly Greek myth.

Dianne L. Cox, editor, *William Faulkner's As I Lay Dying: A Critical Casebook,* Garland Publishing, Inc., 1985.
    This important collection includes many valuable essays examining such topics as Faulkner's narrative design, language, characterization, and major themes.

Philip Hanson, "Rewriting Poor White Myth in *As I Lay Dying,*" *Arkansas Quarterly,* Vol. 2, No. 4, 1993, pp. 308-24.

Employing the economic, cultural, and political environment of the Bundrens, Hanson explores Faulkner's treatment of beast imagery in relation to poor white Southerners.

Elizabeth Hayes, "Tension Between Darl and Jewel," *Southern Literary Journal,* Vol. 24, No. 2, Spring, 1992, pp. 49-61.
    Hayes analyzes the centrality of Darl and Jewel's relationship to the novel. In contrast to many critics, she denies that Darl hates Jewel, contending that he sees Jewel as a means to verifying his own identity.

Robert Hemenway, "Enigmas of Being in *As I Lay Dying,*" *Modern Fiction Studies,* Vol. 19, Summer, 1970, pp. 133-46.
    Hemenway analyzes Darl's most important philosophical monologues and conversations.

Lynn Gartrell Levins, *Faulkner's Heroic Design: The Yoknapatawpha Novels,* University of Georgia Press, 1976.
    In her study of the novel, Levins finds similarities in the Bundrens' trip and epic and Christian journeys.

Robert Merrill, "Faulknerian Tragedy: The Example of *As I Lay Dying,*" *Mississippi Quarterly,* Vol. 47, No. 3, Summer, 1994, pp. 403-18.
    Merrill contends that Faulkner blends comedy and tragedy in the novel, but that tragedy ultimately prevails.

Michael Millgate, *The Achievement of William Faulkner,* Random House, 1966.
    Millgate provides a general introduction to Faulkner's novel.

Stephen M. Ross, *Fiction's Inexhaustible Voice: Speech and Writing in Faulkner,* University of Georgia Press, 1989.
    Ross examines Faulkner's narrative techniques.

Patricia R. Schroeder, "The Comic World of *As I Lay Dying,*" in *Faulkner and Humor,* edited by Doreen Fowler and Ann J. Abadie, University Press of Mississippi, 1986, pp. 34-46.
    Schroeder surveys the variety of humor in the novel as well as Faulkner's overall comic vision.

John K. Simon, "What Are You Laughing At, Darl?: Madness and Humor in *As I Lay Dying,*" *College English,* Vol. 25, November, 1963, pp. 104-11.
    In his respected study of Darl, Simon closely analyzes the character's madness and final speech.

Hyatt Waggoner, *William Faulkner: From Jefferson to the World,* University of Kentucky Press, 1959.
    Waggoner offers a Christian interpretation of the text, examining many of its elements from this perspective.

The Brothers Karamazov

Fedor Mikhailovich Dostoevsky

1881

At the heart of *The Brothers Karamazov* is a murder mystery surrounding the homicide of a family patriarch, Fyodor Karamazov, and the role of his sons in the crime. The book is also a novel of ideas: Fedor Dostoevsky debates the existence of God, the role of religion in modern societies, and the consequences of class differences on the individual.

On its publication in 1881 readers were shocked by the controversial nature of the novel, in particular the frank discussions of religion and class division. Today, *The Brothers Karamazov* is considered one of the greatest novels in world literature; moreover, Dostoyevsky is renowned as one of the preeminent figures in Russian literature, along with such authors as Nikolai Gogol, Leo Tolstoy, and Alexander Pushkin. His work has influenced many important writers and thinkers of the twentieth century, such as Franz Kafka, Albert Camus, and Sigmund Freud.

Author Biography

Born in Moscow on October 30, 1821, Dostoevsky grew up in a privileged family. His father, a doctor, was a tyrannical disciplinarian; his mother was a pious woman who died before Dostoevsky was sixteen. After her death the family moved to a spacious country estate. To escape the oppressive atmosphere at home, he developed a love for reading, in particular the works of Nikolai Gogol, E. T. A. Hoffmann, and Honore de Balzac.

Fedor Dostoevsky

While attending boarding school, Dostoevsky received word that his father had been murdered by his serfs. The family did not report the murder for fear of losing income; their serfs would undoubtedly have been sent to Siberia for the crime.

According to his father's wishes, Dostoevsky trained as an engineer at the School of Military Engineers in St. Petersburg. With this training, he accepted a commission in the Czar's army in 1843. After a year he resigned and began his career as an author, depending on income from the family estate. His first novel, *Poor Folk* (1846), was published to great critical acclaim but little commercial success.

Dostoevsky's participation in the subversive and socialist Petrashevsky Circle led to his imprisonment. In 1849 he was ordered to die by firing squad. Fortunately, an imperial rider appeared in the nick of time with the message that his sentence had been commuted to ten years of hard labor in Omsk, Siberia.

This traumatic experience prompted Dostoevsky to abandon his interest in humanism, atheism, Western ideas, and liberal thought; instead, he focused his attention on Russian Orthodox dogma and conservative politics. These new interests were fueled by studying the only book allowed prisoners in Siberia—the New Testament. Consequently,

Dostoevsky's works after 1849 are wrought with Gospel images of suffering and redemption.

After four years in the penal colony at Omsk, he was released on the condition that he serve in the army at Semipalatinsk. While in the service, he met and married a widow. In 1859, with a grant of full amnesty, Dostoevsky returned with his wife to St. Petersburg. He set to work immediately and started two political journals. He wrote articles on his belief that Russia should take a religious and conservative course in its development and published them in his magazines. Tragically, he suffered several personal and professional setbacks in the next few years: his wife died in 1864; he became a gambling addict; his brother died; and the authorities shut down his political journals.

In 1867 Dostoevsky married Anna Snitkina, a young woman who had been employed as his stenographer. Soon after they married, they traveled to Europe to escape creditors. Together they raised four children: Sofia, Lyubov, Fyodor, and Aleksei. These years abroad proved very fruitful for Dostoevsky, as he completed several works before his return to Russia in 1871.

In the 1870s he reconciled himself to the liberal elements of Russian politics. He finished *The Brothers Karamazov* in 1880. Within a year of the book's publication, Dostoevsky suffered a hemorrhage in his throat and died on January 28, 1881.

Plot Summary

Part I

The Brothers Karamazov is set over a period of two-and-a-half months in 1866, in a small Russian town near Moscow. A third-person anonymous narrator tells the story thirteen years later after the events of the novel. In Part I, the Karamazov family is introduced: Fyodor and his three sons Dmitri, Ivan, and Alyosha. There is assumed to be a fourth son, Smerdyakov, born illegitimate.

Because their mother is dead, and Fyodor has abnegated his fatherly obligations, the sons are brought up outside the Karamazov home.

Each brother—except for Smerdyakov—appears to represent a particular human aspect: Dmitri is the sensualist (body); Ivan is the intellectual (mind); and Alyosha is the spiritual one (soul). As all three aspects struggle and balance one another in the individual, so too do these three brothers in the family. Although different, they exhibit a characteristic Karamazov trait, like their father: they are passionate, do not consider the consequences of their actions, and compulsively tell what they believe to be the truth.

Two brothers appear to escape the Karamazov destiny. Born illegitimate, Smerdyakov is rational and deceitful. Alyosha is profoundly influenced by two father-figures, in particular Father Zossima, who provides spiritual guidance.

Dmitri and Fyodor visit Father Zossima to have him settle a dispute over Dmitri's inheritance. Zossima is dying, and soon Alyosha will take over this position of mediator, providing a bridge between spiritual and secular worlds. Their mission is a failure.

Although Dmitri is engaged to Katerina, he has fallen in love with Grushenka. Fyodor decides that he wants Grushenka as his wife as well.

Part II

At first Alyosha works to reconcile the hostile factions of his family and community together, but soon he wonders: is he a monk or a Karamazov? Alyosha's dilemma dominates Part II.

Before Zossima dies, he tells his life story to Alyosha. As a youth, Zossima had been a wild young man—much like Dmitri—until he realized God's goodness and the world's beauty. After Zossima felt remorse after slapping a servant, he decided to treat everyone—servants, children, animals—with love and respect.

Perhaps the most well-known passage in the novel occurs in Part II: Ivan's philosophical essay on "The Grand Inquisitor." The poem is set in sixteenth-century Spain during the inquisition when the Church was burning heretics (non-believers) at the stake. It is an imaginary dialogue between a Grand Cardinal and Christ, which parallels the situation of Ivan speaking with Alyosha.

The Cardinal explains his cynical and pragmatic view of humanity, that all a person wants is "someone to bow down to, someone to take over his conscience, and a means for uniting everyone at last into a common, concordant, and incontestable anthill." Because people are hungry, they will accept slavery.

Alyosha is strongly affected by both speeches, but by Ivan's in particular. He experiences a crisis of faith. At the end of Part II, Zossima dies.

Part III

Fyodor is murdered and the investigation begins. Dmitri becomes the prime suspect when it is revealed that he has apparently spent a large amount of Katerina's money on a party with Grushenka, precisely the same amount that Dmitri believes Fyodor owes him. Instead, Fyodor offered this money to Grushenka. Dmitri in fact saved half of the money so that he and Grushenka could leave town and begin a new life elsewhere. In everyone's eyes, Dmitri is insane with jealousy and this is assumed to be his motive for his father's murder.

One night, with Alyosha at the monastery grieving for Zossima, Ivan in Moscow, and Smerdyakov apparently fallen into an epileptic fit, Dmitri goes to his father's house looking for Grushenka. When he discovers that she left with a former lover, Dmitri strikes Fyodor's servant Gregory and leaves him for dead. He chases after Grushenka, who welcomes Dmitri's love and offer of escape. At that climactic moment the police arrive to arrest him for the murder of his father. With so much evidence against him, Dmitri's plans to escape are thwarted.

Part IV

Part IV is set two months later. The scandal has become national news and attracts much attention. A notorious Moscow lawyer has even offered to defend Dmitri. Before the trial begins, Alyosha's maturation into a father-figure to several of the boys in town further develops, and Ivan makes his love for Katerina known.

A number of characters are sick, including Ivan, Smerdyakov, and a young boy, Ilyusha. Ilyusha's relationship with his father contrasts with that of the Karamazovs as Ilyusha and his father lovingly defend one another's honor. Ilyusha also admires the precocious Kolya, who in turn admires Alyosha; these bonds cross class and age barriers.

Smerdyakov admits to Ivan that he killed Fyodor after Dmitri left the house. Smerdyakov commits suicide. Tragically, Ivan has a mental breakdown the night before the trial begins. As a result, this new evidence is never seriously considered. The trial is filled with dramatic tension, and both the prosecutor and the defense attorney deliver convincing arguments on the guilt and innocence of Dmitri Karamazov. There is a collective sense of guilt in the courtroom. According to the narrator's sense of courtroom's reaction just prior to the verdict, Dmitri will be judged innocent. Yet the verdict is guilty.

Epilogue

Alyosha, Ivan, Katerina, Grushenka, and Dmitri plan for Dmitri's escape to America. There

A scene from the movie The Brothers Karamazov, *featuring Yul Brynner (right).*

is some reconciliation amongst the members of the group. Ilyusha dies and, like Dmitri's trial did for the Karamazov family, this event brings the characters together. Alyosha urges them all not to forget these events because, as dark as they were, they proved the importance of love and community.

Characters

Alyosha
See Alexey Karamazov

Father Ferapont
Father Ferapont is an old monk who rarely goes to church and is constantly experiencing religious doubts. Yet in the novel, he represents saintliness. He represents an archaic Christian ascetic and he is adamantly opposed to Father Zossima.

Fetyukovitch
Fetyukovitch is a famous defense attorney. He is attracted by the notoriety of Dmitri's case; in the end, he is unable to save Dmitri.

Gregory
A former serf, Gregory is a religious old man who decides to stay with Fyodor after his emanci-

pation. Deep down, he hates his master, but he believes he is fated to stay with him. He also acts as a surrogate father for Dmitri.

Grushenka
See Agrafena Svyetlov

Anna Hohlakov
Madame Hohlakov is a wealthy widow who suffers from a lack of faith.

Katerina Ivanovna
Daughter of a military officer, Katerina feels obliged to offer herself to Dmitri because he saved her father from prison by providing the money needed to replace embezzled funds. As fate would have it, she later inherits a fortune and repays the debt.

According to Ivan, Katerina is the epitome of the lacerated person, which is defined as someone who suffers a particular humiliation or pain and is incapable of moving beyond that moment. For Katerina, this moment is the offering of herself to Dmitri for money. When he gives her the money without taking advantage of her offer, this act of generosity from a man she thought was base and vile troubles her for years. At first she thinks that marrying Dmitri will ease her mind. She is placated only when she is able to help him later in the novel.

Alexey Karamazov

Alexey, known as Alyosha, is the youngest of the Karamazov brothers and an honest young man. Alyosha's earliest memory is of his mother praying to the Virgin Mary to protect him. After growing up away from home, he returns and visits his mother's grave. Later he decides to become a monk.

According to the narrator, he is the "future" hero of the book and of Russia. (In fact, Dostoevsky had planned a second volume focused on Alyosha.) Alyosha serves as a bridge between the corrupt past and a brighter future, as represented by the closing scene where the previously surly gang of boys surrounds him. The atheist Kolya is chief among them.

Alyosha is not a religious fanatic like Father Ferapont or a mystic like Father Zossima. In fact, Alyosha is considered a realist. The difference between Alyosha and Ivan is simply that Alyosha decides, "I want to live for immortality, and I will accept no compromise."

Dmitri Karamazov

First son of Fyodor, Dmitri is raised by Gregory, the family servant. As a boy, Peter Miusov decides to give him the best education. When he loses interest, Dmitri is passed off on relatives. Having no other prospects, he pursues a military career.

Over the years, his father gives him money, yet never informs him of his net worth. Eventually, he discovers that he has spent all of his inheritance—according to Fyodor. Dmitri's inability to sort out his financial situation and stand up to his father eventually leads to his downfall.

Dmitri's voice can be funny or poetic, swaggering or humiliated. Psychologically, he is a man of passion and the senses, of the earth (Dmitri is from Demeter, goddess of earth, fertility and grain).

The lesson Dmitri learns is that only by the awakening of men like himself to Christian duty, can those in poverty and oppression (as seen in his vision) have a bright, fulfilled life.

Fyodor Karamazov

Modeled upon Dostoevsky's own father, Fyodor is the patriarch of the Karamazov family. A cruel and miserly man, he is also a misanthrope and

Media Adaptations

- *The Brothers Karamazov* was made into a silent film in 1918 by Dmitri Buchowetzki and Carl Froelich in Germany. Irmgard Bern and Fritz Kortner were in the cast.

- The second German adaptation of *The Brothers Karamazov* was directed and scripted by Erich Engels. The 1931 film starred Fritz Kortner (again) as Dmitri and Bernhard Minetti as Ivan.

- William Shatner made his film debut in the 1958 English production of *The Brothers Karamazov*. Adapted by Julius J. Epstein and directed by Richard Brooks, the film also starred Yul Brynner and Maria Schell.

- A Russian production of the novel was made in 1968. Ivan Pyryev wrote the adaptation. Kirill Lavrov and Mikhail Ulyanov directed the film. Ulyanov and Lavrov also starred in the film, which was nominated for a best foreign film Oscar in 1970.

narcissist. He plans to use his formidable fortune to marry Grushenka.

Fyodor embodies "Karamazovism," that family trait of the Karamazovs referred to throughout the novel. It is the ability to throw oneself into dissipation—orgies, alcohol, and blasphemy—with wild abandon. According to Kirillovitch, the Karamazovs are emblematic of that element of Russian society whose spiritual side is undeveloped but which possesses an overwhelming vitality. Fyodor stands in opposition to those who hope to enlighten and reform Russia, like Peter Miusov.

Ivan Karamazov

If Dostoevsky's novel is viewed as a novel of ideas, then Ivan, the middle brother, is the hero. He is a "morose and reserved" young man who recently graduated from the university. Besides the narrator's voice, his voice is the most frequent. Ivan, however, uses other narrative voices to express his thoughts—a devil, an Inquisitor, or a dry recitation of facts.

Ivan gets so caught up in polemics that he ends up in critical condition with a "brain fever." His apparent possession by a demonic being sheds light on the primitive state of neurology just prior to the revolutionary ideas of Sigmund Freud.

Like his father, Ivan prefers logic and facts; they prevent him from falling into a despair brought on by trying to make sense of a world full of absurdities. Therefore he collects facts in a notebook. In this, some critics and biographers assert that he resembles Dostoevsky.

Ivan is responsible for the most famous aspect of the novel, "The Grand Inquisitor." This "poem" is an internal monologue. As Ivan's mental suffering increases, he withdraws from society. He eventually suffers a mental breakdown.

Ippolit Kirillovitch

Kirillovitch is the prosecutor who views this murder case as his swan song. He dies of consumption nine months after the trial.

Kolya Krassotkin

Kolya is a potential Ivan. However, with the intervention of a strong spiritual man like Alyosha, Kolya can become a positive force in the future.

Michael Makarov

Michael Makarov is a police captain. A man of little education and not altogether abreast of the recent judicial reforms, he is loved by the community for his dependability.

Marfa

Marfa is Gregory's wife. A smart woman, she knows some herbal remedies that she uses several times a year when Gregory suffers from lumbago. The remedy consists of alcohol and is sleep-inducing, which is a key fact in Fyodor's murder.

Maximov

Formerly a landowner, Maximov is a silly character down on his luck.

Peter Miusov

A distant relative of Fyodor and Kalaganov, Miusov is a liberal freethinker, reformer, and an atheist. He is a landowner in the district and has spent considerable time abroad, especially in France. Hypocritically, his revolutionary acts benefit his financial interests, not humanity.

Captain Mussyalovitch

Captain Mussyalovitch is a proud Polish officer who dumps Grushenka. Later he tries to reconcile with her in order to spend her money.

Father Paissy

A learned and well-respected man, Father Paissy is a man of reason who assumes the role of Alyosha's spiritual guide.

Peter Perhotin

Dmitri pawns his pistols to Perhotin, a young official who is launched on a bright career because of Dmitri's murder case. Perhotin directs the authorities to Mokroe.

Rakitin

A sycophantic gossip, Rakitin (his name means pliable, like a willow branch) is willing to do anything to be "in the loop." He is a divinity student, but some predict he will eventually be a gossip columnist. He fulfills this destiny during Dmitri's murder trial.

Kuzma Samsonov

Samsonov is an evil merchant who sexually exploits Grushenka. Now old and dying, he tries to encourage Grushenka to marry Fyodor. To facilitate the match he sends Dmitri to a man who would gladly give him the money he needs.

Lizaveta Smerdyastchaya

The mother of Smerdyakov (his name means "the stinker"), Stinking Lizaveta is the town's child. An orphan with a mental disability, she was most likely raped by Fyodor. She dies giving birth to her son in a bathhouse. Gregory takes and raises the child.

Smerdyakov

Smerdyakov is Fyodor's illegitimate son. Given different circumstances, Smerdyakov could have been Ivan's equal. Instead, his thirst for knowledge has been unsatisfied. Like Dmitri, Smerdyakov resents Fyodor. However, he represses his feelings and becomes Fyodor's trusted confidant to gain a better position. He plans out the murder.

Captain Snegiryov

Captain Snegiryov is the town drunk.

Ilusha Snegiryov

Ilusha is the proud son of Captain Snegiryov. He represents the innocent child destroyed by the world in Dmitri's dream. Protective of his family, he is embarrassed by his father's drunken antics. When Dmitri beats his father, the boy is tormented by desires for revenge. When Alyosha tries to befriend him, Ilusha beats him. Alyosha's nonviolent response surprises Ilusha. He races home and comes down with a cold. The cold worsens; before he dies, he reconciles with everyone and becomes a martyr for love and peace.

Stinking Lizaveta
See Lizaveta Smerdyastchaya

Agrafena Svyetlov
Known as Grushenka, she represents the ideal Russian beauty. She is the proper counterpart to the ideal man, Dmitri. Grushenka (whose name means light and bright) is dumped by a Polish officer and spurned by her family. With little to her name, a merchant named Samsonov becomes her protector and she becomes his mistress until he is too old. She also helps him in his business and wisely invests any money that comes her way so that she is an independent woman.

Samsonov advises her to marry Fyodor for the money; however, she wants to marry Dmitri for love. When the Polish officer returns she thinks she is still in love with him but discovers he only wants money. Throughout the novel, Katerina and Grushenka are enemies until Katerina helps Dmitri.

Father Zossima
Born into the upper class, Zossima becomes an officer until, in his haughtiness, he hits his servant. He asks for forgiveness, considered an incredible act. The next day he refuses to return fire in a duel. He resigns his commission and becomes a monk who wanders the country for twenty years. Eventually, he makes his home in the monastery and tries to reinvigorate the institution of the Elder.

Word of his greatness spreads far and wide. Many predict he will be a saint and they unsuccessfully look for evidence of miracles.

Themes

God and Religion
The central theme of the book is the question of God's existence and the role of religion in modern society. At the time he wrote *Brothers Karamazov*, Dostoevsky was deeply religious and felt

that the only true religion was Russian Orthodoxy. Even so, the question of God's existence bothered him to the day he died. In the novel, he employs the narrative technique of two inset works—an article and a story within the novel—in order to debate religious concerns. The former is Ivan's article on the position of ecclesiastical courts, and the latter is Ivan's philosophical essay featuring the Grand Inquisitor.

With the story of the Grand Inquisitor, Ivan doubts the existence of God. Presented as a debate in which the Grand Inquisitor condemns Christ for propagating the belief that man has the choice between good and evil, the essay reflects on redemption, the conflict between intellect and faith, and the role of evil in Christianity. If one is a Christian, one becomes consumed with questions, such as if God is all-powerful and good, why do children suffer as in Dmitri's nightmare?

Alyosha exemplifies the idea that the answers do not matter. He views a belief in God as a way to spread love. Thus, Alyosha is a man of action, a realist working within the system, while Ivan is paralyzed by doubt and fear.

The questions are not decided by the end of the novel. Still, there are definite lessons: love is all-important and people should love freely; life after death should be an integral belief for all; people are capable of evil, especially when they attempt to divorce themselves from their sensuality; and man must be his brother's keeper.

Finally, salvation for mankind—as Alyosha expresses it to the group of boys at the end of the novel—depends upon social solidarity. Isolation of people from each other must end; people must be guided by their spiritual leaders. This last message is almost a prophetic warning to the communists who hoped to create solidarity without spiritual kinship.

Justice and Injustice
There are many instances of injustice in the book—Dmitri beats Ilyusha's father, Fyodor rapes Lizaveta—but none of these injustices are punished or resolved. In fact, the legal system seems to be a mockery of justice. Courts, lawyers, and punishment are for the weak and are often ineffectual. In the novel, the criminals punish themselves and seek their own redemption. For this reason, the role of the church becomes more important; if secular society cannot effectively punish transgressors, then religion must impose a sense of guilt and eventual punishment for sinners.

Topics for Further Study

- Dostoyevsky had a profound impact on many twentieth-century authors like Albert Camus, Richard Wright, and Franz Kafka. Select a novel by one of these authors and write an essay tracing Dostoyevsky's influence.

- There are many references throughout the novel to religious lore. Pick a few of them and research the full stories. How do these references impact the story? Are they relevant to modern American readers, or are these stories ignored?

- Define the concept of the ideal Russian woman. Compare Grushenka and Katerina in terms of this concept.

- Dmitri reluctantly considers escaping to America. What does America represent in this context? Has the impression of America changed?

- How does the story of Ilusha's lost dog reflect the concerns of the novel as a whole?

Artists and Society

Both the prosecution and the defense use the analogy of the novelist for the case of Fyodor's murder. The imaginative artist, Fetiukovich, has a better grasp of the facts than Kirillovich. Yet Kirillovich triumphs because the average man, who sits on the jury, cannot perceive what is "real."

According to Dostoevsky, reality cannot be explained in terms of environmental factors, social facts, and evidence, but in the impossible terms of faith. If the jury can be made to believe that something else might have happened, then Dmitri is innocent.

The trial's debate over reality and Dmitri's fate is allegorical of the debates in the novel as a whole. Dmitri is not as smart as Ivan, but he knows to focus on the important issues. He believes that people are stuck in the trivial concerns of life and give too little attention to immortality. Apparently, the role of the novelist is to accentuate this situation.

Style

Structure

Like many other novels of the nineteenth century, *The Brothers Karamazov* is composed of a diverse array of narrative techniques. These techniques include tales, anecdotes, confessions, digressions, a novella, and a trial transcript. None of these elements can be isolated from the novel without making it incomplete.

The narrator seems omniscient, yet allows various parts of the story to be told by others without clarification. As a result, there are approximately eleven versions of Fyodor's murder.

The multiplicity of voices and layers drive home the themes of the novel through repetition and mirroring. The novel works on thesis and antithesis. Zossima, and his echo Alyosha, counter Ivan's thesis. Fyodor and Miusov foreshadow Ivan's thoughts. Dmitri repeats a portion of Ivan's speech. Ilusha and his friends are mirrors of and responses to Ivan's "rebellion." Kolya's goose is a mirror of Ivan and Smerdyakov.

Symbolism

There is allegorical significance in virtually every aspect and feature composing the fabric of *The Brothers Karamazov*. Dmitri's shame hangs about his neck like an albatross. His redemption is in the form of a small icon that Madame Hohlakov gives to him.

Animals and insects are employed not only to describe character traits, but also as harbingers. For example, cockroaches in the wall emphasize Ivan's horror.

Another symbolic technique is the use of color. The dominant color in the story is black, then red. Black stands for mourning but also for bad choices, such as Grushenka's wearing of a black dress. Blackness, or darkness, also hides Dmitri as he awaits Grushenka or watches his father.

The counterweight to blackness is the pure white of snow. Snow saves Russia from its enemies. Snow is the predominant element in the land of exile, Siberia; it signals redemption and rebirth.

Water is a symbolic force by its very absence. The people of the town, like Alyosha, must leave in order to find fresh water. All water in the town is dirty, except for tears and dew.

Crime Story

The Brothers Karamazov is a crime story. A subgenre of the detective story—a nineteenth-century innovation—crime stories focus on the environment in which the crime was committed. They tend to be told from the perpetrator's point of view.

While a crime story at heart, the novel is far more complex. It is not only concerned with the perpetrator's point of view or with the crime, but also with the concept of original sin as allegorized by the criminal event. Thus, the murder is only a device to explore universal philosophical themes such as religion and the existence of God.

The lack of a reliable version of the crime allows the reader to make his or her own decisions—not just about Dmitri but about those larger themes.

Oedipus Complex

Although the Greek story of Oedipus (in Sophocles' *Oedipus Rex*) has been the subject of many artists, it is best known in the twentieth century through Freud's reworking of the myth as a psychological condition. The Oedipus complex, according to Freud, is common among men who desire the death of their father in order to sleep with their mother. Freud was quite literal about this incestuous desire.

Essentially, the Oedipus story tells the tale of a boy destined to murder his father and sleep with his mother. Knowing this prophecy, extensive precautions are taken to avoid contact with his parents. Yet while traveling as a young man, Oedipus fights and kills a stranger at a crossroads—this stranger turns out to be his father. Later, he arrives in Thebes and solves the riddle of the Sphinx. As a result, he marries Jocasta (his mother). When the truth of his actions are revealed, he blinds himself.

The Oedipal complex is evident in each of the brothers Karamazov. Each brother secretly longs for their father's death—both on behalf of their deceased mother and because their father is very cruel. It is most obvious in the character of Dmitri who was sent away from his father but returns. He falls in love with the woman his father desires. The death of his father enables him to marry Grushenka.

In addition to the Oedipal complex, Dostoyevsky explores other realms of psychology in the novel. In many ways, he was ahead of his time, as he preceded the work of Freud. For example, Dostoyevsky explores several psychological issues: exhibitionism; adolescent perversity; laughter as an unconscious unmasking; the phenomena of the "accidental family"; and the "death-instinct." He also displays the phenomena of split personalities in Dmitri, Katerina, and Ivan.

Historical Context

The Romanovs

In 1689 Peter the Great assumed the throne in Russia. His attempts to modernize Russia were not entirely successful, but he did manage many reforms before his death in 1725. Another reform-minded leader, Catherine the Great, resumed the task of modernization in 1762.

From 1801 to 1825, Alexander I continued in the path of Peter and Catherine. He granted amnesty to political prisoners and repealed many restrictive laws. Under Alexander's reign, Russia increased in size and power. When Napoleon marched on Moscow in 1812, he found the city burned to the ground and, with no supplies and winter setting in, he retreated. The Russian army routed Napoleon's troops using guerrilla tactics.

In 1826 Nicholas I adamantly opposed liberal ideas and Western thought. He instituted secret police, strict censorship, and the removal of all controversial materials from educational institutions. Writers were arrested, university chairs in history and philosophy abolished, and student bodies reduced. Meanwhile, he reformed the economy and compiled the first set of Russian laws since 1649. In 1854 the Russian military forces were defeated by an international army of Turkish, British, French and Sardinian troops in the Crimean War (1854-1856).

In the tradition of Peter, Alexander II reduced restrictions on higher learning. He reformed the judiciary, instituting Zemstvas in 1864. A Zemstva was a system of local self-government responsible for education and public welfare. Throughout the 1870s Russia resumed its struggle with Turkey over the Dardanelles, a struggle it eventually lost.

After 1881, Alexander III reintroduced censorship and strengthened the police force. The Zemstvas were curbed, assimilation was forced on minorities, and assaults began in earnest on the Jewish population through a series of pogroms which kill hundreds.

The last of the Romanovs, Nicholas II, started his reign in 1894. Although he had the best of intentions, the populace assumed that he was under the influence of Rasputin, a mysterious religious leader. After a loss to Japan in 1904, his rule was in danger. On January 22, 1905, his troops fired on thousands of peaceful protesters. Hundreds were killed.

The Russian Orthodox Church of the Resurrection in St. Petersburg, Russia.

Revolution

Under the reign of Alexander I, secret organizations and societies formed and influenced Russian culture and politics. For example, the Decembrists called for an end to Czarist leadership and advocated a constitutional monarchy or a republic. They attempted to take control of Russia when Alexander I died but were crushed by Nicholas I. Another group, the Nihilists, advocated a complete abolition of the present state. Revolutionary activity increased under the tolerant reign of Alexander II.

Revolutionary groups grew more educated, organized, and focused. Industrialism created a class of factory workers open to communist ideas. This group would eventually overthrow the Romanov dynasty in the Russian Revolution of 1917. Though Alexander allowed the revolutionary groups to exist, they were not content with the pace of reform. In 1881, Alexander was assassinated by a revolutionary.

Russian Serfdom

A serf was a person who was legally designated servile to his landlord. Unlike a slave, a serf

Compare & Contrast

- **Late 1800s:** The forefather of Russian communism and Marxist philosopher, Georgy Plekhanov, fled to Western Europe in 1880.

  Today: Russia is developing democratic institutions based on the American model.

- **Late 1800s:** There was a great famine in the agricultural regions of Russia from 1891-1892.

  Today: Agricultural problems are still frequent in Russia due to poor infrastructure, inadequate

resources for private farms, and a lack of credit sufficient to finance farming.

- **Late 1800s:** The United States experienced an industrial revolution that would catapult it to the fore of manufacturing by the twentieth century.

  Today: The United States is in the midst of an information revolution that has created significant economic benefits. These innovations have changed the way people communicate and do business in the twenty-first century.

---

could have inherited property, bequeathed wealth, and bought his way out of serfdom or of some servile duties. Dictated by local custom, service included fighting for the landlord in combat and allowing the landlord to sleep with one's daughters.

With the rise of the merchant class in Europe and evolution of feudal societies into constitutional monarchies, serfdom declined. Descendants of serfs rose to the middle class and social mobility increased. In France, serfs gradually vanished as a result of the French Revolution. Yet the practice survived and grew more repressive in Russia. Spurred by revolutionaries, serfs revolted throughout the first half of the nineteenth century in Russia.

The most notable series of revolts occurred during the disastrous Crimean War in 1854. Finally, forty million Russian serfs were liberated when Alexander II ordered their release in 1861. Even though free by law, many peasants remained second class citizens in reality—an issue explored in *The Brothers Karamazov*.

Critical Overview

When *The Brothers Karamazov* was published in 1881, critics and readers were shocked by the controversial nature of the novel. For example, a negative assessment in *Temple Bar* contends that

the work would "add nothing to [Dostoyevsky's] reputation." Vladimir Nabakov was even less impressed. He deems the novel "quaint" and "weird" though he liked the random phraseology of the chapter headings. Furthermore, a review in *The Spectator* deems the novel "disordered," although it is "the most carefully composed of [Dostoyevsky's] novels, the constructions seems often to collapse entirely; there are the strangest digressions and the most curious prolixities."

Not surprisingly, most of the critical commentary on the novel focuses on the problem of faith and religion. There is quite a bit of commentary discussing the ideas presented by the fable of the "Grand Inquisitor" alone.

D. H. Lawrence, in his *Preface to "The Grand Inquisitor,"* maintains that complete devotion to Christianity is impossible because it expects too much from its followers. Accordingly, Ivan's position is not evil but honest. Ivan rediscovered something "known until … the illusion of the perfectibility of men, of all men, took hold of the imagination of the civilised nations." That something is, "that most men *cannot* choose between good and evil."

Hans Kung, in his "Religion in the Controversy over the End of Religion," views Dostoyevsky as a prophet who "was convinced that the Europe of Western science, technology, and democracy needs Russia's spirituality and conciliating power in order to find its way to a new, free unity."

The novel interests psychologists because they are concerned not with the crime, as Sigmund Freud maintains, but with "who desired it emotionally and who welcomed it when it was done." According to Freud, in *Dostoyevsky and Parricide, The Brothers Karamazov* is the "most magnificent novel ever written."

Freud asserts that the artistic "formula for Dostoyevsky is as follows: a person of specially strong bisexual predisposition, who can defend himself with special intensity against dependence on a specially severe father." Even more profound, "it can scarcely be owing to chance that three of the masterpieces of the literature of all time—the *Oedipus Rex* of Sophocles, Shakespeare's *Hamlet,* and Dostoyevsky's *The Brothers Karamazov,* should all deal with the same subject, parricide."

Besides discussions regarding the novel's themes of religion and psychology, critics consider the characters of the story. Prince Kropotkin contends that with so many characters suffering from "brain and nervous diseases," the novel appears unnatural and fabricated. Further, he asserts that the novel has "here, a bit of morals, there some abominable character taken from a psycho-pathological hospital ... that a few good pages scattered here and there do not compensate the reader for the hard task of reading these two volumes."

Camus views *The Brothers Karamazov* as "a work which, in a chiaroscuro more gripping than the light of day, permits us to seize man's struggle against his hopes." Some critics assert that allegory is more important than characters in the novel. Others note the appearance of the twentieth-century hero—solitary, rebellious, and possibly dangerous.

Critical commentary also focuses on Dostoyevsky's narrative technique. J. Middleton Murray, in *Fyodor Dostoyevsky: A Critical Study,* asserts that The Brothers Karamazov is not "an encyclopedia of Russian life" but a confused and chaotic symbolic tale.

Ralph E. Matlaw disagrees with this assessment in his *The Brothers Karamazov: Novelistic Technique.* He maintains that "the minutiae of the novel are as carefully controlled ... as the thematic and structural lines."

Victor Terras, in *A Karamazov Companion: Commentary on the Genesis, Language, and Style of Dostoyevsky's Novel,* agrees with Matlaw and employs Mikhail Bakhtin's (in *Fyodor Dostoyevsky*) concept of narrative polyphonics. Terras traces the many layers and subtleties of meaning in the novel, asserting that, "the trial of Dmitri ... is an allegory of Dostoyevsky's effort" to persuade the jury of mankind that the "cognitive power of the creative imagination" is the most powerful.

Throughout the years, critics grew to appreciate Dostoyevsky's accomplishments with *The Brothers Karamazov.* In particular, his use of multiple voices is viewed as an effective and innovative narrative technique. Furthermore, his exploration of religious and psychological issues is considered influential for many twentieth century authors and philosophers. Today, *The Brothers Karamazov* is considered one of the more important works of world literature.

Criticism

Logan Esdale

Esdale is a doctoral student in the Poetics Program at SUNY-Buffalo. In the following essay, he explores the role of religious faith in The Brothers Karamazov.

If you have watched any television, you know that murder mysteries and courtroom dramas are popular shows. You also know that real murder trials are televised. The issue with these shows is often not whether the defendant is guilty or innocent, but if the trial is entertaining. Fyodor Dostoevsky's novel, *The Brothers Karamazov,* is an entertaining murder mystery, both for the reader and for the characters in the novel.

The question of whether Dmitri Karamazov is guilty or innocent of his father's murder is treated very seriously. Critics have typically focused on the novel's presentation of the crisis of religious faith in the nineteenth century; in particular, the characters debate the very existence of God and the implications of the answer. For example, if God does not exist, then guilt, innocence, and sin are meaningless. The critics note that Dostoevsky refuses to give a simple answer to this universal question. Instead, there is a compromise: if God's existence cannot be accepted, then people must accept the world as it is.

Dostoevsky attempted to write a novel that incorporated all aspects of Russian society: rich and poor, men and women, believers and nonbelievers. Since the character of Dmitri seems to represent the average Russian, the question of his guilt can be perceived as a question of the nation's guilt. If Dmitri is judged guilty, then all are guilty. If he is judged innocent, then all are innocent.

Dmitri is "wrongly" judged guilty. His attorney maintains that "the overwhelming totality of the facts is against the defendant, and at the same time there is not one fact that will stand up to criticism." In other words, the Russian people are guilty, but the individual is innocent.

Novels influenced by *The Brothers Karamazov* provide insight into Dostoevsky's book. Franz Kafka, for example, loved Dostoevsky's novel; his novel *The Trial* (1925) chronicles the story of Joseph K., or just K., who wakes up one morning to find that he is under arrest. Yet no one can tell him exactly what crime he committed. His attempts to find information are circumvented by a confusing legal system that functions to hinder, not help, defendants.

K. never learns the nature of his crime; therefore, he cannot adequately defend himself. He meets other defendants whose trials drag on for months and years with no final verdict in sight. K. realizes that the court assumes his guilt and that he is in danger of lingering in the complex legal system for years.

However, a certain logic is at play here: if everyone is guilty, then no one person can be held responsible. Since you cannot punish everyone, no one is punished. The final verdict—everyone is under arrest, and also innocent—has for many readers become prophetic, symbolically describing the world today.

Realistically, someone has to be guilty since we always look for someone to blame—usually a person without power. The verdict in *The Trial* contradicts the Christian account of original sin in the first family: after Adam and Eve were exiled from the Garden of Eden for disobedience to God, they became mortal and passed on that mortality to their children. Children are born guilty of their parents' sin. For this reason there is animosity between generations, since many children blame their parents for the burden of guilt. Inevitably, children will rebel against their parents.

According to Sigmund Freud's account of human origins, which describes the tension within the Karamazov family, a son or a group of sons desire to kill the father because the father has exclusive privilege over all women. Competitive instinct governs family interaction. Dmitri is charged, however, with parricide (the killing of a family member), not patricide (the killing of the father). Parricide opens itself to the possibility that any murder is like a family murder.

Adam and Eve's first son, Cain, commits parricide when he kills his brother Abel out of sibling rivalry. And in Shakespeare's *Hamlet,* Claudius kills his brother—Hamlet's father—to gain the throne of Denmark. Parricide emphasizes that a murder affects more than just the victim. It affects the other family members—like the members (people) of a body (nation). So much attention has been given to the family in literature because the family can be regarded as a small community, or miniature nation. What happens in a family can be said to mirror—with the distortions that all mirrors create—the state of a nation.

An account of the world that claims everyone is innocent then argues against Christian scripture, and claims also that God is dead. This conclusion is likely true of *The Trial*, but *The Brothers Karamazov* is more ambiguous. Three characters in Dostoyevsky's novel quote Voltaire, an eighteenth-century French philosopher: "If God did not exist, he would have to be invented." This hypothesis has lingered and turned up in the most unlikely places, such as on the wall of a New Orleans brothel in the 1969 film *Easy Rider.*

The solution to this hypothesis is of course beyond us; we can only speculate. Fyodor, Ivan and young Kolya all invoke Voltaire's popular hypothesis, and all three are mocked at times for their credulity—believing that if it comes from a book, it must be true. Kolya also asks a question at the heart of the novel: "It's possible to love mankind even without believing in God, don't you think?" Ivan provides an answer that each character will test for himself and herself: "it is not God that I don't accept; it is the world that he has created." Ivan despairs that "everything except man is sinless," and with this disavowal in mind decides that "everything is permissible."

As Dmitri is accused of having murdered his (earthly) father, Ivan can be accused of having murdered God the Father. Richard Peace has noted that "Ivan's father becomes a sort of sacrificial substitute for God." Ivan participates in the events of Fyodor's murder and, at least initially, believes himself to have been innocent because it is not possible to be guilty of killing someone who is already dead: Fyodor had effectively killed himself years before when he rejected the responsibilities of fatherhood—like God. If God has forsaken you and

What Do I Read Next?

- *Notes from the Underground* (1864) marks a turning point in Dostoyevsky's thought. It was written in reaction to Nikolay Chernyshevsky's utopian novel, *What Is To Be Done?* Here, Dostoyevsky outlines the moral universe that he will explore in the rest of his writings.

- Dostoyevsky's *Crime and Punishment* was published in 1866. This crime novel chronicles the moral struggles of an impoverished student, Raskolnikov, who kills his landlady for money. This novel is considered a masterpiece.

- Published in installments between 1875 and 1877, Leo Tolstoy's *Anna Karenina* tells the story of a tragic love affair in late nineteenth-century Russia.

- In Russia, a landowner must pay a soul tax on his serfs—though they are dead—until the next census. Such absurdities inspired Nikolay Gogol's 1842 masterpiece, *Dead Souls.* Gogol's satire about an enterprising young man who is trying to buy social mobility through prospecting on such dead souls gave Russian literature garnered critical and commercial popularity.

- Ivan Turgeniev's *Fathers and Sons* (1862) explores the generation gap. The protagonist is a young intellectual nihilist who believes only in the laws of natural science; much to his chagrin, he falls prey to emotions such as love and unhappiness.

---

the generation before you has already killed everything, why should what you do matter?

Enter Smerdyakov, Fyodor's bastard son, a character that in many ways makes this novel relevant today. He represents disaffected youth, those alienated from their parents and from themselves, a demographic that has become so stereotypical in the last few decades. Smerdyakov murders the father who had disowned him from birth, but who had consented to employ him as one of the servants. What might have been a familial relation was reduced to an economic relation. A man without a family and an inheritance, Smerdyakov is aimless until Ivan asserts that "everything is permissible."

This reading of the world permits Smerdyakov to kill Fyodor and then flee to France. It is he who will play God and punish people for their pride—he says to Ivan, "It was your pride made you think I was stupid." Yet to create a new life Smerdyakov would have to erase his terrible crime; he would have to claim that he was innocent.

At the end of the novel, once Dmitri has been convicted and sentenced, a plan is put into motion that would have Dmitri escape to America—the ideal place to start again. Americans killed their symbolic fathers—rules that limit freedom, such as God, class, ethnicity, gender or all origins altogether—and are not obligated to pay the debt of history. Yet does eliminating the patriarchal system also alleviate the obligations of mutual responsibility people feel toward each other, toward animals, and toward the earth? Without a symbolic father figure, will the family implode?

The novel suggests that one method of accepting this mutual responsibility is to treat adults as children, and children as adults, which means that fathers would become brothers, and mothers become sisters. Exchanging positions in the family and becoming mutually responsible for each other dismantles one of the primary hierarchies (the Family) that structure inequalities into the human community.

After Cain kills his brother, he responds to God's question about Abel's existence: "Am I my brother's keeper?" Because Cain failed to recognize his responsibility to his brother, God marked Cain and sent him out of the community (as proof that he was always and already outside)—like Hester Prynne in Nathaniel Hawthorne's *The Scarlet Letter* (1850), who is cursed to wear a scarlet "A" to signify her crime of adultery. The Karamazovs are similarly marked: in Russian, *kara* means "punishment" and *mazov* comes from *mazat,* which means "to daub or smear."

Since one of the central questions at Dmitri's trial is whether all Russians are Karamazovs, the title of the novel is suggestive: *Brothers Karamazov* may include a community larger than a single family. A monk or nun willingly takes on the mark of sin, as Christ did, believing that all have sinned. To believe that "all are guilty" is to take that step nuns and monks take towards participation in the larger brotherhood and sisterhood beyond the family. To believe instead that "all are innocent" is to decide that there is no community. Conforming to society's values and laws then becomes optional, and can lead to anarchy.

To believe both at the same time—and become a sort of monk or nun in the world instead of in the monastery—is a possibility explored in the novel. In doing so, the characters begin to accept degrees of belief and degrees of guilt, and reject absolute belief or guilt. Because laws exist absolutely, however, they exist in conflict with exceptions to those laws. No single explanatory system (such as Christianity) can fully explain the complexity of a world of competing brothers, or competing instincts. You cannot find absolute truth in a book—either in the Bible or *The Brothers Karamazov*. Reading a book is a solitary pursuit. Truth must be constructed in dialogue with others.

One Father would be the author himself, Dostoevsky, and the monument of his great book. In this book Fatherhood is put on trial and the author questions his own authority by employing what his foremost critic, Mikhail Bakhtin, has called *dialogism* ("dia-" is two or more, and "-logue" is to speak). Bakhtin focuses more on the novel's form than its religious philosophy, but the two aspects are related. He has noted that "Capitalism created the conditions for a special type of inescapably solitary consciousness" by alienating us from the things we make and from each other, but that this solitary consciousness is a fantasy and an illusion. A solitary consciousness, or *monologism* ("mono" is one), claims to know the one Truth; it claims that everyone is entitled to her or his own opinion or truth, but in so claiming there is no conversation. No one listens.

Freud's theory of narcissism, which explain how people think only of themselves, offered to the twentieth century a life—not of innocent intentions—but innocent of its own intentions. Freud does not deny guilt, but maintains that there are other, psychological reasons for behavior that go beyond guilt and innocence. The mechanisms that operate the mind, like those that operate a piece of machinery, are neither sinful nor innocent in themselves.

Monologism is natural in capitalist America; in this country you can perhaps too easily claim to be innocent, and that others are to blame. Dialogism instead accepts both guilt and innocence as shared amongst the members of a family or nation. In effect, Dostoevsky kills the author-Father himself by opening up the novel form to multiple or dialogic consciousness, constituted collectively by the author *and* the characters. In this way, the hero in a dialogic novel becomes a collective hero.

Bakhtin says that a Dostoevsky novel develops itself—and cannot finally ever conclude itself—by creating a hero who takes a position on the world, and draws other people into dialogue with that position. Out of that dialogue certain shared truths emerge.

Although Dostoevsky's world is largely mechanistic, without God and innocent of its own intentions, it still demands that we intuit and respect other people's truths and move beyond monologism.

The declared hero of the novel is Alyosha, who describes the events of thirteen years ago to the narrator. Yet the narrator also witnessed many of the events, and often claims to be recording what he or she saw and heard.

With all these methods the book is almost literally composed collectively, and its conclusion is an exemplary instance of a chorus of voices: the young boys are gathered by Alyosha in both a fatherly and brotherly manner, and as they shout tributes of love they are asked to remember always this moment before they go their separate ways. Such moments might happen infrequently in their lives—in our lives too, so the reader is also drawn into the chorus, and we are entreated to remember the experience of having read this book.

Source: Logan Esdale, in an essay for *Novels for Students*, Gale, 2000.

Arnold McMillin

In the following essay, McMillin presents a critical overview of The Brothers Karamazov.

The Brothers Karamazov was Dostoevskii's last great novel, bringing to culmination many of the themes of his earlier fiction, such as the debate between religion and atheism, the battle between good and evil in the hearts of 'broad' Russian characters, clashes of incompatible rival women, the ever-fascinating legal process, and, above all, Dostoevskii's longstanding attempts to create a 'positively good man' capable of leading Russia's spiritual regeneration. Moreover, the three brothers seem to reflect the three main stages of the author's life: Dmitrii, his youthful Romantic period; Ivan, his attachment to atheistic socialist circles; and Alesha, his spiritually reborn post-Siberian period.

The longest of the novels, *The Brothers Karamazov* is also one of the most tightly constructed, topographically exact (the town of Skotoprigonevsk is closely modelled on Staraia Russa where Dostoevskii spent his last years), and chronologically compact: the main action of the book takes place over a period of only three days, but with much interleaving of narration as we follow the lives of the three brothers in long, intercalated sections with a constant feeling of acceleration driving the action on. Each brother in turn, with the aid of significant dreams (and, in Ivan's case, delirium), learns important facts about himself and, for all the narration's pace, the reader shares a strong sense of epiphanic development.

The novel's main theme is the nature of fatherhood. On the one hand we have the saintly elder Zosima, a spiritual father to Alesha, the youngest brother; on the other the irresponsible, scheming, lecherous Fedor Karamazov, a father in the biological sense alone, whose possible murder is a topic of discussion from early in the book. This crime, once committed, provides a source of guilt for all of his sons: Alesha, the novice sent out into the world by Zosima, who for all his Christian goodness cannot avert the parricide; Dmitrii, cheated by his father and a rival for the favours of the amoral Grushenka; and Ivan, the haughty intellectual, spiritual descendant of Raskol'nikov, whose formula 'if God does not exist, then all is permitted' falls onto the receptive ears of his bastard half-brother, the lackey Smerdiakov who, in fact, proves to be the actual perpetrator of the crime.

As a detective story this chronicle of small-town life is handled in masterly fashion with concatenations of circumstances and fatally coincidental sums of money all seeming to impugn the passionate Dmitrii, who is eventually tried and condemned. Rarely, if ever, has the tension of mounting circumstantial evidence been portrayed in such a gripping manner (Dostoevskii was inspired by a comparable real-life case). His response to the new legal system in Russia adds particular vividness to the description of the trial, in which not only Dmitrii, or even the Karamazov family, but effectively the whole of Russia is judged before the world.

The Brothers Karamazov was Dostoevskii's last attempt to create a 'positively good man'. Father Zosima, though charismatic, is, perhaps, too pale and other-worldly for this role, but Alesha, through counselling distressed adults and children, gains authority as the novel progresses, and it is

with him that the book ends. More memorable, however, is his brother Ivan's exposition of the reasons for rejecting God's world: the examples he adduces of gross cruelty to innocent children make his 'returning of the ticket' to God very persuasive. His principal thought is expressed in the 'Legend of the Grand Inquisitor,' a profound and disturbing meditation on Christianity, free will, and happiness, at the end of which Alesha kisses his brother, just as Christ had responded to the Inquisitor with a silent kiss. Subsequently Ivan's brilliant Euclidian mind proves unable to resist a mocking petty bourgeois devil and he falls into insanity. In the world of Dostoevskii's novels Christianity and the intellectual have a purely negative relationship.

Dmitrii, aware that his nature contains elements of both the Madonna and Sodom, shares his father's impulsive, passionate character but none of his cynicism or buffoonery. Dmitrii's romance with Grushenka, who also alternates between satanic pride and self-abasement, voluptuousness and spiritual sublimation, makes this one of the great love stories in all literature. Also fascinating are all three brothers' relations with two other mentally troubled women, Katerina Ivanovna and Liza Khokhlakova, revealing a disturbingly dark side of passion first seen in *Igrok* (*The Gambler*) but also encountered in ensuing novels, particularly *The Idiot* and *The Devils.* The depiction of these women's behaviour together with the parricide itself strongly attracted the professional interest of Sigmund Freud.

The Brothers Karamazov is a rich and fascinating text containing crime, passion, psychology, religion, and philosophy. It is indeed one of the great novels of the world.

Source: Arnold McMillin, *"The Brothers Karamazov,"* in *Reference Guide to World Literature,* second edition, edited by Lesley Henderson, St. James Press, 1995.

Sources

Mikhail Bakhtin, "Toward a Reworking of the Dostoyevsky Book," in *Problems of Dostoyevsky's Poetics,* translated and edited by Caryl Emerson, University of Minnesota Press, 1984, pp. 283-302.

Albert Camus, in *The Myth of Sisyphus* Vintage, 1991, pp. 93-118.

Sigmund Freud, in *Dostoyevsky and Parricide,* translated by D. F. Tait, Basic Books, 1959, pp. 222-42.

Prince Kropotkin, "Gontcharoff; Dostoyevsky; Nekrasoff," in *Russian Literature,* McClure, Phillips & Co., 1905, pp. 151-90.

Hans Kung, "Religion in the Controversy over the End of Religion," in *Literature and Religion: Pascal, Gryphius, Lessing, Holderlin, Novalis, Kierkegaard, Dostoyevsky, Kafka,* edited by Walter Jans and Hans Kung, translated by Peter Heinegg, Paragon House, 1991, pp. 223-42.

Ralph E. Matlaw, in *The Brothers Karamazov: Novelistic Technique,* Mouton & Co., 1957, pp. 20-33.

J. Middleton Murray, in *Fyodor Dostoyevsky: A Critical Study,* Russell & Russell, 1966.

Richard Peace, in *Dostoyevsky: An Examination of the Major Novels,* Cambridge University Press, 1971.

The Spectator, Vol. 109, No. 4396, September 28, 1912, pp. 451-52.

The Temple Bar, Vol. 91, February, 1891, pp. 243-49.

Victor Terras, in *A Karamazov Companion: Commentary on the Genesis, Language, and Style of Dostoyevsky's Novel,* The University of Wisconsin Press, 1981, pp. 100-09.

For Further Study

Albert Camus, *The Stranger,* translated by Matthew Ward, Vintage Books, 1989.
> An ordinary man is drawn into a senseless murder. Camus explores the use of the stranger archetype.

Fyodor Dostoyevsky, *The Possessed,* translated by David Magarshack, Penguin USA, 1954.
> First published in 1871, this is Dostoyevsky's first major novel. Thematically, it concerns politics, atheism, and murder.

Franz Kafka, *The Trial,* Schocken Books, 1998.
> In this novel, Joseph K. is faced with imprisonment, but never informed of his crime. The story explores the psychology of bureaucracy and its impact on the human condition.

Jean Paul Sartre, *The Age of Reason,* Vintage Books, 1992.
> Famous for his theories of existentialism, Sartre examines freedom and responsibility in his philosophical treatise.

Richard Wright, *Native Son,* Harper Perennial Library, 1993.
> A crime novel influenced by Dostoyevsky, Wright debates psychological theories in this story of a young man charged with a crime.

The Call of the Wild

Jack London

1903

The Call of the Wild first appeared in serial form in the popular magazine *The Saturday Evening Post* in 1903. Later that year, an expanded version was published in book form and enjoyed favorable reviews and commercial popularity. The novel's simple style and crude depiction of harsh realities in the frozen Klondike region appealed to a reading public tired of the sentimental, romanticized fiction that dominated the literary marketplace. At the same time, readers were drawn to it as an adventure story, a popular genre in turn-of-the-century America.

In writing the novel, Jack London drew on his experiences in the Klondike gold rush of 1897. In fact, many critics see parallels between the author's and the protagonist's experiences. The novel has been one of the most beloved animal stories ever written precisely because London was able to keep the story of a dog's adventures realistic while allowing readers to relate to Buck's perspective.

Although the novel has long been considered a children's book, many literary scholars have argued that the novel's complexities warrant close analysis. Chief among the topics of interest to scholars is the novel's relationships to the philosophy of the "survival of the fittest" that was in vogue at the turn of the century.

Author Biography

One of America's most prolific and beloved authors, London was born in 1876 in San Francisco,

California. His family was so poor that he went to work as soon as he finished grade school. His early experiences working in a saloon and a factory, hunting seals, tramping on the railroads, and spending thirty days in prison for vagrancy provided London a wealth of material for his gritty, naturalistic fiction.

In 1894 London completed high school, attended the University of California at Berkeley for one semester, and joined the Socialist Party. He immersed himself in the writings of Charles Darwin, Karl Marx, Friedrich Nietzsche, and Herbert Spencer. He was intrigued by socialism and Darwin's concept of the "survival of the fittest," two ideas that would influence his later writings.

In 1897, frustrated with his unsuccessful attempts at starting a literary career, he went with his brother-in-law to the Klondike, in the Yukon territory of Canada. The gold rush in the Klondike was underway, and London hoped to strike it rich. Although he did not discover any gold, he did find subject matter for his fiction. His experiences in the frozen Northland inspired his first stories, which appeared in the nation's leading periodicals. London's fiction was very popular with the public; his stories were new and exciting and very different from the tales of romance that flooded the market during that time.

The most popular book to come out of his Alaskan experiences was *The Call of the Wild* (1903), the story of a dog's difficult transition from the warm, comfortable Southland to the wild, treacherous Northland. Many scholars find autobiographical elements in this novel, in particular London's exciting and dangerous adventures in the Klondike and his short stint in prison. Just as Buck has to learn to accept the "law of the club" and the "law of the fang," London learned how to survive in prison. The novel was one of London's greatest critical and commercial successes. Unfortunately London had accepted $2,000 for the book instead of a share of the royalties. London would not make the same mistake with his subsequent novels and short fiction. He became a wealthy man writing adventure novels. He died at the age of forty of uremia.

Plot Summary

Chapter 1: Into the Primitive

Buck is a dog living with Judge Miller at a sprawling ranch in Santa Clara Valley, California.

Jack London

He lives the life of a country gentleman's dog, beloved by his master and given the run of the property.

Buck's idyllic life is cut short by one of the ranch hands, Manuel, whose gambling habit and large family prompt him to sell Buck on the black market. Buck is taken by rail to a man in a red sweater, a dog breaker, who uses a club for training. Buck's spirit is beaten, but not broken; he learns to adapt to his changing environment. He's bought by two French Canadians, Perrault and Francois, fair men who have a shrewd eye for a good dog and realize Buck's worth.

Chapter 2: The Law of Club and Fang

The law of the club refers to the method humans use to extract obedience from a dog; the law of the fang refers to the method dogs use to subjugate other dogs. Buck learns about the law of the fang when Curly, one of the friendlier sled dogs, makes advances toward another dog. This other dog rips open her face, then jumps aside to avoid retaliation. Curly is then killed by thirty to forty dogs. Buck learns life in the Klondike is violent, survival belongs to the alert, and leadership belongs to the most cunning.

Buck has his first experience as a sled dog and proves to be adept at the job. The team expands to nine dogs, including Spitz, the white husky leader; Dave, an antisocial but hardworking team dog; brothers Billee and Joe, one sweet and the other sour; and Sol-leks, a one-eyed dog whose name means "the Angry One."

Next Buck learns how to survive the night by digging a hole in the snow and curling into a ball. He also learns how to steal food without getting caught and clubbed. This is the only way to ensure survival in a cruel, cold land where a dog runs all day, sleeps to run the next day, and in between might lose his life in a dog fight.

Chapter 3: The Dominant Primordial Beast

As the team works its way up the frozen Thirty Mile River to Dawson, Buck prepares to challenge Spitz. One night when Spitz confronts him, Buck attacks. However, a gang of starving, marauding dogs interrupts the fight and turns the camp upside down looking for food. The team runs off into the woods until they leave. A few days later, due to the strain of the trip, Dolly goes mad, howling like a wolf, chasing Buck until Francois finally axes her to death.

Once in Dawson, Perrault wants to travel back to Dyea. During this trip Buck undermines Spitz's authority by siding with any dissenting dog. Eventually, Spitz is powerless to make the team run as a unit. One night near the Northwest police camp, team dogs and police dogs spot a snowshoe rabbit and give chase, with Buck in the lead. Spitz challenges Buck for the rabbit. This begins their fight to the death. Although Spitz is a formidable fighter, Buck has the greater imagination and wins. As soon as Spitz falls, the other dogs kill him.

Chapter 4: Who Has Won to Mastership

Perrault and Francois promote Sol-leks as the head of the team but Buck pushes him out of place. This happens several times until, finally, Buck's demand to lead is met. With him heading the team, they make a record run. Afterwards, the men and dogs are exhausted, and the team is sold to a man who runs the Salt Water mail from Dawson to Skagway. Due to all the gold rushers, the mail load keeps growing and the dogs are pushed to their breaking point. Along the route, Dave weakens and is cut from the team. However, he refuses to be cut and returns to his place. Finally he is allowed back and, although he stumbles now and then, he does his best to pull his weight. One morning, however, Dave cannot even crawl to his place. He is left

where he is and the team leaves. A few miles out, the man stops the team and walks back. The team hears a gunshot.

Chapter 5: The Toil of the Traces

The team is again sold, this time to a brother and sister and her husband. All three are inexperienced and must be told by the locals how to pack a sled. Unfortunately, they have their own ideas and end up with fourteen dogs pulling an oversized load plus the woman, who insists on riding instead of going on foot. Due to their poor calculations, the trio eventually runs low on food and must ration the dogs. Soon everyone is irritable and the dogs are starved and beaten.

The threesome asks an old, experienced Klondiker, John Thornton, for advice. He tells them they have been lucky to travel so far on a thawing river. Nevertheless, they decide to continue, but Buck will not move no matter how much they beat him. Thornton, enraged at their treatment of Buck, steps in to cut Buck from the traces, saving his life. As the man and dog bond, they watch the team run along the river, hit a thawing patch, and drown.

Chapter 6: For the Love of a Man

Thornton is a loving master, and Buck begins to love him. If not for Thornton, Buck would leave the company of men and join the wild. Buck proves his love by obeying Thornton when he commands Buck to jump over a cliff. At the last second, Buck is saved. Twice Buck saves Thornton's life, once by defending him from a bully and again by rescuing him from drowning. Finally, Buck wins a bet for him by breaking a sled from the ice and dragging its heavy load one hundred yards.

Chapter 7: The Sounding of the Call

The money won from the bet allows Thornton to fulfill his dream of searching for a lost gold mine. When they eventually find it, the men work the mine and Buck has a chance to explore the wild. He even brings down a wounded moose by stalking it for days. When Buck comes back to the camp he finds the men and dogs massacred by the Yeehats. He takes his revenge on the tribe, killing the greatest predator of all, man.

With Thornton's death breaking his last tie to humanity, Buck joins his ancient ancestors, the wolves. With the Yeehats, he gains a reputation as the Ghost Dog, but each year he visits Thornton's grave. This is his only concession to the past.

Characters

Buck

Half St. Bernard, half Scotch shepherd, Buck is a dog and the protagonist of *The Call of the Wild.* The novel is told largely from Buck's perspective, although the narrator interprets his "feelings" and "thoughts" for the reader. Buck is a loyal friend to his owner, Judge Miller, and he "lived the life of a sated aristocrat" on his California ranch. But he is physically strong from hunting expeditions, and his thick coat and strength are exactly what the men going North to seek their fortune in the Klondike gold rush need.

Buck is stolen by the gardener and sold to a group traveling north. Before long Buck knows that he is in a strange land with different rules and expectations. A man in a red sweater teaches Buck his first lesson of the Northland: "a man with a club was a law-giver, a master to be obeyed, though not necessarily conciliated." Buck's first masters are just, but he must make a difficult adjustment to his new life of labor and near-starvation. He even steals food from his master, an act which marks "the decay or going to pieces of his moral nature, a vain thing and a handicap in the ruthless struggle for existence." Although Buck is a dog, his "development (or retrogression)," as London calls it, is depicted in almost human terms. He is losing all the trappings of civilization. "The domesticated generations fell from him," and "instincts long dead became alive again."

Buck is more and more drawn to the wild. He discovers the thrill of the blood hunt, and he defeats his rival, Spitz, for the position of lead dog. But when he meets his third master, John Thornton, a strong relationship develops between man and dog. Buck stays with Thornton because he loves him, not because of the "law of the club." He risks his life for Thornton on more than one occasion. Yet he is still attracted by the call of the wild. He meets a wolf, a "brother," and longs to run off with him, but he stays with Thornton. Only when Yeehat Indians murder Thornton does Buck join the wolf pack, becoming the "Ghost Dog" in Yeehat legend. The wolves are greatly feared, and Buck "may be seen running at the head of the pack."

Charles

Charles is one of Buck's masters. He is searching for gold, but his group is completely unprepared for the harsh, demanding environ-

Charlton Heston in the 1972 movie Call of the Wild.

ment. Through their ignorance, lack of sense, and cruelty, they starve the dogs and nearly work them to death. When they travel on a precarious river trail, they crash through the ice to their deaths.

Dave

Dave is the wheel-dog on the team. His pride in his work is so great that he ends up working himself to death, unwilling to be carried when he becomes ill.

Dolly

Dolly is a dog who goes mad on the trail. She comes after Buck in her madness and is killed by Francois.

Francois

Francois is a dog driver, one of Buck's first masters in the Klondike. He and his partner, Perrault, are mail couriers. They are just masters who treat the dogs fairly, although they get the maximum amount of work out of their dogs with the minimum amount of food.

Media Adaptations

- *Jack London Cassette Library,* read by Jack Dahlby, includes readings of *The Call of the Wild, Martin Eden,* and *The Sea-Wolf.*

- *The Call of the Wild* is read by Arnold Moss on a cassette made by Miller-Brody.

- *The Call of the Wild* was first captured on film in 1935 by United Artists.

- In 1972, a film was made of *The Call of the Wild* starring Charlton Heston as John Thornton. It is available on video.

- *The Call of the Wild* was adapted for television in 1983. This version stars Rick Schroder as John Thornton and is available on video.

Hal

Hal is Charles's brother-in-law. When Buck refuses to lead the dogs further on the trail, he beats him severely. Hal is the one who leads the party to their deaths.

Manuel

Manuel is the gardener who steals Buck and sells him.

Mercedes

Mercedes is Hal's wife and Charles's sister. Because she "had been chivalrously treated all her days," she is particularly ill-suited to the life of the trail. She feels sorry for the hungry dogs, so she gives them more to eat, only to have them run out of food. And she refuses to walk, making the exhausted dogs carry her weight on the sled.

Judge Miller

Judge Miller is Buck's original owner on the California ranch.

Perrault

Perrault is Francois's partner and one of Buck's first masters.

Sol-leks

Sol-leks is one of the sled dogs who shows Buck the ropes. He takes great pride in his job, and Francois and Perrault make him lead dog after Spitz's death. But Sol-leks relinquishes his position when Buck claims it. Sol-leks goes down with the team when Charles, Mercedes, and Hal drive them into the thawed river.

Spitz

Spitz is the lead dog of the team, and he is Buck's nemesis. Buck resents his power and intends to challenge him, knowing that it must be a battle to the death. When Buck, in the full frenzy and "ecstasy" of the "blood lust," closes in on a rabbit, and Spitz steps in to claim the prey for his own, Buck attacks Spitz. After a long and bloody fight Buck is the victor, the "dominant primordial beast."

John Thornton

John Thornton is Buck's last master. He intervenes when he sees Hal beating Buck for refusing to go any further on the trail, and he saves the dog's life. Thornton "was the ideal master. Other men saw to the welfare of their dogs from a sense of duty and business expediency; he saw to the welfare of his as if they were his own children." Buck becomes his loyal friend and loves him more than any human or beast he has ever known.

Thornton tests Buck's loyalty by ordering him to jump off a cliff. Only by jumping in front of Buck does he prevent him from plunging to his death. Although Buck is drawn to life in the wild, he remains with Thornton. When his beloved master is killed by Yeehat Indians, Buck avenges Thornton's death, killing his first human; he then leaves the world of men forever. The bond between Buck and Thornton had been Buck's last and strongest tie to civilization.

Themes

Civilization vs. the Wild

The main conflict in *The Call of the Wild* is the struggle between civilization and the wild. The novel traces Buck's gradual transformation from a domesticated dog to a wild one.

Buck has to learn to adapt to an entirely new way of life and code of conduct in order to survive. He must give up his life of leisure and his trusting nature. He learns "the law of the club and fang," meaning that those who have the greatest physical strength are the rulers. The chain of command is comprised of men with clubs; the lead dogs, who have achieved mastery by wounding or killing dogs that challenge them; and the other dogs, who do most of the work.

Buck starts out on the bottom of this hierarchy, but soon adapts to his new life. He begins to steal food, losing his moral nature. Most of all, Buck is fit, and his superior strength, conditioned by his experiences, allows him to be more aggressive. He challenges the lead dog and wins the coveted top position. His survival instinct leads him to refuse to lead the team any further when they travel on thin ice.

At this point in the narrative, Buck's consistent "development (or retrogression)," as London calls it, from civilization to the wild is halted. When Thornton becomes his master, he discovers a stronger bond—love—than any he has ever experienced. His risks his life for his master, in direct contradiction to the new ethos he has learned on the trail. With Thornton, Buck lives a domesticated life, but he continues to hear the call of the wild. Although he is torn between the two, he remains with Thornton, unable to break the bond between them. When Thornton is killed, he is released, finally able to fulfill his true nature and join the wolf pack. Only then is his transformation from domesticated dog to wolflike wild one complete.

Ancestral Memory

As Buck metamorphoses into a wild creature, he discovers within himself instincts that have been dormant for generations. In *The Call of the Wild,* London glorifies the almost metaphysical element of Buck's nature that allows him to survive in conditions that are completely foreign to him. He does more than learn to adapt, London argues, he draws on his ancestral memory to show him how to behave.

It is this metaphysical aspect of Buck's nature that has led critics to detect a supernaturalist or spiritualist slant to this novel. Even though Buck's experiences determine that he will become wild, leaving civilization behind, after he meets Thornton he is lured back into the domesticated life. Thornton will protect and feed him, treating him more like a beloved member of the family than a mere dog or work animal. Throughout his relationship with Thornton, it is his growing awareness of his ancestral memory that lures him into the wild. The "call of the wild," therefore, refers to the mystical natural forces at work within Buck, making the story more supernatural.

Topics for Further Study

- Research the philosophies of the "superman" and the "survival of the fittest" as espoused by Friedrich Nietzsche and Herbert Spencer, two thinkers who influenced London. Compare them to London's philosophies found in *The Call of the Wild.*

- Read Ralph Waldo Emerson's seminal essay "Self-Reliance" (1841). Write an essay considering whether or not you think it was possible for Buck to be a "self-reliant" individual at the end of the nineteenth century.

- For decades *The Call of the Wild* has been considered by many to be a children's book. Do you think it is an appropriate book for children, and why? Who do you think the intended or most appropriate audience for this book is—children, teens, adult readers, or literary scholars?

- Research changing views of nature and the American wilderness in the nineteenth and early twentieth centuries, studying such figures as Henry David Thoreau, Theodore Roosevelt, and John Muir. Write an essay in which you discuss London's place within these debates/traditions.

Style

Point of View

Point of view is the narrative perspective from which a work is presented to the reader. *The Call of the Wild* is told from a very unusual point of view—that of a dog. Yet a human narrator stands outside of Buck's consciousness and makes sense of the dog's universe to human readers. London also tries to maintain Buck's believability as a dog. So while he explains his motivations, London reminds the reader that Buck does not actually think. After a lengthy passage about Buck's moral decline, explaining why Buck steals food from his master, London writes, "Not that Buck reasoned it out.... unconsciously he accommodated himself to the new mode of life."

Setting

Setting is the time, place, and culture in which the action of a narrative takes place. *The Call of the Wild* is neatly divided into two regions that are diametrically opposed—the Southland and the Northland. The former represents civilization and the latter the wild. In the South, Buck lived a domesticated and perfectly stable life. When Buck arrives in the North, he realizes that survival is the only concern.

The difference between the two regions is typified by their climates. In the South, it is warm, food grows easily, and people enjoy their leisure. In the North, the harsh, cold conditions are very dangerous if one is not prepared, and people must work hard and suffer much to survive.

Allegory

Many critics perceive that *The Call of the Wild* was more than the story of a dog. Many believe that it is an allegory about human society. An allegory tells two stories at once: the surface narrative, which in this case would be Buck's transformation; and the "real" story that is suggested by the literal narrative. As such, then, this novel also tells the story of the savagery of man, who is transported into a hostile world against his will, must confront his inability to determine his own fate, must learn to survive by any means necessary, and who must choose between the bond of love with other humans and his own desire to live outside of human connections.

Earle Labor deems *The Call of the Wild* a "beast fable," because it "provoke[s] our interest—unconsciously if not consciously—in the human situation, not in the plight of the lower animals." Charles N. Watson Jr. provides another assessment of this aspect of the novel: "This is not a matter of observing, as some critics have done, that the dog story involves a human 'allegory,' a term implying that Buck is merely a human being disguised as a dog. Rather, the intuition at the heart of the novel is that the process of individuation in a dog, wolf, or a human child are not fundamentally different."

Naturalism

Although there has been much debate about how much *The Call of the Wild* conforms to naturalism, some of the novel's basic ideas are perfect illustrations of the theory. As an outgrowth of realism, naturalism dawned in the 1890s, when writers like Stephen Crane and Frank Norris produced fiction that examined life with scientific objectivity, concluding that biology and socioeconomic factors

ruled behavior. While local color and sentimental fiction dominated the literary marketplace at that time, these writers promoted a literature that was "real" and "true" in its depiction of the underside of America's burgeoning cities. Influenced by Darwinist theories of biological determinism, they applied such ideas to society, where the struggle for existence was often brutal and dehumanizing.

Buck's fate is in the hands of men. He is unable to decide his own course of action. London underscores this when he writes that Buck found himself where he was "because men had found a yellow metal in the North, and because Manuel was a gardener's helper whose wages did not lap over the needs of his wife and divers small copies of himself." In other words, circumstances well beyond Buck's control are guiding his life. *The Call of the Wild* perfectly illustrates the doctrines of naturalism because Buck "is a product of biological, environmental, and hereditary forces."

Romanticism

Despite the naturalist elements of *The Call of the Wild,* some scholars also perceive romantic tendencies. Although romanticism as a movement peaked in the mid-nineteenth century in America, its central tenets have always been popular in American fiction. In this style, strict adherence to reality is not important. Rather, setting or characters take on mythic or symbolic proportions. As Buck begins to heed the "call of the wild" he hears through his ancestors, the story becomes less realistic and more mythic.

As Earle Labor and Jeanne Campbell Reesman have argued, the novel is a "mythic romance" because "the call to adventure, departure, initiation, the perilous journey to the mysterious life-center, transformation, and apotheosis: these are ... all present in Buck's progress from the civilized world through the natural and beyond to the supernatural world." Although he starts out as a real character, Buck is transformed into the mythical "Ghost Dog" of Yeehat legend. Likewise, the setting of the Northland begins as a real region and ends up a dreamlike, mythical realm.

Historical Context

The Klondike Gold Rush

Many early settlers in North America had migrated in search of the gold that Spaniards had found in Central and South America. Dreams of a

The Klondike gold rush brought fortune-seekers, such as these in an 1897 photo, to the Alaska Territory.

continent paved with gold did not begin to come true until the 1840s, when gold was found in California. In the subsequent decades, gold was found in many regions of the West. Most prospectors that traveled to California never realized their dream. By the 1880s, mining had become big business, making it even more difficult for optimistic individuals to seek their fortunes.

When gold was found in the Klondike region in 1896, part of the Yukon territory of Canada, new dreams were kindled in the minds of many who viewed it as the last opportunity to make it big. This gold rush attracted hoards of people to the Alaska territory, which adjoined the Yukon. This forbidding region had barely been explored, and most had very little idea what to expect. Many were totally unprepared for the harsh conditions, like Charles, Hal, and Mercedes in *The Call of the Wild*. For the first time, towns were established in the interior of Alaska. In 1897, the year Jack London set sail for Alaska, the Klondike yielded $22 million in gold.

Social Darwinism

At the turn of the century, Charles Darwin's theory of evolution was applied to human society by philosophers and a new cadre of social scientists, including Herbert Spencer and William Gra-

ham Sumner. Adapting the notion of natural selection, they argued that life was a struggle for survival and that the "fittest" would come out on top. It was inevitable that only a few individuals would prosper; the rest would suffer in poverty. According to Social Darwinists, these conditions were not only inevitable but a positive process of weeding out those who were unfit, or inferior.

This theory of social evolution seemed to complement the competitive strain of capitalism that was shaping America in the 1890s and 1900s. Wealth was concentrated in the hands of a very few, like Andrew Carnegie, whose book *The Gospel of Wealth* (1900) used Social Darwinist ideas to justify his position in society. The prevailing view was that by extending charity to the needy, one would not only prolong the survival of people who were not fit to live but jeopardize the survival of society as a whole. Nonetheless, Carnegie felt he had a responsibility to use his millions to benefit others, so rather than simply give his money away, he set up trusts for the establishment of universities, art galleries, and public libraries.

For many Americans, among them Protestants and social Progressives, the philosophies of Spencer and Sumner were ruthlessly barbaric and

Compare & Contrast

- **1900s:** Americans recognize the need for conserving or protecting the environment. The U.S. government begins forest preservation efforts in 1891. In 1892 John Muir founded the Sierra Club. In 1903 President Theodore Roosevelt created the National Wildlife Refuge System.

  Today: The Sierra Club still exists and is a major force in the environmentalist movement. Business and environmentalists clash frequently over America's natural resources and endangered species.

- **1900s:** Indigenous to the area, wolves inhabit most of the northwestern United States, Canada, and Alaska.

  Today: Wolves have long ago disappeared from most of the United States. A project to reintroduce wolves to Yellowstone National Park is hotly contested by local ranchers, but is implemented with some success in the 1990s.

- **1900s:** Alaska, which became part of the United States in 1867, was sparsely populated until the gold rushes in Juneau (1880) and the Klondike (1897). The excitement regarding these discoveries brought streams of fortune hunters to settle the interior.

  Today: Alaska became a state in 1959. For many years, oil was the major economic product of the state. But in the 1980s, with the depression of the oil market, Alaska's economy suffered. When the *Exxon Valdez* ran aground in 1989, the oil polluted more than 1,285 miles of shoreline, including the Prince William Sound wildlife sanctuary. Alaska possesses the largest area of unspoiled wilderness in the United States and continues to try to balance its economic and environmental interests.

- **1900s:** In 1901 Theodore Roosevelt became President of the United States. A member of the "Rough Riders," a volunteer cavalry regiment, Roosevelt was a war hero in the Spanish-American War in 1898. He was also an avid sportsman, hunter, and adventurer, and he embodied the robust manliness that set a new standard for American manhood.

  Today: President William Jefferson Clinton was impeached by the House of Representatives in 1998 for lying under oath about an affair he had with a White House intern. Many Americans believe Clinton's affairs and lying to cover them up are a disgrace to America's values and a sign of the deterioration of the presidency.

---

amoral. They accused Social Darwinists of degeneracy and nihilism. Instead of merely accepting that those on the lowest rung of the ladder would simply be weeded out of society, they attempted to level the playing field for all Americans by enacting legislation and providing social services. They rejected the ideas of "rugged individualism" and "survival of the fittest" and promoted the idea of social cooperation.

Some, like the philosopher Lester Frank Ward, maintained that people possessed the capacity to change the world around them. Ward believed that a greater society would result from people's active protection of the weak rather than the laissez-faire doctrine of letting competition take its course.

Arts in the 1900s

Greatly influenced by Social Darwinism, the growth of poverty in urban areas, and labor unrest, writers and artists of the 1900s perceived the world as bleak. These younger writers and artists wanted to remove literature and art from the drawing rooms of genteel society and depict life in the street, in the factory, and the deteriorating farm in all its gritty detail. These writers believed that a kind of natural selection was taking place in society, but they did not share Spencer's and Sumner's optimism about the outcome. Instead, they focused on how the individual (the primary subject of literature) was affected by the unrestrained capitalist forces that drove this new society.

Naturalist writers, such as Theodore Dreiser, Frank Norris, Stephen Crane, and Jack London, created memorable characters who had to learn to survive in an uncaring and amoral society. The title character in Theodore Dreiser's *Sister Carrie* (1900) is lured to Chicago by dreams of big-city sophistication and material prosperity, only to find herself trapped in a low-paying, stifling factory job. She escapes by becoming the mistress of a well-off man, whose demise corresponds to Carrie's rise as an actress. While she adapts to the new economy, he is destroyed by it.

In the visual arts, a new group of artists—called the ash can school—depicted the realities of everyday urban existence. They rejected the credo of earlier artists, who believed that beauty was the only true subject of art. Centered in New York City, this movement eschewed traditional views of technique and training in favor of painting from the gut in an impressionistic style. Their art featured an abundance of brown and gray landscapes crowded with buildings and bridges. But often the work of ash can artists celebrated the life of immigrants and the urban working class, finding aesthetic value in these groups neglected by earlier artists.

Critical Overview

When *The Call of the Wild* was published in 1903, it was a resounding critical and popular success. Reviewers applauded this exciting adventure tale and viewed it as a welcome alternative to the popular fiction of the day. J. Stewart Doubleday, reviewing the novel in *The Reader,* praised London's "suggestion of the eternal principles that underlie [life]," admitting that "it is cruel reading—often relentless reading; ... But we forgive the writer at last because his is true! He is not sentimental, tricky; he is at harmony with himself and nature."

The *Atlantic Monthly* found "something magnificent in the spectacle of [Buck's] gradual detachment from the tame, beaten-in virtues of uncounted forefathers, ... and his final triumph over the most dreaded powers of the wilderness." Overall, the reviewer praised it as "not a pretty story at all, but a very powerful one."

London's reputation also extended overseas, where he was considered one of America's foremost writers. Yet in America, despite the early attention the novel received, *The Call of the Wild* came to be seen as escapist fiction most suitable for children. London was barely mentioned in the literary histories published in the 1920s and after, and he was dismissed by the New Critics, the prominent literary scholars of the 1940s and 1950s.

London's fiction, especially *The Call of the Wild,* continued to be popular with the reading public. It wasn't until the 1960s that scholars reassessed their opinions regarding London's work. Since that time a flood of critical and biographical material on London has been published, elevating him once again as one of America's most important authors.

Critical commentary on *The Call of the Wild* focuses on autobiographical aspects of the story, the nature of the novel's allegory, and the question of whether it can be considered an example of literary naturalism. Joan Hedrick views the novel as London's attempt to deal with his past. "London had consciously closed the book on his working-class past. That self dwelt in a black and slippery pit to be recalled only in dreams. But in *The Call of the Wild* London was able, through his canine hero, to return to the scenes of his past, and, having got in touch with them, to imagine a different future."

Andrew Flink maintains that the novel is London's attempt, "either consciously or unconsciously," to deal with one specific part of his past, namely his stint in prison. He draws extensive parallels between London's experiences as a prisoner and Buck's life in the Klondike.

Most critics agree that the novel functions as an allegory, at least on one level. Abraham Rothberg expresses this view: "London was not only treating animals like human beings, but treating human beings like animals, recognizing no essential difference between man and animal. In *The Call of the Wild* he equated men with dogs and wolves, and equated the harshness of the trail with the harshness of society, implying that force, savagery and cunning were equally the ways to success in both areas."

According to Charles N. Watson Jr., the novel is "about society as well as about the wilderness—or rather, ... it is about the conflict between the two." In other words, the novel is more than a simple allegory about society; it is a complex rendering of competing ideologies. Watson addresses the debate regarding the novel's naturalistic theme. To Watson, *The Call of the Wild* embodies both "Zolaesque naturalism ... —a reversion to savagery, a process of degeneration" and "romantic primitivism," by conveying "the forward movement of an initiation rite, through which Buck attains maturity and even apotheosis as a mythic hero." This dualism is perhaps the most discussed aspect of the novel.

While a few scholars, including Mary Kay Dodson, perceive the novel as a perfect embodiment of naturalism, others, such as Earl J. Wilcox, argue that the "naturalism that characterizes this novel is not consistently developed." Jonathan Auerbach sums up most opinions on the issue when he states, "There is a massive set of contradictions about Buck at the heart of the narrative, which moves in two seemingly opposite directions: toward nature from culture (the standard naturalist plot of decivilization), and a more troubled but also more passionate movement toward self-transcendence, which cannot be fully contained by the conventional naturalistic model."

Watson argues that it is precisely these contradictions that have made this novel appealing to readers and critics. In the novel he perceives "a fruitful tension between the naturalistic impulse, with its emphasis on society and environment, and the romantic impulse, which emphasizes the power of the exceptional individual to act on his own. Such a tension ... is one of the most fundamental themes of American fiction." As critics continue to explore the complexity of *The Call of the Wild,* it is becoming recognized as one of America's most enduring classics.

Criticism

Chloe Bolan

Bolan is an adjunct English instructor at the College of Lake County and Columbia College of Missouri extensions, a playwright, short story writer, poet, and essayist. In the following essay she speculates on why The Call of the Wild *is one of the most popular American novels in the world.*

Jack London's *Call of the Wild,* one of the most widely read American novels in the world, seems a strange choice for this distinction. The setting is the wilderness of the Klondike region, the protagonist is a dog, and the theme of the novel is devolution of the protagonist. Yet these are the same elements that garnered fame for the novel when it was first published in 1903; and these same elements continue to attract readers almost a century later.

In the late 1800s the Klondike region was swept by a gold rush. Gold had been found in California in 1848, and later in British Columbia, South Africa, Australia, and New Zealand. Yet this rush was in Alaska, purchased from Russia thirty years earlier in 1867, and Canada's Yukon Territory, and rivaled all previous gold rushes. It had formidable challenges, though; not only the forbidding cold, but also the uncharted geography made it a treacherous choice for the unprepared prospector. Still, many answered the call of quick money, including the young Jack London.

Although London staked a claim which he later abandoned, he was awed by the natural beauty he found in the ice-locked rivers and snow-encrusted mountains, in the spring thaw and sudden summer blooms, in the abundance of animal life from king salmon in the streams to caribou and bear on the plains to sheep and goats in the highlands. Before a year was up, London returned to his California home with debilitating scurvy. Yet he had found gold: his visions of the Klondike, the tales from the sourdoughs or old-timers, and his own intense experiences gave him enough material to write brilliant stories including his most masterful of all, *The Call of the Wild.*

Most early readers of the novel were content to curl up in a warm corner and read about the inhospitable climate and terrain of America's last frontier. Today, although Alaska attracts tourists, its environment and weather conditions will never attract as many permanent residents as, for example, the Sun Belt states do. The exotic land skirting the Arctic Circle is still forbidding—and if the environmentalists maintain their influence in the region, its pristine and primitive beauty will be preserved for future generations and future readers.

A beautiful, dangerous setting alone does not guarantee a great novel. Character is often paramount. In *The Call of the Wild,* however, the main character is assumed to be enslaved by man and by its own instinct. Both of these considerations would make Buck, the Saint Bernard-Scotch shepherd mix, a poor candidate for a riveting, dynamic character. Yet, by following his instincts, Buck takes his readers to the deepest reaches of the mind; and the readers, following their instincts, immediately translate Buck's canine qualities into human ones. Buck, therefore, becomes a mythic hero, and here lies the real power of the novel.

In the first chapter, "Into the Primitive," Buck meets all the criteria necessary for becoming a mythic hero, according to Joseph Campbell's out-

What Do I Read Next?

- *Social Darwinism in European and American Thought, 1860-1945: Nature as Model and Nature as Threat (1997),* written by Mike Hawkins, explores the way individual thinkers and larger social groups define and interpret the theories of Social Darwinism. It also examines the traditional and revisionist approaches historians have taken with Social Darwinism.

- *Modern Man in Search of a Soul* (1933) summarizes many of Carl Jung's psychoanalytical theories. London discovered Jung's work late in life and found in it an expression of many ideas that corresponded with his own. Most notably, Jung's theory of the "collective unconscious" was anticipated in *The Call of the Wild.*

- Rudyard Kipling's *The Jungle Book* (1895) is a collection of tales featuring Mowgli, a young boy raised by wolves. The stories take place in the jungles of India and include a cast of talking animals who teach Mowgli valuable lessons.

These stories were among the most popular animal stories for children when London wrote *The Call of the Wild.*

- *Martin Eden* (1909) was London's most autobiographical novel. It chronicles the story of a young man who rises from poverty to fame as an internationally-acclaimed author.

- In *The Road* (1907), London describes his early tramping experiences and traces his development from hobo and "blond-beastly" adventurer to an author and a socialist.

- In *White Fang* (1906), considered a companion piece to *The Call of the Wild,* London depicts a wild dog who becomes domesticated, reversing Buck's transformation.

- Frank Norris's *McTeague* (1899) is a classic example of naturalism, as heredity and environment determine the fate of luckless individuals in turn-of-the-century San Francisco.

---

line in *The Hero with a Thousand Faces.* The hero must first answer "[t]he [c]all to [a]dventure"—although Buck is kidnapped instead of called. But since a domesticated dog would rather die than desert his master, only a violent act could wrench the loyal Buck away from the Judge and his happy life in a California valley.

The next step, the "[r]efusal of the [c]all," is fruitless. Buck's attempt to escape from the rope around his neck only tightens the rope and makes him more enraged. After this, "[s]upernatural [a]id" is offered in the form of the saloon keeper removing the rope and checking in on Buck throughout the night. Although "supernatural" is stretching a point, the saloon keeper frees Buck from a dangerous device and allows the dog to suffer alone, foreshadowing the self-reliance he'll need in the hostile environment to come.

"Crossing of the [f]irst [t]hreshold" comes when Buck meets the man in the red sweater, the dog breaker, who teaches Buck to obey by beating him with a club. Some dogs won't adapt, and they die fighting; others adapt with a broken spirit; Buck adapts a spirit that bends without breaking.

The last step is entering the "passage into the realm of night" and here, at the end of the chapter, is where Buck experiences snow for the first time. Despite the beauty of a veil of falling snow or the serenity it lends to a landscape, the snow symbolizes a formidable foe for the sled dogs and their mushers: the dogs need the ice accumulated from the day's run removed from their paws to prevent frostbite; the mushers need to be alert to the poor visibility and the disguised trails that could result in an accident in an environment where carelessness can quickly lead to death. Although Buck is mystified by the snow, it clearly belongs to the darker side of experience.

The following six chapters of the novel fall into place with the hero's "[r]oad of [t]rials." Here

---

Buck learns important things from the other dogs: how to steal food without getting caught, how to sleep outside, how to interact with the other dogs. The friendly Newfoundland, Curly, greets a dog who attacks her in the wolf style—biting her face, then jumping back to avoid retaliation. When she stumbles to the ground because of her wounds, the other dogs tear her apart. Buck learns it's better to be wary, or even antisocial like Dave and Sol-leks. He also learns to deal with Spitz, the pack leader, whom he eventually defeats in a fight to the death, because he has one great advantage—imagination.

"Meeting with the [g]oddess," the next step, suggests the scene where Buck meets Mercedes, who is tenderhearted towards him at first, until her own survival takes precedence. She insists on riding the sled that is already overloaded. Her rationale for her husband and brother beating the dogs is circuitous: if they'd only run faster, they wouldn't get whipped. This is not a woman Buck likes, but she is the only one of the three Yukon greenhorns who could protect the dogs, and she fails.

The following step, "[w]oman as the [t]emptress," is missing because this is a novel without sex. While London never avoided writing about intimate relationships, he did avoid their sexual aspects, due in large part to his Victorian audience. Prostitution was rampant in the Klondike yet is never mentioned in the story. Since the focus is on the dog instead of man, this fact isn't missed; however, Buck is a sexual creature, and that part of his life is never directly addressed.

The next two steps involve Buck's relationship with John Thornton. "Atonement with the [f]ather" casts John Thornton in the fatherly role of the loving master, replacing Buck's former father-figure and master, the Judge. Through Thornton, Buck comes to believe in man again—not man in general, but man in particular. The "[a]potheosis," or elevation to divine status, occurs when Buck has avenged John Thornton's death by killing several Yeehat Indians and gains a reputation as the Ghost Dog. Finally, the "[u]ltimate [b]oon" may well be the markings on the young wolves, evidence of Buck's leadership, accompanying sexual dominance and contribution to the pack.

Campbell concludes that the hero's reintegration into society may be his most difficult task. In *The Call of the Wild,* there is no reintegration into the society of the domestic dog, a creature whose evolution is in the hands of its master. Buck has left that society, has devolved, undone the canine choice made in prehistory and referred to in the

novel: the image of anxious prehistoric man sitting before the fire. Buck has visions of this, but he is moved to follow his deepest instincts: to break the pact with man and join the wolf pack—in fact, to strengthen the pack by broadening the gene pool.

This reversed ending, devolution over evolution, is the one that works best on the narrative level, for Buck has at last found his place. On the analogous level, it suggests the human struggle to answer heroically the wild call within, the call of individualism, a call all the world understands.

Source: Chloe Bolan, in an essay for *Novels for Students,* Gale, 2000.

Leonard R. N. Ashley

In the following essay, Ashley asserts that London should be remembered as more than "a once-popular author, an author of juvenile literature, the master of the dog story," but concludes, "Nonetheless, London's place in literary history depends now and always will depend on the appeal of The Call of the Wild.*"*

In the Soviet Union, Jack London is regarded as one of the greatest of American writers, chiefly because of such sentiments as are found in now-obscure works of his such as "A Night with the Philomaths." There he has a firebrand orating about a revolution of the proletariat.

> Twenty-five millions strong … to make rulers and ruling classes pause and consider. The cry of this army is: No quarter! We want all that you possess. We want in our hands the reins of power and the destiny of mankind…. We are going to take your governments, your palaces, and all your purpled ease away from you, and in that day you shall work for your bread even as the peasant in the field or the starved and runty clerk in your metropolises…. You have failed in your management of society, and your management is to be taken away from you…. This is the revolution, my masters. Stop it if you can.

However, the early poverty and struggle that drew London to Marx and to communist or socialist ideology as he read books in the Klondike winter were followed by success and belief, according to Charles Child Walcutt, in himself as "an epitome of the Darwinian Struggle for Existence, his success an example of the [Herbert] Spencerian Survival of the Fittest." He had also read Nietzsche, and he came to people his prolific output of fiction with supermen, heroes who could succeed without or in spite of either communism or democracy, heroes that were not so much self-sacrificing socialists as rapacious capitalists of the spirit. They conquered by force of will and indomitable courage rather than by cleverness. In the great American tradition, they "hung in there"; and when the going got tough, they got tougher. London liked to think of himself as one of these semi-divine heroes. A newspaper reporter once noticed that his Korean houseboy called London "Mr. God." The reporter added, "Jack liked it."

In London's most popular novel, *The Call of the Wild,* the hero is a dog—the story is told entirely from the dog Buck's point of view—and even when ill treatment causes him to revert to the "dominant primordial beast" he is a symbol of what man can do to overcome obstacles and become the leader of his fellows. A mongrel, a cross between a German Shepherd and a St. Bernard, Buck is uprooted, stolen from his comfortable California home, and sold for work as a sled dog in the Gold Rush of 1897. Then he becomes the companion and eventually the savior of a young prospector. Finally he becomes the leader of a wild pack, and the book ends with these triumphant and famous words:

> When the long winter nights come on and the wolves follow their meat into the lower valleys, he may be seen running at the head of the pack through the pale moonlight or glimmering borealis, leaping gigantic above his fellows, his great throat a-bellow as he sings a song of the younger world, which is the song of the pack.

In some sense Buck is a representation of the author as he would like to see himself. An illegitimate child of a spiritualist (who later married John London, not his father), London quit school at 14, worked in a cannery, became a pirate on the ship *Razzle Dazzle* in San Francisco Bay at 16 and a sailor to Siberia and Japan at 17, tramped around, and went to the Klondike in 1897. There he found more adventure, opportunity for the will to power, risk and challenge and self-fulfillment, freedom from civilization's restraints—the life suited to a man who once said "morality is only an evidence of low blood pressure."

London returned from the Klondike without gold but with a rich vein of wilderness experiences which he industriously mined thereafter. *The Call of the Wild* is but one of his tales of heroism and violence in circumstances of danger. Where Bret Harte told the story of "A Yellow Dog" that became a snob in the gold fields and Eric Knight was to sentimentalize canine faithfulness in *Lassie Come-Home,* London told the tale of a dog who went from snob to superdog. London's was a rousing tale that had a message as well as a love for mankind.

London, who always had more drive than deftness in writing, was extremely clever to focus on Buck rather than on the human world around him. Judge Miller, by whose Santa Clara, California, fireside the young Buck lay in innocence and peace before he was "dognapped," has more of a function than a character in the book. John Thornton, the strong, silent, noble type to whom Buck becomes attached in the Yukon, is a stereotype: we provide his qualities from other reading rather than discover them in the novel. "Black" Burton and other bad guys are also stock characters. So are the greenhorns and the French-Canadians and the other humans. The animals, however, are sufficiently humanized, and if they, too, are stereotypes we are more impressed with the personalities they are given than with their lack of depth. Pike (the thief), Dub (the clumsy one), Dave and Sol-leks (the sled dogs who are dedicated "professionals"), Curly (the amiable Newfoundland dog) who "made advances to a husky dog the size of a full-grown wolf" and was "ripped open from eye to jaw" in an instant—these animals each have their place in the story and can be said to be characters in the fiction in a sense in which the humans are not. Among the dogs are the "bully" personalities so beloved of the Teddy Roosevelt period of American history. Among them is clearly shown "the law of club and fang": "So that was the way. No fair play. Once down, that was the end of you." Among them, also, there are treachery and nobility, faithfulness unto death, and a conviction that moral nature is "a vain thing and a handicap in the ruthless struggle for existence." They learn that "kill or be killed, eat or be eaten, was the law." Towering above all is Buck. "When he was made, the mould was broke," says Pete. And in awkward dialect Hans affirms: "Py jingo! I t'ink so mineself."

That a good deal of the book is given to describing the feelings of the animals is an advantage in the light of London's clumsiness with cliche ("Every animal was motionless as though turned to stone") and dialogue ("Plumb tuckered out, that's what's the matter"). The action moves swiftly; we are seldom aware of the "stoppages" of the sleds or that characters are "lessoned," of the awkward prolepsis or the literary infelicities, as the melodramatic tale unfolds of how Buck "put his name many notches higher on the totem pole of Alaskan fame." We discover that sentiment can exist without a love story; Mercedes, the only woman in the book, is a shadow. Popular writers discover that a riveting story, as of the "kidnapped king" tried in the furnace and emerging pure gold (or "a yellow metal," as London would say), is enough.

Those who want more can see London as a racist, fascist, Social Darwinist; as a predecessor of Jack Kerouac and other "on the road" writers; as a tough-guy writer in the tradition developed by John Dos Passos, Ernest Hemingway, and Norman Mailer, though perhaps best exemplified in Dashiell Hammett and other writers of crime fiction; as a writer about animals (such as Buck and the wolf-dog that seeks civilization in *White Fang*) foreshadowing George Orwell's *Animal Farm* in using them as metaphors of humanity; as a giant in his time—in 1913 the most popular and best-paid writer in the world—who was denigrated in later times; as (to note Andrew Sinclair's argument) a path-finder in areas as different as the boxing novel and sociobiology of the school of Lorenz, Ardrey, and Desmond Morris.

In the biography *Jack* (1977), Sinclair makes a gallant effort to rescue London from too close identification with the message that "a man with a club was a law-giver, a master to be obeyed" and the view of "nature red in tooth and claw." Sinclair does much to bring him to serious consideration as much more than a once-popular author, an author of juvenile literature, the master of the dog story. Nonetheless, London's place in literary history depends now and always will depend on the appeal of *The Call of the Wild.*

Source: Leonard R. N. Ashley, "*The Call of the Wild,*" in *Reference Guide to American Literature,* third edition, edited by Jim Kamp, St. James Press, 1994.

John S. Mann

In the following excerpt, Mann suggests that various doubles, or pairings of antithetical characters and plot elements in the novel, contribute to the enduring popularity of The Call of the Wild *and to the value of the novel as an object of critical study.*

Dogs and men are fundamentally alike in the Klondike world of Jack London's *The Call of the Wild:* There was imperative need to be constantly alert; for these dogs and men were not town dogs and men. They were savages, all of them, who knew no law but the law of club and fang. Dogs and men answer the call of their savage natures and their terrifying environment in a violent, bloody, and continual struggle for survival. The primitive fears and desires which surface in Buck—the splendid animal on whom the story centers—also control his human masters. London describes the dog's development—his regression to instinct—in terms of *human* personality and action, so that by the end

of the tale Buck emerges as a fully-realized character whose motivation can be thoroughly understood. *The Call of the Wild* remains, curiously, a dog story made humanly understandable: it is a story of the transformations that a dog undergoes in the development of a new identity.

London patterns the relationships between dogs and humans with special care, and they strike the reader with clarity and richness. In part this justifies one's discovery in the story of a controlling metaphor, a theme, usually applied to a peculiar facet of human character. The theme of the double in fact illuminates *The Call of the Wild* in several important ways, offering focus for revelations about Buck and his human masters alike. The double as theme, as idea, as complex symbology provides a radiant metaphorical center for the whole landscape of Buck's tale. It encompasses character—the presentations of Buck, men and other dogs, and their necessary relations—but it also touches the action, the points of view involved in the telling of the story, and its atmosphere and setting in significant ways. Doubles and doubling themselves become controlling, almost obsessive preoccupations in London's narrative. Accordingly, a consideration of the double can help to account for the fascination the book has had for readers in the seventy-odd years since its publication in July, 1903. It can also suggest ways in which the book, surely one of London's best, is worthy of continued serious critical attention....

If the theme of the double usually depicts men as deeply divided within themselves, at war with their own natures and with their surroundings, then its first manifestation [in *The Call of the Wild*] is in the opposing values, the polar attractions, of civilized and uncivilized worlds at work on the consciousness of a dog. The story develops through the impact of Buck's new Klondike environment upon his habits and expectations, conditioned as they are by his four-year sojourn in the civilized Santa Clara Valley of California. The logic of Buck's experience is to drive him increasingly, dramatically into the wild, so that even the interruption of this process by the civilizing love of John Thornton is not enough to return him to men and civilization.

London called the process the devolution or decivilization of a dog. Buck's first theft of food from the government courier Perrault early in the book marks the decay or going to pieces of his moral nature, a vain thing and a handicap in the ruthless struggle for existence. Stealing food helps Buck stay alive, and the narrator remarks that the completeness of his decivilization was now evidenced by his ability to flee from the defence of a moral consideration and so save his hide. The remainder of the story parallels the outer conflict between Buck and his new Klondike environment with the inner conflict between the savage character of his buried nature and the patterns of conduct imposed on that nature by civilized society. Like the chief character in O'Neill's *Emperor Jones,* Buck faces experiences that force instincts long dead [to become] alive again. The domesticated generations fell from him.

London dramatizes this split between civilization and savagery in several interesting ways, each involving a kind of double in turn. Though he once commented that God abhors a mongrel, he carefully states that Buck is of mixed breed—half St. Bernard and half Scotch shepherd. This racial split in Buck's physical nature shrewdly underscores the inner conflict between civilized values and their opposites.

More important in defining the antithetical parts of Buck's nature is London's constant use of images of war throughout the book. Civilization and savagery fight a war inside Buck; much of Chapter Three chronicles the secret growth of the dominant primordial beast within him. Marks of war are everywhere in the plot of *The Call of the Wild:* in the huskies' savage killing of the Newfoundland, Curly; in the fight of Buck's team with a pack of starving huskies; in the constant fighting among the dogs on the team; in the murder of John Thornton and his partner by marauding Yeehat Indians; in Buck's battle with the wolf pack at the end of the book. Buck fights a literal war with his rival Spitz, first as a rebellious underling deposing the leader of the dog team, and later in a significant affirmation of his savage inheritance:

> In a flash Buck knew it. The time had come. It was to the death. As they circled about, snarling, ears laid back, keenly watchful for the advantage, the scene came to Buck with a sense of familiarity. He seemed to remember it all, the white woods, and earth, and moonlight, and the thrill of battle. Over the whiteness and silence brooded a ghostly calm.... To Buck it was nothing new or strange, this scene of old time. It was as though it had always been, the wonted way of things.

The war between Buck and Spitz provides London with one of his clearest metaphors for Darwinian struggle and survival. The taste of Spitz's blood remains with Buck, drawn back and waiting for the other dogs to finish off the wounded rival: Buck stood and looked on, the successful champion, the dominant primordial beast who had made his kill and found it good.

Francois, the team driver, notices the change in Buck the next day in a significant phrase: 'Eh? Wot I say? I spik true w'en I say day Buck two devils!' As if in confirmation of that statement, London further dramatizes the theme of the double in an explicit set of controlling oppositions. Each of these projects Buck's inner and outer conflicts in things of opposite value. The original opposition between civilization and the wild encompasses all the others. The civilized world of the Southland, described continually in the book as warm, soft and easy, is opposed to the wild Northland, a terrifying arena of cold, hard brutality and sudden, violent death which yet—in London's most intriguing paradox—is finally seen as life-giving for the transformed Buck. The human world of ethical impulse and civilizing sanctions against violence is placed against the savage world of animals and savage men. More civilized dogs like Newfoundlands and even huskies find primitive counterparts in the wolves whose howl at the end of the story is the very sound of the wild.

Less obviously, London doubles the story into opposing worlds. Buck begins in the waking world of reality and ends in a silent, white wasteland which is also the world of dream, shadow, and racial memory. Buck survives to embrace life at the end of a book informed by death as the horrifying, rhythmic reflex of an entire order of things. Life in *The Call of the Wild* is a survival built on the death of other living creatures.

Between these opposing worlds and these opposing values Buck hovers continually in the action of the tale. Even the call of the wild itself, to which Buck responds with growing intensity throughout, receives double focus, twin definition: it is both lure and trap. In the second chapter, when Buck learns The Law of Club and Fang, he builds his first warm sleeping nest in the snow, to discover the next morning:

> It had snowed during the night and he was completely buried. The snow walls pressed him on every side, and a great surge of fear swept through him—the fear of the wild thing for the trap. It was a token that he was harking back through his own life to the lives of his forbears; for he was a civilized dog, an unduly civilized dog, and of his own experience knew no trap and so could not of himself fear it. The muscles of his whole body contracted spasmodically and instinctively, the hair on his neck and shoulders stood on end, and with a ferocious snarl he bounded straight up into the blinding day, the snow flying about him in a flashing cloud.

The alluring world of snow and silence remains no less a tomb at the end of the book; though Buck is able to respond to it and still survive, John Thornton cannot.

It is impossible to view such doubled worlds and values, such connected oppositions, for very long without returning to London's pairing of dogs and humans with a renewed sense of its interest and complexity. Both Maxwell Geismar and Charles Child Walcutt have pointed to London's skill in keeping the story within an animal point of view while retaining for balance and proportion a wise degree of human perspective. In fact, *The Call of the Wild* does retain a double point of view throughout, and London's cunning alternation of dog and human perspectives becomes the essential mark of his craft in the story.

Source: John S. Mann, "The Theme of the Double in *The Call of the Wild*," in *Markham Review,* Vol. 8, Fall, 1978, pp. 1-5.

Sources

Atlantic Monthly, Vol. 92, November, 1903, pp. 695-96.

Jonathan Auerbach, "'Congested Mails': Buck and Jack's 'Call,'" in *Rereading Jack London,* edited by Leonard Cassuto and Jeanne Campbell Reesman, Stanford University Press, 1966, pp. 25-45.

Joseph Campbell, "The Hero and the God," in *The Hero with a Thousand Faces,* Princeton University Press, 1968, p. 36.

Mary Kay Dodson, "Naturalism in the Works of Jack London," in *Jack London Newsletter,* Vol. 4, No. 3, September-December, 1971, pp. 130-39.

J. Stewart Doubleday, in a review of *The Call of the Wild,* in *The Reader,* Vol. 2, No. 4, September, 1903, pp. 408-09.

Andrew Flink, "'Call of the Wild'—Jack London's Catharsis," in *Jack London Newsletter,* Vol. 11, No. 1, January-April, 1978, pp. 12-19.

Joan D. Hedrick, "*The Call of the Wild*," in *Solitary Comrade: Jack London and His Work,* The University of North Carolina Press, 1982, pp. 94-111.

Earle Labor and Jeanne Campbell Reesman, *Jack London,* Twayne, 1994.

Abraham Rothberg, in the introduction to *The Call of the Wild* and *White Fang,* by Jack London, Bantam Books, 1963, pp. 1-17.

Charles Watson Jr., "Ghost Dog: 'The Call of the Wild,'" in *The Novels of Jack London: A Reappraisal,* The University of Wisconsin Press, 1983, pp. 33-52.

Earl J. Wilcox, "Jack London's Naturalism: The Example of *The Call of the Wild,*" in *Jack London Newsletter,* Vol. 2, No. 3, September-December, 1969, pp. 91-101.

For Further Study

Raymond Benoit, "Jack London's *The Call of the Wild,*" in *American Quarterly,* Vol. 20, No. 2, Summer, 1968, pp. 246-48.

    Benoit contends that *The Call of the Wild* is part of the tradition of "pastoral protest" literature in America and that it embodies the "American dream of escaping from the entangling complexity of modern living."

Jacqueline Tavernier-Courbin, *The Call of the Wild: A Naturalistic Romance,* Twayne, 1994.

    Offers a detailed analysis of the novel's competing ideologies.

————, editor, *Critical Essays on Jack London,* G.K. Hall, 1983.

    This collection contains important early assessments of London's works as well as contemporary critical essays.

Charles Child Walcutt, "Jack London: Blond Beasts and Superman," in *American Literary Naturalism, A Divided Stream,* University of Minnesota Press, 1956, p. 87-113.

    In the chapter on London in his classic study of American naturalism, Walcutt discusses the nature of morality in *The Call of the Wild.*

Earl J. Wilcox, editor, *The Call of the Wild by Jack London: A Casebook with Text, Background Sources, Reviews, Critical Essays, and Bibliography,* Nelson Hall, 1980.

    In addition to the text of the novel, this book contains reviews, helpful essays on the novel, the story "Batard," and nine letters by London pertaining to the novel.

Don Quixote

Miguel de Cervantes Saavedra

1605

In 1605 a novel appeared that has become one of the most beloved stories of European literature. It was the history of Don Quixote, the tall, gaunt knight-errant astride his fallible steed, with his pot-bellied, illiterate squire, Sancho Panza. These eccentric characters are as famous as Sinbad, Tarzan, Odysseus, Hamlet, or Superman. *Don Quixote* was immediately embraced by his countrymen; it is a testament to the novel and Miguel de Cervantes Saavedra's vivid characterization that the character of Don Quixote is still utilized to mock politicians and satirize the self-righteous.

The original story, *El ingenioso hidalgo don Quijote de la Mancha,* was immediately popular—with six editions in 1605 alone—and has never lost its prominence. Cervantes not only created one of the greatest comic figures of world literature, but with his realist and humanist techniques, he originated, some critics assert, the modern novel.

Part I of Don Quixote's story appeared in 1605 and was complemented ten years later—a year after the usurper, Avellaneda, published a false sequel—by Part II. In both parts of the novel, Don Quixote lives in a world created in his imagination, which had been fueled by his obsession with chivalric tales. He longs to resurrect this world he has long read of: chivalry, battles with giants and evil knights, the rescue of virtuous maidens. Instead, Don Quixote deals with windmills, bedclothes, and much disappointment. Along the way, he acquires a sidekick, Sancho, who helps Don Quixote in hopes of getting rich. This dynamic duo has pro-

Miguel de Cervantes Saavedra

vided readers throughout the centuries with humorous, yet poignant, chivalric tales.

Author Biography

Cervantes was born in Alcalé de Henares on September 19, 1547. Little is known about his early childhood, other than that it was an itinerant existence; his father, a barber-surgeon, was constantly moving his family from town to town to find work. It is assumed that Cervantes's education was minimal although he does seem to have received some education from the Jesuits in Seville.

In 1569, his teacher, López de Hoyos, published four of his poems in Madrid. Cervantes then traveled to Italy, possibly as a result of a duel with Don Antonio Sigura. In Rome, Cervantes served the Cardinal-elect Giulio Acquaviva. In 1571 he enlisted in the Spanish militia to fight for Don Juan of Austria against the Ottoman-Turks at Lepanto. During this battle, he received two bullets to the chest and one to his left hand, which left him permanently disabled. In 1572, he joined Don Juan's campaign to fight at Navarino, Corfu, and Tunis. Returning to Spain in 1575, he was captured by Algerian corsairs.

Cervantes fetched a high price for his captors. Cervantes, as is recorded in the *Informacion* (a document based on eyewitness testimony to refute his enemies and avoid the Spanish Inquisition), kept up the spirits of his fellow hostages. He tried unsuccessfully to lead them in several escapes. Finally, in 1580, Trinitarian friars paid his high ransom, probably collected from family and friends. Now free, he returned to Spain a great hero. Despite his fame, he was without a job and his family was destitute.

He was unsuccessful as a playwright, because he was unable to compete with the monopoly of Lope de Vega. He wrote poems, but that brought in little money. His only child, Isabel de Saavedra, was the result of an affair with an actress named Ana Franca de Rojas. In 1584, he married a young woman, Catalina de Salazar y Palacios.

In 1585 Cervantes published *La Galatea.* He became a commissary agent, then a tax collector. Since his salary was often late, he made money by lending out his tax collections at interest. When such a transaction went bad, he was investigated. This landed him in jail several times. During one such jail term in 1597 he conceived of the story that became *Don Quixote.*

With the publication of *El ingenioso hidalgo don Quijote de la Mancha,* Cervantes became famous around the world. Although inadequate copyright protection robbed him of riches, patrons enabled him to settle in Madrid and write more novels. His last works included the second part of the Don Quixote saga and *Los trabajos de Persiles y Sigismunda,* completed three days before he died in April 1616.

Plot Summary

Part I

Don Quixote opens with a prologue. Much of the prologue, however, is devoted to a discussion of what a prologue should include, offering the reader some insight into what a seventeenth-century audience might expect.

Don Quixote is the story of Alonso Quijano, an aging gentleman of La Mancha. He reads so many chivalric romances that he loses his sanity. As the narrator reports: "With virtually no sleep and so much reading, he dried out his brain and lost his sanity."

Don Quixote decides to become a knight-errant, which is a knight who travels the countryside performing good deeds and seeking adventure. He puts on an old suit of armor, mounts a bony old horse he calls Rocinante, and renames himself Don Quixote de La Mancha. He also appoints a peasant woman, Aldonza Lorenzo, as his ladylove, and renames her Dulcinea del Toboso. Like the knights of old, Don Quixote performs good deeds in the name of Dulcinea, although she does not know that she is the object of the older man's attention.

Don Quixote then rides in search of adventure. Just as he considers himself a knight, he imagines that a local inn is a castle and the innkeeper a castellan. As a result of his madness and odd behavior, a group of travelers beat him.

After the beating, he makes his way home, where he is interrogated by the local priest and barber. Concerned, they decide to cure him of his madness by burning his books. Don Quixote attributes the missing books to a thieving wizard.

Soon he sets off on another adventure, this time accompanied by Sancho Panza, a rude peasant. In a very famous scene, Don Quixote mistakes some windmills for giants and rushes at them with his spear. When Don Quixote realizes that he has attacked a windmill, he says that the same magician who has stolen his books has also turned the giants into windmills.

Don Quixote and Sancho have several more adventures, including mistaking two herds of sheep for armies and a funeral for a parade of monsters. Furthermore, they free some prisoners on their way to becoming galley slaves. Don Quixote travels to the mountains to fast and pray for his love, Dulcinea, and sends Sancho Panza with a message to Dulcinea. Don Quixote's friends intercept Sancho and learn his master's whereabouts. They finally lure Don Quixote home, hoping that they can keep him safe.

Part II

Don Quixote's friends are unable to keep him at home for long. Don Quixote and Sancho Panza take off in search of adventure again, this time meeting with the Knight of the Wood (a village student in disguise who had promised to impede Don Quixote's adventures), joining a wedding party, and destroying a traveling puppet show.

The second volume of the novel also includes a long section in which Don Quixote and Sancho Panza stay with a duke and a duchess who have

A scene from a Russian adaptation of Don Quixote, *starring Yuri Tobubeyev and Nikolai Cherkassov, 1957.*

read about the pair's famous adventures. The Duke and the Duchess play a series of tricks on Don Quixote, including the "disenchantment" of Dulcinea and the enthronement of Sancho as ruler of an island.

Next, Don Quixote and Sancho decide to go to Barcelona where they have additional adventures. Finally, the student from the earlier episode finds Don Quixote and challenges him to combat. Don Quixote is defeated. He decides to return home and become a shepherd.

On his return home, Don Quixote falls ill. He instructs his niece and housekeeper, "Take me to my bed because I don't feel at all well, and just remember: whether I'm a knight errant, as now, or a shepherd, later on, I'll never stop doing for you whatever needs to be done, as you will see in the event."

Although his friends try to cheer him up, Don Quixote grows weaker and weaker. Finally he writes his will and apparently returns to sanity:

> I was mad, and now am sane; I was Don Quixote de La Mancha and now, as I have said, I am Alonso Quijano the Good. I pray that my repentance, and my honesty, may return me to the good opinion your graces once held of me.

With this renunciation of chivalry and romance, Don Quixote receives his last rites and subsequently dies. He leaves an inheritance to both Sancho and to his niece, instructing her to marry a man who has never read a book of chivalry.

Characters

The Barber
See Master Nicholas

The Captive Captain
See Perez de Viedma

Cardenio
Cardenio is in love with Luscinda, but Don Fernando tricks him into giving her up. After seeing them wed, he hides in a desolate region of mountains. Found by the Curate and Barber, they find the woman wronged by Don Fernando. Together they fetch Don Quixote and return to the Inn, where Cardenio and Luscinda are reunited.

Sanson Carrasco
Carrasco is a scholar and historian who informs Don Quixote and Sancho Panza about the book that had been written of their adventures. Carrasco seems to encourage Don Quixote to ride again, but then he becomes the Knight of the Mirrors to convince Don Quixote to return home. When Carrasco is vanquished instead, he tries again as the Knight of the White Moon. This time he is successful and commands Don Quixote to return home for one year. Carrasco, unlike the Barber and Curate, really respects and loves Don Quixote, and worries about the old man's safety. Don Quixote thanks him by making him the executor of his will—a position of trust. Carrasco also writes Don Quixote's epitaph.

The Curate
See Pedro Perez

Dulcinea del Toboso
See Aldonza Lorenzo

Don Diego de Miranda
Don Diego is a wise gentleman from La Mancha. He is concerned by Don Quixote's madness and is witness to his conquest of the lion. As a man of sense, he represents what Don Quixote would be if he hadn't become obsessed with chivalric tales.

Gines de Pasamonte
Pasamonte is a notorious criminal freed by Don Quixote. He gives Don Quixote no thanks and even knocks his teeth out with a stone. Later, he steals Sancho's ass.

Perez de Viedma
Maria's companion, Perez de Viedma, the Captive Captain, relates the experience of his slavery in Algeria to Don Quixote. His tale is based somewhat on Cervantes's own captivity experience in Algeria.

Dorotea
Dorotea flees to a convent rather than marry Don Fernando. He retrieves her and is escorting her home when they meet Cardenio and Luscinda.

Duchess
The Duchess is based on Maria Luisa de Aragon, Duchess of Villahermosa. Sancho is her favorite character in the story and she pays much attention to him. At her encouragement, Sancho is made governor of a small village.

Duke
Based on the historical Don Carlos de Borja, the Duke of Villahermosa is a kindhearted, wealthy man. He has read Part I of *Don Quixote* and hopes to play tricks on Don Quixote and Sancho.

Don Fernando
Don Fernando is a rich and selfish man who steals his friend's woman, Luscinda. In the process he affects the life of another woman, his lover Dorotea.

Roque Guinart
Roque Guinart is like Robin Hood; he steals only from the rich. Don Quixote and Sancho travel with Roque's band for three days until they are delivered to a friend of Roque's in Barcelona.

Housekeeper
One of several stock characters, Don Quixote's housekeeper is a woman "about forty" who blames books of chivalry for her master's madness and wants them all burned.

Knight of the Green Cloak
See Don Diego de Miranda

Media Adaptations

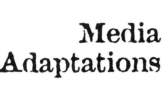

- In 1984, Universal released a laser disc game called "Super Don Quixote." It was similar to *Dragon's Lair,* and the gamester was a knight named Don who had to rescue Isabella from a witch. Sancho Panza even tags along but, as one would expect, does little to help.

- *Don Quixote* has been adapted as a ballet many times. Famous dancers, including Mikhail Baryshnikov, have performed in various productions. Rudolf Nureyev choreographed a production in 1973. He also danced the part of Basilio. The Kirov Ballet performed *Don Quixote* as choreographed by Petopia and Gorsky in 1988. Tatianna Terekhova was the star performer. Nina Ananiashbili starred in a production in 1992.

- *Don Quixote* was made into a silent film a few times. Edward Dillon directed DeWolf Hopper Sr., Fay Tincher, and Max Davidson in 1915. Maurice Elvey filmed another silent version in 1923; his film starred Bertram Burleigh and Sydney Fairbrother.

- Dramatic film adaptations have been produced in Russia. The first, which contained an amazing windmill scene, is known as *Don Quichotte.* Georg Wilhelm Pabst directed the story in three linguistic versions using mostly the same cast: French, English, and German. Feodor Chaliapin Sr. stars as Don Quixote. Several years later, *Don Kikhot* (1957) appeared. This version was directed by Grigori Kozyntsev and starred Nikolai Cherkassov as Don Quixote and Yuri Tolubeyev as Sancho Panza. Oleg Grigorovich directed a version known as *Don Quixote Is Coming Back* (1966). A film version of *Don Quixote* for children was released by Mosfilm Company in 1965. For this production, Yevgeni Karelov directed a cast including Anatoli Papanov, Vera Orlova and Vladimir Korenev.

- There have been many adaptations produced in Spanish. *Don Quijote de la Mancha* was directed by Rafael Gil in 1948. It starred Rafael Rivelles as Don Quixote and Juan Calvo as Sancho Panza. More recently, an animated series was made for TV by Romagosa International Merchandising, S.L., in 1997, entitled *Don Quixote of La Mancha.*

- An Israeli version of the story was released in 1956. *Dan Quihote V'Sa'adia Pansa,* also known as *Don Quixote and Sa'ad Pancha,* was directed by Nathan Axelrod.

- An Australian version of *Don Quixote* (1973) was directed by Robert Helpmann and Rudolf Nureyev.

- Jesus Franco and Patxi Irigoyen finished Orson Welles's black-and-white *Don Quixote* in 1992. The original narrator was Orson Welles, but Constantino Romero narrates in the new version. Jose Mediavilla is Don Quixote and Juan Carlos Ordónez plays Sancho Panza.

- Alvin Rakoff directed *Don Quixote de la Mancha* for BBC-TV in 1973. Rosemary Leach played Dulcinea and Bernard Hepton played Don Quixote.

- Dale Wasserman wrote the original TV play *Don Quixote,* in 1959. This version eventually evolved into the musical *Man of La Mancha.*

- Combining the play by Dale Wasserman with the music of Joe Darion, *Don Quixote* was made into the musical *Man of La Mancha* by United Artists in 1972. Don Quixote was played by Peter O'Toole, but the singing voice was that of Paolo Gozlino. Sophia Loren played Dulcinea and Sancho Panza was acted by James Coco.

- *Don Quixote by Cervantes: A Multimedia Storybook—Windows CD-ROM* was released in 1997 by TDC. With illustrations by Manuel Boix, the interactive story teaches kids about Spain in the time of Don Quixote while telling the story of the famous knight-errant.

Aldonza Lorenzo

To be a full knight requires a ladylove. Don Quixote chooses Aldonza Lorenzo, a local woman, and renames her Dulcinea. She does not have a major role in the novel, but remains the ideal of womanhood in Don Quixote's mind. He resolves to do good deeds in her honor. Dulcinea has three appearances in the novel: the delivery of the letter; the appearance in an "enchanted" form astride an ass outside El Toboso; and finally, in a vision in the Cave of Montesinos.

Luscinda

Having been dumped by Don Fernando for Dorotea, Luscinda runs away to live the quiet life of a shepherd. She is a clever woman who steps in to play the role of a princess and therefore saves the Barber from transvestitism. While playing this role, she is reunited with Don Fernando.

Maria

See Lela Zoraida

Princess Micomicona

See Luscinda

Master Nicholas

Master Nicholas, the village barber, helps to preserve some of Don Quixote's library. He and the Curate work to bring Don Quixote back to his estate and, in the process, amuse themselves. The Barber, like the Curate, is well intentioned but cruel to Don Quixote. In their duplicity, they allegorize humanity's kind inhumanity to man.

The Niece

See Antonia Quixano

Sancho Panza

Sancho Panza is a neighbor of Don Quixote. He is an illiterate laborer who signs on to be Don Quixote's squire in hopes of becoming governor of an island as a reward for some adventure. At first Sancho is a timid character. Gradually, however, Sancho becomes more loquacious, full of proverbs, and a believer in Don Quixote's madness. He also functions as the jester, or the gracioso (the buffoon character of Spanish comedy) archetype.

Although he continues to hope for financial reward from his association with Don Quixote, Sancho admits that he his happy to be with Don Quixote, participating in wild adventures. Eventually, he does receive the position of governor to an island, and his leadership decisions surprise everyone by their wisdom. He is funny, round, and wise.

Pedro Perez

Perez, the Curate, is a friend of the family who preaches good will and "bonhomie." He considers it his duty to help Don Quixote recover his senses. First, the Curate and the Barber undertake a mock Inquisition and burn chivalric books. Later, they take a more active role in Don Quixote's adventure and bring him home in a cage.

Alonso Quixano

See Don Quixote

Antonia Quixano

Don Quixote's niece loathes chivalric tales and her uncle's fascination with them. She pleads with him to stay home and be sane. In an effort to curb Don Quixote, she willingly helps to burn many of his books.

Don Quixote

Alonso Quixano is a fifty-year-old man who reads of chivalric tales until he begins to neglect his domestic affairs. Eventually he decides that for his own honor and that of the state, he must revive the profession of the knight-errant. He therefore dons his armor and becomes Don Quixote, Man of La Mancha and Knight of the Rueful Figure. Not happy with the modern world, he takes it upon himself to bring back the golden age of heroism and chivalry.

In first part of the novel, Don Quixote suffers physical humiliation. In several instances, he is aggressive and rather dangerous. On numerous occasions, he charges into the fray of an adventure, only to come crashing down to earth with his lance in splinters and his body bruised. He is wise in the ways of knight-errantry and his speech on the importance of the scholar is a good example of this.

Resurrected in the second part of the novel, he becomes the gaunt figure towering above the Spanish landscape. Due to the publication of the first part, he had become famous. Unlike his earlier adventures, however, he is gradually regaining his reason. This becomes more obvious as he begins to call an Inn an Inn; in addition, he admits to interpreting reality. "God knows whether Dulcinea exists on earth or not. I contemplate her in her ideal." Don Quixote becomes wiser and less likely to lash out in the fury that surrounded him in part one.

As Don Quixote strives to return to sanity, however, people take advantage of his fame and encourage him in his delusions. His defeat at the hands of the Knight of the White Moon crushes him in mind and body. It leads to his speedy death.

The Ragged One
See Cardenio

Lela Zoraida

Lela Zoraida, known as Maria, is a Moor who escapes with the Captive Captain. She wants to become Christian.

Themes

Love

Love is the major theme of the novel. It functions as the motivating force of knight-errantry. In the several real adventures (for example, Dorotea and Cardenio or Basilio and Quiteria), where there is a question of forced conjugation, love conquers all: "true love cannot be divided, but must be free and uninhibited." In each of these encounters, there are lessons about the nature of love. These lessons are spelled out in ABC fashion in "The Tale of Ill-Advised Curiosity." Love also allows forgiveness, even of murder—as is the case of Claudia and Don Vicente.

The theme of love never really involves the character of Don Quixote. He speaks favorably of true love and prevents a quarrel (as in the situation with Camacho the Rich), but because the theme of love deals with what is true in reality, Don Quixote plays no part in the many reunions that occur in the novel. In fact, in the case of Luscinda and Don Fernando, Don Quixote is asleep and dreaming when their tense reunion occurs.

War and Peace

"There are two roads ... by which men can travel and reach wealth and honor: one is the way of letters, the other the way of arms." Don Quixote has chosen arms. In fact, he believes that fighting for what is right is as important as anything else. He is not a big believer in modern warfare; instead, he prefers the ancient, chivalric duels that pit one man against another.

There is also a desire for peace. Don Quixote, by his words and actions, prefers the Arcadian life. He admirably defends the art of poetry and in the end wishes to lead the simple life of a shepherd

with no mention of revenging his honor. Sancho shows a preference for this quiet alternative when he questions the chase. The Duke tells us that all rulers partake in the exercise of the chase to keep their skills fresh, for "chase is the image of war." But Sancho wonders if it isn't a waste to always be at war "killing an animal that has done no harm to anyone." The same could be said about the other victims of Don Quixote's efforts to revive knight-errantry.

Fear

In the life of a knight-errant, fans, admirers, and squires often broach the topic of fear. Sancho is in constant fear for his own safety and for that of his master. However, as Sancho admits to his wife, such a life makes him happy. For whether he climbs an oak tree or runs away, Sancho is just happy to be a part of the action. And that adventure is the main thing; as both Don Quixote and Sancho believe, it is better to try and maybe fail than not to try at all.

At the height of his powers, right after defeating the Knight of the Mirrors, Don Quixote passes the ultimate test of courage. In the face of this test, Don Quixote reveals a truth about fear. "Fear ... will make [danger] seem bigger by half." Subsequently, he faces and defeats the lion. Everyone is impressed by the feat, although the narrator downplays the event. It is Don Quixote's willingness to face up to his fears that is the true achievement.

Sanity and Insanity

Don Quixote becomes obsessed with the idea of knight-errantry to the point of losing himself. His loss of reason is similar to that of any person who becomes obsessed with something. As he says to his niece, "if these knightly thoughts did not monopolize all my faculties, there would be nothing I could not do...."

Indeed, Don Quixote never quite loses his mind, he simply indulges—to the fullest extent—his imagination. It is a conscious effort, "and that is where the subtlety of my plan comes in. A knight-errant who goes mad for a good reason deserves no credit; the whole point consists in going crazy without cause." That is, if knight-errantry were in fashion, Don Quixote would not be unique. If he succeeds in resuscitating chivalry, he will become famous.

The point of Don Quixote's knight-errantry is to make a fantasy come true. Living a fantasy even for a short time is more than most hidalgos could

Topics for Further Study

- Discuss the importance of reading in the novel and in the lives of the characters. Be sure to examine negative, as well as positive, examples from the story.

- Don Diego believes that "if the laws and ordinances of knight-errantry had been lost, they would be found in your worship's heart, as in their right repository and archive." What does he mean by this? What is the code of the knight-errant according to Don Quixote? How does this compare with the real code of chivalry?

- Find misrepresentations of the Don Quixote character in the media, on film, or in cartoons. Compare these versions with the original character in the book. How has the image of Don Quixote changed throughout time?

- Spain's tenure as a superpower was ruined by extravagant military spending and a lack of investment in business and industry. How does Spain's experience as a superpower contrast with that of the United States? Will the United States suffer the same fate as Spain? Why or why not?

- Investigate the meaning of the story about the madman and the dog experiment at the start of

say. His friends unwittingly bring his wish to fruition better than he could have possibly hoped. Everyone wins, for "what the world needed most of all was plenty of knights-errant" and by acting in his fantasy, his friends help revive the traditions of knight-errantry.

In fact, it is their indulgence—their cooperation with the fantasy—that fulfills Don Quixote's dream and "astonished [him], and for the first time he felt thoroughly convinced that he was a knight-errant in fact and not in imagination." Don Quixote's madness, sadly, is the only way for adults to play in the serious world of Spain's Golden Age.

Style

Structure

Cervantes switches between a style of narration that Boccacio employed in the *Decamaron*—a renowned collection of tales—to a more modern style. Like the *Decamaron, Don Quixote* is a medieval work wherein characters incorporate novellas, old ballads, and legends. Cervantes combines this style with the chivalric genre. This hybrid style is considered innovative.

Another result of Cervantes's unique style is that his characters have independent, interesting stories of their own. To offset this, Cervantes adds the device of the found manuscript; well into the story, the reader discovers the story is part of a manuscript found in the ruins of an old building. In fact, the history is the work of Cide Hamete Berengena, "the author of our true history."

This clever stylistic device does not change the tone of the narration, which is that of an omniscient, omnipresent, and amused narrator. This duplicity of narration only adds to the overall irony of the work. The characters are aware of being characters in a story that is being delivered by a narrator who is quoting, with liberality, from a found manuscript. In addition, there are other narrative viewpoints mixed into the melange. The potential layering—anticipating later Russian narrative forms—is kept at a minimum by the picaresque.

Satire

Don Quixote is a satire on conditions in Spain at the time the novel was written. This is accomplished by rendering Spain's archetype—the knight-errant as formidable, honorable, and above reproach—into realistic terms. For example, at the end of the first section, Don Quixote answers the call of nature—bathroom breaks are not a part of chivalric tales.

Picaresque

Don Quixote transforms the chivalric tale of adventure into the picaresque. This type of narrative chronicles the humorous adventures of a rogue, like Gines de Pasamonte (who has been working on a manuscript about his own adventures), while on the road, often traveling a long distance. The picaresque is often a satiric tale.

Irony

The technique of irony has its roots in the character Eiron. This character in Greek comedy always manages to outsmart Alazon. The term has come to mean a moment when words express something other than their literal meaning. The result is often intentionally humorous. Cervantes employs this technique on many levels.

In the process, Cervantes tears down the barriers between maturity and fantasy. Don Quixote and Sancho are so famous by the beginning of the second part of the novel that they are able to have a man with a degree help them judge the verisimilitude of their story—they are aware of themselves as being fictional characters. This leads to other jokes about whether the character or the narrator or the writer said such and such.

In fact, this occurs at the opening of the second part of the novel. There, Sancho surprises the narrator, and the reader, with his clever speech—or he has been faking his stupidity the whole time. Although the audience should know the truth, in many moments of *Don Quixote* the truth is whatever you wish it to be and therein lies the irony.

Dialogue

In the sixteenth and seventeenth centuries, dialogue was being developed into an artistic technique. At that time, dialogues in histories or "novels" were flat, presenting and debating ideas; then the techniques of the playwright were incorporated into dialogue, and the technique was used to show characterization and motivation, as well as propel the action of the story. Cervantes's practice as a playwright enabled him to utilize dialogue in an engaging, non-pedantic manner.

Don Quixote is an excellent example of an early effort to inject depth of psychology into a character through conversation. Two hundred years before the first psychological thriller, psychology—usually shown in mannerisms and action—could be revealed and confessed by the character.

Historical Context

The First Global Empire: Philip II

The marriage of King Ferdinand and Queen Isabella in 1469 unites the kingdom of Spain. After defeating the Moors in 1492, as well as financing the expedition of Christopher Columbus, Spain becomes a global empire. Spain also benefits from an early form of capitalism amongst its merchant classes—a force Spain weakens by deporting its

The title page from an early edition of Don Quixote.

Jewish citizens. The remaining Moors fill the void, however, and Spain flourishes.

Using the influx of wealth from the New World, Spain remains a superpower for more than one hundred years. Consolidated and powerful, leadership is passed to Philip II in 1556. He commands fifty thousand soldiers, the best generals, a navy of 140 vessels, and collects an annual revenue ten times that of England.

In addition, Philip reigns over all of Central America and parts of North and South America; also the Netherlands, several kingdoms in Italy, the Philippines, protectorates in Europe, and the West Indies. The Spanish court is the most splendid, its nobles are the proudest, and its architecture is on display on five continents.

Philip II nearly doubles the size of the empire when he absorbs Portugal and its holdings in 1580 (Portugal regains independence in 1640). However, despite his meticulous attention to detail, Spain's economy begins to decline. Prices skyrocket and wages fail to catch up. Industry, never a strong part of Spain's economy, simply grinds to a halt.

To compound these dire circumstances, wars grow more costly. Philip II grows so intolerant of the Protestants in England harassing his convoys

Compare & Contrast

- **1600s:** In 1615, 40,000 people demonstrate in favor of the doctrine of the Immaculate Conception of the Virgin (which contended that the Virgin Mary was without Original Sin). Once approved, this doctrine becomes a central tenet of Catholicism.

  Today: Devotion to Mary is still central to the practice of Roman Catholicism. Around the world there are many holy sites where she is believed to appear to believers.

- **1600s:** As the most powerful nation on Earth, Spain ignores its industrial and agricultural sectors, leading to their eventual decay.

  Today: With one of the healthiest economies in the European Union, Spain exports 63% of its industrial production. It is also the center for small car manufacturing in Western Europe. With 29 million acres in permanent crops, Spain's agricultural base is larger than the United States'.

- **1600s:** Spain ruins its economy building armadas to win the naval war against England.

  Today: The United States and Russia, after spending trillions of dollars on an arms race, are still affected by the economic repercussions. In particular, Russia has a difficult time adapting to a capitalist economy and suffers a near financial collapse.

- **1600s:** Moralists bemoan the corrupting influence of chivalric tales on the young.

  Today: Commentators blame television, video games, music, and absent parents for a youth culture viewed as irresponsible and immoral. Dramatic incidents of youth violence prompt a widespread debate on how society raises its youth.

- **1600s:** The land that would eventually become the United States is claimed by Spain, although it is inhabited by native peoples.

  Today: The United States is a world superpower. Ownership of the land is still contested by native people in various parts of the American hemisphere.

---

that he bankrupts his government to finance a formidable armada. The Spanish Armada sails in 1588 and is destroyed by winds and storms. The loss is so disastrous that Spain is in denial of the repercussions. The economic situation worsens as Philip tries to rebuild his armada. As a result, the Spain of Don Quixote is a superpower in decline.

Phillip III

Taking power in 1598, Philip III is weak and totally unable to manage even one-tenth of the empire left by his father. He appoints the Duke of Lerma to govern in his stead.

The Duke of Lerma funnels more money into war supplies, in particular the Spanish Armada. Failure on all fronts prompts him to search for scapegoats. In 1609 the Moriscos are shipped to Africa (where many are killed as Christians and others die of starvation). The loss of the best members of the industrial, merchant, and banking classes weaken Spain even more. By 1618 Spain is in ruins.

Religion

While the rest of Europe is undergoing a period known as the Renaissance, Spain clings to its medieval values. The Roman Catholic Church is second only to the monarchy in terms of power. Spain is virtually ruled by Catholic laws and philosophies.

Thousands of young men enter the priesthood—approximately 32,000 men comprise the Dominican and Franciscan orders during this time. A number of these men form a secret, very powerful group: the Inquisition. This group behaves like police, enforcing the highest standards of morality; in fact, they punish sinners with a range of punishments from 100 lashes to execution. The

Spanish Inquisition also persecutes those of other faiths, especially Jews and Protestants. As a result, many people of these faiths convert to Roman Catholicism out of fear.

Hidalgo

Originally a term used to describe the minor nobility of Spain, the number of hidalgos explodes as Spain reaches her zenith as a superpower. A hidalgo is anyone with papers proving he descends from a noble family. Such a heritage meant, to the hidalgo, that he deserved the honor due to a person of nobility. Consequently, a whole segment of the population refuses to work and aspires to an aristocratic lifestyle; this, along with the expulsion of those who did work, is another factor in Spain's downfall.

Critical Overview

Readers have always loved *Don Quixote*. Critics, however, have offered mixed assessments of the novel. For example, Lord Byron asserted that Cervantes was responsible for finally extinguishing the flame of chivalry in Europe. This charge was repeated by the English author Ford Madox Ford. Other negative reviewers, like Miguel de Unamuno and Giovanni Papini, consider *Don Quixote* a brilliant novel but deem its author a disorganized hack.

Yet, these authors are in the minority. Most critics appreciate the achievement of the novel and the author. Highest praise for the author came from Victor Hugo: "Cervantes sees the inner man."

Don Quixote's popularity spread throughout Europe soon after the first English translation of the first part of the novel appeared in 1612. By the eighteenth century, Cervantes was a literary icon. In his biography of the author, Tobias Smollet recalled that dignitaries visiting Spain were appalled by the idea that Cervantes was not financially supported for his contribution to Spanish literature. Summarily, said Smollett, "Cervantes, whether considered as a writer or a man, will be found worthy of universal approbation and esteem."

William Hazlitt, in his "Standard Novels and Romances," examined a very popular subject of Cervantes criticism—the delightful characters. "The characters in Don Quixote are strictly individuals; that is, they do not belong to, but form a class of themselves." Hazlitt applauded the lin-

guistic play of the author and the insights into human nature. Furthermore, Cervantes "furnished to the whole of civilized Europe" a great "number of allusions" useful for conversation and for sermonizing. Hazlitt ranked Cervantes with Le Sage as one of the great writers of the ages and ahead of Fielding, Richardson, Smollett and Sterne on the local English stage.

Unlike Lord Byron, many commentators were thankful that Cervantes had, as Heinrech Heine contended, "uprooted the tales of chivalry." Heine asserted that after *Don Quixote* the "taste for such books died." Indeed, "Cervantes founded the modern novel by introducing into the knightly romance the faithful delineation of the lower classes—by giving the life of the people a place in it."

Carlos Fuentes maintained that if *Don Quixote* is the first modern novel then his "debt to tradition is enormous." Another critic, the noted author Vladimir Nabokov, agreed:

> I wish to stress the fact that in romances of chivalry all was not Ladies and Roses and Blazons, but that scenes occurred in which shameful and grotesque things happened to those knights and they underwent the same humiliations and enchantments as Don Quixote did—and that, in a word, Don Quixote cannot be considered a distortion of those romances but rather a logical continuation, with the elements of madness and shame and mystification increased.

Cervantes is often compared with his English contemporary, William Shakespeare. For example, Wyndham Lewis compared the character of Don Quixote to Falstaff. Ivan Turgeniev, in "Hamlet and Don Quixote" made a more immediate comparison: While Hamlet represents the Northern European archetype, Don Quixote represents the Southern European man. This man is characterized by his affinity for a romantic view of the Middle Ages. Perhaps Don Quixote is more limited than Hamlet but he "reflects all that is human ... [he is a] deep river quietly flowing [with which] the reader, slowly carried by its transparent waves, looks with joy at that really epic tranquility."

Believing that Cervantes was sent by God solely to give us Don Quixote, Miguel de Unamuno asserted, "Cervantes never existed but Don Quixote did." As if that were not clear enough, Unamuno categorically declared, "I have no doubt in my mind but that Cervantes is a typical example of a writer enormously inferior to his work, to his *Don Quixote*." However the novel came into being, Unamuno admitted that *Don Quixote* is as much an artifact for meditation as anything Homeric or, for the English, anything Shakespearean.

The master of magic realism, Jorge Luis Borges, considered Don Quixote his muse. His remarks, characteristically, analyze the theme of reality: "Every novel is an ideal depiction of reality." He asked the troublesome question, "Why does it make us uneasy to know that the map is within the map ... that Don Quixote is a reader of the *Quixote,* and Hamlet is a spectator of *Hamlet?*" The answer is such: "Those inversions suggest that if the characters in a story can be readers or spectators, then we, their readers or spectators, can be fictitious."

The theme of madness is a recurring subject of Cervantes commentary. Recent criticism of the psychological vein has been insightful. Caroll B. Johnson speculated on the relationship between Don Quixote and his loyal sidekick, Sancho. He perceived homoerotic elements in their friendship; moreover, he considered the relationship a life-affirming example of how men can be friends with men.

Carroll summarized his view of Quixote: "Don Quixote's madness propels him backward into life. It enables him to have a life, to engage in purposeful and meaningful activity, and to enjoy a fulfilling, evolving relationship with another human being. That is, in the psychological as well as the existential sense already observed by Unamuno, our fiftyish hidalgo's only meaningful life is his life as a madman Don Quixote ... [therefore, readers] are saddened by his recuperation of sanity and his swift death."

Criticism

Diane Andrews Henningfeld

Henningfeld is an associate professor at Adrian College. She holds a Ph.D. in literature and writes widely for educational publishers. In this essay, she views the novel Don Quixote *as postmodern.*

In 1605, Miguel de Cervantes Saavedra wrote the first part of his ingenious novel, *El ingenioso hidalgo don Quijote de la Mancha,* known in English as *Don Quixote.* Written because Cervantes was in financial trouble and he needed to make some money, *Don Quixote* met with immediate commercial success.

Indeed, the novel was so popular that in 1614, another writer imitating Cervantes's subject and style published a book called *Segundo tomo del ingenioso hidalgo Don Quixote de la Mancha.* While

imitation might be the most sincere form of flattery, Cervantes was not amused. Already working on the second volume of *Don Quixote,* he wrote into the book a chapter castigating the impostor and denigrating the imitative work. This second volume was published in 1615, and once again met with both critical and popular approval.

Since the seventeenth century, *Don Quixote* has grown to be one of the most regarded and highly influential novels in the western world. It continues to generate critical study and controversy, and has been called the most important novel ever written, particularly by South American writers. Indeed, important writers such as Michel Foucault and Jorge Luis Borges have both discussed *Don Quixote* at length.

What is there about the novel that makes it the subject of so many literary studies, centuries after its first publication? Perhaps it is because the novel offers readers nearly endless possibilities for interpretation. As Harold Bloom argues in *The Western Canon:* "No two readers ever seem to read the same *Don Quixote....* Cervantes invented endless ways of disrupting his own narrative to compel the reader to tell the story in place of the wary author."

Further, a number of critics believe that it is the first modern novel. Carlos Fuentes, for example, in a foreword to the Tobias Smollet translation of *Don Quixote,* tells the reader that for him, "[T]he modern world begins when Don Quixote de la Mancha, in 1605, leaves his village, goes out into the world, and discovers that the world does not resemble what he has read about it."

P. E. Russell, in his book *Cervantes,* also traces the connections between *Don Quixote* and the modern novel. Most interesting, however, are Russell's statements concerning how the book is *not* like the modern novel. For example, he argues that "A parodic or even a more generally comic stance is hardly the norm in the modern novel." Russell continues, "The ambiguity of the book is another feature that we scarcely associate with the modern novel."

The problem, of course, is how to reconcile Cervantes' multi-layered, highly ironic, playful text with the modern novel, which tries to preserve the illusion of the reality of its fictive world. Russell might meet with more success if he were to connect *Don Quixote* with the postmodern novel, what Russell refers to as "experimental fiction."

Postmodern literature is concerned with narrative and the disruption of narrative; with the connection between naming and reality; and with

What Do I Read Next?

- Cervantes's first book, *La Galatea* (1684), is one of the few books in Don Quixote's library to escape the fire. The work is a pastoral novel.

- Cervantes's *Exemplary Novels* is comprised of stories that depict examples of exemplary behavior. Some tales, like "Lady Cornelia," are traditional cloak-and-dagger romances. Others are Kafkaesque; "Doctor Glass Case" chronicles the story of a servant boy who gets to attend school. He goes mad when he falls in love, and in his madness he believes he is made of glass.

- Cervantes's final novel was completed three days before his death. Published posthumously, *Los trabajos de Persiles y Sigismunda* is a scathing denunciation of reason and science in favor of the idylls of the golden age of Spain. The story itself is a quest, as several characters leave an imperfect society and eventually arrive at superior wisdom.

- Voltaire's classic satire, *Candide,* is a picaresque adventure that unmasks many of the pretensions of 1750s Europe. The principal characters are engaged in a quest for understanding.

- R. E. Raspe wrote a collection of stories based loosely on the tales of the adventurer Karl Friedrich Hieronymus (Baron von Munchhausen) in 1785. The volume is titled *Baron Munchausen's Narrative of His Marvellous Travels and Campaigns in Russia.*

- Published at approximately the same time as *Don Quixote,* Shakespeare's *Hamlet* is the tale of a prince trying to solve the mysterious death of his father. Under the ruse of madness, he succeeds in exposing the perpetrator.

- An excellent example of a chivalric tale is *Acts of King Arthur and His Noble Knights,* by John Steinbeck. The story retells the exploits of the legendary King Arthur and the tragic Lancelot.

- Charlotte Lennox wrote *The Female Quixote, or the Adventures of Arabella* to warn young women against reading novels. In her story, set just outside of colonial Philadelphia, Arabella pays so much attention to novels that she is unable to attract a husband. In fact, she goes mad as a result of so much reading. A family friend finally works out a romantic ruse by which to cure her.

- *Gulliver's Travels* is Jonathan Swift's satire of Europe, set in the first half of the eighteenth century. Gulliver visits many strange lands, and as a result gains a new perspective on his own country. Upon his return home, he is pronounced mad and spends his remaining days talking to his horses.

---

fiction that self-reflexively calls attention to itself as fiction. By examining each of these in turn, readers may find that Cervantes anticipates the postmodern moment in *Don Quixote.*

A narrative is, according to *The Harper Handbook of Literature,* an account of real or imaginary events, and a narrative perspective is the standpoint from which a story is told. A narrative demands a narrator, that is, a teller of the story. While this may seem self-evident, postmodernism has rendered the entire relationship between the narrator and the narrative problematic. Like a postmodernist himself, Cervantes plays with the relationship as well.

As the novel opens, Cervantes introduces himself to the reader through his prologue. Readers thus expect that Cervantes will be the voice narrating the tale. As E. Michael Gerli in his book *Refiguring Authority: Reading, Writing, and Rewriting in Cervantes* notes, however, "[T]he narrative structure of *Don Quijote* is exceedingly complex." The voice that opens the novel, introduces the characters, and recounts the action remains consistent for the first eight chapters.

Suddenly, however, Cervantes disrupts his own narrative, and informs the reader that he has been reading from a text that has suddenly come to an end, right in the middle of a battle. This disruption of the narrative throws the reader into confusion. Does this mean that Cervantes is not the narrator of his own story? Or that he is not the author of this text?

At the beginning of chapter nine, the battle suspended, the narrator goes in search of the rest of the story. He tells the reader that he is "always reading, even scraps of paper [he] finds in the street...." He finds a set of notebooks, written in Arabic. Although the narrator is a voracious reader, he is unable to read the Arabic and must find a translator. He finds a Moor in the marketplace who translates the notebooks, which are, it appears, the work of the Arab historian Sidi Hamid Benengeli, who is the writer of the *History of Don Quijote of La Mancha.* With the translation finished, the original narrator resumes his story.

However, the disruption has served several purposes. First, it undermines the reliability of the narrator and of the text itself. Although the reader *thought* that the narrator and Cervantes were one and the same, clearly this is not the case. In addition, the text that the narrator reads from is located *within* the larger text Cervantes creates. Second, the disruption forces the reader to consider the reliability of sources and of history itself. Whose story is this anyway? What does it mean that the story was originally written in Arabic, translated by someone the narrator finds in the market, written in Spanish by Cervantes, and translated into English by any one of several translators?

Certainly, the layering of text upon text serves to distance Cervantes from his story. However, at the same time, it calls attention to Cervantes as a writer of fiction. The disruption in the narrative reminds the reader that Don Quixote is a character in a novel, not a real human being. It also reminds the reader that the narrator, the translator, and Sidi Hamid Benengeli are all fictional characters, created by Cervantes for his novel.

In addition, the fictional Moorish translator forces readers to consider the role of the real English translators who undertake to interpret and render meaningful texts separated from their readers by culture, space, and time. How does reading a novel in translation differ from reading it in the original language? What is the relationship between the text itself and the translation? For that matter,

what is the text itself? These are questions that postmodern writers and readers find most intriguing.

Postmodernism is also concerned with the process of naming. As Brenda Marshall suggests in *Teaching the Postmodern,* "Naming must occur from a position 'outside' of a moment, and it always indicates an attempt to control.... Only from a fictional, removed, and separate point of perspective do we name (identify) the framework or paradigm within which people have lived in the past."

Cervantes calls attention to the power of naming by first creating doubt over the name of his fictional character: "It's said his family name was Quijada, or maybe Quesada: there's some disagreement among the writers who've discussed the matter. But more than likely his name was really Quejana." By introducing this moment of doubt, Cervantes suggests that he has less control over his story than one might think. Always there is the possibility of not being able "to tell things as faithfully as you can."

As Michel Foucault argues in *The Order of Things, Don Quixote* is a novel about the rupture between words and meaning, between names and identity. Reality depends on the ability to name, to identify, and to tell a story faithfully. The rupture evident in the novel suggests that there may be more than one reality.

Brenda Marshall continues, "But the traditional process of naming—a belief in the identity of things with names, so that 'reality' may be known absolutely—provides a space of interrogation for postmodernism, which asks: whose 'reality' is to be represented through the process of naming?"

The importance of names is especially clear when Alonso Quejana renames himself, his servant, his lady, and his horse. In so doing, he creates identities for them that have meaning within the "framework or paradigm within which people have lived in the past." Cervantes makes it clear that names have consequences: once Don Quixote becomes Don Quixote, he enters into a different reality and becomes a knight-errant. Don Quixote, through the process of naming, creates a reality that requires particular action on his part. Likewise, the naming of Don Quixote as "mad" requires a different understanding of reality on the part of his friends.

The kind of fiction described above can be called "metafiction." Metafiction asks readers to recognize that what they are reading is fiction, not reality, in order to help readers explore the relationship between fiction and reality. Throughout *Don Quixote,* Cervantes says as much about the nature of fiction as he does about the adventures of Don Quixote. For example, at the beginning of chapter twenty-four, he tells the reader,

> He who translated this great history from its Arabic original, written by its primal author, Sidi Hamid Benengeli, tells us that, when he got to this chapter about the adventure in Montesinos' Cave, he found, written in the margins, and in Sidi Hamid's own handwriting, "I cannot persuade myself nor quite believe that the valiant Don Quixote in fact experienced literally everything written about in the aforesaid chapter, because everything else that has happened to him, to this point, has been well within the realm of possibility and verisimilitude, but I find it hard to accept as true all these things that supposedly happened in the cave, for they exceed all reasonable bounds."

This intrusion reminds the reader that the translator, the Arabic original, the marginal notes, and Sidi Hamid Benengeli are also fictional creations of Cervantes, just as Don Quixote is a fictional creation. In addition, while a fictional text may seem to be true because of verisimilitude, that is, its imitation of reality, all fictional texts "exceed all reasonable bounds." In other words, a text that *seems* true is no truer than a fictional text that does not seem true; both only exist in the world of fiction.

Don Quixote, then, is a work that continues to speak to its readers. Through its play with narration, its exploration of the power of naming, and its attention to metafictional concerns, the novel seems acutely appropriate for reading in the postmodern moment. Nevertheless, if, as Harold Bloom contends, no two readers ever read the same *Don Quixote,* future readers will also find much to interest them, for with each reading, the novel grows in richness and complexity.

Source: Diane Andrews Henningfeld, in an essay for *Novels for Students,* Gale, 2000.

Miguel de Unamuno

In the following excerpt from an essay originally published in 1905, Unamuno, one of the most influential Spanish writers and thinkers of his era, argues that Cervantes "extracted Don Quixote from the soul of his people and from the soul of all humanity."

[Today], there is scarcely a literature that yields less individual and more insipid works than that of Spain, and there is scarcely a cultured nation—or one that passes for such—where there is such a manifest incapacity for philosophy. This

[This] philosophical incapacity which Spain has always shown, as well as a certain poetic incapacity—poetry is not the same as literature—has allowed a host of pedants and spiritual sluggards, who constitute what might be called the school of the Cervantist Masora, to fall upon *Don Quixote.*

The Masora was, as the reader will doubtless remember, a Jewish undertaking, consisting of critical annotations to the Hebrew text of Holy Scripture, the work of various rabbis of the school at Tiberias during the eighth and ninth centuries. The Masoretes, as these rabbis were called, counted all the letters which compose the Biblical text and determined the incidence of each letter and the number of times each one was preceded by one of the others, and other curious matters of this type.

The Cervantist Masoretes have not yet indulged in such excesses with *Don Quixote;* but they are not far off. As regards our book, all manner of unimportant minutiae and every kind of insignificant detail have been recorded. The book has been turned upside down and considered from every angle, but scarcely anyone has examined its entrails, nor entered into its inner meaning.

Even worse: whenever anyone has attempted to plumb its depths and give our book a symbolic or tropological sense, all the Masoretes and their allies, the pure *litterateurs* and the whole coterie of mean spirits, have fallen upon him and torn him to bits or have ridiculed him. From time to time, some holy man from the camp of the wise and shortsighted pedants comes along and informs us that Cervantes neither could nor would mean to say what this or that symbolist attributed to him, inasmuch as his sole object was to put an end to the reading of books of chivalry.

Assuming that such was his intent, what does Cervantes' intention in *Don Quixote,* if he had any intention, have to do with what the rest of us see in the book? Since when is the author of a book the person to understand it best?

Ever since *Don Quixote* appeared in print and was placed at the disposition of anyone who would take it in hand and read it, the book has no longer belonged to Cervantes, but to all who read it and feel it. Cervantes extracted Don Quixote from the soul of his people and from the soul of all humanity, and in his immortal book he returned him to his people and all humanity. Since then, Don Quixote and Sancho have continued to live in the souls of the readers of Cervantes' book and even in the souls of those who have never read it. There scarcely exists a person of even average education who does not have some idea of Don Quixote and Sancho.

Cervantes wrote his book in the Spain of the beginnings of the seventeenth century and for the Spain of that time; but Don Quixote has traveled through all the countries of the world in the course of the three centuries that have passed since then. Inasmuch as Don Quixote could not be the same man, for example, in nineteenth-century England as in seventeenth-century Spain, he has been transformed and modified in England, giving proof thereby of his powerful vitality and of the intense realism of his ideal reality.

It is nothing more than pettiness of spirit (to avoid saying something worse) that moves certain Spanish critics to insist on reducing *Don Quixote* to a mere work of literature, great though its value may be, and to attempt to drown in disdain, mockery, or invective all who seek in the book for meanings more intimate than the merely liberal.

If the Bible came to have an inestimable value it is because of what generations of men put into it by their reading, as their spirits fed there; and it is well known that there is hardly a passage in it that has not been interpreted in hundreds of ways, depending on the interpreter. And this is all very much to the good. Of less importance is whether the authors of the different books of the Bible meant to say what the theologians, mystics, and commentators see there; the important fact is that, thanks to this immense labor of generations through the centuries, the Bible is a perennial fountain of consolation, hope, and heartfelt inspiration. Why should not the same process undergone by Holy Scripture take place with *Don Quixote,* which should be the national Bible of the patriotic religion of Spain?

Perhaps it would not be difficult to establish a relation between our weak, soft, and addled patriotism and the narrowness of vision, the wretchedness of spirit, and the crushing vulgarity of Cervantist Masoretism and of the critics and *litterateurs* of this country who have examined our book.

I have observed that whenever *Don Quixote* is cited with enthusiasm in Spain, it is most often the least intense and least profound passages that are quoted, the most literary and least poetic, those that least lend themselves to philosophic flights or exaltations of the heart. The passages of our book which figure in the anthologies, in the treatises of rhetoric—they should all be burned!—or in the selections for school reading, seem specially picked out by some scribe or Masorete in open warfare

with the spirit of the immortal Don Quixote, who continues to live after having risen again from the sepulcher sealed by Don Miguel de Cervantes Saavedra, after the hidalgo had been entombed there and his death certified.

Instead of getting to the poetry in *Don Quixote,* the truly eternal and universal element in it, we tend to become enmeshed in its literature, in its temporal and particular elements. In this regard, nothing is more wretched than to consider *Don Quixote* a language text for Spanish. The truth is that our book is no such thing, for in point of language there are many books which can boast a purer and more correct Spanish. And as regards the style, *Don Quixote* is guilty of a certain artificiality and affectation.

I have no doubt in my mind but that Cervantes is a typical example of a writer enormously inferior to his work, to his *Don Quixote.* If Cervantes had not written this book, whose resplendent light bathes his other works, he would scarcely figure in our literary history as anything more than a talent of the fifth, sixth, or thirteenth order. No one would read his insipid *Exemplary Novels,* just as no one now reads his unbearable *Voyage to Parnassus,* or his plays. Even the novellas and digressions which figure in *Don Quixote,* such as that most foolish novella, *Foolish Curiosity,* would not warrant the attention of any reader. Though Don Quixote sprang from the creative faculty of Cervantes, he is immensely superior to Cervantes. In strict truth, it cannot be said that Don Quixote is the child of Cervantes; for if Cervantes was his father, his mother was the country and people in which he lived and from which Cervantes derived his being; and Don Quixote has much more of his mother about him than of his father.

I suspect, in fact, that Cervantes died without having sounded the profundity of his *Don Quixote* and perhaps without even having rightly understood it. It seems to me that if Cervantes came back to life and read his *Don Quixote* once again, he would understand it as little as do the Cervantist Masoretes, and that he would side with them. Let there be no doubt that if Cervantes returned to the world he would be a Cervantist and not a Quixotist. It is enough to read our book with some attention to observe that whenever the good Cervantes introduces himself into the narrative and sets about making observations on his own, it is merely to give vent to some impertinence or to pass malevolent and malicious judgments on his hero. Thus, for example, when he recounts the beautiful exploit wherein Don Quixote addresses a discourse on the Golden Age to some goatherds who could not possibly understand it in the literal sense—and the harangue is of a heroic order precisely because of this incapacity—Cervantes labels it a purposeless discourse. Immediately afterwards he shows us that it was not purposeless, for the goatherds heard him out with openmouthed fascination, and by way of gratitude they repaid Don Quixote with pastoral songs. Poor Cervantes did not attain to the robust faith of the hidalgo from La Mancha, a faith which led him to address himself to the goatherds in elevated language, convinced that if they did not understand the words they were edified by the music. And this passage is one of many in which Cervantes shows his hand.

None of this should surprise us, for as I have pointed out, if Cervantes was Don Quixote's father, his mother was the country and people of which Cervantes was part. Cervantes was merely the instrument by which sixteenth-century Spain gave birth to *Don Quixote*. In this work Cervantes carried out the most impersonal task that can be imagined and, consequently, the most profoundly personal in another sense. As author of *Don Quixote*, Cervantes is no more than the minister and representative of humanity; that is why his work was great.

The genius is, in effect, an individual who through sheer personality achieves impersonality, one who becomes the voice of his country and people, one who succeeds in saying what everybody thinks though they have never been able to say it.

There are lifelong geniuses, geniuses who last throughout their lives and who manage during all that period to be ministers and spiritual spokesmen for their country and people, and there are temporary geniuses, who are geniuses only once in their lives. Of course, that one occasion may be more or less long-lasting and boast greater or lesser import. And this fact should serve as consolation to us earthenware mortals when we consider those of finest porcelain. For who has not at some time been, even if only for a quarter hour, a genius of his people, and even though his people only number three hundred neighbors? Who has not been a hero for a day or for five minutes? And thanks to the fact that we can all be temporary geniuses, though it be only for a few moments, we can understand the lifelong, the lifetime geniuses, and be enamored of them.

Cervantes was, then, a temporary genius; and if he appears to us an absolute and lasting genius, as greater than most of the lifelong geniuses, it is because the work he wrote during his season of genius is a work not merely lifelong but eternal.

Consider what there is of genius in Cervantes, and consider what his inward relation is to his *Don Quixote*. Such considerations should indeed move us to leave Cervantism for Quixotism, and to pay more attention to Don Quixote than to Cervantes. God did not send Cervantes into the world for any other purpose than to write *Don Quixote*; and it seems to me that it would have been an advantage for us if we had never known the name of the author, and our book had been an anonymous work, like the old ballads of Spain and, as many of us believe, the *Iliad*.

I may indeed write an essay whose thesis will be that Cervantes never existed but Don Quixote did. In any case, inasmuch as Cervantes exists no longer, while Don Quixote continues alive, we should all abandon the dead and go off with the living, abandon Cervantes and follow Don Quixote.

Before finishing I must make a declaration to the effect that everything I have said here about Don Quixote is applicable to his faithful and most noble squire Sancho Panza, even worse known and more maligned than his lord and master. This disfavor blighting the memory of the good Sancho Panza descends to us directly from Cervantes, who, if he did not rightly understand his Don Quixote did not even begin to comprehend his Sancho, and if he was sometimes malicious as regards the master, he was almost always unjust to the servant.

One of the obvious truths which leaps to our attention while reading *Don Quixote* is the incomprehension shown by Cervantes of the soul and character of Sancho, whose sublime heroism was never understood by his literary father. Cervantes maligns and ill-treats Sancho without rhyme or reason; he persists in not seeing clearly the motivations behind his acts, and there are occasions when one feels tempted to believe that, impelled by incomprehension, he alters the facts and makes the good squire say and do things he never could have said or done, and which, therefore, he never did say or do.

So cunning was malicious Cervantes in twisting Sancho's intentions and shuffling his purposes that the noble squire has gotten an unmerited reputation, from which we Quixotists will redeem him, I trust, since a good Quixotist has to be a Sanchopanzist as well.

Fortunately, since Cervantes was, as I said, only in part—and in very small part—the author of *Don Quixote,* all the necessary elements to reinstate the true Sancho and give him the fame he deserves remain at hand in the immortal book. For if

Don Quixote was enamored of Dulcinea, Sancho was no less so, with the difference that the master quit his house for love of glory and the servant did so for pay; but the servant began to get a taste for glory, and in the end he was, in the heart of him, and though he would have denied it, one of the most unmercenary men the world has ever known. And by the time Don Quixote died, grown sane again, cured of his madness for glory, Sancho had gone mad, raving mad, mad for glory; and while the hidalgo was cursing books of chivalry the good squire begged him, with tears in his eyes, not to die, but to go on living so they might sally forth along the roads in search of adventure.

Inasmuch as Cervantes did not dare kill Sancho, still less bury him, many people assume that Sancho never died, and even that he is immortal. When we least expect it, we will see him sally forth, mounted on Rocinante, who did not die either, and he will be wearing his master's armor, cut down to size by the blacksmith at El Toboso. Sancho will take to the road again to continue Don Quixote's glorious work, so that Quixotism may triumph for once and all time on this earth. For let there be no doubt that Sancho, Sancho the good, Sancho the discreet, Sancho the simple, Sancho who went mad beside the deathbed of his master dying sane, Sancho, I say, is the man charged by God definitively to establish Quixotism on earth. Thus do I hope and desire, and in this and in God do I trust.

And if some reader of this essay should say that it is made up of contrivances and paradoxes, I shall reply that he does not know one iota about matters of Quixotism, and repeat to him what Don Quixote said on a certain occasion to his squire: Because I know you, Sancho, I pay no attention to what you say.

Source: Miguel de Unamuno, "On the Reading and Interpretation of *Don Quixote*," in *Selected Works of Miguel de Unamuno: Our Lord Don Quixote*, Vol. 3, edited by Anthony Kerrigan and Martin Kozick, translated by Anthony Kerrigan, Bollingen Series LXXXV, Princeton University Press, 1967, pp. 445-66.

Havelock Ellis

Ellis was a pioneering sexual psychologist and a respected English man of letters. In the following excerpt, he favorably compares Don Quixote *to other literary masterpieces and also emphasizes the indelibly Spanish nature of the work.*

There can be no doubt, *Don Quixote* is the world's greatest and most typical novel. There are other novels which are finer works of art, more exquisite in style, of more perfect architectonic plan. But such books appeal less to the world at large than to the literary critic; they are not equally amusing, equally profound, to the men of all nations, and all ages, and all degrees of mental capacity. Even if we put aside monuments of literary perfection, like some of the novels of Flaubert, and consider only the great European novels of widest appeal and deepest influence, they still fall short of the standard which this book, their predecessor and often their model, had set. *Tristram Shandy,* perhaps the most cosmopolitan of English novels, a book that in humour and wisdom often approaches *Don Quixote,* has not the same universality of appeal. *Robinson Crusoe,* the most typical of English novels, the Odyssey of the Anglo-Saxon on his mission of colonising the earth—God-fearing, practical, inventive—is equally fascinating to the simplest intellect and the deepest. Yet, wide as its reputation is, it has not the splendid affluence, the universal humanity, of *Don Quixote. Tom Jones,* always a great English novel, can never become a great European novel; while the genius of Scott, which was truly cosmopolitan in its significance and its influence, was not only too literary in its inspirations, but too widely diffused over a wilderness of romances ever to achieve immortality. *La Nouvelle Héloïse,* which once swept across Europe and renewed the novel, was too narrow in its spirit, too temporary in its fashion, to be enduring. *Wilhelm Meister,* perhaps the wisest and profoundest of books in novel form, challenges a certain comparison, as the romance of the man who, like Saul the son of Kish, went forth to seek his father's asses and found a kingdom; it narrates an adventure which is in some sense the reverse of Don Quixote's, but in its fictional form it presents, like the books of Rabelais, far too much that is outside the scope of fiction ever to appeal to all tastes. *The Arabian Nights,* which alone surpasses *Don Quixote* in variety and universality of interest, is not a novel by one hand, but a whole literature. *Don Quixote* remains the one great typical novel. It is a genuine invention; for it combined for the first time the old chivalrous stories of heroic achievement with the new picaresque stories of vulgar adventure, creating in the combination something that was altogether original, an instrument that was capable of touching life at every point. It leads us into an atmosphere in which the ideal and the real are equally at home. It blends together the gravest and the gayest things in the world. It penetrates to the harmony that underlies the violent contrasts of life, the only harmony which in our moments of finest insight we feel to be possible, in the same manner and, indeed, at the same moment—for *Lear* appeared in the same year as *Don Quixote*—that Shakespeare brought together the madman and the fool on the heath in a concord of divine humour. It is a storybook that a child may enjoy, a tragicomedy that only the wisest can fully understand. It has inspired many of the masterpieces of literature; it has entered into the lives of the people of every civilised land; it has become a part of our human civilisation.

It was not to be expected that the author of such a book as this, the supreme European novel, an adventure book of universal human interest, should be a typical man of letters, shut up in a study, like Scott or Balzac or Zola. Cervantes was a man of letters by accident.

He was a soldier, a man of action, who would never have taken up the pen, except in moments of recreation, if a long chain of misfortunes had not closed the other avenues of life. Before he wrote of life he had spent his best years in learning the lessons of life.

Seldom has any great novel been written by a young man: *Tristram Shandy*, *Robinson Crusoe*, *Tom Jones*, *La Nouvelle Héloïse*, *Wilhelm Meister*, were all written by mature men who had for the most part passed middle age. *Don Quixote*—more especially the second and finer part—was written by an old man, who had outlived his ideals and his ambitions, and settled down peacefully in a little home in Madrid, poor of purse but rich in the wisdom garnered during a variegated and adventurous life. *Don Quixote* is a spiritual autobiography. That is why it is so quintessentially a Spanish book.

Cervantes was a Spaniard of Spaniards. The great writers of a nation are not always its most typical representatives. Dante could only have been an Italian, and Goethe only a German, but we do not feel that either of them is the representative man of his people. We may seek to account for Shakespeare by appealing to various racial elements in Great Britain, but Shakespeare—with his volubility and extravagance, his emotional expansiveness, his lightness of touch, his reckless gaiety and wit— was far indeed from the slow, practical, serious Englishman. Cervantes, from first to last, is always Spanish. His ideals and his disillusions, his morality and his humour, his artistic methods as well as his style—save that he took a few ideas from Italy—are entirely Spanish. Don Quixote himself and Sancho Panza, his central personages, are not

only all Spanish, they are all Spain. Often have I seen them between Madrid and Seville, when travelling along the road skirting La Mancha, that Cervantes knew so well: the long solemn face, the grave courteous mien, the luminous eyes that seem fixed on some inner vision and blind to the facts of life around; and there also, indeed everywhere, is the round, wrinkled, good-humoured face of the peasant farmer, imperturbably patient, meeting all the mischances and discomforts of life with a smile and a jest and a proverb. Don Quixote! I have always exclaimed to myself, Sancho Panza! They two make Spain in our day, perhaps, even more than in Cervantes's day; for, sound as Spain still is at the core, the man of heroic action and fearless spirit, the *conquistador* type of man, is nowadays seldom seen in the land, and the great personalities of Spain tend to become the mere rhetorical ornaments of a rotten political system. Don Quixote, with his idealism, his pride of race and ancestry, his more or less dim consciousness of some hereditary mission which is out of relation to the world of to-day, is as inapt for the leadership of the modern world as Sancho Panza, by his very virtues, his brave acceptance of the immediate duty before him, his cheerful and uncomplaining submission to all the ills of life, is inapt for the ordinary tasks of progress and reform. The genius of Cervantes has written the history of his own country.

Even in the minute details of his great book we may detect the peculiarly national character of the mind of Cervantes, and his thoroughly Spanish tastes. To mention only one trifling point, we may observe his preference for the colour green, which appears in his work in so many different shapes. Perhaps the Moors, for whom green is the most sacred of colours, bequeathed this preference to the Spaniards, though in any case it is the favourite colour in a dry and barren land, such as is Spain in much of its extent. Cervantes admires green eyes, like many other Spanish poets, though unlike the related Sicilians, for whom dark eyes alone are beautiful; Dulcinea's eyes are *verdes esmeraldas* [green emeralds]. Every careful reader of *Don Quixote*, familiar with Spain, cannot fail to find similar instances of Cervantes's *Españolismo*.

And yet, on this intensely national basis, *Don Quixote* is the most cosmopolitan, the most universal of books. Not Chaucer or Tolstoy shows a wider humanity. Even Shakespeare could not dispense with a villain, but there is no Iago among the six hundred and sixty-nine personages who, it is calculated, are introduced into *Don Quixote*. There is no better test of a genuinely human spirit than an ability to overcome the all-pervading influences of religious and national bias. Cervantes had shed his blood in battle against the infidel corsairs of Algiers, and he had been their chained captive. Yet— although it is true that he shared all the national prejudices against the Moriscoes in Spain—he not only learned and absorbed much from the Eastern life in which he had been soaked for five years, but he acquired a comprehension and appreciation of the Moor which it was rare indeed for a Spaniard to feel for the hereditary foes of his country. Between Portugal and Spain, again, there was then, to an even greater extent than to-day, a spirit of jealousy and antagonism; yet Cervantes can never say too much in praise of Portugal and the Portuguese. If there was any nation whom Spaniards might be excused for hating at that time it was the English. Those pirates and heretics of the north were perpetually swooping down on their coasts, destroying their galleons, devastating their colonial possessions; Cervantes lived through the days of the Spanish Armada, yet his attitude towards the English is courteous and considerate.

It was, perhaps, in some measure, this tolerant and even sympathetic attitude towards the enemies of Spain, as well as what seemed to many the ridicule he had cast upon Spanish ideas and Spanish foibles, which so long stood in the way of any enthusiastic recognition by Spain of Cervantes's supreme place in literature. He was for some centuries read in Spain, as Shakespeare was at first read in England, as an amusing author before he was recognised as one of the world's great spirits. In the meanwhile, outside Spain, *Don Quixote* was not only finding affectionate readers among people of all ages and all classes; it was beginning to be recognised as a wonderful and many-sided work of art, a treasure-house in which each might find what he sought, an allegory, even, which would lend itself to all interpretations.... It is not alone the pioneer in life, the adventurous reformer, the knight of the Holy Ghost, who turns to *Don Quixote,* the prudent and sagacious man of the world turns thither also with a smile full of meaning, as the wise and sceptical Sydenham turned when an ambitious young practitioner of medicine asked him what he should read: Read *Don Quixote.* It is a good book. I read it still. And when we turn to the noble ode—etania de Nuestro Señor Don Quijote—which Ruben Dario, the most inspired poet of the Spanish-speaking world of to-day, has addressed to Don Quixote, we realise that beyond this Cervantes has created a figure with even a religious significance for the consolation of men. *Don Quixote* is not only the type

and pattern of our greatest novels; it is a vision of the human soul, woven into the texture of the world's spiritual traditions. The Knight of La Mancha has indeed succeeded in his quest, and won a more immortal Dulcinea than he ever sought.

Source: Havelock Ellis, "Don Quixote," in *The Soul of Spain,* Houghton Mifflin Company, 1908, pp. 223-43.

Sources

Harold Bloom, "Cervantes: The Play of the World," in his *The Western Canon,* Harcourt, Brace, 1994, p. 128.

Jorge Luis Borges, "Partial Enchantments of the 'Quixote,'" in his *Other Inquisitions: 1937-1952,* translated by Ruth L.C. Simms, University of Texas Press, 1964, pp. 43-6.

Miguel de Cervantes Saavedra, in *Don Quixote,* translated by Burton Raffel, edited by Diana de Armas Wilson, W.W. Norton & Company, 1999.

Manuel Duran, *Cervantes,* Twayne, 1974.

Carlos Fuentes, "When Don Quixote left his Village, the Modern World Began," in *The New York Times Book Review,* March 23, 1986, p. 15.

————, "Foreword," in *The Adventures of Don Quixote,* translated by Tobias Smollet, Farrar, Strauss & Giroux, 1986, p. xi.

E. Michael Gerli, *Refiguring Authority: Reading, Writing, and Rewriting in Cervantes,* The University Press of Kentucky, 1995, p. 62.

William Hazlitt, "Standard Novels and Romances," in his *The Collected Works of William Hazlitt,* edited by A. R. Waller and Arnold Glover, McClure, Philips & Co., 1904, pp. 25-44.

Heinrech Heine, "Heine on Cervantes and the 'Don Quixote',." in *Temple Bar,* Vol. XLVIII, October, 1876, pp. 235-49.

Victor Hugo, "Men of Genius," in his *The Works of Victor Hugo,* Vol. X, The Jefferson Press, n.d., pp. 23-65.

Caroll B. Johnson, *Madness and Lust: a Psychoanalytical Approach to Don Quixote,* University of California Press, 1983, 230 p.

Brenda Marshall, *Teaching the Postmodern: Fiction and Theory,* Routledge, 1992, p. 3.

P. E. Russell, *Cervantes,* Oxford University Press, 1985, p. 117.

Tobias Smollet, "The Life of Cervantes," in *The History and Adventures of the Renowned Don Quixote, Vol. I, by Miguel Cervantes,* translated by Tobias Smollet, A. Millar, 1755, pp. i-xx.

Ivan Turgeniev, "Hamlet and Don Quixote," translated by Josef Firi Kral and Pavel Durdik, in *Poet Lore,* Vol. IV, No. 4, April 15, 1892, pp. 169-84.

Miguel de Unamuno, *Selected Works of Miguel de Una-muno: Our Lord Don Quixote,* Vol. 3, edited by Anthony Kerrigan and Martin Nozick, translated by Anthony Kerrigan, Bollingen Series, LXXXV, Princeton University Press, 1967, 553 p.

For Further Study

Jean Canavaggio, *Cervantes,* translated by J. R. Jones, W. W. Norton, 1990.
    Originally published in Paris, this biography of Cervantes is considered one of the best. Also contains bibliographical references.

Brenda Knox and Joe Main, *Don Quixote de la Mancha Exhibit,* at the Milton S. Eisenhower Library at the Johns Hopkins University, http://milton.mse.jhu.edu:8006/tour1.html.

The Don Quixote Exhibit contains historical illustrations of the novel and some background information.

Felix Martinez-Bonati, in *Don Quixote and the Poetics of the Novel,* translated by Dian Fox, Cornell University Press, 1992.
    This critical work examines past criticism and trends for reading *Don Quixote.*

Melveena McKendrick, in *Cervantes,* Little Brown, 1980.
    A comprehensive biography of Cervantes.

Ian Watt, *Myths of Modern Individualism: Faust, Don Quixote, Don Juan, Robinson Crusoe,* Cambridge University Press, London, 1997.
    Watt examines four hero archetypes of the modern West: Faust, Don Juan, Don Quixote, and Robinson Crusoe. He traces their historical influence and considers their continued relevance in our society.

Empire of the Sun

J. G. Ballard

1984

When *Empire of the Sun* was published in 1984, it quickly became a critical and commercial success. Many commentators regard it as one of the finest war novels ever written. In the novel, Ballard chronicles the semi-autobiographical experiences of an eleven-year-old British boy named Jim living in China during World War II.

When the fighting comes to Shanghai, Jim is separated from his parents and sent to a prison camp. It is there that he faces the harsh realities of war and learns important lessons about human nature. The novel has been praised for its vivid portrayal of the devastating effects of war and the psychology of survival as seen through the eyes of a young boy. In this moving coming-of-age tale, Jim lets go of his innocent ideas about war and heroism and in the process reveals the meaning of courage, tenacity, and faith in the endurance of the human spirit.

Author Biography

J. G. Ballard was born on November 15, 1930, in Shanghai. Like Jim, the protagonist of *Empire of the Sun,* Ballard was a child when World War II began; and, like Jim, he wandered the city of Shanghai after being separated from his parents. However, he was eventually reunited with them in Lunghua prison camp, where the three remained prisoners until the camp was liberated by the American army.

J. G. Ballard

Ballard left China when he was sixteen and later studied medicine at Cambridge University from 1949 to 1951. He became a regular contributor to *New Worlds* magazine. From 1954 to 1957 he served as a pilot for the Royal Air Force.

Ballard married Helen Matthews in 1953 and had three children. Her death in 1964 devastated him and death became a recurring theme in his writing. He began writing science fiction in the mid-1950s and, by the 1960s, he became associated with the "New Wave" movement in science fiction, which introduced experimental literary techniques and more sophisticated subject matter into the genre. Initially his novels did not garner much critical or commercial success. Eventually, he was recognized as an innovative writer of science fiction, especially in England and Europe.

Ballard departed from the science fiction genre in several of his short stories and in *Empire of the Sun* and its sequel, *The Kindness of Women* (1991), which deals with Ballard's life in England after the war. *Empire of the Sun* was a popular and critical success, earning a Guardian Fiction Prize in 1984, a nomination for the Booker Prize in 1984, and the James Tait Black Memorial Prize in 1985. Adapted into a movie in 1987, the film was produced and directed by Steven Spielberg. Ballard's fifteen novels and numerous short stories have established him not only as a first-rate science fiction writer, but also as an accomplished novelist and short story writer of works that explore intricate psychological landscapes.

Plot Summary

Part I

The novel opens on the day Japan attacked Pearl Harbor, December 7, 1941, in Shanghai's International Settlement. Eleven-year-old Jamie—or Jim as he prefers to be called—his father and his mother live in a wealthy European area within the city.

With the threat of war, most of the European women and children have been evacuated to Hong Kong and Singapore. Jim's family remains. While riding his bicycle through the streets of Shanghai, he dreams of being a fighter pilot like the Japanese pilots that fly over the city.

On the morning of the 7th, Jim witnesses the Japanese attack on British and American warships docked at Shanghai (which occurred at the same time as the attack on Pearl Harbor), and in the ensuing turmoil he becomes separated from his parents.

After the attack, the Japanese intern the Europeans living in the city. For the next few months, Jim roams the city on his bicycle in constant search for food, shelter, and a recognizable face. Exhausted from long trips around the city and a lack of food, he decides to give himself up to the Japanese.

As he roams the city, Jim meets Frank and Basie, two American sailors. The three are soon captured and Basie and Jim are sent to a detention center. On arrival at the camp, Jim becomes seriously ill. With Basie's help, he learns how to get enough food to keep himself alive.

Part II

Jim and Basie are transported outside the city to the prison camp at Lunghua. During his three years there, Jim faces hunger, disease, and death. As the American bombing raids intensify, their meager rations are reduced.

Jim spends his time running errands for Basie, Dr. Ransome, and others. He tries to ingratiate himself with both prisoners and guards to gain company, food, and gifts, like a shiny pair of golf shoes. However, his boundless energy and unflagging determination to survive sometimes annoy the other prisoners.

He enjoys visiting the American prisoners, and reads copies of *Reader's Digest* and *Popular Mechanics*. He plays chess and does homework problems assigned by Dr. Ransome. Over time, he forgets what his parents looked like.

In August 1945, after American air attacks become a daily event, the Japanese evacuate the camp to the Olympic Stadium outside Shanghai. Jim finds it hard to leave the relative security of the camp. During the difficult journey there, many of the prisoners die. At one point, Jim becomes seduced by the idea of death, and decides to stop along the side of the road. Mr. Maxted, however, coaxes him on, insisting, "we need you to lead the way."

Mr. Maxted dies after they are herded inside the stadium. Jim acknowledges that "he had been trying to keep the war alive, and with it the security he had known in the camp. Now it was time to rid himself of Lunghua, and face up squarely to the present, however uncertain, the one rule that had sustained him through the years of the war."

Part III

That night the Japanese soldiers vanish and Jim sees a strange flash of light that floods the stadium. Later he is told the light came from the atomic bomb explosion at Nagasaki, reflected across the China Sea. Not knowing where to go, Jim decides to walk back to Lunghua.

As he walks back to Lunghua, American planes drop canisters of food and magazines that contain tales of the heroic exploits of the American soldiers. Jim devours the food and eagerly reads the magazines; the cans of Spam and candy bars make the "most satisfying" meal of his life. Back in the camp, unsure of what to do next, he notes that "peace had come, but it failed to fit properly." At times he is not sure that the war is really over.

Jim soon leaves with Lieutenant Price, an American who had taken control of Lunghua. Price, however makes a detour to the Olympic Stadium, hoping to steal some looted cars and furniture. After they arrive, a Chinese soldier shoots Price. As a threatening gang of bandits surrounds Jim, he recognizes Basie among them. After Basie and the gang strand him on a mud flat, he returns to the camp where he is reunited with Dr. Ransome.

Two months later Jim has been reunited with his parents and is preparing for his departure for England. As his parents slowly recover from their years at a prison camp in Soochow, Jim returns by bicycle to his old haunts in the city. He realizes that "only part of his mind would leave Shanghai. The rest would remain there forever, returning on the tide like the coffins launched from the funeral piers at Nantao."

Characters

Basie

Basie is an American sailor. Jim meets him before the two of them are sent to the prison camp and describes Basie as having a "bland, unmarked face from which all the copious experiences of his life had been cleverly erased." Basie is a player and tries to make money off of the war by trading anything he can. As a result, he acquires "a complete general store" at the camp.

Jim has ambivalent feelings about Basie, perceiving him as "a parasite" feeding "on the succulent terrain of the prison camps." Yet he is sometimes generous to Jim. For instance, he is the only one who gives him presents on his birthday. In addition, his confidence in the future is encouraging. However, when Jim runs into Basie and a group of bandits outside the stadium, he recognizes

Christian Bale tries to escape a holding facility in Steven Spielberg's 1987 movie Empire of the Sun.

that "Basie had been prepared to see him die, and only Jim's lavish descriptions of the booty waiting for the bandits in the stadium … sustained Basie's interest in Jim."

At the end of their relationship, Basie remains "the same small, finicky man … ignoring everything but the shortest-term advantage. His one strength was that he never allowed himself to dream, because he had never been able to take anything for granted." That is why he survives so long, because the entire experience of the war had "barely touched" him.

Father

Jim's father, a serious man, tries to remain calm in the face of threats to his firm from the Communist Labor Unions, his concern for his work with the British Residents Association, and fears for Jim and his mother.

Frank

An American sailor Jim meets as he wanders around Shanghai looking for his parents, Frank introduces Jim to Basie.

Vera Frankel

Vera is Jim's nanny at Amherst Avenue, who usually follows Jim everywhere "like a guard dog." She is "a calm girl who never smiled and found everything strange about Jim and his parents." Her family fled Poland after Hitler's invasion. They now live with thousands of Jewish refugees in "a gloomy district of tenements and faded apartment blocks." The fact that she and her parents all live together in one room amazes and fascinates Jim.

Jim

The novel, opening from the eve of the Japanese attack on Pearl Harbor on December 7, 1941, focuses on the story of Jim, an eleven-year-old British boy who lives with his family in Shanghai. Before the Japanese take over Shanghai, Jim lives a comfortable life in the city's suburbs. He has seen some of the devastating results of the war, but seems to be detached from them. Completely absorbed in his own privileged world, he spends his days riding his bicycle around the city, dreaming of being a fighter pilot like the Japanese pilots he sees flying overhead. When he is separated from his parents after the Japanese take over the city, his world drastically changes.

At the detention center, Jim's bravery emerges as he learns important survival skills. On his way to the prison camp, Jim "already felt himself apart

Media Adaptations

- *Empire of the Sun* was adapted as a film in 1987. Tom Stoppard and Menno Meyjes (uncredited) wrote the screenplay and Steven Spielberg produced and directed it for Warner Bros.

---

from the others, who had behaved as passively as the Chinese peasants. Jim realized that he was closer to the Japanese, who had seized Shanghai and sunk the American fleet at Pearl Harbor," pilots "ready to chance everything on little more than their own will." At this point, Jim retains his romantic dreams of heroism.

During his three years at the prison camp, Jim exhibits his strength, his curiosity, his energy, and his eagerness to please. Early on, he decides he won't allow himself to become too ill and so is able to perform countless errands for others. He enjoys the idea that his errands help keep the others alive. He works hard in order "to keep the camp going." Dr. Ransome often refers to him as a "free spirit" roving across the camp, "hunting down some new idea in his head."

He is curious about everything, including the war. He discovers what it takes to survive, learning how to get extra food and how to fight those who would try to take his rations. While trying to keep himself alive, he sometimes takes food meant for others and feels guilty, acknowledging that "parts of his mind and body frequently separated themselves from each other."

Jim's experiences in the camp change him from an innocent boy to an experienced man. He learns to accept the cruelty he sees around him and comes to understand the true horror of war. Yet he also learns that "having someone to care for was the same as being cared for by someone else."

Private Kimura

A Japanese guard at the camp who sometimes invites Jim into his bungalow and allows him to wear his armor.

Dr. Lockwood

Dr. Lockwood is the Vice-Chairman of the British Residents Association. He throws elaborate parties, including the "fancy-dress Christmas" party Jim and his family go to at the beginning of the novel.

Mr. Maxted

Mr. Maxted is the father of Jim's closest friend, Patrick. Jim admired this architect-turned-entrepreneur who had designed the Metropole Theater and numerous Shanghai nightclubs. He imagined himself growing up like Mr. Maxted, "the perfect type of the Englishman who had adapted himself to Shanghai, something that Jim's father, with his seriousness of mind, had never really done."

Mr. Maxted is also sent to Lunghua Camp where he helps distribute food to the prisoners. Jim runs errands for him in the camp and cares for him during the trek to the Olympic Stadium "out of nostalgia for his childhood dream of growing up one day to be like him." Mr. Maxted is also kind to Jim at the camp and encourages him to continue on the march when Jim is about to give in to death. Mr. Maxted dies soon after they get there.

Mother

Jim's mother is "a gentle and clever woman whose main purposes in life, he had decided, were to go to parties and help him with his Latin homework." After the war, when she and Jim's father return to Amherst Avenue, they take a long time to recover from their experience at the prison camp. When Jim is reunited with his parents, he decides they are too worn out from their own experiences in the camp to hear about his experiences.

Lieutenant Price

Price takes over Lunghua Camp after the Japanese leave. He shoots Private Kimura.

Dr. Ransome

When Jim first meets Dr. Ransome, the British doctor in the camp, Ransome is in his late twenties, with "the self-assured manner of the Royal Navy officers" Jim had seen at the parties. At first, Jim distrusts him and perceives Ransome as selfish and arrogant. On the way to the camp, Jim notices that the doctor is "less interested in the dying old people than he pretended."

In the camp, however, Jim's opinion of him changes. He still considers him selfish, but on occasion the doctor begins to reveal his generosity and spirit of self-sacrifice when he often gives Jim some of his own food. He also takes an interest in Jim's education, always coming up with homework problems for him to complete. Due to this kindness, Jim is determined to keep Dr. Ransome alive. While he shows obvious affection for Jim, he "resented [him] for revealing an obvious truth about the war, that people were only too able to adapt to it."

Mr. Tullock

Mr. Tullock is the chief mechanic at the Packard agency in Shanghai. He lets Jim come back into the camp and keeps him out of Price's way.

Mrs. Vincent

Jim shares a room at the camp with Mrs. Vincent, her husband, and their six-year-old son. She resents his presence and makes him feel unwelcome. In fact, she seems detached from everything around her, even her own son. Jim often has adolescent sexual fantasies about her. By the end of their stay at the camp, Jim grants her a certain respect, deciding she is "one of the few people in Lunghua Camp who appreciated the humor of it all." Mrs. Vincent dies in the march back from the stadium.

Yang

Yang is Jim's "fast-talking" chauffeur.

Topics for Further Study

- Research the internment of European civilians in China by the Japanese during World War II. Can you find reports of experiences similar to or different from those of Jim's?

- Investigate what psychologists say about the relationship between prisoners and guards. Compare their findings to the dynamics of Jim's relationship with his guards. Find examples in the novel.

- View the film *Empire of the Sun.* What differences do you find between the book and the movie? What effect do those differences have on the themes? Characters?

- Investigate the culture of Japan and China. Compare your findings to Jim's descriptions of the different cultures.

Themes

Coming of Age

The main focus of *Empire of the Sun* is Jim's maturation from child to man during World War II. After the war begins and he is separated from his parents, he spends the remainder of the book trying to reunite with them. He learns to survive the brutal conditions he faces in detention and prison camps. As a result of these experiences, he learns important lessons about himself and human nature.

Change and Transformation

As Ballard traces Jim's maturation, he explores the transformations he experiences. The biggest change occurs when Jim is wrenched from his comfortable, privileged life in Shanghai and forced to live, as do the Chinese, with deprivation and the constant threat of death. This experience brings Jim to new levels of self-discovery as he realizes his ingenuity, courage, and resilience in the face of tragedy.

Alienation and Loneliness

Jim must learn to cope with the alienation and loneliness that result when he is separated from his parents. As an only child, Jim had used his imagination to fill lonely days, envisioning himself as a Japanese fighter pilot. His imagination also helped Jim combat the loneliness he suffered after losing his parents.

While in camp, Jim tries to erase his sense of alienation through his interaction with the other prisoners. He considers the prisoners to be almost an extended family, and thus comes to feel a measure of safety while he is interned there. In this way, he tries to create order in a chaotic and dangerous world.

Strength and Weakness

Jim's ability to cope with his harsh surroundings reveals his strength of character and the nature of human adaptability. While others escape through death, Jim resolves to survive. In order to do this, he learns how to eat insects and to ingratiate himself with his captors.

Violence and Cruelty

Jim is able to recognize the capacity for violence and cruelty in others as well as himself. After seeing so much cruelty, Jim comes to understand its causes. For example, "Jim knew that Lieutenant Price would have liked to get him alone and then beat him to death, not because he was cruel, but because only the sight of Jim's agony would clear away all the pain that he himself had endured."

Jim often struggles with his own capacity for cruelty. In order to survive, he obtains extra food, which sometimes means less for others. He also learns how to defend himself against others trying to take food from him. As a result, "few boys of his own age dared to touch" him and "few men." Sometimes stealing food makes him feel guilty and he acknowledges that "parts of his mind and body frequently separated themselves from each other."

Appearances and Reality

By the end of the novel, Jim has let go of his innocent ideas about the nature of war. As a child, he had considered war to be "an heroic adventure filled with scenes of sacrifice and stoicism, of countless acts of bravery" like those detailed on the newsreels he watches and the magazines he reads. By the end of the novel, however, Jim recognizes the devastating reality of war.

Style

Point of View

One of the novel's most interesting and successful qualities is its use of point of view. The events unfold through the eyes of Jim, the protagonist, as he experiences the horrors of life in China during World War II. While providing a vivid depiction of the destruction that surrounds him, Jim remains the detached observer, a survival skill he learns at the prison camp. That same sense of detachment is evident in the novel's early scenes before Jim is separated from his parents.

While he enjoys the benefits of his upper class life in Shanghai, this lonely boy observes with an ironic eye the stark contrasts between European and Chinese life. He notes the "dances and garden parties, the countless bottles of scotch consumed in aid of the war effort" while beggars are whipped in the streets by limousine drivers. Jim sees that "all over the western suburbs people were wearing fancy dress, as if Shanghai had become a city of clowns."

Genre

Although this novel is concerned with the devastating impact of war, it does contain elements found in the science fiction genre. In their review published in *Newsweek,* David Lehman and Donna Foote maintain that the novel has "more in common with [Ballard's science fiction novels] than immediately meets the eye. Like its predecessors, the book explores the zone of 'inner space' that Ballard sees as 'the true domain of science fiction.'" John Gross echoes this assessment in his review for *The New York Times,* viewing many of its scenes "lurid and bizarre, so very nearly out of this world."

Symbol

In the novel, Ballard uses abandoned buildings and drained swimming pools as symbols of Jim's predicament and psychological state. As he searches for his parents in Shanghai, Jim comes across the abandoned homes and drained swimming pools, symbols of the privileged lives of the Europeans who once resided there. These empty images foreshadow the world Jim will face in the prison camp, a world where social hierarchies reverse and eventually collapse.

Historical Context

World War II

The rise of totalitarian regimes in Germany, Italy, and Japan during the 1930s tipped the scales toward a world war. These dictatorships—known as the Axis power when they became allies—began to forcibly expand into neighboring countries. For instance, in 1936 Benito Mussolini's Italian troops took over Ethiopia, which gave them a strong foothold in Africa. In 1938 Germany annexed Austria; a year later, German forces occupied Czechoslovakia. Italy took control of Albania in 1939.

On September 1, 1939, Germany invaded Poland and World War II began. On September 3, 1939, Britain and France declared war on Germany after a U-boat sank the British ship *Athenia* off the

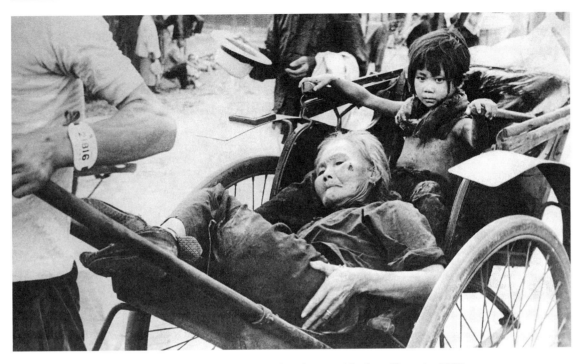

A woman and her granddaughter, injured in the bombing raid of a village in 1937.

coast of Ireland. Another British ship, *Courageous,* was sunk on September 19. All the members of the British Commonwealth, except Ireland, soon joined Britain and France in their declaration of war.

By 1940, Japan controlled a large part of China, including Northern China, the coastal areas, and the Yangtze valley. During the years before World War II, the Japanese met resistance from the Chinese Communists. After Japan attacked U.S. and British bases in 1941 and World War II broke out in Asia, China received U.S. and British aid.

By the end of the war, however, China was in full civil war. Hostilities between the Chinese nationalist forces and the communist troops intensified into a full-scale war as both sides vied for occupancy of the territories evacuated by the Japanese. By April 1950, China was a communist country.

In August 1937 the Japanese attacked Shanghai, which fell under Japanese control by November. The foreign zones of the city were occupied by the Japanese after December 7, 1941, the date *Empire of the Sun* opens. In 1943 Great Britain and the United States gave up their claims in Shanghai. China regained control of the city at the end of World War II. In May 1949, Shanghai fell to the Communists.

Critical Overview

Published in 1984, *Empire of the Sun* was highly acclaimed by critics and became a best-seller in England. In their review of the novel appearing in *Newsweek,* David Lehman and Donna Foote place the book "on anyone's short list of outstanding novels inspired by the second world war…. [It] combines the exactness of an autobiographical testament with the hallucinatory atmosphere of twilight-zone fiction."

Most reviews focus on the novel's serious subject matter. John Calvin Batchelor, in his essay, "A Boy Saved by the Bomb" in *The New York Times Book Review,* asserts that Ballard "has reached into the events of his childhood to create a searing and frightening tale of wartime China. Yet this novel is much more than the gritty story of a child's miraculous survival in the grimly familiar setting of World War II's concentration camps. There is no nostalgia for a good war here, no sentimentality for the human spirit at extremes…. He aims to render a vision of the apocalypse, and succeeds so well that it can hurt to dwell upon his images."

In his review of the novel for *The New York Times,* John Gross contends that the book "sets out to raise large issues and stir deep feelings, and for the most part it succeeds remarkably well." After criticizing what he considers to be Ballard's editorializing at the end of the book, Gross claims "that is the only real weakness in an outstanding novel."

Gross also praises the novel's style: "The detail of life both in the city and in the camp is brilliantly rendered by Mr. Ballard—with swift, economic strokes where there could easily have been clutter, with a plain, terse style where rhetoric would have been counterproductive."

In *Books and Bookmen,* William Boyd claims that "what makes [this] Ballard's best novel is that on this occasion style and narrative fuse." Boyd praises the author's pace, structure, character development and use of symbols. While he asserts that the novel contains "flaws" like "shaky" dialogue and repetition in some parts, he states that "the mix is otherwise extremely—and uniquely in his work—impressive."

Many critics maintain that the novel has strong ties to the science-fiction genre. Lehman and Foote note that the novel has earned Ballard the kind of critical acclaim denied his earlier work, "since it has more in common with them than immediately meets the eye. Like its predecessors, the book explores the zone of 'inner space' that Ballard sees as 'the true domain of science fiction.'"

Although the novel is clearly more realistic than Ballard's past work, Gross "still hesitates to call [it] a conventional novel ... because many of the scenes in it are so lurid and bizarre, so very nearly out of this world. Among other things, they help to explain why in his work up till now Mr. Ballard should have been repeatedly drawn to apocalyptic themes."

Considering Ballard's future, David Pringle in *Earth Is the Alien Planet: J. G. Ballard's Four Dimensional Nightmare* determines that "Ballard's reputation will grow in the decades to come, and he is likely to become recognized as by far and away the most important literary figure associated with the field of science fiction. More than that, he will be seen as one of the major imaginative writers of the second half of the 20th century—an author for our times, and for the future."

Criticism

Wendy Perkins

Perkins is an Associate Professor of English at Prince George's Community College in Mary-

land and has published several articles on British and American authors. In the following essay, she examines how the point of view utilized in Empire of the Sun *complements the anti-war theme of the novel.*

In Charles Platt's *Dream Makers: The Uncommon People Who Write Science Fiction,* J. G. Ballard asserts, "Conventional life places its own glaze over everything, a sort of varnish through which the reality is muffled. In Shanghai, what had been a conventional world for me was exposed as no more than a stage set whose cast could disappear overnight; so I saw the fragility of everything, the transience of everything, but also, in a way, the reality of everything." Jim also sees "the reality of everything" in Ballard's semi-autobiographical novel *Empire of the Sun.* Through this young British boy's observant perspective, Ballard rejects traditional notions of the glories of war and instead reveals the true nature of its brutality and futility.

At the beginning of the novel, Jim is protected from the realities of war by the privileges of his race and class. "Life in Shanghai was lived wholly within an intense present," especially for the Europeans who lived in the affluent suburbs of the city. This intense present was created in part by the impending threat of war, but the Europeans remained curiously detached from its reality. Jim observes his parents and the parents of his friends fill their days with "dances and garden parties," and watches them consume "countless bottles of scotch ... in aid of the war effort." He notes that "all over the western suburbs people were wearing fancy dress, as if Shanghai had become a city of clowns." The newsreels they all watch give Jim the impression that the British were "thoroughly enjoying the war."

At one of the parties, Jim watches Mr. Maxted, his friend's father, drink his whiskey by the drained swimming pool, a symbol of the impending death of the old order that Jim does not yet recognize. He imagines himself growing up like Mr. Maxted, an architect-turned-entrepreneur who had designed the Metropole Theater and numerous Shanghai nightclubs, "the perfect type of the Englishman who had adapted himself to Shanghai."

Separated and protected by their sense of superiority, the Europeans view the casualties of the early stages of the war with a cold objectivity as evidenced when they tour bombed airfields in "silk dresses" and "gray suits, strolling through the debris arranged for them" and stepping over "the bodies of dead Chinese soldiers."

Jim, more than the others, sees the suffering that surrounds him. He observes the extremes of affluence and poverty in the city as his chauffeur runs over or whips beggars in the streets. He sees the "regatta of corpses" on the waterfront, surrounded by paper flowers, wash back in with the tide. He also has glimpsed the results of the Japanese presence in Shanghai, how the "bones of the unburied dead rose to the surface of the paddyfields" along with the "bloody heads of Communist soldiers mounted on spikes along the Bund."

Yet, at this point, his innocence and his sense of his own superiority separate him and thus prevent him from empathizing with the suffering he sees. Soon, however, the realities of war will touch everyone in Shanghai, and the hierarchies they have benefited from will be reversed and finally smashed. As a result, Jim and the other Europeans in China will no longer be able to maintain an objective distance.

Jim is forced to confront the horror of war when he is separated from his parents after the Japanese attack British and American ships in the Shanghai harbor. After wandering through the deserted homes in his neighborhood, a scared, sick, and starving Jim meets a shady American sailor named Basie, who teaches Jim how to survive in this new, harsh environment.

Jim notes that his "entire upbringing could have been designed to prevent him from meeting people like Basie, but the war had changed everything…. All his experience of the previous two months told him not to trust anyone, except perhaps the Japanese." Even after experiencing the deprivation and despair of the detainment and prison camp, Jim will retain his respect for the Japanese, an attitude that sets him apart from most of the Europeans who have demonized the enemy.

Jim goes through enormous changes even before he reaches the Lunghua prison camp. The deprivation and despair he has experienced in the detention center and on the long route to the camp has exposed him to a world from which he had previously been detached.

Before he reaches the camp where he thinks his parents will be, "to his surprise he felt a moment of regret, of sadness that his quest for his mother and father would soon be over. As long as he searched for them he was prepared to be hungry and ill, but now that the search had ended he felt saddened by the memory of all he had been through and of how much he had changed. He was closer now to the ruined battlefields and this fly-

What Do I Read Next?

- *Anne Frank, The Diary of a Young Girl* (1947) chronicles the courageous life of its author, a gifted Jewish teenager, after she and her family are forced into hiding in Nazi-occupied Amsterdam. Anne later died in a German concentration camp.

- Written by James Jones, *From Here to Eternity* (1951) concerns the story of Private Robert E. Lee Prewitt, a young American who rebels against the conformity of military life in Pearl Harbor during World War II.

- In *The Kindness of Women* (1991), J. G. Ballard continues the story chronicled in *Empire of the Sun*. In this sequel, he focuses on Jim's life in England after the war.

- *Night* (1958) is Elie Wiesel's semi-autobiographical tale of a teenager's internment in a Nazi concentration camp.

infested truck, to the nine sweet potatoes in the sack below the driver's seat, even in a sense to the detention center, than he would ever be again to his house in Amherst Avenue." When they are turned away from the first camp, "he felt a strange lightness in his head, not because his parents had rejected him, but because he expected them to do so, and no longer cared."

Jim's attitude also changes toward the British as he observes their behavior in the camp. He becomes annoyed "with their constant talk about prewar London." Now he condemns them for claiming "a special exclusiveness." He also reveals how much he has changed when he recognizes that "naming the sewage-stained paths between the rotting huts after a vaguely remembered London allowed too many of the British prisoners to shut out the reality of the camp, another excuse to sit back when they should have been helping."

Jim understands the reality of the camp and so works hard to keep himself and others alive. In a strange twist, while learning these survival skills, Jim learns to "enjoy the war." He appreciates the relative safety of the camp, and doesn't want to venture into the unknown or known terrors he has seen. Time ceases at the camp, and a "curious vacuum" sets in as he focuses on the day-to-day task of survival.

Jim's experiences force him to view things from the perspectives of others, even those who have been cruel to him. When he returns to the camp, he lies down on Mrs. Vincent's straw mattress in the room that he had shared with her and her family. "Seen from Mrs. Vincent's vantage point, the past three years appeared subtly different; even a few steps across a small room generated a separate war, a separate ordeal for this woman with her weary husband and sick child."

Jim also comes to understand the cruelty of those affected by war. After observing Lieutenant Price, the officer who takes over the camp after the Japanese leave, Jim notes "that Lieutenant Price would have liked to get him alone and then beat him to death, not because he was cruel, but because only the sight of Jim's agony would clear away all the pain that he himself had endured."

After three years in the camp, Jim's notions of war have changed. When he sees prisoners collaborate with the Japanese guards, he realizes that "patriotism meant nothing. The bravest prisoners—and collaboration was a risky matter—were those who bought their way into the favor of the Japanese and thereby helped their fellows with small supplies of food and bandages."

When Dr. Ransome notes Jim's previous fascination with the machinery of war and his determination that the Japanese are the bravest soldiers in the world, Jim now admits, the war "had nothing to do with bravery. Two years earlier when he was younger, it had seemed important to work out who were the bravest soldiers, part of his attempt to digest the disruptions of his life. Certainly the Japanese came top, the Chinese bottom, with the British wavering in between.... However brave, there was nothing the Japanese could do to stop" the American warplanes.

When Jim returns to the camp, he reads the magazines dropped by the American planes. He realizes "they described an heroic adventure on another planet, filled with scenes of sacrifice and stoicism, of countless acts of bravery, a universe away from the war that Jim had known at the estuary of the Yangtze." While reading a *Life* magazine he finds, "he studied a photograph of American marines raising the flag on the summit of Mount Suribachi after their battle for Iwo Jima. The Americans in these magazines had fought a heroic war, closer to the comic books that Jim had read as a child. Even the dead were glamorized, the living's idea of the dead." He recognizes that "unlike the war in China, everyone in Europe clearly knew which side he was on, a problem that Jim had never really solved." Jim has discovered that there are no clear victors or enemies in war.

At the end of the book, his recognition of the realities of war fills him with despair. This feeling is reflected in his thoughts after he comes across a dead Japanese fighter pilot, who he thinks is the same one he used to watch at the camp: "for so long he had invested all his hopes in this young pilot, in that futile dream that they would fly away together, leaving Lunghua, Shanghai, and the war forever behind them. He had needed the pilot to help him survive the war, this imaginary twin he had invented, a replica of himself whom he watched through the barbed wire. If the Japanese was dead, part of himself had died. He had failed to grasp the truth that millions of Chinese had known from birth, that they were all as good as dead anyway, and that it was self-deluding to believe otherwise."

Jim is reunited with his parents, but he will never be able to return to his prewar innocence. Back at Amherst Avenue, his home "now seemed as much an illusion as the sets of the Shanghai film studios." When he leaves, he recognizes that "only part of his mind would leave Shanghai. The rest would remain there forever, returning on the tide like the coffins launched from the funeral piers at Nantao."

He leaves his childhood behind in the final scene as he sees a child's coffin float in the stream, surrounded by a garland of paper flowers, taken out but then swept back by the incoming tide, "driven once again to the shores of this terrible city."

Source: Wendy Perkins, in an essay for *Novels for Students,* Gale, 2000.

John Calvin Batchelor

In the following essay, Batchelor praises Ballard's courage in revealing events of his childhood.

The first-rate science-fiction author, J. G. Ballard, has reached into the events of his own childhood to create a searing and frightening tale of wartime China. Indeed, Mr. Ballard declares in a foreword that this novel is based on his experiences in the Lunghua Civilian Assembly Center near Shanghai from 1942 to 1945. He has performed a heroic feat of memory to recover feelings that must have been tormenting to live through and can have been no less painful to relive in fiction.

Yet this novel [*Empire of the Sun*] is much more than the gritty story of a child's miraculous survival in the grimly familiar setting of World War II's concentration camps. There is no nostalgia for a good war here, no sentimentality for the human spirit at extremes. Mr. Ballard is more ambitious than romance usually allows. He aims to render a vision of the apocalypse, and succeeds so well that it can hurt to dwell upon his images. For Mr. Ballard seems to be against all armies and the ideologies that mobilize troops; he seems also to believe that the horror of his youth ended only when World War III began with a nuclear sunburst over Nagasaki.

The story opens in Shanghai's International Settlement the day before the Japanese attack on Pearl Harbor. Eleven-year-old Jim is everything one could want in a hero—affectionate, tireless, brave and more curious about life than a research biologist. Jim is the only child of a British textile industrialist who has kept his family on in Shanghai long after many British dependents have fled the threat of the Japanese domination of China. Yet even with the Japan-China war going on all around, Jim continues to enjoy the luxuries of the European community—chauffeurs, swimming pools, lawn parties, private schools. He is not unaware of the staggering desperation of the China that presses legless beggars against the front gate and daily exhibits public stranglings; but he has learned to accept cruelty as the real world. Meanwhile, Jim has a secret life, in which he roams Shanghai on his bicycle, and a life of daydreams in which he soars in a fighter plane. He aches to fly, and can identify both with the Spitfire pilots in the propaganda films about the Battle of Britain he sees after church and with the Japanese pilots he has seen swooping over Shanghai in Zeros emblazoned with the Rising Sun.

The war crashes upon Jim and the Europeans in China as the Martians fell to Earth in H. G. Welles's *The War of the Worlds*. Jim awakens Monday morning to study for an examination only to witness, accidentally, the Japanese sneak attack on British and American warships on the Shanghai waterfront that was timed to coincide with the raid on Pearl Harbor. Instantly, the panic that follows makes Jim the fair equal of all adults, and in a short time he is alone, separated from his parents.

For four months, Jim struggles in a netherworld, grubbing for food in abandoned homes, fleeing slavery and death on his bicycle. Slowly, he realizes that the Japanese are his only protectors in China. And with the hope of an innocent, Jim submits to the detention camps. His opinion of the Japanese is ambivalent. He admires their courage and fears their brutality; he also knows that the Japanese are capable of mercy toward children. In fact, Jim has understood very early on that in a real war no one knew which side he was on, and there were no flags or commentators or winners. In a real war there were no enemies.

In the second and third parts of the novel, Mr. Ballard reaches beyond the survivor's manuals, like those of James Clavell and Aleksandr Solzhenitsyn, that have become this century's obligatory reading. On one level, Jim grows for three years into a resourceful prisoner who can thrive in a world turned upside down, learning how to hoard food, hustle for favors and ingratiate himself with the moral and immoral authorities of the camp. But on a deeper level, in the closing months of the war, Jim is precocious enough to recognize the emergence of a new specter of mass extinction. If the Japanese were like the Martians conquering Earth at the war's opening, they become helpless victims like everyone else as the battlefronts collapse and China descends into famine, slaughter and chaos.

In complete control of his awesome material, Mr. Ballard is able to evoke the panorama of the apocalypse and then to plunge Jim and the reader into a genuine nightmare. Here is the stench of the dead stacked like wood, the brackish taste of river water polluted by corpses floating nearby, the strange singsong of peasants crying in frustration because they know they are about to be beaten to death. And here are scenes that are not believable except that they feel entirely real. Jim sees teenage Kamikaze pilots crawl into their shabby planes without any more ceremony than the bored farewell of three other teen-age soldiers. He watches shallow graves deteriorate, exposing corpses that tempt the starving remnant as meat. And in August 1945, after a death march to the Olympic Stadium outside Shanghai, with the guards and the prisoners alike envying the sleep of the dead, Jim watches what he recognizes as the birth of a new empire of the sun that usurps Japan's setting star. In the sky to the northeast of Shanghai, he sees a flash that momentarily overwhelms the dawn and floods the stadium with an odd light. Five hundred miles across the China Sea, Nagasaki has just been annihilated by the atomic bomb.

It would be comforting to say that Jim's story closes happily when he once again embraces his parents by their drained swimming pool. He has survived the war by luck, and he has survived the end of the Japanese because canisters of Spam and powdered milk were dropped by the same kind of American airplane that dropped the bomb. However, Jim is not persuaded that the war is really over. He is equally uncertain what kind of world awaits him as he sails from China. The most optimistic thing one can say is that Mr. Ballard, with a splendid and powerful talent, has written a novel that makes haunting fictional sense of what happened to Jim 40 years ago. And with the wisdom born of having actually witnessed the potential of Armageddon, Mr. Ballard has now passed on the opinion that his own survival, and the world's, remain tentative.

Source: John Calvin Batchelor, "A Boy Saved by the Bomb", in *New York Times Book Review*, November 11, 1984, p. 11.

John Gross

In the following essay, Gross notes Ballard's departure from the science fiction genre in Empire of the Sun.

J. G. Ballard is a famous name among science-fiction fans, but many of his admirers, most notably Anthony Burgess, have argued that science fiction is too constricting a label for his work. Now, for the first time, Mr. Ballard has abandoned fantasy—though not the fantastic—and produced a straightforward, naturalistic narrative. As he explains in his foreword, it is closely based on his own experiences as a young boy in China during World War II.

If one still hesitates to call *Empire of the Sun* a conventional novel, it is only because many of the scenes in it are so lurid and bizarre, so very nearly out of this world. Among other things, they help to explain why in his work up till now Mr. Ballard should have been repeatedly drawn to apocalyptic themes. But this time the prophet of doom has become a historian of doom.

The story opens on the very eve of Pearl Harbor. We are in Shanghai—the old, garish, cosmopolitan Shanghai of the International Settlement and the Bund, with its extremes of luxury and misery and apathy. Chauffeurs lash out at beggars with riding crops; coffins decked with paper flowers are cast adrift from the funeral piers and swept back by the tide; members of the Graf Zeppelin club set off on expeditions to beat up Jewish refugees. Outside the Cathay, the biggest cinema in the world,

200 hunchbacks in medieval costume parade up and down advertising *The Hunchback of Notre Dame.*

All this is seen through the eyes of an 11-year-old English boy called Jim, whose father runs a local textile firm. He also sees the attack on the American and British gunships with which the Japanese go into action. In the turmoil that follows he is separated from his parents and left to fend for himself. For two months or so he roams round the city, scavenging in deserted villas and then falling into the dangerous company of a shady American sailor called Basie and his sidekick (Jim's entire upbringing could have been designed to prevent him from meeting people like Basie). Eventually he realizes that he will be safer if he surrenders to the Japanese.

The next three years are spent in a prison camp outside the city. Living on close terms with brutality, deprivation and death, he is sustained by his frenetic energy and by a determination (not always appreciated) to make himself as useful as he can to the other prisoners. When the camp is evacuated he manages to get away, but he still has to undergo some terrifying hazards and ordeals before the war ends.

If it ends, that is, since there is a good deal of foreboding in the closing pages that the next war has already begun. Hiding in the Olympic stadium in Shanghai, Jim sees a strange flash light up the sky—the distant glow of Nagasaki. It has been preceded in the book by many other images of light, of deadly glitter and sinister incandescence. But until this point the empire of the sun could reasonably be thought to refer, first and foremost, to the empire of the Rising Sun. Subsequently it takes on a more general and even more threatening significance.

The detail of life both in the city and in the camp is brilliantly rendered by Mr. Ballard—with swift, economic strokes where there could easily have been clutter, with a plain, terse style where rhetoric would have been counterproductive. And binding it all together is the skill with which we are made to enter into Jim's thoughts and feelings, into his self-absorption, his eagerness, his confusion, his schoolboy fancies, his forced coming of age.

Much of the time he seems to be living through a dream. The newsreels he watches become confused with the newsreel running inside his head (movies are one of the leitmotifs of the book); his suffering self is someone else, a double he catches sight of in a mirror. And where death is commonplace, the boundaries between the living and the dead become blurred. There are moods when Jim finds death seductive and comforts himself with the thought that he is nothing. Perhaps he is dead already—the simple truth known to every Chinese from birth.

When he feels himself being dragged down, he identifies with the Chinese. In the fantasies where he reasserts himself, he hero-worships the Japanese, their airmen in particular; he wishes he could have taken part in the attack on Pearl Harbor. Ultimately, though, this, too, turns out to be a death fantasy, and he ends up with visions of himself as a kamikaze pilot.

But in the real world he is a survivor. He knows that the word is not always meant to be a compliment—when it is applied to the unscrupulous Basie, for example. Still, without his intelligence and resourcefulness he would be lost. At the beginning of the book one of his hobbies is compiling a manual called "How to Play Contract Bridge," based on conversations he has had with his mother; he has never played a hand himself. He is keen to master the rules of a world he never made. It is a quality that is to stand him in good stead in less cozy circumstances.

At one level this is a classic adventure story— Jim could be a descendant of Jim Hawkins in *Treasure Island.* At another level it sets out to raise large issues and stir deep feelings, and for the most part it succeeds remarkably well. Toward the end, when he makes Jim start brooding about World War III, Mr. Ballard editorializes a little too much, but that is the only real weakness in an outstanding novel.

Source: John Gross, "A Survivor's Narrative," in *New York Times,* October 13, 1984, p. 18.

Sources

John Calvin Batchelor, "A Boy Saved by the Bomb," in *The New York Times Book Review,* November 11, 1984, p. 11.

William Boyd, "Unique Vision," in *Books and Bookmen,* September, 1984, pp. 12-13.

John Gross, "A Survivor's Narrative," in *The New York Times* October 13, 1984, p. 18.

David Lehman and Donna Foote, in a review in *Newsweek,* January 28, 1985, p. 69.

David Pringle, in *Earth Is the Alien Planet: J. G. Ballard's Four Dimensional Nightmare,* Borgo Press, 1979.

For Further Study

Jonathan Cott, "The Strange Visions of J. G. Ballard," in *Rolling Stone,* November 19, 1987, p. 76.
   In this interview, Ballard discusses how the novel relates to the science fiction genre.

Edward Fox, "Goodbye, Cruel World," in *The Nation,* Vol. 240, No. 3, January 26, 1985, pp. 89-90.
   This review explores the theme of survival in the novel.

Roger Luckhurst, "Petition, Repetition, and 'Autobiography': J. G. Ballard's *Empire of the Sun* and *The Kindness of Women,*" *Contemporary Literature,* Vol. 35, Winter, 1994, pp. 688-708.
   Luckhurst examines the autobiographical significance in both novels.

Luc Sante, "Tales from the Dark Side," *The New York Times Magazine,* September 9, 1990, p. 58.
   Sante explores the "complex, obsessive, and disquieting" themes in the novel.

John Simon, in a review in *National Review,* February 5, 1988, p. 59.
   Simon finds the cinematic adaptation a poor version of the novel.

The Hobbit

J. R. R. Tolkien

1937

J. R. R. Tolkien's fantastic novel *The Hobbit; or There and Back Again* was first published in 1937. The enchanting story of tiny, furry-footed Bilbo Baggins and his adventures in Middle-earth ultimately served as the prelude to Tolkien's epic *The Lord of the Rings,* which was published in three volumes during the 1950s. These novels are perhaps the most beloved works of fantasy in the twentieth century.

An eminent Oxford philologist, Tolkien's translation of ancient myths inspired him to create a world of his own, known as Middle-earth. He spent a great deal of his life developing his own language and mythology for this imaginary realm.

Although the *The Hobbit* garnered favorable reviews on its publication, it wasn't initially a commercial success. However, the novel became extremely popular over the years, eventually selling over one million copies in the United States alone.

Author Biography

Tolkien was born in Bloemfontein, South Africa, on January 3, 1892. His father, Arthur, was an Englishman who had left the Birmingham branch of Lloyds Bank to work for the Bank of Africa. Tolkien and his younger brother were sickly children. Hoping to improve her sons' health, Tolkien's mother, Mabel, took the boys to England in 1895. Arthur remained in Africa to work until

his sons sufficiently recovered or he could find a position back in England. Unfortunately, only a few months later, Arthur died of acute peritonitis. Mabel and the boys remained in England.

Tolkien was interested in languages at an early age. His mother began teaching him Latin and Greek when he was seven years old. He also inherited his mother's love for nature and the Catholic church. In 1903 Tolkien won a scholarship to the prestigious King Edward VI School in Birmingham, where his studies included not only the mandatory Latin and Greek, but also Welsh, Old and Middle English, and Old Norse. Tragically, his mother died of diabetes when he was only twelve. A Catholic priest, Father Francis Morgan, cared for the Tolkien brothers after Mabel's death.

At sixteen Tolkien met his future wife, Edith Mary Bratt. Later, his burgeoning love of languages led him to pursue a degree in comparative philology at Exeter College, Oxford University, in 1911. He graduated with honors in 1915, and one year later, he and Bratt married. Shortly after, Tolkien was commissioned a second lieutenant in the English army and left his new bride to fight in World War I. Enclosed in the trenches during the Battle of the Somme, Tolkien contracted a severe case of trench fever and had to be evacuated in 1916.

After returning from the war, Tolkien spent the next several decades building a reputation as a noted scholar and professor at Oxford. He published several esteemed essays, including "Beowulf: The Monsters and the Critics" (1936) and "On Fairy Stories" (1947). Along with C. S. Lewis and Charles Williams, he was an important member of the literary group "The Inklings."

The Hobbit; or There and Back Again was published in 1937 to favorable reviews. It took Tolkien seventeen years before the hobbits returned in *The Lord of the Rings,* a trilogy consisting of *The Fellowship of the Ring* (1954), *The Two Towers* (1954), and *The Return of the Ring* (1955). Although Tolkien's bibliography contains many great works, *The Hobbit* and *The Lord of the Rings* represent the heart of his literary accomplishments. He produced few writings after the success of his 1950s masterpiece. Tolkien died from complications resulting from a bleeding gastric ulcer and a chest infection on September 2, 1973, in Bournemouth, England. However, several of his works were published posthumously, including *The Silmarillion* (1977). Tolkien's work continues to be popular with readers and critics alike.

J. R. R. Tolkien

Plot Summary

The Beginning of the Quest

The Hobbit is set in the imaginary world of Middle-earth. The unidentified narrator begins the tale with a description of hobbits:

> They are (or were) a little people, about half our height, and smaller than the bearded Dwarves. Hobbits have no beards.... They are inclined to be fat in the stomach; they dress in bright colours (chiefly green and yellow); wear no shoes, because their feet grow natural leathery soles and thick warm brown hair like the stuff on their heads (which is curly); have long clever brown fingers, good-natured faces, and laugh deep fruity laughs (especially after dinner, which they have twice a day when they can get it).

The main character, Bilbo Baggins, is a fifty-year-old hobbit living a quiet, comfortable life. This situation is changed by Gandalf, a mysterious wizard, who is looking for someone to go on an adventure with him. Bilbo wants no part of any adventures and quickly excuses himself to go back into his hobbit-hole. Gandalf, secretly amused, scratches a sign into Bilbo's door as it closes.

The next day, Gandalf and a band of thirteen dwarves visit Bilbo. Thorin Oakenshield, the leader of the dwarves, tries to recruit the reluctant hobbit to help recover his father's treasure from the wicked dragon, Smaug. Aided by a map, the group plans to cross the Misty Mountains and the Mirkwood Forest to reach Smaug's hideout. Bilbo is promised a share of the treasure if he will help them. Bilbo eventually concedes.

Along the way, it begins to rain and the group of adventurers lose a large amount of food when one of their ponies, which becomes frightened, jumps into the river. When Bilbo is sent to investigate a light on the side of the road, he finds three trolls sitting by a fire. Bilbo is caught trying to pick one of their pockets, but later escapes into the woods when the trolls begin to argue. The rest of the dwarves are captured as they approach the fire.

Gandalf cleverly uses his magic to cause the trolls to fight amongst themselves. Losing track of time, the trolls turn to stone at dawn. Bilbo and the dwarves search the cave of the trolls, where they discover some food and coins to help them on their journey. Gandalf and Thorin find two jeweled swords, and Bilbo takes a small blade for himself.

After a brief rest, the adventurers continue their journey toward the mountains. Upon reaching the valley of Rivendell, they are greeted by singing elves. They stop at the Last Homely House, where Elrond, chief of the elves, resides. Elrond identifies the blades carried by Gandalf and Thorin; they are magical, powerful goblin-killers. Elrond, also familiar with the runes on Thorin's map, finds a clue regarding an entrance to the Lonely Mountain, where Smaug resides with the treasure. The travelers rest for two weeks before heading into the mountains.

The Misty Mountains

The adventurers are trapped on a narrow pass high in the mountains. As a storm begins, they see stone giants playing with boulders in the pouring rain. Frightened, the dwarves hide in a nearby cave. However, a passage opens in the rear of the cavern, though which goblins enter and abduct them. In the confusion, the dwarves are separated from Gandalf.

Bilbo and the dwarves are brought before the Great Goblin, who is infuriated when he recognizes Thorin's sword. The Great Goblin is ready to execute them. Suddenly, the torches are extinguished, and Gandalf murders the Goblin king. The adventurers flee, fighting off goblins as they escape. They each take turns carrying Bilbo on their backs because he cannot keep up. Bilbo is eventually knocked unconscious.

When Bilbo regains consciousness, he is alone in the cave. Groping through the darkness, he finds a ring on the cavern floor and pockets it. He also discovers that his blade is magical; it glows dimly in the darkness. He wanders to an underground lake, where a slimy, lizard-like creature called Gollum lives. Gollum and Bilbo trade riddles. If Bilbo wins, Gollum agrees to show him the way out. If he loses, Bilbo becomes Gollum's dinner.

After a series of riddles, Bilbo cleverly stumps Gollum by asking him to guess what he has in his pocket. He does not realize that the ring belongs to Gollum and that it has the power to make its wearer invisible. Gollum cannot guess, and when he goes to fetch his ring, he realizes the answer to Bilbo's riddle. Enraged, he chases Bilbo, but Bilbo slips on the ring, becomes invisible, and sneaks out of the cave.

Bilbo finds Gandalf and the dwarves and surprises them with his sudden appearance. He earns their respect when he tells them the story of his encounter with Gollum and of his escape, but he keeps the secret of the ring to himself. The group travels through a wooded area and, as the sun begins to set, they arrive at a clearing. Frightened by the howls of wolves, they climb up trees to hide.

The Wargs, evil wolves allied with the goblins, appear in the clearing. Gandalf magically lights pine cones on fire and launches them at the Wargs, setting many aflame. However, the goblins appear and build fires at the base of the trees. Meanwhile, the Lord of the Eagles hears the commotion and brings his minions to the rescue. The flock of eagles carries the group to safety.

Gandalf informs his band that he will accompany them to one final destination before they reach the great forest of Mirkwood. He introduces them to Beorn, an enormous shape-shifter of great strength who has the ability to communicate with animals and change into a bear. Beorn provides food for the weary travelers and allows them to rest in his home. He sends them on their way with ponies, food, and water for their journey through the forest, and warns them to keep to the path.

The Forest of Mirkwood

The adventurers leave Gandalf and travel through the forest for several days and nights, slowly exhausting their food and water supply. One night, they see many fires off the path. Hungry, they ignore Beorn's warning and heard for the warm glow of the forest's campfires.

As they approach, everything goes dark. Bilbo falls into an enchanted slumber and giant spiders seize the rest of his comrades. Bilbo recovers and uses his ring to trick the spiders and to release his friends from the webs. A terrific battle ensues and the adventurers escape, only to notice that Thorin is missing.

The next day, the group—except for Bilbo, who wears his ring—is captured by wood elves and brought before their king. The king imprisons the dwarves in his dungeon because they refuse to tell him any information about their mission. Bilbo, discovering that Thorin is also a captive, filches keys from a drunken guard and frees the dwarves. They escape to Long Lake by hiding in barrels used to move goods up and down the river to the town of Esgaroth.

Smaug and the Battle of Five Armies

The group stops in Esgaroth, a town built in the middle of Long Lake and inhabited by men. Thorin, whose grandfather was once a king allied with the townsmen's ancestors, is greeted warmly. The adventurers are provided food and ponies, and continue their journey by water toward the Lonely Mountain, where Smaug the dragon resides. Once they arrive, they discover a secret opening. Bilbo sneaks into the dragon's lair, steals a cup, and brings it back to the dwarves to prove his worth as a burglar.

The disturbed dragon leaves his lair to find the thief. Bilbo and the dwarves take cover, but they are unable to save their pack animals. Smaug devours the ponies and returns to his lair. Bilbo agrees to sneak back into Smaug's lair for further investigation. Bilbo, now invisible, intrigues the dragon with flattery and riddles. He discovers that Smaug has a weak point in his breast. After Bilbo flees the lair, Smaug leaves and attacks the town of Esgaroth. The adventurers enter the unguarded cave and locate the stolen treasure. Bilbo finds the Arkenstone of Thrain, the great jewel of the dwarves.

Meanwhile, Smaug sets Esgaroth on fire. Bard, a human, finds Smaug's weak point and shoots an arrow into the dragon's heart, killing him. Upon learning of the dragon's death, the King of the Wood Elves and his army join the humans and together they set off for the Lonely Mountain to claim the treasure.

A raven informs Thorin that Smaug is dead and that the humans and the elves are coming for the treasure. The dwarves fortify the only open entrance to the mountain. Thorin sends the raven to fetch his cousin's army. The men and elves arrive and demand a share of the treasure; Thorin refuses. The men and elves decide to camp around the mountain, but Bilbo sneaks out with the Arkenstone.

Hoping to avoid bloodshed, Bilbo gives Bard and the King of the Wood Elves the Arkenstone to use in bargaining with Thorin. They offer Bilbo sanctuary, but he is loyal to the dwarves and determined to rejoin them. On his way back, he is heartened to discover that Gandalf has returned and is camping with the men.

The next morning, the humans and elves show the Arkenstone to Thorin. When Bilbo admits that he gave the jewel to the men, Thorin accuses Bilbo of treachery and threatens to throw him off the mountain. Thorin releases Bilbo, but still refuses to share the treasure. Thorin's cousin Dain arrives.

An army of goblins and Wargs descends upon both warring groups, however, and the two sides are compelled to join forces. Even Thorin overcomes his greed and bravely joins the fight. A fierce battle ensues, and the goblins appear to have the upper hand. However, Bilbo's spirits are lifted when he sees the Lord of the Eagles arriving with a huge flock. Bilbo is once again knocked unconscious when a rock hits his head.

The End of the Tale

Bilbo awakens to a deathly quiet until he hears a man calling for him. Bilbo removes his ring and is brought to a tent where Thorin lays dying. Thorin apologizes for treating Bilbo badly and commends the hobbit's wisdom and bravery. Bilbo weeps when Thorin dies; he also discovers that Beorn arrived after the eagles to help turn the tide of the battle. The hobbit accepts a share of the treasure and leaves with Gandalf and Beorn, heading for home.

The story ends with a short epilogue a few years later when Gandalf and the dwarf, Balin, visit Bilbo. Bilbo learns that the dwarves are content and prosperous, and that Bard has led many of the men of Esgaroth to rebuild Dale, a city destroyed by Smaug.

Characters

Bilbo Baggins

A short, peaceful hobbit, Bilbo Baggins is the protagonist of the novel. He considers himself a typical hobbit; that is, until Gandalf and the dwarves appear at his door. Although he initially

A scene from the animated film version of The Hobbit.

hesitates, Bilbo joins the adventure to find the stolen treasure.

As the story progresses, Bilbo proves himself to be a clever burglar and resourceful companion. He proves his courage when he cuts the dwarves from the webs in Mirkwood and battles the spiders. He later frees the dwarves from the prison of the wood elves. His keen observation of Smaug ultimately reveals the dragon's weak point. One of his most valiant acts is giving the Arkenstone, Thorin's beloved jewel, to the men and elves in a bold attempt to avoid bloodshed. Out of loyalty he returns to the dwarves even though he knows he risks Thorin's wrath.

Balin

Balin is one of the band of thirteen dwarves led by Thorin. Years later he visits Bilbo.

Bard

A courageous human, Bard slays the dragon. Afterward, he goes to the mountain to claim the treasure. He attempts to bargain fairly with Thorin, but the dwarf is blinded by greed. A war over the treasure is avoided only when the goblins attack. After the forces of good defeat the goblins, Bard rebuilds Dale and the city becomes prosperous under his leadership.

Beorn

Beorn is a shape-shifter. A peaceful creature, he allows the band of adventurers to stay in his cabin. He helps turn the tide of the Battle of Five Armies when he appears and kills the goblin general. He also protects Gandalf and Bilbo on part of their journey home.

Bifur

Bifur is one of the band of thirteen dwarves led by Thorin.

Bofur

Bofur is one of the band of thirteen dwarves led by Thorin.

Bombur

Bombur is one of Thorin's band of dwarves. He slips into the enchanted river in Mirkwood Forest and falls into a magical sleep, forcing the party to carry him along.

Dain

Dain is Thorin's cousin from the Iron Hills. Thorin sends a raven to summon Dain and his army to help defend the treasure under the Lonely Mountain from the men and elves after Smaug is slain, and Dain joins forces with the men to defeat the evil creatures. He is crowned King under the Mountain after Thorin dies in the Battle of Five Armies.

Dori

Dori is one of the band of thirteen dwarves led by Thorin.

Dwalin

Dwalin is a member of Thorin's band of dwarves.

Elrond

Elrond is the master of the Last Homely House of Rivendell. He gives Bilbo, Gandalf, and the dwarves sanctuary. A mix of elf and human, he is the peace-loving chieftain of all the elves in the valley. He identifies the swords carried by Gandalf and Thorin, and he is able to read the runes on Thorin's map.

Fili

Fili and his brother Kili are the youngest of the dwarves. He perishes defending Thorin during the Battle of Five Armies.

Gandalf

A mighty wizard, Gandalf convinces the dwarves to recruit Bilbo Baggins for the adventure to reclaim the treasure. Ageless and wise, he alone recognizes the potential greatness in Bilbo. Gandalf is also brave, as evidenced by his decapitation of the Great Goblin. He tends to appear at the most opportune moments and is familiar with all aspects of Middle-earth.

Gloin

Gloin is one of the band of thirteen dwarves led by Thorin.

Goblins

Goblins are evil creatures. After Gandalf slays the Great Goblin with a magical sword, the elves hunt down the adventurers. The goblin army almost defeats the forces of good in the Battle of Five Armies, but the Lord of the Eagles and Beorn turn the tide of the conflict. At the end of the story, most of the goblins in the region have been annihilated.

Gollum

Gollum is a slimy, lizard-like creature living on a rock in the middle of a cold lake underneath the Misty Mountains. He possesses the powerful ring of invisibility. (How it came into his

Media Adaptations

- *The Hobbit* was adapted into an animated film for television by Jules Bass and Arthur Rankin in 1978. The film features the voices of Orson Bean as Bilbo, John Huston as Gandalf, and Richard Boone as Smaug. It is available on videotape.

- There are several audiotape versions of *The Hobbit,* including a 1992 BBC adaptation from Bantam Doubleday.

possession is revealed in *Lord of the Rings*). Bilbo accidentally discovers the ring and wins a war of riddles with Gollum. It is only when Gollum attacks Bilbo in a rage that the hobbit actually discovers the power of the ring. Bilbo leaves Gollum, pathetic and weeping over the loss of "his precious" ring, in the tunnels below the Misty Mountains.

Kili

Kili and his brother Fili, Thorin's nephews, are the youngest of the dwarves. He is killed defending his uncle during the Battle of Five Armies.

King of the Wood Elves

The King of the Wood Elves captures Thorin and the rest of the dwarves when they leave the beaten path in the forest of Mirkwood. He demands to know the purpose of their journey. Bilbo frees the dwarves before he can find out, but the King soon learns of their intentions after Smaug's demise. He gathers an army of elves to earn a piece of the treasure. He recognizes Bilbo's wisdom when the hobbit offers the Arkenstone.

Lord of the Eagles

The Lord of the Eagles leads his flock to save Bilbo, Gandalf, and the dwarves when they are trapped in the trees by goblins and Wargs. Later, they join the humans, elves, and dwarves in the Battle of Five Armies to defeat the goblins. Dain rewards their efforts with golden collars.

Nori

Nori is one of the band of thirteen dwarves led by Thorin.

Thorin Oakenshield

Thorin is the brave leader of a band of thirteen dwarves. His grandfather was the King under the Mountain until Smaug drove the dwarves away and destroyed the human city of Dale. At the start of the novel he seeks to reclaim the treasure of his ancestors and take his throne. When Smaug is finally defeated, Thorin's greed for the treasure, especially his lust for the Arkenstone, almost leads to a disastrous war with the humans and elves. He even banishes Bilbo from his camp when the hobbit gives away the Arkenstone. Thorin is redeemed when the goblins and Wargs attack in the Battle of Five Armies. He joins the humans and elves to fight the wicked creatures and dies from his wounds.

Oin

Oin is one of the band of thirteen dwarves led by Thorin.

Ori

Ori is one of the band of thirteen dwarves led by Thorin.

Smaug

Smaug is a wicked, fire-breathing dragon. He is extremely powerful, intelligent, and cruel. Years before, he destroyed the peaceful, wealthy community of dwarves under the Lonely Mountain and the human city of Dale. The dwarves and humans were trading partners and enjoyed a friendly relationship. The human survivors built Esgaroth, a town in the middle of the Long Lake.

When Bilbo and the dwarves arrive at the Lonely Mountain, Smaug has been in hibernation for quite some time. Wearing the ring of invisibility, Bilbo awakens the evil monster; fortunately, he is clever enough to find Smaug's vulnerabilities. Later Smaug attacks Esgaroth and Bard kills the dragon.

Spiders

Giant, intelligent spiders lurk in the forest of Mirkwood. Bilbo frees the dwarves from webs when he distracts the spiders; once free, the group slaughters the spiders.

Trolls

The trolls are described as large, nasty, and strong. At one point, they capture the dwarves and plan to eat them. Gandalf saves the day by spreading dissension amongst the trolls; as a result, they argue until dawn and turn to stone.

Wargs

The Wargs are evil wolves. They take part in the Battle of Five Armies.

Themes

Good vs. Evil

The conflict between good and evil is the main theme of Tolkien's *Hobbit*. The good creatures strive for a peaceful existence, while the evil creatures cause suffering. In the novel, the quest to reclaim the treasure is considered a righteous cause. Even Bilbo, a gentle hobbit reluctant to get involved, is ultimately convinced to join the quest because he believes it to be a noble mission.

The wizard Gandalf also believes in a good cause. He is a wise and just being who wanders the realm improving the quality of life. A decent judge of character, he recognizes Bilbo's resourcefulness. Elrond, Beorn, and Bard are also examples of the many good and courageous beings who live in Middle-earth.

Evil creatures constantly threaten the forces of good. The mighty dragon Smaug destroys towns and kills their inhabitants. The goblins and Wargs are sneaky, cruel, and vicious. Horrible, enormous spiders lurk in the forests of Mirkwood, preying upon those who venture away from the main path.

There are shades of gray, as in real life. Good characters also can do bad things. For example, although most would consider stealing immoral, Bilbo is recruited as a thief. Thorin, a brave and honorable dwarf, is temporarily blinded by greed and he almost causes a war over the treasure before he redeems himself in the Battle of Five Armies. In any case, the conflict between good and evil is a major theme in the novel. Ultimately the virtuous are triumphant.

Fate and Chance

The roles of fate and chance are addressed in *The Hobbit*. While many of the events in the novel seem to occur by chance, especially Bilbo's discovery of the ring of power that grants him invisibility, the characters ostensibly are ruled by fate. For example, at the end of the book, Bilbo refers to the "prophecies of old songs" that turn out to be true. Gandalf replies:

> Surely you don't disbelieve the prophecies, because you had a hand in bringing them about yourself? You don't really suppose, do you, that all your adventures and escapes were managed by mere luck, just for your sole benefit?

In this passage Gandalf implies that fate partly determined the course of Bilbo's adventures.

While Tolkien did not ignore the importance of free will and chance in *The Hobbit,* he also recognized prophecy and fate as core elements of mythology. Thus, as a modern myth-maker, he worked these themes into the framework of his fantasies.

Friendship

In the novel, friendship often results from peculiar alliances. At first, Bilbo and the dwarves do not trust each other: Bilbo finds the dwarves rude and coarse; the dwarves believe that Bilbo is timid and meek. Yet Bilbo eventually gains their respect with his cleverness, courage, and wisdom. He learns that the dwarves, however brusque and ill-mannered they may be, are loyal and brave friends. At the end of the novel Bilbo is officially made an "elf-friend."

Gandalf befriends any creature on the side of good, particularly hobbits, dwarves, and elves. He recruits Beorn, the mighty shape-shifter, as a valuable ally.

Even evil creatures have friends, as exemplified by the alliance between the goblins and Wargs.

Death

In *J. R. R. Tolkien: Architect of Middle-earth,* Daniel Grotta quotes Tolkien, who once stated that the principle theme of his work was death:

> If you really come down to any really large story that interests people and holds their attention for a considerable time, it is practically always a human story, and it is practically [always] about one thing all the time: *death.* The inevitability of death.

Although Tolkien was referring to his epic novel *The Lord of the Rings,* death is also an important theme in *The Hobbit.* The good characters in this novel risk death at almost every turn. They encounter incredibly vicious creatures such as trolls, goblins, wolves, spiders, and a fire-breathing dragon. They almost end up as meals for the giant spiders and trolls.

They also face such natural hazards as storms, treacherous mountain passes, and the seemingly

Topics for Further Study

- Tolkien composed songs and verses for the creatures of Middle-earth to sing. Choose an event from the novel, such as the Battle of Five Armies or Bilbo's fight with the spiders, and write a verse based on the event. Add music, prerecorded or original.

- Do some research into Norse or Greek mythology. What elements do the various myths share with the Middle-earth of *The Hobbit?*

- Explain what happens between Bard and the Master of Esgaroth after Smaug's death. Are there examples in contemporary world politics that reflect the dynamics of this situation?

- Using computer graphics, painting, sculpture, or another type of artistic media, create a character or scene from *The Hobbit.*

endless forest of Mirkwood. They are often in danger of starvation. Fortunately, they have powerful allies like Gandalf and Beorn on their side. In addition, the adventurers also have magical items to aid them: the swords they take from the trolls and Bilbo's ring of power.

It is not until the end of the story that death claims any of the major characters. Thorin's nephews, Fili and Kili, are killed during the Battle of Five Armies. Thorin is mortally wounded during this battle.

War

War plays an important part in the climax of *The Hobbit.* When Thorin fortifies the Lonely Mountain after the death of Smaug, a war between the forces of good appears imminent. The men and elves are in a stalemate with Thorin's band over the treasure.

However, armies of goblins and Wargs attack the humans, elves, and dwarves camped at the mountain. Thorin overcomes his greed and the forces of good unite to fight evil in the Battle of the Five Armies. Although the losses are great, the forces of good are victorious with the help of Beorn and the Lord of the Eagles.

The end of the war signals the close of the novel. Most of the goblins and Wargs have been driven away. Thorin dies, and Dain is made King under the Mountain in Thorin's place. The treasure is divided to everyone's satisfaction. Bard rebuilds the city of Dale, and both Dale and Esgaroth prosper. Finally, Bilbo returns to the peace and quiet of his hobbit-hole.

Style

Fantasy and Mythology

The Hobbit is considered a masterpiece of fantasy. There is often a tendency among scholars of literature to deride genres such as fantasy and science fiction; however, Tolkien's books are so imaginative and brilliantly conceived that he has earned a great deal of critical respect.

Tolkien's imaginary world was derived from mythology. He believed that myth was a tool that cultures use to build bridges of understanding between generations.

Although Tolkien invented hobbits, most of the creatures that populate Middle-earth were borrowed from the myths of other cultures. Beings akin to *The Hobbit*'s dwarves, elves, and trolls, as well as Smaug the dragon, can be found in many ancient legends and myths. In addition, magic and magical objects are incorporated within the plot of the story, as in so many other fantastic tales. The quest motif advances the narrative, as it does in Arthurian legend. Virtue, embodied in the heroism and humility of the characters, is ultimately triumphant as it is in most classic mythology.

Narration

The story is told in the third person, mostly from Bilbo's point of view. However, the narrator acts as a storyteller familiar with the history, geography, language, and demographics of Middle-earth. The telling is informal, as if it were a campfire or bedtime story.

The narrator also knows how the story is going to end and functions as a link between Middle-earth and the present.

Setting

The Hobbit is set in the enchanted realm of Middle-earth, which has a topography much like that of Earth, with forests, rivers, mountains, etc. Tolkien wanted the world of the novel to be somewhat familiar to readers. Thus, he drew from his childhood experiences—particularly those of his hometown of Sarehole, which inspired the Shire of the hobbits—to construct some of the geographies of Middle-earth. His memories of a climbing expedition in the Swiss Alps during his youth inspired the Misty Mountains.

Humor

Although much of *The Hobbit* is dark, humor is often used to break up the tension. Bilbo's meek and fussy behavior in the beginning of the novel is one example. The dwarves, as they clean up the mess they have made in Bilbo's hobbit-hole, sing a song about breaking plates, because "That's what Bilbo Baggins hates...."

There is humor in even the most dangerous situations. The scenes when Bilbo is threatened by Gollum, or when he flatters Smaug, are good examples.

Historical Context

Pre-World War II England

When *The Hobbit* was published in 1937, Europe was in turmoil. The German dictator Adolf Hitler made no secret of his plan to expand German territory and rid his country of certain minorities, in particular the Jewish people. Many English politicians, including Winston Churchill, recognized the potential danger of Hitler's regime. However, British Prime Minister Neville Chamberlain sought to avoid conflict with Hitler. In March 1938, Hitler's forces annexed Austria and created a crisis throughout Europe.

Chamberlain's controversial response was a policy of "appeasement," which allowed Hitler certain territories like Austria. He signed the Munich Pact with Hitler after the Austrian annexation to avoid war and proclaimed, "I believe it is peace in our time." A month later, Germany occupied the Czech Sudetenland. Yet when Germany invaded Poland on September 1, 1939, Great Britain and France declared war on Germany two days later. Chamberlain was forced to resign in May, 1940; Churchill took over and led the country through the difficult years of World War II.

With the start of World War II, constant air raids and threats of invasion from the European

Compare & Contrast

- **Late 1930s:** Hitler occupies Austria and the Czech Sudetenland in 1938. British Prime Minister Neville Chamberlain adopts his controversial "appeasement" policy in an effort to mollify Hitler. The strategy is doomed when Hitler's aggression leads Germany to invade Poland on September 1, 1939. Two days later Great Britain and France declare war on Germany.

  Today: The European Economic Community (EEC) is an economic powerhouse. A new European currency, the Euro, is issued. However, political events threaten economic progress for Europe as the conflict in Yugoslavia wreaks havoc in the Balkans. Also, Serbian aggression in Kosovo leads to the NATO bombing of Belgrade.

- **Late 1930s:** In South Africa, Tolkien's birthplace, the Native Laws Amendment Act is passed. This law extends the long-established system of pass laws, which require blacks to carry special papers to stay in the cities. This law is only one in a series over many years establishing the apartheid (apartness) system in South Africa.

  Today: Nelson Mandela retires as President of South Africa. Imprisoned in 1961 for protesting the apartheid system, he was freed in 1988 and elected president of South Africa. Apartheid has been dismantled for many years, yet the effects of the policy are still evident throughout South African society.

- **Late 1930s:** With the advent of World War II, military production provides a spark for American manufacturing and industrial production. As a result, the United States begins to reverse the economic collapse of the Great Depression.

  Today: The economies of the United States and Europe are strong. Due to the government's efforts to adopt a more democratic system, the Russian economy experiences a difficult transition. Japan suffers from a recession because of various factors, including a banking crisis.

---

continent endangered the English. Meanwhile, English casualties mounted and the German forces (as well as Benito Mussolini's Italian army) gained much ground early in the war. Tolkien believed that fantasy literature comforted people in such anxious and difficult times, and certainly *The Hobbit* serves as an excellent example of escapist literature.

Oxford University and the Inklings

Oxford University is the oldest English-speaking university in the world. Since 1096 teaching has existed at Oxford in some form. The university is comprised of thirty-nine independent, self-governing colleges, including Exeter College, which Tolkien entered in 1911.

At Oxford, Tolkien studied the classics, including Greek and Roman languages, literature, art, history, and philosophy, as well as modern languages, literature, and philosophy. He was awarded a degree with first-class honors in English Language and Literature just before he left for France to fight in World War I.

After the war Tolkien returned to Oxford to work as a teacher and tutor for the English School. Over the next several years, he established a reputation as a brilliant philologist and linguist. From the mid-1930s until 1962, Tolkien was part of an informal literary club at Oxford known as the Inklings. The group included several famous English writers, poets, essayists, and critics of the time, including Tolkien's close friend C. S. Lewis, as well as Owen Barfield, Hugo Dyson, and Charles Williams.

The Inklings would read and discuss their writings with each other. Many of the members encouraged Tolkien to publish *The Hobbit*. Tolkien also read most of *The Lord of the Rings* to the group years before it was published. The Inklings dissolved when Lewis became ill in 1962 and died the following year.

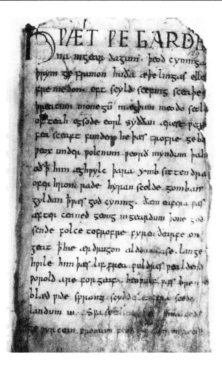

A page from an early Beowulf *manuscript. This work was among Tolkien's inspirations for* The Hobbit.

Critical Overview

Perhaps the most important critique of *The Hobbit* came from ten-year-old Raynor Unwin, the son of English publisher Sir Stanley Unwin. According to Daniel Grotta, in his biography *J. R. R. Tolkien: Architect of Middle-earth,* young Unwin earned between a shilling and a half-crown for reviewing children's literature. His assessment of *The Hobbit* is as follows:

> Bilbo Baggins was a hobbit who lived in his hobbit hole and *never* went for adventures, at last Gandalf the wizard and his dwarves persuaded him to go. He had a very exciting time fighting goblins and Wargs. At last they got to the lonely mountain: Smaug, the dragon who guards it, is killed and after a terrific battle with the goblins he returned home—rich!
>
> This book, with the help of maps, does not need any illustrations. It is good and should appeal to all children between the ages of 5 and 9.

Raynor Unwin said years later, "I wouldn't say my report was the best critique of *The Hobbit* that has been written, but it was good enough to ensure that it was published."

The Hobbit was published in 1937, and most reviewers concurred with Unwin's positive assessment. Although the book was primarily viewed as children's literature, several reviewers emphasized the book's appeal to older readers. A reviewer (believed to be C. S. Lewis) in the London *Times Literary Supplement* wrote, "It must be understood that this is a children's book only in the sense that the first of many readings can be undertaken in the nursery."

In the *New York Times,* Anne T. Eaton asserted, "Boys and girls from 8 years on have already given *The Hobbit* an enthusiastic welcome, but this is a book with no age limits." Because Tolkien believed that mythology and fairy tales helped bridge the gap between generations, he would have been pleased with these assessments.

Despite the excellent reviews, *The Hobbit* was not initially a financial success for Tolkien. However, the commercial success of *The Lord of the Rings* trilogy during the 1950s also affected the sales of its predecessor. Tolkien lived to see *The Hobbit* sell over a million copies in the United States alone. It continues to be one of the best-selling fantasy titles in print.

Tolkien's work has generated a great deal of scholarly criticism, primarily concentrating on *The Lord of the Rings.* Much commentary focuses on the creation, history, and languages of Middle-earth. Several authors, including Edmund Fuller, have looked for allegory (characters or events used to represent things or abstract ideas to convey a message or teach a lesson) in Tolkien's work. However, the author vehemently denied the use of allegory in his books. In his introduction to the Ballantine edition of *The Lord of the Rings,* he wrote:

> I cordially dislike allegory in all its manifestations, and always have done so since I grew old and wary enough to detect its presence. I much prefer history, true or feigned, with its varied applicability to the reader. I think that many confuse applicability with allegory; but the one resides in the freedom of the reader, and the other in the purported domination of the author.

The Hobbit is first and foremost a grand adventure, a tale of good overcoming evil.

Criticism

Don Akers

Akers is a freelance writer with an interest in fantasy literature. In the following essay, he examines the creative philosophy of Tolkien and the continuing influence of The Hobbit *on contemporary fantasy literature and popular culture.*

J. R. R. Tolkien's *The Hobbit* is sometimes dismissed as a mere children's story by critics and readers, especially when compared to his *Lord of the Rings.* Obviously, *The Lord of the Rings* is a much more sophisticated and elaborate work than its predecessor.

However, as simple as the novel may seem, *The Hobbit* is an important work in its own right. Tolkien finally realized his vision of an imaginary world and history he had been creating for years before the book was published in 1937. More significantly, Tolkien established the groundwork of his theories on the creation—and usefulness—of mythology and fantasy in culture as he wrote *The Hobbit.* His work continues to serve as a bridge between cultures of the past and the present.

Tolkien often denied that he wrote *The Hobbit* only to entertain children. As one of his biographers, Daniel Grotta, maintains in *J. R. R. Tolkien: Architect of Middle-earth,* Tolkien's purpose in writing *The Hobbit* can be found in a statement he made about *The Lord of the Rings:* "In *The Lord of the Rings,* I have tried to modernize the myths and make them credible."

Tolkien knew the importance of mythology to language and culture. He believed that people needed myths to link them with the past, thus helping them cope with the uncertainties of the present and giving them hope for the future. Grotta makes an analogy between the roots of a plant and the myths of a culture to explain this concept:

> In an era of unprecedented change, the links to the past are stretched to the breaking point, and a people without roots are likely to become, analogously, a people without branches or flowers. The roots of the past—mythology—are no longer acceptable in their traditional form and have to be recast in a more contemporary, relevant mode.

Therefore, Tolkien created a mythology that was accessible to people in the twentieth century. His most famous lecture, "On Fairy-Stories" (1947), detailed his thoughts on the importance of fantasy and mythology to culture. He noted that in a world filled with wars, poverty, and disease, people turned to fantasy for comfort. He used the powerful metaphor of a prisoner confined in jail to illustrate this longing for "far away and long ago." The wish to escape is reasonable in this context; similarly, the reader of fantasy literature wishes to escape to a better world.

In "On Fairy-Stories," Tolkien also developed his theory of the "sub-creator." He believed that stories and myths, regardless of how fantastic, should contain components of the real world in order to help the reader "suspend disbelief." For example, the geography of Middle-earth is similar to that of the Earth with forests, rivers, and mountains. While there are strange races and amazing creatures, there are also humans and familiar animals such as horses and birds. These familiar elements allow the reader to accept, at least temporarily, the fantastic elements. Grotta explains the dynamics of sub-creation:

> When a fantasy world is consistent with the real world—with variations and differences of course—the storyteller or mythmaker is less a creator than a *sub-*creator. He *discovers* rather than *invents* a never-never land that is at once similar to and unlike our own.

This concept explains the narrator's familiarity with Middle-earth in *The Hobbit.* The narrator is like a professor or historian who has discovered Bilbo's chronicle of his adventures, the *Red Book of Westmarch.* The narrator shares the evidence of this fantastic world with the reader.

Tolkien freely borrowed from the myths of the past. This practice made sense, not only because he was a scholar intimately familiar with ancient myths, but also because he was trying to link past and present. He was especially proficient at plundering Norse mythology. For example, the names of all the dwarves in *The Hobbit* were lifted directly from *The Elder Edda,* a group of poems from a thirteenth-century Icelandic text. The names of Gandalf and the forest of Mirkwood also came from Norse mythology.

Of course, Tolkien didn't limit himself to Norse mythology. *The Hobbit* also shares many of the characteristics of Arthurian legend. Gandalf plays a role similar to that of Merlin. The dwarves are on a quest, much like the Knights of the Round Table. There are powerful artifacts in both stories: the Holy Grail in Arthurian legend and the ring of power in *The Hobbit.* Tolkien was captivated by the dragons, or dragon-like beasts, that he found in the myths of many cultures; in fact, Smaug the dragon is one of his most fascinating creations.

Tolkien, along with Robert E. Howard and Fritz Leiber, profoundly influenced contemporary fantasy. All of these authors used the elements of mythology in their works, and the fantasy, horror, and science-fiction writers of today are building from their strong foundation.

A study of the character of Beorn in *The Hobbit* demonstrates this continuity. Beorn is a shape-shifter, a man who can change into a bear. Tolkien was aware that shape-shifting creatures have been part of the mythology of many cultures. Several of the Greek gods changed form at will, and the Europeans of the Middle Ages feared vampires and werewolves. Beorn is essentially a good creature, but several contemporary writers have continued this thread of past mythology by using shape-shifters as villains.

For example, in Peter Straub's *Ghost Story* (1979) an evil shape-shifter seeks vengeance on a group of old men. The shape-shifter in Stephen King's *It* (1986) terrorizes a small town by taking the forms of various movie monsters.

Another element of myth that serves as a thread from ancient mythology to contemporary fantasy is the magical artifact. Perhaps the most famous of these items is the Holy Grail of Arthurian legend. The Holy Grail was the cup used by Jesus Christ at the Last Supper. The Knights of the Round Table searched for it to save King Arthur. There are several magical items in *The Hobbit,* the most obvious being the ring of power discovered by Bilbo in Gollum's lair. The adventurers also find three enchanted blades made by elves in the cave of the trolls.

There are many examples of magical items in contemporary fantasy as well. In Michael Moorcock's *Elric* (1970s) series, the albino elf Elric brandishes a mighty sword called Stormbringer. Elric has a symbiotic relationship with the sword, which is capable of stealing the souls of its victims. Another interesting example of a "magical" relic is in Gene Wolfe's *Book of the New Sun* (1980-83) series. The protagonist, Severian, is an apprentice torturer who finds the Claw of the Conciliator. The Claw is capable of healing people and even bringing them back from the dead.

The influence of Tolkien and his contemporaries on modern fantasy literature is obvious. However, there have also been some unexpected effects on popular culture. The phenomenon of the fantasy role-playing game is a perfect example. "Dungeons and Dragons" is probably the most popular of these games. Using fantasy literature and mythology as its basis, the game allows players to choose from a variety of races (human, dwarf, elf, etc.), classes (fighter, wizard, etc.), and "alignments" (good, neutral, or evil) to create characters. Each different type of character has various strengths and weaknesses. A referee, known as the

Dungeon Master, designs adventures for the players using a number of resources, including manuals, maps, and charts. The outcome of each adventure is determined by the choices the players make and the roll of several different types of die. The game is limited only by the imagination of the Dungeon Master and the players.

A quick study of the game's guidelines reveals Tolkien's influence. The "halfling" character race is blatantly patterned after Tolkien's hobbits. In the game, halflings perform best as thieves because of their ability to move silently, hide quickly, and sneak into tight spaces. Of course, these are the characteristics that prompt the dwarves in *The Hobbit* to recruit Bilbo Baggins.

"Dungeons and Dragons" was popular with teenagers and college students during the 1970s and 1980s; however, the game has received some bad press over the years due to some unfortunate incidents of players taking it to extremes. The popularity of "Dungeons and Dragons" has also decreased because of the increased availability of video, computer, and on-line fantasy games.

Tolkien's work, and fantasy literature in general, remains very popular. At this writing, plans for a live-action film version of *The Lord of the Rings* are underway. It seems as if the modern world still has a place in its heart for Tolkien's fantastic realm.

The most successful writers of fantasy have followed Tolkien's pattern: they *discover* their worlds rather than create them. In the 1973 introduction to *The Hobbit,* Peter S. Beagle wrote:

> For in the end, it is Middle-earth and its dwellers that we love, not Tolkien's considerable gifts in showing it to us. I said once that the world he charts was there long before him, and I still believe it.

Tolkien died two months after Beagle's introduction was written. One hopes he had the chance to read it; he would have been pleased.

Source: Don Akers, in an essay for *Novels for Students,* Gale, 2000.

C. W. Sullivan III

In the following essay, Sullivan considers The Hobbit *in terms of its impact on children's literature.*

When it was first published in 1937, J.R.R. Tolkien's *The Hobbit* was an immediate success. Reviewers noted its ties to ancient northern European myths and legends, especially *Beowulf* and the Eddas, and praised it for its strong component of

What Do I Read Next?

- Tolkien's epic *The Lord of the Rings* is essential reading for those interested in Middle-earth. The novel contains three volumes: *The Fellowship of the Ring* (1954), *The Two Towers* (1955), and *The Return of the King* (1955). It chronicles the adventures of Frodo, Bilbo's nephew, and his quest to destroy the ring of power discovered in *The Hobbit*.

- *The Silmarillion* (1977) was published after Tolkien's death. His son, Christopher, compiled the book from various fragments written before *The Hobbit* and *The Lord of the Rings*. It details the ancient history of Middle-earth.

- C. S. Lewis wrote a seven-volume children's fantasy series called *The Chronicles of Narnia*. The series follows the adventures of four children who discover a magical world of talking animals, witches, and dwarves behind a wardrobe in an old house. The first book published in the series, *The Lion, the Witch, and the Wardrobe* (1950), is a good place to start.

- Daniel Grotta's *J. R. R. Tolkien: Architect of Middle-earth* (1976) is a compelling account of Tolkien's life and works. Grotta discusses the influences on Tolkien's fiction and provides an in-depth analysis of his major works.

- Fritz Leiber wrote dozens of stories featuring his Fafhrd, a barbarian, and the Gray Mouser, a cynical thief. Their adventures in the world of Newhon are exciting and original. *Ill Met in Lankhmar* (1995) contains the first two collections of his Fafhrd and Gray Mouser stories. It is a good introduction to the fascinating realm of Newhon.

- Author Michael Moorcock's *Elric* series is captivating for those readers interested in fantasy literature. The protagonist, Elric, is an evil elf whose sword, Stormbringer, steals souls. *Elric of Melnibone* (1972) is the first novel in the series.

---

adventure, its humor, its imaginative scope, and its intelligent presentation. At least one reviewer asserted that the book was destined to become a classic of children's literature. Allen and Unwin, who published the book, must have agreed, for they were soon urging Tolkien—who really wanted to work on the mythological materials that would eventually be published, some years after his death, as *The Silmarillion*—to produce "another Hobbit." But history has denied *The Hobbit* the status it deserves as an important children's book. World War II, Tolkien's work on the *Silmarillion* materials, and the length to which *The Lord of the Rings* eventually grew—in addition to familial and professorial duties—prevented Tolkien from publishing his "next Hobbit" until 1953-1954. *The Lord of the Rings* then eclipsed *The Hobbit;* the sequel became the main work, and *The Hobbit* was relegated by many—critics and readers alike—to prequel status. In fact, the Ballantine paperback edition of *The Hobbit* announces, on the front cover, that this book is the "enchanting prelude to *The Lord of the Rings.*" Instead of being recognized as a touchstone of children's literature, *The Hobbit* became an additional, but somewhat less important, part of a larger adult work.

In the mid-1960's, when Tolkien's books became a cultural (and also a counter-cultural) phenomenon, *The Hobbit*'s status as a children's book was pushed even further into the background. The controversial Ace Books' paperback publication, followed by the highly-publicized and "authorized" editions from Ballantine Books, created a much larger interest in Tolkien's fiction than had previously existed. At that time, publishers were responding to a renewed interest by adults in fantasy literature by reissuing, in paperback, classics of fantasy by everyone from William Morris to Robert E. Howard; this fantasy-hungry market devoured Tolkien. That led to everything from college courses about Tolkien specifically and fantasy in general (which, in turn, resulted in an explosion of articles and books on Tolkien and fantasy), to the creation of a large group of adults with money to spend on Tolkien-related paraphernalia, and time to spend in Tolkien clubs or at Tolkien or fantasy conventions.

In and of itself, none of this activity is bad; but it has taken attention away from *The Hobbit* as a children's book. Most of the articles and books listed in Richard C. West's *Tolkien Criticism: An Annotated Checklist* deal with aspects of *The Lord of the Rings* or with aspects common to both *The Lord of the Rings* and *The Hobbit.* Few articles and no books deal solely with *The Hobbit,* and much of what does focus on *The Hobbit* concerns itself with identifying some of the ancient sources on which Tolkien drew. While those who have discussed *The Hobbit* in its own right have noted some of the aspects which suggest that it was aimed at young readers, very few have discussed it, first and foremost, as a children's book.

In *Tolkien's World,* Randel Helms deals with *The Hobbit* as a learning experience for its author, through which he prepared himself to write *The Lord of the Rings:*

> Taken in and for itself, Tolkien's children's story deserves little serious, purely literary criticism. But we cannot take *The Hobbit* by itself, for it stands at the threshold of one of the most immense and satisfying imaginative creations of our time, *The Lord of the Rings.*

More recently, in *Tolkien and the Silmarils,* Helms has suggested that *The Hobbit* is important as a "mid-wife" to the birth of *The Lord of the Rings* out of *The Silmarillion,* commenting that "*The Hobbit* could be called *The Silmarillion* writ small." While this latter observation may increase the critical importance of *The Hobbit,* it does not bring us any closer to understanding it as a children's book. Helms does, however, recognize and enumerate three major characteristics which separate *The Hobbit* from *The Lord of the Rings,* and which also help to identify it as a children's book: intrusions by the narrator, a plot about growing up, and word or language play. These characteristics are not found only in *The Hobbit,* of course; as Lois Kuznets notes in "Tolkien and the Rhetoric of Childhood," they are a part of a general rhetoric found in various classics of children's literature.

There are more than three dozen incidents in *The Hobbit* of direct intrusion by the narrator— intrusions such as "I must say" or "I can tell you," in which the narrator refers to himself in the first person singular before going on to give the reader some information or to offer his own opinion on the events taking place, and other intrusions such as "that comes at the end of the tale" or "as you have heard," in which the narrator directs the reader's attention to some other events in the story. In addition, of course, there are various explanations of or comments on the story which any omniscient author might make, but which are written in the same tone as the more direct narrator intrusions and must, therefore, also be credited to the narrator.

As Jane Nitzsche points out in *Tolkien's Art: A Mythology for England,* the narrator's intrusions have "annoyed readers and critics" alike. And because Tolkien later repudiated the technique (by example in *The Lord of the Rings* as well as in interviews and in critical articles about writing fantasy), most of these annoyed critics and readers have passed over the narrator's intrusions as merely a way one writes for children or as the sort of flaw one often finds in an early work. A few critics, however, have suggested that the narrator's intrusions were not a mistake in narrative style—regardless of Tolkien's later comments. Nitzsche, for example, likens the narrator in *The Hobbit* to the narrator in Chaucer's *The Canterbury Tales,* and suggests that Tolkien's narrator, like Chaucer's, is quite separate from the author and must be treated as another character in the novel. And Kuznets sees the narrator as someone who "promises protection and companionship even when one is reading alone."

But the sources for the narrator's intrusions may be quite different from the ones that these critics suggest. There are similar moralizing comments by the narrator of *Beowulf,* many of which occur in the digressions but are actually comments on actions in the main story. And in the main story itself, the narrator occasionally makes a direct evaluative comment. When Wiglaf finally comes to Beowulf's aid against the dragon, for example, the narrator says, "so should a man be / a thane in need" (lines 2708-2709). Even closer in narrative style to *The Hobbit,* however, is *Sir Gawain and the Green Knight,* in which there are numerous first person narrator intrusions. After describing some of Arthur's Christmas feast, for example, the narrator of that poem says, "Now will I of their service tell you no more, / for everyone well knows that no lack was there" (lines 103-131). It is possible, then, that Tolkien took his narrative pose not from other children's literature or from a sense of having to talk down to an imagined naive listener, but from two poems (and from other ancient and medieval works like them) with which he was very familiar, and in whose image he may well have been casting many aspects of *The Hobbit.* Tolkien's debt to Celtic and Scandinavian sources has been established in other matters and should certainly be considered here.

About the second major element which marks *The Hobbit* as a children's book, its plot about growing up, there is little debate. Every critic recognizes that Bilbo Baggins "grows up" as a result of his adventures, that he matures and accepts responsibilities toward the end of the novel which he could not have even imagined in the first chapter, and that by the last chapter it is a much more competent hobbit who returns to the Shire and puts things back into order there. The hobbit who left home without even a pocket handkerchief has become the friend of eagles and elves, has rescued his companions time and again, has faced and conquered his own doubts and fears, and has returned home with a magic ring and bags of gold. As Bilbo and Gandalf approach the Shire, Bilbo recites some new verses to "Roads Go Ever Ever On," and Gandalf comments, "Something is the matter with you! You are not the hobbit that you were."

But there is some debate over how to analyze this plot. As already noted, Helms sees *The Hobbit* as Tolkien's learning experience and, like many other critics, comments on the close parallels between the episodic structures of both works, concluding that "*The Lord of the Rings* is *The Hobbit* writ large." In addition, of course, he notes the real and important differences between the two works, especially those which make one a children's book and the other a work for adults. Helms also offers a more or less tongue-in-cheek Freudian analysis of *The Hobbit* which, focusing on caves and swords and the like, reduces the story to a psychological ritual of emerging manhood. Timothy R. O'Neill, however, in *The Individuated Hobbit,* presents a serious Jungian analysis of Bilbo's journey as a journey into his own subconscious.

Most other critics, like Helms, have set up their discussions of *The Hobbit* to balance, if not directly preview, their discussions of *The Lord of the Rings.* Nitzsche discusses *The Hobbit* as a children's story, similar to but less complex than *The Lord of the Rings,* which she discusses as an epic. In *One Ring to Bind Them All: Tolkien's Mythology,* Anne Petty suggests that "the most profound and ominous elements of *LOTR* are quarried from [*The Hobbit*]," and she employs Propp's morphological analysis

as a means of illustrating just how similar the two works are. And Katharyn Crabbe, in *J.R.R. Tolkien,* deals with *The Hobbit* as a fairy tale before dealing with *The Lord of the Rings* as legend and *The Silmarillion* as myth.

A third major characteristic of children's literature, word or language play, is an important part of *The Hobbit,* and it seems to me that it exists on at least three levels. On the most obvious and simplest level, there are the puns, sound effects, silly songs, and made-up words which have most annoyed the critics and which, quite probably, have most delighted the children. The broadest pun, perhaps, involves the beheading of the goblin king, Golfimbul, which not only won a battle but also, when the head went down a rabbit hole, began the game of golf.

Also on this level are the sound effects, from the *ding-dong-a-ling-dang* of Bilbo's doorbell in the Shire to the *swish, smack!* of the goblins' whips far under the Misty Mountains. At various points in *The Hobbit,* the reader encounters the songs of the goblins and the elves. All of these songs are so whimsical that they undercut the basic natures of the singers; that is, the reader finds the goblins less fearsome and the elves less wondrous after hearing their respective songs. (In *The Lord of the Rings,* Tolkien wrote much more serious songs and poetry.) And finally, there are words such as "confusticate" and "bebother," which Bilbo uses when he is annoyed with the dwarves. If nothing else, these words, songs, sounds, and puns should catch the ears of children and, perhaps, make them more attentive to all of Tolkien's words.

The second level of word or language play involves various traditional uses of language, much of which a child would recognize and be familiar with. The riddling contest between Bilbo and Gollum is probably Tolkien's most dramatic use of traditional language, and except for Bilbo's last riddle (which is not actually a riddle at all), all of them are traditional riddles, some of which a child might have already heard. Thus, Bilbo's riddling session with Gollum could catch the interest of children, and, by acquainting and re-acquainting them with traditional riddles which have variants in their own world, prepare them for the riddling Bilbo does with Smaug, a session in which the riddles belong primarily to Middle Earth and have no close variants in the child's world. Similarly, Tolkien's use of proverbs is both traditional and original. Proverbs such as "Third time pays all" have variants such as "Third time's the charm" in the reader's world; but Bilbo's proverbs, "Every worm has his weak spot" and "Never laugh at live dragons," while they are structured like familiar proverbs, belong essentially to Middle Earth.

Tolkien includes other language-based activities with which children would be familiar. Gandalf's mimicking of the trolls' voices to save Bilbo and the dwarves and Bilbo's name-calling to lure the spiders away from the dwarves are both activities which have their parallels in the child's world. And a child, much more than an adult, understands the effectiveness of mimicry and name-calling. Also, Tolkien's use of runic writing and maps would be familiar, at least in principle, to young readers. To be sure, most children are not familiar with runic writing as such, but they do invent various kinds of secret codes and maps which use otherwise meaningless symbols to stand for letters and which show the way to a secret camp. The concept of a secret runic writing or a special map, then, would not be all that strange to young readers.

The third level of word or language play in *The Hobbit* introduces the reader to some fairly sophisticated linguistic concepts. One such concept involves the nature of names as symbols. Bilbo is merely polite to the old man who appears in front of his hobbit hole in chapter one, but when that old man announces that "I am Gandalf, and Gandalf means me" Bilbo becomes quite excited. It is the old man who has the power, but Bilbo reacts to the name, the symbol, more strongly than to the old man, the object for which the symbol stands. The symbol has aroused something in Bilbo that the object did or could not.

Other incidents involving names as symbols abound in *The Hobbit*. At one point, Bilbo asks Gandalf why Beorn calls an unusual geological formation a "Carrock;" Gandalf answers that Beorn "calls things like that carrocks, and this one is *the* Carrock because it is the only one near his home and he knows it well." Rather than a symbol of meaning, the name is a point of reference, a way for someone—in this case, Beorn—to locate himself in his world. It is also, of course, a sign of ownership; giving something a name is an assertion of the right to give it a name. Tolkien also suggests that names can be relative. The swords found among the trolls' spoils are called *Orcrist,* "Goblin-cleaver," and *Glamdring,* "Foe-hammer," by the dwarves and the elves, but the goblins, against whom they were used, call them *Biter* and *Beater.*

Knowing the names of people, places, and things is important for more than merely functional reasons; Tolkien strongly suggests that, in addition to a knowledge of languages being power (as in the case of Elrond's knowing how to read the runes and, thereby, giving Bilbo and the dwarves the power to open the secret door), the languages themselves may be magical. Certainly there are magic spells, mostly Gandalf's, which open doors and make either friendly or destructive fire, but Tolkien does not stop there. He suggests that there is power inherent in language and that words, used effectively, can move people in ways they do not fully understand.

In the first chapter, for example, the dwarves sing about a dragon who killed dwarves to get their gold and harps, and about a quest to win back those treasures. The dwarves' song has a profound effect on Bilbo:

> As they sang the hobbit felt the love of beautiful things made by hands and by cunning and by magic moving through him, a fierce and jealous love, the desire of the hearts of dwarves. Then something Tookish woke up inside him, and he wished to go and see the great mountains, and hear the pine-trees and waterfalls, and explore the caves, and wear a sword instead of a walking stick.

And later in the book, when Bilbo is talking to Smaug, he feels "an uncomfortable desire ... to rush out and reveal himself and tell all the truth to Smaug." Bilbo has almost fallen under a "dragon-spell," and although Tolkien says no more about it, Smaug's language is an example of language which has power far beyond its denotative or connotative value. This language is magical.

Although these three characteristics—an intrusive narrator, a plot about growing up, and word or language play—may help identify a story as one aimed at a young reader, their presence alone does not identify it as a classic. But they can be a guide. I have dealt with the word or language play of *The Hobbit* in some detail to illustrate that Tolkien put a lot of care and craftsmanship into the writing, the actual language, of this book. This feature may, in fact, be the key to *The Hobbit*'s stature. Tolkien was, after all, a philologist, and he knew the historical and cultural depths of words. Simonne d'Ardenne, Tolkien's student, friend, and colleague in philology, asserts that "Tolkien belonged to that very rare class of linguists, now becoming extinct, who like the Grimm brothers could understand and recapture the glamour of 'the word.'" In his essay, "On Fairy-Stories," Tolkien himself said that it was "in Fairy Stories that I first divined the potency of words" and suggested that it is the power of language that creates the fantasy world. In other critical works, especially "Beowulf: The Monsters and the Critics" and "Chaucer as a Philologist: *The Reeve's Tale,"* he illustrated that a knowledge of the individual words themselves, in as much of their original and contextual meaning as we can establish, is invaluable to understanding a literary work as a whole. Thus, it comes as no surprise when Verlyn Flieger suggests, in the preface to *Splintered Light:*

> Above all, he gives us back words, those tired old counters worn with use, and makes them new again in all their power, variety, and magic. He remembers for us what we have forgotten, that *spell* is both a noun and a verb, that it means incantation as well as the formation of a word by letters, and that to use it in either sense inevitably involves using it in both senses.

And because of Tolkien's language, the reader retains vivid pictures from *The Hobbit* long after the actual reading has been completed, pictures which make him always slightly dissatisfied with the renderings on the Tolkien calendars or the interpretations of various illustrators and animators. The reader draws his pictures directly from Tolkien's language, a language in which any word may be used in many senses simultaneously. Gandalf alerts us to this early in the book when he asks Bilbo what he means by "Good Morning!" "Do you wish me a good morning, or mean that it is a good morning whether I want it or not; or that you feel good this morning; or that it is a morning to be good on?" And Bilbo replies that it is all of that and more.

Almost all fantasy writers and critics agree that it is its language upon which a fantasy novel stands or falls. In "From Elfland to Poughkeepsie," Ursula LeGuin argues that the heroes of High Fantasy must speak as if they are from Elfland—and not from Poughkeepsie or Washington, D.C. The style is important, she continues, acknowledging Tolkien, "because in fantasy there is nothing but the writer's vision of the world … A world where no voice has ever spoken before; where the act of speech is the act of creation. The only voice that speaks here is the creator's voice. And every word counts."

When all of those words are woven together, they make a story. As a term of literary criticism, "story" has fallen on hard times. In "On Stories," C.S. Lewis suggests that critics have paid much more attention to literary works in which the story, "the series of imagined events," is there as a vehicle for something else—social criticism, for example—than they have to literary works "in which

everything else is there for the sake of the story." This, it seems to me, strikes right to the heart of the critics' problems with *The Hobbit;* the novel is first and, perhaps, foremost a good story, and those who refuse to deal with it on that level—or who are ignorant of that level—have little recourse but to try to deal with the source materials, the psychological patterns, or the stirrings of an imagination which would not reach full fruition until *The Lord of the Rings.*

The Hobbit is a touchstone, finally, because it is a very good story, and it is a good story primarily because Tolkien was a philologist. This means, as I have already suggested, that Tolkien knew about words and knew how to choose them effectively. But he was also a philologist of his time, a time in which, as Flieger notes, "philology, mythology, and anthropology were coming to be seen as formed from the same matrix." And so *The Hobbit,* a children's book, reverberates with mythic and legendary resonances from its connections to Tolkien's own mythological creation, *The Silmarillion,* as well as from its connections to northern European, especially Scandinavian and Celtic, myths and legends. The novel opens with dwarves from *The Elder Edda* and a wizard close to druidic traditions, and it does not close until after the vanquishing of a dragon (certainly kin to the Midgard Serpent) right out of *Beowulf.*

But Tolkien was not merely borrowing materials from ancient sources, he was telling a traditional story. This, too, was a result, in part, of his being a philologist. As a philologist, Tolkien studied not only the ancient words, but also the documents in which they appeared—*Beowulf, The Mabinogion, The Elder Edda, Sir Gawain and the Green Knight,* and the rest. He knew, from those studies, that the traditional story teller was less an inventor of new materials that a refiner of old ones. In *The Celts,* Gerhard Herm notes that, among many other materials, the Bards had to learn "all of the old stories circulating that the public invariably wished to hear again and again, in the same traditional form." Tolkien, then, took the traditional materials he knew and retold them as *The Hobbit.*

Tolkien's fiction, while written in the twentieth century, is more closely patterned after mythic and heroic narrative (in both content and style) than it is after more recent literatures. And judged as a traditional narrative, as a "good story" carefully crafted by a master of language, *The Hobbit* is clearly one of the classics of children's literature.

Source: C. W. Sullivan III, "J. R. R. Tolkien's *The Hobbit*: The Magic of Words," in *Touchstones: Reflections on the Best in Children's Literature,* Children's Literature Association, 1985, pp. 253-60.

Dorothy Matthews

In the following excerpt, Matthews discusses The Hobbit *from a psychoanalytic perspective.*

J.R.R. Tolkien's *The Hobbit* has received very little serious critical attention other than as the precursor of *The Lord of the Rings*. It has usually been praised as a good introduction to the trilogy, and as a children's book, but anyone familiar with psychoanalysis cannot avoid being tantalized by recurrent themes and motifs in the three stories. Bilbo's story has surprising depths that can be plumbed by the reader who is receptive to psychoanalytic interpretations.

The central pattern of *The Hobbit* is, quite obviously, a quest. Like so many heroes before him, Bilbo sets out on a perilous journey, encounters and overcomes many obstacles (including a confrontation with a dragon) and returns victorious after he has restored a kingdom and righted ancient wrongs. However, this pattern is so commonplace in literature that it is not a very helpful signpost. But it may help in other ways.

Let us first look briefly at *The Hobbit* for its folk ingredients, that is, the common motifs or story elements which it shares with folk narratives. There are, of course, the creatures themselves: dwarves, elves, trolls, animal servants, helpful birds and, the most frequently recurring of all folk adversaries, the treasure-guarding dragon. There are magic objects in abundance: a ring of invisibility, secret entrances into the underworld, magic swords, and doors into mountains. Dreams foretell and taboos admonish, the violation of which could bring dire results.

There are tasks to be performed, riddles to solve, and foes to be outwitted or outfought. Folk motifs form the very warp and woof in the texture of this tale, which is not surprising since Tolkien, as a medievalist, is immersed in folk tradition, a tradition that gives substance not only to the best known epics but to most medieval narratives and to fairy tales.

In fact, it is probably its resemblance to what today's readers see as the nursery tale that has resulted in *The Hobbit* being relegated to elementary school shelves....

But even if *The Hobbit* is only a children's story, it should be analyzed more closely for deeper levels of meaning, for it is the kind of story that has provided the most profound insights into the human psyche....

Bilbo Baggins' journey [is] a metaphor for the individuation process, his quest ... a search for maturity and wholeness, and his adventures ... symbolically detailed rites of maturation....

... [At] the beginning of the tale, Bilbo's personality is out of balance and far from integrated. His masculinity, or one may say his Tookish aggressiveness, is being repressed so that he is clinging rather immaturely to a childish way of life. He has not even begun to realize his full potential. The womblike peace and security of his home is disturbed with the arrival of Gandalf, who may be seen as a projection of the Jungian archetype of the wise old man since he resembles the magic helper of countless stories....

At the outset of their adventure, Bilbo, like a typical young adolescent, is uncertain of his role, or persona, to use a Jungian term....

One of the most crucial incidents of the story takes place when Bilbo finds himself unconscious and separated from the dwarves within the mountain domain of the goblins. In this underground scene he must face an important trial; he must make a decision whose outcome will be a measure of his maturity.... With unprecedented courage he decides to face life rather than to withdraw from it. This decision marks an important step in his psychological journey.

The danger he decides to face at this time, of course, is Gollum, the vaguely sensed but monstrous inhabitant of the underground lake. The association of this adversary with water and the attention given to his long grasping fingers and voracious appetite suggest a similarity to Jung's Devouring-Mother archetype, that predatory monster which must be faced and slain by every individual in the depths of his unconscious if he is to develop as a self-reliant individual. The fact that the talisman is a ring is even more suggestive of Jungian symbology since the circle is a Jungian archetype of the *self*—the indicator of possible psychic wholeness. The psychological importance of this confrontation is further supported by the imagery of the womb and of rebirth which marks the details of Bilbo's escape....

Whether the spider with whom Bilbo battles is interpreted as a Jungian shadow figure, embodying evil, or as the Devouring-Mother facet of the anima is immaterial. The symbolism is clear without specific terms: a lone protagonist must free himself from a menacing opponent that has the power to cripple him forever. With the aid of a miraculously acquired sword and a magic talisman, he is able to face the danger and overcome it....

From this point on, Bilbo has the self-esteem needed to fulfill his responsibilities as a mature and trustworthy leader. It is through his ingenuity that they escape from the dungeon prisons in the subterranean halls of the wood-elves. This last episode also reveals telling symbolic details in that the imprisonment is underground and the escape through a narrow outlet into the water is yet another birth image.

The climactic adventures of Bilbo are of course the episodes with Smaug, who, like the traditional dragon of folklore, has laid waste the land and is guarding a treasure. If viewed in the light of Jungian symbology, the contested treasure can be seen as the archetype of the self, of psychic wholeness. Thus this last series of events marks the final stages of Bilbo's quest of maturation....

A truly critical question arises in considering [the incident where Bilbo acquires the Arkenstone] and the remainder of the story. I have taught this work many times and am constantly hearing complaints of dissatisfaction from students who feel that the last part of the book is both puzzling and anticlimactic. Many report that they felt a real loss of interest while reading the final chapters. Why does Bilbo keep the Arkenstone without telling the dwarves and then use it as a pawn in dealing with their enemies? Why, they ask, did Tolkien have a rather uninteresting character, rather than Bilbo, kill Smaug? Why is Bilbo, the previous center of interest, knocked unconscious so that he is useless during the last Battle of Five Armies? Isn't it a fault in artistic structure to allow the protagonist to fade from the picture during episodes when the normal expectation would be to have him demonstrate even more impressive heroism?

Answers to these questions are clear if the story is interpreted as the psychological journey of Bilbo Baggins. It stands to reason that Tolkien does not have Bilbo kill the dragon because that would be more the deed of a savior or culture hero, such as St. George, or the Red Cross Knight, or Beowulf. The significance of this tale lies in fact in the very obviously anti-heroic manner in which Tolkien chooses to bring Bilbo's adventures to a conclusion. As a result, Bilbo emerges as a symbol of a very average individual, not as a figure of epic proportion. Bilbo has not found eternal glory, but, rather, the self-knowledge that a willingness to meet challenge is not necessarily incompatible with a love of home.... [At] the conclusion of his adventures Bilbo finds the greatest prize of all: a knowledge of his own identity. In maturing psychologically, he has learned to think for himself and to have the courage to follow a course he knows to be right in spite of possible repercussions.

Source: Dorothy Matthews, "The Psychological Journey of Bilbo Baggins," in *A Tolkien Compass,* edited by Jared Lobdell, Open Court, 1975, pp. 29-42.

Sources

Peter Beagle, in an introduction to *The Hobbit,* by J. R. R. Tolkien, Houghton Mifflin, 1973.

Anne Eaton, in the *New York Times,* March 13, 1938, p. 12.

Daniel Grotta, in *J. R. R. Tolkien: Architect of Middle-earth,* Running Press, 1976, pp. 85–105.

Times Literary Supplement, October 2, 1937, p. 714.

For Further Study

David Day, in *A Tolkien Bestiary,* Random House, 1998, 286 p.
  Surveys the beasts, deities, and other creatures that exist in Middle-earth.

Karen Wynn Fonstad, in *The Atlas of Middle-earth,* Houghton Mifflin, 1991, 210 p.
  Detailed maps of Middle-earth, including war and other thematic maps.

Robert Foster, in *A Guide to Middle-earth,* Ballantine Books, 1974, 291 p.
  A directory to all the proper names appearing in *The Hobbit, The Lord of the Rings, The Adventures of Tom Bombadil,* and *The Road Goes Ever On.*

Neil D. Isaacs and Rose A. Zimbardo, in *Tolkien and the Critics,* University of Notre Dame Press, 1968, 296 p.
  A collection of essays analyzing Tolkien's *The Lord of the Rings,* including contributions from C. S. Lewis and W. H. Auden.

Paul H. Kocher, in *Master of Middle-earth: The Fiction of J. R. R. Tolkien,* Houghton Mifflin Co., 1973, 247 p.
  A comprehensive study of Tolkien's major works.

J. R. R. Tolkien, in *The Tolkien Reader,* Ballantine Books, Inc., 1974, 200 p.
  Contains some of Tolkien's lesser-known fiction and poetry.

Kindred

Octavia Butler

1979

Prior to the publication of her fourth novel, *Kindred,* Octavia Butler was primarily known only to fans of science fiction. While her first three novels—all part of the "Patternmaster" series—received favorable reviews, her work was marginalized as genre fiction. Since the 1979 publication of *Kindred,* however, Butler's work is known to a wider audience.

The novel focuses on many of the issues found in Butler's fiction: the abuse of power, the limits of traditional gender roles, and the repercussions of racial conflict. The science-fiction elements of the story are limited, however, to the unexplained mechanism that permits a twentieth-century African American woman to travel into the past. Each time Dana Franklin is drawn back into the early 1800s to save the life of her white ancestor, she learns more about the complex nature of slavery and the struggles of African Americans to survive it. The result is a powerful and accessible story that resembles a historical slave narrative—but one told from a modern perspective and in a modern voice.

Butler's exploration of this era has led many new readers to discover her work, from feminist critics to students of African American literature. These individuals have learned what fans of science fiction have long known: Butler crafts some of the most imaginative and thought-provoking fiction today. "In *Kindred,*" Robert Crossley wrote in his introduction to the novel, "Octavia Butler has designed her own underground railroad between

past and present whose terminus is the reawakened imagination of the reader."

Author Biography

Butler was born in Pasadena, California, in 1947, and grew up in a racially mixed neighborhood. An only child, she was very young when her father died, and her mother worked as a maid to support the two of them. She was raised as a strict Baptist, a faith that forbade dancing or makeup. For solace and escape, she turned to reading. She became a fan of science fiction magazines; inspired by the possibilities of the genre, she was only twelve when she began writing the first version of what would eventually become her "Patternmaster" novels.

Butler received an associate's degree from Pasadena City College in 1968 and entered California State University in Los Angeles the following year. She left school, however, after discovering there was no creative writing major. She attended several workshops in the late 1960s, including the Writers Guild of America. There she met noted science-fiction writer Harlan Ellison, who became Butler's mentor and helped her gain admittance to the Clarion Science Fiction Writers Workshop in 1970. The six-week course introduced her to several well-known writers.

She supported herself with the kinds of menial jobs that Dana Franklin describes in *Kindred.* In 1976 she published her first novel, *Patternmaster,* the first in a series of works describing a society whose members have developed telepathic powers over the course of centuries. Butler went on to publish five novels in this series.

While in the midst of exploring the "Patternmaster" universe, Butler began to write a novel examining the pain and fear African Americans had to live through in order to endure and succeed in American society. The resulting novel was *Kindred* (1979), a unique exploration of slavery as experienced through a modern woman's eyes.

Butler has been awarded several of science fiction's highest awards for her short fiction, including the Hugo and Nebula Awards. She continues to write science fiction, including the three-volume "Xenogenesis" series and two volumes in her "Earthseed" series. Her protagonists are usually women coming from a black or biracial background, which provides a different perspective to a field dominated by white males for many years.

Octavia Butler

Plot Summary

The River

On her twenty-sixth birthday, Dana, the protagonist of *Kindred,* is overcome by nausea and finds herself on the bank of a river. When she sees a young boy drowning in the river, she jumps in and saves him. She is shocked when the boy's father points a gun at her head; it is clear that he is suspicious of Dana, a young black woman. Suddenly, she finds herself back in her living room. Although she was by the river for minutes, she has been away from home for only a few seconds.

Traumatized by the event, she calms down and begins to recover her wits. Suddenly she finds herself next to the same boy, named Rufus, in a burning bedroom. As she saves him again, Dana realizes that Rufus is calling her when his life is in danger. She discovers that the year is 1815, and although he is a white, Southern slave-owner, he is the future father of the first woman listed in her family records—Hagar Weylin. The woman listed as Hagar's mother, Alice Greenwood, is a free black child and Rufus' friend. Dana realizes that she has just saved the life of her ancestor.

Dana decides to visit Alice, but ends up watching as patrollers drag Alice's father out and whip him. He is a slave, and has come to visit his family without permission. A patroller grabs Dana and tries to rape her. She hits him and returns to her life in 1976. When she shares her experiences with her husband, Kevin, he has a hard time believing her. He realizes that Dana can only come back to the present when her life is in danger.

The Fall

The next time that she begins to disappear, Kevin is pulled back in time too. They arrive in a clearing next to Rufus, now twelve years of age, who has a broken leg. Rufus' father, Tom Weylin, arrives. Kevin—a white man—invents a cover story to explain their presence, asserting that Dana is a literate slave whose job is to help him with his writing. Rufus insists on having Dana by his side in the sickroom, which leads to tension with his unstable mother, Margaret.

Dana makes friends with the other slaves and Tom hires Kevin to teach his son. They settle into a routine, until Dana becomes uncomfortable with how easy it is. She realizes that slavery is a mental degradation, not just a physical one. When Tom discovers her teaching slave children to read, he knocks her to the ground and beats her. Before Kevin can reach her, she is returned to 1976.

The Fight

After eight days Dana is dragged back to a clearing where Rufus is fighting for his life. He has attempted to rape Alice Greenwood, and her husband Isaac is beating him to death. When Dana intervenes, Isaac and Alice flee the scene. She and Rufus return to the house—a large, wealthy Maryland plantation—and she learns that Kevin has been gone for two years, and Margaret has left. Dana nurses Rufus back to health, and he mails a letter to Kevin for her.

Alice and Isaac are caught, and his ears are cut off before he is sold. Rufus buys Alice and brings her home near death. Dana nurses her back to health. There is still no word from Kevin, and Dana sends more letters. Rufus gives Dana a horrible ultimatum—either she makes Alice consent to having sex with him, or he will have her beaten into submission. Alice, weary and terrified, agrees.

Discovering that Rufus never sent any of her letters to Kevin, Dana escapes, but is caught and whipped. Tom sends for Kevin, and he arrives as Dana reaches her breaking point. Riding away, Rufus shoots at them, and they are dragged back to the present.

The Storm

Back in 1976, Kevin finds it impossible to adjust. Dana finds herself pulled back again. Rufus is very ill. Dana helps him recover, but is unable to help Tom when he collapses with a heart attack. Blaming her, Rufus sends her into the fields, and then pulls her back out to help his mother, now a laudanum addict.

Alice and Rufus have a child, Joe. She teaches Joe to read, and Rufus begins to love his son. Alice has a daughter, Hagar—Dana's ancestor. Dana agrees to help Alice escape as soon as Hagar is old enough. When Rufus sells a slave as a punishment for being too friendly with Dana she tries to stop him, but he punches her in the face. She slits her wrists and awakes in 1976.

The Rope

Fifteen days later, on the Fourth of July holiday, Dana is pulled back for the last time. She finds Rufus on the brink of suicide because Alice is dead. As a punishment for trying to run, Rufus moved their children to Baltimore, and told Alice that he'd sold them. Despairing, she took her own life.

After the funeral, tension mounts between Dana and Rufus, culminating in a confrontation in which he tries to rape her. She stabs him, and he dies clutching her. She is pulled back to the present with her arm crushed in the wall. Everything below her elbow—where Rufus grabbed her—is pulverized.

Epilogue

Dana recovers; she and Kevin discover that Weylin plantation was burnt to the ground the night Dana killed Rufus, and his death was attributed to the fire. The slaves were all sold. They realize that the murder was covered up, and accept that they will never know the rest.

Characters

Carrie

A mute slave, Carrie is a good friend to Dana. Most people believe that she is mentally impaired because of her handicap, but she is not. Carrie comforts Dana after Tom's death and explains that the slaves are better off under Rufus' ownership; if Rufus were dead, the slaves would be separated from their friends and families. She also comforts Dana when she is derided as being more white than black. Dana appreciates and values her friendship.

An illustration depicting a slave woman and child being attacked in their cabin.

Jake Edwards

Jake Edwards is one of the overseers hired to manage the field hands. "It was amazing how much misery the man could cause doing the same job Luke had managed to do without hurting anybody," Dana observes. He forces Dana to do laundry by threatening her with a whipping.

Evan Fowler

Evan Fowler is the second overseer Dana encounters on the Weylin plantation. At first she believes that he is harmless, but his brutality proves that he is a cruel and unforgiving man.

Dana Franklin

An aspiring African-American writer, Dana Franklin is shocked when she is suddenly transported back into the past to save the life of her white ancestor, Rufus Weylin. Nothing in her life has prepared her for experiencing the South in the early nineteenth century. She witnesses the whipping of Alice Greenwood's father on her second visit, and the vivid sounds and smells make her realize that "I was probably less prepared for the reality [of violence] than the child crying not far from me."

As she later tells Kevin, "the more I think about it, the harder it is for me to believe I could survive even a few more trips to a place like that." She considers herself—a black woman—"the worst possible guardian" for Rufus, for "I would have all I could do to look after myself." She does not shrink from the task, however, because she knows her family's existence depends on her success. In addition, she thinks "I would … maybe plant a few ideas in [Rufus'] mind that would help both me and the people who would be his slaves in the years to come."

As her visits to the past become longer and more involved, Dana enjoys a privileged status in the Weylin household. She is disturbed by how easily she seems to acclimate to her new role, but realizes that this is because most of the time she can act as an observer. As time goes on, however, she is drawn more deeply into the pain of slavery.

When Rufus convinces Dana to persuade Alice to sleep with him in order to avoid a beating, she wonders if she has become "submissive"—the "white nigger" Alice accuses her of being. Yet as Carrie reassures her, the black "doesn't come off."

Dana eventually comes to understand that she is like the other slaves. All of them "have to do things they don't like to stay alive and whole." In the end, however, Dana realizes that although it would be "so easy" to submit to Rufus' advances, "A slave was still a slave. Anything could be done to her." She is unable to submit, and kills Rufus. Although she returns to the present, she loses an arm on the journey: her escape, like everything else about her experience, has exacted a high cost.

Edana Franklin

See Dana Franklin

Kevin Franklin

Kevin is Dana's husband. He is an "unusual-looking white man, his face young, almost unlined, but his hair completely gray and his eyes so pale as to be almost colorless." His pale eyes make him "seem distant and angry whether he was or not," but he has a winning grin that "completely destroyed the effect of his eyes."

When Dana meets him at the temp agency, she enjoys his sense of humor, and recognizes that this fellow writer "was like me—a kindred spirit crazy enough to keep on trying." After four months together Kevin proposes, and the two marry despite the objections of their families.

Kevin is a kind and thoughtful husband. After Dana's second trip into the past, although he has little understanding of what has happened to her, he prepares a survival kit and ties it to her waist while she is sleeping. When she begins to disappear a third time, he embraces her and is pulled back into the past as well. Although she knows she will be safer with him there, Dana fears what it will do to his mind: "I didn't want this place to touch him except through me."

There are signs that perhaps her fears are valid. Dana is upset by how easily they both seem to adjust to their new roles as slave and master, and how Kevin sometimes finds the idea of living in the past interesting. Kevin is not really suited to the past, as Sarah observes: "He'd get in trouble every now and then 'cause he couldn't tell the difference 'tween black and white." The five years he spends in the past scar him terribly.

When they finally return to the present, he seems colder, angrier, and more solitary. Nevertheless, while the long separations have not helped the couple's relationship, in some ways they have reinforced their sense of being kindred spirits. As Dana notes, "It was easy for us to be together, knowing we shared experiences no one else would believe."

Alice Greenwood

Dana has already figured out that Alice Greenwood is her ancestor when she meets the child on her second trip to the past. Rufus considers Alice his friend, and notes that she is a free black, "born free like her mother." Alice obviously knows the pains of slavery, however, for her father is a slave on the Weylin plantation who is brutally whipped when he is discovered visiting his wife without a pass.

Dana does not meet her ancestor again until her fourth visit, when Isaac almost kills Rufus. Although Alice is furious over Rufus' attempt to rape her, she persuades Isaac not to kill him, knowing it would mean Isaac's death if he were captured. Instead she tries to escape with him.

Alice and Isaac are captured, however, and the penalty for helping him to escape is a beating, after which she is sold into slavery. Rufus buys her, paying twice the market price. Dana nurses her back to health and tells Alice the truth about what happened when she cannot remember it.

Alice and Dana become close friends. The two women look alike, and Rufus considers them two halves of one woman. Alice's "erratic" relationship with Dana is sister-like: "sometimes needing my friendship, trusting me with her dangerous longings for freedom … ; and sometimes hating me, blaming me for her trouble."

As the years pass, Alice becomes hard and bitter. She loses two of her first three children to illness, and the other slaves shun her because of her relationship with Rufus. After the birth of Hagar, Alice resolves to escape. Alice commits suicide after Rufus moves her children away.

Alice Jackson

See Alice Greenwood

Isaac Jackson

Isaac Jackson is Alice's husband. When he discovers Rufus trying to rape his wife, he beats him, which brings Dana into the past for the fourth time. After the incident, he and Alice attempt to escape. They are captured, however, and Isaac is sold after being beaten and mutilated.

Sam James

Sam James is a big, muscular slave who attempts to get Dana to dance with him at Christmas. She warns him not to speak to her after Rufus threatens to sell any slave she might want to "jump the broom" with. After Rufus allows Dana to teach some of the young slave children to read, Sam James asks her to teach his brother and sister as well. When Sam is sold three days later, Dana's anger with Rufus leads her to attempt suicide and return to the present.

Liza

Liza is a slave who is sent into the fields after Alice has healed enough from her beating to take her job. Her resentment of Alice—and by extension Dana, who healed Alice—leads her to betray Dana. Alice, Tess, and Carrie perceive this as a betrayal of the slave community, and beat her severely as a warning. "Now she's more scared of us than of Mister Tom," Alice says.

Luke

Luke is Nigel's father. Dana meets Luke after Rufus breaks his leg. He is the "driver" of the plantation, a type of black overseer whose job it is to manage the field hands. She learns later that Tom grew tired of his attitude and sold him.

Aunt Mary

Aunt Mary's job is to look after the children; unfortunately, she is senile. Yet people are more likely to rely on her knowledge of herbal medicine than on the white doctor.

Nigel

Nigel is a slave and Rufus' playmate. As an adult, he becomes a house slave—one with a privileged position. He grows into a big, handsome man like his father, with the same desire for freedom. After an attempt to run away, he is severely whipped.

Nigel has enough influence with Rufus to stand up to the overseer Jake Edwards. After he marries Carrie and starts a family with her, the Weylins feel assured that Nigel will not make another attempt to run away. He still dreams of freedom, however. As he tells Dana, "It's good to have children.... But it's so hard to see them be slaves."

Sarah

Sarah is the plantation cook. She is kind and patient with Dana and is fond of Rufus. Nevertheless, she resents him for selling away most of her children. She does not trust whites, for she learned from her first master—the father of her first child—that even promises made in love are "just another lie."

Sarah is outspoken and opinionated. After Luke is sold, however, Sarah appears more cautious. "She had done the safe thing—accepted a life of slavery because she was afraid." Dana comes to appreciate the warnings and wisdom Sarah shares with her.

Tess

Tess is a young slave Dana meets on her fourth trip into the past. Dana helps Tess with her work because Tom injured her during a sexual experience. Tess loses her laundry job after Tom discards her, leaving her to the attentions of Jake Edwards. Edwards sends her to the fields so he can keep watch over her. Eventually she is sold. Her experiences exemplify the inhuman conditions slaves face. As Tess says, "You do everything they tell you ... and they still treat you like an old dog."

Doctor West

Doctor West is the Weylin family doctor. He is "pompous, condescending, and almost as ignorant medically as I was," as Dana describes him. His use of such methods as bleeding and purging, despite his good intentions, is harmful to his patients. Doctor West serves as another reminder to Dana that she is living in a very different age from her own.

Joe Weylin

Joe is the oldest surviving child of Alice Greenwood and Rufus Weylin. Initially a sickly child, he is also lively and bright. He is a good student and excels at his lessons. Rufus gradually comes to recognize his son, allowing him to call him "Daddy" after Alice's death.

Margaret Weylin

Margaret Weylin is the second wife of Tom Weylin. At first, she is ignorant and mean-spirited. Margaret hates Dana not only because she is an educated black but also because she is jealous that Dana has both Kevin's and Rufus' favor. Dana comes to understand that a great part of Margaret's problem is boredom—she has nothing to occupy her time, and so spends it supervising and criticizing people in order to prove her worth.

After giving birth to stillborn twin boys, Margaret has a mental breakdown and is sent to stay with her sister in Baltimore. Rufus brings her back to the plantation after his father's death and asks Dana to care for her. While Margaret still insists on having things a certain way, she is calmer and introspective. Dana and Margaret eventually become friends.

Rufus Weylin

Dana finds Rufus a complex and contrary figure. He is an oddly appealing child, accepting of Dana and adventurous enough to help her escape on her second visit. Even as a boy, Rufus shows signs of a cold, possessive temper. When Margaret interrupts Dana, he berates her, just as his father Tom does: "His mouth was drawn into a thin straight line and his eyes were coldly hostile." As an adult, he tends to drink too much and will "pick a fight just out of meanness."

Rufus loves his childhood friend Alice, but it is a "destructive single-minded love" that is more about power than love. After she marries Isaac, Rufus attempts to rape her—an act that ironically leads to his purchase of Alice and the sale of her husband. He is "erratic, alternately generous and vicious," but Dana does not quite believe Sarah's warning that Rufus "says what will make you feel good—not what's true"; that is, until she discovers he has lied about sending her letters to Kevin. "I kept thinking I knew him, and he kept proving to me that I didn't."

Somehow Dana is able to forgive him for his possessiveness and cruelty. She recognizes that his behavior comes from pain, anger, or fear. His attempt to replace Alice with Dana, however, is the last straw for her. "I could accept him as my ancestor, my younger brother, my friend, but not as my master, and not as my lover."

Tom Weylin

Initially, Dana finds Tom Weylin a brutal and fearsome figure. He beats his son, Rufus; moreover, when his son breaks his leg his only concern seems to be what it will cost him. He shows no hesitation in whipping slaves and has no qualms about separating slave families.

Tom sometimes demonstrates a sense of fairness and gratitude. He allows Dana to choose whether to stay on the plantation or search for Kevin after her fourth arrival. He gives Dana a whipping after she makes an escape attempt, but "he didn't hurt you nearly as much as he's hurt others," Rufus tells her. After he discovers that Rufus broke his promise to let Kevin know of Dana's arrival, he sends word himself.

"Daddy's the only man I know," says Rufus, "who cares as much about giving his word to a black as to a white." As Dana comes to understand, Tom Weylin "wasn't a monster at all. Just an ordinary man who sometimes did the monstrous things his society said were legal and proper."

Themes

Human Condition

As Dana soon discovers, the reality of slavery is even more disturbing than its portrayal in books, movies, and television programs. Before her journey into the past, Dana called the temp agency where she worked a "slave market," even though "the people who ran it couldn't have cared less whether or not you showed up to do the work they offered."

This turns out to be an ironic contrast to life at the Weylin plantation, where a slave who visits his wife without his master's permission is brutally whipped. Perhaps a more painful realization for Dana is how this cruel treatment oppresses the mind. "Slavery of any kind fostered strange relationships," she notes, for all the slaves feel the same strange combination of fear, contempt, and affection toward Rufus that she does.

At first she has difficulty comprehending Sarah's patience with a master who has sold off three of her children. Likewise, she observes that Isaac Greenwood "was like Sarah, holding himself back, not killing in spite of anger I could only imagine. A lifetime of conditioning could be overcome, but not easily."

"After being beaten following her attempt to run away, however, Dana is tormented by doubts about her own resistance: "Why was I so frightened now—frightened sick at the thought that sooner or later, I would have to run again? ... I tried to get away from my thoughts, but they still came. *See how easily slaves are made?* they said."

In the end, however, Dana realizes that she cannot bring herself to accept slavery, even to a man who would not physically hurt her. "A slave was a slave. Anything could be done to her," Dana thinks as she sinks the knife into Rufus' side.

Choices and Consequences

The whole reason behind Dana's travels into the past is survival. Dana finds herself driven to save Rufus not just to ensure his existence but also that of her whole family. Despite her modern education, Dana doubts that she has the strength and endurance that her ancestors had: "To survive, my ancestors had to put up with more than I ever could," she tells Kevin.

On her second trip to the past, her squeamishness keeps her from defending herself from a patroller. The next time, however, she is ready to maim to escape: "I could do it now. I could do anything." Nevertheless, she finds it ironic that her job is to protect a white man: "I was the worst possible guardian for him—a black to watch over him in a society that considered blacks subhuman, a woman to watch over him in a society that considered women perennial children."

Despite her doubts, she manages to save Rufus on several different occasions, and learns more about survival in the process. As she listens to the field hands talking in the cookhouse and observes the other house slaves, she gains information: "Without knowing it, they prepared me to survive."

The drive for survival is very strong, and for slaves this means making many painful choices. "Mama said she'd rather be dead than be a slave," Alice recalls, but Dana disagrees: "Better to stay alive.... At least while there's a chance to get free." Because she thinks she will have a better chance of survival if she befriends the Weylins, she accepts the role of slave during her stay on the plantation. As long as this is her choice and she still has some semblance of control over her life, she finds she can endure more than she ever anticipated.

Accepting this role, however, means that Dana must make some very painful choices. For instance, she agrees to convince Alice to sleep with Rufus willingly because she does not want to see her suffer another beating. She is a quiet and compliant worker, even though this makes the other slaves look at her suspiciously. As she explains to Sam, the field hands "aren't the only ones who have to do things they don't like to stay alive and whole." It is only when Rufus tries to take away the final bit of control she has—control over her body—that Dana kills him.

Appearances and Reality

The strange nature of their time travels causes Dana and Kevin to examine how much their perceptions truly reflect reality. When Dana returns from her first visit, Kevin has difficulty accepting her explanation of where she has been. Yet he has no alternate explanation for her sudden disappearance. "I know what I saw, and what I did—my facts," Dana tells him. "They're no crazier than yours."

After Dana's second trip, however, Kevin admits, "I wouldn't dare act as though I didn't believe. After all, when you vanish from here, you must go someplace." That he finally gets proof when he accompanies Dana on one of these trips does not lessen his point: to communicate with others, sometimes you must accept their perceptions of reality—no matter how strange—as valid.

While Dana and Kevin are living together in the past, they discover another aspect of the con-

Topics for Further Study

- Write a short story in which you travel to the future. Describe this world. What has changed? Does racism still exist in this society?

- Read an original slave narrative of the 1800s, such as Frederick Douglass's *Narrative of the Life of Frederick Douglass* (1845) or Harriet Jacobs's *Incidents in the Life of a Slave Girl* (1861). Use the details of slave life to write a mock diary entry describing a typical day in the life of a slave.

- As an interracial couple, Kevin and Dana Franklin face legal obstacles to their marriage in the nineteenth century and social opposition in the twentieth. Do some research into interracial marriages: trace the history of miscegenation laws (laws regulating interracial relationships) and look up statistics. Are interracial marriages on the increase? Are they more or less likely to end in divorce? Write an essay discussing your findings.

- The Missouri Compromise of 1820 established a precedent for how the United States would deal with the issue of slavery. Research the history of laws and Supreme Court decisions concerning slavery between 1820 and 1860. Create a timeline tracing these developments, and accompany it with a map illustrating the addition of new slave and free states during the same period.

nection between appearances and reality: sometimes when you fake an appearance, it begins to feel like reality. At first, Dana is only "pretending" to play the part of a slave, one who sleeps with her master because she has no choice. Although she knows in her heart that she and Kevin are married equals, she nevertheless feels strange when she sneaks in his room: "I felt almost as though I really was doing something shameful, happily playing whore for my supposed owner."

Later she realizes that she cannot continue to be just a modern observer playing the "role" of slave. She becomes involved: she quietly teaches Nigel to read, befriends Carrie and Alice, and plans her escape after being beaten. In the end she cannot fully accept the reality of life as a slave, however, and leaves the past by killing Rufus.

Difference

As a modern woman living in the past, Dana is different in experience and perspective from everyone around her. She is bound to feel alienated because she is so out of place. Ironically, however, it may be a shared sense of alienation that attracts her to others. When she wonders why she is drawn into the past to save Rufus, for instance, she thinks that their blood relationship does not quite explain it: "What we had was something new, something that didn't even have a name. Some matching strangeness in us that may or may not have come from being related."

Her relationship with Kevin is based on a similar sense of shared difference. When they first meet, Dana thinks he "was as lonely and out of place as I was." As she gets to know him, she understands that this loneliness makes him "like me— a kindred spirit crazy enough to keep on trying." On the plantation, Dana's closest friends are people who are similarly alienated from the slave community: Carrie because of her muteness, and Alice because of her role as Rufus' mistress.

Returning home does not cure Dana and Kevin of feeling out of place; it takes them a while to readjust to the twentieth century. Again, however, this alienation brings them together: "It was easy for us to be together, knowing we shared experiences no one else would believe."

Style

Narrator/Point of View

Kindred uses a first-person narrator, which means that Dana is telling her story from her own perspective. She relates her own thoughts, feelings, perceptions, and experiences. Other characters—such as Rufus, Alice, and Kevin—are known to the reader only through her perceptions of them.

An advantage of first-person narration is that the reader can really identify with Dana. In addition, much of the plot is comprised of Dana's attempts to understand the society and the people of

the past. Her perspective is paramount; in fact, if the reader did not know her thoughts and feelings, it could be difficult to perceive this type of "action."

Another important advantage of a first-person narrator is that it makes the story resemble the historical slave narratives of the past. In creating her own version of the slave narrative, Dana is echoing and extending these historical stories.

Flashback

A flashback is a literary device used to relate events that occurred before the beginning of the story. After a brief prologue, the main action of the story begins with Dana's first journey back into the past. The first two chapters are used to reveal the basic plot of the novel: Dana is being called back in time to rescue her ancestor.

The third and fourth chapters, however, open with a flashback to Dana and Kevin's courtship. This helps flesh out Kevin's character, as well as Dana and Kevin's relationship. This added depth is essential for the reader to understand their devotion to each other. Butler could have presented this information chronologically by describing the courtship at the very beginning of the novel. By presenting it in flashbacks, Butler can focus the opening on Dana's adventure and is thus able to immediately draw the reader into the action of the book.

Foreshadowing

Foreshadowing is a literary device used to hint at future events before they actually happen. In *Kindred,* the prologue actually takes place after the main action of the story, and thus provides the reader with a glimpse of the result of Dana's travels. "I lost an arm on my last trip home," Dana recalls in the first sentence of the novel. Her conversation with Kevin also reveals that the truth of what has happened to her is unbelievable.

This prologue prepares reader for two things: first, that Dana is about to recount events that are strange and unexplainable; second, it alerts readers that Dana's experience will involve serious violence that will permanently scar her.

Denouement

Sometimes called falling action, the *denouement* refers to the resolution of a story's conflict. (*Denouement* is a French word which means "the unknotting.") The *denouement* follows the climax of the conflict and traditionally provides a resolution to the primary plot situation as well as an explanation of secondary plot complications. This outcome does not always have to consist of a physical action; it can also involve a character's recognition of his or her state of mind or moral condition.

The *denouement* of *Kindred* does not strictly fit this definition, however. There is a resolution, for Dana returns to the present after her fight with Rufus, ending the essential conflict of the novel. Yet many secondary questions are never resolved. How was Dana pulled into the past in the first place? Why and how did she lose an arm on her last trip? What happened to Rufus and Alice's children—were they sold or freed?

Dana's search for answers at the end of the novel yields nothing. Critic Robert Crossley has suggested that this open-ended *denouement* serves a specific purpose. "Leaving the novel's ending rough-edged and raw like Dana's wound," he wrote in the introduction to the novel, "Butler leaves the reader uneasy and disturbed by the intersection of story and history rather than comforted by a tale that 'makes sense.'"

Science Fiction

While Butler maintained that *Kindred* is not really science fiction—there is no scientific explanation for Dana's voyages to the past—the time travel story is a staple of the genre. The first novel by English writer H. G. Wells, long considered one of the fathers of science fiction (along with Frenchman Jules Verne), was *The Time Machine* (1895).

Wells also used the device of time travel to dramatize human inequalities. Journeying into the distant future, Wells' traveler encounters two races, the Eloi and the Morlocks. The relationship between the pleasure-loving Eloi and the subterranean Morlocks serves as an ironic comment on the conflict between ruling and working classes of the late-nineteenth century's newly industrialized society.

In *Kindred* it is never explained *how* Dana is transported into the past, or why her arm should be severed upon her final return. While the novel contains elements of science fiction, it also works from the tradition of the slave narrative and the historical novel. As Crossley concluded, "Butler's novel is an experiment that resists easy classification by blurring the usual boundaries of genre."

Historical Context

The Missouri Compromise

The Missouri Compromise marked the first serious debate over the status of slavery in the growing United States, and provides an interesting look at how slavery was perceived at the time. In 1819 the territory of Missouri applied for admission to the Union. During the review process, Representative James Tallmadge of New York added an amendment that would outlaw slavery in Missouri. The House and Senate were divided over the amendment.

Eventually a compromise was reached: Missouri would be admitted as a slave state; Maine would be admitted as a free state; and slavery would be prohibited in the remaining portions of the Louisiana territory north of latitude 36 degrees 30 minutes north.

The debate over slavery was an important turning point in American history. Not because Northerners wanted to eliminate slavery—they were more concerned with limiting it than with eradicating it. Instead, it was the Southern attitude that showed a marked change from previous debates on the issue. In previous years, Southerners were defensive about the institution, and seemed only to tolerate it as a necessary evil.

However, during the debate over the Missouri Compromise, Southerners began to justify and even glorify slavery as a moral system. Attacks on it were considered attacks on the South itself. Attempts to limit slavery were similarly considered attacks on the sovereignty of Southern states.

The Missouri Compromise eased the tensions created by the slavery issue for several years, and set a precedent for further political settlements. Yet it wasn't long before the United States entered into a bloody Civil War.

Rebels and Abolitionists

Several highly publicized slave rebellions in the early nineteenth century reinforced the resolve of Southern slave owners to protect the institution of slavery. While there had been a few slave revolts in the 1700s, the largest occurred in the years just before the events of *Kindred*. In 1800, a revolt by more than one thousand slaves in Virginia was delayed by rainstorms; the leaders were captured before the revolt could be continued.

The largest U. S. slave rebellion occurred in 1811 in Louisiana, when some three to five hundred slaves marched from plantation to plantation gathering recruits and weapons. The rebellion ended when the slaves, led by freeman Charles Deslondes, encountered militia and U.S. military troops.

CASH!

All persons that have SLAVES to dispose of, will do well by giving me a call, as I will give the

HIGHEST PRICE FOR

Men, Women, & CHILDREN.

Any person that wishes to sell, will call at Hill's tavern, or at Shannon Hill for me, and any information they want will be promptly attended to.

Thomas Griggs.

Charlestown, May 7, 1835.

PRINTED AT THE FREE PRESS OFFICE, CHARLESTOWN.

An 1835 handbill offering "the highest price" for slaves.

Another rebellion, which is mentioned in *Kindred* as one that frightened many slave owners, was the 1822 insurrection planned by Denmark Vesey. A former slave who bought his freedom with lottery winnings, Vesey and nine thousand recruits planned to invade Charleston, South Carolina. Vesey's plans were betrayed, however, and he was captured and hanged before his plans could be carried out.

In *Kindred*, Kevin Franklin mentions that he was suspected of helping slaves to escape. Both whites and free blacks were involved in the Underground Railroad in the 1810s and 1820s, help-ing slaves to escape north. Nevertheless, the abolitionist movement—the drive to eliminate slavery completely—did not really get off the ground until the 1830s.

Most historians date the beginning of abolitionism to 1831, when William Lloyd Garrison began publishing his journal *The Liberator*. Before this time, most opponents of slavery proposed moderate solutions, such as compensating slave owners for emancipation or the emigration of free blacks to Africa. Garrison's journal, however, advocated immediate eradication of slavery everywhere in the United States. The American

Anti-Slavery Society was founded in 1833, and was an important voice in the debates over slavery that led up to the Civil War.

Black Power and Black Pride

The "Black Power" movement of the late 1960s and 1970s grew out of the movement for civil rights. As efforts to integrate America were slow to progress, some African Americans came to believe that working within the white-dominated system was not an effective way to achieve their goals. Black Power advocates believed that blacks should celebrate their own heritage and culture. They should not depend on whites to help change the system, but should instead rely on their own communities for political and economic success.

Sometimes the rhetoric of the Black Power Movement was angry and polemic. For instance, many advocates believed that no whites were to be trusted. African Americans—often of older generations—who supported working within the system were often accused of being collaborators. It was this atmosphere of mistrust between different activist camps that was one of Butler's inspirations in writing *Kindred.*

There were groups within the Black Power movement, however, that were less radical and more willing to work within the system to affect political and social change. Their promotion of "Black Pride" led to an increased visibility of African American heritage and culture. In the 1970s African Americans had a growing influence on television, movies, and literature.

The most notable of these successes was the 1977 television miniseries *Roots.* Based on the novel by Alex Haley, this eight-part saga of one African American family captivated nearly 130 million viewers and spawned a new interest in genealogy (the study of family history). Thousands of Americans were inspired to research their own family backgrounds—just as Dana Franklin had to do to survive in Butler's novel.

Critical Overview

Although Butler's *Kindred* was only her fourth novel, published a mere three years after her 1976 debut, it did not take long for critics to praise its unusual qualities. In an early review of the novel, Joanna Russ asserted in the *Magazine of Fantasy and Science Fiction* that "*Kindred* is more polished than [Butler's] earlier work but still has the author's

stubborn, idiosyncratic gift for realism." In particular, Russ hailed how the author "makes new and eloquent use" of the time-travel idea, and pointed out her skilled characterizations and fast-paced style.

While *Fantasy Review* contributor John R. Pfeiffer deemed *Kindred* a novel "of such special excellence that critical appreciation of [it] will take several years to assemble," such in-depth analyses soon followed.

In 1982 Beverly Friend examined how the time-travel plot of the novel served to highlight important feminist issues. "No one would intellectually argue against the proposition that life is better today for both men and women," the critic wrote in *Extrapolation,* "but few realize what … [this novel has] didactically presented: that contemporary woman is not educated to survive, that she is as helpless, perhaps even more helpless, than her predecessors."

Subsequent analyses of *Kindred* have explored how Dana's experiences as a twentieth-century writer and nineteenth-century slave have illuminated issues of sex, race, and history. Margaret Anne O'Connor, for instance, observed that it is not just the stark contrasts between Dana's two lives that are educational, but also the parallels: "Slowly [Dana and Kevin] also come to see the situations of virtual slavery in their own technological, twentieth-century culture," the author wrote in the *Dictionary of Literary Biography.* "Drawing an analogy between power relationships of the early nineteenth century and the home, office, and bedroom of contemporary America, *Kindred* offers readers a chance to evaluate the racial and sexual dimensions of both cultures."

Dana's experiences also allow her insight into the power that has allowed black women—supposedly powerless in a sexist and racist society—to persevere. According to Thelma J. Shinn, Dana learns to survive the travails of slavery by learning from black female mentors such as Sarah, an archetypal figure Shinn called "the wise witch." As the critic stated in *Conjuring: Black Women, Fiction, and Literary Tradition,* "*Kindred* shows that Butler's wise witches, her compassionate teachers armed with knives and cast-iron skillets, have survived and will survive, whether or not they are accepted by their society."

Not only does *Kindred* emphasize the power of those who are oppressed, it also reclaims history from the dominant culture, according to Adam McKible. In a 1994 *African American Review* article, the critic argued that *Kindred,* like other tales of African American women enduring slavery, forces the reader to reassess historical "truth" just by making a black woman the heroine. As a result, "the perspective of the black female slave, who finds herself at the bottom of the hierarchies of race, class, and gender … can in fact become a powerful site of rebellion and self-assertion."

In addition, McKible underscored the way in which names can similarly become symbols of resistance. In *Kindred,* not only does Alice name her children after biblical survivors of slavery, but the protagonist asserts control by choosing to call herself Dana rather than Edana. Thus names "are crystallizations—constant reminders—of resistance and the will to freedom," according to McKible.

The analysis that *Kindred* attracts, even twenty years after its publication, seems to justify Robert Crossley's belief that "if any contemporary writer is likely to redraw science fiction's cultural boundaries and to attract new black readers—and perhaps writers—to this most distinctive of twentieth-century genres, it is Octavia Butler. More consistently than any other black author, she has deployed the genre's conventions to tell stories with a political and sociological edge to them, stories that speak to issues, feelings, and historical truths arising out of Afro-American experience."

Criticism

Tabitha McIntosh-Byrd

Tabitha McIntosh-Byrd is a doctoral candidate at the University of Pennsylvania. In the following essay, she perceives Kindred *as a dark allegory exploring the impossibility of racial and sexual equality in the United States.*

After she has returned from her first trip into the antebellum South, Dana says to her husband, "I don't have a name for the thing that happened to me, but I don't feel safe anymore." The "thing that has happened to her" is history—as it is understood both literally and metaphorically.

On one level, *Kindred* is about literal history—early nineteenth-century life as seen by the protagonist through time travel. Dana is transported into this world by a violent process that has clear parallels to the seizure and transportation of slaves from Africa. The destabilizing experience of the past will cause her to lose an arm because of a problem with the physical act of time travel.

On a deeper level, the history that has "happened to her" is a metaphor; a figurative representation of the cultural meaning and construction of gender and race in her society. In this reading, Dana's time travel is symbolic of memory—a literalized version of one woman's reminder of the inequitable basis of the culture and marriage in which she considers herself an equal. In its metaphoric interpretation, the loss of her limb therefore signifies something much stronger and darker. It acts as a powerful comment on the sacrifices that black Americans, especially black female Americans, have to make in order to coexist in a hostile world.

Dana and her husband Kevin live in an intellectual world that enables them to avoid discussing race and class. Their relationship is based on the careful exclusion of voices that threaten to disrupt this veneer, exemplified by their marriage ceremony. Confronted by hostile and betrayed families, Dana and Kevin marry alone in Las Vegas. A coworker has left them a present when they return—"a blender." In these few sentences we can see a perfect encapsulation of the themes of repressed memory that run throughout Butler's novel.

Their decision to marry without the presence of their families stands for the cultural amnesia that is forced upon mixed race couples. Their literal ties to history—the older generations—must be cut off from the experience. At the same time, this rejection inevitably takes on a symbolic quality, forced by interpretations like that of Dana's uncle, who sees the marriage as a rejection of personal, social and racial identity.

Both excluded as well as voluntarily removed from her own cultural history, Dana gets married in Las Vegas. The choice of cities is significant. Las Vegas is the most modern of modern American cities, a place with no memories. Having married in a place without history, in a ceremony that excludes their familial roots, and in a relationship that optimistically ignores cultural history, Kevin and Dana return home.

Dana narrates without comment that they were greeted by a blender from her best friend and a check from the *Atlantic Monthly.* These objects suggest the uneasy balance of hope and pessimism that remains unresolved at the close of the novel. Dana has her check—her long awaited professional reward and acceptance. At the same time she has a blender—a physical symbol of her expected duties as a wife, as well as a slur on her racially "blended" marriage. She and Kevin settle into their marriage with history purged from everything but the bookshelves.

The trips to Maryland represent a forceful awakening for both of them, but especially for Dana. As she is drawn further and further into a life of slavery, the parallels between the 1800s and the 1970s provide a subtle reevaluation of her relationship to Kevin, irrevocably revealing the cultural history attached to the hierarchic relationship between men and women, and blacks and whites.

In order to make this possible, Butler first enacts a series of skillful defamiliarizations. For Dana as well as the reader, the historical and cultural concept of slavery must be stripped of its modern associations before it can be investigated more closely.

In the process of telling Dana's story, *Kindred* "unpacks" the metaphorization of enslavement in twentieth-century culture. The narrative records the ways in which slavery is used to stand in for any number of exploitative situations, such as the temporary agency, of which Dana says, "we regulars called it the Slave Market."

The narrator's description of her entrance into the Weylin compound marks an authorial attempt to defamiliarize the history of slavery, confounding Dana's expectations of the reality of slave life by shaking it out of its filmic and televisual representations. Dana and Kevin have a shelf-full of books on the subject and a close historical knowledge. Most importantly, they have absorbed the iconography of slavery—the visual and narrative conventions that are used to convey the American slavery story, from *Uncle Tom's Cabin,* to *Gone With The Wind, Mandingo,* and *Roots.* It is this iconography which must be undermined in order for serious critique to occur.

Roland Barthes's analysis of the Hollywood version of ancient Rome suggests that directors rely on three things to instantly create the illusion of classical life—the Caesar haircut, togas, and a pair of sandals. As he points out, during the heyday of these films, American audiences were happy to believe that any actor looked authentically Roman so long as this visual shorthand was in place.

Dana experiences a powerful lesson on the inadequacy of such shorthand. Traveling to the Weylin house, she is continually shocked by the reality of life in the antebellum South. She had expected horrors, and to a certain extent prepared for them as soon as she realized what was happening. Instead, she is shocked by the *lack* of horror—by

the mundane, relatively benign situation that she thinks she sees around her. None of her visual expectations were correct. As she says:

> I looked around for a white overseer and was surprised not to see one. The Weylin house surprised me too when I saw it in daylight. It wasn't white. It had no columns, no porch to speak of. I was almost disappointed.

Before Dana can learn the *true* nature of brutality she must unlearn what she thinks she knows about it. She must learn instead that the first and worst impact of enslavement is in the mind, and that it is this enslavement which makes the rest possible.

This in turn enables a major part of the problematizing impact that the past has on Dana and Kevin's present. If slavery is more than just chains and whippings, if it is greater than legal rights and physical emancipation, then the possibility must exist that Dana and Kevin are not entirely free from the legacy of mental enslavement—Kevin as master, Dana as chattel. The most terrifying thing for both of them is not the alienating unfamiliarity of the antebellum South, but its comfortable familiarity. As they are transported back to Maryland they are both horrified to realize that they are relieved. It feels like going home.

The familiarity of Maryland only compounds the suggestion that Dana is still trapped in mental slavery, a suggestion signaled throughout *Kindred* by the parallels between the heroine and the female slaves. Her apparent compliance with the Weylins causes the field workers to compare her to Sarah—the "Mammy" of the novel—on a constant basis.

On a basic level, punishment and fear make her reconsider the distance that separates her from her 1800s counterparts. Perhaps most powerfully, the blood relationship that Dana has with Alice cements the metaphoric linkage between the two time periods, Alice becoming not so much Dana's forbear as she is her alternate self. Dana's trips to the past can thus be read as an interrogation of a symbolized version of her life. As Rufus Weylin says when he looks at the two women:

> Behold the woman ... You really are only one woman. Did you know that?

The parallels between life in the early nineteenth and late twentieth centuries are not confined to race. Gender distinctions figure as an even greater boundary—cutting across race lines and enabling comparisons between otherwise very disparate groups. Alice, it seems, is not so different from Margaret Weylin, who is herself trapped in a period and place when "women were considered as children."

Like the slave girl who betrays Dana's escape to Tom Weylin, Margaret is caught in a horrible trap forged of self-protection, love, dependency and powerlessness. Margaret viciously defends her roles of wife, mother, and mistress because they are the only careers available to her, just as the looming specter of being sent into the fields, or sold down the river, ensures that the house slaves are unwary and distrustful, their well-being dependent on the bad luck of others.

As Butler's novel makes clear, gender, race, and social class form an intertwined set of prescriptive circumstances that cannot be separated from each other, and the lessons that Dana learns are not confined to those of race. A series of encounters, leading on from Rufus' bewildered exclamation, "But you can't be married!" hammer the point home. Sarah tries to understand Dana and Kevin's relationship to one another, and assumes it was like hers with her "husband"—an owner and lover who beat her. Margaret meets her outside Kevin's room and accuses her of being a whore. When Tom Weylin sees her, he winks in acknowledgment. This all just is business as usual.

Refusing to use slavery as a metaphor for marriage—a rhetorical technique common in some white feminist writing of the seventies—Butler illustrates the very real function of marriage as a constitutive part of the working dynamics of oppression. As all of the slaves and owners know, marriage ensures that a slave will not run away by promoting bonds of affection and family that ties them to the land. Having established this, the structure of the novel allows a metacommentary on the legacy of that race-gender/marriage-control dynamic in Kevin and Dan's marriage.

Kevin's cover story for the Weylins is that Dana is his slave—a literate black woman that works as his secretary. Too close to the truth of their situation, his story is symptomatic of his insensitivity to the injustices of American culture. A few pages later this is compounded when he expresses a wish to "go west" and Dana has to remind him about the existence of Native Americans.

Though the possible implications of his historical blindness and his cover story are clear, their meaning becomes shocking when Dana returns to 1976. As at the beginning of every section, their past is intercut with the immediate past of the narrator, foreshadowing and being commented upon the history sections. This time, the flashback is to Kevin's proposal. Without interpretive comment, Dana describes a relationship of need and economic necessity as well as love. She was broke and unemployed, and in this context Kevin offered to marry her. Putting the job and the marriage in one package, he concluded his proposal with the words, "I'd let you type all my manuscripts."

Dana's history is the forced remembering of the discriminatory thinking that lies behind Kevin's innocuous marriage proposal. History is the silence in Kevin and Dana's marriage—the power issues that they cannot talk about. They may love each other, but, as her amputated arm shows, if they fail to respect the reality of the power issues that divide them they run the risk of destroying themselves.

Source: Tabitha McIntosh-Byrd, in an essay for *Novels for Students,* Gale, 2000.

Robert Crossley

In the following essay, Crossley examines Kindred *as a "new slave narrative," a work that could no longer be written from personal experience and would instead require a narrative technique which allows a modern-day person to travel back in time, as Dana does in the novel. Crossley concludes that* Kindred, *"like all good works of fiction, ... lies like the truth."*

The American slave narrative is a literary form whose historical boundaries are firmly marked. While first-person narratives about oppression and exclusion will persist as long as racism persists, slave narratives ceased to be written when the last American citizen who had lived under institutionalized slavery died. The only way in which a new slave-memoir could be written is if someone were able to travel into the past, become a slave, and return to tell the story. Because the laws of physics, such as we know them, preclude traveling backwards in time, such a book would have to be a hybrid of autobiographical narrative and scientific fantasy. That is exactly the sort of book Octavia Butler imagined when she wrote *Kindred,* first published in 1979. Like all good works of fiction, it lies like the truth.

Kindred begins and ends in mystery. On June 9, 1976, her twenty-sixth birthday, Edana, a black woman moving with her white husband Kevin Franklin to a new house in a Los Angeles suburb, is overcome by nausea while unpacking cartons. Abruptly she finds herself kneeling on a riverbank; hearing a child's screams, she runs into the river to save him, applies artificial respiration, and as the boy begins breathing again she looks up into a rifle barrel. Again she sickens and is once more in her new house, but now she is soaked and covered in mud. This is the first several such episodes of varying duration which make up the bulk of the novel. Sometimes Dana (the shortened form of her name she prefers) is transported alone, sometimes with Kevin; but the dizzy spells that immediately precede her movements occur without warning and she can induce her return to Los Angeles only at the hazard of her life. To her horror Dana discovers during a second and longer episode of disorientation that she is moving not simply through space but through time as well—to antebellum Maryland, to the plantation of a slaveowner who is her own distant (though not nearly distant enough) ancestor. These trips, like convulsive memories dislocating her in time, occupy only a few minutes or hours of her life in 1976, but her stay in the alternative time is stretched as she lives out an imposed remembrance of things past. Because of this dual time level a brief absence from Los Angeles may result in months spent on the Maryland plantation, observing and suffering the backbreaking field work, persistent verbal abuse, whippings, and other daily cruelties of enslavement. Eventually Dana realizes that Rufus Weylin, the child she first rescues from drowning, periodically "calls" her from the twentieth century whenever his life is in danger. As he grows older he becomes more repugnant and brutal, but she must try to keep him alive until he and a slave woman named Alice Greenwood conceive a child, to be named Hagar, who will initiate Dana's own family line. Only at Weylin's death does Dana return permanently to 1976.

But she returns mutilated. The narrative comes full circle to the book's strange and disturbing opening paragraph: "I lost an arm on my last trip home. My left arm." Although the novel illuminates the paradoxes of Dana's homecoming—the degree to which her comfortable house in 1976 and the Weylin plantation are both inescapably "home" to her—Butler is silent on the mechanics of time travel. We know that Dana's arm is amputated in the jaws of the past, that time is revealed to be damaging as well as healing, that historical understanding of human crimes is never easy and always achieved at the price of suffering, that Dana's murderous relative, like Hamlet's, is "more than kin and less than kind." The loss of her arm becomes in fact, as Ruth Salvaggio has suggested, "a kind of birthmark," the emblem of Dana's "disfigured heritage." The symbolic meanings *Kindred* yields are powerful and readily articulable. The *literal*

truth is harder to state. In *The Time Machine* (1895) H. G. Wells had his traveler display the shiny vehicle on which he rode into the future to verify the strange truth of his journey; in *Kindred* the method of transport remains a fantastic given. An irresistible psychohistorical force, not a feat of engineering, motivates Butler's plot. *How* Dana travels in time and *how* she loses her arm are problems of physics irrelevant to Butler's aims. In that respect *Kindred* reads less like Wellsian science fiction than like that classic fable of alienation, Kafka's *Metamorphosis,* whose protagonist simply wakes up one morning as a giant beetle, a fantastic eruption into the normal world.

Perhaps Butler deliberately sacrificed the neat closure that a scientific—or even pseudo-scientific—explanation of telekinesis and chronoportation would have given her novel. Leaving the novel's ending rough-edged and raw like Dana's wound, Butler leaves the reader uneasy and disturbed by the intersection of story and history rather than comforted by a tale that "makes sense." Certainly, Butler did not need to show off a technological marvel of the sort Wells provided to mark his traveler's path through time; the only time machine in *Kindred* is present by implication: it is the vehicle that looms behind every American slave narrative, the grim death-ship of the Middle Passage from Africa to the slave markets of the New World. In her experience of being kidnapped in time and space, Dana recapitulates the dreadful, disorienting, involuntary voyage of her ancestors, just her employment in 1976 through a temporary job agency—"we regulars called it a slave market," Dana says with grouchy irony—operates as a benign ghostly version of institutional slavery's auction block.

In many ways *Kindred* departs from Octavia Butler's characteristic kind of fiction. Most of her work, from her first novel *Patternmaster* (1975) through *Clay's Ark* (1984), has been situated in the future, often a damaged future, and has focused on power relationships between "normal" human beings (*Homo sapiens*) and human mutants, gifted with extraordinary mental power, who might generically be named *Homo superior*. More recently, in her prize-winning story "Bloodchild" (1984) and her novel *Dawn* (1987), Butler has shifted her attention to the intricate web of power and affection in the relationships between human beings and alien species. In all her science fiction she has produced fables that speak directly or indirectly to issues of cultural difference, whether sexual, racial, political, economic, or psychological. *Kindred* shares with Butler's other works an ideological interest in exploring relationships between the empowered and the powerless, but except for *Wild Seed* (1970), *Kindred* is her only novel situated in the past. And even *Wild Seed*—set in seventeenth-century Africa, colonial New England, and antebellum Louisiana—is strongly mythical in flavor and is populated by some of the same long-lived, psychically advanced characters who appear in her futuristic novels. *Kindred* is technically a much sparer story; the psychic power that draws the central character back in time to the era of slavery remains in the novel's background, and the autobiographical voice of the modern descendant of, witness to, victim of American slavery is foregrounded. Moreover, apart from the single fantastic premise of instantaneous movement through time and space, *Kindred* is consistently realistic in presentation and depends on the author's reading of authentic slave narratives and her visits to the Talbot County, Maryland, sites of the novel. Butler herself, when interviewed by *Black Scholar,* denied that *Kindred* is science fiction since there is "absolutely no science in it."

The term "science fiction" is, however, notoriously resistant to definition and is popularly used to designate a wide range of imaginative literature inspired and patterned by the natural sciences (chemistry, physics, geology, astronomy, biology), by such social sciences as anthropology, sociology, and psychology, and by pseudo-sciences like parapsychology and scientology. The proportion of science-fictional texts based on scrupulously applied scientific principles rather than on faulty science, pseudo-science, or wishful science is probably quite small. If, for instance, all the narratives and films premised on "starships" and the fantastic notion of faster-than-light travel were denied the title of "science fiction," the canon would shrink dramatically. By the most conservative of definitions—those which emphasize the natural sciences, rigorously applied to fictional invention—*Kindred* is not science fiction. Butler's own preferred designation of *Kindred* as "a grim fantasy" is a more precise indicator of its literary form and its emotional tenor. The exact generic label we assign *Kindred* may be, however, the least important thing about it. Like Kafka's *Metamorphosis* or Anna Kavan's *Ice,* Butler's novel is an experiment that resists easy classification by blurring the usual boundaries of genre. Inevitably, readers will wonder what provoked the author to adapt the form of a fantastic travelogue to a restoration of the genre of slave-memoir.

When she enrolled in a summer workshop for novice science fiction writers in 1970 at the age of twenty-three, Octavia Estelle Butler took a decisive step toward satisfying an ambition she had cherished since she was twelve. An only child whose father died when she was a baby, Butler was aware very early of women struggling to survive. Her maternal grandmother had stories to tell about long hours of work in the canefields of Louisiana while raising seven children. Her mother, Octavia M. Butler, had been working since the age of ten and spent all her adult life earning a living as a housemaid. As the author told Veronica Mixon in an interview just before *Kindred* appeared, the experiences of the women in her family influenced her youthful reading and her earliest efforts at writing: "Their lives seemed so terrible to me at times—so devoid of joy or reward. I needed my fantasies to shield me from their world." The powerful imaginative impulse that produced *Kindred* had its origin in the escapist fantasies of a child who needed to find or invent alternative realities. By temperament and by virtue of the strict Baptist upbringing her mother enforced, Butler was reclusive; imaginary worlds solaced her for the pinched rewards of the actual world, and books took the place of friends.

Kindred, however, is not an escapist fantasy. If as a girl Butler needed to distance herself from the grimness of her mother's life, she nevertheless always had her eyes open. What she saw as a child she later confronted and reshaped as a novelist. When her mother couldn't find or afford a babysitter, young Octavia was often taken along to work, as she told the interviewer from *Black Scholar.* Even then she observed the long arm of slavery: the degree to which her mother operated in white society as an invisible woman and, worse, the degree to which she accepted and internalized her status. "I used to see her going in back doors, being talked about while she was standing right there and basically being treated like a non-person, something beneath notice.... And I could see her later as I grew up. I could see her absorbing more of what she was hearing from the whites than I think even she would have wanted to absorb." Some of these childhood memories infiltrated the fiction she produced in her maturity; certainly, they shaped her purpose in *Kindred* in imagining the privations of earlier generations of black Americans who were in danger of being forgotten by the black middle class as well as ignored by white Americans. Butler's effort to recover something of the experience of the nineteenth-century ancestors of those who, like herself, grew up in the heady days of the 1960s civil rights movement was a homage both to those women in her family who still struggled for an identity and to those more distant relations whose identities had been lost. "So many relatives that I had never known, would never know," the contemporary black woman from California muses sadly early on in *Kindred* as she thinks of the bare names inked in her family Bible.

Although Dana's experiences when she is hurled into the midst of slave society are full of terror and pain, they also illuminate her past and freshen her understanding of those generations forced to be nonpersons. One of the protagonist's—and Butler's—achievements in traveling to the past is to *see* individual slaves as people rather than as encrusted literary or sociological types. Perhaps most impressive is Sarah the cook, the stereotypical "mammy" of books and films, whose apparent acceptance of humiliation, Dana comes to understand, masks a deep anger over the master's sale of nearly all her children: "She was the kind of woman who would be held in contempt during the militant nineteen sixties. The house-nigger, the handkerchief-head, the female Uncle Tom—the frightened powerless woman who had already lost all she could stand to lose, and who knew as little about the freedom of the North as she knew about the hereafter." Here we see literary fantasy in the service of the recovery of historical and psychological realities. As fictional memoir, *Kindred* is Butler's contribution to the literature of memory every bit as much as it is an exercise in the fantastic imagination.

The artfulness of *Kindred* is the product of a single-minded and largely isolated literary apprenticeship. In her younger years Butler's relatives paid little attention to what she read, as long as it wasn't obscene. Her teachers were baffled by and unreceptive to the science fiction stories she occasionally submitted in English classes. Her schoolmates simply thought her tastes in reading and writing strange, and increasingly Butler kept her literary interests to herself. In her adolescence she immersed herself in the science-fictional worlds of Theodore Sturgeon, Leigh Brackett, and Ray Bradbury, and the absence of black women writers from the genre did not deter her own ambitions: "Frankly, it never occurred to me that I needed someone who looked like me to show me the way. I was ignorant and arrogant and persistent and the writing left me no choice at all."

In the 1940s and 1950s no black writers and almost no women were publishing science fiction.

Not surprisingly, few black readers—and, we can assume, very few black girls—found much to interest them in the science fiction of the period, geared as it was toward white adolescent boys. Some of it was provocatively racist, including Robert Heinlein's *The Sixth Column* (1949), whose heroic protagonist in a future race war was unsubtly named Whitey. The highest tribute paid to a character of color in such novels was for the author to have him sacrifice his life for his white comrades, as an Asian soldier named Franklin Roosevelt Matsui does in *The Sixth Column,* as does the one black character in Leigh Brackett's story "The Vanishing Venusians" (1944). Other books tried resolutely to be "colorblind," imagining a future in which race no longer was a factor; such novels often embodied the white liberal fantasy of a single black character functioning amiably in a predominantly white society. Jan Rodricks, the last survivor on earth in Arthur C. Clarke's *Childhood's End* (1953), is a representative instance of the black character whose blackness supposedly doesn't matter; but the novel's one overt comment on race is a flippant allusion to a future reversal of South African apartheid in which whites are the victims of black discrimination—the stereotypical white conservative fantasy.

A diligent reader in the 1950s, searching for science fiction novels with something more than a patronizing image of black assimilation on white terms, could have turned up only a few texts in which black characters' blackness was acknowledged and allowed to shape the novel's thematic and ideological concerns. Perhaps the most interesting example is a chapter in a book that Butler read in her youth, Bradbury's *The Martian Chronicles* (1950). Titled "Way in the Middle of the Air," the chapter describes a mass emigration of black Southerners to Mars in the year 2003. The Southern economy and the cultural assumptions of white supremacy are devastated when the entire black populace unites to ensure that all members of the community can pay their debts and arrive at the rocket base in time for the great exodus. Barefoot white boys report in astonishment this unanticipated strategy for a black utopia: "Them that has helps them that hasn't! And that way they *all* get free!" In a speech that ironically skewers the myt' of progress in the history of black America, one petulant white man complains:

> I can't figure why they left *now.* With things lookin' up. I mean, every day they got more rights. What they *want,* anyway? Here's the poll tax gone, and more and more states passin' anti-lynchin' bills, and

What Do I Read Next?

- The five novels in Octavia Butler's "Pattern-master" series explore the history of the Patternists, human mutants with telepathic powers. In the first novel of the series, *Patternmaster* (1976), the Patternists battle the "Clayarks" and each other for control of the world.

- Butler's "Xenogenesis" trilogy, like *Kindred*, is a complex exploration of the relationship between rulers and subjugated. After a nuclear holocaust, Earth's few surviving humans are offered rescue by a race of alien traders in exchange for their genetic material. The moral questions that are faced by both humans and first-and second-generation hybrids are related in *Dawn: Xenogenesis* (1987), *Adulthood Rites* (1988), and *Imago* (1989).

- Butler's recent "Earthseed" series is set in a violent America of the early twenty-first century. Lauren Oya Olamina is a young African-American teen with the ability to feel other people's pain. She "discovers" her own religion, called Earthseed, and begins to gather followers. Lau-

ren's story begins in *Parable of the Sower* (1993) and continued in *Parable of the Talents* (1998).

- Gayl Jones's *Corregidora* (1975) is another tale of the psychological effects of slavery on a modern woman. Blues singer Ursa Corregidora comes from a line of women sexually abused by a Portuguese slaveholder named Corregidora—the father of both Ursa's mother and grandmother. The novel relates her efforts to reconcile her heritage with her present life.

- Marge Piercy's *Woman on the Edge of Time* (1976) uses the device of time travel to provide a view of a utopian future. During her stay in a mental hospital, a woman makes periodic trips into the future, where she finds a cooperative society.

- Slave narratives such as Harriet Jacobs's *Incidents in the Life of a Slave Girl* (1861) and Frederick Douglass's *Narrative of the Life of Frederick Douglass* (1845) supplied Butler with essential background details for her novel.

---

all kinds of equal rights. What *more* they want? They make almost as good money as a white man, but there they go.

"Way in the Middle of the Air" may be the single most incisive episode of black and white relations in science fiction by a white author. But its very rarity demonstrates how alien the territory of American science fiction in its so-called golden age after the second world war was for black readers and for aspiring writers like Octavia Butler.

Butler's formative years and her early career coincide with the years when American science fiction took down the "males only" sign over the entrance. Major expansions and redefinitions of the genre have been accomplished by such writers as Ursula K. LeGuin, Joanna Russ, Pamela Sargent, Alice Sheldon (writing under the pseudonym of James Tiptree, Jr.,), Pamela Zoline, Marge Piercy, Suzy

McKee Charnas, and Butler herself. The alien in many of the new fictions by women has been not a monstrous figure from a distant planet but the invisible alien within modern, familiar, human society: the woman as alien, sometimes more specifically, the black woman, or the Chicana, or the housewife, or the lesbian, or the woman in poverty, or the unmarried woman. Sheldon's famous story "The Women Men Don't See" (1974), about a mother and daughter who embark on a ship with extraterrestrials rather than remain unnoticed and unvalued on earth, is a touchstone for the reconception of the old science-fictional motifs of estrangement and alienation. In a writers' forum Butler has commented on the paradoxical poverty of imagination in science-fictional representations of the human image: "Science fiction has long treated people who might or might not exist—extraterrestrials. Unfortunately, however, many of the same science fiction writers who started us thinking about the possibility of extraterrestrial life did nothing to make us think about here-at-home human variation." As American women writers have abandoned the character types that predominated in science fiction for a richer plurality of human images, they have collectively written a new chapter in the genre's history.

But the dramatic numbers of women writers subverting and transforming the conventions, stereotypes, and thematic issues of science fiction have not been matched by an influx of black writers of similar proportions. Samuel R. Delaney, the first and most prolific black American writer to publish science fiction, beginning in 1962 with *The Jewels of Aptor,* has specialized in stylish and complexly structured fictions more closely tied to European literary theory than to black experiences. Another of the handful of black North Americans writing in the allied genres of science fiction and heroic fantasy is Charles Saunders, a Pennsylvanian transplanted to Canada. Saunders's most distinctive literary innovation has been his effort to write fantasies set in Africa and based on historical research into precolonial cultures and myths. His hero Imaro appears in several novels and is meant to replace the Tarzan-image of the white noble savage with an authentic African hero; he has also produced some engaging short stories centered on a woman warrior of Dahomey named Dossouye. Most recently Jewelle Gomez has begun publishing a loosely connected set of fantasies about an escaped slave from 1850 who becomes a vampire and extends her life over the next several centuries; the character functions, according to Gomez, as "a super heroic black woman who interprets our lives through a phenomenal perspective."

In an essay called "Why Blacks Don't Read Science Fiction," Saunders proposes that black writers of science fiction and fantasy remain few because the black readership has grown little since the 1950s. New readers of science fiction, he suggests, frequently come to the fiction by way of the nonprint media, and science fiction television and cinema remain overwhelmingly white and uninviting to young black audiences. Furthermore, black readers

who share the common demographic characteristics of white science fiction readers (i.e., young, educated, middle-class) tend to be more interested in political and sociological works along with the fiction of black writers like James Baldwin and Toni Morrison. To them, science fiction and fantasy may well seem irrelevant to their main concerns.

Saunders concludes that, despite his own interests in African-based heroic fantasy, the prospects of black science fiction are dim. While welcoming the enlargement of the genre's racial horizons—and he singles out Butler's early fiction as the chief instance of a black presence in science fiction—he fears that a specifically black science fiction will share the fate of so-called blaxploitation movies of the 1970s and be justifiably short-lived.

Perhaps Saunders would have been more sanguine about the possibility of serious black science fiction if *Kindred* had been available when he wrote his essay. If any contemporary writer is likely to redraw science fiction's cultural boundaries and to attract new black readers—and perhaps writers—to this most distinctive of twentieth-century genres, it is Octavia Butler. More consistently than any other black author, she has deployed the genre's conventions to tell stories with a political and sociological edge to them, stories that speak to issues, feelings, and historical truths arising out of Afro-American experience. In centering her fiction on women who lack power, suffer abuse, and are committed to claiming power over their own lives and to exercising that power harshly when necessary, Butler has not merely used science fiction as a "feminist didactic," in Beverly Friend's term, but she has generated her fiction out of a black feminist aesthetic. Her novels pointedly expose various chauvinisms (sexual, racial, and cultural), are enriched by a historical consciousness that shapes the depiction of enslavement both in the real past and in imaginary pasts and futures, and enact struggles for personal freedom and cultural pluralism.

At the same time, Butler has been eager to avoid turning her fiction into polemic. Science fiction is a richly metaphorical literature. Just as Mary Shelley in *Frankenstein* invented a monstrous child born from a male scientist's imagination as a metaphor for the exclusion of women from acts of creation, and just as Welles's *Time Machine* used hairy subterranean Morlocks and effete aboveground Eloi as metaphors for the upstairs-downstairs class divisions of Victorian England, so Butler has specialized in metaphors that dramatize the tyranny of one species or race or gender over another. But her work does not read like fiction composed by agenda. White writers, she has pointed out, tend to include black characters in science fiction only to illustrate a problem or as signposts to advertise the author's distaste for racism; black people in most science fiction are represented as "other." All her fiction stands in quiet resistance to the notion that a black character in a science fiction novel is there *for a reason.* In a Butler novel the black protagonist is there, like the mountain, because she is there. Although she does not hesitate to harness the power of fiction as fable to create striking analogies to the oppressive realities of our own present world, Butler also peoples her imagined worlds with black characters as a matter of course. Events and lives are usually in crisis in her books, but she celebrates racial difference.

While Butler's frequent use of black women as protagonists has often been noticed, it is also important that there are always numbers of characters of color in her novels. There is enough of a critical mass of racial and sexual and cultural diversity in any Butler novel to make reading it different from the experience of reading the work of almost any other practicing science fiction writer. One of the exciting features of *Kindred* is that so much of the novel is attentive not to the *exceptional* situation of an isolated modern black woman in a white household under slavery but to her complex social and psychological relationships with the community of black slaves she joins. Despite the severe stresses under which they live, the slaves constitute a rich human society: Dana's proud and vulnerable ancestor Alice Greenwood; the mute housemaid Carrie; Sarah, the cook who nurses old grievances while kneading down the bread dough; young Nigel, whom Dana teaches to reach from a stolen primer; Sam James the field hand, who begs Dana to teach his brother and sister; Alice's husband Isaac, mutilated and sold to Mississippi after a failed escape attempt; even Liza the sewing woman, who betrays Dana to the master and is punished by the other slaves for her complicity with the white owners. Although the black community is persistently fractured by the sudden removal of its members through either the calculated strategy or the mere whim of their white controllers, that community always patches itself back together, drawing from its common suffering and common anger a common strength. It is the white characters in the novel who seem odd, isolated, pathetic, alien, problematic.

In some ways the most problematic white man in *Kindred* is not the Maryland slaveowner but the liberated, modern Californian married to Dana. Kevin Franklin is a good man. He loves Dana, loathes the chattel system that governs every feature of antebellum life in Maryland, and works on the underground railroad during the period when he is trapped in the past. Yet he is by gender and race implicated in the supremacist culture.

Throughout the novel Butler ingeniously suggests parallels between Rufus Weylin and Kevin Franklin: their facial expressions, their language, even after a time their accents merge in Dana's mind so that at times she mistakes one for the other. One of the novel's subtlest touches is the chapter in which Dana is obliged to become Rufus Weylin's secretary and handle his correspondence and bills; in 1976 Kevin had, unsuccessfully but still revealingly, tried to get his wife to type his manuscripts and write his letters for him. When both Kevin and Dana are in nineteenth-century Maryland at the same time the only way they can spend a night together is for them to make a public pretense of being master and slave and seemingly to accept the ethos of black women as the sexual property of white men. But as Dana realizes, the more often one plays such a role, the nearer the pretending comes to reality: "I felt almost as though I really was doing something shameful, happily playing whore for my supposed owner. I went away feeling uncomfortable, vaguely ashamed." And, she fears, Kevin begins to fit into the white, male, Southern routines far too easily. Shuttling between the two white men in her life, she is aware not only of the blood link between herself and Rufus but of the double link of gender and race that unites Rufus and Kevin. The convergence of these two white men in Dana's life not only dramatizes the ease with which even a "progressive" white man falls into the cultural pattern of dominance, but suggests as well an uncanny synonymy of the words "husband" and "master."

The date of Dana's final return to Los Angeles is July 4, 1976, the bicentennial of the founding of the United States. Her fantastic journey becomes an occasion for meditating on American cultural history. What has been forgotten or trivialized or sentimentalized in the public celebrations of the past reemerges unvarnished in Dana's homecoming on the fourth of July. Dana comes back to southern California with a truer understanding of black history in America than the sanitized versions in the popular media had ever given her. Predictably, she scorns the image of the plantation derived from *Gone with the Wind,* but she also learns the inadequacy of even the best books as preparation for the first-hand experience of slavery. Dana's literacy, her education, and her historical knowledge sometimes lull her into a false sense of security. In one passage, she records her pleasure in the friendly atmosphere of the cookhouse where the slaves gather to eat and talk, usually free from white oversight. There she observes "a girl and boy, sitting on the floor eating with their fingers. I was glad to see them there because I'd read about kids their age being rounded up and fed from troughs like pigs. Not everywhere, apparently. At least, not here." Although she does not name her literary source, almost certainly Dana is recalling an episode from chapter 5 of Frederick Douglass's 1845 *Narrative* (a work Butler read carefully as part of her research for *Kindred*) where Douglass describes feeding time at Colonel Lloyd's plantation:

> Our food was coarse corn meal boiled. This was called *mush*. It was put into a large wooden tray or tough, and set down upon the ground. The children were then called, like so many pigs, and like so many pigs they would come and devour the mush; some with oyster-shells, others with pieces of shingle, some with naked hands, and none with spoons.

Mistakenly, because the food and the treatment of children is better than Douglass's *Narrative* seemed to promise, Dana behaves as if the cookhouse is a sanctuary. That error in judgment leads to her first vicious flogging when she is detected in the act of teaching slave children to read. After her second shipping by Rufus Weylin's father following her attempted flight from the plantation, she reflects angrily as another slave woman tries to salve her wounds, "Nothing in my education or knowledge of the future had helped me to escape." Books had not taught her why so many slaves accepted their condition, nor had books defined the kind of bravery possible in the powerless and humiliating situation of being owned and in the face of the ruthless means by which owners protected their investments.

Films, Dana finds, are an even less reliable guide to the past. About the tendency of Hollywood production values to insulate viewers even from material filmed with purported historical or documentary intent, Dana is withering. She recalls witnessing the beating of a slave hunted out one night by white patrollers and how she crouched in the underbrush a few yards away from the man's young daughter. The slave's crime was being found in bed with his own free-born wife without written permission from his owner:

> I could literally smell his sweat, hear every ragged breath, every cry, every cut of the whip. I could see his body jerking, convulsing, straining against the rope as his screaming went on and on. My stomach heaved, and I had to force myself to stay where I was and keep quiet. Why didn't they stop!
>
> "Please, Master," the man begged. "For Godsake, Master, please ...."

> I shut my eyes and tensed my muscles against an urge to vomit.
>
> I had seen people beaten on television and in the movies. I had seen the too-red blood substitute streaked across their backs and heard their well-rehearsed screams. But I hadn't lain nearby and smelled their sweat or heard them pleading and praying, shamed before their families and themselves. I was probably less prepared for the reality than the child crying not far from me.

At such moments of first-person intensity, *Kindred* reveals its own literary kinship with the memoirs of ex-slaves published in the nineteenth century, for Butler's greatest achievement in the novel is her collapsing of the genres of the fantastic travelogue and the slave narrative. Her incorporation into *Kindred* both of narrative strategies of the classic memoirs of former slaves and of occasional deliberate verbal and situational echoes of those texts establishes a degree of authenticity and seriousness rarely attained by contemporary writers mining the conventions of the Wellsian time-travel story.

Reconstructing Womanhood, Hazel V. Carby's feminist revision of the traditions of American black women's writing, contrasts the image of the slave woman as victim in men's slave memoirs with a very different image that emerges in such autobiographies as Harriet Jacobs's *Incidents in the Life of a Slave Girl,* Lucy Delany's *From the Darkness Cometh Light,* and Mary Prince's *The History of Mary Prince, a West Indian Slave.* In such narratives, Carby argues, women define themselves as agents rather than as mere victims, and they record the brutality of their treatment by their owners in order to emphasize their resistance to victimization and their claim to freedom. Butler's fictive autobiographer Dana extends that ideology and aesthetic of the slave woman's memoir into the late twentieth century. Much of *Kindred* is a record of endurance, but there are also numerous acts of heroism and humanity, culminating in the act of manslaughter in self-defense which finally liberates Dana, at terrible cost, from her tyrannical ancestor.

As she discovers the terrible link to her own past which requires her to keep the oppressive slavemaster alive until her own family is inaugurated, Dana works out the ethic of compromise which Harriet Jacobs tolerated to safeguard her children and herself. Despite personal repugnance and culturally induced shame, Jacobs compromised the sexual standards imposed on nineteenth-century women in order to maintain a central core of integrity and freedom of will; she reluctantly practiced a situational ethics dictated by the extreme circumstances which constrained the ethical choices of black women under slavery. As several black feminist commentators on Jacobs's memoir have recently argued, the crucial sentence around which our understanding of *Incidents in the Life of a Slave Girl* must be fashioned is her retrospective revision of the ethical norms that govern a woman's choices and behaviors under systematic oppression: "Still, in looking back, calmy, on the events of my life, I feel that the slave woman ought not to be judged by the same standard as others." Butler's Dana must move painfully toward a similar ethical relativism as she discovers that the moral choices of a late twentieth-century black feminist cannot be exercised with impunity in the world of the slave state. At earlier stages of her experience in Maryland, she tells her white husband, she is able to cling precariously to the ethical imperatives of her own world, though even then her perspective and choices are bound to be fundamentally different from his:

> You might be able to go through this whole experience as an observer…. I can understand that because most of the time, I'm still an observer. It's protection. It's nineteen seventy-six shielding and cushioning eighteen nineteen for me. But now and then … I can't maintain the distance. I'm drawn all the way into eighteen nineteen, and I don't know what to do.

The longer she remains in the nineteenth century, the thinner the protective cushioning becomes until Dana finds herself five years later (in Maryland time) divided against herself, torn between absolute standards and pragmatic choices. The Dana of 1976 California finds it unthinkable that she would assist in the sexual exploitation of another black woman by a white man, but the Dana of 1824 Maryland finds herself in a moral trap. Rufus Weylin asks her to persuade Alice Greenwood, her own great-great-grandmother, to go to bed with him without compulsion. Although she knows that her family tree is traceable to a child that Rufus will one day father on Alice, Dana initially finds Rufus's proposal that she act as pander repulsive, and she angrily rejects it. But when Rufus threatens Dana that he will beat Alice—perhaps even beat her to death—if she refuses his advances and if Dana does not try to change Alice's mind, she is caught in Harriet Jacobs's dilemma: "He had all the low cunning of his class. No, I couldn't refuse to help the girl—help her avoid at least some pain. But she wouldn't think much of me for helping her this way. I didn't think much of myself." The choice demanded by the situation will satisfy nei-

ther Dana's own internal standards nor the larger feminist principle of sisterhood; she suffers the same shame that Jacobs felt, but she also adopts the compromise.

In the end, what may be most powerful and valuable for readers of *Kindred* is the simple reminder that all that history is not so very long ago. In foreshortening the distance between now and then, Butler focuses our attention on the continuity between past and present; the fantasy of traveling backwards in time becomes a lesson in historical realities. We may also be reminded that historical progress is never a sure thing; in one of her brief respites in 1976 between bouts of enslavement in the nineteenth century, Dana reads the memoirs of Jewish survivors of the Nazi death camps: "Stories of beatings, starvation, filth, disease, torture, every possible degradation. As though the Germans had been trying to do in only a few years what the Americans had worked at for nearly two hundred." The systematic horrors of American slavery, we must remember, provide a model for later programmed oppression and genocide. Like Dana and Kevin, the reader of *Kindred* may discover a closer kinship with the characters and events of the antebellum South than we often care to admit. And just as Dana feels compelled in the novel's epilogue to travel to contemporary Maryland and "touch solid evidence that those people existed," readers of this fantastic invention may also find their understanding of history enriched and deepened. In *Kindred* Octavia Butler has designed her own underground railroad between past and present whose terminus is the reawakened imagination of the reader.

Source: Robert Crossley, Introduction to *Kindred,* Beacon Press, 1988, pp. ix-xxiii.

Beverly Friend

In the following excerpt, Friend asserts that Kindred *reveals weaknesses in modern women and inequities in their treatment that have not been eliminated despite the relatively better conditions of contemporary society.*

[Dana, the] heroine of *Kindred,* is … at the mercy of an outside force. An unpublished writer, she is working at a mind-stultifying job with a temporary employment firm when she meets and marries co-worker and fellow author Kevin. They are just setting up housekeeping in a new residence when Dana is suddenly pulled back to the year 1815 to save a little boy, Rufus Weylin, from drowning. But this tale goes far beyond a mere recitation of twentieth-century woman facing nineteenth-century life, for while Kevin and Rufus are white, Dana is black. Even more important, Rufus, son of a tyrannical plantation owner and his hysterical, ill-natured wife, is also one of Dana's ancestors; and he has a link with her so powerful that it calls her back from the present to save him from intense moments of danger throughout his entire lifetime. Thus, a contemporary black woman comes to experience the life of a slave on a Maryland plantation, although she does return to the twentieth century sporadically and briefly throughout the novel at those moments of absolute terror when the belief in her own imminent death triggers an involuntary return.

All in all, she makes six trips into the past, called each time by Rufus's near encounter with death. Each return Dana makes to the present is triggered by the possibility of her own death. Once she returns during a hideous beating; another time she causes the return by desperately slitting her own wrists. Each visit to the plantation accounts for from a few minutes to several days in Dana's own time, but comprises months to years of the past. Thus, she follows Rufus from childhood to adulthood while she scarcely ages herself. Throughout, she feels a moral responsibility for Rufus: "Someday, he would be the slave-holder, responsible in his own right for what happened to the people who lived in those half-hidden cabins. The boy was literally growing up as I watched—growing up because I watched and because I helped to keep him safe." Dana goes on to question her role as the guardian for Rufus: "A black to watch over him in a society that considered blacks subhuman, a woman to watch over him in a society that considered women perennial children."

Dana's role in this society, as subhuman and perennial child, is reinforced in the third trip when Kevin, who has been embracing Dana, unwittingly transfers with her. In Rufus's world, they cannot admit to being man and wife and are forced to enact the role of master and slave. And Dana fears the corruptive potential of such a civilization, even on her husband, if he should be stranded there....

How does Dana keep it from marking her? She doesn't. It marks her, although she manages to hang onto her sanity through continual reexamination of her situation....

But living does not always look better. Dana's third trip ends with her being beaten so badly that she suddenly returns to the present without Kevin.

When she next visits the plantation (on the fourth trip), eight days have elapsed for her, and five years have gone by for Kevin. He has left the plantation, gone north, and Dana must now send for him and await his return. At one point, when the waiting becomes unbearable and she discovers that Rufus has never mailed her letters to Kevin, she attempts to run away. She is caught. Nothing in her twentieth-century education or experience had prepared her to succeed....

Perhaps the twentieth century does not help her because she does not utilize it effectively. Dana ... [is] able to carry material into the past. In fact, she has a bag tied to her, ready to go the moment she is transported. And what is in the bag? All the things she needs and misses from civilization: toothbrush, soap, comb, brush, knife, aspirin, Excedrin, sleeping pills, antiseptic, pen, paper and pencil, and spare clothing. Prior to one of the trips she also packs a history of slavery and maps of Maryland, but this outrages Rufus, who demands that she burn them.

And so Dana works and survives as a slave, learning all the skills necessary to survive as a house worker, but not showing sufficient stamina to succeed as a field hand. Her twentieth-century ability to read antagonizes Rufus's father, who fears education for his slaves, and causes danger to herself and others when she teaches the slave children to read. Her knowledge of history is no help and only stands her in good stead by preventing her from killing Rufus until he has raped her black great-grandmother, assuring the inception of Dana's family tree.

Finally, when Dana does act, there are repercussions. She murders Rufus (who well deserves it), but justice does not then triumph. His death causes the end of life on that plantation, and the slaves are then sold off. Dana does not get away unscathed, either, losing an arm in her final wrench from past to present.

No one would intellectually argue against the proposition that life is better today for both men and women, but few realize what ... [this novel has] didactically presented: that contemporary woman is not educated to survive, that she is as helpless, perhaps even more helpless, than her predecessors. Just as Philip Wylie pointed out in *The Disappearance,* a world of men might be strife-ridden, but it would go on; a world of women would grind to a halt, sans transportation (no pilots, bus drivers, train engineers), sans full grocery shelves (no farmers or truckers), sans adequate health care (no ambulance drivers, paramedics, few doctors). Men understand how the world is run; women do not. Victims then, victims now.

Source: Beverly Friend, "Time Travel as a Feminist Didactic in Works by Phyllis Eisenstein, Marlys Millhiser, and Octavia Butler," in *Extrapolation,* Vol. 23, No. 1, Spring, 1982, pp. 50-5.

Sources

Robert Crossley, in an introduction to *Kindred,* by Octavia Butler, Beacon Press, 1988, pp. ix-xxvii.

Beverly Friend, "Time Travel as a Feminist Didactic in Works by Phyllis Eisenstein, Marlys Millhiser, and Octavia Butler," in *Extrapolation,* Vol. 23, No. 1, Spring, 1982, pp. 50-5.

Adam McKible, "'These Are the Facts of the Darky's History': Thinking History and Reading Names in Four African American Texts," in *African American Review,* Vol. 28, No. 2, 1994, pp. 223-35.

Margaret Anne O'Connor, "Octavia E. Butler," in *Dictionary of Literary Biography,* Vol. 33: *Afro-American Fiction Writers After 1955,* edited by Thadious M. Davis and Trudier Harris, Gale Research Company, 1984, pp. 36-40.

John R. Pfeiffer, "Latest Butler a Delicious Confection," in *Fantasy Review,* Vol. 7, No. 6, July, 1984, p. 44.

Joanna Russ, in *Magazine of Fantasy and Science Fiction,* Vol. 58, No. 2, February, 1980, pp. 96-7.

Thelma J. Shinn, "The Wise Witches: Black Women Mentors in the Fiction of Octavia E. Butler," in *Conjuring: Black Women, Fiction, and Literary Tradition,* edited by Marjorie Pryse and Hortense J. Spillers, Indiana University Press, 1985, pp. 203-15.

For Further Study

Frances M. Beal, "Black Women and the Science Fiction Genre: Interview with Octavia M. Butler," in *Black Scholar,* Vol. 17, March-April, 1986, p. 14.
    An interview with Butler in which she discusses her childhood and other influences.

Teri Ann Doerksen, "Octavia E. Butler: Parables of Race and Difference," in *Into Darkness Peering: Race and Color in the Fantastic,* edited by Elisabeth Anne Leonard, Greenwood Press, 1997, pp. 21-34.
    Views Butler's novels as works that "have the potential to lead the once typical white or male reader into some (perhaps uncomfortable) realizations about his or her own society."

Sandra Y. Govan, "Homage to Tradition: Octavia Butler Renovates the Historical Novel," in *MELUS,* Vol. 13, Nos. 1-2, 1986, pp. 79-96.
    Provides a stylistic examination of Butler's novel, praising innovative aspects of her work.

Patricia Maida, "*Kindred* and *Dessa Rose:* Two Novels That Reinvent Slavery," in *CEA Magazine,* Vol. 4, No. 1, 1991, pp. 43-52.
    Traces the portrayal of slavery in both novels.

Veronica Mixon, "Futurist Woman: Octavia Butler," in *Essence,* Vol. 15, April, 1979, pp. 12-13.
    A biographical article on Butler containing an interview with the author.

Burton Raffel, "Genre to the Rear, Race and Gender to the Fore: The Novels of Octavia E. Butler," in *Literary Review,* Vol. 38, Spring, 1995, pp. 453-61.
    Provides a thematic overview of Butler's novels, in particular the treatment of race and gender issues.

Hoda M. Zaki, "Utopia, Dystopia and Ideology in the Science Fiction of Octavia Butler," in *Science Fiction Studies,* Vol. 17, No. 2, 1990, pp. 239-51.
    Surveys the major themes of Butler's science fiction.

The Master and Margarita

Mikhail Bulgakov
1967

The Master and Margarita by Mikhail Bulgakov is considered one of the best and most highly regarded novels to come out of Russia during the Soviet era. The book weaves together satire and realism, art and religion, history and contemporary social values. It features three story lines. The main story, taking place in Russia of the 1930s, concerns a visit by the devil, referred to as Professor Woland, and four of his assistants during Holy Week; they use black magic to play tricks on those who cross their paths. Another story line features the Master, who has been languishing in an insane asylum, and his love, Margarita, who seeks Woland's help in being reunited with the Master. A third story, which is presented as a novel written by the Master, depicts the crucifixion of Yeshua Ha-Notsri, or Jesus Christ, by Pontius Pilate.

Using the fantastic elements of the story, Bulgakov satirizes the greed and corruption of Stalin's Soviet Union, in which people's actions were controlled as well as their perceptions of reality. In contrast, he uses a realistic style in telling the story of Yeshua. The holy life led by Christ in this book is more ordinary than the miraculous one told in the Scriptures. Because the book derides government bureaucracy and corruption, the manuscript of *The Master and Margarita* was hidden for over twenty years, until the more lenient Khrushchev government allowed its publication.

Mikhail Bulgakov

Author Biography

In his final weeks, as he lay dying of nephrosclerosis, Mikhail Bulgakov continued to dictate changes for *The Master and Margarita* to his wife. He had been working on the book for twelve years, through eight versions, and he meant it to be his literary legacy.

Bulgakov was born in Kiev on May 3, 1891. His father was a professor at the Kiev Theological Seminary, an influence that appears in the novel through mentions of the history and philosophy of religious matters. Bulgakov graduated with distinction from the University of Kiev, and after attaining his medical degree from St. Vladimir's University, he went into the army, which sent him to a small town in the province of Smolensk. It was 1916, and Russia was involved in the First World War. The autobiographical stories in Bulgakov's collection *A Country Doctor's Notebooks* are based on his experiences in Smolensk.

Bulgakov returned to Kiev in 1918, but was drafted into the White Army to fight in Russia's civil war against the communist Red Army. On a train trip home from Northern Caucasus, where the army had sent him, he sat up all night writing his first short story, and when the train stopped he took the story to the local newspaper office, which promptly published it. The following year, 1920, Bulgakov gave up medicine and moved to Moscow to write full time. He had several books published and several plays produced. His greatest success was the play *Days of the Turbins,* which was his adaptation for the stage of his own novel *The White Guard.* The story features a family that suffers at the hands of the Communists during the revolution, a depiction that would earn Bulgakov the suspicion of the Communists, who by then controlled the government. Despite the Communist reaction, Soviet Union audiences would applaud the play. From 1925 to 1928, the author was affiliated with the Moscow Arts Theater, where he had an uneasy relationship with the theater's founder and director, Konstatin Stanislavsky, who is known today for developing the theatrical technique referred to as "Method acting."

In 1929, the Russian Association of Proletarian Writers became the official government agency overseeing the political content of literary works. Bulgakov found himself unable to publish because his ideologies did not conform to those of the Communists. In frustration, he burned many of his manuscripts in 1930. He wrote an appeal directly to Joseph Stalin, the secretary general of the Communist Party and leader of the country. Stalin had been a fan of *Days of the Turbins,* and by his order Bulgakov was reinstated into the Art Theater. For the next ten years, Bulgakov wrote, directed, and sometimes acted, and he worked on *The Master and Margarita.*

Upon his death in 1940, he instructed his wife to hide the manuscript of *The Master and Margarita,* because he was afraid that it would be confiscated and destroyed by government censors. It was not published for another twenty-seven years, when the government of the Soviet Union had become more open to intellectual differences to the party line. Until the publication of *The Master and Margarita* in an English translation in 1967, few people outside of the Soviet Union had ever heard of Bulgakov. In subsequent years, his other novels, short stories, plays, essays, and his autobiography have been published, as well as numerous publications about his life and works.

Plot Summary

Bulgakov's *The Master and Margarita* is split into three different, yet intertwined, versions of reality: events in present-day Moscow, including the adventures of satanic visitors, events concerning the crucifixion of Yeshua Ha-Notsri, or Jesus Christ, in first-century Yershalaim, and the love story of the Master and Margarita.

Wednesday

Mikhail Alexandrovich Berlioz, an important literary figure, and Ivan Nikolayevich Ponyryov, a poet who is also known as Bezdomny, which means "homeless," meet at Patriarch's Ponds to discuss a commissioned poem that Berlioz had asked Ivan to pen. Berlioz would like Ivan to rewrite the poem because he believes the poem makes Jesus too real. He goes on to explain why he believes Jesus never existed, providing Ivan with a brief history of religion. Berlioz is eventually interrupted by a mysterious man named Professor Woland, who assures them that Jesus did indeed exist. When Berlioz objects, Woland begins the story of Pontius Pilate, but not before he tells Berlioz he will be decapitated before the day is out.

The story shifts to Yershalaim, where Pilate is hearing Yeshua's case. Yeshua is accused of inciting the people to burn down the temple, as well as advocating the overthrow of Emperor Tiberius. Pilate is forced to try him, and Yeshua is sentenced to death. Back in Moscow, Berlioz is indeed later decapitated by a streetcar. After Berlioz is killed, Ivan confronts and chases Woland and his gang—a choirmaster, Korovyov, and a huge tomcat, Behemoth—through the streets to no avail. When he tries to relate the happenings of the day, he is taken to the asylum.

Thursday

Styopa Likhodeyev, Berlioz's flat mate and director of the Variety Theater, awakes with a hangover to find Woland waiting for him. Woland apprises Likhodeyev that he has agreed to let Woland make seven performances of black magic at his theater. Likhodeyev does not remember having made this agreement. Contracts do contain Likhodeyev's signature; it seems that Woland is manipulating the situation, but Likhodeyev is bound to the agreement. Once a dazed Likhodeyev realizes that he must allow Woland to perform, Woland introduces the theater director to his entourage—Behemoth, Korovyov, and the single-fanged Azazello—and announces that they need apartment number 50, which has a reputation for being cursed (tenants of the apartment usually end up missing after a while). It is revealed that Woland and his group do not think highly of Styopa; they

believe people like him in high places are scoundrels.

Styopa soon finds himself transported to Yalta. The satanic gang spread mayhem throughout the building, and the manager has foreign money planted on him and is taken away by the police. The manager of the Variety Theater, Ivan Savelyevich Varenukha, attempts to find Styopa, who has been sending desperate telegrams from Yalta. At the same time, he, with the help of others, is trying to ascertain the identity of the mysterious Woland. To prevent inquiries by Varenukha, Woland sends a new infernal creature, Hella, to Varenukha, and she turns him into a vampire.

At the Variety Theater, Woland and his entourage give a black magic performance, during which the master of ceremonies is decapitated, and bewitched money—which later turns into bottle labels, kittens, and sundry objects—is rained over the crowd. Meanwhile, back at the asylum, Ivan meets his neighbor—the hero of the tale, the Master. He tells him about the previous day's events, and the Master assures him that Woland is Satan. The Master then tells him about his own life. He is an aspiring novelist and married, but he reveals he is in love with his "secret wife," Margarita, who is also married. His novel—the Pontius Pilate story—was their obsession, but critics lambasted it after it was offered for publication. Maddened, the Master had burned the manuscript, and ended up at the asylum.

Later, Ivan dreams the next part of Pilate's story: Condemned men are walking to their executions; Levi Matvei watches them hang and feels responsible. Then he grows angry and curses God. A storm comes, and the prisoners are put humanely to death by a guard stabbing them under the pretext of giving them water.

Friday

Woland and his group are still wreaking havoc in Moscow, and Margarita is pining over her love, the Master, and she rereads what is left of the Master's novel. She then goes to a park where she sees Berlioz's funeral and meets Azazello, who sets up a meeting between Margarita and Woland. He also gives Margarita some cream, telling her it will make her feel better. After she smears the cream over her body, she becomes a witch. Azazello contacts her and tells her to fly to the river for the meeting with Woland. She flies naked over the city and, on the way, destroys the critic Latunsky's apartment for he had been the one who ruined the Master. Her maid Natasha, now a witch, and Nikolai Ivanovich, now a pig, join her after using the cream.

They meet Woland and his followers, and Satan's ball takes place with Margarita as the hostess. A parade of both famous and commonplace evil people attend, and the ball climaxes with the murder of Baron Maigel. Margarita drinks blood, and opens her eyes to find the ball is over. Woland grants Margarita a wish for being the hostess of the ball. She chooses to be reunited with her lover, the Master. He soon appears before Margarita. The Master is confused at first, but he soon realizes that he is reunited with the woman he loves. Woland also has a copy of the Master's entire manuscript even though the Master had burned it, and he gives it to the Master. He then returns the Master and Margarita and other characters, including Nikolai Ivanovich and Varenukha, back to their lives as they wish. Natasha however chooses to remain a witch.

The Pilate story continues and Pilate meets with the chief of the secret police, Afranius. He premonishes that Judas of Kerioth, the man who betrayed Yeshua, will be murdered, and indeed, he is later lured outside of the city and murdered. Afranius reports the murder of Kerioth to Pilate, as well as the burial of the criminals. In a conversation with Levi (who was found to have taken Yeshua's body after the execution), Pilate reveals that it was he who killed Kerioth.

Saturday

An investigation into the strange events incited by Woland and his group begins, while Ivan is possessed by visions of Pilate and the bald hill on which Yeshua and the two other criminals had been executed. A shoot-out occurs in apartment number 50 between the investigators and Behemoth, but, surprisingly, no one is hurt. Instead, the building burns. Behemoth and Korovyov continue to perform more pranks that leave many areas of Moscow burning.

Levi comes to Woland with a message from Yeshua: he requests that Woland give the Master "peace." Woland agrees, and Azazello gives poisoned wine to the Master and Margarita. Their bodies die and the couple flies off with the infernal creatures, who, as they fly, return to their real figures. They soon come upon a man and his dog. Woland states that the man is the hero of the Master's novel: Pontius Pilate. He claims that Pilate has been sitting in the same spot for the past two thousand years with his dog, Banga. The Master is allowed to set Pilate free from his immortal insomnia by creating and stating the final line of his novel; he yells, "Free! Free! He is waiting for you!" Pi-

late and Banga are finally able to leave their static existence and be with Yeshua. The Master and Margarita are not given enlightenment, but they are allowed to spend the rest of eternity together in a small cottage.

Characters

Azazello

Azazello is the harshest and most sinister member of Woland's band, the one who will physically attack an opponent rather than simply play tricks. He is a short, broad-shouldered disfigured man with a bowler hat and red hair. His face is described as being "like a crash" and a fang protrudes from his mouth. It is Azazello who is sent to recruit Margarita to host the devil's ball, although he is not comfortable with this responsibility: he is awkward around women and thinks that one of the other servants who has more charm should have been sent to talk to her. He gives Margarita the cream that she rubs onto her body to become a witch. His true character, revealed in the parting scene, is that of "the demon of the waterless desert."

Behemoth

Behemoth, one of the novel's most memorable figures, is a huge black cat who walks on his hind legs and has many humanlike qualities: he pays for his trolley fare, drinks brandy from glasses, fires guns, and more. At the black magic show at the Variety Theater, it is Behemoth who twists the head off of the master of ceremonies. When the apartment at 302B Sadovaya Street is raided by police, Behemoth takes a gun and stages a shoot-out with them; although it is later determined that, even after the firing of hundreds of bullets, nobody on either side was injured. Behemoth burns the apartment with kerosene, and then does the same to Griboyedov House, the headquarters of MASSOLIT. In the end he is revealed to not really be a cat at all, but "a slim youth, a page demon, the greatest jester there had ever been."

Mikhail Alexandrovich Berlioz

Mikhail Alexandrovich Berlioz is the editor of one of Moscow's most fashionable literary magazines and a member of the management committee of MASSOLIT, the most prominent literary association in Moscow. The novel opens with Berlioz in the park discussing the historical evidence of Jesus Christ with Ivan. Woland interrupts with his own story about Pontius Pilate, and minutes later

A scene from a film adaptation of The Master and Margarita.

he prophesies that Berlioz will not make it to the meeting to which he is going; instead, he will have his head cut off by a woman. Leaving the park, Berlioz slips and falls under a trolley car, driven by a woman, and the wheels cut his head off. Later, during the devil's ball, his head is brought in on a platter, still alive and aware.

Bezdomny

See Ivan Nikolayich Ponyryov

Nikanor Ivanovich Bosoi

Nikanor Ivanovich Bosoi, whose surname means "barefooted," is the chairman of the tenants'

association of 302B Sadovaya Street, the building where Berlioz and Likhodeyev shared an apartment. After signing a one-week lease with Woland, Bosoi accepts a bribe, and takes it home and hides it in an air duct in his apartment. Woland calls the police to report the bribery, and Bosoi is arrested.

Fagot

See Korovyov

Yeshua Ha-Notsri

In the version of the crucifixion told by Woland and the Master in this book, Jesus has a different name; he is known as Yeshua Ha-Notsri.

Yeshua is presented as a simple man, not braver nor more intelligent than most, but more moral. Like the Jesus of Biblical tradition, he fascinates Pilate with the meek humanity of his ideas, but unlike the Jesus of the Bible he does not display a sense of security about the overall rightness of his death. The most striking aspect of Yeshua's conversation is that he believes in the goodness of all humans, even those who are cruelly persecuting him: "There are no evil people on earth," he tells Pilate.

Nikolai Ivanovich

Nikolai Ivanovich is a neighbor of Margarita's who also rubs the special cream on himself that had turned Margarita into a witch. Instead of taking on witchlike qualities, he is turned into a hog.

Jesus

See Yeshua Ha-Notsri

Homeless

See Ivan Nikolayich Ponyryov

Korovyov

Korovyov is one of Woland's associates, who identifies himself as Woland's interpreter. He first appears at Patriarch's Ponds, near the place where Berlioz dies. He is described as a lanky man wearing pince-nez glasses, a jockey cap, and a plaid suit. It is Korovyov who gives a bribe to Bosoi, and then calls the authorities to report him. As Woland and his entourage prepare to leave Moscow, it is revealed that Korovyov is not the buffoon he has presented himself as, but is a knight who once made "an ill-timed joke" and has been sentenced to serve Woland in this form because of it.

Stepan Bogdanovich Likhodeyev

The manager of the Variety Theater, Stepan Bogdanovich Likhodeyev, wakes up one morning after a night of drinking and finds that he has signed Woland to a week-long engagement at the theater.

Margarita Nikolayevna

Margarita Nikolayevna is the mistress of the writer known as the Master. In the past, when he was distraught about the novel, she comforted and nursed him. He gave all of his money to her for safekeeping, but then was arrested and taken away to the asylum. At a certain point, Margarita is asked to be the hostess of the devil's ball. Once she has a taste of witchcraft—invisibility and the ability to fly—she is glad to perform this duty. In return for her help, Woland offers to grant Margarita a wish. She wishes to be reunited with her beloved Master.

Master

The Master is an author who has written a book about Pontius Pilate. "I no longer have a name," he tells Ivan when they meet at the mental hospital, where they both are incarcerated. While there, the Master explains his past to the poet. He once was an historian (which is the same profession that Ivan settles into at the end of the book), but when he won a large sum in the lottery, he quit his job to work on his book. One day he met Margarita, with whom he fell hopelessly in love. When she took the novel around to publishers, it came back rejected, and then, even though it was unpublished, the reviewers attacked it in the newspapers. In a fit of insanity, imagining that an octopus was trying to drown him with its ink, the Master burned his book. He gave what was left of his savings to Margarita for safe keeping, but he was soon arrested and put in the asylum, and he never saw her again.

In the mental hospital, the Master has a stolen set of keys that allows him to escape, but he has nowhere to go. Margarita's reward for helping with the devil's ball is her reunion with the Master. Woland arranges for them to return to the Master's old apartment, for his bank account to be restored, for him to receive identification papers and, miraculously, for the burned novel to return to its original condition. In the end, at the request of Jesus, Woland takes the Master with him when he leaves the world: Jesus cannot take him because "He has not earned light, he has earned peace." Margarita joins him, of course, and they are never separated again.

Levi Matvei

Unlike the traditional stories of Jesus in the New Testament of the Bible, Yeshua has only one disciple in this story. Levi Matvei follows the philosophical vagabond Yeshua Ha-Notsri around, writing down what he says, usually without much accuracy. "This man follows me everywhere with nothing but his goatskin parchment and writes incessantly," Yeshua explains to Pilate. "But once I caught a glimpse of that parchment and I was horrified. I had not said a word of what was written there. I begged him, 'Please burn this parchment of yours!' But he tore it out of my hands and ran away." Levi is the one who later brings the message to Woland that Yeshua would like to give the Master "peace."

Natasha

Natasha is Margarita's maid who witnesses Margarita's transformation into a witch after she rubs special cream over her body. Natasha then rubs the cream on herself and turns into a witch as well.

Pontius Pilate

Pontius Pilate is presented as a tormented figure in this novel. He is in Jerusalem during the Passover holiday and is forced to pass a death sentence on a man who he thinks is a tramp and a fool, but not dangerous. After the crucifixion, Pilate assigns soldiers to guard the man who betrayed Jesus, fearing religious followers might try to take revenge on him. However, in this novel, there is no evidence that Yeshua actually has followers. Later, Pilate reveals that he himself had the traitor murdered. Throughout the story there is evidence that Pilate has become fascinated with Jesus from his brief encounter with him, and at the end of the book, Pilate is united with Yeshua.

Ivan Nikolayich Ponyryov

Ivan Nikolayich Ponyryov is a young, twenty-three-year-old poet, who writes under the pen name Bezdomny, which means "homeless" in Russian. This character is present in the first chapter of the novel and the last, as well as appearing intermittently throughout the story. When the novel begins, Ivan is meeting with Berlioz, a magazine editor, at Patriarch's Ponds. They are discussing the historical accuracy of Jesus when Woland, who is the devil, interrupts their conversation and tells them the story of the crucifixion as he witnessed it. He goes on to foretell the bizarre circumstances of Berlioz's death. When Berlioz dies in this exact same way a few minutes later, Ivan chases Woland and his accomplices across town, bursting through apartments and diving into the river. When he ends up at the headquarters of the writers' organization in his underwear, Ivan is arrested and sent to the mental ward. At the asylum, the Master is in a neighboring room; he is able to visit Ivan at night because he has stolen a set of keys that open the doors on their floor of the hospital. The Master explains that Ivan actually did encounter the devil, and he goes on to recount his own life story to the poet. Before he is released from the clinic, Ivan decides to stop writing poetry. By the end of the story, years after the events that make up the bulk of the book, Ivan has become an historian, but continues to be plagued by strange visions every time the moon is full.

Media Adaptations

- *The Master and Margarita* was adapted for video in 1988. This version was directed by Alexandra Petrovich and released by SBS.

- The video *Incident in Judea,* directed by Paul Bryers and released by SBS in 1992, is based on material from Bulgakov's *The Master and Margarita.*

- A Polish version, *Mistrz i Malgorzata (The Master and Margarita*—with English subtitles—of *The Master and Margarita* was released on four video cassettes by Contal International in 1990. This version was directed and written by Maciej Wojtyszko.

- *The Master and Margarita* was adapted for audio cassette by IU Liubimov, and released by Theater Works in 1991.

- An audio compact disc called *Master and Margarita: Eight Scenes from the Ballet* was released by Russian Discs in 1995.

Grigory Danilovich Rimsky

The treasurer of the theater, Grigory Danilovich Rimsky, is visited by the ghost of Varenukha the night of Woland's performance, but manages to escape to the train station.

Professor Woland

Woland is frequently referred to in the book as a foreigner. He is mischievous and cunning, but also noble and generous. The contradictions in his personality show in his looks: "his left eye was completely mad, his right eye black, expressionless and dead." He claims to have been present when Pontius Pilate sentenced Jesus and he can foretell the future, but people rationalize his supernatural powers as illusions or else they, like Ivan and the Master, end up in the psychiatric ward. Woland and his associates wreak havoc in Moscow. They put on a show of black magic at the Variety Theater, at which gorgeous new clothes are given to all of the ladies and money falls from the ceiling: soon after, the women are found to be walking the streets in their underwear and the money that looked authentic proves to be meaningless paper. At the devil's ball, Woland drops his disguise as a visiting professor and reveals his true identity as the devil. On the day after the ball he and his associates ride off to the netherworld on thundering black stallions.

Themes

Absurdity

The actions taken by the devil, Woland, and his associates in Moscow seem to be carried out for no reason. From the beginning, when Woland predicts the unlikely circumstances of Berlioz's beheading, to the end, when Behemoth stages a shootout with the entire police force, there seems to be no motivation other than sheer mischief. After a while, though, their trickery reveals a pattern of preying upon the greedy, who think they can reap benefits they have not earned. For example, when a bribe is given to the chairman of the tenants' association, Bosoi, Woland tells Korovyov to "fix it so that he doesn't come here again." Bosoi is then arrested, which punishes him for exploiting his position. Similarly, the audience that attends Woland's black magic show is delighted by a shower of money only to find out the next day that they are holding blank paper, while the women who thought they were receiving fine new clothes later find themselves in the streets in their underwear. These deceptions appear mean-spirited and pointless, but the victims in each case are blinded by their interest in material goods.

Guilt and Innocence

The story of Pontius Pilate serves to raise fundamental questions about guilt. As the Procurator of Judea, the representative of the Roman government in Israel, Pilate is responsible for passing judgment on people the Israelis have arrested and brought before him. In Yeshua's case, he feels guilty having to sentence Yeshua to death. Pilate's conscience is awakened during his interview with Yeshua; he shows a fascination with the idea of acceptance, but because of his position he is not able to completely believe in it nor is he able to forget about the idea of evil. The subsequent feelings of guilt over having sent an innocent man to death are compounded when it is reported that, at his death,

Yeshua blamed no one for what happened to him, and "that he regarded cowardice as one of the worst human sins." To lighten his guilt, Pilate orders the death of Judas, the man who turned Yeshua over to the authorities. However, Pilate is left eternally discontent; "there is no peace for him by moonlight and … his duty is a hard one."

Good and Evil

The traditional understanding of the devil is that he is the embodiment of evil, and that any benefits one might expect from an association with him are illusory. In *The Master and Margarita,* the devil is portrayed slightly different. In the story he does take advantage of the people with whom he comes into contact, offering them money and goods that later disappear; however, he does not send any souls to hell. In fact, Bulgakov's depiction of the devil has him catering to a request made by Yeshua: he leaves the world with the souls of the Master and Margarita and in the afterlife the two souls are given a cottage in which they are united forever. Far more evil than the devil in this book is the literary establishment, which ruins the Master, indulges in gluttonous behavior, and aligns with the controlling Soviet government. By comparison, the actions of Woland and his associates can be looked at positively as they may actually lead people to better themselves. However, most of the victims of Satan attribute their experiences to hypnotism, putting the responsibility for their woes on the devil, not on themselves.

In the case of Jesus, the novel portrays him as an obscure figure, a pawn in a political struggle. Whereas Jesus of the Bible is a celebrated prophet, with a dozen disciples and crowds of thousands who would come to hear him speak and welcome him, Yeshua has one follower, Levi Matvei, who is so mentally unstable that Yeshua himself is uneasy around him. Rather than a gospel of love, Yeshua's message is the more psychological observation that "there are no evil people on earth."

Artists and Society

Both of the true artists in this book, the Master and Ivan, end up in the mental institution under Dr. Stravinsky's care, while less talented people feast on opulent meals and listen to dance bands at Griboyedov House. The damage caused by false artists goes beyond greed and laziness: when the Master produces his novel the established writers mock him and his book before the public has a chance to see it. This negative reaction does not harm the Master financially—he is independently wealthy from having won the lottery-but it crushes his artistic sensibilities and drives him to madness. As a result, he burns his work and wanders aimlessly in the cold. He is then admitted to the asylum. Even in his insanity, though, the Master knows himself: he realizes that he has lost his identity and that he probably could not survive outside if he escaped the asylum. He suffered so greatly for having created a work of true art that in the end, when Woland restores his burned manuscript, he is hesitant to take it: "I have no more dreams and my inspiration is dead," he says, adding that he hates the novel because "I have been through too much for it."

As for Ivan, the Master, during their initial meeting, tells the writer he should write no more poetry, a request Ivan agrees to honor. Later, as the Master leaves, he calls Ivan "my protégé." By the end of the story, Ivan becomes a historian, which is the position that the Master held before his novel about Pontius Pilate dramatically changed his life.

Style

Structure

This book uses a complex version of the story-in-story structure, weaving the narrative about Pontius Pilate in through the text of the story that takes place during the twentieth century in Moscow. The chapters about Pilate are continuous, following the same four-day sequence of events, and they are coherent, with the same tone of seriousness in the voice throughout the Pilate story. In one sense, their cohesion shows Bulgakov breaking the rules of narrative, because these chapters spring from the minds of different characters. Chapter two is presented as a story told by Woland to Berlioz and Ivan, chapter sixteen is supposed to be Margarita's dream, and chapters twenty-five and twenty-six are allegedly from the Master's novel. Bulgakov tells the events in all of these with one voice because doing so strengthens readers' senses of how much these characters are alike in their thinking.

Mennipean Satire

Critics have noted that this book follows the tradition of Mennipean Satire, named after Mennipus, the philosopher and Cynic who lived in Greece in the third century BC. Cynics were a school of Greek thinkers, founded by Diogenes of Sinope, who felt that civilization was artificial and unnatural, and who therefore mocked behaviors that were

Topics for Further Study

- Explain why you think that Woland's associate Behemoth is presented as a cat, while Pilate's closest companion is his dog. List the characteristics of these animals that make them fit the roles that Bulgakov has given them here.

- Study the treatment of writers in the Soviet Union in the 1930s through the 1960s. Report on the standards to which writers were held by the government, and the punishments that were given to those who disobeyed.

- Read *Faust,* by Johann Wolfgang von Goethe, which is openly acknowledged as one of the inspirations for *The Master and Margarita.* Compare Goethe's version of the devil with Bulgakov's Woland. Which do you think is more dangerous? Which is written to be the more sympathetic figure? Why do you think Bulgakov made the changes to the devil that he made?

- Study the specific political role played by the Procurator of Judea. How did this position come into existence? What would have been the extent of his powers and responsibilities?

considered socially "proper." Diogenes is best remembered for carrying a lantern through Athens in broad daylight looking for an "honest man," but he also is said to have pantomimed sexual acts in the streets, urinated in public, and barked at people (the word "cynic" is believed to come from the Greek word meaning "dog-like"). Cynics are remembered for being distrustful of human nature and motives: even today, people use the word "cynical" to describe someone who expects the worst of people.

The satires of Mennipus, written in a combination of prose and verse, made fun of pretensions and intellectual charades. The elite were also ridiculed in Mennipus' plays, as they are in *The Master and Margarita.* The Roman scholar Marcus Tarentius Varro, living in the first century BC, took up this style when he wrote his *Saturarum*

Mennipearum Libri CL (150 Books of Mennipean Satires, c. 81-67 BC). The form has continued through the centuries, distinguished from other satires by the wide range of society it derides and the harshness with which it mocks. From the eighteenth century, Alexander Pope's ruthless *Dunciad* is considered a Mennipean Satire, as is Aldous Huxley's *Brave New World,* from 1932. In the 1960s and 1970s, around the time that *The Master and Margarita* was published, the form proved useful for Russian writer Aleksandr Solzhenitsyn to express his outrage with the Soviet system.

Symbolism

The symbolic aspects of this novel serve to both render a clear vision of the action while also linking the spirit of the different plot lines together. Of these, the most notable are the sun and the moon, which are mentioned constantly throughout, giving the sense that they are the true observers of the action. The first page of the novel, with Berlioz and Ivan at Patriarch's Ponds, begins "at the sunset hour," and goes on to introduce the devil as the sun recedes. Pontius Pilate's headache is worsened by the blaring sun, as is, the following day, Yeshua's suffering on the cross. In contrast, the Master and Ivan are both tormented by moonlight, which plays with their sanity. Traditionally, sunlight is associated with logic and rationality, while the light of the moon is often related to the subconscious. Another major symbol is the mention of thunderstorms, which appear in the most significant places in the book. The storm that gathers while Yeshua is on the cross and breaks upon his death is notable for its ferocity, as is the storm that washes over Moscow at the end, while Woland and his associates settle their business and leave. Writers often use a thunderstorm to symbolize the release of one character's pent-up emotions. In *The Master and Margarita,* the storms can be seen as the crying out of whole cultures, ancient and modern, as they become aware of how diseased their social systems are.

The book has numerous other events and objects that can be seen as symbolic because they refer one's thoughts to broader philosophical issues than those at hand. Foreign currency, for instance, can be equated with non-Soviet ideas, with value that the government tries to suppress; the blood-red wine that Pilate spills does not wash away, like the sins on his soul; and the empty suit that carries on business, as well as the Theatrical Commission staff that finds itself unable to stop singing "The Song of the Vulga Boatmen," all represent the mindlessness of the bureaucratic system. These are just a few of the elements that add meaning to the story if read as being symbolic as well as actual.

Historical Context

The Stalin Era

Bulgakov's writing career, particularly the twelve-year period between 1928 and 1940 when he worked on *The Master and Margarita,* was marked by Russia's transition from the monarchic empire ruled by Nicholas II, who was overthrown in the Russian Revolution in 1917, and the totalitarian Communist government that ruled the country throughout most of the twentieth century. The first post-revolutionary head of the country, Vladimir Lenin, had the practical concern of protecting the country from enemies and establishing the Soviet power base. He guided the country through the 1918 to 1921 civil war and kept the economy mixed, partially nationalized and partially privatized.

In 1922, two years before Lenin's death, Joseph Stalin rose to be the secretary general of the Communist Party, and he used this position to gain control of the Soviet Union when Lenin died. Stalin felt that the country was far behind the world's more industrialized nations—at least a hundred years behind, in fact. He put forward programs, all part of what he called his "Five Year Plan," intended to increase production quickly. One place he pushed for change was agriculture. There were about twenty-five million farms in the Soviet Union in the mid-1920s, but few produced enough food to feed anyone but the families who lived on them. Successful farmers who made a profit were called "kulaks." Stalin proposed state-run agricultural collectives, which would produce enough to feed the whole country. The kulaks resisted. In 1929, he called for the "liquidation" of the kulaks, and in fighting to keep their farms they destroyed crops, livestock, and farming tools. Nearly one-third of Russia's cattle and half of the horses were destroyed between 1929 and 1933. Successful farmers were taken away to prisons. Soldiers were sent out across the land, arresting farmers who owned private land. In 1928, only 1.7 percent of Soviet peasants lived on collective farms, but that number grew rapidly with the military action: 4.1 percent of the peasants were on collective farms in October of 1929, a number that jumped to 21 percent just four months later and then 58 percent three

Compare & Contrast

- **1968:** Viewing the Vietnam War on television, Americans became more and more suspicious of their government. Atrocities, such as the massacre of hundreds of Vietnamese men, women, and children in the village of My Lai, made Americans feel as distanced from their government as the citizens of Moscow in *The Master and Margarita.*

  Today: Americans are still suspicious of the government's honesty and competence, so that any military initiative is met with distrust.

- **1968:** The newly appointed secretary of the Communist Party of Czechoslovakia, Alexander Dubcek, refused to attend conferences in Warsaw and Moscow. In order to keep control of the satellite Communist countries, the Soviet Union sent 200,000 troops into Czechoslovakia.

  Today: Czechoslovakia no longer exists. After the breakup of the Soviet Union, it divided into two republics: The Czech Republic, with a capital city of Prague, and Slovakia, whose capital is Bratislava.

- **1968:** Race riots swept many of the country's major metropolitan areas after Martin Luther King Jr. was shot dead in Memphis. A total of 21,270 arrests were made across the country. Forty-six people died in the riots.

  Today: Many social scientists consider the continued divisions between the races to be America's greatest social failure.

---

months after that. By the end of the decade, 99 percent of the Soviet Union's cultivated land was collective farms, while millions of kulaks who had been taken from their farms labored in prison camps.

Stalin's Five Year Plan also reorganized Soviet industry. The government organization "Gosplan," with half a million employees, had the task of planning productivity goals for all industries and checking with factories to see if they were meeting their goals, all with the intent of raising Russia's annual growth rate by 50 percent. Factory managers and workers who were seen as holding back progress, even for safety or economic reasons, were arrested and sent off to labor camps. Fearing punishment, many workers stayed at their jobs twelve and fourteen hours a day, while other factories, with no hope of reaching their assigned production levels, took the chance of falsifying paperwork. From 1928 to 1937 Russian steel production rose from 4 to 17.7 million tons; electricity output rose 700 percent; tractor production rose 40,000 percent. The country's national income rose from 24.4 billion rubles to 96.3 billion. The price, of course, was freedom, and readers of Bulgakov can see the dangers of being in a closed, controlling society with limited resources.

The Brezhnev Years

Tension between the Soviet Union and the United States was at its greatest between the mid-1940s and the mid-1960s. At the time, these were the world's two leading "super power" nations, and they competed against each other for technological superiority in the race to put humans on the moon and military superiority in the buildup of nuclear arms. In 1964, Nikita Khrushchev, the Soviet leader most identified with the Cold War, was forced from power in a coup d'etat, and was replaced by the duo of Leonid Brezhnev as the Communist Party leader and Aleksei Kosygin as Soviet Premier. The early part of their rule, from 1964 to 1970, was a period of reformation and stabilization. Brezhnev had risen up through the ranks of the Communist Party and was not interested in changing the social system, just in making the system function more smoothly within the structure set by the Soviet governing body, the Politburo.

The year 1967, when *The Master and Margarita* was finally published, was a time of youth

In The Master and Margarita, *the devil wreaks havoc on Communist Russia. In this illustration, which appeared in a Moscow newspaper, a Communist conquers the devil and the entire kingdom of Heaven.*

rebellion in the United States, but the same spirit of rebelliousness pervaded in other countries across the world as well. One of the most notable instances of riots against the government came in Czechoslovakia, where, during the "Prague Spring" of 1968, protesters almost shut down the country's Communist government. Because Czechoslovakia was an ally of the Soviet Union, Brezhnev sent Soviet troops across the border, into Czechoslovakia, to defeat the protesters and to keep control of the country for the Communists. It was a turning point in Soviet history, showing the world that the Soviet Union would go to great lengths to defend Communism.

The fact that Bulgakov's book was finally published after nearly thirty years should not be taken as an indicator that the government was relaxing its policies toward artistic works judged to be critical of the political system. Writers were regularly arrested for spreading "anti-Soviet propaganda" if their work showed any flaws in the system, and convicted writers were sent to work in forced labor camps or to languish in mental asylums for "paranoid schizophrenia." Only a writer who man-

aged to sneak his works out of the country and reach an international audience could avoid a harsh punishment from the government, which had its reputation within the international community to protect. This happened to Aleksandr Solzhenitsyn, who won the Nobel Prize for Literature in 1970 and was expelled from the country in 1974.

Critical Overview

Bulgakov was reviewed with respect during his lifetime, although it was not until the world saw *The Master and Margarita,* published almost thirty years after his death, that he came to be generally recognized as one of the great talents of the twentieth century. During his lifetime, his literary reputation stood mostly on the quality of the plays that he wrote for the Moscow theater, and, because of the totalitarian nature of Soviet politics, critics were at least as concerned with the plays' political content as their artistic merit. In the years after his death, Bulgakov's reputation grew slowly.

Writing about Bulgakov's novel *The White Guard* in 1935's *Soviet Russian Literature,* Gleb Strave was unimpressed, noting, "As a literary work it is not of any great outstanding significance. It is a typical realistic novel written in simple language, without any stylistic or compositional refinements." Strave went on in his review to express a preference for Bulgakov's short stories, which were unrealistic and fanciful. In 1968, when *The Master and Margarita* was released in the West, Strave was still an active critic of Soviet literature. His review of the book in *The Russia Review* predicted the attention that it would soon obtain, but Strave did not think that it was worth that attention, mainly because of the story line with Margarita and the Master, which he felt "somehow does not come off." True to his prediction, though, critics welcomed the novel with glowing praise when it was published. Writing in *The Nation,* Donald Fanger predicted that "Bulgakov's brilliant and moving extravaganza ... may well be one of the major novels of the Russian Twentieth Century." He placed Bulgakov in the company of such literary giants as Samuel Beckett, Vladimir Nabakov, William Burroughs, and Norman Mailer.

Many critics have focused their attention on the meaning of *The Master and Margarita.* D. G. B. Piper examined the book in a 1971 article for the *Forum for Modern Language Studies,* giving a thorough explanation of the ways that death and murder wind through the story, tying it together, illuminating the differences between "the here-and-now and the ever-after." In 1972 Pierre S. Hart interpreted the book in *Modern Fiction Studies* as a commentary on the creative process: "Placed in the context of the obvious satire on life in the early Soviet state," he wrote, "it gains added significance as a definition of the artist's situation in that system." While other writers saw the book as centering around the moral dilemma of Pilate or the enduring love of the Master and Margarita, Hart placed all of the book's events in relation to Soviet Russia's treatment of artists. Edythe C. Haber, in *The Russia Review,* had yet another perspective on it in 1975, comparing the devil of Goethe's *Faust* with the devil as he is portrayed by Bulgakov.

That same year, Vladimir Lakshin, writing for *Twentieth-Century Russian Literary Criticism,* expressed awe for Bulgakov's ability to render scenes with vivid details, explaining that this skill on the author's part was the thing that made it possible for the book to combine so many contrasting elements. "The fact that the author freely blends the unblendable—history and feulleton, lyricism and myth, everyday life and fantasy—makes it difficult to define his book's genre," Lakshin wrote, going on to explain that, somehow, it all works together. In the years since the Soviet Union was dismantled, the potency of *The Master and Margarita*'s glimpse into life in a totalitarian state has diminished somewhat, but the book's mythic overtones are as strong as ever, making it a piece of literature that is every bit as important, if not more, than it was when it was new.

Criticism

Tabitha McIntosh-Byrd

McIntosh-Byrd is a doctoral candidate at the University of Pennsylvania. In the following essay she looks at Mikhail Bulgakov's The Master and Margarita *as a commentary on the nature and politics of writing.*

Mikhail Bulgakov's *The Master and Margarita* is a novel about novels—an argument for the ability of literature to transcend both time and oppression, and for the heroic nature of the writer's struggle to create that literature. The story's hero, the Master, is an iconographic representation of such writers. Despite rejection, mockery and self-censorship, he creates a fictional world so power-

ful that it has the ability to invade and restructure the reality of those that surround him. Indeed, it has a life beyond authorial control. Despite his attempts to burn it, the story of Pontius Pilate refuses to die. As Woland remarks, "Manuscripts don't burn." This transcendence of message over physical form—the eternal power of narrative over the mundane reality of flammable paper—is in itself an idea that "escapes" from Bulgakov's novel, becoming a commentary on his contemporary Soviet society and the role of authors like Bulgakov within it.

Readers first meet the Master in Dr. Stravinsky's mental hospital, as he says when asked about his identity, "I am a master ... I no longer have a name. I have renounced it, as I have renounced life itself." His identity subsumed into his role as Great Author, the Master's symbolic status is sign-posted from his first appearance. Both the details of his creative process as well as the story he has created will be presented throughout Bulgakov's novel as powerful, almost occult forces, that are greater than material reality, just as the infernal visitors are greater than the rationalist society upon which they wreak havoc. The multiple narrative strands of the novel—the Master and Margarita's story of creation, the story-within-a-story of the master's novel, the dry world of state controlled literature exemplified by MASSOLIT (a literary club in Moscow), and the rule-less world of the satanic gang—perform both individually and in their entirety as a commentary on the nature and power of narrative.

As the hero explains to his fellow inmate, it was the creation of his novel that caused his transcendence to the status of Master—the act of writing forcing a kind of personal transformation upon him. He and his lover, Margarita, were completely consumed in one other and in his work-in-progress—the two consummations fed into and from one another. The novel enabled their romance at the same time as their romance enabled the novel—it is Margarita who oversees its creation and bestows the name "Master" upon its author, and it is she who keeps faith in it when the publishing world rejects it. When the Master burns his manuscript, throwing it in the wood stove, he is attempting to reverse the alchemical process of creation. The unclean text must be transformed into ashes in the "purifying" flames, just as he was transformed into An Author by the purifying act of creating it.

In his story we can see a metaphorized version of the struggles of all authors, the master's story presenting a sort of extended meditation on the nature of being an author. The completion of the novel is the culmination of everything he was working toward and the expression of his personality, an "alternative self" in which his dreams reside. His rejection of writing thus becomes a rejection of his own mind, an act that is literalized by his self-committal to the asylum: he has literally "lost his mind." When Woland returns the manuscript to him, the Master rejects it, saying, "I hate that novel." Woland's reply encapsulates the crippling effects of such self-censorship. As he asks, "How will you be able to write now? Where are your dreams, your inspiration?" The Master replies, "I have no more dreams and my inspiration is dead … I'm finished." Of course, by the end of the novel, the Master has re-embraced his story, completing the final line as he flies off to his eternal cottage with Margarita. This pattern of creative struggle, rejection, self-doubt and transcendence represents a simultaneous exploration and rejection of glorification through pain. It is creation, not rejection, that turns a simple author into a Master. In just the same way, the Master's version of the crucifixion stresses joy over suffering. It is forgiveness that allows Pontius Pilate to ascend to Heaven, not a proscribed period of torment; just as Margarita's compassion frees Frieda the infanticide from the eternal cycle of suffering. Both the literal Purgatory of Catholic theology and the metaphoric purgatory of authorial trial are rejected in favor of Grace and acceptance.

This rejection of suffering-as-purity acts as a nuanced critique of literary life in Soviet culture. The writers of "acceptable" literature—the members of MASSOLIT—are forgettable idiots not worthy of serious critique. The authorial voice, represented by the all-powerful satanic gang, dismisses them with a capricious amusement exemplified by the fate of Berlioz, who simply has his head cut off to shut him up. Similarly, the proprietors of the Variety Theater are subjected to various Byzantine tortures befitting their production of terrible art. In this way, *The Master and Margarita* presents not so much an indictment of Socialist Realism as a disgusted mockery of it. Instead, the more serious and sensitive exploration is reserved for "real" authors, those who are outside state approval and whose work is marginalized and banned. Again, the Master is used to exemplify such authors. Subjected first to dismissal and then to active persecution, he gradually embraces the logic of MASSOLIT and burns his own book. As Woland says, "They have almost broken him," and they have done so by causing him to

break himself. When this is taken into account, the rejection of suffering as a creative aesthetic must be read as a powerful call to an artistic community under siege rather than to the forces besieging it. The story of the Master's suffering acts as a parable which warns of the dangers inherent in heroizing struggle.

To Bulgakov and his contemporaries, heroizing struggle was an attractive option, very difficult to resist. Soviet writers of the Stalinist period were subjected to extreme levels of censorship, and faced with a choice between living in fear, writing what they were told to write, or never attempting to get published. In *The Master and Margarita,* Bulgakov creates an artistic world that acknowledges these conditions, and negotiates a different intellectual and philosophical approach to them. The danger of accepting that struggle purifies is presented by the fate of the Master. Struggling does not purify him—rather it represents an acceptance of the forces ranged against him; a voluntary erasure of self that serves the purposes of the state. When he embraces the power of his narrative, he embraces a form of resistance, which says that joy, creation and the telling of stories must be an end in themselves, since—like the Master's novel—they may well be truly finished only after the death of the author. As Bulgakov bitterly said of his own work:

> I have heard again and again suspiciously unctuous voices assuring me, 'No matter, after your death everything will be published.'

The most difficult task facing The Master, Bulgakov, and Soviet writers in general is to accept that fact while refusing to consign themselves to purgatory.

The power of narrative to create belief, and the concurrent power of belief to restructure reality, is a major thematic aspect of the novel. This works in a multi-layered way, with many versions of narrative playing against each other and providing commentaries on one another. In the most obvious, structural instance, the novel-within-a-novel motif allows Bulgakov to comment on the role of literature in the life of the society and author that produces it. A common genre in Russian literary history, the book within a book appears in such works as Pushkin's *Eugene Onegin* and Zamiatin's *We.* Bulgakov's innovation is the relationship between the two books. Though the story of Pontius Pilate is indeed a story within a story, and though it is indeed the Master's novel, discrete boundaries between the two texts are constantly blurred until it is no longer clear which story is taking place within which. Only once is an excerpt from the Master's novel presented as an excerpt—when Margarita sits down to read the charred fragment. The rest of the time, Pilate's story comes from the minds and mouths of others—from Woland at Patriarch's Ponds and the dreams of Homeless at the asylum. It becomes just as real as the story that seems to contain it, a parallel reality that reaches into contemporary Moscow and reshapes it according to its needs. Everything in the Moscow reality revolves around the Yershalayim reality that the Master's book set in motion, culminating in a scene in which it becomes apparent that the Master now exists, like Bulgakov's frame narrative, to resolve the painful reality of Pontius Pilate's story. What started as an author's attempt to achieve—to transform his life by the creation of literature—has been entirely reversed. The author exists in the service of literature, and not the other way round.

The role of literature within the culture that produces it is similarly configured: it literally has the power to change the past, present, and future. The interaction of the Yershalaim and the Moscow realities complicates the relationship of cause and effect through the manipulation of chronology, and in doing so suggests that art transcends time. Chapter twenty-six of *The Master and Margarita* marks the end of the Master's story of Pilate, but in chapter thirty-two Pilate himself reappears, this time within the Moscow narrative. Woland tells the Master:

> We have read your novel, and we can only say that unfortunately it is not finished. I would like to show you your hero. He has been sitting here for nearly two thousand years … He is saying that there is no peace for him … He claims he had more to say to [Ha-Notsri] on that distant fourteenth day of Nisan.

The meeting of the master and his hero Pilate in the 'eternal now' of the afterlife completes the link between past and present. The two concurrent story lines finally intersect physically, after they have touched upon each other throughout the novel. The Master frees Pilate from his eternal torment, and is himself granted peace by one of his own creations—his version of Levi Matvei who arrives as Yeshua's messenger to Woland. Narrative, this would seem to suggest, is so powerful that it is not only incapable of destruction, but also the very means by which reality is constructed. In this way, Pilate is paradoxically "created," millennia before his creator, the Master, was even born.

When the Master wrote about Pilate, he effectively changed the past, and his characters gained the ability to walk into his present and change his life and the life of his society. In an extended chronological and narrative game, Bulgakov suggests that it is what we read that makes us believe, and what we believe that makes us who we are. Woland and his followers wreak havoc on Moscow by dropping millions of rubles into the audience of the Variety Theater, rubles that turn into foreign bills, soda bottles, and insects, infesting the economy with a supply of worthless money. As Bulgakov makes clear, money—no less than fiction and religion—is dependent on faith, on the willingness to believe that objects of material culture are greater than the sum of their parts. When that belief is lost, reality becomes a set of meaningless, valueless artifacts of no use to anyone. In the final analysis, *The Master and Margarita* represents an absolute rejection of "reality" as it is understood by Soviet materialist culture. Instead, the novel says, fiction is reality and reality is fiction. Everything is dependent on stories.

Source: Tabitha McIntosh-Byrd, in an essay for *Novels for Students,* Gale, 2000.

A. Colin Wright

In the following essay, Wright presents an overview of The Master and Margarita.

The Master and Margarita was essentially completed in 1940 but its origin goes back to 1928, when Bulgakov wrote a satirical tale about the devil visiting Moscow. Like his literary hero, Gogol (as well as the Master in his own novel), Bulgakov destroyed this manuscript in 1930 but returned to the idea in 1934, adding his heroine, Margarita, based on the figure of his third wife, Elena Sergeevna Shilovskaia. The novel went through a number of different versions until, aware that he had only a short time to live, he put other works aside in order to complete it, dictating the final changes on his deathbed after he had become blind. It remained unpublished until 1965-66, when it appeared in a censored version in the literary journal *Moskva,* immediately creating a sensation. It has since been published in its entirety, although the restored passages, while numerous, add comparatively little to the overall impact of the novel. It has been translated into many other languages. (In English, the Glenny translation is the more complete, while the Ginsburg translation is taken from the original *Moskva* version.)

The novel's form is unusual, with the hero, the Master, appearing only towards the end of the first part, and Margarita not until Part Two. It combines three different if carefully related stories: the ar-

What Do I Read Next?

- This book's use of fantasy elements to lampoon social behavior is reminiscent of Lewis Carroll's ever-popular Alice books, *Alice's Adventures in Wonderland* (1865) and *Through the Looking-Glass* (1872). Bulgakov refers to these books, in fact, in the beginning of chapter eight, when Ivan finds a cylinder in the mental ward labeled "Drink," similar to the mysterious bottle labeled "Drink Me" that Alice finds at the start of her adventure in Wonderland.

- Many of Bulgakov's ideas, especially his conception of Woland, the devil, are taken directly from German poet Johann Wolfgang von Goethe's two-part poem *Faust* (published in 1808 and 1832), which he wrote over a span of fifty years.

- Salman Rushdie's novel *The Satanic Verses* created a sensation when it was released in 1988, causing an Iranian religious leader to offer a reward for the "blaspheming" author's death. Rushdie himself acknowledged the similarities between his book and *The Master and Margarita*, noting that "the echoes are there, and not unconsciously." Like Bulgakov's novel, it is the retelling of an ancient religious story within a contemporary story.

- Aleksandr Solzhenitsyn is a Russian novelist of a generation after Bulgakov's, who grew up within the repression of Lenin's reformed government. He won the Nobel Prize for literature in 1970 and was expelled from Russia in 1974 for denouncing the official government system. Critics consider some of his early fictional works about the Soviet government to be his most powerful, including *One Day in the Life of Ivan Denisovich* (1962) and *The First Circle* (1968).

- Critics have pointed out that the modern trend of "magical realism" in fiction has much in common with *The Master and Margarita*. This style has been most evident in Latin America since the 1960s, in the works of such writers as Alejo Carpenter, Carlos Fuentes, and Mario Vargas Llosa. The most preeminent novel in this genre is *One Hundred Years of Solitude,* by Gabriel García Márquez, who won the 1982 Nobel Prize for Literature.

---

rival of the devil (Woland) and his companions in contemporary Moscow, where they create havoc; Margarita's attempt, with Woland's assistance, to be reunited with her love after his imprisonment and confinement in a psychiatric hospital; and an imaginative account of the passion of Christ (given the Hebrew name of Yeshua-Ha-Nozri) from his interrogation by Pontius Pilate to his crucifixion. Differing considerably from the gospels, the latter consists of four chapters which may be regarded as a novel within a novel: written by the Master, related by Woland, and dreamed of by a young poet (Ivan Bezdomnyi, or 'Homeless') on the basis of 'true' events. Correspondingly, the action takes place on three different levels, each with a distinct narrative voice: that of Ancient Jerusalem, of Moscow of the 1930s (during the same four days in Holy Week), and of the 'fantastic' realm beyond time. The book is usually considered to be closest in genre to Menippean satire.

Despite its complexity, the novel is highly entertaining, very funny in places, and with the mystery appeal of a detective story. In the former Soviet Union, as well as in the countries of Eastern Europe, it was appreciated first of all for its satire on the absurdities of everyday life: involving Communist ideology, the bureaucracy, the police, consumer goods, the housing crisis, various forms of illegal activities and, above all, the literary and artistic community. At the same time it is obviously a very serious work, by the end of which one feels a need for more detailed interpretation: what, in short, is it all about? The problem is compounded by the fact that it is full of pure fantasy and traditional symbols (features associated with devil-lore, for example), so that the reader is uncertain what is important to elucidate the meaning. Leitmotifs (such as sun and moon, light and darkness, and many others) connect the three levels, implying the ultimate unity of all existence.

Soviet critics tended to dwell initially on the relatively innocuous theme of justice: enforced by Woland during his sojourn in Moscow, while Margarita tempers this with mercy in her plea to release a sinner from torment. Human greed, cowardice, and the redemptive power of love are other readily distinguishable themes. More fundamental ones are summed up in three key statements: 'Jesus existed' (the importance of a spiritual understanding of life, as opposed to practical considerations in a materialistic world that denied Christ's very existence); 'Manuscripts don't burn' (a belief in the enduring nature of art); and 'Everything will turn out right. That's what the world is built on': an extraordinary metaphysical optimism for a writer whose life was characterized by recurring disappointment. There is indeed a strong element of wish-fulfilment in the book, where characters are punished or rewarded according to what they are seen to have deserved.

Thus the novel's heroes, the Master and Margarita, are ultimately rescued, through the agency of Woland, in the world beyond time. They are, however, granted 'peace' rather than 'light', from which they are specifically excluded: a puzzle to many critics. Here, on a deeper philosophical level, there is an undoubted influence of gnosticism with its contrasting polarities of good and evil—which, as I have argued elsewhere, are reconciled in eternity, where 'peace' represents a higher state than the corresponding polarities of light and darkness. Another influence is the Faust story, with Margarita (a far more dynamic figure than either the Master or Goethe's Gretchen) partly taking over Faust's traditional role, in that she is the one to make the pact with Woland, rejoicing in her role as witch. A major scene is 'Satan's Great Ball', a fictional representation of the *Walpurgisnacht* or Black Mass.

Bulgakov, however, reinterprets his sources— *Faust,* traditional demonology, the Bible, and many others—in his own way, creating an original and entertaining story which is not exhausted by interpretation. His devil is helpful to those who deserve it and is shown as necessary to God's purposes, to which he is not opposed. Bulgakov's Christ figure, a lonely 'philosopher', has only one disciple (Matthu Levi) although eventually Pontius Pilate, 'released' by Margarita from his torments after 2,000 years, is allowed to follow him as well.

Woland too has his disciples: Azazello, Koroviev, and a huge, comical tomcat called Behemoth. So has the Master, with Ivan Bezdomnyi. Like Faust, the Master is the creative artist, 'rivalling' God with the devil's help; like Yeshua he is profoundly aware of the spiritual plane, but is afraid, cowed by life's circumstances.

Endlessly fascinating, the novel indeed deserves to be considered one of the major works of 20th-century world literature.

Source: A. Colin Wright, "*The Master and Margarita,*" in *Reference Guide to World Literature,* second edition, edited by Lesley Henderson, St. James Press, 1995.

Donald Fanger

In the following excerpt, Fanger praises The Master and Margarita *as one of the major novels of the twentieth century, comparing Bulgakov to a number of other authors.*

Bulgakov's brilliant and moving extravaganza [*The Master and Margarita*] may well be one of the major novels of the Russian 20th century…. For the Western reader, the novelty of Bulgakov's genre can only be relative after Joyce and Beckett, Nabokov, Burroughs and Mailer; yet the novelty of his achievement is absolute—comparable perhaps most readily to that of Fellini's recent work in the cinema….

[This] is a city novel, the enormous cast of characters (largely literary and theatrical types) being united by consternation at the invasion of Moscow by the devil—who poses as a professor of black magic named Woland—and his three assistants, one of whom is a giant talking cat, a tireless prankster and expert pistol shot….

On its satirical level, the book treats the traditional Russian theme of vulgarity by laughing at it until the laughter itself becomes fatiguing, ambivalent and grotesque. But there is more: thematically, the novel is put together like a set of Chinese boxes. A third of the way through, in a mental hospital, the hack poet Ivan Bezdomny meets the Master, whose mysterious presence adds a new dimension to the narrative—the dimension in which art, love and religion have their being. Ivan has been taken, protesting, to the hospital; the Master, significantly, has voluntarily committed himself, rejecting the world. He is a middle-aged historian turned novelist who, after winning 100,000 rubles in the state lottery, devotes himself, an egoless Zhivago, to the twin miracles of love and art. Aided by the beautiful Margarita, whom he has met by chance in the street, he writes a novel about Pontius Pilate—which she declares to be her life—only to become the object of vicious critical attack in the press and, in a fit of depression, burns the precious manuscript....

What, then, becomes of the manuscript? The answer is the key to Bulgakov's work. Echoes of Gogol, Goethe, Dostoevsky, Hoffmann and a dozen others are not hard to find, but they are internal allusions; to account for the form of the book—and its formal significance within Soviet literature—one must mention Pirandello, and the Gide of The Counterfeiters. Bulgakov's characters, in the common Russian phrase, are out of different operas. The story of the disruption of Moscow by Woland and company is *opéra bouffe;* the story of the Master and Margarita is lyrical opera. But there is a third and epical opera, richly staged and in a style that contrasts sharply with the styles of the other two. The setting is Jerusalem, the main subject Pontius Pilate, the main action the crucifixion of Christ.

This narrative is threaded through the whole of the book, in a series of special chapters....

By merging [the question of what happened to the Master's novel] with Woland's account and Ivan's dream, Bulgakov seems to be suggesting that truth subsists, timeless and intact, available to men with sufficient intuition and freedom from conventional perception. The artist's uniqueness in particular lies in his ability to accept miracle—and this ability leads him, paradoxically, to a truth devoid of miracle, a purely human truth. I am simplifying what I take to be implicit, though complex and unclear, in Bulgakov's book, but there is a clue, easily overlooked, that would seem to support this interpretation. When the Master first appears to tell Ivan his story, Margarita is waiting impatiently for the promised final words about the fifth Procurator of Judea, reading out in a loud singsong random sentences that pleased her and saying that the novel was her life. Now, Bulgakov's own novel ends precisely with the phrase about the cruel Procurator of Judea, fifth in that office, the knight Pontius Pilate. Is the novel we read then, to be identified with the Master's?

The answer is clearly (but not simply) yes. The perspectives turn out to be reversible. Bulgakov's novel had appeared to include a piece at least of the Master's; now at the end it appears that the Master's novel has enlarged to include Bulgakov's. The baffling correspondences, in any event, make the case for mystery, and the heart of mystery is transfiguration—*quod erat demonstrandum.* Mar-

garita's faith in the Master's art is thus justified in ways which she could not have anticipated—and becomes a symbol of Bulgakov's similar faith in his own work. The Master's novel is Margarita's life in one sense as Bulgakov's novel is in another....

[*The Master and Margarita*] is a plea for spiritual life without dogmatic theology, for individual integrity based on an awareness of the irreducible mystery of human life. It bespeaks sympathy for the inevitably lonely and misunderstood artist; it opposes to Philistinism not good citizenship but renunciation.

Source: Donald Fanger, "Rehabilitated Experimentalist," in *Nation,* January 22, 1968, pp. 117-18.

Sources

Mikhail Bulgakov, *The Master and Margarita,* translated by Diana Burgin and Katherine Tiernan O'Connor, Vintage Books, 1995.

Donald Fanger, "Rehabilitation Experimentalist," in *The Nation,* January 22, 1968, pp. 117-18.

Edythe C. Haber, "The Mythic Structure of Bulgakov's 'The Master'," in *The Russia Review,* October, 1975, pp. 382-409.

Pierre S. Hart, *"The Master and Margarita* as Creative Process," in *Modern Fiction Studies,* Summer, 1973, pp. 169-78.

Vladimir Lakshin, "Mikhail Bulgakov's *The Master and Margarita,"* in *Twentieth-Century Russian Literary Criticism,* Yale University Press, 1975, pp. 247-83.

D. G. B. Piper, "An Approach to Bulgakov's *The Master and Margarita,"* in *Forum for Modern Language Studies,* Volume VII, No. 2 April, 1971, pp. 134-37.

Gleb Strave, *Soviet Russian Literature,* The University of Oklahoma Press, 1935.

Gleb Strave, "The Re-Emergence of Mikhail Bulgakov," in *The Russia Review,* July, 1968, pp. 338-43.

For Further Study

J. A. E. Curtis, *Manuscripts Don't Burn: Mikhail Bulgakov, a Life in Letters and Diaries,* Overlook Press, 1992.
    A noted Bulgakov scholar presents the history of Bulgakov's life in the author's own words, filling in gaps where appropriate but for the most part presenting long-lost personal papers.

Arnold McMillian, "The Devil of a Similarity: *The Satanic Verses* and *Master i Margarita,"* in *Bulgakov: The Novelist-Playwright,* edited by Leslie Milne, Harwood Academic Publishers, 1995, pp. 232-41.

Compares *The Satanic Verses* to *Master and Margarita.*

Nadine Natov, *Mikhail Bulgakov,* Twayne Publishers, 1985.
Examines the life of Mikhail Bulgakov.

Ellendea Proffer, *Bulgakov,* Ardis Press, 1984.
A comprehensive study of Bulgakov, his life, and his works available.

Joel C. Relihan, *Ancient Mennipean Satire,* Johns Hopkins University Press, 1993.
Discusses the history of Mennipean satire.

Kalpana Sahni, *A Mind in Ferment: Mikhail Bulgakov's Prose,* Humanities Press, Inc., 1986.
Analyzes Bulgakov's writing, including *The Master and Margarita.*

The Old Gringo

Carlos Fuentes
1985

The Old Gringo is one of Carlos Fuentes's best-known works. It is a complex novel that intertwines psychology, mythology, and political events to examine the culture of modern Mexico. At the core of the story is the disappearance of Ambrose Bierce, an American newspaperman and short-story writer. Bierce, who is most remembered for his brutally sardonic parody *The Devil's Dictionary* and the often-anthologized short story "An Occurrence at Owl Creek Bridge," left his job and home in 1913 at age seventy-one and disappeared, never to be heard from again. Speculation has held that he went to Mexico to join Pancho Villa in fighting the revolution, but there has never been conclusive evidence to support this. Bierce is the old gringo referred to in this novel's title. The story focuses on the relationships the character forms in Mexico with Harriet Winslow, a schoolteacher from Washington, DC, and with General Tomás Arroyo, leader of the revolutionary band that is on its way to meet up with Villa's army. The three form a triangle, exploring questions of love, respect, and sensuality in ways that highlight the differences between Mexican and American ways of thinking. A few years after the book was published, it was adapted into a motion picture starring Jane Fonda, Jimmy Smits, and Gregory Peck as the old gringo.

Author Biography

Carlos Fuentes is considered one of the pre-eminent voices in Mexican literature in the last

half of the twentieth century. He was born in Panama City, Panama, in 1928, and is the son of a Mexican diplomat. Throughout his childhood, he moved from one country to another, living in Chile, Argentina, and the United States. In his early years, he spent much time in Washington, DC, which is described vividly in *The Old Gringo.* He attended high school in Mexico City and received degrees from the National University of Mexico and the Institut des Hautes-Etudes in Geneva, Switzerland.

Fuentes's writing career developed after he already had a successful career in the diplomatic corps. Even after he was an internationally recognized novelist, he remained in politics, holding such positions as the chief of the Department of Cultural Relations of Mexico's Ministry of Foreign Affairs, and, from 1975 to 1977, as his country's ambassador to France. His development as a writer coincided with the emergence of a Latin American avante garde during the late 1950s and early 1960s. This movement also included Julio Cortazar and Nobel laureate Gabriel García Márquez.

Fuentes's fiction has developed throughout the years. His first novels, *The Good Conscience* and *Where the Air Is Clear,* reflect the author's concern with Mexican identity, using the magical realism techniques that came to be associated with him and his peers. Fuentes's prose is so richly luxurious that readers find it hard to distinguish between actions that are presented as reality and those that are the dreams or fantasies of the characters. The same features have appeared in Fuentes's later books, but over the years his novels have become less rooted in the imagination and increasingly more representative of reality. Fuentes has also written extensively about politics, exploring Mexico and Latin America's place in the world culture as well as his country's identity in relation to the United States. Since the publication of *The Old Gringo* in 1985, his nonfiction writings have vastly outnumbered his fictional works. Fuentes's most recent novel is 1995's *Diana, The Goddess Who Hunts Alone,* which was based on his affair in the 1960s with the actress Jean Seeberg.

Carlos Fuentes

mentioned until the final pages of the book. The novel takes place within the frame narrative—an old lady remembering. Bracketed by her act of memory, the story of Tomás Arroyo, Harriet Winslow, and the old gringo is pieced together in a dizzying series of multi-layered perspectives, voices, and times. It starts with the gringo's corpse being disinterred so it can be sent back to the United States. As they uncover his desiccated body, the diggers share their memories of him. He had come to Mexico to die, and no one ever found out who he was.

The Old Gringo Arrives

With the railway bridge burning behind him, the old gringo buys a horse at El Paso and rides off across the border into the deserts of Mexico. He is looking for Pancho Villa and the revolution. He is looking for death. The narrative shifts to the perspective of the revolutionaries, watching him approach. They immediately understand that he has a death wish. Introduced to the General, Tomás Arroyo, the gringo offers his services as a fighter, and is mocked until he proves his marksmanship by shooting a tossed peso through the center. Pedro— then a boy, later one of the voices that remembers the gringo as his body is dug up—is given the peso. Arroyo agrees to let the old gringo stay.

Plot Summary

The Old Lady Remembers

Though the protagonist of *The Old Gringo* is Ambrose Bierce, and the novel an extended meditation on his possible fate, Bierce's name is not

General Tomás Arroyo

The gringo rides with Arroyo in a lavish train carriage—plunder from the revolution. On their way to the Miranda Hacienda, Arroyo's current base and his past home, the general explains the nature of Mexican history and his right to reclaim the Mirandas' property. He carries with him a set of ancient papers, sealed by the King of Spain, that granted perpetual land rights to his people. As he explains, he cannot read, so the papers act as an icon that validates and represents his hereditary memory. As they arrive at the hacienda, it is burning to the ground.

Harriet Winslow

The hacienda is decorated with hanged bodies and jubilant crowds. The only thing left standing is the mirrored ballroom, and in a thematically vital moment, the peasants gaze at their reflections, realizing for the first time that they are whole, physical individuals. In the midst of the mayhem is Harriet Winslow—a prim, responsible spinster from Washington, DC, who had been hired by the Mirandas as a governess. Her Protestant work ethic, she says, compels her to stay and finish the job for which she has been paid—"improving" children. Through a series of flashbacks and conversations with the old gringo, we learn that she is genteelly impoverished—she and her mother have lived on a military pension after her father disappeared during the action in Cuba.

The First Campaign

The old gringo and Harriet have begun to enter each other's dreams. The troops ride off to fight the Federales, and the gringo leads the decoy charge across the plains. As the gringo rides out, he is lost in a version of one of his most famous stories, a tale of patricide in the U.S. Civil War, and this image of a son killing a father is reworked as a symbol of revolution throughout the novel. Hailed as a hero, he returns to the hacienda, which Harriet has been ordering the peasants to rebuild. Undermining her unwillingness to comprehend, a series of voices from the past and present explain the reasons for the revolution to her. She and the gringo drink together, and she learns his identity, but does not name him. She understands that he has rejected that name in favor of the generic term "gringo."

The Federales

During the second engagement, Arroyo's troops take many prisoners. Those who refuse to join the cause will be killed, and Arroyo demands that the old gringo be the one who shoots them. Arroyo says that a man as brave as the gringo is dangerous, and must prove his loyalty. The gringo deliberately misses the captain of the opposing troops, and Arroyo kills him instead. As they ride back, the gringo realizes that though he came here to die, he has rediscovered life, fear, and his need to write. Back at the hacienda, Harriet has spent the day exhorting the revolutionaries to establish a new society, and trying to teach them "Christian virtues." When a string of pearls goes missing, she dismisses the revolutionaries as larcenous. Later, Arroyo will show her that the necklace has been taken to the chapel and placed on a statue of the Virgin Mary. Harriet knows herself to be alien, and has uneasy dreams in which Mexican voices speak to her, and her father's death is revealed as something other than what she had said.

Tomás and Harriet

Arroyo and Harriet make love in the mirrored ballroom, and Harriet knows that she is experiencing life and love for the first time. As she said in the first pages of the novel, she will always hate Arroyo for showing her what she could never be. Afterwards, he explains his relationship to the hacienda. He grew up there as a servant. She tells the old gringo what happened, and says that she did it to protect the gringo from Arroyo. The gringo tells her he loves her, but it's too late—she and Arroyo are like his children to him now. Harriet reveals that her father didn't die at all, but stayed in Cuba to live with "a negress." Now that Harriet has experienced physical love, she understands her father better.

The Old Gringo Dies

Arroyo returns. The old gringo goes into the train car, and Arroyo follows him. Shots are fired, and the gringo stumbles out, Arroyo following and shooting. The gringo is holding Arroyo's talismanic papers—they are burning. The gringo dies facedown in the dirt, and the burnt words send echoes through the desert. Now another story begins. The narrative switches to a point later in time, where Pancho Villa is being interviewed by the U.S. press. They ask him about a U.S. citizen murdered by Arroyo and buried in the desert. Harriet Winslow has claimed that the old gringo is her father, and is demanding the return of his body.

The End—The Death of General Arroyo

The exhumation of the old gringo's body is juxtaposed with Arroyo's final conversation with

Harriet. While the corpse is dug up and shot in the front for the sake of military etiquette, we learn that Arroyo was a Miranda—the son of the hacienda owner. Shocked, Harriet accuses him of being merely a disgruntled heir. Back at the grave, Villa asks Arroyo to deliver the coup de grace to the gringo's body. As he does so, Villa's troops open fire. Arroyo dies shouting "Viva Villa!" The gringo's corpse is buried in Arlington Cemetery. In the final pages, Harriet says his name—Ambrose Bierce—and returns to the point at which the novel began: "Now she sits alone and remembers."

Characters

Doroteo Arango

See Pancho Villa

Tomás Arroyo

Tomás Arroyo is the general of the revolutionaries. The plan is supposed to be that Arroyo will lead his band of soldiers across the northern state of Mexico and meet up with the forces of Pancho Villa later to attack Mexico City. In reality, though, Arroyo is hesitant to leave his encampment at the Miranda hacienda. The Mirandas were a wealthy family, "owners of half the state of Chihuahua and parts of Durango and Coahuila as well." Arroyo is the illegitimate result of a union between the head of the Miranda family and one of the servants, and though he was raised on the estate, he has never been recognized as a relative. Now that the revolution has driven the Mirandas out, Arroyo seems to relish his position as master of the household, and he hesitates leading his troops' departure.

Arroyo has a box of documents in his possession that was given to him by another servant on the estate, Graciano, an old man who died soon after turning the papers over. Arroyo explains that the ancient documents grant the land to his people, by order of the King of Spain, but as Bierce points out, Arroyo is illiterate and does not really know what is written on the papers.

Arroyo develops an intimate relationship with Harriet on the night that the revolutionaries are celebrating a victory over the federal forces, a victory due in large part to Bierce's reckless bravery. In part, Arroyo wants her because she is someone to whom he can explain his people's struggle, as well as someone cultured and sophisticated who can recognize him for more than a greedy criminal. How-

ever, his actions toward Harriet are also motivated by jealousy for the admiration that she shows Bierce.

When Bierce destroys the documents toward which Arroyo had been so reverent, Arroyo kills him in frustration. Harriet, angry with him, shouts out, "You poor bastard. You are Tomás Miranda," humiliating him by implying that he has the same values as his land-owning father. After having the corpse of the old gringo executed "properly," Pancho Villa tricks Arroyo into standing near the gringo's body against the wall: "Give him the coup de grace," he tells Arroyo, "you know you're like a son to me. Do it well. We have to do everything aboveboard and according to the law. This time I don't want you to make me any mistakes." He then gives the firing squad the order to shoot Arroyo, and fires the final, lethal bullet into Arroyo himself.

Ambrose Bierce

Part of the story of the old gringo—his death— is based on the fate of William Benton, a British citizen who was beaten to death by Pancho Villa's men, and whose body was later dug up, formally executed, and sent home. The rest of the gringo's story is based on what is known about the last days of the writer Ambrose Bierce. Most of the details given about the character in the book fit with the facts of Bierce's life: he was a satirist, short-story writer, and journalist, who lived in San Francisco for much of his life and wrote for the newspaper chain owned by William Randolph Hearst. In 1913, at the age of seventy-one, Bierce left everything he had and went to Mexico to join Pancho Villa and his band. There is no historical record of what happened to Bierce after he crossed the border, and this is where the novel picks up his story.

A well-known cynic, the old gringo is tired of the hypocrisy of American life, and of life in general: he describes himself to Harriet Winslow as "[a] contemptible muckraking reporter at the service of a baron of the press as corrupt as any I denounce in his name. I attack the honor and dishonor of all men, without distinction. In my time, I was feared and hated." Having traveled to Mexico to die in the revolution, Bierce has the advantage of not fearing death in battle. This attitude earns him the admiration of the revolutionary band he joins after he rides straight into the enemy's gunfire.

The old gringo's relationship with the schoolteacher Harriet Winslow, however, gives him something for which to live. His relationship with

A scene from the 1989 film The Old Gringo, *starring Jimmy Smits as General Tomás Arroyo and Gregory Peck as Ambrose Bierce.*

Harriet is complex. To a certain degree they are lovers: the narrator explains that she gives him, not Arroyo, the right to dream about her. However, their relationship never becomes a physical one, like the relationship Harriet has with Arroyo. To both Harriet and Arroyo, Bierce is a father figure, replacing the fathers that rejected them both in childhood. The old gringo, however, is later killed by Arroyo after the gringo burns Arroyo's precious papers.

Frutos Garcia

Frutos Garcia is a colonel in the revolutionary army; he is one of the people responsible for digging up the old gringo's body in the opening scene. He appears periodically throughout the novel, expressing opinions about the actions of the three main characters and explaining Mexican customs to Harriet. At a certain point, Harriet recalls that it was Colonel Garcia who gave the order to kill his friend Mansalvo after Mansalvo was caught stealing gold coins from a derailed train car in Charco Blanco.

La Garduña

La Garduña joined the revolution from a house of prostitution in Durango. She plans to be buried in holy ground when she dies; her family is going to tell the priest that she is her virginal Aunt Josefa. Harriet saves La Garduña's two-year-old child from choking by sucking the phlegm out of her mouth and earns La Garduña's gratitude.

Graciano

An old man on the Miranda hacienda while Arroyo was growing up, Graciano was responsible for winding all of the clocks, and so was entrusted with keys to all of the rooms. When he took young Tomás Arroyo with him on his rounds one day, and let the boy carry his key ring, the master of the house severely admonished him. Graciano taught the boy about dignity and refusing charity. Before he died, he gave the box of ancient papers with the seal of the King of Spain to young Arroyo to watch over.

La Luna

La Luna is one of Arroyo's lovers. She met him when he hid in the basement of her house in a small town in Durango. Her husband was a moneylender, and when the revolutionaries came through town they took him out to the corral and shot him. Arroyo was trapped in the basement when Federal troops came chasing the revolutionaries—

Media Adaptations

- *The Old Gringo* was adapted for film and released by Columbia Pictures in 1989. The motion picture was directed by Luis Puenzo and starred Gregory Peck, Jane Fonda, and Jimmy Smits.

- The video titled *Carlos Fuentes* was released by Ediciones del Norte and Television Productions and Services Inc. in 1983.

- *Carlos Fuentes: Bridging the 20th and 21st Centuries,* another video, was released by Metropolitan State College in 1998.

- *Bill Moyers' A World of Ideas, Volume 8: Carlos Fuentes* was released on video by Films for the Humanities in 1994.

- *Carlos Fuentes: A Video* was released by Lannan Foundation in 1989.

- The video *Carlos Fuentes: A Man of Two Worlds* was released by A. J. Casciero in 1988.

- *Crossing Borders: The Journey of Carlos Fuentes* was released on video by Home Vision Video in 1989.

- The audio cassette *Faces, Mirrors, Masks: Twentieth Century Latin American Fiction* was released by National Public Radio in 1984.

- *Carlos Fuentes: An Interview in Spanish* was released on audio cassette by Ediciones del Norte in 1988.

- *Carlos Fuentes Reads from* Distant Relations was released on audio cassette by In Our Times Arts Media in 1986.

---

the moneylender had nailed boards over the basement door. La Luna pulled the boards up after the troops left, saving Arroyo's life.

Inocencio Mansalvo

Inocencio Mansalvo is a Mexican peasant who is traveling with the revolutionary band. He was a peasant field-worker before he joined them. At the end, after the death of Arroyo and Bierce, it is Mansalvo who is responsible for escorting Harriet back to the American border. There, she takes her first good look at him: "He was a thin man, with green eyes and hair black as an Oriental's; two deep clefts furrowed his cheeks, two marked the corners of his mouth, and two crossed his forehead, all in pairs, as if twin artisans had hurriedly hacked him out with a machete, the sooner to thrust him out in the world.... Until this minute, she had never *looked* at this man." In her last moments with Mansalvo, Harriet comes to understand the Mexican people better.

Old Gringo

See Ambrose Bierce

Pedrito

See Pedro

Pedro

Pedro is the eleven-year-old boy who first talks to Bierce and leads him into the camp of the revolutionaries. He gains respect for Bierce when the old man shoots a peso in the air, and Arroyo lets Pedro keep the peso as a souvenir. Pedro's last words to the old gringo's corpse as it is shipped across the border are, "The way you wanted it, old man. Pancho Villa himself gave you the coup de grace."

Pancho Villa

Pancho Villa was a real person in the Mexican revolution. In the book, he is presented as a showman who knows how to manipulate the American reporters who follow him. When the press asks about the person who was shot in the back by his people, Villa has the body of Bierce dug up out of his grave and shot again, from the front, so that the revolutionaries will not get a bad reputation. Then he has his soldiers kill Arroyo for

---

embarrassing the revolution with the shooting of the old gringo.

Raul Walsh

Raul Walsh is the photographer traveling with Pancho Villa. Walsh is one of the novel's actual historical personalities: he was one of the pioneers of silent movies.

Harriet Winslow

A thirty-one-year-old woman from Washington, DC, Harriet lived with her mother and was engaged to marry a corporate lobbyist, Mr. Delaney, who idealized her and would not have sex with her until after they married. Her father had left to fight in the army in Cuba when Harriet was sixteen, and she never saw him again: for years, Harriet and her mother lived on the pension the government sent them because it was thought her father was killed in the war. However, Harriet knew from a letter he had sent that he actually had moved in with another woman.

An older Harriet moves to Mexico to become the schoolteacher for the Miranda family. However, when she arrives, the wealthy family has abandoned their huge home and it has been taken over by Arroyo and his band of revolutionaries. Harriet decides to stay because she feels responsible for the Mirandas' house, having received a month's salary in advance from them. She also intends to teach American ways to the children of the revolutionaries. In Bierce, Harriet finds a substitute for the father who abandoned her, and in Arroyo, she finds the promise of romantic adventure, and also a sympathetic figure who understands what it is like to be rejected by one's father. Harriet explains to Bierce that her sexual relationship with Arroyo is only to keep him from taking the old gringo's life, although the satisfaction she feels during the experience is real and profound.

After Arroyo kills Bierce, Harriet returns to Washington and tells reporters that Arroyo shot down an officer in the American army. This news brings political pressure on the revolutionaries which results in Arroyo's death. Harriet also tells U.S. government officials that the old gringo was her father, who had actually survived the Cuban invasion and had come to Mexico to rescue her. Thus, Bierce is buried in her father's grave at Arlington National Cemetery. The novel begins and ends with Harriet as an old woman, sitting alone in her apartment in Washington, remembering the events of her trip to Mexico.

Themes

Identity

All three of the principal characters in this novel have mixed feelings of both love and hatred toward their fathers. When Ambrose Bierce, the old gringo, charges recklessly toward the guns of the Federal troops and is triumphant, his first words are "I have killed my father." He imagines himself, having grown older and increasingly bitter, as having "invented myself a new family, a family of my imagination, through my Club of Parenticides, the target of destruction." He has even lost his chance to identify with his own children because one son became an alcoholic and the other took his own life, mirroring Bierce's own cynical attitude.

Harriet Winslow's sense of herself is based on her idea of honor, which is both supported and offended by memories of her father. The official story that is accepted by the war department is that he died serving his country during the 1898 invasion of Cuba, and in his honor, the U.S. government has sent his pension checks to Harriet and her mother. Harriet's secret shame is that she knows her father did not die in battle but abandoned his family to live with a woman who, because she was a Negro, was considered to be from a lower social order in early twentieth-century America. In a way, Harriet's affair with the Mexican peasant Tomás Arroyo is based on her identification with her father.

Arroyo's father would not acknowledge his illegitimate son's existence: Arroyo remembers an incident from when he was nine years old, when a trusted servant allowed him to hold the ring of keys that opened all of the doors of the house, and the father shouted at the servant to "take those keys from the brat." Arroyo's strong sense of self comes from the mysterious documents that he cannot read, which he counts on to establish his legitimate claim to the land. This situation puts him in the odd position of being a Mexican revolutionary who counts on the authority of the King of Spain to give him a sense of self. For Arroyo's followers, taking over the Miranda estate is a victory of the poor over the rich, but for him it represents an ascension to his rightful place in the world, as heir to his father's possessions.

Culture Clash

Ambrose Bierce goes to Mexico to die in this novel, because to him Mexico is a strange and dangerous frontier. He knows that it is a place where he can die fighting, and not just wallow away in corruption as he would in America. "Let me imagine for you a future of power, force, oppression, pride, indifference," Bierce tells General Arroyo. When the general relates these words to the fate of the revolution, Bierce makes another statement that applies equally to the country and to the man: "The only way you will escape corruption is to die young."

The novel presents the Mexican revolution as a product of uncorrupted society, probably the only place on the continent where hope is earned fairly. The Mexican establishment, represented by landowners like Miranda and the Federal troops that guard them, is well on its way to moral impurity. The height of corruption is represented by wealthy Americans, such as William Randolph Hearst, Leland Stanford, and Harriet's fiancé, Delaney, who is false to his business associates and false to himself about their relationship. The lower-class Mexicans, however, do not see the differences between the two countries as being about corruption and violence. To them, the United States represents the kind of wealth for which they can dare to hope. As Harriet leaves the peasant Inocencio Mansalvo, the novel explains, "she knew that he would always keep an eye on the long northern border of Mexico, because for Mexicans the only reason for war was always the gringos." One culture is violent and the other refined, one corrupt and the other pure: "what mattered was to live with Mexico in spite of progress and democracy," Harriet thinks at the end, "that each of us carries his Mexico and his United States within him, a dark and bloody frontier we dare cross only at night: that's what the old gringo had said."

Death

Death is not feared by the characters in *The Old Gringo*. The Mexicans who encounter Bierce early in the novel acknowledge the fact that he came to Mexico to die. In the novel, the gringo quotes the real Ambrose Bierce in explaining why he welcomes death on his trip: "To be a gringo in Mexico, ah, that is euthanasia." Going to Mexico is Bierce's way of putting himself out of his misery, of freeing himself from the complications of American life that he knows are false. He gains the respect of Arroyo's men by riding straight into enemy gunfire because the possibility of death does not frighten him. Arroyo himself is quite fearless, fully aware that success in the revolution would eventually make him as corrupt as the heartless, passionless men he is fighting to overthrow, like President Diaz, who, he points out, was once a revolutionary like himself.

Topics for Further Study

- Read Ambrose Bierce's famous short story "An Occurrence at Owl Creek Bridge," which is mentioned in this novel. What does that story tell you about the character of Bierce as Carlos Fuentes portrays him here?

- Pancho Villa's reputation is still controversial: many people see him as a hero of the revolution, while many others see him as a criminal who manipulated the media. Research his life story and explain whether you think he did more good or harm for the development of Mexico.

- Many Americans are familiar with songs that were popular in 1914, such as "St. Louis Blues" or "Peg O' My Heart." Research some Mexican music that was popular at the time, and compare it to popular music of Mexico today.

- How has the relationship between the United States and Mexico changed since the passage of the North American Free Trade Agreement in 1994? Do you think it will it help or hinder Mexican economic development? Explain what you think one of the three main characters of this novel (Bierce, Harriet, or Arroyo) would say about it and why.

Perhaps the most stirring symbol of death in this story is the open grave at Arlington National Cemetery that is waiting for the body of Harriet Winslow's father. According to one story, Major Winslow was a war hero who died serving his country, but another story holds that he lived out his life in a cheap apartment with his mistress. Either way, the same open grave awaits him. In the end, the grave is filled with the body of Ambrose Bierce, an exalted resting place for someone who went to Mexico to die in anonymity. Bierce states throughout the story that he wants to leave a good-looking corpse: having been shot, exhumed and shot again, his corpse is not in good physical shape, but it is given a hallowed resting place, while the corpse of Tomás Arroyo is put out in the desert to be forgotten.

Style

Structure

The action in *The Old Gringo* is structured within a framing device; that is, the main part of the novel is "framed" by scenes of Harriet Winslow described in the present tense, sitting in her apartment in Washington and reflecting on events long past. Periodically throughout the course of the novel this present-tense Harriet is mentioned briefly, reminding readers that the story being told is not being narrated directly but is a summary of one character's memories. Many novels use a framing device to contain their story within a particular context, but *The Old Gringo* has an even more complex structure: it presents a frame within a frame. The first and last settings are in Harriet's apartment, but the second and second-to-last actions happen after the death of the gringo, with the exhuming of his body coming in chapter two, and the story of how Arroyo was executed—which should come right after the exhumation chronologically—coming in the last chapters. This makes Harriet's final days in Mexico a frame that is in itself framed by her sitting in her apartment.

Symbolism

Fuentes writes in a way that makes the most of the objects with which his characters interact, raising them to a symbolic level beyond their role in the telling of the story. One example of this is the way that Arroyo talks about the worm in the bottle of tequila in chapter five: "The worm eats some things and you eat others. But if you eat things like I was in El Paso … then the worm will attack you because you don't know him and he doesn't know you, Indiana General." Obviously, Arroyo's speech has greater significance than just a worm, which is drowned in liquor, and so readers are led to assume that his point about familiarity and different types of foods relates to Mexicans and Americans.

Fuentes's use of symbolism is not subtle, and should be clear even to those readers who do not approach novels as puzzles. The mirrors in the ballroom represent self-awareness: if this is not clear from Bierce's oft-repeated question, "Did you look at yourself in the mirrors when you entered the ballroom?," the point is hard to avoid when General Arroyo explains that he left the ballroom unburned so that his men could see themselves. Another object in the story that is too mysterious to have less-than-symbolic value is the packet of ancient documents that Arroyo handles with such tenderness. The reader is never told whether they actu-

ally give legitimacy to Arroyo's claim to land, though it is implied that they do not. The important thing is not their actual worth, but what they mean to Arroyo: they represent his social legitimacy, and he believes in the documents so much, even though he cannot read them, that he kills Bierce out of frustration when they are burned. One final obvious symbol is the "open grave" in Arlington National Cemetery: of course, the cemetery would not leave a hole in the ground waiting for someone who disappeared, but the phrasing of this item reminds readers of the chasm, the empty void, waiting for everyone at death.

Oedipus Complex

The father of psychoanalysis, Sigmund Freud, coined the term "Oedipus complex." It refers to the ancient Greek myth of Oedipus, who was sent away as an infant and, running into his birth father years later, did not recognize him and killed him, later marrying the man's wife—Oedipus's mother. In psychiatry, the Oedipus complex refers to the unconscious desire that makes a person wish to eliminate the parent of his or her own gender and replace the missing parent. In this story, Bierce is the acknowledged father figure, and the feelings that both Harriet Winslow and Tomás Arroyo have for him are nearly textbook examples of the psychoanalytic design. Arroyo sees himself in sexual competition with Bierce for Harriet's love, and it is for psychological reasons that he ends up shooting Bierce, who could otherwise have been an asset to his revolutionary cause. Harriet is attracted to Bierce as a father, as indicated in her near-panic regarding his relationship with his own daughter: after asking twice about his daughter during their most intimate conversation, she nearly screams out, "And your daughter?," as the narrator explains, "with a stubborn, controlled coldness." In the end, she adopts Bierce as her father and has him entombed under her father's name for all time.

In addition to their father-son-daughter triangle, each of the main characters has a desire to replace lost fathers. Even the old man, Bierce, thinks often about how much he is like his father: "The gringo thought how ironic it was that he the son was traveling the same road his father had followed in 1847." Arroyo never manages to move his troops out of the hacienda where his father—who had been violently chased away—ignored him throughout his childhood. And Harriet spends much time musing on the probable sex life of her father and his probable mistress.

Journalist Ambrose Bierce, who is believed to have disappeared in Mexico.

Historical Context

Before the Revolution

Long before the revolution, which serves as the context for this novel, Mexico was a country steeped in political turmoil. In the early sixteenth century, conquerors from Europe overcame the indigenous peoples who lived there, notably the Maya, Aztecs, Olmecs, and Toltecs. Spain ruled the country as a colony from 1535 to 1821, when revolutionary forces were able to gain independence, in part because Spain itself was occupied by France.

Independence was followed by a series of revolts, as the country struggled to establish a unified national identity. President Antonio Lopez de Santa Anna, elected in 1933, tried to bring the numerous provinces that made up the country under one central government, which raised the question of who controlled Texas, leading to the Mexican-American war of 1846 to 1848. America won the war, and, in turn, Texas, and the border between the two countries was established as the Rio Grande River (which the old gringo crosses at the beginning of the novel).

Compare & Contrast

- **1914:** The assassination of archduke Franz Ferdinand, heir to the Austrian throne, sets off a chain of political events that draws most of the countries of the world into the First World War.

  1985: Many of the countries that had formerly been in the Austro-Hungarian empire before the start of World War I are members of the Soviet Union.

  Today: After the Soviet Union's dissolution in 1991, some countries are struggling to cope with independence and establish their own identities.

- **1914:** Feminist Margaret Sanger is forced to leave the United States for England to avoid prosecution for printing her pamphlet, "Family Limitation," which dealt with the subject of birth control.

  1985: U.S. abortion rights, which were established by the Supreme Court in the 1973 decision in *Roe v. Wade,* constitute one of the most talked-about political issues. Candidates for national offices endure tremendous pressure to de-

  clare themselves supporters for either the "pro-life" or "pro-choice" sides of the debate.

  Today: Scientific advances, such as time-released implants and "morning-after" pills, have made birth control a commonplace concern in the United States.

- **1914:** President Victoriano Huerta of Mexico, who had come to power by having his predecessor murdered, is forced to leave the country for exile. One of the decisive elements in his leaving was a military occupation of Mexico's main seaport, Veracruz, by the U.S. Atlantic fleet.

  1985: The administration of President Ronald Reagan, opposed to the leftist government of Nicaragua, arranges illegal arms shipments to guerrilla revolutionaries.

  Today: The U.S. government's intervention into the affairs of other countries is severely limited by its own laws and by United Nations supervision.

After the war, the balance of power in Mexico shifted several times. Estate owners, many of whom did not live near their lands but only reaped the benefits of them, struggled against the peasantry who worked the lands. Uprisings broke out at different times, in different parts of the country. The liberal Benito Pablo Juarez led the fight for a new constitution in 1858, which included such benefits for the citizenry as freedom of speech and the right to vote for all males. He was elected president in 1861, but he incurred the wrath of Spain, France, and Great Britain by refusing to pay interest on loans from them: those countries sent invading forces to Mexico, and as a result, Juarez and his cabinet fled into exile for several years, during which a conservative government favoring the land owners took power. Juarez returned to power in 1865.

In 1877, Porfirio Diaz was elected president, a post that he held, with one brief interruption, until he was ousted by the revolution in 1910. Diaz had been a soldier during the political turmoil and ran unsuccessfully for the presidency twice, in 1867 and 1871. He led military uprisings after each defeat. During Diaz's tenure, Mexico became an active participant in the world economy, but the peasantry were discontent, left unable to share in the wealth that was generated.

The Mexican Revolution: 1910-1920

In 1910, the Republic of Mexico was actually run as a dictatorship under President Diaz's control. Diaz had brought stability to the country and helped build its economy early in his long presidency, but he and his followers became increasingly totalitarian as the years went by. In order to

build up the country's infrastructure and to provide government contracts for his friends, Diaz had to raise money by turning over more and more land to foreign interests, taking it out of the control of poor Mexicans. In 1910, Francisco I. Madero led a successful revolution against Diaz, sending him into exile, and in 1911 Madero was elected president.

Madero, however, did not deliver the country back to the people, and he became unpopular by allowing corruption to fester. In 1913, one of his generals, Victoriano Huerta, a former Diaz supporter, led a counterrevolution, took control of the government, and had Madero killed. Although Madero had been unpopular, the people deeply resented his murder. Several branches of revolution broke out across the country. The governor of Coahuila, Venustiano Carranza, led one; Emaliano Zapata led the revolution in the southern state of Morelos; and in Chihuahua, the revolution was led by Francisco ("Pancho") Villa, who appears as a character in *The Old Gringo*. The American press portrayed the media-savvy Villa as a modern-day Robin Hood.

In July of 1914, with his own people and the international community opposing him, Huerta resigned and left the country. The capital was taken over by followers of Carranza. Soon, Carranza was at odds with the other leaders of the revolution; in 1915, his forces fought against Villa's, and by 1916, Villa had lost any official claim on the government and was leading a band of outlaws in making raids across the Texas border. President Woodrow Wilson sent U.S. troops under the command of General John "Blackjack" Pershing into Mexico to capture Villa. A new constitution in 1917 established Carranza as the country's president, but he was ousted and murdered in 1920, replaced by a former ally, General Alvaro Obregon.

Critical Overview

The Old Gringo has remained one of Carlos Fuentes's most widely read novels, in part because of the star-studded Hollywood movie adaptation that followed shortly after its publication. Many of the early reviews of the book expressed admiration for the story and for Fuentes as an author and as a writer. At the same time, though, many reviewers held back their praise, unsure about the novel's cool style. Earl Shorris's review in *The New York Times Review of Books* showed deep respect for the is-

sues that Fuentes touches upon in *The Old Gringo:* "It is the work of an integrated personality, the artist who contains and illuminates all of the times and cultures of a nation." Shorris had difficulty finding fault. "The only serious flaw for me is that the book may be too concise. I wished for details to more fully realize the characters, to limit them less by their symbolic roles."

Gloria Norris mentioned in her review of *The Old Gringo* in *America* that "Fuentes uses the approach of the poet rather than the novelist." She went on to praise his rendering of Washington, DC, over his descriptions of the Mexican settings, adding that, "surprisingly, his Mexican figures are more like statuesque figures in a mural, while Bierce and Harriet are given more depth." Neither of Norris's comments are negative, but they both touch upon the most frequent causes of discomfort among reviewers: that this novel about Mexico is too distant from both its characters and its country.

John Seabrook, writing for *The Nation,* said early in his review that "*The Old Gringo* is a fascinating novel to reflect on, though at times a dense, bewildering one to read." Like Norris, Seabrook was more impressed with Fuentes's handling of his American characters, feeling that the Mexican characters functioned as symbols, as explanations for the mind of modern Mexico, rather than as people. Thomas R. Edwards picked up on the same idea in his review. After explaining the symbolic positions of Arroyo, Winslow, and Bierce, he pointed out that their symbolic functions were sometimes too simplistic, that the author was trying too hard to convey ideas about sociology. "This triptych of characters risks being too obvious a device to show the distance between Mexican and American minds," Edwards wrote in *The New York Review of Books,* "but Fuentes sometimes forces the point he wants to make about them on the reader—there are a few too many remarks like 'each of us carries his Mexico and his United States within him' or 'be us and still be yourself' or 'I want to learn to live with Mexico. I don't want to save it.'"

Michiko Kakutani took an opposite view, explaining in *The New York Times* that Fuentes's cultural and racial myths actually bring life to the love triangle the novel is centered around, making it "as inevitable as it is real." One of the least forgiving reviews was written by noted novelist, poet, and playwright John Updike, for *The New Yorker.* Updike expressed admiration for what Fuentes was trying to achieve, but even more pressing for him was his regret that, in his opinion, *The Old Gringo* is "a very stilted effort, static and wordy, a series of tableaux costumed in fustian and tinted a kind of sepia I had not thought commercially available since the passing of Stephen Vincent Benet." While other reviewers appreciated the novel's enchanting, heavily stylized tone, Updike could not accept the falseness of what is presented: he could not suspend his disbelief long enough to find much to admire in the book. "Fuentes is certainly intelligent," he concludes, "but his novel lacks intelligence in the sense of a speaking mind responsively interacting with recognizable particulars. Its dreamlike and betranced gaze, its brittle grotesquerie do not feel intrinsic or natural: its surrealism has not been earned by any concentration on the real."

Criticism

Tabitha McIntosh-Byrd

McIntosh-Byrd is a doctoral candidate at the University of Pennsylvania. In the following essay she looks at Carlos Fuentes's The Old Gringo *as a critique of the Western-European traditions of philosophy and narrative.*

The Old Gringo is a novel about borders—about the boundaries that demarcate countries, separate minds and cultures, and mark the edges and turning points of linear history. It is also a novel about the falsity of those borders—presenting a structural and textual collapse of distinctive chronologies, viewpoints, identities, and narratives. Carlos Fuentes's book takes on form among the multitudes of discrete stories and histories. It generates itself at the points of impact between nineteenth-century U.S. novels and Mexican peasant oral history, between journalism and fiction, playing with the harmonies that are produced from the simultaneous speech of disparate voices.

Even on its most basic level, that of plot, *The Old Gringo* is a hybrid text, combining fact—Ambrose Bierce—and fiction—a version of what may have happened to him—in its choice of subject matter. Just as in the work of the Hearst journalists, from whose ranks Bierce had himself recently escaped, fictional invention is allied to historical fact, and the personal agendas of writers, storytellers, and historians are brought to the forefront. In creating the alliance between fact and history; in providing border crossings for the frontier that seems to separate them; Fuentes makes a powerful case

for the contingent, poetic, and socially constructed nature of life, history, and writing. In doing so, he offers a powerful alternative to the tradition of Western-European literature, and a critique of the assumptions that underlie its structures.

Perhaps the single most powerful recurring image in Fuentes's novel is that of "the self" reflected in a mirror. If the ramifications of this image are traced, the critique that Fuentes is offering becomes much easier to understand, as do the structural purposes of his complex narrative style. Within the Western psychoanalytic tradition associated with the French philosopher Lacan, this mirror image has pivotal importance in understanding how human personalities are constructed. According to Lacanian theory, the turning point in human development comes when a child sees his or her reflection in a mirror and understands for the first time that the person reflected is not a stranger, but him- or herself. In other words, the child first objectifies and then accepts herself as an individual—a physical and social entity separate and removed from others, who are also understood to be individuals. With this separation comes a full awareness of personal identity, need and desire—the Ego, which literally translates as, "I am." To put it another way, the Western tradition understands human development as the successful imposition of a series of boundaries, especially the mental boundary that creates a line of demarcation between "self" and "other." As the Old Gringo says, the greatest and final frontier is not that which marks the border between the United States and Mexico, but the "frontier" within our own minds.

Fuentes's novel can be read as an extended examination of this way of thinking, an attack on Western theories of individuality and the kind of reality they construct. Nowhere is this clearer than in his reworking of Lacan's mirror theory. Western individualism of the kind outlined above is exemplified in the characters of the Old Gringo and Harriet Winslow. Before they begin to lose their coherence and blend into one another, realizing that "each of us exists only in the imagination of another," they reach out to each other by sharing their life stories. This formalized exchange of individual, narrative accounts of themselves is predicated on very specific understandings of history and personality from which certain cultures and peoples are excluded. Inocencio Mansalvo's voice interjects itself into their conversation to point this out, in a narrative moment typical of the novel's methods. "They live a life we don't understand," he says:

Do they want to know more about our lives? Well, they will have to make them up, because we're still nothing and nobody.

The Americans' gradual realization that their identities are neither so contained nor so separated as they have been taught to believe is figured throughout the novel by the image of the mirror. The question that haunts Harriet throughout the text is the Gringo's insistent need to know if she looked at her reflection. Turning up again and again throughout the book in fragments and ellipses, the Gringo asks her, "Harriet, when we entered the ballroom, did you look at yourself in the mirror?" When she makes love to Tomás Arroyo in the ballroom and embraces the continuum of life and love for the first time, Harriet is surrounded by mirrors at which she doesn't look. In effect, she must deny the validity of Western individualism in order to live. The fact that she cannot stay is linked to her awareness of the roomful of reflections that surround her—this will be only a temporary respite from isolation. In the first and last lines of the novel she is returned to her "bordered" self—"Now she sits alone and remembers."

As Inocencio Mansalvo's words, quoted above, make clear, the Mexican peasant voices of *The Old Gringo* express no sense of personal individuality—not as it is understood by the Gringo and Harriet. The North-American sense of self-contained identity that makes life-story telling possible is absent. Prior to the revolution, the peasants are caught in an unstriated and perpetual "pre-mirror" stage. As illustrated by their astonishment in front of the mirrors, the revolution represents a psychological revolution that is as great as the simultaneous socio-political one. Arroyo explains the peasants' reaction to their reflections—silence and subsequent jubilation—to Harriet in terms that are strongly resonant of Lacanian theory:

> They had never seen their whole bodies before. They didn't know their bodies were more than a piece of their imagination or a broken reflection in a river. Now they know.

The identities of the oppressed and the colonized are here shown to be hybrid self-compositions of history, imagination, and partial viewing—just like the novel itself. Resistance and self-determination conversely require an initial understanding of the powers and limitations of people as individuals. Arroyo's fatal weakness and his greatest source of power are the same thing—his possession of a sense of self as clearly defined as that of the gringos. In this way, it is his need for *personal* revenge on his father, Miranda, that leads

him to stay too long at the hacienda and then to murder Bierce when his documented rights to the hacienda are destroyed. Both of these acts of proprietary self-interest doom him—placing him in opposition to the Villa-established revolutionary principle of movement. As he says, he is fighting because he understands injustice as it relates to *him,* because he understands himself as an individual who can resist. It is:

> All because one day I discovered the ballroom of mirrors and I discovered I had a face and a body. I could see myself. Tomás Arroyo.

All of the leaders of the revolution, especially Pancho Villa, need to establish themselves as individuals in this way in order to revolt. In so doing they begin to mimic the cheap political expediency of the "yellow journalists," as the symbiotic association of Villa with the Hearst press corps makes clear. What Fuentes's novel as a textual whole presents is an attempt to "freeze" the process of movement into one narrative moment—a blend of perspectives, realities, and times that the Gringo understands as part of the process of revolution— the principle of revolution, as it were. Caught between an unknowing "pre-mirror" stage, and a self-interested individualist stage, the novel's technique of assemblage allows the characters to be always "becoming"—always moving restlessly forwards, backwards, and sideways in time, with narrative history as a principle of movement instead of a delimiting act of definition.

The expression of this idea can be seen clearly in Fuentes's literalization and use of the metaphor "to burn one's bridges." Bierce, the product of a linear culture, leaves the El Paso railway bridge burning behind him when he crosses into Mexico. He has come here to die and there is no turning back. When Harriet returns to Washington, she too leaves behind a crossing in flames. For both of them, return across chronological or developmental boundaries is impossible. Significantly, the Gringo crosses his burning bridge with a copy of *Don Quixote* in his suitcase. A powerful satire of quest narratives, this text serves as a commentary on the Western culture and personalities of Bierce and Winslow. As a book that is often credited with the creation of the modern novel, the presence of *Don Quixote* signals that the nature and history of Western narrative is being called into question. At the same time, the text's major theme, that heroic quests are a symptom of madness, subtly undercuts the Gringo's heroism and his stated mission.

As all of the Mexican characters realize, Bierce's bravery in battle, his fearlessness, is the product of a kind of narrative derangement. His obsession with the end of the story, the fact that he has "come to Mexico to die" by offering his services to Villa's troops, is as much a deluded product of Romance literature as Don Quixote's "tilting at windmills." The bridge burning behind the Gringo thus becomes symptomatic of his inability to understand life as anything other than a linear narrative with a beginning, middle, and end. Only later, when it's too late for him to stop what he has set in motion, will he start to realize that his obsession with his "ending" has prevented him from living. His Calvinist sense of Predestination—the fated nature of individual lives—is contrasted with the populist Catholicism of the Mexican lower classes. Where Calvinism offers no alternative to the prescribed ending, stating that individual souls are bound either for heaven or hell and can do nothing to alter their fate, Catholicism offers an endless process of change and redemption through confession and acts of contrition.

In this way, the Gringo's quest—his initial belief that his life will be ended in Mexico and that his fate is decided by a determined set of actions—is linked to his Calvinism, and both are tied to his role as an author. His trained, conscious mind turns his shifting dreams into "an elaborate plot peopled with details, structures, and incidents." The power of the story he has invented for himself, the power of storytelling, and the impact of his religious childhood make him unable to embrace the multitude of possibilities that revolutionary Mexican culture offers. As Harriet says, in their way of thinking they have crippled themselves by folding "death into life"—allowing "the end" to take over the story. When Arroyo arrives at the Mirandas' hacienda, the buildings are burning *before* him. In effect, "the end" precedes him. His bridges are burnt before he comes to them, undermining normative narrative conventions of cause and effect, just as the secret of his motivation comes out only in the final pages of the novel.

By positioning it this way, Fuentes allows us to question the logic of traditional novels, the conventions of the nineteenth-century bildungsroman that demand an orderly, logical progression of character development and motivation. In dissolving the first and greatest boundary of the Western-European tradition, the boundary between ourselves and others, *The Old Gringo* dissolves all of the philosophical and social boundaries that govern literary representation. In so doing, the novel calls into question the abiding myths of Western culture itself. They too are "figments of someone else's imagination," and the only real border is in the mind—"a dark and bloody frontier we dare cross only at night."

Source: Tabitha McIntosh-Byrd, in an essay for *Novels for Students,* Gale, 2000.

Kenneth E. Hall

In the following excerpt, Hall examines Fuentes's handling of the female perspective in The Old Gringo *and illustrates parallels between the novel and "elegiac Western" films "which are characterized by a quality of lament for the passing of the hero, and by extension, of the heroic age of the American West."*

The opening of *The Old Gringo* (1985), by Carlos Fuentes, sets in place the chief organizing principle of the novel, the narrated memories of Harriet Winslow, an unmarried schoolteacher from Washington, D.C., who, the reader discovers, once came to Mexico to instruct the children of the rich *hacendado* Miranda family and there became embroiled in the Revolution. Her contacts with the *uillista* general Tomas Arroyo and the Old Gringo polarize her experiences between an apparent infatuation with Arroyo and an attempt to substitute the Gringo for her lost father. In her memories of the incidents which led her to place the body of the Old Gringo in her father's empty tomb in Arlington, an elegiac tone—one of mourning for lost experience as well as a questioning of the value of that experience—is clearly discernible. Like the heroine of a classic Western film such as *The Virginian* (1929), Harriet, as the "Eastern schoolmarm" character type, confronts the heroic Westerner, in this case "doubled" into the figures of the Old Gringo and Arroyo, and in the process re-examines her own preconceptions about civilization. She becomes conscious of her marginalization from the society around her, as an intellectual woman who questions her past and present. One concern of the discussion here will be the importance of the female perspective in the elegiac Western narrative: rather than a mere foil or pretext for the hero's actions, the female character serves a critical function in clarifying the degree and nature of the hero's loss of relevance in present-day society. The heroic figures themselves, the Old Gringo and Arroyo, can lay strong claim to kinship to the heroes (and villains) of Western film and fiction. Equally larger-than-life and ironically viewed, the Old Gringo has the superhuman marks-manship and courage of classic Western heroes such as the Ethan Edwards of John Wayne or the Shane of Alan Ladd. But he carries about him a cynicism and world-weariness which, though mir-roring his real-life source in Ambrose Bierce, yet recall the elegiac musings of the aging gunfighters J. B. Books of *The Shootist,* Steven Judd of *Ride the High Country,* and Pike Bishop of *The Wild Bunch.*

The term "elegiac Westerns" has been applied by popular culture and film critics such as Michael Marsden and John Cawelti to Western films which are characterized by a quality of lament for the passing of the hero, and by extension, of the heroic age of the American West. These Westerns share the central element of a frequently poetic treatment, anywhere on a scale from ironic to tragic, of the myths and heroes of the Old West as cultural icons whose time has passed, usually with some indica-tion of the influence of technology on their pass-ing. They share the quality of nostalgia found in the literary Western as typified by Zane Grey and Owen Wister. The motif of the gunfighter cog-nizant that "his days are over," as the titular hero of *Shane* is told, is frequent, as is the tendency for many of the heroes of these films to be aging. The element of the now vulnerable hero, an erstwhile near-superman with a six-shooter, may be tragic, as in *Ride the High Country* or *The Man Who Shot Liberty Valance,* or it may be savagely, even mor-bidly ironic, as in *The Wild Bunch.* But in all cases, the once invincible hero of dime-novel Westerns has become a complex representation of a member of an age which has passed and whose violent so-lution to once simple situations has now become either outmoded, as in *The Man Who Shot Liberty Valance,* or merely criminal, as in *The Wild Bunch:* Pike and Bishop could at an earlier stage of their development (or decline) have been Stephen Judd and his friend Gil.

Much as the aging, sick, and outdated hero of *The Shootist* (1976), played with understated sen-sitivity and power by John Wayne, wishes to die with self-respect, so too does the Old Gringo wish to die in a moment and manner chosen by him. Both characters shun their reputations. The Old Gringo avoids mentioning his name or revealing significant autobiographical data, such as his asso-ciation with William Randolph Hearst, to anyone but Harriet. Similarly, Books, the aging shootist, is reluctant, at least at first, for the truth about his identity to get around the small town to which he

has come, as he does not wish to give fame-hun-gry guns a chance to prove themselves. He even forces a Ned Buntline-like newspaperman to leave his boarding house at gunpoint after hearing his publicity scheme.

Important to *The Shootist* is the discrepancy between the myths or legends which have formed around Books and in general around the figure of the gunfighter, as opposed to the historical reality of such figures as well as, in this case, the personal biographical facts about J. B. Books. In *The Old Gringo,* a similar conflict between historical fact, legend, and falsification of history is established, since the character of the Gringo is based on the historical figure Ambrose Bierce: their "biogra-phies." as Joaquin Roy has shown, tend to intersect in several ways, the chief of which is their journey to Mexico with the intention of dying or disap-pearing.

The picture given of Books and of the Gringo is well-removed from "history." The Fuentes nar-rative, filtered through the recollections of Winslow, presents a picture of the Gringo, who only slowly comes to be revealed as Ambrose Bierce; his anonymity is maintained during the ear-lier part of the novel, until he begins to reveal him-self to Harriet. The Gringo character, presented in legendary proportions (as in the battle scenes or the early incident of heroic "proof," in which the Gringo demonstrates his marksmanship), is in part derived from legends about Bierce, especially the tale about his disappearance in Mexico. As Joe Nickell has suggested in his "Biography: The Dis-appearance of Ambrose Bierce" [*Literary Investi-gation: Texts, Sources, and "Factual" Substructs of Literature and Interpretation,* UMI Press, 1987] this tale may have been fabricated by Bierce to cover his withdrawal from society, perhaps to live in Colorado until his expected death, probably from suicide. In any case, the Gringo, or Bierce, becomes as much a part of Winslow's perspectivist recol-lections as does the portrait of the Mexican Revo-lution which emerges from such mythmaking works as *Vámanos con Pancho Villa!* [*Let's Go with Pancho Villa!*] (1949), by Rafael Luis Muñoz.

Similarly, J. B. Books is placed into parallel in an interesting manner with the filmic image, that is, the mythic or fictionalized image, of John Wayne. The film opens with clips from some of Wayne's earlier movies, all showing him in heroic or dynamic sequences. Here the effect is not, as Marsden and Nachbar have stated [in "The Mod-ern Popular Western: Radio, Television, Film and

What Do I Read Next?

- *Don Quixote,* the book that the old gringo says he intends to read some time, was written by Spanish novelist Miguel de Cervantes Saavedra and published in 1615. It is the classic story of idealism and of standing up to unbeatable odds.

- *The Complete Short Stories of Ambrose Bierce* is available in a 1985 paperback, edited by Ernest Jerome Hopkins. Among the most notable pieces referred to in Fuentes's novel are "A Horseman in the Sky," about a Union soldier who kills his father, a member of the Confederacy; and Bierce's most famous work, "An Occurrence at Owl Creek Bridge."

- Mexico's most honored contemporary poet was the late Nobel Prize laureate Octavio Paz. The most comprehensive volume of his work is 1987's *The Collected Poems of Octavio Paz 1957-1987.* This volume contains both English and Spanish versions of his poems.

- Most of Fuentes's novels received critical acclaim. Readers interested in his work may want to contrast the intellectualism of this book with the vigor of his first published novel, *Where the Air Is Clear* (1958).

- Carlos Fuentes is almost as well known for his essays as for his fiction. He frequently explores the character of his homeland. His 1996 collection *A New Time for Mexico* revisits themes ex-

plored in his book from twenty-five years earlier called *Tiempo mexicano* ("Mexican Time").

- Gabriel García Márquez is a Nobel Prize laureate from Columbia and one of Fuentes's contemporaries. His book *One Hundred Years of Solitude* (1969) is recognized as his masterpiece, and stylistically it resembles the work that Fuentes was doing in the 1960s. Like Fuentes, though, Marquez's style evolved, and his 1985 novel *Love in the Time of Cholera* is closer in style and tone to *The Old Gringo.*

- One of the most striking and influential novels by a Latin-American writer of Fuentes's generation was Argentine author Julio Cortazar's 1963 book *Hopscotch,* about international intrigue. Though the book's subject matter is not much like that of *The Old Gringo,* Cortazar's style is similar, and this book is widely praised as one of the best of the century.

- Reviewers have pointed out that British writer Malcolm Lowrey's 1947 novel *Under the Volcano* is one of the best examples of a non-Mexican capturing the country's essence. It is the fevered, nightmarish story of an English counsel's spiritual collapse.

- E. L. Doctorow's 1975 novel *Ragtime* shows the life of three American families in New York at roughly the same time as this story takes place. At the end of Doctorow's book, one of the characters runs away to join Pancho Villa and his bandits.

Print," in A Literary History of The American West, Texas Christian University Press, 1987], to "suggest that Books and Wayne are identical," but rather on the one hand (1) to show the character of Books as derived from a corpus of myth; (2) to imply that the public image of Books as heroic may be as much of a fiction as was the image of Wayne as a frontier hero; and (3) to emphasize the elegiac core of the film, since the clips lead us to remember the past deeds of Books.

The sense of loss and marginalization felt by the Old Gringo is mirrored in Harriet Winslow, who has never, at least until the unfolding of the narrative here, become reconciled with her father's abandonment of her and her rather domineering mother and has in fact collaborated or acquiesced in fictionalizing the desertion into a heroic death for her father at San Juan Hill. Harriet, like the Gringo, and like Ned Buntline or any other popularizer of the Western hero, is engaged in "mythmaking," that is, lying and the falsification of history.

Or perhaps, one might say, in rationalization, since Harriet would rather eschew mention of her fixated concentration on her father, an undeserving object of such attention. The Electra motif here is similar to the less clearly expressed, but nonetheless central complex dramatized in *True Grit,* novel and film (1969), in which Mattie Ross (Kim Darby), a stubborn adolescent girl, enlists an aging marshal. Rooster Cogburn (John Wayne), to help her bring to justice the murderer of her father. She is inordinately determined to punish the killer, driving Rooster and a Texas Ranger who accompanies them sometimes to exasperation. One of the more interesting aspects of *True Grit,* clearer in the Charles Portis novel than in the more emotionally diffuse Henry Hathaway film, is the gradual transference of Mattie's affection from her father—who soon drops into the background of the narrative, becoming only a motivating plot element—to Rooster, whose "cussedness," at first repellent to the arch Mattie, gradually becomes endearing to her. Harriet Winslow, on the other hand, does not see the Old Gringo as repellent so much as she recoils from his cynicism; nevertheless, as does Mattie with Cogburn, she becomes fascinated with the Gringo and literally supplants her father with him. An interesting sidelight on *The Old Gringo* and *True Grit* is their narrative technique, as both are told in flashback (on much differing levels of sophistication, however) by their female protagonists.

The female perspective is often quite important to the elegiac Western. Just as Mattie criticizes and ironizes the action around her (especially in the novel), so Marian (Jean Arthur) in *Shane* provides a reasonable perspective on the rivalry between ranchers and homesteaders. It is she who perceives the truth about Shane's vulnerability and about his incapability of fitting into present-day society and who points up the absurdity of the hard-driving male solutions to range problems. Similarly, in *High Noon* (Fred Zinnemann, 1952) Amy (Grace Kelly) acts as a balance to her husband's sense of perhaps misplaced duty by questioning the morality of violence as a solution. Such female characters are not merely stereotypical "voices of civilization" who try to restrain male depredations: more than this, they serve as surrogates for a critical perspective on the essential absurdity of the hero myth. Thus, Laurie (Vera Miles), in *The Searchers,* generally treats Edwards and Pauley in a rather indulgent manner, as if they were irresponsible adolescents who refuse to let the past alone and who thus jeopardize their present.

One should not make the error of seeing the elegiac elements in *The Old Gringo* as positively nostalgic (as, perhaps, one could see *Ride the High Country*); if nostalgia is an element here, its core of loss is emphasized. Or it is shown as nostalgia without basis, as in the fond stories propagated by Harriet about her father. As *The Man Who Shot Liberty Valance* reveals the lie behind the fame of Ranse Stoddard and calls into question as well the myth of the Western hero (who, as Robert Ray has noted [in *A Certain Tendency of the Hollywood Cinema, 1930-1980,* Princeton University Press, 1985], is shown to be the other side of the outlaw coin), so too *The Old Gringo* questions and criticizes the revolutionary past of Mexico—Frutos Garcia dies a comfortable, scarcely heroic death in his house in Mexico City in 1964—while still not sparing the Porfiriato. Arroyo's fantasy about the Indians' land title is deflated by the criticisms of the Gringo concerning the lack of worth of the written word and by the inability of Arroyo to read, and is finally exploded by the Gringo's burning of the papers. The legalistic appeal by Arroyo is shown to be just as fruitless, one might suggest, as has been the sad appeal to treaties by the wronged original inhabitants of North America. The heroic myths about the U.S. Civil War are questioned by references to the ironic stories of Bierce about that war, in which its "glory" is deflated. Thus, *The Old Gringo* demonstrates its affinity less to autumnal elegies like *Ride the High Country* or to pastoral hymns like *Shane* than to more corrosive and demystificatory critiques such as *The Wild Bunch, Little Big Man* (1970), and, occupying a middle ground, *The Man Who Shot Liberty Valance.* Like Pike Bishop in *The Wild Bunch,* the Old Gringo wishes to emend his compromised past with heroic action—however futile—and as do Pike, Tom Doniphon, and J. B. Books, he dies an outsider, only finding an ironic re-integration into the community after his death.

Source: Kenneth E. Hall, "*The Old Gringo* and the Elegiac Western," in *University of Dayton Review,* Vol. 23, No. 2, Spring, 1995, pp. 137-47.

Joseph Chrzanowski

In the following essay, Chrzanowski analyzes Fuentes's use of the "double" or "doppelgänger" literary device as well as the theme of patricide in El gringo viejo *(The Old Gringo), and asserts that the author's employment of both "has imbued his novel with remarkable structural coherence and has touched upon human issues which transcend history, geography, and culture."*

In reading Carlos Fuentes's *El gringo viejo,* (1985; *The Old Gringo*) one is struck by the masterful way in which he has conjoined fictionalized biography, dramatic action, and ideological concerns. It also becomes evident that it is a novel in which character psychology has a dominant thematic and structural role. Central to the psychological component are father-child conflict and the concomitant motif of patricide. This study examines Fuentes's use of literary doubling in his treatment of these themes and in his portrayal of the novel's three principal characters.

The "gringo viejo," of course, is a fictionalized Ambrose Bierce—the controversial American journalist and short-story writer of the late nineteenth and early twentieth centuries. In 1913, at the age of seventy-one, the historical Bierce set out for revolutionary Mexico, aware of the likelihood of dying there. Although he did maintain some written correspondence with a friend in the United States, it was not long before Bierce disappeared without a trace. In *Gringo viejo,* Fuentes presents an imaginary account of the writer's experience in Mexico.

A second main character is Harriet Winslow, a young American who meets the "gringo viejo" in Mexico and whose recollections of him form the novel's organizational frame. In contrast to the disillusioned and cynical old man, she is portrayed as naive and idealistic. Contracted to tutor the grandchildren of a wealthy landowner, Harriet is present at his estate when it is over-run by a group of revolutionaries who have allowed the "gringo viejo" to join them.

The third major character is Tomás Arroyo, the leader of a band of insurgents and the illegitimate son of the owner of the estate where Harriet is employed. Also an idealist, Arroyo embodies the spirit of protest that has motivated the revolutionaries to rebel against a system and a history of oppression and injustice.

Readers familiar with Ambrose Bierce's life and works will recognize the biographical accuracy and inaccuracy of various situations, statements, and persons presented in the novel. They will also readily perceive Fuentes's allusions to some of Bierce's short stories. The most important of these references are to "A Horseman in the Sky," a story whose title is evoked in the following descriptive passage. "At this early hour the mountains seem to

await the horsemen in every ravine, as if they were in truth horsemen of the sky."

Set in the United States Civil War, "A Horseman in the Sky" begins with a description of a young Federal soldier who has fallen asleep while on guard duty. A flashback provides information about him. The only son of a wealthy Virginia couple, the boy had unexpectedly decided to join a Union regiment that was passing through his hometown. Acquiescing to his son's betrayal of the State of Virginia, the father stoically advises him: "Well, go, sir, and whatever may occur do what you conceive to be your duty." [*The Complete Short Stories of Ambrose Bierce,* compiled by Ernest Jerome Hopkins, Doubleday, 1970]. The reader is then returned to the war scene to witness the young man awakening to the sight of a horseman on a distant ridge that borders a cliff. A grey uniform indicates that he is a Confederate scout who has discovered the presence of the Union force. For several moments, the young man anguishes over whether to kill his enemy. Recalling his father's parting counsel, he finally takes aim at the rebel's horse and fires. The scene immediately shifts to a Federal officer who observes "a man on horseback riding down into the valley through the air" [*The Complete Short Stories of Ambrose Bierce*]—obviously the Confederate soldier upon whom the sentry has fired. Another shift in scene occurs as a Federal sergeant approaches the young guard and asks if he discharged his weapon. The boy acknowledges that he shot at a horse and observed it fall off the cliff. Responding to the sergeant's inquiry as to whether anyone was on the horse, the young guard hesitatingly states: "Yes … my father" [*The Complete Short Stories of Ambrose Bierce*].

A common treatment of decomposition or fragmentation in literature involves the creation of several characters, all of whom represent a single concept or attitude. This technique has been referred to as "doubling by multiplication." Borrowing the motifs of parental conflict and patricide from "A Horseman in the Sky," Fuentes employs doubling by multiplication to link his ostensibly dissimilar characters and to introduce the presence of psychological conflict in the novel. In doing so, he alters and simultaneously commingles historical fact and the fictional antecedent of Bierce's story. The "gringo viejo," who, like Bierce himself, had been a Union soldier, is described as experiencing a dream in which his father served in the Confederate army. Without elucidating the nature of the father-son conflict, Fuentes introduces the patricidal motif by attributing the following thought to the "gringo viejo": "He wanted what he had dreamed of—the revolutionary drama of son against father."

Juxtaposed with this dream is a dramatic battle scene in which the "gringo viejo" single-handedly attacks a group of Mexican Federal soldiers. Reinforcing the dream's psychological symbolism, the narrator clarifies that the American's inordinate act of bravery was in reality the externalization of unconscious rage directed at his father's memory: "it was toward this horseman, flashing his anger from the mountaintop, the gringo rode, not toward them, their machine gun lost now." The thematic and structural importance of the "gringo viejo"'s dream and its patricidal implication is apparent in Fuentes's allusion to it on five other occasions in the novel. The conflictual nature of the paternal relationship is also underscored by the following description of the "gringo viejo"'s father: "a hell-fire Calvinist who also loved Byron, and who one day feared his son would try to kill him as he slept."

Harriet Winslow's father, like the "gringo viejo"'s, was a military man. Because of him, she too bears the burden of psychological scarring. The narrator singles out two circumstances that have had lasting impact on her: (1) her discovery of her father's licentiousness and infidelity with a black servant and; (2) his abandonment of his wife and daughter in order to live in Cuba with another woman. Recurring references to her father attest to Harriet's psychological struggle in dealing with her loss of him on both the ideal and real levels. Paralleling the characterization of the "gringo viejo," her latent patricidal inclination is also expressed symbolically. When Harriet and her mother are overwhelmed by the economic necessity occasioned by the father's disappearance, they declare him dead in order to obtain a government pension. Harriet's lexical choice in referring to the incident has obvious psychological significance in the context of the patricidal theme: "We killed him, my mother and I, in order to live."

Arroyo's father, while not in the military, was also an authoritarian figure by virtue of the absolute power emanating from his socioeconomic standing Like Harriet's father, he was licentious. In fact, Arroyo is a produce of his abuse of power and position to sexually exploit a family servant. Arroyo's hatred for his father stems from that circumstance, as well as from the latter's refusal to recognize him legally. Even as a child, he would have readily killed his father if given the opportunity: "I spied him as he was drinking and fornicating, not know-

ing his son was watching him, waiting for the moment to kill him." The intensity of his hatred only increased over the years, as evidenced in his virulent declaration to Harriet toward the end of the novel.

As these references indicate, the patricidal motif is developed in *Gringo viejo* in a concrete, insistent manner. A further examination of textual evidence points to the presence of a psychological paradigm that is less obvious, yet fully consistent with the motif as employed by Fuentes in his portrayal of all three characters. In his recent study, *The Son-Father Relationship from Infancy to Manhood: An Intergenerational Inquiry,* Peter Blos underscores the Freudian notion that usurpation of the father's position can be interpreted as an unconscious attempt to "annihilate" him. Interestingly, Blos uses the term "patricide" figuratively to describe such usurpation. Reflecting this phenomenon, there is a moment or circumstance in *Gringo viejo* in which each protagonist duplicates some important trait of his or her father and, moreover, is identified with him at that moment. (Consistent with the basic premise of psychological criticism that textual evidence can point to unconscious as well as conscious motivation in characterization, none of the protagonists in *Gringo viejo* perceives the psychological significance of these details.) In the "gringo viejo"'s case, it is repeating his father's trip to Mexico more than fifty years earlier and distinguishing himself as a brave soldier: "The gringo thought how ironic it was that he the son was travelling the same road his father had followed in 1847." For Harriet, it is her rejection of her cultural and religious values through surrender to her most primitive sexual desires with Arroyo. In doing so, she consciously identifies with her father: "Don't you know that with Arroyo I could be like my father, free and sensual." In Arroyo's case, it is returning to the Miranda ranch and acting with the same arrogance and violence as did his father. The parallel between the two is underscored by Harriet's admonition of Arroyo: "you provoked yourself to prove to yourself who you are. Your name isn't Arroyo, like your mother's; your name is Miranda, after your father." If it is true, as Jean-Michel Rabaté asserts, that "a father is not a 'problem' but a nexus of unresolved enigmas, all founded on the mysterious efficacy of a Name," then Arroyo's choice of surname and Harriet's comment have particular significance in the patricidal context. Similarly, it should be remembered that the "gringo viejo" does not reveal his family name to anyone except Harriet while in Mexico. These details substantiate that, even on the unconscious level, the patricidal wish is central to Fuentes's depiction of all three characters.

As the plot of *Gringo viejo* unfolds, the paternal issue has profound effect on the manner in which the three protagonists relate and respond to one another and to events. In this regard, the "gringo viejo"'s role as father figure for Harriet and Arroyo merits special discussion. Their disposition toward relating to him as such is consistent with their figurative orphanhood: "General Tomás Arroyo, who, like her, had no father, both were dead or unaware, or what is the same as dead, both unaware of their children, Harriet and Tomas." The "gringo viejo"'s role as surrogate father is compatible with his advanced age, position of respect among the revolutionaries, and the paternal affection and behavior he demonstrates toward both characters on several occasions.

As a father figure, the "gringo viejo" facilitates Arroyo's and Harriet's resolution of the psychological conflict they experience as a consequence of their individual relationships with their fathers. It is well to clarify, however, that neither father has any active contact with his offspring in the historical present recreated in the novel, and that Harriet's and Arroyo's fatherlessness, as is often the case in literature, "is not so much the absence of relationship as a relationship to an absence."

In relating to the "gringo viejo" as a substitute father, Harriet and Arroyo each embody one pole of a basic endopsychic conflict: the love-hate relationship of child to father. Consequently, Fuentes has drawn his characters by also utilizing the literary device of doubling by division: "the splitting up of a recognizable, unified psychological entity into separate, complementary, distinguishable parts represented by seemingly autonomous characters."

Arroyo, of course, represents the negative pole of the paradigm. The principal issues in his psychic struggle are lack of identity stemming from his father's refusal to acknowledge him, the hatred it engenders and the need to express that hatred and to avenge his father's treatment of him. (On a conscious level, the latter need is one factor which explains Arroyo's participation in the Revolution.) These issues play a decisive role in the culminating action of the novel: Arroyo's murder of the "gringo viejo." As the plot unfolds, a number of references are made to papers which Arroyo is safeguarding on behalf of his corevolutionaries. The papers date from the colonial period and constitute a legal claim to the land that Arroyo's family had

appropriated. They also represent a de facto affirmation of personal and social identity: "The papers are the only proof we have that these lands are ours. They are the testament of our ancestors. Without the papers, we're like orphans."

The "gringo viejo"'s eventual burning of the papers therefore acquires profound psychological significance. On the one hand, the papers are symbolic of Arroyo's identity and claim to legitimacy within the social system. On the other, the man who destroys them is, at this point in the novel, a substitute for his father. Consequently, the childhood trauma of the son being reduced to a nonperson is symbolically recreated and relived on an unconscious level. The destruction of the papers provokes the hatred underlying Arroyo's previously mentioned patricidal wish and is externalized and expressed through his murder of the "gringo viejo." The psychological dynamics of the act mirror the drama of the Revolution itself: the socially and economically disenfranchised striking out against the fatherland that has denied them their patrimony and identity. Hence, with consummate artistry, Fuentes intertwines the personal drama of his characters with the historical drama of the Revolution.

Harriet's relationship with the "gringo viejo" as a hypostatic father is developed more fully in the novel, and in a way which suggests her awareness of it. The exclusively positive nature of the relationship corroborates Fuentes's presentation of her and Arroyo as a "composite character." Having been deprived of a father from the age of sixteen, Harriet finds in the "gringo viejo" a person with whom she can openly share her innermost thoughts and feelings; an object of tenderness, concern, and love; and, ultimately, a literal replacement for her absent father. Her awareness of what the "gringo viejo" signifies for her is first alluded to in a conversation in which he states: "I thought a lot about you last night. You were very real in my thoughts. I think I even dreamed about you. I felt as close to you as a ...." Before he completes the thought, Harriet interrupts by asking: "As a father?" In a subsequent exchange, she explicitly and dramatically communicates to him that he indeed represents a father to her: "Don't you know ... that in you I have a father? Don't you know that?" Similarly, when Harriet senses Arroyo's determination to kill the "gringo viejo," she begs him not to the kill "the only father either of them had known."

It is Arroyo's murder of the "gringo viejo," however, that provides Harriet a lasting solution for her psychological conflict. Having returned to the United States after his death, Harriet publicly states that she had gone to Mexico in order to visit her father, and that she had witnessed *his* assassination at the hands of Arroyo: "She says she saw him shoot her daddy dead." Some time later, when his body is disinterred, she identifies it as her father's and has it buried in the family plot next to her deceased mother. Her words to the lifeless body of the "gringo viejo" confirm the presence of unconscious as well as conscious psychological motivation in the novel: "An empty grave is waiting for you in a military cemetery, Papa." The abandoned child has fulfilled her need to have and love a father.

In sum, *Gringo viejo* is a multifaceted novel that deftly combines dramatic action, historical verisimilitude, and ideological statement. It is also a work of profound psychological dimension and implication. In utilizing the literary device of the double and developing the patricidal motif which he borrowed from Ambrose Bierce, Carlos Fuentes has imbued his novel with remarkable structural coherence and has touched upon human issues which transcend history, geography, and culture.

Source: Joseph Chrzanowski, "Patricide and the Double in Carlos Fuentes's *Gringo viejo*," in *International Fiction Review,* Vol. 16, No. 1, Winter, 1989, pp. 11-16.

Sources

Thomas R. Edwards, "Pathos and Power," in *The New York Review of Books,* December 19, 1985.

Carlos Fuentes, *The Old Gringo,* translated by Margaret Sayers Peden, Farrar, Straus, 1985.

Michiko Kakutani, "The Old Gringo," in *The New York Times,* October 23, 1985, p. C21.

Gloria Norris, "The Old Gringo," in *America,* May 17, 1986, p. 416.

John Seabrook, "One of the Missing," in *The Nation,* January 18, 1986.

Earl Shorris, "To Write, to Fight, to Die," in *The New York Times Review of Books,* October 27, 1985, p. 1.

John Updike, "Latin Strategies," in *The New Yorker,* February 24, 1986, p. 98.

For Further Study

Alfonzo Gonzalez, *Carlos Fuentes: Life, Work and Criticism,* York Press, 1987.
    Written soon after the publication of *The Old Gringo,* this book is by an eminent researcher in Third-World studies.

Lanin Guyrko, "Twentieth-Century Literature," in *Mexican Literature: A History,* edited by David William Foster, University of Texas Press, 1994.
    Contains sections about various genres in different eras of Mexican history. A good reference source for putting Fuentes in an historical context.

Kristine Ibsen, *Author, Text and Reader in the Novels of Carlos Fuentes,* Peter Lang Publishing, 1996.
    Ibsen, the editor of a book about female authors in Mexico in the 1980s and 1990s, gives a detailed analysis of Fuentes's works and the ways in which they involve readers more than traditional fiction.

John Rutherford, *Mexican Society during the Revolution: A Literary Approach,* Oxford University Press, 1971.
    Examines the revolution and its leaders as they are depicted in literature written at the time.

Cynthia Steele, *Politics, Gender and the Mexican Novel, 1968-1989: Beyond the Pyramids,* University of Texas Press, 1992.
    Steele's work covers Fuentes's most active time as a novelist, and reviews the social attitudes that affected him and his contemporaries.

Maarten Van Delden, *Carlos Fuentes, Mexico and Modernity,* Vanderbilt University Press, 1997.
    Van Delden explores the schism between Fuentes's differing visions of Mexico.

Raymond Leslie Williams, *The Writings of Carlos Fuentes,* University of Texas Press, 1996.
    Focused principally on Fuentes's major novel *Terra Nostra,* this study examines the treatment of Mexican culture throughout the author's works.

On the Road

Jack Kerouac

1957

The literary movement known as the Beat Generation exploded into American consciousness with two books in the late 1950s. The first, *Howl and Other Poems* by Allen Ginsberg, was published in 1956. The book achieved notoriety when poet and bookstore owner Lawrence Ferlinghetti went to trial for selling it in San Francisco. The second book had an even more profound cultural effect when it was published. Jack Kerouac's *On the Road,* published in 1957, was viewed as nothing less than a manifesto for the Beat Generation.

On the Road is the story of two young men, Sal Paradise and Dean Moriarty, who travel frantically back and forth across the American continent seeking thrills. The novel is actually a thinly veiled account of Kerouac's own life in the late 1940s, when he fell under the spell of a charismatic drifter named Neal Cassady (represented by Moriarty in the novel). Every episode in the novel was inspired by real-life events. The book, which would probably be considered rather tame today, shocked readers in 1957 with its depiction of drug use and promiscuous sex. Many critics attacked the work as evidence of the increasing immorality of American youth. Other critics saw it as a groundbreaking work of originality. American readers, fascinated with the bohemian lifestyle of the characters, turned the novel into a best-seller.

The Beat literary movement was short-lived. Most of the work Kerouac published in the 1960s had been written during his creative peak in the 1950s. Beat literature retains its popularity decades

later because the writers of the Beat Generation must ultimately be judged by their work, not by any real or imagined influence on popular culture. Allen Ginsberg's poetry is still revered. The nightmarish visions of William Burroughs continue to influence post-Modern writers. Finally, Kerouac's *On the Road* is still a campus favorite, and continues to draw scholarly criticism.

Author Biography

Kerouac was born on March 22, 1922, in Lowell, Massachusetts. His parents, Leo and Gabrielle, were French-Canadian immigrants. "Ti Jean" (Little Jean), as he was known as a child, lived in the shadow of his sickly, angelic brother, Gerard. Gerard was barely ten years old when he died of rheumatic fever, and his death had such a profound effect on Kerouac that he later wrote a novel about his brother entitled *Visions of Gerard*. Kerouac had a lively imagination as a boy. He scripted his own "movies" and acted them out in front of the family Victrola and later illustrated them in his own comic books. He created a complex baseball game with an ordinary deck of playing cards that he would play throughout his life. In the early years of his life, Kerouac was a solitary child with few friends. However, he soon grew into a handsome, athletic young man.

Kerouac excelled at football in high school and attracted the attention of coaches from several major colleges. An athletic scholarship to Columbia brought him to New York City. He dropped out of Columbia when World War II started and enlisted in the navy, but he was quickly discharged for "indifferent character" because he refused to follow orders. He ended up enlisting in the merchant marine and worked on a ship that crossed the treacherous, submarine-infested waters of the North Atlantic. After the war, he returned to New York City to write and study. It was during this period that he met other bohemians, such as Allen Ginsberg and William Burroughs. It was at this time that the literary phenomenon known as the Beat Generation was born.

The Beat Generation espoused freedom, individuality, and experimentation in living and in literature. Kerouac discovered what he believed was an icon for this generation when he met Neal Cassady, a wild, magnetic, young drifter from Denver, in 1946. Although Kerouac recognized that Cassady was a manipulative pseudo-intellectual, he ad-

Jack Kerouac

mired Cassady's zest for life and hunger for learning. Cassady ultimately inspired the character of Dean Moriarty in *On the Road*. Kerouac spent the next several years traveling across the country, both with and without Cassady.

In 1950, Kerouac's first novel, *The Town and the City,* was released to lukewarm reviews. The indifferent reaction to his first novel, although discouraging, did not prevent him from writing. Although his second (and most popular) novel, *On the Road,* was not published until 1957, the fifties were his most creative years. He wrote several novels in furious spurts between his first two published books. For example, he wrote *The Subterraneans* in a thirty-six hour, amphetamine-fueled marathon. The success of *On the Road* enabled him to publish, in quick succession, several of the books he had already written. Buddhism influenced some of his later work in much the same way jazz did. Unfortunately, the pressures of fame and the debilitating effects of his alcoholism affected his work in the 1960s. Although he was sometimes brilliantly lucid and clever during interviews for print and television in the late sixties, his drunken behavior often made him a sad caricature of himself. Complications from alcoholism led to his death in St. Petersburg, Florida, on October 21, 1969, at the age of forty-seven.

Plot Summary

Part One

In part one of *On the Road,* Sal Paradise, the narrator, is a young writer living with his aunt in Paterson, New Jersey, during the late 1940s. Sal is writing his first novel as he recovers from a failed marriage. In the opening of part one, Sal describes how he comes to meet a charismatic, exciting drifter and con artist from Denver named Dean Moriarty. Sal's curiosity is first piqued when he reads the interesting, lively letters that Dean wrote during his stay in a New Mexico reformatory to their mutual friend Chad King. By the time Dean arrives in New York City with his child-bride, Marylou, Sal is anxious to meet him. Sal describes Dean as "trim, thin-hipped, blue-eyed, with a real Oklahoma accent—a sideburned hero of the snowy West." Soon after the two young men meet, Dean leaves Marylou when she files a false police report after an argument. Dean goes to Sal to learn how to write. Although Sal recognizes that Dean is a con artist, he is inspired by him; he cannot resist Dean's zest for life and his endless search for "kicks" (defined here as almost any powerful sensory experience). Sal introduces Dean to his friend, poet Carlo Marx, and Dean and Carlo become inseparable. However, Dean and many of Sal's other friends head west to Denver in the spring of 1947. Carlo soon follows.

Sal saves up enough money to go west himself in July of 1947. He plans to ship out on an around-the-world liner from San Francisco with his friend Remi Boncoeur after a short visit in Denver. Sal's first attempt to travel west ends in frustration when he realizes he has chosen the wrong route. To make up for lost time, Sal spends half his money on buses to get to Joliet, Illinois. Once there, he begins to hitchhike, and he meets a variety of eccentric people on his way to Denver. He looks up his friend Chad King when he reaches Denver, and he learns that his clique of university friends has somewhat ostracized Dean and Carlo because of their weird, unpredictable behavior. Sal stays with Roland Major, a young journalist, in an apartment owned by the traveling parents of another friend. When Sal finally finds Dean and Carlo, he finds out that Dean plans to divorce Marylou (with the understanding that they will still see each other) in order to marry a woman named Camille. Sal's stay in Denver is a frenetic, ten-day whirlwind of revelry culminating in a wild trip to the Central City Opera. He finally leaves for San Francisco, realizing that he has spent very little time with Dean.

In San Francisco, Sal lives with Remi Boncoeur and Lee Ann, Remi's shrewish girlfriend. Remi, claiming to know a Hollywood director, asks Sal to write a screenplay. Sal becomes bored after finishing the screenplay and takes a job with Remi guarding the temporary barracks for overseas construction workers waiting to ship out to Okinawa. Sal spends more time drinking with the workers than he does guarding the barracks, and Remi makes a practice of burglarizing the cafeteria. After Remi is unsuccessful in selling Sal's script, the relationship between the three roommates deteriorates. Remi and Lee Ann end up having a ferocious fight and, afterwards, as one last favor, Remi asks Sal and Lee Ann to be on their best behavior when they take Remi's visiting stepfather out for dinner. The dinner turns into a disaster when Sal gets drunk and sees Roland Major, who is also drunk, and invites him to their table. Sal regretfully leaves the shack in the morning while Remi and Lee Ann are asleep.

Sal heads for Los Angeles after he leaves Remi's place. He meets a pretty Mexican girl named Terry on a bus and begins a bittersweet, two-week love affair. They plan to hitchhike together back to New York City after saving enough money. After unsuccessful attempts to get jobs in Los Angeles and Bakersfield, they go to Terry's hometown of Sabinal to work in the cotton fields. Terry is reunited with her young son. Sal becomes frustrated because he cannot earn enough in the fields to support Terry and her son. Terry tells him she will join him later in New York. He leaves, knowing he will never see her again. Tired and depressed, he returns to New York City, and ends up in Times Square. He panhandles enough change for bus fare to get to his aunt's home in Paterson. He arrives to find that he just missed Dean, who is on his way to San Francisco, by two days.

Part Two

Sal doesn't see Dean for over a year. He finishes his book and goes back to school. He visits his brother, Rocco, in Virginia on Christmas in 1948. Dean shows up in Virginia in a car with his ex-wife, Marylou, and his friend Ed Dunkel. Dean has left Camille behind in San Francisco with a baby daughter. Although Ed's new wife, Galatea, had originally joined them on the trip, they abandoned her in Tucson because they found her troublesome. Sal and Dean move furniture from Virginia to Paterson, and return to Virginia to pick up Sal's aunt, all in thirty hours. They discover that Galatea Dunkel has appeared in New Orleans at

Old Bull Lee's home. Old Bull Lee, an odd mentor to Sal, Carlo, and Dean, is not pleased and wants the men to come and get Galatea. After a brief stay in New York, Sal goes on the road again with Dean, Ed, and Marylou to retrieve Galatea in New Orleans and, from there, go on to San Francisco.

In New Orleans, the group stays at the home of Old Bull Lee and his wife, Jane. Lee is a middle-aged, well-educated, peculiar drug addict who tells bizarre, humorous stories and has strange, yet interesting, theories. Ed is reunited with Galatea and they decide to stay in New Orleans when Sal, Dean, and Marylou leave. The travelers drive west across Texas, New Mexico, and Arizona, turn north in California, and finally reach San Francisco. Dean, in a hurry to get to Camille, deserts Sal and Marylou on O'Farrell Street. They have no money. For a few days, the two wander around the city, bumming money and sleeping in cheap hotels. Marylou grows weary of Sal and abandons him. Sal is depressed and miserable when Dean finally finds him again. They spend the rest of Sal's stay in San Francisco hopping from one jazz club to the next. Sal begins to get uncomfortable staying with Camille and Dean, so he returns home after receiving his GI check.

Part Three

Sal goes back on the road in the spring of 1949. He returns to Denver, but none of his old friends live there anymore. He works in a fruit market for awhile, but he soon becomes lonely. A rich girl he knows gives him one hundred dollars to travel to France; instead, Sal takes it and spends eleven dollars to get to San Francisco to see Dean again. Sal finds Dean in an awful state; when he isn't arguing with Camille, he is stalking Marylou around the city. He has broken his thumb in a fight with Marylou and his overall health is not good. Camille throws both men out of the house. They decide to go back to New York, and perhaps Rome and Paris after that. On the way to New York, they stop in Denver. Sal gets angry with Dean in a diner, but apologizes to him. They stay with Okie Frankie, a single mother that Sal knows, and Dean causes trouble when he tries to seduce the neighbor's daughter. Later that night, Dean steals several cars, one of them belonging to a local police detective. Sal and Dean flee Denver in fear the next morning. They make their way back east, with stops in Chicago and Detroit. Dean finds yet another girlfriend named Inez in New York City.

Part Four

Sal sells his book in the spring of 1950, and goes on the road again. At first, Dean stays behind with the pregnant Inez, but he later catches up with Sal in Denver. Dean easily convinces Sal to drive to Mexico City with him so Dean can get a Mexican divorce from Camille. They are joined by another friend, Stan Shephard. Driving through Mexico, they stop at a bordello and sleep in the jungle. Once they arrive in Mexico City, Sal gets sick with dysentery. Dean abandons him there to return to his women in the United States. Sal is hurt by Dean's behavior, but he understands the "impossible complexity" of Dean's life.

Part Five

Part Five is the epilogue of the novel. Sal returns to New York City and falls in love with a woman named Laura. They plan to move to San Francisco to live near Dean and Camille. Dean arrives in New York almost six weeks early, and Sal and Laura have no money to move. Dean turns back for San Francisco almost immediately. Sal senses that Dean is close to the edge of a breakdown when he sees him for the last time in a melancholy scene on the winter streets of New York City.

Characters

Remi Boncoeur

Remi Boncoeur is a friend of Sal's living in San Francisco with his nagging girlfriend, Lee Ann. Sal takes his first trip west, planning to ship out and work on a luxury liner with Remi. Instead, after writing a screenplay, Sal and Remi get a job guarding the temporary barracks of construction workers waiting to go overseas. The relationship between Remi, Lee Ann, and Sal begins to deteriorate when Remi is unable to sell Sal's screenplay. As one last favor, Remi asks Sal and Lee Ann to accompany him out to dinner, a futile attempt to impress his visiting stepfather. Sal gets drunk and runs into his friend Roland Major, who is also drunk, and they embarrass Remi. Sal, feeling terribly guilty, sneaks away from Remi's shack the next morning. At the end of the novel, Remi visits New York City and is with Sal and Laura the last time that Sal sees Dean.

Ed Dunkel

Ed Dunkel is one of Dean's friends. He works with Dean on the railroad in San Francisco. When

Kerouac based his character Dan Moriarty on Beat Generation writer Neal Cassady, shown here.

they are both laid off, they decide to travel east to see Sal. Ed marries his girlfriend Galatea so she will accompany them and foot the bill. They abandon her in Tucson because she spends all her money staying in hotels. In New York City, Ed tells Sal that he feels like a ghost walking through Times Square. Ed discovers that Galatea is in New Orleans at Old Bull Lee's home and he travels with Sal, Dean, and Marylou to get her. Ed and Galatea live in New Orleans before moving to San Francisco and finally Denver. The last time Sal sees

him in the novel, Ed plans to take sociology classes.

Galatea Dunkel

Galatea is Ed Dunkel's wife. Ed marries her in order to get her to finance the trip he and Dean are taking across the country to visit Sal. They desert her in Tucson when she runs out of money. She travels on to New Orleans and stays at the home of Old Bull Lee until Ed comes to get her. She and Ed decide to live in New Orleans. Later, they move on to San Francisco, where she tells Sal that Dean will one day go on one of his road trips and never come back. She ends up living with Ed in Denver.

Frankie

Frankie is the single mother with whom Sal and Dean stay for a brief period when they stop in Denver on their way to New York City. Frankie is a coal-truck driver with four children who likes to drink like a man. Dean tries to convince her to buy a car, but she refuses, angering him. He also creates a scene when he tries to seduce her neighbor's daughter. The men are later forced to flee her home when Dean steals a local detective's car.

Chad King

Sal is introduced to Chad King through the letters Dean writes to Chad from a New Mexico reformatory. Sal describes Chad as being a "Nietzschean anthropologist." Chad is the first friend Sal calls on when he reaches Denver for the first time.

Laura

In the epilogue, Sal meets Laura when he calls to one of his friends from the street outside her apartment building. Laura invites him up to her room for hot chocolate and they fall in love. Sal and Laura agree to move to San Francisco in order to live near Dean and Camille, but Dean arrives in New York City six weeks earlier than planned. Nobody has the money to actually make the move at that time, and Dean is forced to turn around and go back alone. Laura and Sal are on a date with Remi Boncoeur and his girlfriend the last time they see Dean. Dean is in pathetic condition and Laura pities him. Sal tells her that Dean will be all right.

Jane Lee

Jane Lee is the Benzedrine-addicted wife of Old Bull Lee. They have two children. Benzedrine and polio have affected her health. She hallucinates regularly. Sal describes the odd relationship between Jane and Old Bull Lee:

> Something curiously unsympathetic and cold between them was really a form of humor by which they communicated their own set of subtle vibrations. Love is all; Jane was never more than ten feet away from Bull and never missed a word he said, and he spoke in a very low voice, too.

Old Bull Lee

Old Bull Lee is the strange, well-educated, drug-addicted mentor to Sal, Dean, and Carlo Marx. He has traveled all over the country and the world. He cherishes individual freedom and despises bureaucracy and the police. He is living in New Orleans with his wife, Jane, and their two children when Sal, Dean, Marylou, and Ed Dunkel arrive to retrieve Ed's wife, Galatea. He is glad to see Sal when the group arrives at his home, and he shares his odd theories and beliefs with him. He is curious as to what motivates Sal and Dean to travel back and forth across the country, but neither can give him an answer. He confides in Sal that he thinks Dean is going mad and he invites Sal to stay with him in New Orleans instead of continuing west. However, Sal leaves with Dean and Marylou when his GI check arrives. Sal later writes letters to him from Denver.

Lee Ann

Lee Ann is Remi Boncoeur's nagging girlfriend. Although Sal is attracted to her, he never acts on his desire. She and Remi argue constantly. The only time she is happy is when Remi takes her out to lavish dinners, which they really cannot afford. She is with Remi and Sal when Remi takes his stepfather out to dinner, and she is mortified by the drunken behavior of Sal and Roland Major. She is no longer Remi's girlfriend when he appears at the end of the novel.

Roland Major

Sal shares an apartment with Roland Major during his first visit to Denver. Roland and Sal spend many nights drinking and discussing author Ernest Hemingway. Roland believes that Dean is a "moron and a fool." Later, Sal sees him in San Francisco while he is out to dinner with Remi, Lee Ann, and Remi's stepfather. Both Sal and Roland are roaring drunk, and they embarrass Remi.

Carlo Marx

Carlo Marx, a New York City poet, is one of Sal's many friends. Sal introduces Carlo to Dean,

Media Adaptations

- There are two audio-book versions of *On the Road.* The first is an abridged version read by actor David Carradine available on Penguin Audiobooks (1993). The second is a complete version, recorded in 1995 and read by Tom Parker.

and they become close friends as well. Carlo follows Dean to Denver near the beginning of the book. In an amusing scene, Sal listens as Carlo and Dean spend hours in a Benzedrine-driven analysis of everything they say and do. Carlo and Dean later visit Old Bull Lee, who is living in Texas at the time. Carlo makes a few other appearances in the novel, most notably in New York, where he poses the famous question: "I mean, man, whither goest thou? Whither goest thou, America, in thy shiny car in the night?" Neither Dean nor Sal can answer. "The only thing to do was go."

Camille Moriarty

Camille is Dean's second wife. Dean meets her in Denver and divorces Marylou to marry her. They end up living in San Francisco and having children. Dean regularly leaves her to go on the road. At one point, she throws him out of the house shortly after Sal arrives in San Francisco. Dean later divorces her to marry Inez, but he later returns to her.

Dean Moriarty

Dean Moriarty is the pivotal character of *On the Road.* His arrival in New York City changes Sal's life. Dean is handsome, charismatic, and exciting. His zest for life and learning is infectious. He finds something to "dig" about every person and circumstance. He dreams of being a writer like Sal or a poet like Carlo, but he can rarely sit still long enough to create anything substantial. However, he serves as inspiration to both Sal and Carlo. Sal believes Dean is a "new kind of American saint" and a "HOLY GOOF." Sal appreciates Dean's instinctive refusal to conform and his philosophy of living in the moment.

Dean also has a dark side. He lived on skid row in Denver with his drunken father through his childhood, and most of his teen years were spent in reformatories. He is a con man, a thief, and an unrepentant womanizer. He can be selfish, deserting his friends when he finds it in his own best interests. His behavior is often dangerous, but of course this is one of the qualities that makes him attractive to so many people. Dean's crazed energy ultimately consumes him. As early as part two, Old Bull Lee suggests that Dean may be going mad. By the end of the novel, Dean is barely able to put together a coherent sentence. He is a pitiable figure at the end of the story. The last time Sal sees him, Dean is wandering in rags on the frozen streets of New York City.

Inez Moriarty

Inez is Dean's third wife. He meets her in New York City when he and Sal arrive from San Francisco. Dean goes to Mexico to get a divorce from Camille in order to marry Inez, who is pregnant. After Dean gets the divorce in Mexico, he leaves the feverish Sal to return to New York City to marry Inez. He promptly leaves her after the ceremony to return to Camille in San Francisco.

Marylou Moriarty

Marylou is Dean's young, flirtatious first wife. Dean meets her in a diner after being released from the reformatory and falls in love with her. Marylou continues to have a relationship with Dean after he divorces her to marry Camille. After the divorce, Dean picks her up in Denver when he decides to meet Sal in Virginia. She travels with them to New Orleans and on to San Francisco. She has an affair with Sal after Dean leaves them on a sidewalk in San Francisco, but she leaves him because he can't support her. Even after marrying Camille, Dean stalks Marylou in San Francisco. He watches her bring home a different sailor every night. Marylou finally marries a used-car dealer. The last time Dean sees her, he gives her a gun and asks her to kill him. When she refuses, he attempts to strike her and breaks his thumb.

Sal Paradise

Sal Paradise is the narrator of *On the Road*. At the beginning of the novel, he is living with his aunt in New Jersey and writing a book. Sal is an intelligent, romantic idealist with many friends. He meets a charismatic drifter from Denver named Dean Moriarty in New York City. Although Dean is five years younger than Sal, he shares Sal's love

for literature and jazz and they quickly become close friends. Sal recognizes that Dean is a shameless manipulator, but he longs to travel and Dean's manic energy inspires him to wander around America in the search of "kicks."

The novel covers approximately four years in Sal's life; during that period, he travels thousands of miles. His travels to Denver, San Francisco, Los Angeles, New Orleans, and Mexico City. Along the way he is introduced to many eccentric and interesting characters, and he falls in love more than once. The cross-country journeys that he takes, alone and with Dean, seem pointless to many of the other characters. However, to Sal, each trip itself is far more important than any actual destination. He learns from Dean that the quest to live in the moment is a spiritual one. He searches for meaning in all of his experiences and in all the people he meets on the road because, as Dean tells him, "Everybody's kicks, man!" Sal and Dean see that all of America is "like an oyster for us to open; and the pearl was there, the pearl was there."

Sal's friendship with Dean is, of course, at the center of the novel. Even when Sal isn't with Dean, Dean is never far from Sal's thoughts throughout the book. Although Dean has many weaknesses and faults, Sal loves and admires him in spite of them. Even after Dean abandons him in Mexico City, Sal still considers moving to San Francisco with his girlfriend Laura to live near Dean and Camille. Sal's capacity for love is one of the qualities that make him such a likable character. It is this quality that makes the final scene in the novel, when Sal sees Dean on the cold streets of New York for the last time, so poignantly sad.

Sal's Aunt

Sal lives with his aunt in Paterson, New Jersey, at the beginning of the novel. She nurtures Sal when he returns home from his trips on the road. She bails Dean out when he is caught speeding in Washington, D.C., while he is moving furniture for her from Virginia to New Jersey. At the end of the novel, she is living in Long Island and she advises Dean to take better care of his children.

Stan Shephard

Stan Shephard leaves his parents in Denver to travel with Sal and Dean to Mexico City. He is stung by an unidentified insect as they drive out of Colorado, and his arm swells up. Dean stops in San Antonio to take him to a clinic to get a shot of penicillin and they continue on to Mexico City. Sal never tells what happens to Stan after Dean abandons them.

Terry

Sal meets Terry, a pretty Mexican girl, on a bus in Los Angeles. They have a short, bittersweet romance. They plan to get jobs and save money so they can move to New York City together. When they fail to find jobs in Los Angeles, they go to Sabinal, California, Terry's hometown, to get her son and work in the cotton fields. Sal is frustrated by his inability to earn enough in the fields to support Terry and her son and he decides to return home. Terry promises to meet him in New York City, but Sal knows that they will never see each other again.

Themes

Friendship

There are entire paragraphs listing the names of Sal Paradise's friends in *On the Road*. The nature of friendship is an integral theme of the novel. Sal, being a good-natured person, has a diverse collection of friends. Some are artistic types, such as the bizarre poet Carlo Marx. Others, like Old Bull Lee, are wildly eccentric. Surprisingly enough, Sal even has some ordinary, everyday friends, like Chad King. Sal also has many brief yet memorable friendships on the road. Of course, the most important friendship in the novel is between Sal and Dean Moriarty.

The powerful bond between Sal and Dean drives the story. Soon after Dean arrives in New York City, Sal becomes addicted to Dean's effervescent personality. Sal recognizes that Dean is manipulating him, but Dean's relentless energy captivates him:

> As we rode in the bus in the weird phosphorescent void of the Lincoln Tunnel we leaned on each other with fingers waving and talked excitedly, and I was beginning to get the bug like Dean. He was simply a youth tremendously excited with life, and though he was a con man, he was only conning because he wanted so much to live and to get involved with people who would otherwise pay no attention to him. He was conning me and I knew it (for room and board and "how-to-write," etc.), and he knew I knew (this has been the basis of our relationship), but I didn't care and we got along fine—no pestering, no catering; we tiptoed around each other like heartbreaking new friends. I began to learn from him as much as he probably learned from me.

What Sal learns from Dean is to live completely in the moment, to savor every experience. Sal's friendship with Dean is at first so strong that he is willing to follow Dean anywhere without a second thought. As they travel back and forth across the country, they share each other's life stories, dreams, philosophies, and visions. Together, they work themselves into a music-driven frenzy in countless jazz clubs, and they wallow in drunken debauchery in a Mexican bordello. Sal wants to be with Dean just to see what will happen next.

Of course, like most true friends, they have stormy moments. Sal is slightly jealous after he introduces Dean to Carlo and they become close. Sal also actually makes Dean cry during a petty argument they have in a diner. However, Dean is much more selfish than Sal. He abandons Sal on the road twice. The first time, he leaves him on the streets of San Francisco with Marylou, and with no money. Even worse, Dean later abandons Sal in Mexico City while he is feverish with dysentery. But Sal, ever the understanding friend, always forgives Dean. Ultimately, Sal comes to pity Dean. At the end of the novel, Sal is settling down with a new lover in New York City. Consumed by his wild compulsions, Dean is ragged and nearly incoherent the last time Sal sees him. Although Sal knows he will never forget Dean, the scene is a depressing finale to an extraordinary friendship.

Rebellion

Youthful rebellion in American literature can be traced back to Mark Twain's *The Adventures of Huckleberry Finn*. The rebellion of the characters in *On the Road* is a bit different from the revolt of sixties youth against the establishment (although a very convincing argument can be made that people like Kerouac's characters influenced that upheaval). It is not a violent or political rebellion; it is a rebellion of mind and spirit. It isn't that Sal, Dean, and the others don't believe in the "American Dream"; they simply don't buy into the popular conception of it. These characters rebel by disassociating themselves from society rather than directly attacking it. They embrace the role of the outsider through their use of drugs, their promiscuous sex, and their general disdain for traditional, middle-class American values. Freedom to live in the moment is their goal, and damn the consequences. For example, Old Bull Lee has a "sentimental streak" for the America of 1910 because:

> you could get morphine in a drugstore without prescription and Chinese smoked opium in their evening

Topics for Further Study

- Kerouac sought to write as some of the great jazz musicians played. Listen to some of the great jazz musicians, such as Charlie Parker or Miles Davis. What, if anything, does this music share with *On the Road?* Was Kerouac successful in emulating his musical heroes?

- Research other American literary movements, such as the Transcendentalists of the mid-nineteenth century and the Lost Generation of the 1920s, and write an essay comparing them to the Beat Generation.

- Discuss the female characters in *On the Road.* Several critics have complained that Kerouac's work is misogynistic. Do you agree or disagree and why? Rewrite a scene in the book from the viewpoint of one of the female characters.

- Discuss the religious allusions in the novel. Create a hypothetical religion centering on Dean Moriarty. What would be the major beliefs of such a religion? What kind of ceremonies would this religion practice?

- Use a map of North America to plot out Sal's travels throughout the book. Use different colored markers as a key for each trip. See if you can locate a map of the United States from the late 1940s to determine what roads existed at this time and estimate the mileage. Discuss the creation of the interstate highway system during the Eisenhower administration. What effects did the system have on American culture?

windows and the country was wild and brawling and free, with abundance and any kind of freedom for everyone.

Dean especially seeks this "wild and brawling" freedom. He rebels against any kind of responsibility. Dean doesn't want to overthrow the government, but he doesn't want a government, or anyone else for that matter, to have control over

him, even if it means becoming a denizen of skid row. In a memorable passage, he describes these feelings to Sal:

> You see, man, you get older and troubles pile up. Someday you and me'll be coming down an alley together at sundown and looking in the cans to see.
>
> You mean we'll end up bums?
>
> Why not, man? Of course we will if we want to, and all that. There's no harm ending that way. You spend a whole life of non-interference with the wishes of others, including politicians and the rich, and nobody bothers you and you cut along and make it your own way.

Thus, their rebellion is passive. They seek not to quash authority, but ignore it completely.

Time

Time, and the individual's subjective relationship to it, is an important theme in *On the Road.* Sal mentions few dates in the novel; time is kept more by season than anything else. The events of the novel run into each other and blur, as events do in real life. People pop up and disappear, only to reappear, again as they do in real life. Dean tells Sal several times that "we know time." By this, he means that they know they have no real control over time, and thus they should live as completely as possible in the moment.

This is why Dean's insistence on punctuality is a great joke throughout the novel. He is always on some sort of "schedule." One example of his ostensibly diligent timekeeping is when he schedules his next rendezvous with Camille after Sal arrives in Denver for the first time:

> It is now exactly one-fourteen. I shall be back at exactly *three*-fourteen, for our hour of reverie together, real sweet reverie, darling … so now in this exact minute I must dress, put on my pants, go back to life, that is to outside life, streets and what not, as we agreed, it is now one-*fifteen* and time's running, running—
>
> Well, all right, Dean, but please be sure and be back at three.
>
> Just as I said, darling, and remember not three but three-fourteen. Are we straight in the deepest and most wonderful depths of our souls, dear darling?

The irony in this passage, and in several others where Dean maps out his detailed schedules, is that Dean is a man who strives to live totally in the present, thereby denying the existence of his painful past and his apparently hopeless future. Because Dean "knows time," he believes that the present moment is all he has.

Style

Setting

The characters in *On the Road* travel through countless cities across the United States and Mexico. Major portions of the novel take place in New York City, Denver, San Francisco, southern California, New Orleans, and Mexico. Although Sal's constant traveling gives some of his place descriptions a generic feeling, many of his depictions are vivid. For example, when he first arrives in Mexico City, he sees:

> thousands of hipsters in floppy straw hats and long-lapeled jackets over bare chests padded along the main drag, some of them selling crucifixes and weed in the alleys, some of them kneeling in beat chapels next to Mexican burlesque shows in sheds. Some alleys were rubble, with open sewers, and little doors led to closet-size bars stuck in adobe walls. You had to jump over a ditch to get your drink, and in the bottom of the ditch was the ancient lake of the Aztec. You came out of the bar with your back to the wall and edged back to the street. They served coffee mixed with rum and nutmeg. Mambo blared from everywhere. Hundreds of whores lined themselves along the dark and narrow streets and their sorrowful eyes gleamed at us in the night.

However, the roads of America are the main setting of the novel. Sal hitchhikes with oddballs, rides on flatbed trucks with cowboys, and haunts bus stations with bums. Sal and Dean spend most of part two driving across the southern United States in a dilapidated Hudson that Dean buys in San Francisco. They later ride across the western prairies in a Cadillac limousine obtained through a travel bureau. Thus, the title of the novel is the most accurate description of the novel's setting.

Roman à Clef

A *roman à clef* (translated from French to mean "novel with a key") is a novel in which the characters are real people with fictitious names. *On the Road* is a thinly fictionalized account of Kerouac's life in the late 1940s. Sal Paradise is Kerouac's alter ego. Kerouac was a recently divorced writer who traveled back and forth across the country with an energetic and charismatic drifter from Denver named Neal Cassady (Dean Moriarty). Kerouac counted among his friends the wildly eccentric poet Allen Ginsberg (Carlo Marx), and the decadent bohemian William Burroughs (Old Bull Lee). Al Hinkle (Ed Dunkel), Carolyn Cassady (Camille Moriarty), and Henri Cru (Remi Boncoeur) are just a few of the many other friends and acquaintances of Kerouac making appearances in the novel.

Sal's travels throughout the book closely parallel Kerouac's real-life adventures. Like Sal, Kerouac fell in love with a Mexican girl in southern California; like Sal, he was forced to flee Denver because his friend stole five cars in one night. Kerouac was abandoned on the streets of San Francisco and in Mexico City by Cassady, a man he considered to be like a brother, the same way Sal was deserted by Dean. Kerouac was disappointed by Cassady in the same way that Sal is disillusioned with Dean at the end of the book. One only has to read a biography of Kerouac to find the "key" to this novel.

Anti-hero

Dean Moriarty is a classic example of an anti-hero in American literature. Anti-heroes lack the established traits (bravery, honesty, selflessness, etc.) of traditional heroes. Although Dean is intelligent, likable, and bold like many heroes, his total rejection of responsibility marks him as an anti-hero. Dean is an inveterate thief; although he has spent most of his life in reformatories, he continues to steal throughout the novel. He is a con man who has no qualms about manipulating even his best friends. He is a womanizer who marries and plans adultery in the same sentence. He betrays friends without a second thought, as he does when he twice deserts Sal. However, Dean remains a sympathetic character because of Sal's sensitive portrait of him.

"Spontaneous Prose"

Although Kerouac's later works were much more experimental in terms of style and narrative, *On the Road,* his second novel, was a breakthrough for him. He discovered his voice while writing the novel, and he began to develop his practice of "spontaneous prose." (He later wrote two short essays on his methods at the request of Allen Ginsberg and William Burroughs, "Essentials of Spontaneous Prose" and "Belief and Technique for Modern Prose.") Kerouac wanted to write in the same manner that a great bop jazz musician, such as Charlie Parker, played his instrument, and thus he invented a form of writing he called "bop prosody." Improvisation, passion, and spontaneity were the most important elements in this technique; traditional grammar and punctuation were irrelevant. Several passages in *On the Road* are early demonstrations of this method. A powerful example is the last paragraph in the book, an elegiac passage mourning the end of the road for Sal and Dean:

So in America, when the sun goes down and I sit on the old broken-down river pier watching the long, long skies over New Jersey and sense all that raw land that rolls in one unbelievable huge bulge over to the West Coast, and all that road going, all the people dreaming in the immensity of it, and in Iowa I know by now the children must be crying in the land where they let the children cry, and tonight the stars'll be out, and don't you know that God is Pooh-Bear? the evening star must be drooping and shedding her sparkler dims on the prairie, which is just before the coming of complete night that blesses the earth, and darkens all rivers, cups the peaks and folds the final shore in, and nobody, nobody knows what's going to happen to anybody besides the forlorn rags of growing old, I think of Dean Moriarty, I even think of Old Dean Moriarty the father we never found, I think of Dean Moriarty.

This passage demonstrates Kerouac's technique. It is one long run-on sentence, with a few pauses (as a saxophone player must pause for breath), filled with vivid, poetic imagery. Kerouac continued to use these methods, sometimes with radical effects, in his later work.

Historical Context

Post-World War II America

The last part of World War II was the birth of the atomic age. The United States dropped atomic bombs on Hiroshima and Nagasaki, forcing Japan to surrender. The United States emerged from the wreckage of the war as the leader of the Western world. Veterans returned to their homes, families, schools, and jobs. The United States was poised to become one of the greatest economic powers in history. However, there was an increasing anxiety caused by the atomic bomb and the beginning of the Cold War with the Soviet Union.

On March 5, 1946, Winston Churchill, the prime minister of Great Britain, gave a speech at Westminster College in Fulton, Missouri, in which he declared: "From Stettin in the Baltic to Trieste in the Adriatic an iron curtain has descended across the Continent." Churchill warned that the United States and its allies had to be on guard against Soviet expansionism. His remarks seemed prescient when, in June 1948, the Soviet Union began the Berlin blockade, cutting off Berlin from the West. The United States began a vast airlift to keep Berlin supplied with food and fuel. In August 1949 tensions increased even further when the Soviet Union detonated its first atomic device. The events of the late 1940s led to the anti-communist witch-hunts engineered by Senator Joseph McCarthy.

On the Road is not a political novel, but it is hard to imagine that Kerouac was not influenced by the atmosphere in America at the time. The horrors of the war, the Holocaust, the atomic bomb, and the growing sense of intolerance in the United States had to offend his sensibilities. If anything, these events pushed him even further into his disassociation from the values of the society in which he lived. There are a few passages in the novel that hint at Kerouac's concerns, for example when Old Bull Lee discusses with Sal the possibility of mankind one day communicating with the dead:

> When a man dies he undergoes a mutation in his brain that we know nothing about now but which will be very clear someday if scientists get on the ball. The bastards right now are only interested in seeing if they can blow up the world.

Here it is demonstrated that even these characters, living outside of "respectable" society, cannot escape the shadow of the bomb.

The Beat Generation

In his book, *The Birth of the Beat Generation,* Steven Watson writes:

> By the strictest definition, the Beat Generation consists of only William Burroughs, Allen Ginsberg, Jack Kerouac, Neal Cassady, and Herbert Huncke, with the slightly later addition of Gregory Corso and Peter Orlovsky. By the most sweeping usage, the term includes most of the innovative poets associated with San Francisco, Black Mountain College, and New York's Downtown scene. Using the broad definition, the Beat Generation is marked by a shared interest in spiritual liberation, manifesting itself in candid personal content and open forms, in verse and prose, thus leading to admiration for Walt Whitman, William Carlos Williams, and other avant-garde writers.

According to Ann Charters, editor of *The Portable Beat Reader,* the word "beat" was "primarily in use after World War II by jazz musicians and hustlers as a slang term meaning down and out, or poor and exhausted." The word's street usage was introduced to Kerouac by a Times Square hustler and drug addict named Herbert Huncke. Kerouac was attracted to what he believed to be the elusive, mysterious quality of the word. In a later conversation with his friend, writer John Clellon Holmes, Kerouac first coined the phrase that captured the essence of the vision he shared with Ginsberg, Burroughs and others. Charters writes:

> As Holmes recalled the conversation, Kerouac replied, "It's a kind of furtiveness ... Like we were a generation of furtives. You know, with an inner knowledge that there's no use flaunting on that level, the level of the "public," a kind of beatness—I mean,

Beatniks in a Greenwich coffeehouse in 1959.

being right down to it, to ourselves, because we all *really* know where we are—and a weariness with all the forms, all the conventions of the world.... So I guess you might say we're a *beat* generation."

Holmes went on to write an essay for *The New York Times,* "This Is the Beat Generation," in an attempt to describe the disaffiliation with society that many young people, such as Kerouac, felt in post-World War II America. However, it wasn't until Kerouac published *On the Road* in 1957, shortly after Ginsberg published *Howl and Other Poems,* that the Beat Generation and the Beat literary movement captivated the American public. There was some public backlash (for example, *San Francisco Chronicle* columnist Herb Caen snidely coined the word "beatniks" in reference to the West Coast youth involved in the movement), and in reply Kerouac wrote that "beat" also had a deeper spiritual meaning, as in "beatific." However, Kerouac himself had little patience with the "hipsters" wearing their goatees and berets; he thought many who jumped on the Beat bandwagon were poseurs, even conformists. Later, in the sixties, Kerouac disassociated himself from the "beatniks" as they evolved into "hippies."

Compare
&
Contrast

- **1946:** The Nuremberg trials end in the conviction of fourteen Nazi war criminals.

  1995: Several Serbian leaders are indicted by the United Nations for war crimes committed in Bosnia. Further indictments are expected when Yugoslavia's armies march into the province of Kosovo in an effort to drive out ethnic Albanians in 1999, yet another instance of "ethnic cleansing."

- **1947:** The House Un-American Activities Committee begins hearings and indicts the "Hollywood Ten" for contempt, leading to a blacklist of alleged communist sympathizers in this era of "McCarthyism."

  1999: A controversy erupts when the Academy of Motion Picture Arts and Sciences gives an honorary "Oscar" to film director Elia Kazan. Kazan, the director of classics, such as *On the Waterfront* and *East of Eden,* gained notoriety when he named several colleagues as communist sympathizers. Many in the audience refuse to applaud when the award is presented to him.

- **1948:** The Soviet Union begins the Berlin block-
ade, cutting Berlin off from the West. The United States begins a massive airlift to provide Berlin with food and fuel. The Berlin Wall is ultimately erected, and it serves as a symbol of the division between the freedom of the West and the totalitarianism of the East.

  1999: Torn down in 1989, the Berlin Wall is only a memory. Germany is unified as one country in 1990 for the first time since World War II. The Soviet Union collapses and its various republics declare independence. Today, the United States and its allies draw some of the Soviet Union's former satellites into NATO. Russia's attempts to evolve into a more democratic society throw the country into economic chaos and it turns to the United States and the world community for support.

- **1949:** The American Cancer Society and the National Cancer Institute warn that cigarette smoking may cause cancer.

  1990s: The tobacco industry is forced to settle dozens of class-action lawsuits when it is found liable for the effects its products have had on public health.

Critical Overview

When Viking published *On the Road* in 1957, the *New York Times* gave it a rave review and the book rose to number seven on the best-seller list. In his *New York Times* review, Gilbert Millstein announced that the book's publication was a "historic occasion." Millstein accurately predicted that many other critics would not agree. Indeed, the critics were divided; some, like Millstein, thought the book was extraordinarily original. Others, like Norman Podhoretz, claimed that the novel was an adolescent, even incoherent, work. There were also critics somewhere in the middle who believed that although Kerouac exhibited flashes of true talent in the book, the novel as a whole had too many weaknesses to be considered a masterpiece.

Critics like Millstein stressed the spiritual qualities of Kerouac's novel. Millstein wrote that the "frenzied pursuit of every possible sensory impression" by the various characters in the novel are "excesses ... made to serve a spiritual purpose, the purpose of an affirmation still unfocused, still to be defined, unsystematic." In other words, the characters are on a quest for belief in something, anything. Ralph Gleason, in *Saturday Review,* touched on the search for affirmation and spiritual dimension of the novel when he denied that *On the Road* is a "beat" novel:

> Even though Kerouac himself—and many of his admirers—speaks of "the beat generation," this is not true. To be beat means to be "beat to the socks," down and out, discouraged and without hope. And not once in *On the Road,* no matter how sordid the situation nor how miserable the people, is there no hope. That

is the great thing about Kerouac's book, and incidentally, this generation. They swing. And this ... means to affirm.... And, unlike a member of a generation that is really beat, Kerouac leaves you with no feeling of despair, but rather of exaltation.

Of course, many other critics found Kerouac's novel to be tedious and morally bankrupt. Norman Podhoretz accused Kerouac of being a solipsist (a person who believes that the self is the only existent thing) in his essay "The Know-Nothing Bohemians," published in the collection *Doings and Undoings.* He claimed that *On the Road* is so "patently autobiographical in content" that it is "impossible to discuss [it] as a novel." Edmund Fuller, in *Man in Modern Fiction: Some Minority Opinions on Contemporary American Writing,* wrote:

> *On the Road* is Kerouac's Hell. Dante once took us on a tour through Hell. The difference is, that Dante knew where he was—Kerouac doesn't.

Podhoretz and others charged that Kerouac's use of hipster slang and spontaneous prose was nothing more than meaningless babble, an "inability to express anything in words." Herbert Gold called Kerouac a "Pseudo-Hipster" in his review published in *The Nation.* In an article in *The Antioch Review,* Freeman Champney attacked what he recognized as misogyny (hatred of women) in the novel:

> it is [hard] to see the beat way of life as holding much joy for its women. They have a very rough time. Their only real functions are as audience and as erotic furniture (sometimes as providers and meal tickets). They may come along for the ride, but they don't dig the deeper secrets of life, and their demands for attention and consideration can be a real nuisance. And they turn out badly. They flip and they suicide; they become whores. Or they turn into nagging shrews who challenge the very basics of beatness by demanding regular hours and incomes from their men.

Many critics approached the work much more thoughtfully; that is, they weren't overwhelmed by the sheer exuberance of the work, nor were they offended by its lack of convention. They were thus better suited to delineate the novel's strengths and weaknesses. David Dempsey, in his *New York Times Book Review* article, pointed out that:

> Jack Kerouac has written an enormously readable and entertaining book but one reads it in the same mood that he might visit a sideshow—the freaks are fascinating although they are hardly part of our lives.

His final statement in that article was probably the most even-handed summation of *On the Road* made at the time of its publication:

> As a portrait of a disjointed segment of society acting out of its own neurotic necessity, *On the Road* is

a stunning achievement. But it is a road, as far as the characters are concerned, that leads nowhere—and which the novelist himself cannot afford to travel more than once.

Critics continue to write about the novel and, as when it was published, there are a variety of opinions as to its literary merit. Many of the articles written since the book's initial publication go a bit further than mere reviews. For example, several articles discuss the influence of jazz on Kerouac's style, and several others have noted the influence of Kerouac's study of Buddhism in *On the Road* and his other novels. The book's enduring popularity with both critics and readers suggests that the novel has already been accepted as a major work of the twentieth century.

Criticism

Don Akers

Akers is a freelance writer with an interest in Beat literature. In the following essay, he discusses the early criticism, cultural impact, and contemporary relevance of On the Road *and the Beat literary movement.*

When it was published in 1957, *On the Road* fascinated America with its seemingly aimless outcasts seeking thrills across the continent. It is the autobiographical account of Jack Kerouac's life in the late 1940s. Kerouac was recognized as the father of the Beat Generation with the publication of his novel. The Beat literary movement actually started with a small group of bohemians living in New York City during the mid-1940s. The group included Kerouac, poet Allen Ginsberg, and professional eccentric William Burroughs. The men were trying to define a "New Vision" in literature, and they discussed and criticized various works of literature and theories of writing. Kerouac met a charismatic drifter from Denver named Neal Cassady during this period. Cassady ultimately inspired the character of Dean Moriarty in *On the Road,* and he inspired Kerouac himself to go on the road. The manic movement of Sal Paradise in *On the Road,* with and without Dean Moriarty, is directly patterned after Kerouac's real-life travel during the same period. The novel shocked many readers of the late 1950s with its depictions of pointless travel, drug use, and promiscuous sex. And although some critics were excited by Kerouac's style, many thought Beat literature was adolescent, even immoral. However, the novel continues to be popular both as a critical subject and with readers (especially college students). It is interesting to review the novel and its early criticism with the hindsight of knowing the impact it had on American culture after its publication.

Both Gilbert Millstein and, to a lesser extent, David Dempsey, wrote favorable reviews for *On the Road* in *The New York Times* when the book was first published. Millstein believed that the novel depicted a quest for spiritual affirmation. The characters behave excessively, he wrote, because "the search for belief is very likely the most violent known to man." Because of this theme, and what he believed to be the beauty of the writing, Millstein insisted that *On the Road* was a major novel. Millstein's colleague at the *Times,* Dempsey, agreed that the novel was a "stunning achievement," but he believed that the characters acted out of a "neurotic necessity" rather than a spiritual one. Like Dempsey, many critics were impressed with Kerouac's raw talent, but still found flaws in the novel. For example, they noted the lack of characterization. Dempsey wrote that Kerouac's characters "are not developed but simply presented; they perform, take their bows and do a hand-spring into the wings." Gene Baro, in the *New York Herald Tribune,* also pointed out that the novel's characterizations are "given and illustrated rather than developed." These critics, and several others, considered Kerouac to be a major talent despite the flaws in his second novel.

Of course, there were many who were not infatuated with Kerouac's style. In his book *The Birth of the Beat Generation,* Steven Watson noted that "[a]fter the rave in the *New York Times* [for *On the Road*], the positive reviews were more temperate, and the negative reviews outdid one another in bile." The attack on the novel, and on the Beat literary movement in general, was led by intellectual Columbia graduates Herbert Gold and Norman Podhoretz. In an essay published in *The Nation,* Gold claimed that Kerouac had "appointed himself prose celebrant to a pack of unleashed zazous." Podhoretz, who was Ginsberg's contemporary at Columbia, fervently scorned Kerouac's work. He could be especially vicious in his criticism, as when he stated in his essay "The Know-Nothing Bohemians," first published in the *Partisan Review,* that he believed Kerouac's manifesto to be: "Kill the intellectuals who can talk coherently, kill the people who can sit still for five minutes at a time, kill those incomprehensible characters who are capable of getting seriously involved with a woman, a job, a cause." It should be noted here that Kerouac was never convicted of murder.

The problem with Kerouac's most vehement critics was their inability to criticize *On the Road* strictly on its literary merit. Podhoretz treated *On the Road* as if it were a threat to Western civilization rather than a uniquely stylized autobiographical novel about people on the fringe of society. What Podhoretz really seemed to resent was Kerouac's spontaneity, which, in his opinion, was a lack of control. Podhoretz has been quoted as saying, "Creativity represents a miraculous coming together of the uninhibited energy of the child with its apparent opposite and enemy—the sense of order imposed on the disciplined adult intelligence." In this quote, he indicates that while the exuberance of a child is welcome in the creative process, adult supervision is required. Kerouac certainly did not subscribe to this, as shown by several items on his "list of essentials" in his "Belief & Technique for Modern Prose":

> 1. Scribbled secret notebooks, and wild typewritten pages, for yr own joy … 2. Submissive to everything, open, listening … 7. Blow as deep as you want to blow … 28. Composing wild, undisciplined, pure, coming in from under, crazier the better …

Kerouac imposed no restrictions on his creative "child," and this is perhaps what offended Podhoretz more about *On the Road* than anything. Podhoretz was unable to recognize any of the intelligence and poetry of the novel because he not only disapproved of Kerouac's lifestyle, he also found Kerouac's creative philosophy abhorrent. Currently, Podhoretz is a senior fellow at a conservative think tank, the Hudson Institute. It is strange to consider that Kerouac, who became friends with conservative icon William F. Buckley, Jr. and supported the Vietnam War in the 1960s, was closer to Podhoretz in political ideology than in artistic theory.

Despite some lukewarm reviews and the furor of conservative intellectual critics, *On the Road* was a popular success. Several books Kerouac wrote during the 1950s were quickly published and he became a celebrity. Kerouac tried to explain the Beat phenomenon to middle-class America in various print, radio, and television interviews. He emphasized the spiritual dimensions of his work and the word "beat." Kerouac was credited with an entry in the Random House dictionary with the definition of the Beat Generation:

> Members of the generation that came of age after World War II, who, supposedly as a result of disillusionment stemming from the Cold War, espouse

mystical detachment and relaxation of social and sexual tensions.

Much to Kerouac's dismay, mainstream culture trivialized his work with "beatnik" clichés. The commercialization of Beat culture included several awful "B" movies and many paperback novels with beatnik themes. Perhaps the most egregious example of this fad was in the television series *The Many Loves of Dobie Gillis* (1959-1963). One of the characters on the series, Maynard G. Krebs (played by Bob Denver, whose later claim to fame was as the title character in *Gilligan's Island*), was a perfect illustration of the beatnik cliché. Krebs wore a goatee, used hipster slang, played the bongos, and avoided work whenever possible. The "beatnik" craze in American culture was, thankfully, short-lived. Of course, the passive beatnik evolved into the active hippie. *On the Road* was one part of the social and cultural forces that led to the youth revolution of the 1960s.

However, the continued popularity of *On the Road* can't be explained as mere nostalgia. Recently, the book was ranked number 624 in sales on the Internet bookstore Amazon.com. This is actually very impressive considering that the store has hundreds of thousands of titles. Young people are the book's most avid fans. Thus, Millstein's early praise of the book's "spirituality," embodied in the characters' "search for belief," has proven to be prescient. The search for identity or belief is a universal experience, and it is especially pertinent to young people. For example, it is hard to deny the youthful energy of the following passage from the novel:

> the only people for me are the mad ones, the ones who are mad to live, mad to talk, mad to be saved, desirous of everything at the same time, the ones who never yawn or say a commonplace thing, but burn, burn, burn like fabulous yellow roman candles exploding like spiders across the stars.

It is this yearning, this desire to have "everything at the same time," that attracts so many readers. Sometimes, Sal's search for meaning seems futile, and instead of joy there is melancholy, as when he arrives in Times Square after one of his western sojourns:

> I had traveled eight thousand miles around the American continent and I was back on Times Square; and right in the middle of a rush hour, too, seeing with my innocent road-eyes the absolute madness and fantastic horror of New York with its millions and millions hustling forever for a buck among themselves, the mad dream—grabbing, taking, giving, sighing, dying, just so they could be buried in those awful cemetery cities beyond Long Island City.

The strength of *On the Road* is in its vivid portrayal of both the joy and the pain of being young. It is one thing to criticize Kerouac's verbosity, repetitiveness, and sentimentality; it is quite another to dismiss his work entirely because his characters lead unconventional lifestyles, or because his creative philosophy involved using emotion rather than "craft." Even after forty years, *On the Road* remains a vital work.

Source: Don Akers, in an essay for *Novels for Students,* Gale, 2000.

Carole Gottlieb Vopat

In the following excerpt, Vopat defends Kerouac against critics who deem him unworthy of consideration as an important American writer.

Nothing has been published about Jack Kerouac for seven years. Most of what has been written is either hostile or condescending or both. While it may perhaps be true, as Melvin W. Askew suggests, that to speak of Jack Kerouac in the same breath with Melville, Twain and Hawthorne is to leave a smirch on the configuration of classic American literature, Kerouac has, as they have, provided an enduring portrait of the national psyche; like Fitzgerald, he has defined America and delineated American life for his generation. Certainly, Kerouac is not a great writer, but he is a good writer, and has more depth and control than his critics allow. *On the Road* is more than a crazy wild frantic embrace of beat life; implicit in Kerouac's portrayal of the beat generation is his criticism of it, a criticism that anticipates the charges of his most hostile critics. For example, Norman Podhoretz' assertion that the Beat Generation's worship of primitivism and spontaneity ... arises from a pathetic poverty of feeling, parallels Kerouac's own insights in *On the Road.*

In that novel Kerouac makes it clear that Sal Paradise goes on the road to escape from life rather than to find it, that he runs from the intimacy and responsibility of more demanding human relationships, and from a more demanding human relationship with himself. With all their emphasis on spontaneity and instinct, Sal and his friends are afraid of feeling on any other than the impassive and ultimately impersonal wow level. For Sal especially, emotion is reduced to sentimentality, role-playing and gesture. His responses are most often the blanket, indiscriminate wow! or the second-hand raptures gleaned from books and movies; he thrills to San Francisco as Jack London's town and melodramatically describes leaving his Mexican mistress:

> Emotionlessly she kissed me in the vineyard and walked off down the row. We turned at a dozen paces, for love is a duel, and looked at each other for the last time.... Sal is continually enjoying himself enjoying himself, raptly appreciating his performance in what seems more like an on-going soap-opera than an actual life: She'd left me a cape to keep warm; I threw it over my shoulder and skulked through the moonlit vineyard.... A California home; I hid in the grapevines, digging it all. I felt like a million dollars; I was adventuring in the crazy American night.

Sal's self-conscious posturing undercuts his insistence on the life of instinct and impulse, and indicates his fear of emotions simply felt, of life perceived undramatically and unadorned. He responds to experience in a language of exaggeration; everything is the saddest or greatest or wildest in the world. Although on page 21 he meets a rawhide oldtime Nebraska farmer who has a great laugh, the greatest in the world, a few pages later he encounters Mr. Snow whose laugh, I swear on the Bible, was positively and finally the one greatest laugh in all this world. Reality is never good enough; it must be classified, embroidered and intensified; above all, the sheer reality of reality must be avoided. Sal's roleplaying shelters him from having to realize and respond to actual situations, and to the emotions and obligations, whether of others or of himself, inherent in those situations. He is protected from having to face and feel his own emotions as well as from having to deal with the needs and demands of other people. What Sal enthuses over as a California home Kerouac reveals as a place of poverty, frustration, anger and despair, but Sal's raptures cushion him from recognizing the grimness of the existence to which he is carelessly consigning his mistress and her small son, a child he had called my boy and played at fathering. By absorbing himself in the melodramatics of a renunciation scene, Sal is protected from the realities of Terry's feelings or her future, nor must he cope with his own emotions at parting with her.

Kerouac's characters take to the road not to find life but to leave it all behind: emotion, maturity, change, decision, purpose, and, especially, in the best American tradition, responsibility; wives, children, mistresses, all end up strewn along the highway like broken glass. Sal refuses responsibility not only for the lives of others but for his own life as well. He does not want to own his life or direct his destiny, but prefers to live passively, to be driven in cars, to entertain sensations rather than emotions. A follower, Sal is terrified of leading his own life; he is, as Kerouac points out, fearful of the wheel and hated to drive; he does not have a driver's license. He and Dean abdicate self-control in a litany of irresponsibility: It's not my fault, it's not my fault ..., nothing in this lousy world is my fault. Both of them flee from relevance and significance, telling long, mindless stories and taking equally pointless trips. They avoid anything—self-analysis, self-awareness, thinking—which would threaten or challenge them, for with revelation comes responsibility for change and, above all, they do not want change. They demand lives as thin and narrow as the white lines along the road which so comfort and mesmerize them, and are content with surfaces, asking for no more. Thus they idolize Negroes as romantic and carefree children, seeing in the ghetto not the reality of poverty and oppression, but freedom from responsibility and, hence, joy.

Sal and his friends are not seeking or celebrating self, but are rather fleeing from identity. For all their solipsism, they are almost egoless. They do not dwell on the self, avoid thinking or feeling. They run from self-definition, for to admit the complex existence of the self is to admit its contingencies: the claims of others, commitments to society, to oneself. Solipsism rather than an enhancement of self is for them a loss of self, for the self is projected until it loses all boundaries and limits and, hence, all definition. Sal in the Mexican jungle completely loses his identity; inside and outside merge, he becomes the atmosphere, and as a result knows neither the jungle nor himself. For Sal and Dean, transcendentalism, like drugs, sex, liquor, and even jazz, leads not to enlightenment but to self-obliteration. Erasing both ego and world, nothing remains save motion and sensation, passive, self-effacing and mechanical. Only the sheer impetus of their frantic, speeding cars holds their scattered selves together.

Their selves have no definition and their lives no continuity. Nothing is related, neither self nor time; there is no cause and effect, life is not an ongoing process. Rather, there is only the Eternal Now, the jazz moment, which demands absolutely nothing. Their ideals are spontaneity and impulse because both are independent of relation to what has gone before and what may come after. Spontaneity and impulse are the ethic of disjunction, recognizing neither limit, liability or obligation. Their emphasis on spontaneity is a measure of their fear of life. In their cars they are suspended from life and living, as if in a capsule hurtling coast-to-coast

What Do I Read Next?

- Kerouac's *The Dharma Bums* (1958) is the chronicle of two men searching for the Zen meaning of Truth as they travel the West Coast. Kerouac used his friendship with Buddhist poet Gary Snyder as the basis for this novel.

- *The Subterraneans* (1958) is the story of a writer's interracial relationship amid the backdrop of New York City hipsters. Kerouac based the novel on a real-life romance he had with Alene Lee, a beautiful young black woman who mingled with the denizens of Greenwich Village.

- For those interested in a "key" to *On the Road*, as well as the novels mentioned above, there is an excellent critical biography of Kerouac by Gerald Nicosia, *Memory Babe* (1983).

- Kerouac was deeply influenced by Southern author Tom Wolfe, whose first two novels, *Look Homeward, Angel* (1929) and *Of Time and the River* (1935), were autobiographical accounts of his early life in North Carolina and his later travels to Harvard, New York City, and Paris. The novels are expansive and romantic, filled with lush imagery and humor.

- *The Portable Beat Reader* (1992), edited by Ann Charters, is a great collection of work by dozens of beat poets and writers. It includes excerpts from three of Kerouac's novels, as well as some of his poetry. It also includes "Howl" by Allen Ginsberg, and several pieces by William Burroughs.

- Another great novel of youthful alienation is J. D. Salinger's *The Catcher in the Rye* (1951). The protagonist, sixteen-year-old Holden Caulfield, is one of the most beloved adolescents in American literature. The story details three days in Caulfield's life after he flunks out of prep school. It is a sad, funny, and deeply touching novel.

- Ken Kesey's *One Flew Over the Cuckoo's Nest* (1962) is a classic anti-establishment novel. Small-time con artist Randle McMurphy feigns mental illness to avoid prison. When he is committed to a mental hospital, he winds up in a power struggle with the head nurse. The book was also made into an Oscar-winning film in 1975 starring Jack Nicholson.

- A proponent of the New Journalism of the 1960s, Tom Wolfe (not the same writer mentioned above), spent several months with novelist Ken Kesey and his band of Merry Pranksters as they rolled across the country in their bus. *The Electric Kool-Aid Acid Test* (1968) by Wolfe is an intriguing documentation of the psychedelic era. Neal Cassady and Timothy Leary are among the many oddball occupants of the bus they called "Further."

---

above the earth. They seek out not truth nor values but this encapsulated almost fetal existence as an end in itself, an end that is much like death.

For even their much touted ideal of Freedom is in reality a freedom from life itself, especially from rational, adult life with its welter of consequences and obligations. Dean is utterly free because he is completely mad. He has defied maturity and logic, defied time with its demands that he grow up to responsibility. Like Nietzsche's superman, he is beyond good and evil, blame and expectation, nor must he justify his existence through work and duty, a state Sal sorely admires: Bitterness, recriminations, advice, morality, sadness—everything was behind him, and ahead of him was the ragged and ecstatic joy of pure being. Sal's own longing for freedom is embodied in a mysterious Shrouded Traveler, a figure who unites the road and death. In many avatars, he pursues Sal in his headlong flight down the highway, offering, through solitary travel, the lost bliss which is the death of the self: The one thing that we yearn for

---

in all our living days, that makes us sigh and groan and undergo sweet nauseas of all kinds, is the remembrance of some lost bliss that we probably experienced in the womb and can only be reproduced (though we hate to admit it) in death.

Free love is rather freedom from love and another route down that same dark deathwish. For Sal the lovebed is the deathbed, where he goes to obliterate himself and to find the safe lost bliss of the womb, blindly seeking to return the way he came. But Sal is only able to find this particular version of lost bliss when he has reduced his partner to the non-threatening role of fellow child. He has trouble succeeding with adult women; he fills Rita with nothing but talk and is convinced Theresa is a whore until he discovers with relief that she is only a baby, as fragile and vulnerable as he:

> I saw her poor belly where there was a Caesarian scar; her hips were so narrow she couldn't bear a child without getting gashed open. Her legs were like little sticks. She was only four foot ten. I made love to her in the sweetness of the weary morning. Then, two tired angels of some kind, hung-up forlornly in an LA shelf, having found the closest and most delicious thing in life together, we fell asleep …

Sex here is not a wild explosion but the desperate, gentle solace two babes in the woods haltingly offer each other…. Sal says he ought to be seeking out a wife, but his true search is, as is Dean's, not for lover but for father, for someone to shelter him from life and responsibility. He turns to Terry not for ecstasy or even sensation, but as a respite from his search, an escape from the demands of life: I finally decided to hide from the world one more night with her and morning be damned.

In short, for all their exuberance, Kerouac's characters are half in love with easeful death. And this Sal Paradise and his creator well know. Neither is deceived about the nature of beat existence. Kerouac is able to step back from his characters to point out their follies; to show, for example, Dean's pathetic justification of life on the road…. Sal himself is able to articulate his own fear of feeling and responsibility and his resultant, overwhelming emptiness:

> Well, you know me. You know I don't have close relationships with anybody anymore. I don't know what to do with these things. I hold things in my hand like pieces of crap and don't know where to put it down…. It's not my fault! It's not my fault! … Nothing in this lousy world is my fault, don't you see that? I don't want it to be and it can't be and it *won't* be.

He realizes that he has nothing to offer anybody except my own confusion, and marks the deaths of his various illusions with the refrain, Everything is collapsing.

Kerouac further points out that the shortcomings of his characters parallel the shortcomings of the country to which they are so intimately connected. Kerouac's response to America is typically disillusioned. America is a land of corruption and hypocrisy, promising everything and delivering nothing, living off the innocence and opportunity, the excitement and adventure of the past. In particular Kerouac indicts America for failing to provide his searching characters with any public meaning or communal values to counteract the emptiness of their private lives. Sal looks to America much as he looks to Dean, to provide him with direction, purpose and meaning, to offer him a straight line, an ordered progression to a golden destination, an IT of stability and salvation. But IT never materializes, and the straight line itself becomes an end; the going, the road, is all. Dean's response to continual disillusionment is to forsake the destination for the journey: Move! Sal follows his leader but eventually becomes disgusted with the purposeless, uncomfortable jockeying from coast to coast, just as he becomes disgusted with Dean. Unlike Dean, Sal is able to recognize and identify his despair and, ultimately, to act on the causes of it; where for Dean change is merely deterioration, Sal undergoes true development.

In addition to Sal's growing insight, Kerouac equips his narrator with a double vision, enabling Sal to comment on the people and events of the novel as he saw them when they happened, and as he views them now that they are over, a sadder-but-wiser hindsight which acts as a check upon his naive, undiscriminating exuberances and provides a disillusioned alternative view of the beatifics of the beat generation.

While the younger Sal idolized Dean upon first meeting him, the older Sal reminds the reader that this is all far back, when Dean was not "the way he is today … ," and notes that the whole mad swirl of everything that was to come began then; it would mix up all my friends and all I had left of my family in a big dust cloud over the American night. He observes the sad effect of Time upon his old friends who once rushed down the street together, digging everything in the early way they had, which later becomes so much sadder and perceptive and blank. He corrects himself when his earlier view of Dean intrudes upon the more precise voice of his older self: Dean … had finished his first fling in New York. I say fling, but he only worked like a dog in parking lots. Sal continually checks and repudiates his youthful self, and deflates his naive view of Dean and life on the road: I could hear a new call and see a new horizon, and believe it at my young age; and a little bit of trouble or even Dean's eventual rejection of me as a buddy, putting me down, as he would later, on starving sidewalks and sickbeds—what did it matter? I was a young writer and I wanted to take off.

Sal's double vision does more than correct his impulses. It projects the reader forward in time and provides the sense of continuity the disjunctive characters, including the younger Sal, lack. This older voice offers relations and connections, causes and effects, connects past with present and projects into the future. It firmly anchors reader and narrator to the familiar world of change and conjunction. It knows the discrepancy between appearance and reality and realizes sadly that Time eventually captures even frantically speeding children. It is the view of a man who has, in Dean Moriarty's words, come to know Time, it prepares the reader for Sal's eventual disillusionment with beat life and the sordid hipsters of America.

Sal's double vision is proof of his eventual recapitulation to time and change, a recapitulation which he battles for most of the novel. It is this battling, perhaps, so constant and monotonous, which has infuriated readers used to traditional novels of development and makes them wonder, indeed, whether anything happens to anyone in the novel at all. Sal alone of the characters continually perceives the futility and insanity of his journeys, yet continually makes them, always with the same childlike innocence and expectation, always to follow the same pattern of hopefulness ending in disillusionment as he learns and relearns the same weary lessons about America and Dean Moriarty. Nonetheless, Sal does finally accept the obligations of his insights and revelations, decides to bear the heavy weight of change and responsibility, and grows up to understand, evaluate and finally repudiate Dean Moriarty, the American Dream, and life on the road.

Dean offers Sal more than direction and meaning; he simultaneously provides both a quest and an escape, a hiatus from adult life and adult feelings, a moratorium on maturity. Sal associates Dean with his own childhood: "... he reminded me of some long-lost brother ..., made me remember my boyhood.... And in his excited way of speaking I heard again the voices of old companions and brothers under the bridge...."

Indeed, although Sal is older than Dean, he regards Dean at first not so much as long lost brother but as Father whom he passively follows, trusting to be protected, loved and directed. Sal is disenchanted with Dean at the end of Part Two not because Dean has proven himself a poor friend, but because he has turned out to be yet another bad father: Where is Dean and why isn't he concerned about our welfare?

Sal's emotional maturation is evident in his first lover's quarrel with Dean. Enraged by Dean's casual reference to his growing old (You're getting a little older now), Sal turns on him, reducing him to tears, but immediately afterwards realizes that his anger is directed at aging rather than at Dean: I had flipped momentarily and turned it down on Dean. He takes responsibility for hurting Dean, and apologizes to him, humbly and lovingly: Remember that I believe in you. I'm infinitely sorry for the foolish grievance I held against you.... He sees that his present anger springs from sources buried in his youth (Everything I had ever secretly held against my brother was coming out ...). This insight into himself helps him to understand Dean, who is, like him, mired in a past whose anger and frenzy he is compelled to act out, but, unlike Sal, without benefit of apology or insight: "All the bitterness and madness of his entire Denver life was blasting out of his system like daggers. His face was red and sweaty and mean." Regarding his friend without desperate idealism, Sal sees that Dean's frantic moving and going is not a romantic quest for adventure or truth but is instead a sad, lost circling for the past, for the home and the father he never had. He sees that both he and Dean are as frightened and lost as the Prince of Dharma, going in circles in the dark lost places between the stars, searching for that lost ancestral grove. The road on which they run is all that old road of the past unreeling dizzily as if the cup of life had been overturned and everything gone mad. My eyes ached in nightmare day. True to his vow, he takes Dean back to New York with him, yet knows that for them a permanent home is impossible. Their marriage breaks down; Dean returns to his crazy welter of wives and children, Sal to his aunt and his disillusionment.

In Mexico Sal hopes to escape from the self, civilization, and their discontents. At the bottom of his primitivism is a desire to confront the primal sources of pure being, to discover life as it was—shapeless, formless, dark—before being molded into self or society; in short, to find once and for all the womb he has been seeking all his life. If nothing else, he hopes to search out his final, true and ultimate parents among the Indians who are the source of mankind and the fathers of it.

But the strange Arabian paradise we had finally found at the end of the hard, hard road is only a wild old whore house after all. The Indians are coming down from the mountains drawn to wristwatches and cities. They and the Mexicans welcome Sal and Dean not as brothers or fellow children, but as American tourists to be exploited. The brothel where they converse for their ultimate mind-and time-blowing fling is a sad, frantic, desperate place, full of eighteen-year-old drunks and child whores, sinking and lost, writhing and suffering.... Their great primitive playground is no more than a sad kiddy park with swings and a broken-down merry-go-round ... in the fading red sun.... And in that sad kiddy park Sal leaves behind his faith in the possibility of an infantile paradise and, with it, his faith in Dean.

Dean first induced Sal to accompany him over the border with the happy announcement that ... the years have rolled severally behind us and yet you see none of us have really changed.... In Mexico Sal finds this denial of time not a reprieve but a condemnation. Dean cannot change and he cannot rest, not even in the great and final wild uninhibited Fellahin childlike Mexico City. Wedded forever to his terrible, changeless compulsions, not the love of his friend nor the possibility of paradise can stay him from his rounds. He leaves the delirious and unconscious Sal to return to all that again, for, as he himself announces, the road drives *me*. Sal understands and pities him ("I realized what a rat he was, but ... I had to understand the impossible complexity of his life, how he had to leave me there, sick, to get on with his wives and woes"), realizing his friend is the least free of anyone. Dean leads not a primitive life of spontaneity and instinct but instead a sorry, driven existence of joyless sweats and anxieties. Sal has a vision of Dean not as sweet, holy goof but as the Angel of Death, burning and laying waste whatever he touches....

Returning to America, Sal meets up once more with the Shrouded Traveler, a symbol of the fatal lure of the road and the restless, nomadic beat life. Sal wonders if this tall old man with flowing white hair ... with a pack on his back is a sign that I should at last go on my pilgrimage on foot on the dark roads around America. He wonders, in short, if he ought to become the Ghost of the Susquehanna, to enter the darkness from which the old man appeared and into which he vanished. He responds to the romance of this suggestion, but is haunted by its loneliness. Later, in New York, he calls out his name in the darkness and is answered by Laura, the girl with the pure and innocent dear eyes that I had always searched for and for so long. Settling his dreams of paradise and salvation in her, he gives up the road.

In a sense, Sal's growth as an adult can be measured through his responses to Dean and in the changing aspects of their relationship. Sal moves from idolatry to pity, from a breathless, childlike worship of Dean as alternately Saint and Father, to a realization of Dean's own tortured humanity, marked by Sal's attempt to be brother, then Father, to his friend, sensitive to Dean's needs without melodrama, facing responsibility and decision, allowing himself to feel blame and love, yet, eventually, for the sake of his own soul, rejecting, deliberately and sadly, his lost, perpetually circling friend.

When Dean arrives to rescue him once more from the world of age and obligation, Sal refuses to go. He discards Dean's plan to leave for San Francisco before he himself is absolutely ready (But why did you come so soon, Dean?), and, deciding that he wasn't going to start all over again ruining [Remi's] planned evenings as I had done ... in 1947, he pulls away from Dean and leaves him behind.

In the course of his scattered journeys Sal has learned, perhaps to his regret, what rather tentatively might indeed finally matter, and to this tenuous value he cautiously decides to commit himself, giving up the ghost of the Shrouded Traveler, of Dean Moriarty and Old Dean Moriarty and dead America, and accepting in their place feeling, responsibility, and roots—not in a place but in another person, Laura. Sal's relationship with Dean has served as an apprenticeship during which he has learned how to accommodate to intimacy, as his disillusionment with America has prepared him to look beyond the road for salvation and paradise. Neither America nor Dean can successfully order his life, provide him with direction or meaning. Neither can father him; ultimately, he must father himself, must look inward for purpose and belief. For America has lost her innocence and her sense of purpose just as Dean has and, like Dean, is continually making bogus attempts to pretend it still has all the potential and grace of its youth....

On the Road ends with an elegy for a lost America, for the country which once might have been the father of us all, but now is only the land where they let children cry. Dean Moriarty is himself America, or rather the dream of America, once innocent, young, full of promise and holiness, bursting with potential and vitality, now driven mad, crippled, impotent (We're all losing our fingers), ragged, dirty, lost, searching for a past of security and love that never existed, trailing frenzy and broken promises, unable to speak to anybody anymore.

Source: Carole Gottlieb Vopat, "Jack Kerouac's *On the Road:* A Re-evaluation," in *Midwest Quarterly,* Vol. XIV, No. 4, Summer, 1973, pp. 385-407.

Sources

Freeman Champney, "Beat-Up or Beatific?," *The Antioch Review,* Vol. XIX, No. 1, Spring, 1959, pp. 114-21.

Ann Charters, "Introduction: Variations on a Generation," in *The Portable Beat Reader,* edited by Ann Charters, Penguin Books, 1992, pp. xvii, xix-xx.

David Dempsey, "In Pursuit of Kicks," *The New York Times Book Review,* September 8, 1957, p. 4.

Edmund Fuller, in *Man in Modern Fiction: Some Minority Opinions on Contemporary Writing,* Random House, 1958, p. 154.

Ralph Gleason, "Kerouac's Beat Generation," *Saturday Review,* Vol. XLI, January 11, 1958, p. 75.

Herbert Gold, "Hip, Cool, Beat—and Frantic," *The Nation,* Vol. 185, No. 16, November 16, 1957, pp. 349-55.

Jack Kerouac, *On the Road,* Viking, 1957.

Gilbert Millstein, review in *The New York Times,* September 5, 1957, p. 27.

Norman Podhoretz, "The Know-Nothing Bohemians," (1958) in his *Doings and Undoings,* Farrar, Straus & Giroux, 1964, pp. 143-58.

Steven Watson, in *The Birth of the Beat Generation,* Pantheon Books, 1995, pp. 5, 256.

For Further Study

Lee Bartlett, "The Dionysian Vision of Jack Kerouac," in *The Beats: Essays of Criticism,* edited by Lee Bartlett, McFarland, 1981, pp. 115-23.
    Lee uses psychoanalyst C. G. Jung's theories to illuminate the connection Kerouac makes between the jazz musician and the Dionysian writer.

Jim Burns, "Kerouac and Jazz," in *The Review of Contemporary Fiction,* Vol. III, No. 2, Summer, 1983.
    Explicates the references to jazz pieces and musicians in *On the Road* and other Kerouac works.

Carolyn Cassady, *Off the Road: My Years with Kerouac, Cassady, and Ginsberg,* New York, 1990.
    The memoirs of Neal Cassady's wife.

Ann Charters, *Kerouac: A Biography,* Straight Arrow Books, 1973, 419 p.
    The first biography of Jack Kerouac.

Warren French, *Jack Kerouac,* Twayne, 1986, 147 p.
    Analyzes the novels that comprise "The Duluoz Legend" as an extended effort by Kerouac to recast his life in the form of a literary legend analogous to the Stephen Dedalus novels of James Joyce.

Barry Gifford and Lawrence Lee, *Jack's Book,* St. Martin's Press, 1978, 339 p.
    An oral history of Kerouac and his friends.

John Clellon Holmes, "The Philosophy of the Beats," in *Esquire* Vol. 99, No. 6, June, 1983, pp. 158-67.
    Early analysis originally published in the February 1958 issue of *Esquire* that emphasizes the importance of the spiritual quest to the Beats.

Granville H. Jones, "Jack Kerouac and the American Conscience," in *Lectures on Modern Novelists,* edited by Arthur T. Broes, et. al., Books for Libraries Press, 1972, pp. 25-39.
    Defines the individualistic philosophy Kerouac advocated in his fiction and life as a distinctly American phenomenon.

Jack Kerouac, *Selected Letters 1940-1956,* edited by Ann Charters, Viking, 1995.
    Annotated letters from Kerouac's pre-fame period.

Gerald Nicosia, *Memory Babe: A Critical Biography of Jack Kerouac,* Grove Press, 1983, 767 p.
    The most exhaustive Kerouac biography. Includes critical analysis of his novels.

Sister Carrie

Theodore Dreiser

1900

Sister Carrie shocked the public when Doubleday, Page and Company published it in 1900. In fact, it was so controversial, it almost missed being printed at all. Harpers refused the first copy, and the book went to Frank Doubleday. After the Doubleday printers typeset the book one of the partners' wives read it and so strongly opposed its sexual nature that the publisher produced only a few editions.

In addition to the book's theme of sexual impropriety, the public disliked the fact that Theodore Dreiser presented a side of life that proper Americans did not care to acknowledge. Even worse, Dreiser made no moral judgements on his characters' actions. He wrote about infidelity and prostitution as natural occurrences in the course of human relationships. Dreiser wrote about his characters with pity, compassion, and a sense of awe.

While the book appalled Americans, the English appreciated it. William Heinemann published an English version of the book in 1901. While the book sold well in England, *Sister Carrie* did not enjoy much success in the United States, even though B. W. Dodge & Co. had reprinted it. In order to make ends meet Dreiser worked at other literary jobs. In 1911, when the magazine where he was employed stopped publication and he was out of work, he began to write nonstop to complete his next novel, *Jennie Gerhardt.* Critics liked *Jennie Gerhardt* so much that they began to reconsider the merits of *Sister Carrie.* A new edition of *Sister Carrie* was published, and it became Dreiser's most successful novel.

Author Biography

Theodore Dreiser was born in Terre Haute, Indiana, on August 27, 1871. Dreiser's father, John Paul, fled to America from Germany to avoid the draft. Although the elder Dreiser had mastered weaving in Germany, he found that employers in his new country did not appreciate his skill. He tried to earn a living in Terre Haute while his wife and children moved from place to place looking for other work and more affordable living. Mr. Dreiser and his wife of Moravian descent raised their family on very little money, with the stringent morals and rules of the old country. They communicated with each other in German and followed strict Catholic practices.

One of ten children, next-to-the-youngest Theodore Dreiser felt the influence of his older brothers and sisters who seemed to always find themselves in trouble. For example, one brother, Paul, robbed a saloon in his teens, kept company with a brothel madam, and died of alcoholism and related depression. Two of Theodore's sisters were prostitutes. Because Theodore saw his father's distress over his children's antics, the younger Dreiser learned early how to avoid being caught for his many misadventures. Fortunately, Dreiser loved reading. His fondness for words led him to writing; writing kept him fed and out of trouble. When Dreiser turned sixteen, he left the family and began working at a variety of odd jobs to try to support himself. He lived for a while with a brother in Chicago, then returned to Indiana to attend Indiana University. He left after a year, however, returning to Chicago where, in 1892, he made his writing debut as a reporter for the *Daily Globe*. After having been a reporter in Chicago, St. Louis, and Pittsburgh, Dreiser began to discover that he was better at writing impressions than he was at reporting the facts. While working in New York, Dreiser wrote several short stories that quickly sold. Slightly encouraged by this success and the urging of a friend, Dreiser penned *Sister Carrie*. Based on his sisters' lives, the novel became Dreiser's best-known work. Critics today credit Dreiser with being the first writer to portray nineteenth-century American life in a realistic way. Dreiser died in Los Angeles, California, in 1945.

Plot Summary

Part I

Sister Carrie opens in 1889 with eighteen-year-old Caroline Meeber on her way from her

Theodore Dreiser

small hometown to the big city of Chicago. She is frightened to leave home, but determined to make her way in the city. An attractive, yet naive young woman, Carrie finds herself in the company of Charles Drouet, a "drummer," or traveling salesman. Drouet, well dressed and flashy, engages Carrie in a long conversation. When they part at the train station, they agree to meet the following week in Chicago.

After Drouet leaves, Carrie, feeling alone and bereft in this big city, waits for her sister Minnie to meet her at the station. Carrie will stay with Minnie and her husband Sven Hanson, who live in a small, meagerly furnished apartment. They expect Carrie's wages to help them make their rent payments. Carrie sits in their rocking chair sorting out her thoughts—a position of repose she will often repeat throughout the novel. Realizing how small the apartment is, Carrie then writes to Drouet telling him she cannot see him because there is no room for visitors.

Carrie finally finds a job but the wages are low and when she wants to go to the theatre or enjoy life in the city, her sister disapproves. Carrie's job on the assembly line is dreadful and nearly all her wages go to her sister at the end of each week. Without enough money to buy warm clothes, when the cold weather comes she turns ill and loses her job. When Carrie recovers from her illness she searches for a new job, but without much success. By accident, she bumps into Drouet, who gives her twenty dollars for new clothes; when she decides to leave her sister's home, Drouet establishes her in a furnished room of her own in another part of the city. After several days of sightseeing and shopping, Carrie and Drouet begin living together.

Drouet invites his friend George Hurstwood, the manager of a prosperous saloon, to visit their home. The visit goes well for Carrie and Hurstwood, who is unhappy with his home life. They seem attracted to each other and Drouet suffers by comparison with the older man. Carrie continues to interest Hurstwood and he decides to pursue her when he sees Drouet out with another woman. When he turns his full attention to courting Carrie he ignores his own wife and family.

Meanwhile, Drouet promises his lodge brothers that he will find an actress for their upcoming stage show. He convinces Carrie to take the part. Although the other actors are not good, Carrie herself rises to the occasion and turns in an excellent performance. This renews both Drouet's and Hurstwood's interest in her; Carrie agrees to leave Drouet if Hurstwood will marry her and he agrees.

Hurstwood's wife, aware of the affair with Carrie, hounds him for money and begins divorce proceedings. At the time the novel is set, a man exposed as an adulterer would not only lose his marriage, he would also lose his job and social standing in the community. As Hurstwood ponders what his next step should be, he discovers a large sum of money in the saloon's safe and steals it. He then goes to Carrie telling her that Drouet has been injured and persuades her to board a train that will supposedly take her to Drouet. However, once on board, Hurstwood reveals his true purpose.

Part II

Carrie and Hurstwood marry illegally under the assumed name of Wheeler and move to New York City. Carrie soon comes to realize that she does not love Hurstwood, and has used him to escape her life in Chicago. Nonetheless, she stays and keeps house for Hurstwood, who buys an interest in a New York saloon. As the years pass, their routine becomes predictable and monotonous, and Carrie grows increasingly discontented with her shabby clothes and frugal lifestyle.

Mrs. Vance, an elegant and wealthy woman who befriends Carrie, begins to take her to the the-

atre and helps her pick out new clothes. Carrie then meets Mrs. Vance's cousin, Bob Ames, who convinces her that wealth is not necessarily the means to all happiness. Carrie comes to see Ames as the ideal man.

Meanwhile, Hurstwood grows older and more depressed. He loses the lease on his business and spends his days in hotel lobbies, watching the rich and famous pass by him. This, and reading the morning and afternoon papers, comprise his entire routine. When money grows increasingly scarce the couple move into a cheaper apartment and Hurstwood gambles away the last of their cash.

Carrie then decides to find a job in the theatre. Under the name Carrie Madenda, she takes a job in a chorus line at the Casino theatre and is soon promoted and earning good money. Preferring to spend her time with theatre friends, Carrie increasingly stays away from the apartment and Hurstwood.

Hurstwood eventually finds work as a scab, working on a Brooklyn trolley line where workers are striking. Although he is not seriously wounded, he is shot and beaten but the experience causes him to sink ever deeper into depression. On the other hand, Carrie wins a speaking part in her show and earns more money. She is tired of supporting Hurstwood, and leaves him.

Carrie's career continues to grow. She moves into a new hotel with her friend Lola Osborne and lives the life she has always dreamed yet still finds herself unhappy. Meanwhile, Hurstwood continues to sink. He works in a hotel as an errand boy where he catches pneumonia and takes many months in the hospital to recover.

Around this time, Drouet appears, hoping to win Carrie back, but sees that she has changed and they are no longer on the same level. Following Drouet's appearance, Hurstwood approaches Carrie after a performance asking for money. She gives him all that she has with her. Finally, when Ames comes to New York, telling her she ought to consider other roles, she becomes troubled. Carrie takes to her rocker, where she rocks and trys to sort through her life.

In the final chapter, Dreiser briefly revisits his characters. Hurstwood is now a homeless, itinerant man whose mind has gone. Carrie can be seen reading a serious novel—one that Ames recommends. And Drouet is in the lobby of a grand hotel. Dreiser also describes the Hurstwood family on their way to a vacation in Italy and then returns to Hurstwood himself and the final scene where he commits suicide in a Bowery flophouse by turning on the gas jet and going to sleep.

Characters

Bob Ames

Carrie meets Bob Ames at Mrs. Vance's. Ames has a high forehead and a rather large nose, but Carrie finds him handsome. She likes even more his boyish nature and nice smile. Mr. and Mrs. Vance and Carrie and Ames have dinner together, and Carrie enjoys Ames's scholarly manner. He discusses topics that seem of great importance to Carrie, and admits to her that money possesses little value to him. Carrie is intrigued by this unusual person and views her own life as insignificant in comparison.

Charles Drouet

Charles Drouet travels around the country as a salesman, or drummer, for a dry goods firm. He meets Carrie on the train on her first venture from the farm to the city. Drouet perceives himself as quite a lady's man. Dressed in a vested suit with shiny gold buttons on his sleeves, he fits the 1880 slang term of a "masher," or a person who dresses to attract young women. He starts a conversation with Carrie, and she cannot help but notice his pink cheeks, mustache, and fancy hat. In addition to his fine dress and good looks, he possesses an easygoing nature that puts people, especially women, at ease. Drouet manages to learn where Carrie is going and to arrange to meet her on the following Monday.

Although the two do not meet on that Monday, Drouet thinks of Carrie often while he enjoys his clubs, the theatre, and having drinks with friends, such as George Hurstwood. He brags to Hurstwood one night about meeting Carrie, "I struck a little peach coming in on the train Friday." Drouet vows to Hurstwood that he will see Carrie again before he goes out of town.

Drouet runs into Carrie on the street and takes her out to dinner. He impresses her with his lavish spending and worldliness. He gives Carrie money to buy clothes. Carrie sees him as a kind person; Drouet simply enjoys women. He finally convinces Carrie to move in with him. He is thrilled with his "delicious ... conquest."

Unable to keep his conquest to himself, Drouet introduces Hurstwood to Carrie. When Hurstwood and Carrie become too involved with

New York's Broadway, circa 1900.

one another, though, Drouet shows his jealousy. He cannot understand why Carrie would be interested in Hurstwood when he, himself, has done so much for her. Carrie resents this and threatens to leave. Drouet leaves instead, angry that Carrie has used him.

Drouet and Carrie do not meet again until he arrives at her dressing room in New York. He tries to act as if nothing has happened, expecting to be able to win back Carrie's fond regard. Carrie, however, ignores his advances and leaves town without telling him. He tries to tell himself that he does not care, but he feels a new sense of rejection.

Mrs. Hale

Mrs. Hale lives with her husband in the apartment above the one Carrie and Drouet occupy. Mrs. Hale is an attractive, thirty-five-year-old woman who is Carrie's Chicago friend. Carrie often accompanies Mrs. Hale on buggy rides to view the mansions neither of them can afford. Mrs. Hale gossips frequently, and Carrie becomes an object of her gossip when Mrs. Hale sees her with Hurstwood while Drouet is out of town.

Minnie Hanson

Minnie, Carrie's sister, meets Carrie at the train station when Carrie arrives in Chicago. Minnie dresses plainly and shows the wear and tear of a woman who has to work hard. Her face is lean and unsmiling. Only twenty-seven years old, Minnie appears older. She views her lot in life as duty to her family and sees no room for the pleasures that people around her enjoy. She disapproves of Carrie's desire to experience the many distractions that Chicago offers. When Carrie leaves Chicago, Minnie is angry at first and then concerned for her sister's welfare.

Sven Hanson

An American son of a Swedish father, Sven Hanson is Minnie's husband and Carrie's brother-in-law. He works hard cleaning refrigerator cars at the stockyards and intends to provide a better life for his family in the future. The money he makes goes toward payments on a piece of property where he will someday build their home. Sven expects Carrie to not only do her share of work, but also to contribute to the family's well-being. While he generally demonstrates a serious nature, he handles his baby gently and patiently. He is a caring and ambitious person who sees no room for nonsense in his life.

George Hurstwood Jr.

George Hurstwood Jr., the twenty-year-old son of George Sr. and Julia, works for a real-estate firm but still lives at home. He does not contribute to household expenses and communicates infrequently with his parents. He comes and goes as he pleases, doing little as a family member but reaping the benefits of free room and board.

George Hurstwood Sr.

At the beginning of the novel, Hurstwood imagines himself a man of distinction. While not yet forty years old, he has managed to achieve a certain level of success as the manager of Fitzgerald and Moy's, an elaborately appointed saloon where the best clientele come to socialize. Given his position in the establishment, Hurstwood knows all the right people and can greet most of them in an informal manner. He dresses the part of an important person, too. His tailored suits sport the stiff lapels of imported goods, and his vests advertise the latest patterned fabrics. He complements his suits with mother-of-pearl buttons and soft, calf-skin shoes; he wears an engraved watch attached to a solid gold chain. Hurstwood exudes a sense of self-confidence and notoriety.

Hurstwood impresses Carrie the first time they meet. Not only does Hurstwood's appearance hint at class, but he also charms Carrie with his gentlemanly deference and refined manners. Carrie feels an immediate attraction to Hurstwood.

While Hurstwood associates with Drouet and Carrie as freely as if he were single, he does have a wife and children. At home, Hurstwood displays little of his public geniality although he is always the gentleman. The family revolves about him, generally intent on their own matters but enjoying the status Hurstwood provides for them.

Hurstwood's downfall begins when Carrie discovers that he is married. Shortly after that, upset that Carrie wants nothing to do with him, he has a brief lapse of integrity and takes money from his employer's safe. He tricks Carrie into leaving Chicago with him, and the two eventually settle in New York.

New York life brings Hurstwood the realization that he will not enjoy the same preference he had known in Chicago. The status to which he was accustomed in Chicago would cost him more in New York. When he looks for jobs, Hurstwood finds nothing comparable to his position in Chicago. He goes into business with a man whom he later finds to be less than desirable. The business begins failing. With it, Hurstwood's confidence begins to flag, and his conscience nags him about his crime.

Hurstwood's business fails, and he squanders the money he stole. The stress begins to wear on him, and he shows signs of depression. As money becomes tighter and Hurstwood acts more strangely, Carrie feels more dissatisfied. After meeting Bob Ames, a man who represents an entirely different ideal than the men she has always known, Carrie begins to imagine a different life than the one she has with Hurstwood. At the same time, Hurstwood's psychological state further deteriorates. Eventually, he finds no reason to get dressed. When a friend offers to share an apartment with Carrie, Carrie moves out. After Carrie leaves him, Hurstwood wanders aimlessly through life, one of New York's homeless, until he can no longer will himself to live.

Jessica Hurstwood

Seventeen-year-old Jessica, daughter of George and Julia, displays too much independence to suit her parents. Accustomed to having the latest fashions, she insists on replenishing her wardrobe with the change of the seasons. She has high aspirations for herself, picturing a future wherein she will be loved and further pampered by a rich husband.

Mrs. Julia Hurstwood

A vain person, Mrs. Hurstwood dresses in the latest fashions and enjoys all the luxuries her husband's success allows her. She is not an overly affectionate woman and finds pleasure in her relationship with her children rather than with her husband. She oversees the housework done by a succession of maids with whom she always finds fault. Mrs. Hurstwood has little faith in mankind and does not hesitate to point out people's faults. She knows, however, that finding fault with her husband will do nothing to serve her position in life, even though much of the family's property is in her name.

Carrie Madenda

See Caroline Meeber

Caroline Meeber

Carrie, the main character of the story, allows others to guide her actions. This is particularly true of her relationships with men. At the opening of the novel, eighteen-year-old Carrie sits on a train bound for Chicago from the rural Midwest. A Wisconsin farm girl, Carrie dresses true to her ordinary circumstances. She wears a plain blue dress and old shoes, and demonstrates a reserved, lady-like nature. She feels slightly regretful at telling her parents good-bye and leaving the only home and safety she has known, but she looks forward with curiosity and anticipation to her new life in the city.

When a salesman named Charles Drouet starts a conversation with her on the train, Carrie does not know how to be coy and is, instead, simply direct in her responses to him. It is this first bold encounter with Drouet that establishes Carrie's fate in the world that exists beyond her farm home. Her exchange with Drouet sets the precedent for her relationship with him and other men she meets.

Carrie lives with her sister and brother-in-law until they are no longer willing to support her. Having run into Drouet on the street and renewed her acquaintance with him, Carrie accepts his invitation to take care of her. While her upbringing rings a cautionary bell in her subconscious, Carrie can see only the advantages to having Drouet provide her with room and board. Drouet offers all that Carrie desires—nights at the theatre, beautiful clothes, and delicious restaurant dinners. Carrie ignores her misgivings and enjoys Drouet's attentions.

These same enticements guide Carrie's actions after she meets George Hurstwood. His expensive dress and money impress her. At about the same

Media Adaptations

- Blackstone Audio Books offers *Sister Carrie* on audiocassette, which was produced in 1989.

time, she has her first acting experience under the stage name Drouet has given her, "Carrie Madenda." Carrie gains confidence in herself through Hurstwood's attentions and the response she gets from her first audience. She eventually leaves Drouet behind.

Carrie and Hurstwood settle in New York. From this point on in the story, Carrie lives for the good things in life that money and fame can bring her. When Hurstwood fails to provide her with these, she leaves him. As Carrie Madenda, the actress, she lives for herself.

Sister Carrie

See Caroline Meeber

Mrs. Vance

Mrs. Vance is Carrie's New York friend. She lives with her husband across the hall from Carrie and Hurstwood, and Carrie delights in Mrs. Vance's piano playing. She and Mrs. Vance visit one another and often walk along Broadway to see and be seen. Mrs. Vance introduces Carrie to Bob Ames.

Carrie Wheeler

See Caroline Meeber

Themes

American Dream

Each of Dreiser's characters in *Sister Carrie* search for their own "American Dreams"—the ones offered by a growing and prosperous democratic country. Carrie, a poor country girl, arrives in Chicago, filled with the expectations of acquiring the finer things in life. She imagines the elegant clothes she will wear, the exciting places to which she will go, and the fashionable people with whom she will associate, thinking that everyone who lives beyond the boundaries of her Midwestern state has achieved that higher status. Drouet seeks his own version of the American Dream. He has achieved a certain station in life and wears the clothes to prove it. He frequents the important establishments in town and has befriended many of the right people. Yet, he pursues the other appointments that represent his dream, such as a beautiful woman to adorn his arm and his own home. Hurstwood has the woman, the established home and family, and a good position. He, though, wants more. He knows that his employers leave him out of important decision making, and he knows his friends like him for his position. He seeks love, appreciation, and more prestige.

Change and Transformation

Carrie and Hurstwood undergo dramatic changes from the beginning of the novel to the end. Though gradual, their transformations create immediate repercussions along the way. Carrie's metamorphosis takes her from country bumpkin to glamorous actress. In her wake, she leaves her disillusioned sister, an angry suitor, and a broken-down man. Hurstwood's transition moves him from prominent and trusted businessman, husband, and father to homeless street beggar. Behind him survive robbed employers, a dysfunctional family, and a self-satisfied woman.

Choices and Consequences

Hurstwood makes one choice that dramatically affects the rest of his life. While all choices result in consequences, those consequences can be positive or negative. Hurstwood's decision to take the money from his employer's safe starts his downward spiral to his eventual suicide.

Wealth and Poverty

Industrial growth brought the United States a period of prosperity during the late 1800s and early 1900s. With factories flourishing, job opportunities were abundant. People made good money in factory management positions and other white-collar jobs. Factory workers, however, not only earned low incomes, but they also worked long hours. Consequently, a wide division existed between the wealthy and the poor.

Carrie comes from a lower-middle-class background and determines that she will rise above it.

Her sister's family, however, maintain the same struggling existence Carrie has always known. They have no time to enjoy leisure activities and no money to spend on them. Carrie wants more for herself.

Throughout *Sister Carrie,* the distinction between social classes is obvious. The clothes people wear, the homes in which they live, and the activities in which they are involved distinguish the rich from the poor. The wealthy wear stylish clothes and attend elaborate performances of the arts. The poor buy factory-made clothes and jeans and are lucky to go to the penny arcade or the local dance pavilion. In the final chapter, the description of Hurstwood's last days offers a vivid picture of the ultimate plight of the poorest.

Identity

Experiences contribute greatly to shaping people's identities. Carrie's transformation from the beginning of the novel to the end occurs as a result of her responses to her experiences. The Carrie who boards the train in Columbia City sits primly, trying to ignore the glances of the man seated near her. Having certain morals, Carrie hesitates to acknowledge Drouet's presence. Yet, she responds quickly to his initial comments to her and makes direct eye contact with him when she senses his interest in her. From this point on, Carrie allows herself to act in whatever manner benefits her. Leaving her sister's home and moving in with Drouet, for example, goes against all propriety her parents have taught her. She sees, though, that this action will get her closer to having what she wants. As she understands her value to others, she changes her identity accordingly. As a result, she never really has an identity but adjusts her "act" to fit the situation. In the end, this ability gains her recognition as an acclaimed actress but does not result in her achieving happiness.

Sex

In the early 1900s, the morals and virtues of the Victorian era still guided people's actions. People with proper upbringing did not speak of sex. The public was shocked that Dreiser's characters so openly participated in explicit relationships and that Dreiser seemed to condone it.

Carrie uses sex to gain status for herself. She sees nothing wrong in living with Drouet to get the clothes she wants and to have opportunities to move in Chicago's affluent circles. Later, Carrie sees that Hurstwood can offer her an even higher standard of living. She ignores the fact that he is already

Topics For Further Study

- Andrew Delbanco notes in his introduction to the 1999 Modern Library's Edition of *Sister Carrie* that "Carrie's fate ... has been set in motion ... by her failure to understand ... that a woman does not look a strange man steadily in the eye without signaling to him that she is ready to be included in the system of exchange." Psychologists today would call Carrie's eye contact a form of nonverbal communication. Research the forms of nonverbal communication psychologists have identified. Give examples of the types of messages psychologists believe people are sending when they use different nonverbal clues. What kind of nonverbal clue could Carrie have sent if she did not want to interact with Drouet?

- Today, critics credit Dreiser with paving the way for writers who came after him to write realistically about life in America. Research late nineteenth-century life in America. Make at least three comparisons between Carrie's life and the life of a typical nineteenth-century American that would support critics' view of Dreiser's realistic portrayal of the American way of life.

- Carrie was most impressed by the clothes people wore. During the late 1800s, fashions actually did make a statement about a person's socioeconomic status. Read about fashion and social status in the late nineteenth century. Write a paper that discusses the differences in clothes among lower, middle, and upper class people; the changes in the clothing industry that allowed for new looks in clothing; and the changes in women's fashions in particular.

- Draw three portraits of Carrie that portray the three distinct periods in her life: before Drouet's influence, as a kept woman, and as an actress. Your drawings must accurately reflect both knowledge of Carrie's life and an understanding of the relationship between fashion and a person's status.

- Depict through illustrations Carrie's rise to and Hurstwood's fall from social acceptance. Be sure that your drawings are accurate representations of the time in which events took place.

- Dreiser is said to have been an "agnostic." What is an agnostic? What personal beliefs do you find in Dreiser's biographical sketches that would support his being an agnostic? How do you see Dreiser's agnosticism influencing his work in *Sister Carrie?*

- Many reviewers describe Dreiser's work using such descriptive nouns as Darwinian, pessimistic determinism, naturalism, and agnosticism. Compare and contrast these terms. Describe specific events from *Sister Carrie* that would support or repudiate the use of any of these terms in describing this work.

- Carrie often felt the effects of gender inequity in her endeavors. While women's rights were just beginning to be an issue at the time this book was published, there were certain events occurring that brought the idea of equal rights for women to the forefront. Trace the history of the women's rights movement beginning with the first political convention held in 1848 at Seneca Falls, New York, and ending with the current decade.

---

married and the two of them will be committing adultery. With no regard for Drouet's emotions, she breaks off their relationship and pursues one with Hurstwood. After living with Hurstwood for some time, she realizes she can no longer benefit from the arrangement and leaves him, too.

Style

Point of View

Dreiser uses a third person omniscient point of view to tell the story of his heroine, Carrie. Through this point of view, Dreiser provides readers with insight into not only Carrie's thoughts but also those of all his characters. One example of this is found in chapter twenty-seven, when Hurstwood discovers a note from Carrie and later steals money from his employer's safe. Dreiser portrays Hurstwood's distorted thinking as well as Carrie's confusion over Hurstwood's actions.

Setting

Early twentieth-century, newly urbanized America provides the backdrop for *Sister Carrie.* At the start of the story, Carrie travels by train to Chicago, a city of opportunity for not only country girls like herself, but also for immigrants from all over the world. The Chicago that Carrie finds offers an abundance of factory jobs for both men and women. In addition, numerous opportunities for enjoyment of the arts present themselves in the form of theatre, opera, symphonies, and so on. Carrie enjoys the fashionably dressed people around her and her own ownership of the latest styles. The same prosperity exists in New York City, where Carrie and Hurstwood find themselves at the end of the story. Yet here, the less fortunate in this materialistic culture appear more obviously, begging on street corners and seeking refuge in homeless shelters. While upper- and middle-class Americans are envisioning a future full of promise, those at the lower end of the spectrum are suffering the negative repercussions of a stratified society.

Structure

Critics recognize Dreiser for the extensive detail he uses in his writing. The hallmark of Dreiser's fiction, his journalistic style, receives criticism for being an "endless piling up of minutiae," H. L. Mencken notes in his Commentary to *Sister Carrie.* Mencken goes on to say that he wonders if Dreiser actually enjoys creating his collections of words that do not reflect any beauty or even a particular style.

Although Dreiser recieves negative appraisal for his rambling style, he earns accolades for his ability to write realistically. Mencken acknowledges that Dreiser's writing reflects the influences of Thomas Hardy and Honoré de Balzac in its ability to portray drama in the most mundane of life's daily routines. A greater strength, though, is that Dreiser goes beyond the drama of the moment to immerse his characters in humankind's eternal struggles. The portrayal of Carrie's obsession with fashion, for example, merely demonstrates her attempts to escape from physical miseries in her search for true happiness. Dreiser's descriptions,

set in underlying universal themes, arouse readers' emotions. As a result, Dreiser is viewed as a pivotal force in changing the direction of twentieth-century literature.

Realism

Many late nineteenth- and early twentieth-century writers tried to portray life as it actually existed. Their scenes, characters, and actions reflect daily activities in people's lives, whether noteworthy or not. Literary experts call these writers "realists." Realists who take their writing to the extreme—discussing even life's coarse, brutal, or disgusting aspects—are "naturalists." Critics categorize Dreiser as a naturalist. Sister Carrie's blatant prostitution and supposed marital infidelity shocked people when the novel first appeared. Also shocking is that Dreiser makes no attempt to apologize for his heroine's actions. He sympathizes with Carrie's efforts to survive in a modern world given her lower-middle-class background and less-than-genteel upbringing. Dreiser's Carrie and the settings in which he put her render a vivid and realistic picture of a newly urbanized America populated by people from all walks of life.

Determinism

Dreiser writes from a philosophic doctrine known as "determinism." Determinists believe that man's actions are not his own; they are determined by inherited or environmental influences. Viewed from this philosophy, Carrie cannot avoid her experiences; her world runs on sex and chance. Neither does Hurstwood deserve his fate. His downfall results only from circumstances around him. The two characters' destinies have nothing to do with morals: They simply happen.

Tragedy

Tragedy describes characters who have survived numerous struggles only to fail in the end. They fail, however, in such a way as to become heroes and heroines, evoking sympathy from readers. Dreiser's Carrie and Hurstwood both portray tragic characters. Carrie struggles to overcome her meager existence and her naivete. Though she gains security, ease, and a taste of the finer things in life, Carrie never fully realizes the happiness she seeks. Hurstwood, on the other hand, represents the average middle-class American struggling to maintain his place in a mercurial class system. One moment of poor judgment ruins the rest of his life. The tragedy of Hurstwood's life is his undeserved punishment.

Historical Context

Late-Nineteenth-Century Industrialism

The United States experienced a huge growth in manufacturing in the late 1800s that resulted in prosperity for many but virtual poverty for others. As a result of improved technology and an increase in the number of people in the workforce, including experienced businessmen, factories could produce more goods at a faster rate than ever before. In addition, changes in government policy and the availability of resources contributed to the expansion of manufacturing. Factory jobs were plentiful, but the wages were not always sufficient. Many workers enjoyed a better standard of living, while others struggled to make ends meet.

Factory conditions varied from workplace to workplace, yet the challenge of the type of work remained the same. First, the work was boring. A factory worker generally stood at an assembly line performing the same job repeatedly and to a degree of perfection. Factory work also meant long hours. Workers often averaged ten hours per day, six days per week with few breaks and little flexibility. People who were accustomed to working on farms or to creating their own handcrafted goods found factory schedules a difficult adjustment. Next, the factories themselves lacked safe working conditions and were often dark, dirty, and poorly ventilated. Illnesses, injuries, and even death were not uncommon. Finally, factory workers' wages varied. Often, women, like Carrie, and children worked at factory jobs because they agreed to lower wages than men did. As a result, men moved from workplace to workplace seeking better conditions and wages or joined labor unions to try to improve their lives at work.

From Tradition and Gentility to Modernism

The last years of the 1800s ushered in a sense of optimism and confidence felt by most Americans in the beginning of the twentieth century, the time period of *Sister Carrie*. The United States enjoyed a position as a leading world power, and the country's industrial growth and resulting stable economy provided the American people with a great measure of security. They believed that the 1900s would continue to offer them the best of that which had occurred in the previous century. Continued technological advances would make life even easier. Work would take less of people's time; play could take more. People would nurture the same genteel morals, and the arts would reflect

The Waldorf-Astoria Hotel on Fifth Avenue in New York City, opened in 1897.

their refined tastes. Americans felt that nothing could shake the status quo.

While many Americans basked in their country's success, others lived a less comfortable existence. The cities were comprised of distinct socioeconomic classes: highbrow, middlebrow, and lowbrow. The very technology that had made the country prosperous also created a huge division between the "haves" and the "have nots." The upper and middle classes, secure in their positions and comforts, were content to continue their lives as they had always known them; they ignored the less fortunate people around them and supported the same traditions in the arts and letters that they had in the past. At the same time, some members of the arts community began to address the realities of the twentieth century and to gain an audience for works that depicted the facts of life. These creative people—painters, writers, musicians, and architects—began the movement that would mark the beginning of modernism in America.

Social Class and Status

Social class distinction revealed itself not only through the disparity in wages earned but also through the kinds of leisure activities people en-

Compare
&
Contrast

- **Late 1800s:** Women's fashions favor Victorian styles. Dress indicates a woman's status. Upper- and middle-class women wear constrictive underclothing (corsets), high-heeled shoes, and elaborate, vividly colored dresses made of luxurious fabrics.

  Early 1900s: As women become more involved in leisure activities, such as sports, and take on new roles in society, such as office workers and students, their fashions evolve to freer, less structured styles. The styles include loose bloomers instead of corsets, less bulky skirts, and shirtwaist blouses. Shoes are flatter and more feminine.

  Late 1900s: Women become more health conscious and involved in professional careers; they begin to define their own unique styles of fashion. Clothing varies from jeans to pants to short and full-length skirts. Form-fitting clothes that show off a woman's figure are popular.

- **Late 1800s:** The arts become a popular form of entertainment. Drama, musical comedy, and vaudeville acts proliferate. Modern art and architecture reflect simplicity and realism. A movement from tradition and gentility begins.

  Early 1900s: The Progressive Era begins. Artists bring social relevancy to their work.

  Blacks, immigrants and women contribute in unprecedented ways, breaking color, cultural, and gender barriers.

  Late 1900s: Art becomes a bigger cultural presence: bigger in scope, ambition, theme, budget, and promotion. Media coverage makes all forms of art more accessible than ever before. People have more money to spend as a result of the healthy economy, and they are ready to enjoy themselves. They buy fine art and electronic gadgets; they enjoy huge film and television productions. Overall, arts and leisure of the late 1900s reflect America's obsession with wealth and success.

- **Late 1800s:** The United States is considered the leader in manufacturing and has the largest economy in the world.

  Early 1900s: Automotive leader Henry Ford introduces the moving assembly line, which results in greater productivity, more consistent quality, higher wages for workers, and lower prices for the consumer.

  Late 1900s: Advanced technology, such as computers, aid in greater information access and allow for expansion of commerce and economy.

---

joyed and the fashions they wore. In *Sister Carrie,* Carrie strove to attend the events of the wealthier set as well as wear their fashions, hoping she would one day be part of high society.

As technology in the early twentieth century helped create a variety of paying jobs for workers and production methods improved, workers were allowed more time to pursue leisure activities. Sports and show business became amusement favorites for everyone; the kinds of events people attended reflected their socioeconomic status. In addition, the trend towards healthy activities dictated clothing styles.

Organized sports heralded amusement activities for the wealthy. Baseball, the most popular sport for years, was enjoyed only by upper and middle classes until 1876. After that, spectators and participants of all classes became involved in it, although it appealed more to men than to women. Women preferred croquet and bicycling. Croquet and bicycling allowed middle- and upper-class men and women to socialize. Tennis and golf appealed to the wealthy of both sexes. Football began as a sport for privileged college students but soon became as popular as baseball. Women became more involved in sports such as rowing, track, swimming, and basketball as a result of being exposed to these sports in college.

While sporting events drew the interest of mostly wealthy people, show business entertained the common people. As railroad travel improved, circuses reached small towns across the country and prospered. In the cities, popular drama, musical comedy, and vaudeville provided Americans with a means of escape from their daily trials.

Very early on, fashions made a statement about social status. As the times changed, though, the clothes people wore said less about them and more about changes in society. Before the Civil War, only the wealthiest people could afford finely tailored clothes; others wore hand-sewn clothes. Because of changes in the textile industry to accommodate the mass production of Civil War uniforms, however, clothing became more available and affordable to everyone. Clothing continued to indicate social status. Department stores appeared and catered to the wealthy. Chain stores, like the "five and dime," met the needs of the general public. In order to look like everyone else, poorer people bought cheap factory-made clothes. The working poor wore the first blue jeans. The wealthy, though, stood out. The men wore three-piece suits in somber colors; the women wore restrictive underclothes and elaborate dresses and hats made of bright, luxurious fabrics.

As women became increasingly involved in sports and new occupations, clothing became more comfortable and sensible. Women needed freedom to move, so Victorian-style dresses and tight corsets gave way to "shirtwaist" styles, loose undergarments, and shoes with shorter heels. No longer did plain dress indicate low socioeconomic status.

Critical Overview

Dreiser wrote successfully for years as a newspaper reporter. Yet readers appreciated his stories not for their exact reporting of the events, but for their relating of personal impressions about people, places, and happenings. Dreiser grew to understand that providing his readers with realistic impressions was his strength and began to cultivate it. When critics read his early fiction, they did not at first appreciate his truthful portrayal of life in America. Only later did they applaud this in Dreiser's writing. Critics did, however, immediately praise his sensitivity and viewed it as a powerful storytelling

tool. While reviewers did not particularly like his style of writing, they did like the content.

The very characteristic that disturbed the public about *Sister Carrie* when the book first came out is the same characteristic that critics now recognize as a strength in Dreiser's work. That characteristic is Dreiser's realistic treatment of real-life occurrences. At the time that *Sister Carrie* appeared, fiction seldom touched upon the darker side of human endeavors and relationships. Prostitution, for example, might occur in the real world, but authors did not make it an overt part of their plots. For Dreiser's Carrie, though, prostitution was a way of life. She would not have been able to survive without using men to get to her next level of existence. Dreiser writes about Carrie's lifestyle in a matter-of-fact manner. The public was appalled that Dreiser viewed it so lightly. Today, however, readers are not as shocked by Carrie's way of life. While readers may not approve of it, they understand how a woman of that period might feel compelled to seek her independence in this manner.

In addition to being known for his realistic treatment of topics that most other writers of his time considered taboo, Dreiser also receives acclaim for his sensitivity to his characters' predicaments. H. L. Mencken says in his Commentary in the 1999 Modern Library Edition of *Sister Carrie* that what Dreiser lacks in style in comparison to other novelists, he makes up for in his serious consideration of human nature. Mencken says, "What they lack, great and small, is the gesture of pity, the note of awe, the profound sense of wonder … which even the most stupid cannot escape in Dreiser."

Dreiser started *Sister Carrie* at the urging of his friend, Arthur Henry. While Dreiser had written for years as a newspaper reporter, and had recently completed and sold four short stories, he doubted that he had the talent to write a novel. He sat down to write *Sister Carrie* with the image of his own siblings in mind. His sister, Emma, who had run away with her married lover, served as Dreiser's model for Carrie. Dreiser wrote about Carrie from a sense of feeling, rather than from a sense of purposeful problem-solving. That is, he wrote as if he were experiencing the events and their effects as they occurred. Critics have often noted this artistic passion in Dreiser's writing. For example, Mencken compares Dreiser to Franz Schubert. Mencken says that Schubert knew little of the technique of music but had such an artistic sense of the music he was able to create musical works of art. Dreiser, says Mencken, has the same ability to create stories from his sense of the world around him.

While Dreiser possessed a sense of the world around him and could write about it realistically, he lacked the ability to create beauty with his words. His writing style is highly criticized by experts as being too verbose, and the words too commonplace. Mencken, even as one of Dreiser's first advocates, agrees with this assessment. In his *Commentary* he describes Dreiser's writing as a "dogged accumulation of threadbare, undistinguished, uninspiring nouns, adjectives, verbs, adverbs, pronouns, participles, and conjunctions." Most writers work to find the perfect words to communicate ideas to their readers. Dreiser does not appear to bother. Critics see this as a fault in Dreiser's works. They consider his writing less precise and less elegant than the works of other writers. Not only do experts discredit Dreiser's style, they also disapprove of his contradictory conveyance of a deterministic philosophy. While Dreiser believed that life results from blind chance, he still evoked sympathy for this characters.

Even though Dreiser did not immediately find success as a writer, he did not get discouraged. Dreiser wrote prolifically for more than forty years. Over the years, critics saw more value in Dreiser's writing. They set aside their problems with his style to appreciate the lasting influences his messages portrayed. Today, critics note that Dreiser's greatest influences were to pave the path for writers to convey realistic images of American life and to help launch modern naturalism. Jack Salzman said in *Theodore Dreiser: The Critical Reception,* that Dreiser's "significance in the history of American letters is no longer a matter for dispute. We may continue to debate his merits as an artist, but his importance to American literature has been well established."

Criticism

Diane Andrews Henningfeld

Henningfeld is an associate professor at Adrian College. She holds a Ph.D. in literature and writes widely for educational publishers. In this essay she examines Sister Carrie *as a tragic novel, focusing on Carrie's use of sex as capital.*

Sister Carrie, written by Theodore Dreiser from 1899 to 1900, was published by Doubleday,

Page in 1900. The novel created a stir from the moment of its publication, caused in part by a supposed attempt by the publisher to suppress the novel. The truth behind the "suppression" of *Sister Carrie* is difficult to uncover. Regardless, the novel met with mixed reviews from contemporary readers, who found the book unpleasant and gloomy. Some critics suggest that these initial negative reviews were because *Sister Carrie* was a novel ahead of its time. The novel has grown in stature over the years until it has come to be considered one of the most important American novels of the twentieth century.

Sister Carrie is the story of young Carrie Meeber, who comes to Chicago in 1889 to make her fortune. Chicago is not as she envisions it, however. In her desire for material possessions and success, she begins and leaves two different illicit affairs. By the close of the book, she is in New York, having embarked on a highly successful stage career. Even this success does not bring her happiness; the novel closes with Carrie rocking in her chair, considering her sense that there is more to life than she has experienced.

While the book received many negative reviews upon publication, it nonetheless attracted the attention of the literary establishment, igniting a controversy that still has fire. Stuart P. Sherman, in the famous and much-anthologized essay "The Barbaric Naturalism of Mr. Dreiser," takes Dreiser to task for his naturalism. He distinguishes between realism and naturalism, finding realism an acceptable form of literature and naturalism unacceptable. He writes,

> A realistic novel is a representation based upon a theory of human conduct. If the theory of human conduct is adequate, the representation constitutes an addition to literature and to social history. A naturalistic novel is a representation based upon a theory of animal behavior. Since a theory of animal behavior can never be an adequate basis for a representation of the life of man in contemporary society, such a representation is a blunder.

H. L. Mencken, one of Dreiser's earliest supporters, wrote at length in response to Sherman and about *Sister Carrie* and its contribution to American literature. He writes of Sherman's criticism in "The Dreiser Bugaboo," "Only a glance is needed to show the vacuity of all this irate flubdub," before going on to connect Dreiser's realism with the classical Greek writers. He argues, "In the midst of democratic cocksureness and Christian sentimentalism, of doctrinaire shallowness and professorial smugness, he stands for a point of view which at least has something honest and courageous about it; here, at all events, he is a realist."

It is important to understand what these writers mean when they use the term "naturalism." *The Harper Handbook to Literature* states that naturalism, a literary movement of the late nineteenth century, grew out of realism, but preferred to focus on "the fringes of society, the criminal, the fallen, the down-and-out, earning as one definition … the phrase *sordid realism*." Further, naturalism grew as an interest in science and Darwinism grew. "Darwinism was especially important, as the naturalists perceived a person's fate as the product of blind external or biological forces, chiefly heredity and environment, but in the typical naturalistic novel chance played a large part as well." Dreiser's novels are nearly always critiqued through the naturalistic lens. Critics point to Carrie's upward rise and Hurstwood's downward spiral as the result of forces beyond their control. The chance event, such as the open safe at Hurstwood's saloon, lead him to take actions resulting in negative consequences. Carrie's chance meeting with Drouet on the street when she is out of money and looking for a job leads to her involvement with both Drouet and Hurstwood.

Although it cannot be denied that *Sister Carrie* is a good example of early twentieth-century naturalism, it is also possible for the novel to be read in different ways. Karl F. Zender, for example, argues, in *Studies in the Novel,* that the emphasis on circumstance and the de-emphasis on character "is adequate neither to the artistic power nor to the culture implications of *Sister Carrie.*" Zender goes on to examine the novel as a tragedy of character caused by emotional repression. Other critics have examined the tragic nature of the novel as well. However, in general, critics see the novel as the story of Hurstwood's tragedy. It is possible to examine the novel as a tragedy in another way, one that focuses on Carrie as capitalist, engaged in the exchange of goods.

The circumstances that swirl Carrie through the novel are largely economic. The great life she imagines for herself in Chicago centers on the attainment of material goods. It is this desire that drives her away from her small town in Wisconsin and toward the bright lights of Chicago. Once in Chicago, she discovers that her sister and her husband see her as the means for their own economic security. In exchange for her small room, Carrie must produce enough capital to help her sister meet their rent.

Carrie has few resources to produce this capital. She hits the streets of Chicago, looking for work. She finally finds a job, producing shoes on an assembly line. The assembly line, as a means of production, removes the worker from the product. She is responsible for running a machine that punches the lace holes in the right upper half of a man's shoe. She becomes a machine herself, fitting leather to machine, over and over. In exchange for the mechanization of her life, she receives four dollars and fifty cents per week. She must turn over four dollars per week to her sister, leaving her with little capital or hope for economic advancement.

If, therefore, it is economic forces that allow a person to rise or fall in the culture presented in the novel, Carrie's problem becomes one of economics. What does she have that can be exchanged for the goods she wants? Clearly the money she earns at the factory will never keep up with her material desires. When Carrie accepts the astronomical sum of twenty dollars from the drummer Drouet, she is doing more than accepting a loan. She is embarking on an economic arrangement, the first step in an exchange of capital. Quite simply, Carrie discovers that she has capital in the form of sex. In a materialistic society, sex becomes a commodity, something that can be bought, sold, and exchanged for goods.

Carrie's rise, then, is directly linked to the way she barters her sexual capital. Her appearance in the lodge theatre performance offers her the opportunity to market her sexual capital. The men in the audience all represent potential buyers. The competition for Carrie's capital renders her as a more attractive commodity to Hurstwood. As a result of her appearance on stage, Carrie finds that she can trade upward. Hurstwood offers better material conditions than those she enjoys with Drouet.

While it is true that Carrie continues to trade in on her own sexual capital throughout the book, leading eventually to her rise as a famous stage star, the story is nonetheless a tragedy. Looking at the novel as Hurstwood's tragedy, however, is too limiting. The novel as a whole can be read as the tragic results of making sex a commodity.

Dramatic literature can usually be divided into two categories, comedy and tragedy. Comedy is characterized by young love, sex, fertility, marriage, spring, and birth. Tragedy, on the other hand, is characterized by sterility, waste, and death. While comedy rejoices in each new generation, tragedy marks the end of the generation without progeny. The tragedy of *Sister Carrie* is one of

What Do I Read Next?

- Like *Sister Carrie,* Dreiser's second novel, *Jennie Gerhardt,* draws from experiences in Dreiser's sisters' lives. Published in 1911, the story centers on Jennie, the poor and immoral daughter of an immigrant who detests the methods by which his daughter tries to achieve happiness.

- *Jennie Gerhardt* has been compared to Thomas Hardy's 1919 classic, *Tess of the D'Urbervilles,* if only because of the similarities between their main characters. Like Jennie, Tess comes from a common background. She admits to her husband that she has had a child out of wedlock, who died in infancy. Her husband leaves her. In order to save her family, she goes to live as the mistress of the wealthy Alec D'Urberville, the father of the dead child.

- *Jude the Obscure,* another of Thomas Hardy's books, is similar to *Sister Carrie.* Published in 1919, the story is about a young man and his unhappy experiences with love, sex, destiny, and social status.

- *The Awakening,* Kate Chopin's highly controversial novel published in 1899, tells the story of Edna Pontellier, a married woman who experiences a summer romance and returns to the city a changed woman. She turns her back on her old life—family, social involvement, and traditional morals—to search for self-fulfillment through new love, life ventures, and sexual activity.

sterility and death. Although sex is at the foundation of the novel, there are no pregnancies and no births. Carrie's sister and her husband are childless, and Carrie remains childless and unmarried throughout the novel. Carrie's rocking chair, in this reading, takes on new significance. Rocking chairs are often associated with nursing mothers. Carrie, however, rocks incessantly in her chair without purpose. While she wants marriage, what she obtains in exchange for her sexual capital is a place to live

and clothes to wear. Her liaisons with Drouet and Hurstwood are sterile. Although there is a hint that she would like to start a relationship with Ames, that relationship remains platonic. Indeed, it is Ames himself who tells Carrie that he sees her more as the star of a drama than of the comedies she has been playing. Ames reads Carrie well. As the novel ends, Carrie is in her rocking chair, reading a tragic novel. While Hurstwood's suicide seems the more apparent tragedy, Carrie, too, is a tragic figure, locked in sterile longing and futile hope.

In sum, it is possible to read *Sister Carrie* as a cautionary tale, a lesson in what happens when a culture reduces all human interactions to the exchange of capital. In such a culture, intimate emotional and physical bonds are reduced to tradable commodities, sex can be traded for material goods, and comedy is no longer possible. Instead, what remains is a bleak and desolate picture of a fallen society, a landscape of waste and sterility.

Source: Diane Andrews Henningfeld, in an essay for *Novels for Students,* Gale, 2000.

Martin Bucco

In the following essay, Bucco presents an overview of Sister Carrie.

In *Sister Carrie* Theodore Dreiser went beyond the Hoosier romanticism of Meredith Nicholson's "Alice of Old Vincennes" (1900) and the genteel realism of Booth Tarkington's *The Gentleman from Indiana* (1899). Growing up poor in Indiana, the daydreamy Dreiser envied the escape to the metropolis of his older brothers and sisters. Later, he drifted from one newspaper to another—Chicago, St. Louis, Pittsburgh. Charged with Balzac's *Comedie humaine,* Herbert Spencer's *First Principles,* and his own vivid memories, Dreiser began *Sister Carrie* in New York in 1899. The author based his first novel partly on his sister, Emma, who in 1886 had fled from the law with a saloon clerk. Because of the novel's sexual frankness, Dreiser's own publisher (Doubleday Page) did not promote it; but the senior reader, the writer Frank Norris, zealously sent out review copies. When B.W. Dodge (in 1907) and Grosset and Dunlap (in 1908) reissued the controversial book, *Sister Carrie* reached a larger public.

The novel has an hourglass structure. Carrie Meeber—pretty, eighteen, penniless, full of illusions—leaves her dull Wisconsin home in 1889 for Chicago. On the train Charles Drouet, a jaunty traveling salesman, impresses her with his worldliness and affluence. In Chicago, Carrie lives in a cramped flat with her sister and brother-in-law. Her job at a shoe factory is physically and spiritually crushing. After a period of unemployment, she allows Drouet to "keep" her. During his absences, however, she falls under the influence of Drouet's friend, a suave, middle-aged bar manager. George Hurstwood deserts his family, robs his employers, and elopes with Carrie, first to Montreal and then, after returning most of the money, to New York, where they live together for several years. As Hurstwood declines, Carrie develops. To earn money, she goes on stage, rising from chorus girl to minor acting parts. When Hurstwood, failing to find decent work, becomes too great a burden, Carrie deserts him. In time, she becomes a star of musical comedies. Meanwhile, Hurstwood sinks into beggary and suicide. In spite of her freedom and success, Carrie is lonely and unhappy.

Critics have labeled the novel's biological-environmental determinism, graphic fidelity, and compassionate point of view as the work of, respectively, a "naturalist," a "realist," a "romanticist." Consistently, Dreiser intermingles the world-as-it-is, -seems, and -should-be. Like Stephen Crane, Frank Norris, and Jack London, he creates characters caught in the web of causation and chance. In one of his numerous philosophical asides, the narrator informs us that physico-chemical laws underlie all activity: "Now it has been shown experimentally that a constantly subdued frame of mind produces certain poisons in the blood called katastates, just as virtuous feelings of pleasure and delight produce helpful chemicals called anastates." To evoke the illusion of mechanical motion and spiritual drift, Dreiser relies on metaphor and symbol—Carrie attracted to the magnetic city, Carrie tossed about in the sea of humanity, Carrie rocking in a chair. Against baffling forces, she is a "half-equipped little knight," a "little soldier of fortune." And as fortune propels Carrie upward, so it spins Hurstwood downward. Though the narrator avows glorious reason at the end of human evolution, at the end of the novel he pictures a discontented Carriefated to remain in the clutch of her powerful opportunistic instincts.

Dreiser's network of dramatic contrasts, parallels, foreshadowings, and ironies (not to mention the cryptic chapter headings his publishers requested) help unify this episodic novel. The sheer mass of detail obscures the chiasmic symmetry of Carrie's rise and Hurstwood's fall, as it screens somewhat the improbability of Hurstwood's "accidental" theft of money and his calculated "abduction" of Carrie. Still, Hurstwood's destitution and matter-of-fact death seem less melodramatic than

the tacked on apostrophe sentimentalizing Carrie as no Saved Sinner or Lost Soul but rather as the Beautiful Dreamer. The awkwardness, repetition, and cliches of Dreiserian prose often grate on fine-tuned sensibilities—as when the narrator informs us that Carrie had "four dollars in money" or when a chapter begins: "The, to Carrie, very important theatrical performance was to take place at the Avery on conditions which were to make it more noteworthy than was at first anticipated." For all this, the author retains the power to endow his factories, hotels, department stores, slums, theaters, and restaurants with an extraordinary sense of life.

At first, *Sister Carrie* (in the 1901 abridged Heinemann edition) was better received in Britain than in America, though the myth of its "suppression" contributed to later interest both in America and abroad. Through *Sister Carrie* Dreiser led socio-literary novelists in the first decade of the 20th century into the creation of closer ties between American life and American literature. Although Dreiser did not receive the Nobel Prize, *Sister Carrie* and *An American Tragedy* are among the truly important novels in American literature. *Sister Carrie* is now available in the Pennsylvania edition (1981), which restores the novel as closely as possible to the author's more complex original manuscript. Whatever one might say about Dreiser's graceless genius, the raw integrity of *Sister Carrie* helped pave the way for the more candid, more crafted American masterpieces of the 1920s.

Source: Martin Bucco, "*Sister Carrie,*" in *Reference Guide to American Literature,* third edition, edited by Jim Kamp, St. James Press, 1994.

Sources

Theodore Dreiser: The Critical Reception, edited by Jack Salzman, David Lewis, 1972.

H. L. Mencken, Commentary in *Sister Carrie,* Modern Library Paperback Edition, 1999, pp. xxxvii-lxxx.

H. L. Mencken, "The Dreiser Bugaboo," in *The Stature of Theodore Dreiser,* edited by Alfred Kazin and Charles Shapiro, Indiana University Press, 1955, pp. 84-91.

"Naturalism," in *The Harper Handbook to Literature,* edited by Northrup Frye, et. al., Longman, 1997, pp. 313-14.

Stuart P. Sherman, "The Barbaric Naturalism of Mr. Dreiser," in *The Stature of Theodore Dreiser,* edited by Alfred Kazin and Charles Shapiro, Indiana University Press, 1955, pp. 71-80.

Karl F. Zender, "Walking Away from the Impossible Thing: Identity and Denial in *Sister Carrie,*" in *Studies in the Novel,* Vol. 30, No. 1, Spring, 1998, pp. 63-76.

For Further Study

Theodore Dreiser, *Letters of Theodore Dreiser,* edited by Robert H. Elias, University of Pennsylvania Press, 1959.

Contains Dreiser's communications with friends over the years. Especially pertinent are the references to Doubleday's suppression of *Sister Carrie* after it was already in print.

Theodore Dreiser, *Sister Carrie,* University of Pennsylvania Press, 1981.

This work expands characters Carrie and Hurstwood through a research team's efforts to reconstruct portions of the novel that reviewers edited in the publishing process.

Philip L. Gerber, *Plots and Characters in the Fiction of Theodore Dreiser,* Archon, 1977.

A quick reference for students providing a synopsis of every short story and novel by Dreiser as well as details about every character.

Philip L. Gerber, *Theodore Dreiser,* Twayne, 1964.

A good introduction to the life and literature of Dreiser, providing biographical detail as well as critical analysis.

Herbert G. Gutman, *Work, Culture, and Society in Industrializing America,* Knopf, 1976.

As a historian, Gutman offers a critical view of the beliefs and behaviors of various labor groups throughout American history in relationship to class, race, religion, and ideology.

New Essays on Sister Carrie, edited by Donald Pizer, Cambridge University Press, 1991.

A collection of late-twentieth-century essays on *Sister Carrie,* including a useful bibliography.

Donald Pizer, *Realism and Naturalism in Nineteenth-Century American Literature,* revised edition, Southern Illinois University Press, 1984.

An important study of a literary period by a major scholar of Dreiser's work.

Joan L. Severa, et. al., *Dressed for the Photographer: Ordinary Americans and Fashion, 1840-1900,* Kent State University Press, 1997.

The author presents fashions through photographs arranged by decades and comments on the effects of material culture, expectations of society, and socioeconomic conditions that affected choices of style.

Song of Solomon

Toni Morrison
1977

Toni Morrison's third novel, *Song of Solomon,* established her as a major American writer. The story of a Black man's search for his identity through a discovery of his family history, it became a best-seller and drew praise from readers and critics when it was published in 1977. The novel has been especially admired for the beauty of its language and its grounding of universal themes in the particularity of the African-American experience, as well as for its use of folklore.

Song of Solomon is based on an African-American folktale about slaves who can fly back to Africa when they choose. Morrison fictionalizes this folktale through the character of Solomon, the great-grandfather of the story's protagonist, Milkman Dead. Through his discovery of the story of Solomon and his ability to fly, Milkman learns to take pride in his ancestry and to value his connections to family and community. *Song of Solomon* won the National Book Critics Circle Award for fiction in 1977. It is now widely taught, and appeared again on best-seller lists when it was chosen by Oprah Winfrey for inclusion in her book club. Beloved by readers for more than twenty years, it is still considered one of Morrison's best books.

Author Biography

Like her character Milkman Dead, Toni Morrison came of age in a family that had only recently left the South and moved to the Midwest. Her

Toni Morrison

mother's family migrated north from Greenville, Alabama, around the turn of the century as part of the Great Migration of southern Blacks to the urban North. Morrison was born Chloe Anthony Wofford in 1931—the same year as Milkman Dead's birth—in Lorain, Ohio, where her first book, *The Bluest Eye,* is set. She recalled a childhood in which she was "intimate with the supernatural," and read the classics of the Western tradition.

Morrison graduated from Howard University and took a master's degree at Cornell, then returned to Howard to teach, including among her students Claude Brown and Stokely Carmichael. While at Howard, she married a Jamaican architectural student named Harold Morrison, the father of her two sons. After a later divorce, she started her first novel, *The Bluest Eye,* which was published in 1970. Also that year, Morrison began work on *Sula,* her second novel, and took a job as an editor at Random House, where she worked with some of the prominent Black authors of the 1970s. After publishing *Sula,* she produced her third novel, *Song of Solomon,* which established her as a major American writer and won her the National Book Critics Circle Award.

This was followed by *Tar Baby* in 1981, and the book considered her masterpiece, *Beloved,* in 1987.

When *Beloved* failed to win either a National Book Award or a National Book Critics Circle Award, a group of Black writers and intellectuals decried the lack of national recognition given to Morrison. *Beloved* did win the Pulitzer Prize, and in 1993, following the 1992 publication of *Jazz,* Morrison was awarded the Nobel Prize for literature. The first African-American woman to win the Nobel, her acceptance speech in Stockholm, in which she spoke about the power of, and necessity for, language, prompted a standing ovation. In recent years, Morrison has turned out several works of nonfiction, writing *Playing in the Dark: Whiteness and the Literary Imagination* and publishing essays on the Clarence Thomas/Anita Hill hearings, the O. J. Simpson case, and other current events. Two of her novels, *Song of Solomon* and her most recent, 1998's *Paradise,* have been chosen for Oprah Winfrey's book club, making her both a popular, best-selling author and a critical favorite. Having given up her editing position in 1987, Morrison currently holds an appointment at Princeton University.

Plot Summary

Part I

Song of Solomon begins with the flight of Robert Smith, an insurance agent, from the roof of Mercy Hospital. Smith appears on the roof of the hospital with two handcrafted wings on his back. A small crowd gathers to witness the impending jump. Many believe he won't jump, but to the amazement of some and horror of others, Smith does jump. Because of Smith's attempt to fly, Ruth Foster Dead is able to deliver her child inside the hospital instead of on its steps. Negro women during this time are not allowed to give birth inside the hospital due to segregation. Thus Macon Dead becomes the first Negro child to be born inside Mercy Hospital.

Four years later, young Macon acquires his nickname, Milkman, when his father's tenant Freddie catches Ruth nursing Macon at age four. Milkman's father, Macon, Sr.—who is a harsh landlord to other Blacks—does not know the origins of this nickname, but he thinks it must have something to do with Ruth, of whom he can think only with disgust. The elder Macon is also estranged from his sister, Pilate, but on a night that he mercilessly evicts one of his poor tenants, Mrs. Bains, Macon stands outside Pilate's house to hear her singing.

Time goes on and Morrison details certain events in Milkman's growing up. As a young boy, Milkman and his family go on Sunday afternoon drives. On a particular Sunday, Milkman accidentally urinates on his sister Lena, a memory that Lena remembers years later. When Milkman is twelve, he and his friend Guitar Bains approach his Aunt Pilate. Milkman knows his father would disapprove of him approaching his aunt, but he decides to anyway. The two boys inquire as to whether or not she has a navel. She responds no, and invites them in for a snack. While inside, Pilate relates the history of the Dead family, and when her daughter, Reba, and her granddaughter, Hagar, come home, they are introduced to Milkman. Everyone has a nice time engaging in conversation that afternoon. However, when Milkman's father hears of Milkman's encounter with his Pilate, he is upset. He reminds Milkman that he does not want him consorting with his sister. Milkman asks his father why, and in response his father relates more of the family history. He then concludes by saying his sister is a "snake," and that he wants Milkman to stay away from her.

Following their discussion, Macon tells Milkman that he is to start working with him. Milkman's responsibilities include running errands in his aunt's part of town. Thus, he has even more opportunities to visit his relatives. A couple of years later, Milkman realizes that one of his legs is shorter by about half an inch. He tries not to dwell on what he believes is a deformity.

When Milkman is twenty-two, his father hits Ruth, and Milkman throws his father against the radiator in defense of his mother. He threatens to kill his father if he ever touches his mother again. Macon never hits his wife again, but he does explain to his son the reasons behind his poor relationship with Ruth. He claims Ruth and her father had had an inappropriate relationship; he even describes an incestuous scene he witnessed between Ruth and her dead father. After this incident, Milkman finds Guitar at the barbershop, where the men are listening to a report about the murder of Emmett Till. The news about Till reminds them of the atrocities suffered by the returning Black veterans of World War I and spurs Guitar to greater involvement in politics.

When Milkman is thirty-one, he ends a long-standing intimate relationship that he has had with Hagar, and she begins regular attempts on his life. Meanwhile, Freddie tells Milkman that Guitar has been hanging around another man, Empire State, whom he believes has murdered a white boy found dead in a schoolyard. He tells Milkman to pay close attention to Guitar from now on.

One night, Milkman lays waiting another attack from Hagar, and he recalls the recent night he followed his mother to her father's grave. Upon confronting his mother at the cemetery, Ruth explains her version of the rift between herself and Macon; she accuses Macon of lying about her relationship with her father. She denies any incestuous behavior, but does say that she felt her father was the only person who ever really cared about her. She also describes Pilate's efforts to restore sexual relations between herself and Macon and to protect Ruth's resulting pregnancy (which would result in the birth of Milkman) from Macon's violence. After pondering his recollections of his encounter with his mother, Milkman hears Hagar trying to enter Guitar's apartment; after she makes her way in, she is emotionally unable to kill Milkman. When Ruth finds out that Hagar has been trying to kill Milkman, she goes to confront Hagar. Pilate finds Ruth with Hagar, and to distract her she tells Ruth about her childhood and her travels across the country.

Meanwhile, Milkman finally asks Guitar about his relationship with Empire State. Guitar hesitates at first but then reveals that he has become a member of the Seven Days, an organization of seven Black men who murder whites chosen at random in retaliation for lynchings and other atrocities. Milkman does not approve of Guitar's involvement in this group and fears for his friend's safety, but Guitar is deeply committed to the cause.

Later, while talking to his father, Milkman mentions that Pilate has a green sack hanging from her ceiling that she calls her inheritance. Macon is surprised by this news and tells Milkman that as children he and Pilate had found some gold in a cave when they were hiding from the whites who killed their father, gold he believes belonged to a white man Macon had killed in the cave. Macon believes the green sack could contain the gold from the cave. With this knowledge, Milkman, with urging from his father and help from Guitar, steals the sack. Guitar's motives for stealing the gold include giving him the means to avenge the deaths of the four little girls in the church bombing in Birmingham.

At the beginning of chapter nine, the story shifts to Milkman's sister Corinthians, who is secretly working as a maid and having an affair with a man named Henry Porter. She has just returned from her first night of lovemaking with him when she is startled by the sounds of male voices in her kitchen. Milkman and Guitar have been arrested after they were pulled over without cause and found to have human remains in the car with them. The green sack that they had taken from Pilate's home had actually contained rocks and human bones, not gold. Pilate had to bail them out of jail by humbling herself to the police and saying that the bones are those of her dead husband.

Later, Milkman, who has figured out that Corinthians is having an affair with Porter, realizes that Porter is a member of the Seven Days. Worried for his sister, he decides to tell his father about the affair. His sister Lena does not understand Milkman's actions against their sister; she confronts him, saying that he has a habit of pissing on others (which also refers back to the time he urinated on her as a child). After this confrontation, Milkman decides to leave home.

Part II

Milkman has embarked on a solo quest for the gold, though he still intends to split the proceeds with Guitar. Milkman starts by going to Danville,

Pennsylvania, the site of the cave. He asks about a mysterious woman named Circe, who sheltered Macon and Pilate after their father's death, and is directed to the house of Reverend Cooper, who knew his father when he was a boy. Milkman learns that the Butlers, the same people Circe worked for, were responsible for his grandfather's death and never brought to justice. While Reverend Cooper's car is being repaired, Milkman meets the old men of the town, who tell him stories about his father's family.

Milkman soon encounters Circe, who looks incredibly old but speaks with the voice of a twenty-year-old girl. She tells him that his grandmother's name was Sing, his grandfather's original name was Jake, and that his grandfather's body floated up from its shallow grave and ended up being dumped in the cave. When Milkman gets to the cave there is no gold, and no body. Milkman decides that Pilate has taken the gold to Virginia during her travels around the country.

After Milkman arrives in his ancestral town of Shalimar, Virginia, he sees some children singing a song and playing, and remembers that he had never had friends as a child, until he met Guitar. However, Guitar's friendship has not lasted. While on a hunting trip with the old men of the town, Milkman fights off Guitar's first attempt to take his life. (Guitar believes Milkman has taken the gold for himself; thus he wants to kill him so he can obtain the gold.)

As the old men skin the bobcat they've caught on their trip, Milkman learns that his grandmother is one of the Byrds, related to a woman named Susan who lives in the town. After a magical night with a woman named Sweet, he goes to see Susan Byrd, who is evasive with him about their shared ancestry because of the presence of her gossipy friend Grace. Later, Milkman realizes that his ancestors are named in the song that the children of Shalimar sing; he then goes to see Susan Byrd again, excited by his discovery.

Chapter thirteen shifts the focus back to Hagar, who is profoundly depressed, rising from her bed only to go on a manic shopping spree. She then spikes a fever. Shortly afterwards, she dies, and Macon pays for her funeral.

When Milkman returns to Susan Byrd's house, she tells him all she had not told him earlier: that Sing left Shalimar with Jake, and that Jake was the youngest child of a man named Solomon who flew back to Africa. The story is that Heddy, Sing's mother, found Jake on the ground when Solomon dropped him and raised him after Ryna, Solomon's wife, lost her mind.

Having pieced together the story, Milkman returns home and tells Pilate that she has her father's bones, not those of the white man Macon killed. Milkman and Pilate return to Shalimar to bury her father's bones, but after they do, Guitar—who has been hiding nearby—shoots her. The novel ends on an image of flight, as Milkman jumps in attack from the ridge "into the killing arms of his brother [Guitar]."

Characters

Guitar Bains

Guitar is Milkman's best friend. As a child, his father was killed in a terrible industrial accident, and his mother abandoned the family when she couldn't cope. Because his mother gave him candy after his father's death, sweets make Guitar sick. After Guitar's grandmother took responsibility for him, Macon Dead evicted Guitar's family from their home for nonpayment of rent. Later, Guitar befriends Milkman after defending him in a fight, and introduces him to Pilate and the community of Southside. As an adult, Guitar is the Sunday man of the Seven Days, responsible for choosing white victims at random in retaliation for white atrocities against Blacks. He tries to kill Milkman because he believes that Milkman has cut him out of their plot to recover the gold from the cave. At the end of the novel, he kills Pilate after she and Milkman bury her father's bones at Solomon's Leap.

Susan Byrd

Susan Byrd is the daughter of Milkman's great uncle, his grandmother Heddy's brother Crowell. She lives in Shalimar and is not very helpful to Milkman the first time he sees her because she does not want her friend Grace Long to know about their shared ancestry. When he visits again, she tells him more about the history of his grandmother, including the story that Heddy's husband Jake, who becomes the first Macon Dead, was the son of a flying African named Solomon.

Circe

Circe is the woman who hides Pilate and Macon after their father's murder. She works as a maid for the same family who killed the first Macon Dead, and she hides his children in the Butler mansion, in rooms the Butlers do not use. Milkman meets her when he goes to Danville. She is living in the Butler house and tending to their Weimaraners, allowing them to destroy the house for which the Butlers killed, stole, and lied. She directs Milkman to the cave and tells him that his grandfather's body was dumped there after he floated up from his shallow grave.

Reverend Cooper

Reverend Cooper is a childhood friend of Macon's in Danville. His father made Pilate's snuff-box earring. He is the first person Milkman finds on his trip to Danville, and he introduces Milkman to the old men of the community, who tell him stories about his people.

Corinthians Dead

Corinthians Dead is the second of the two daughters of Macon and Ruth Dead. She is raised to be a good catch for a professional man of color, but after college and a trip abroad, is a little too elegant for the few professional men of color that she meets. Instead, she stays home with her sister Lena and makes rose petals. When she wakes up one morning realizing that she is a forty-two-year-old maker of rose petals who still lives with her parents, she gets a job as a maid and begins an affair with Henry Porter. After Porter tries to break off their affair, Corinthians realizes that she will die of loneliness if he leaves her, and she hangs on to the hood of his car until he relents, taking her home with him. After Milkman discovers that Porter is a member of the Seven Days, the Black terrorist organization, he tells Macon about the affair, and Macon responds punitively. Eventually, though, Corinthians moves to a small house in Southside with Porter.

Lena Dead

See Magdalene Dead

Macon Dead

Macon Dead is the father of Milkman, Lena, and Corinthians Dead. An owner of houses and apartments, Macon believes that owning things enables you to own yourself, and others too. With Pilate, he grew up on a farm in Pennsylvania called Lincoln's Heaven. At sixteen, he sees his father killed by whites who want the family's land, and he and Pilate are protected by Circe, a midwife and maid who shelters them in unused rooms of the Butler house. Macon and Pilate run away from the Butler place, and while hiding in a cave for the night, encounter a white man. After Macon kills the man, they find his cache of gold, which Pilate prevents Macon from taking, leading to their estrangement.

After Macon flees to Michigan, he marries Ruth Foster, having two daughters with her before her father's death and their subsequent estrangement. Macon believes that he has seen Ruth naked in bed with her dead father, kissing him, and almost kills her as a result. They have not had sexual relations in many years when Pilate uses magic to compel Macon to have intercourse with Ruth. A pregnancy results, which Macon wants to abort. When Milkman—the product of the controversial pregnancy—is a child, Macon grows richer, buying land on Honore Island and evicting tenants who can't pay their rent. When Milkman grows up, he works in Macon's office with him. Milkman's decision to leave the office results in his disclosure about Pilate owning a green sack that he has heard contains her inheritance, and Macon tells his son to steal the gold he believes the sack contains. Milkman's subsequent journey, and discovery of the family's mythic past, does not heal Macon's estrangements with his sister and his wife, but Macon does enjoy hearing Milkman's stories about Danville and the old men who still fondly remember him.

Macon Foster Dead III

See Milkman Dead

Magdalene Dead

Lena is the elder daughter of Macon and Ruth. As a child, Milkman accidentally urinates on her, and many years later she confronts him about it, saying that he has been cruel to Corinthians and to her. Lena's anger with Milkman spurs him to leave home for the first time.

Milkman Dead

Milkman Dead is the son of Ruth Foster Dead and Macon Dead. Milkman acquires his name when his father's employee, Freddie, catches Ruth nursing him when he is four years old. Later, we find out that Ruth nurses her son in part because she has been sexually deprived after a rift between her and Macon. Macon, who has come to her as a result of his sister Pilate's spells, tries to end Ruth's pregnancy before Milkman is born and afterwards speaks to him only "if his words held some command or criticism." Milkman grows up cowed by his father, and disobeys him for the first time only after he meets his aunt, Pilate, who teaches him how to make an egg and shows him the sky. In response, Macon tries to lessen Pilate's influence on

his son by putting Milkman to work in his office. While running errands for Macon, Milkman learns about Southside, the working class Black area of town, and develops a relationship with Pilate and her family. When he is seventeen, he begins a sexual relationship with his cousin Hagar. At twenty-two, he hits Macon in response to Macon's violence toward Ruth, and learns Macon's version of the rift between his parents. At thirty-one, he breaks off his relationship with Hagar in a letter, and she tries to kill him several times as a result.

An essentially passive person, Milkman gravitates toward those who inspire fear, and until he is thirty-two, lives with his parents and works for his father. It is only after he breaks into Pilate's house and has a confrontation with his sister Lena that he decides to leave home, travelling to Danville, Pennsylvania, and then Shalimar, Virginia, in search of stolen gold. Instead, he discovers the mythic history of his family, a history that teaches him his obligations to others and makes him an adult.

Pilate Dead

Pilate, Macon's sister, is a maker of home-brewed wine who lives with her daughter and granddaughter in Southside. A woman without a navel who fought her way out of her mother's dead body at birth, Pilate is widely believed to have magical powers. She helps Ruth to restore sexual relations with her husband and to protect her unborn child from Macon's attempts to kill it. Pilate wears her mother's snuffbox as an earring; the box contains the only word her father ever wrote: her name, which he copied from the Bible onto a piece of paper. Pilate has traveled all over the country with her daughter Reba, finally settling in Michigan when her grandchild Hagar is two years old. She is uneducated yet intelligent, full of wisdom about human relationships and generous to all who come to her door. She also has a warm posthumous relationship with her father, the first Macon Dead. Unbeknownst to her, she has been carrying her father's bones in her green sack, the sack which she believes contains the bones of a white man her brother Macon killed, and which Milkman and Guitar steal from her, believing it contains gold. Milkman tells her that she has been carrying her father's bones, and together they bury those bones on Solomon's Leap, where Pilate is fatally shot by Guitar.

Ruth Foster Dead

Ruth Foster Dead is the daughter of the first Black doctor in the city and the wife of Macon

Dead. After her estrangement from her husband, Ruth undergoes a long period of sexual deprivation, broken only by the brief time when Pilate's spells are working on Macon. Pilate also helps Ruth protect her unborn child from Macon's violence. After her son is born, Ruth nurses him until he is four years old, when her husband's employee Freddie discovers her. Ruth also indulges in overnight visits to her father's grave; on one of these visits, her son Milkman follows her and she tells him her version of her behavior at her father's deathbed. In contrast to Macon, she says that she was only kneeling at her father's bed while she was in her slip, kissing his fingers. Though Ruth seems resigned to her fate, she does confront Hagar when she learns of Hagar's attempts to kill Milkman, and she forces Macon to give her money for Hagar's funeral. Morrison calls her "a pale but complicated woman given to deviousness and ultra-fine manners."

Freddie

Freddie is Macon's employee. He is the one who broadcasts news of Robert Smith's death to the Black community, catches Ruth nursing Milkman, tells Macon that Milkman has been at Pilate's house, and tells Milkman that Guitar has been hanging around with a dubious character, Empire State.

Hagar

Hagar is Pilate's granddaughter. Five years older than Milkman, she has a relationship with him for fourteen years. When Milkman breaks off their relationship, she tries to kill him, then sinks into a deep depression. Believing that Milkman prefers pale, white-looking women, Hagar goes on a manic shopping spree to try to acquire the dominant culture's standards of beauty. After most of what she buys is ruined in a downpour, Hagar falls into a fever from which she never recovers, and dies soon afterward.

Grace Long

Grace is a friend of Susan Byrd's. Her presence prevents Susan from telling Milkman all she knows about their shared ancestry. She flirts with Milkman, then steals his watch.

Henry Porter

Porter is one of the Seven Days. He has a nervous breakdown on the same day that Macon evicts Guitar's grandmother from her house. Later, he becomes Corinthians's lover.

A family tree designed for African Americans, allowing them to trace their heritage before and after the Civil War.

Reba

Reba is Pilate's daughter and Hagar's mother. She has extraordinary luck, winning contests, lotteries, and raffles. She lives "from orgasm to orgasm" and is described as looking "as though her simplicity might also be vacuousness."

Robert Smith

One of the Seven Days, Robert Smith jumps to his death from Mercy Hospital at the beginning of the novel.

Empire State

Empire State is an elective mute, and one of the Seven Days. He stopped speaking when he found his French wife in bed with another man, and he gets his name because he just stands around and sways.

Hospital Tommy

Hospital Tommy, the other owner of the barbershop, is also one of the Seven Days. A veteran of World War I, he talks "like an encyclopedia."

Railroad Tommy

Railroad Tommy, also a veteran of World War I, owns the barbershop, and is one of the Seven Days. Early in the novel, he tells Guitar and Milkman all the things they will never experience when they complain about not being served a beer.

Themes

Coming-of-Age

In some respects, Milkman's story is a classic *Bildungsroman,* a coming-of-age story about the moral and psychological development of the main character. However, Milkman is thirty-two when he finally comes of age, unlike traditional heroes and heroines of the *Bildungsroman.* In part, Milkman postpones his adulthood because he is comfortable as the pampered only son of an upper-middle-class family. But Milkman also resists the sense of connection and commitment to others that are required of adults. As he seeks the lost gold, he discovers instead his family's history: the ambivalent legacy of his great-grandfather, who abandons his family to fly back to Africa, the injustice of his grandfather's murder, the Indian roots of his grandmother, and the child his father had been. He begins to define himself as the descendant of a man who could fly, but also to recognize the costs of his great-grandfather's transcendence. In so doing, he learns his duty to his family and community. One major turning point occurs when he is lost in the woods, and he realizes that "[a]pparently he thought he deserved only to be loved— from a distance, though—and given what he wanted. And in return he would be … what? Pleasant? Generous? Maybe all he was really saying was: I am not responsible for your pain; share your happiness with me but not your unhappiness." Milkman's growth into maturity depends on his realization that in order to share the happiness of others, he must also share their unhappiness and that in some cases he is in fact responsible for the pain of others. It is this lesson that he learns throughout the course of the novel, ultimately becoming a mature, responsible adult.

Atonement and Forgiveness

Closely related to Milkman's coming-of-age is his quest for atonement and forgiveness. He begins to see how selfish he has been, taking from his mother and his sisters, coldly casting his lover off, feeling like he doesn't deserve the few things people ask of him. In order to get the gold, he had been prepared to assault Pilate, a woman who has only been generous to him, an intention of which he is deeply ashamed. But Pilate also teaches him how to seek atonement, for it is Pilate who has returned to the cave for the bones of the man her brother killed, knowing that once you take another human life, you own it. Milkman tries to live up to this, taking a box of Hagar's hair home with him as a way of seeking to atone for his actions. He also hopes to reconcile his fractured family, inspiring forgiveness among them, but he cannot. Morrison shows the limits of atonement and forgiveness when she writes that Milkman's newfound knowledge does not change those around him.

Class Conflict

The class conflict in the novel manifests itself in the relationships of those in the novel. Macon Dead feels ashamed of his lower-class status in relation to his wife and father-in-law. Milkman feels estranged from other Blacks by virtue of his privileged position. Macon feels that his sister threatens his newfound propriety. Guitar's killing rage is in part directed toward Milkman's inherited advantages, and toward Milkman's blase attitude to life. Corinthians feels ashamed of her poor lover, Porter. Class jealousy, superiority, and shame prevent the characters from having close relationships with each other; although in relation to whites, they are only recognized as having one status: being colored, which is something brought home to Milkman when he is picked up by police for no particular reason other than his race.

Language and Meaning

A continuing preoccupation in the novel is language and meaning, particularly with regard to names and naming. The Deads get their name because of the mistake of a drunk Yankee soldier, yet they claim it anyway. Milkman eventually discovers his family history through his interpretation of the words of a childhood game. Pilate's name comes from the Bible, and she keeps it in a box that dangles from her ear. The Blacks of Southside try to claim the power of naming by calling Mains Avenue Doctor Street. When they are told that it is not Doctor Street, they call it Not Doctor Street, continuing to honor Doctor Foster while acknowledging their powerlessness to name the streets of the city. Language, then, is a double-edged sword: it is imposed on African Americans, but they must claim it, make it their own, and find meaning in it.

Style

Motif

The main motif in *Song of Solomon* is flying: the novel begins with Robert Smith's flight from the roof of Mercy Hospital and ends with Milkman's flight from Solomon's Leap. The motif of flight is a complicated one: it represents transcendence as well as loss. Milkman's great-grandfather Solomon was able to transcend his circumstances by flying back to Africa, but in doing so he abandoned his wife and children. Milkman finds a better example of flight in Pilate, who can fly without leaving the ground.

Narration

Though the main focus of *Song of Solomon* is Milkman's story, the narrator repeatedly turns to other stories to show how they intersect with Milkman's story. The narrative jumps back and forth in time to give the reader the necessary background for understanding the current situation being discussed. For example, in chapter nine the narrative shifts to the story of Corinthians and her affair with Henry Porter. When Milkman realizes that Porter is a member of the Seven Days, he tells his father about the affair, and Macon reacts punitively, forbidding Corinthians from leaving the house and evicting Porter and garnishing his wages. This provokes Lena to confront Milkman, which in turn spurs him to leave home.

Another aspect of the narration is the point of view of the narrator, which, as Catherine Rainwater noted in *Texas Studies in Literature and Language,* sometimes merges "with that of a character, but later undercuts or problematizes this point of view by presenting its alternatives." Though the narrator of *Song of Solomon* seems omniscient, all-knowing, in fact the narrator does not present any absolute truths, only the narrow perspectives of the characters. In this way, readers are forced to interpret the history and the meaning of the story's events and the character's lives for themselves, just as Milkman does when he hears the song of Solomon.

Bildungsroman

The *Bildungsroman* is the classic Western coming-of-age novel. The *Bildungsroman* usually presents a young hero struggling to find his identity. In Milkman's case, he is at thirty-two much older than the classic *Bildungsroman* hero, but Morrison shows how Milkman's race, class, and natural inclination to passivity keep him trapped in

Topics for Further Study

- One of the catalysts for Guitar's increased involvement in politics is the Emmett Till case. Discuss the impact of Emmett Till's lynching on the political involvement of Blacks at the time.

- *Song of Solomon* appeared at the same time that the miniseries *Roots* was playing on television. Compare Morrison's text to Alex Haley's book, *Roots,* considering a topic such as the authors' treatment of African-American folklore, portrayal of male characters, or characterization in general.

- Choose one of the scenes in the book, and write about how you would stage it as a scene from a play.

- Imagine that Milkman has researched his mother's family history, and write an imaginary history of the Fosters.

his carefree boyhood until events in the story compel him to grow up. Cynthia A. Davis writes in *Toni Morrison* that "Milkman's life follows the pattern of the classic hero, from miraculous birth ... through quest journey to final reunion with his double" as Milkman comes of age. The *Bildungsroman* is sometimes called the "novel of education" or "apprenticeship novel." In this case, Milkman's education is not the formal education he learns in school, but an education in his family's mythic past. He apprentices himself to his mythic great-grandfather and learns to fly as a result.

Historical Context

Post-World War I America

Though *Song of Solomon* is set during the 1950s and 60s, much of its action results from events that happened at the turn of the century, including the Great Migration and World War I and its aftermath. The Great Migration involved the movement of millions of southern Blacks to the ur-

African-American infantrymen of the 15th Regiment, in France circa 1918.

ban North in search of jobs and freedom in the first few decades of the nineteenth century. In her novel, Morrison gives voice to one of those families, the Deads, showing their progression from Virginia to Pennsylvania to Michigan. Likewise, Guitar has left the South with his family after his father's death, and no doubt many of the other inhabitants of Southside are relatively recent migrants from the rural South. The Great Migration, though it represented marginal material progress, is also portrayed by Morrison, among others, as representing the loss of a traditional rural culture. Certainly her characterization of Macon Dead, whose loss of his father and his rural lifestyle makes him emotionally stingy and materially greedy, represents this loss.

In addition to heading north, many Blacks enlisted in the armed forces during World War I as a way to improve their status in society. They were subject to discrimination even during their time in the armed forces, but they hoped that the war's end would bring new opportunities in economic life and in civil rights. After all, the war had been waged ostensibly to protect and extend democracy. Instead, the war's end marked a renewal of Ku Klux Klan activities; some Black soldiers were lynched while still in their uniforms. The summer of 1919, after the end of the war, marked the greatest period of interracial strife in the nation's history. In part,

the violence escalated because Blacks were more willing to defend themselves from racist attacks. Morrison echoes this in her treatment of the Seven Days, the older members of which are World War I veterans who speak bitterly of their mistreatment on their return. Other Blacks fought back against racism by increasing their level of activism; some historians credit the period immediately following World War I with the birth of the modern-day civil-rights movement.

Civil Rights Movement

One of the important moments in *Song of Solomon* is the moment when Milkman finds Guitar in the barbershop listening to a report about the murder of Emmett Till. Till was a fourteen year old from Chicago visiting Mississippi in 1955. He allegedly whistled at a white woman and was murdered by whites. No one was ever convicted for his murder, but it was one of the catalysts for a renewal of the civil-rights movement. The National Association for the Advancement of Colored People (NAACP) had been arguing against the legality of segregation in the courts, and Martin Luther King, Jr. and others began using nonviolent direct action to desegregate facilities in the South. In 1963, King gave his "I Have a Dream" speech, which inspired many Americans. Shortly there-

Compare & Contrast

- **1963:** President Kennedy is assassinated, plunging all Americans into mourning.

  1970s: President Nixon resigns after being implicated in the Watergate scandal.

  Today: President Clinton is impeached, becoming the butt of jokes because of his affair with Monica Lewinsky.

- **1963:** Civil rights leader Medgar Evers is assassinated and his assailant brags about the murder before being acquitted by an all-white jury.

  1970s: Americans of all colors are inspired by

the television miniseries *Roots*.

  Today: Byron de la Beckwith, the murderer of Medgar Evers, is sentenced to life in prison by a mixed-race jury.

- **1963:** Many schools are still racially segregated by law.

  1970s: Because of "white flight" to the suburbs, many schools become resegregated.

  Today: Some Blacks begin to question the value of integration and instead work to strengthen all-Black institutions.

---

after, though, whites bombed a Black church in Birmingham, Alabama, killing four young girls. This would later be described as a pivotal moment in the struggle, a moment when many Blacks began to despair that freedom would never be attained. Some civil-rights workers became radicalized, no longer believers in nonviolent action. This is echoed in the character of Guitar, whose violence becomes more acute—and misdirected—after the little girls are killed.

Critical Overview

Song of Solomon, the first of Toni Morrison's works to become a best-seller, also established her as a major American writer. As Carol Iannone wrote in *Commentary,* "[i]n *Song of Solomon* Miss Morrison at last permits herself to work her material through." The novel won Morrison the National Book Critics Circle Award in 1977, and though most critics found flaws in the book, on the whole they praised Morrison's blend of fantasy and reality and her use of myths and folktales to portray Black life. In an early review, Anne Tyler commented, "I would call the book poetry, but that would seem to be denying its considerable power as a story. Whatever name you give it, it's full of

magnificent people, each of them complex and multi-layered, even the narrowest of them narrow in extravagant ways." Other critics have also praised the power of her language; Vivian Garnick, in *The Village Voice,* wrote that "[t]he world she creates is thick with an atmosphere through which her characters move slowly, in pain, ignorance and hunger. And to a very large degree Morrison has the compelling ability to make one believe that all of us ... are penetrating that dark and hurtful terrain—the feel of a human life—simultaneously." *New York Times Book Review* contributor Reynolds Price praised the novel's "negotiations with fantasy, fable, song and allegory" as "organic, continuous and unpredictable," while Maureen Howard noted in *The Hudson Review* that *Song of Solomon* is both "rich in its use of common speech" and "sophisticated in its use of literary traditions and language."

Song of Solomon was the first of Morrison's books to have a male hero, but some critics, including Vivian Garnick, have written that Milkman never really comes to life as a character. Some scholars, including Reynolds Price and Bill Moyers, have also wondered at Morrison's exclusion of white characters, but as Cynthia Price wrote, "the destructive effect of the white society can take the form of outright physical violence, but oppression in Morrison's world is more often psychic violence.

She rarely depicts white characters, for the brutality here is less a single act than the systematic denial of Black lives." Price noted that Morrison's artistic challenge is one in which her characters must act in spite of the limitations placed on them, and that Morrison turns to myth because of, as Roger Rosenblatt suggested, its "acknowledgement of external limitation and the anticipation of it."

Critics have also commented on the "diffuse" nature of the narrative; as Rainwater pointed out, "Chapter 4, for example, skips to Milkman's adulthood, some twelve years after the events of the previous chapter. However, almost immediately, the narrator begins to search backward through time to account for the present. This attempt, however, laterally deflects attention onto the stories of other characters. Before the chapter concludes, the narrative has taken at least four different directions in an effort to amass information convergent upon, and apparently explanatory of, Milkman's life." Some early critics, such as *Newsweek*'s Margo Jefferson, saw "a structural conflict between these embellishments and the demands of Macon's tale which weakens the focus" but later critics have seen, with A. Leslie Harris of *MELUS,* that the plot is not "meandering and confused" but rather "enhanced by its very discontinuity." Harris called Morrison's subplots "meticulously articulated," and with other later critics, saw Morrison's inclusion of the stories of other characters as enriching the novel as a whole.

In addition to noting the parallels between Milkman's story and the myth of Icarus, recent critics have examined the implications of Morrison's use of an African-American folktale as a source for her flying African, Solomon. As Michael Awkward noted in *Negotiating Difference: Race, Gender, and the Politics of Positionality,* the most common variants of this tale present a group of flying Africans, who undertake a communal exodus. By contrast, Morrison's version of the myth presents a solitary flyer and, "while the narrative suggests that the offspring of the legendary Solomon do not perceive themselves as adversely affected by his act—they, in fact, construct praise songs in recognition of his accomplishments—his mate Ryna, who bears his twenty-one children, is so aggrieved by her loss that she goes mad." As Cynthia A. Davis maintained in *Toni Morrison,* this artistic choice makes Morrison's version of the Icarus story a conflict "between 'absolute' freedom and social responsibility," suggesting Morrison's alteration of Western ideas and forms to fit the concerns of the Black community.

Song of Solomon remains one of Morrison's most well-regarded works, as well as a novel beloved by readers. In the twenty-three years since its publication, its positive critical reputation has grown even stronger, and it continues to be read, taught, and studied.

Criticism

Jane Elizabeth Dougherty

Dougherty is a Ph.D. candidate at Tufts University. In the following essay, she discusses Morrison's depictions of the male characters in Song of Solomon.

In *Toni Morrison,* Cynthia A. Davis writes that the narrative trajectories of Toni Morrison's novels are driven by "the Black characters' choices within the context of oppression." In *Song of Solomon,* as Jill Matus notes in her *Toni Morrison,* Morrison investigates "how Black men in America survive and how they position themselves in relation to dominant social and political structures" as well as to their own families and communities. Morrison presents the limited array of choices available to Black men through her portrayals of three living Black men, Milkman and Macon Dead and Guitar Bains, and through her mythic evocation of Dead ancestors, the first Macon Dead and his father, Solomon. As Matus notes, each man must either choose between "fight" and "flight" or find some way to combine the two alternatives. In this essay, I will examine each of the "choices within the context of oppression" that the Black male characters make as a way of illuminating Morrison's concerns in *Song of Solomon.*

Though Morrison's novel is a coming-of-age story, it follows the coming-of-age of a character, Milkman Dead, who is thirty-two years old and has been able to avoid making any choices about his life. Milkman is trapped by the circumstances of his life: within his family and the Black community, he is privileged and pampered, but in the larger world, he is limited by his race. He is separated from the Black community by his class, and hindered from advancing in the larger world by his race. As a result, Milkman avoids making choices or commitments, and is disconnected from his community. As Guitar notes, "[y]ou don't live nowhere. Not Not Doctor Street or Southside." Milkman doesn't "live" on Not Doctor Street, the home of his family, because of the negative history between his parents, but he is also disconnected from Southside, the working class Black community, because of his privilege. Indeed, Milkman's father, Macon, owns rental property in Southside and does not hesitate to evict tenants who have not paid their rent, as he does to Guitar's grandmother in one early scene.

Macon is portrayed by Morrison as angry and harsh, but throughout the course of the story we develop some sympathy for him. We learn that Macon's father valued many of the same things that Macon does, but that his death perverted Macon's values. Morrison writes of Milkman's realization that

> [a]s the son of Macon Dead the first, he paid homage to his own father's life and death by loving what his father loved: property, good solid property, the bountifulness of life. He loved these things to excess because he loved his father to excess. Owning, building, acquiring—that was his life, his future, his present, and all the history he knew. That he distorted life, bent it, for the sake of gain, was a measure of his loss at his father's death.

Milkman's father, the second Macon Dead, loves what his father loved, but he also makes choices to try to keep himself safe from his father's fate. Instead of competing with whites, as the first Macon Dead did, he exploits his fellow Blacks. This is a historically accurate portrait of the Black middle class during this period; unlike today, the Black middle class of the 40s, 50s and 60s mostly worked in, and earned their living from, the Black community. But Macon's harshness toward the members of that community also separates him from it, in contrast to his father. An early scene in the novel has Macon listening to his estranged sister singing, emphasizing the joy and life that Macon has given up for the sake of propriety. Unlike the men of his father's community, the Blacks of Southside do not see Macon's success as belonging to them in any way, perhaps because his success comes at their expense. By contrast, the first Macon Dead was an example to all, as Milkman learns when he journeys to Danville and meets his grandfather's contemporaries:

> He had come out of nowhere, as ignorant as a hammer and as broke as a convict, with nothing but free papers, a Bible, and a pretty black-haired wife, and in one year he'd leased ten acres, the next ten more. Sixteen years later he had one of the best farms in Montour County. A farm that colored their lives like a paintbrush and spoke to them like a sermon. "You see?" the farm said to them. "See? See what you can do? Never mind you can't tell one letter from another, never mind you born a slave, never mind you lose your name, never mind your daddy dead, never

mind nothing. Here, this here, is what a man can do if he puts his mind to it and his back to it. Stop sniveling," it said. "Stop picking around the edges of the world. Take advantage, and if you can't take advantage, take disadvantage. We live here. On this planet, in this nation, in this country right here. *No*where else! We got a home in this rock, don't you see! Nobody starving in my home; nobody crying in my home, and if I got a home you got one too!"

The first Macon Dead's triumph tells the men of Danville to "stop picking around the edges of the world." By contrast, his son Macon knows that "as a Negro he [isn't] going to get a big slice of the pie" and is content with the "bit of pie filling oozing around the edge of the crust." Macon's caution comes from the trauma of his father's death: the first Macon Dead was killed by whites who wanted his farm. Though he sat with a shotgun for five days and nights, willing to fight for his farm and his family, the first Macon Dead still couldn't protect himself or what he owned. In a world in which whites control both the courts and the culture, Macon's choice to fight resulted in his death, a death which haunts his descendants.

The first Macon Dead's choice to fight is contrasted with the choice of his father, Solomon, who chooses flight. The first Macon Dead claims his right to an American life, while his father has despaired of ever being accepted into American society and flown back to Africa. This action, which Morrison bases on an African-American folktale, is both a celebration and a loss; as Michael Awkward notes in his *Negotiating Difference: Race, Gender, and the Politics of Positionality,* "the empowered Afro-American's flight, celebrated in a blues song whose decoding catapults Milkman into self-conscious maturity, is a solitary one … He leaves his loved ones, including his infant son Jake, whom he tries unsuccessfully to carry with him, with the task of attempting to learn for themselves the secrets of transcendence." In giving up the fight for a place in American society, Solomon also abandons his American-born offspring. This corresponds with Milkman's own quest for flight, in which he abandons his lover Hagar and abdicates his familial and communal responsibilities.

Throughout the novel, in fact, Milkman's friend Guitar Bains reminds Milkman that he should feel a sense of connection to his community. Guitar himself takes the "fight" strategy to its logical extreme; he defines "self-defense" as defense of the community, and charges himself with keeping the ratio of Blacks and whites constant through "eye for an eye" justice. Yet Guitar also rejects love and familial ties, and in what A. Leslie

Harris calls "his total commitment to death," ultimately tries to kill his "brother" Milkman. Guitar justifies his violence by arguing that it comes from love, but he separates himself from the very community he claims to be protecting. In her portrayal of Guitar, Morrison suggests that the "fight" strategy costs too much, just as in her portrayal of Solomon, she suggests that "flight" comes at too high a price.

In her portrayal of Milkman, Morrison begins to suggest a viable strategy for Black men struggling in a racist society. Milkman honors both the "fight" and "flight" strategies, as Matus notes when she writes that "the alternatives of flight and fight come together in the final scene of the novel" when "as fleet and bright as a lodestar [Milkman] wheeled toward Guitar and it did not matter which one of them would give up his ghost in the killing arms of his brother." Milkman has learned to honor both strategies by coming to respect his ancestors, who were forced to choose between the two, and through his love for Pilate, who has fought for his life and who could fly without leaving the ground. He has also learned a deep appreciation for the power of language, which Morrison seems to argue is the most effective strategy of both fight and flight. It is through language that the past can be acknowledged, mourned, celebrated, resisted, and transcended. Milkman realizes that names, words and stories can keep the past alive in spite of death: "Shalimar left [his children], but it was the children who sang about it and kept the story of his leaving alive." It is through a sense of commitment and respect for the past, then, that Milkman, unlike his ancestors, can both fly and fight.

Source: Jane Elizabeth Dougherty, in an essay for *Novels for Students*, Gale, 2000.

Jill Matus

In the following essay, Matus considers the significance of father figures, and particularly the theme of the loss of fathers, in Song of Solomon.

Song of Solomon (1977) is a novel about fathers, or more specifically, the loss of fathers. At its heart are two revelatory incidents of traumatic loss which govern the novel's investigation of the history and future of African American men in relation to society and their own families. A brother and sister, Pilate and Macon Dead (the second), witness their father being shot to death by greedy white neighbours who resent his prosperity and covet his land. But this father himself experienced the traumatic loss of his father, who, legend has it,

decided to fly away from America and his condition of enslavement. He attempted to take his baby son Jake with him, but dropped the child a few moments after he took off in flight back to Africa. His bereft wife lost her mind through grief and the child was reared by others. Knowledge of the second of these traumas, withheld almost to the close of the novel, explains not only the riddle on which the novel turns, but reveals the generational transmission of traumatic effects that hampers all the Dead men, descendants of Jake, who is also known as the first Macon Dead. The multivalent meanings of Solomon's flight in the novel allow Morrison to celebrate an early and marvellous escape from slavery, while also registering the trauma of those who must function without the father. Though Solomon's flight may offer inspiration as a version of the celebratory legend of the Flying African, the novel also emphasises the grief and mourning of those who were abandoned.

The trauma of the father's abandonment or death infects the descendants of Solomon—as it does the text—with a series of distortions in memory and obstacles to interpretation. Among these, for example, is the cryptic admonition that Pilate's father utters when he appears to her on a number of occasions after his death. Guiltily, she interprets his saying that you can't just fly off and leave a body as an injunction to return to the bones of the man she and Macon left dead in the cave. When we later learn the history of Jake, we understand that his poignant refrain relates repeatedly the central loss of his own childhood—the fact that he was the body left when his father flew off. Another example is the name of Macon Dead, created by a slip of the pen. Failing to fill the information in the correct boxes, the Yankee clerk at the Freedmen's Bureau takes the place of origin as the first name, writing the condition of the father in the box for the surname. Though one point about this history of naming is that a careless drunk official has the power to change the name of a family, another, and more significant, point is that the new name further emphasises the death of the father. Like the riddle of the children's song, which tells the story of Solomon's flight but cannot be understood until Milkman can hear it properly, the name 'Dead' is a riddle, which also draws attention to the question of the father's survival. In Milkman's world, the 1930s to the 1960s, the father is 'already Dead'. Milkman tells his friend Guitar about the naming:

'Say, you know how my old man's daddy got his name?'

'Uh uh. How?'

'Cracker gave it to him.'

'Sho 'nough?'

'Yep. And he took it. Like a fuckin sheep. Somebody should have shot him.'

'What for? He was already Dead.'

In the genealogy of the Deads, the trauma of paternal loss reveals one father who flew away and one who died violently at the hands of whites while trying to make good in America. The two instances record different responses to life in racist America, each of which entails traumatic consequences—Solomon miraculously flies off, becoming a symbol of transcendence and escape, but bequeathing also a legacy of bereavement, loss and forgetting; Jake stands his ground but is cut down, leaving his family similarly bereft. Both modes raise the question of how black men in America survive and how they position themselves in relation to dominant social and political structures. In confronting the loss of the father, Morrison's novel looks at the ways in which the history of its consequences might be rewritten.

The extent to which the novel is focused on the traumatic loss of the father may be gauged in the narrator's accounts of Macon Dead's death. Early in the novel, after Milkman has returned from talking with his strange aunt Pilate, whom his father has forbidden him to visit, Milkman raises the question of his grandfather's death. In the course of this clandestine visit, Pilate has given Milkman her account of her father's violent death and now Macon is moved to remember and talk about the event:

> His son's questions had shifted the scenery. He was seeing himself at twelve, standing in Milkman's shoes and feeling what he himself had felt for his own father. The numbness that had settled on him when he saw the man he loved and admired fall off the fence; something wild ran through him when he watched the body twitching violently in the dirt.

The death of the first Macon Dead affects not only his son, but, as Milkman later learns, an entire community of men who took Macon as an exemplum of success and self-improvement. Talking to the men of his father's generation in Danville, Pennsylvania, Milkman functions as

> the ignition that gunned their memories. The good times, the hard times, things that changed, things that stayed the same—and head and shoulders above all of it was the tall, magnificent Macon Dead, whose death, it seemed to him, was the beginning of their own dying even though they were young boys at the time. Macon Dead was the farmer they wanted to be,

the clever irrigator, the peach-tree grower, the hog slaughterer....

Macon Dead seems to preach to them in the same style in which Baby Suggs in [Morrison's] *Beloved* will speak to the feed slaves. Whereas she tells black folk that they have to love themselves because no one else is going to love their flesh, Macon's farm and attitude to life speak of helping oneself:

> We live here. On this planet, in this nation, in this country right here. Nowhere else! ... Grab it. Grab this land. Take it, hold it, my brothers, make it, my brothers, shake it, squeeze it, turn it, twist it, beat it, kick it, whip it, stomp it, dig it, plow it, seed it, reap it, rent it, buy it, sell it, own it, build it, multiply it, and pass it on—can you hear me? Pass it on!

But, the narrator continues, 'they shot the top of his head off and ate his fine Georgia peaches. And even as boys these men began to die and were dying still'.

Macon Dead (the second) takes to heart that injunction to 'rent it, buy it, sell it, own it' by becoming a heartless landlord. Setting great store by the symbols of power and success—the keys in his pocket, the big Packard in which he takes the family for a joyless Sunday ride—he relentlessly pursues the bourgeois dream. Only his visit to Pilate, secretly at night in order to hear her sing with her daughter and granddaughter, suggests the vestigeal remains of an emotional life. 'As Macon felt himself softening under the weight of memory and music, the song died down'. For the most part, Macon Dead has spent his life suffering from a dissociation of feeling. Milkman meditates on his father's life:

> And his father. An old man now, who acquired things and used people to acquire more things. As the son of Macon Dead the first, he paid homage to his own father's life and death by loving what that father had loved: property, good solid property, the bountifulness of life. He loved these things to excess because he loved his father to excess. Owning, building, acquiring—that was his life, his future, his present, and all the history he knew. That he distorted life, bent it, for the sake of gain, was a measure of his loss at his father's death.

The loss of the father as a central concern of the novel is also expressed in the case of Guitar Bains—'my father died when I was four. That was the first leaving and the hardest'. Bains's father dies from traumatic amputation—his body is sawn in half in an accident that exposes the exploitation of 'coloured' workers in unsafe working conditions. The children are given a sack of 'Divinity'—candy to recompense them for the loss of their father, and forever afterwards Guitar is sick to his stomach at the thought, let alone the taste, of sweet things. However, he confesses later in the novel that it was not really the candy that made him sick but his mother's smiling gratitude for the four ten-dollar bills that the foreman gave her. Guitar recalls the horrific sight of his father, lying in the coffin, his body sliced vertically in two halves, and the fact that his mother bought the children peppermint rock with some of the money the sawmill owner gave her. In Guitar's reckoning there are no blandishments, no sweet things capable of buying off black claim and rage. 'Don't let them Kennedys fool you' is the warning that concludes this account of his father. His desire for the gold that Milkman believes now hangs in a sack in Pilate's house is not cupidity but vengeance—he wants it to fund the Seven Days' reprisal activities.

The quest motif in the novel, to which critics have drawn much attention, is specifically a quest to understand the father's trauma and the genealogy of the paternal line. By following the trail that brings him to understand the fate of his grandfather and great-grandfather, Milkman feels 'on his own skin', as it were, the inextricability of personal and public history. To understand the trauma of the lost father in the Dead genealogy is to recognise the forces of history that have produced that trauma. If history is 'precisely the way we are implicated in each other's traumas' then the personal, quotidian, mythological history of Milkman's family is not just Dead history; it implicates a wide range of others and it is relevant not only in the context of the novel, but also to the 1990s. Morrison engages Milkman in his people's collective history by sending him on a quest for his own familial, paternal past. It is indeed a quest to raise the Dead fathers. When Milkman is alone in the forest during the night of hunting, it is as if he is protected and aided by a mothering grandfather: 'Down either side of his thighs he felt the sweet gum's surface roots cradling him like the rough but maternal hands of a grandfather'. The quest functions as quests traditionally do, and Milkman predictably recovers pride in his heritage, wisdom to face difficult tasks, and a newly crystallising sense of identity. '"My great granddaddy could fly! Goddam! ... He didn't need no airplane. Didn't need no fuckin tee double you ay. He could fly his own self!"'

Milkman was born, we recall, to discover the meanings of flight. His mother went into labour at the time that Robert Smith leapt from the top of a building in what appears initially to be a suicidal imitation of Icarus. Smith's cryptic note, 'I will take off from Mercy and fly away on my own wings. Please forgive me. I loved you all' cannot be decoded until much later in the novel when we understand his involvement with the Seven Days, but it serves usefully at the outset of the novel to raise questions about flying, and in particular, flying away. Milkman's governing desire as a child is to fly, to the extent that when he learns humans are not fitted for it, he is profoundly disappointed: 'To live without that single gift saddened him and left his imagination so bereft that he appeared dull even to the women who did not hate his mother'. Flight, however, as Morrison gradually reveals in the novel, is not always what it seems. Whereas Robert Smith looked like a 'nutwagon', an Insurance Agent who had flipped out, he turns out to be a member of the Seven Days, strained to the point of suicide because he is unable to deal with the pressures of his commitment. The Seven Days is a group that responds in kind to racial violence, representing the 'fight' rather than 'flight' alternative to oppression and persecution. Milkman's grandfather, Solomon, represents the alternative of 'flight'. The alternatives of flight and fight come together in the final scene of the novel as Milkman leaps into the air to grapple with Guitar—an act of confronting, surrendering and soaring.

Yet even as Morrison allows Milkman to experience elevation and pride in the legends of his flying ancestor, the text does not lose sight of the loss on the other side of celebration. For every joyous escape, every transcendent flyer, there is a grounded wife and mother. For every Leap there is a Gulch, a Ryna for a Solomon. The quintessential 'blue note' in the Solomon myth is Ryna, whose weeping and wailing symbolises the distress of those left behind. Morrison therefore uses the myth of the flying African both to celebrate and to mourn. As Milkman discovers that he is the successor of his flying forebear, the reader begins to see the hapless Hagar as a latter-day incarnation of her ancestor, Ryna. When Milkman hears the song the children are singing in the playground, his recriminations about Hagar are associated with the line that bemoans Solomon's leaving: 'And she stood there like a puppet strung up by a puppet master who had gone off to some other hobby. *O Solomon don't leave me here*'. And when Susan Byrd is telling Milkman the history of Solomon and Ryna she remarks,

> You don't hear of women like that anymore, but there used to be more—the kind of woman who couldn't live without a particular man. And when the man left

they lost their minds, or died or something. Love, I guess, but I always thought it was trying to take care of the children by themselves, you know what I mean?

Hagar is the price of Milkman's ticket to self-understanding and maturation, just as Ryna and her children were the price of Solomon's triumphant flight.

In the light of ongoing debates about father-lessness in relation to African American families (debates initiated to a large extent by the Moyni-han report of the 1960s and manifested in the 1990s in Louis Farrakhan's orchestration of a 'million man march' on Washington) Morrison's novel speaks to concerns about male commitment and re-sponsibility. In some ways, *Songs of Solomon* can be characterized as a mythologising of desertion. Solomon gives leaving a good name because his reasons for escape are inarguable and his mode of leaving is spectacular enough to command awe, in-spiration and celebration. Rather than pathologise the father who leaves, Morrison recovers the his-tory of good reasons for taking flight. The flying African myth also functions her as a consolatory myth—men leave, but they do so in response to in-tolerable pressures and constraints.

In its multiple versions, the myth of the flying African does not necessarily focus on the father. There are many myths dealing with escape from slavery: the Ibo version is that the people who ar-rived in America took one look at what life would be like there and simply turned round and walked back over the water to Africa. Paule Marshall's *Praisesong for the Widow* draws on this version. Virginia Hamilton's *The People Could Fly: Amer-ican Black Folktales* has a tale about the power of flight in which a young slave woman successfully flies away with her baby. With the magic words, *'Kum … yali, kum buba tambe'* she takes to the air and escapes the cruelty of the overseer. Morrison's particular deployment of this well-known escape myth is therefore significant. She *chooses* to make her flying African the father of twenty-one sons, who leaves his wife and family. Instead of invok-ing only the familiar blues theme—a woman be-moaning her abandonment; a man leaving a woman—Morrison puts a new and favourable spin on the history of male peripateticism.

At the same time, however, that Morrison's version of the myth places emphasis on the man's miraculous flight and on the woman's loyalty and love, she also draws attention to the fact that women are left to bear the brunt of the desertion. Though Susan Byrd affirms that women who die of grief for their men are few and far between—'You don't hear of women like that anymore, but there used to be more'—she certainly has a point in her initial understanding of the grief and madness of women like Ryna: 'I always thought it was trying to take care of the children by themselves, you know what I mean?'. The myth of the flyaway father offers a grand drama of male escape and female pining, but in more quotidian terms, whatever the provocation to escape, Solomon does leave Ryna holding the baby—twenty-one of them, in fact.

Once in touch with his history, Milkman's pride in his flying ancestor alerts him now to the significance of the place names: 'He read the signs with interest now, wondering what lay beneath the names. The Algonquins had named the territory he lived in Great Water, *michi gami*. How many dead lives and fading memories were buried in and be-neath the names of the places in this country'. He can now make sense and knowledge of the random facts he knows: 'He closed his eyes and thought of the black men in Shalimar, Roanoke, Petersburg, Newport News, Danville, in the Blood Bank, on Darling Street, in the pool halls, the barbershops. Their names. Names they got from yearnings, ges-tures, flaws, events, mistakes, weaknesses. Names that bore witness'. Possessing some history, and aware of how much more awaits excavation, Milk-man is newly and appropriately empowered. It is as if the rekindling of memory, fading but embed-ded in oral histories, has animated those dead lives and consequently the Dead fathers come to life in Milkman's possession. He now presents the strongest contrast to his increasingly desperate friend Guitar, who is also struggling to memori-alise a dead father and to vindicate the dead, the casualties of racism….

When Milkman returns from the quest that has presumably altered his relationship to his history, his family and himself, we learn that his mother is thankful that he is unhurt, and Lena, 'though un-forgiving as ever, was civil enough to him since Corinthians had moved to a small house in South-side, which she shared with Porter'. Although Milkman returns from his quest having experienced a wonderful reciprocal relationship with Sweet, his new-found awareness of female needs and entitle-ments seems superficial. He berates himself for the death of Hagar and realises that the women in his life have done so much for him and that he has never so much as made them a cup of coffee, but there is not much to suggest that the situation of women is altered. The law of the father—even, of course, the Dead father—is that women serve, love, wait and suffer abuse or abandonment.

Unsurprisingly, mothers are marginally significant in this novel about fathers: Ruth's father is her only important parent; Pilate's mother dies giving birth and is little remembered by her elder brother, Macon Dead. Her only significance is her name 'Sing' and her Native American status, which allows Morrison (through Susan Byrd and her friend Grace Long) to give a condensed account of hybridity and intermixing in African American genealogy. Pilate is an exception in the novel as a free-standing woman, whose knowledge and way of seeing the world provides a contrast to the bourgeois values Macon has adopted, and who represents a matrilineal line. Although there is something free and exciting about her household of women, its nutritional and other eccentricities, wonderful singing, and hand-to-mouth existence, Pilate's line neither thrives nor survives. Her descendants become less independent and self-possessed. Her daughter Reba, who shares many qualities with Hannah Peace in *Sula,* lives for pleasure, and although wonderful, winning and generous, is never quite an adult. As she lies dying, Pilate enjoins Milkman to look after her daughter. And whether we see Hagar as constrained by a crude determinism in the novel that constitutes her as an incarnation of her grieving, mind-tossed maternal ancestor, Ryna, or whether we see her as a version of Pecola in her absorption of white consumer culture, she too is an increasingly pathetic, doomed woman. Whereas Milkman's quest serves to raise the Dead fathers through possession of paternal history, the mothers, daughters and wives associated with the Dead are yet to be raised. The ways of Pilate, who could fly without leaving the ground, are an inspiration for Milkman— 'There's got to be at least one more woman like you'—but in the world of the novel, there are no others like her; nor does she have female descendants who will raise and possess her for their futures.

Source: Jill Matus, "Song of Solomon: Raising Dead Fathers," in *Toni Morrison,* Manchester University Press, 1998, pp. 72-84.

A. Leslie Harris

In the following essay, Harris asserts that "Morrison's success in making one black man's struggle for identity universal is partly explained by her structural use of myth to show man's constant search for reassurance in myths."

In *Song of Solomon* Toni Morrison has faced the tale-spinner's recurring problem—making contemporary, localized events and characters speak to those who cannot share her characters' background or experiences. Morrison's solution in this dilemma is not new. She turns to myth to underpin her narrative, but does so without transforming her novel into pure fantasy or overloading her story with literary allusions. Morrison's success in making one black man's struggle for identity universal is partly explained by her structural use of myth to show man's constant search for reassurance in myths.

According to Mircea Eliade, myth is sacred history, the breakthrough of the supernatural or divine into the human to explain the origins, destiny, and cultural concerns of a people. Man, then, has always turned to myth to explain the inexplicable and to tie narratives into a larger cultural and perceptual framework. We would expect our modern predilection for scientific fact, psychological speculation, and historical verification to have supplanted the role of myth in explaining reality. In fact, genuine myth, living myth, has traditionally been associated with primitive societies in which the myth presupposes not "a tale told but a reality lived." Even our sophistication, however, does not preclude our depending on myth for more than entertainment. If we no longer look to myth for reality, we are still drawn to mythopoesis, where gods, heroes, and supernatural conflicts exist on a purely symbolic level, trying us to our past and showing us our origins. Myths become "agents of stability," not restricting us to a specific place or even to a specific culture but using the specific to ponder the enduring questions of all men. Perhaps mythic absolutes reassure us because, as Kerenyi proposes, the constant themes of myth involve not the "why?" (the causes) but the "whence?" (the groundwork of human nature, belief, and endeavor), which remains as timely as it is timeless.

In Toni Morrison's *Song of Solomon,* we have genuine mythopoesis, the mythic impulse shaped and translated into symbolic art. Morrison fuses Afro-American myth with the cultural, moral, and religious beliefs of both the Judeo-Christian and the Greco-Roman heritages to fashion her own myth. She does not simply rework archetypes but blends the natural with the supernatural and the historically factual with the fantastic. More particularly, she selects one of the oldest and most pervasive mythic themes, the hero and his quest, to inform and control her narrative structure.

In *Song of Solomon* Morrison creates a world both realistic and dreamlike, peopled with amusing, endearing, quirky, and frightening characters. Her deft handling of high drama, low comedy, and dialogue have all been commended. Her structure,

What Do I Read Next?

- *Beloved*, Toni Morrison's 1987 novel of a former slave haunted by the ghost of her daughter, won the Pulitzer Prize for Literature.

- Paule Marshall's *Praisesong for the Widow* (1983) is the story of a woman who discovers her family's origins on a small island on the Atlantic Coast.

- *Cane*, a 1923 work by Jean Toomer, lyrically records the demise of traditional Black Southern life.

- Based on Shakespeare's *King Lear*, *A Thousand Acres* (1991) by Jane Smiley tells the tale of a family unraveled by its secrets.

- Published in 1952, *Invisible Man* by Ralph Ellison is the classic modernist novel of an African American in search of his identity.

- *Rule of the Bone* (1996), by Russell Banks, is a coming-of-age novel about a teenager who journeys from upstate New York to Jamaica.

however, has not been as widely appreciated. *Song of Solomon* is undeniably episodic, but whether the plot is "meandering and confused," lacks linear development, or is enhanced by its very discontinuity is open to question. If we follow Morrison's lead and concentrate on the growth of Macon Dead, known as Milkman because his mother nursed him too long, we find that her novel is cohesive, following the clear pattern of birth and youth, alienation, quest, confrontation, and reintegration common to mythic heroes as disparate as Moses, Achilles, and Beowulf. Such a mythic chronology emphasizes the hero's rejection of and eventual assimilation into his society. Slochower has argued that the hero's victory lies in curbing his early rebelliousness without submitting completely. An Oedipus or a Hamlet attains both tragic and mythic stature by remaining true to himself even as he becomes an agent of the social consciousness. As we watch Milkman grow up and reject the restrictions of his Southside life, we see him undergoing not only psychological and physical maturation but an approximation of the development of a true hero, so that by the end of the novel he knows himself and his obligations to both present and past, to himself and his world.

Western man has always looked to childhood as the mythic time, when the individual is closest to his origins. In the novel's opening Morrison toys with this idea by describing Milkman's birth in terms of signs, omens, and portents, and by presenting Milkman's childhood in a rapidly-passed-

over series of narrative events resonating with symbolic and archetypal significance. The second stage in Morrison's structure and Milkman's maturation is the period of alienation. Milkman, thirtyish, resentful of, yet dependent on his father, wants to leave home but lacks the resolution to do so. His home, Southside, is both reassuringly familiar and confining, like Milkman's own comfortable but loitering and wasted life. His recognition that he is just drifting and lacks both internal and external coherence in his life directs him toward his third stage of development—a quest. Searching for the gold his father and his Aunt Pilate had found hidden in a Pennsylvania cave many years before becomes less important for Milkman than unraveling his family's tangled and confusing genealogy, meeting those who remember his father and Pilate as children, and, finally, realizing that the song he had heard Pilate sing, the "Song of Solomon" of the title, is a children's retelling, a mythologizing, of his own heritage. In his journey through Pennsylvania and Virginia, Milkman rediscovers himself. However, he cannot complete the final stage of his growth into heroic stature, the return and reintegration into a world whose values he can champion, until he defeats the enemy. This enemy is his boyhood friend and adult nemesis, Guitar, who objectifies Milkman's own denial and despair. The confrontation with Guitar in the Pennsylvania woods represents Milkman's complete reintegration and triumph, so that the Lady-or-the-Tiger quality of an ending that stops as the two combatants meet for a fight to the death is less ambivalent than it appears. The novel does not end with a cliff-hanger; the final battle is both a confrontation and a confirmation, marking Milkman's emergence as a champion who understands and will defend his world.

By examining key passages and symbolic turning points in each of these major stages, we will see how Morrison adopted—but adapted—mythic themes and images in her narrative structure. If the brief summary above indicates that the structure of the novel is chronological, it is a chronology imposed through reordering the events of the novel. The textural richness of the novel derives from a present which spans three generations, with each narrative tied back into the development of the novel's hero. The digressions, explanations, and expansions which interrupt Milkman's own story suggest not a serial or chronological unfolding but an interlace, in which the dominant narrative is embellished and enhanced through meticulously articulated subplots and images threading their way through Milkman's life. It is these embellishments which carry much of the burden of the myth.

The opening pages give us the mandrel on which Morrison forms her own myth. Although many of his observations on living myth in primitive societies do not touch directly on mythopoesis, Otto Rank's discussion of the birth and childhood of the mythic hero illustrates the clear connection of Morrison's hero with a mythic heritage. The young hero is traditionally born after a long period of barrenness, and subterfuge is frequently involved in both his conception and his delivery. Milkman's mother seduces her husband, who had not touched her in thirteen years, with a love potion given her by Pilate and later saves her unborn child's life only through Pilate's intervention. Pilate, a moonshiner and a social outcast, certainly qualifies as a member of the humbler orders, whom Rank identifies as significant attendants at the hero's birth. This interference and trickery make the baby the focus of the father's hostility against his wife.

These mythic parallels are, however, only the basis for Morrison's highly allusive narrative. Milkman is born, the first black baby admitted to Southside's Mercy Hospital, on the day after Mr. Smith, the North Carolina Mutual Life Insurance agent, leaps from the roof of Mercy. As we learn later, Mr. Smith is also one of the Seven Days, a black secret society pledged to avenge any black's murder by the random slaying of a white. Smith tumbles headlong from the roof, vainly flapping homemade blue silk wings as he falls, Icarus-like,

to his death. His death signals Milkman's birth. Henceforth, the motifs of Icarus and flight are inextricably connected to the vengeance of the Seven Days. The hero's birth is accompanied by ritualized celebration—his Aunt Pilate singing in the street, and virgins (Milkman's elder sisters) strewing rose petals as a black Icarus dies. But also in attendance is Guitar, the boyhood friend who becomes the Sunday man of the Seven Days and avenges any black slain on a Sunday—until he turns from killing whites to ambushing Milkman. Morrison offsets the Fury-like society of the Seven Days by pairing her Icarus motif of failure and death with references to Lindbergh, drawing together two famous soarers but suggesting that an Icarus' doomed escape must always be balanced by a Daedalus' success. As a child, Milkman yearned to fly and "lost all interest in himself" when he discovered "the same thing Mr. Smith had learned earlier—that only birds and airplanes could fly." The novel follows his attempt to overcome this disaffection and learn to fly again, figuratively, if not literally.

Through the use of the Icarus motif, the opening of the book draws together the thematic concerns of a novel, but the second stage of Milkman's growth, the period of both explanation and alienation, illustrates one of the enduring concerns of myth, the need to create order and bring understanding out of apparent chaos. Milkman's heritage is explained in family histories which he tries, resentfully, to shrug aside. His family's past is dead for Milkman, and he feels increasingly stifled by the greed, anger, and frustration of his home. He remains isolated, alienated from his family, his culture, even from Hagar, his cousin who has been his lover since he was seventeen. One morning,

> Milkman stood before his mirror and glanced, in the low light of the wall lamp, at his reflection. He was, as usual, unimpressed with what he saw. He had a fine enough face…. But it lacked coherence, a coming together of the features into a total self. It was all very tentative, the way he looked, like a man peeping around a corner of someplace he is not supposed to be, trying to make up his mind whether to go forward or to turn back. The decision he made would be extremely important, but the way in which he made the decision would be careless, haphazard, and uninformed.

Milkman's decisions during this period are indeed haphazard and uninformed. He strikes his father for slapping his mother, tries to break up the one love affair of his forty-year-old, unmarried sister, and determines to send Hagar a Christmas present and farewell letter at once. Rather than acting from any belief or commitment to another, Milkman only reacts. Each event is a rejection—of parental authority, of family ties, of love. He realizes that his "life was pointless, aimless, and it was true that he didn't concern himself an awful lot about other people. There was nothing he wanted bad enough to risk anything for, inconveniencing himself for." Moreover, he thinks constantly of escape, of slamming the door of his father's house and never returning, of flying away. He tells Guitar that he feels increasingly off-center, disaffected by his family and society, and detached from the racial tensions which increasingly control Guitar, who is moving more completely into the circumscribed world of the Seven Days. Milkman accuses Guitar, "You mad at every Negro who ain't scrubbing floors and picking cotton. This ain't Montgomery, Alabama." To which Guitar responds,

"You're right, Milkman. You have never in your life said a truer word. This is definitely not Montgomery, Alabama. Tell me. What would you do if it was? If this turned out to be another Montgomery?"

"Buy a plane ticket."

"Exactly. Now you know something about yourself you didn't know before: who you are and what you are."

"Yeah. A man that refuses to live in Montgomery, Alabama."

"No. A man that can't live there."

But, of course, without knowing what is worth risking everything for, Milkman cannot live anywhere yet. He is like Joyce's young Stephen Daedalus, wanting only to fly away.

The single moment during this period of Milkman's life which best illustrates both his yearnings and his vacillation occurs when Milkman and Guitar see a white peacock perched on the roof of a defunct Buick in Southside. The bird, at once beautiful and ludicrous, cannot fly because, as Guitar says, it has "too much tail. All that jewelry weighs it down. Like vanity. Can't nobody fly with all that shit. Wanna fly, you got to give up the shit that weights you down." For Guitar, this means abandoning family, friends, and society, and channeling himself completely into the vengeance of the Seven Days. Although Milkman laughingly accedes to Guitar's jeering interpretation, he is fumbling toward a more positive significance for the peacock—escape into adventure. But he does not see that the incongruous juxtaposition of the peacock and used cars suggests how the exotic appears unexpectedly out of the prosaic, just as his quest rises out of Southside and his family. The way to escape Southside is to get money, the gold his Aunt Pilate and father stumbled across in a Pennsylvania cave.

His quest leads Milkman to Pennsylvania and then to Virginia, where he traces his father's and Pilate's youthful wanderings. He meets his father's boyhood friends, who remember the elder Macon Dead as an almost superhuman figure and who accept the success of the father in Southside real estate as an inevitable extension of his youthful exploits and talents. Milkman drinks in their tales of Lincoln's Heaven, the Edenic Pennsylvania farm which still represents to these old men an ideal world, a flourishing, rich farm hacked out of the woods by an ex-slave, Milkman's grandfather. Milkman finds himself continuing the myth, spinning out, to the wonder and delight of his audience, his own elaborate version of his father's efforts to buy the Erie-Lackawanna Railroad.

He next visits the old plantation where his father and aunt had been hidden by a house servant, Circe, after their father was murdered by whites jealous of a black man's success and greedy for Lincoln's Heaven. The narrative becomes progressively eerier when he finds the ancient servant still alive and presiding over the ruins of the estate, supervising its decay, a witch in the land of the dead. More a Sibyl than her siren namesake, Circe guards this entrance into the past. She initiates Milkman into his own past, showing both the power and the destructiveness of his heritage, and channels his rebelliousness into a quest for his own identity. He could not reach the dream-like core of his quest, his journey into Virginia, without direct contact with the world of the past and the dead. Lincoln's Heaven, Circe, and the decayed plantation all represent the past which still exerts its influence on Milkman. Like Aeneas, like Ulysses, Milkman needs to look into his, his family's, and his people's past before he can move into the future. Circe tells Milkman where the cave holding the gold was, how Pilate and Milkman's father argued and opened the rift which has lasted for decades, where Pilate wandered, and where Milkman's grandfather originally came from—Shalimar, Virginia.

Just as contact with the underworld has traditionally meant knowledge for the living, so Circe's revelations turn Milkman south to Virginia where he abandons the search for the missing gold to regain his self-esteem. Shalimar offers new skills to measure self-worth—hunting, fighting, and surviving, the only prowess these Virginians acknowledge. The city man adapts to their code and participates in a midnight cougar hunt where he suddenly realizes that *he* is being hunted by Guitar, who wants a part of the long-lost gold for the Seven Days and thinks Milkman has found the gold and refuses to share it.

Guitar, the hero's antagonist, threatens the particular virtues and values of the world and the past that Milkman is slowly coming to accept. He is not as much Milkman's opposite as his double, an extension of the very negations Milkman has practiced. Guitar has abandoned his family and his heritage in the South. More importantly, he has rejected love and ties just as Milkman has spurned his family and Hagar. The only brotherhood Guitar acknowledges is the Seven Days, a brotherhood based on death. He is total sterility, wintry and steely in his dedication to vengeance. His name, Guitar, comes from a childhood love of creativity and music which he has denied; Milkman's name suggests the fertility and life which he has been running from. In the dark woods Milkman suddenly understands Guitar and himself. Guitar's total commitment to death is only the logical extension of Milkman's constant attempts to fly away.

Milkman is still not ready to challenge the enemy, and when Guitar's ambush in the Virginia woods fails, the protagonist runs. His return to his own world is thus ambivalent. Although Milkman's relationship to his family and his world improves, his trip brings about no reconciliation between his father and his aunt. The traditional pattern of reintegration and defense of the society cannot be effected, perhaps because he has recognized his own weakness and the values which he tried to deny, but he has not yet fought for them. He returns to Virginia with Pilate to bury his grandfather's bones at Lincoln's Heaven, and there Guitar shoots Pilate, the novel's clearest representative of personal and racial heritage and continuity with the past. The novel ends as Guitar steps from hiding to try, once again, to kill Milkman.

Although the final confrontation offers two possible resolutions, its thematic unity is not ambivalent. If Milkman kills Guitar, then he will return home the conqueror, the hero who has bested his and his society's opponent. If, however, he falls to Guitar, he remains a hero. Milkman himself tells us that he thinks he can beat Guitar in a straight fight but stands little chance if Guitar has a gun, which he has. But success is not the measure of the mythic hero's stature. More frequently than not, he dies in his last battle. The death is less important than its symbolic affirmation of his and his world's values. Hector and Achilles fall, and Beowulf dies to save his people from the dragon. Milkman, too,

has to face, within himself, the dragons of despair, nihilism, and sterility. When Milkman leaps toward Guitar, he has already fought and won his battle.

One of Morrison's strengths is the subtlety with which she ties together the stages of her hero's development through imagery, specifically imagery of flight. If the opening consciously evokes the classical myth of Icarus, her subsequent use of this pattern makes it her own. On the one hand, we have Guitar, who says that only by shedding the burden of personal and past responsibilities can one fly. On the other hand is the "Song of Solomon" which weaves its way through the novel. Rather than a Judeo-Christian love song, Morrison creates an Afro-American history of a slave, Solomon, who flew away, quite literally, from Virginia to Africa. The song becomes a celebration of a family's and, by extension, a people's past. By the time Milkman realizes, at the novel's close, that he must face Guitar, accept and love him, even if he kills him or is killed by him, flight has become soaring:

> Without wiping away the tears, taking a deep breath, or even bending his knees—he leaped. As fleet and bright as a lodestar he wheeled toward Guitar and it did not matter which one of them would give up his ghost in the killing arms of his brother. For now he knew what Shalimar knew: If you surrendered to the air, you could ride it.

This is the control, the coherence, he has sought—acceptance of his past in both its historical and its supernatural aspects and acceptance of himself. When Solomon of the song flew back to Africa, he tried to carry away his favorite son, Milkman's grandfather, but dropped him. However, rather than picking up the Icarus motif of escape and doomed flight, Morrison creates her own myth of those who fumble in their efforts to fly and then soar higher—more Daedaluses than Icaruses. The structure of the novel is not then confusing, nor is it circular, simply moving from one black man's attempted flight to another's. Whether he kills Guitar or is killed by him, Milkman's joyful acceptance of the burden of his past transforms his leap toward Guitar into a triumphant flight.

Source: A. Leslie Harris, "Myth as Structure in Toni Morrison's *Song of Solomon*," in *MELUS*, Vol. 7, No. 3, Fall, 1980, pp. 69-76.

Sources

Michael Awkward, "'Unruly and Let Loose': Myth, Ideology and Gender in *Song of Solomon*," in his *Negotiating Difference: Race, Gender, and the Politics of Positionality*, University of Chicago Press, 1995, pp. 137-55.

Cynthia A. Davis, "Self, Society and Myth in Toni Morrison's Fiction," in *Toni Morrison,* edited by Harold Bloom, Chelsea House Publishers, 1990, pp. 7-26.

Vivian Garnick, "Into the Dark Heart of Childhood," in *The Village Voice,* August 29, 1977, p. 41.

A. Leslie Harris, "Myth as Structure in Toni Morrison's *Song of Solomon, MELUS,* Vol. 7, No. 3, pp. 69-76.

Maureen Howard, a review in *The Hudson Review,* Vol. XXXI, No. 1, Spring, 1978.

Carol Iannone, "Toni Morrison's Career," in *Commentary,* Vol. 84, No. 6, December, 1987, pp. 59-63.

Margo Jefferson, "Black Gold," *Newsweek,* September 12, 1977, p. 93.

Jill Matus, "*Song of Solomon:* Raising Dead Fathers," in her *Toni Morrison,* Manchester University Press, 1998, pp. 72-85.

Toni Morrison, *Song of Solomon,* Knopf, 1977.

Reynolds Price, "Black Family Chronicle," in *The New York Times Book Review,* September 11, 1977, pp. 1, 48.

Catherine Rainwater, "Worthy Messengers: Narrative Voices in Toni Morrison's Novels," in *Texas Studies in Literature and Language,* Vol. XXXIII, No. 1, Spring 1991, pp. 96-113.

For Further Study

Bertram D. Ashe, " 'Why Don't He Like My Hair?': Constructing African-American Standards of Beauty in Toni Morrison's *Song of Solomon* and Zora Neale Hurston's *Their Eyes Were Watching God,*" *African American Review,* Vol. 29, Winter 1995, pp. 579-92.

    Ashe discusses how Black women deal with white standards of beauty by using examples from novels by Morrison and Hurston.

Susan L. Blake, "Folklore and Community in *Song of Solomon,*" *MELUS,* Vol. 7, No. 3, pp. 77-83.

    Blake discusses the tensions between community and individuality in *Song of Solomon.*

Joseph A. Brown, "To Cheer the Weary Traveler: Toni Morrison, William Faulkner, and History," *The Mississippi Quarterly,* Vol. 49, Fall, 1996, pp. 709-26.

    This essay contrasts William Faulkner's *Absalom, Absalom!* with Morrison's *Song of Solomon.*

David Cowart, "Faulkner and Joyce in Morrison's *Song of Solomon,*" *American Literature,* Vol. 62, No. 1, March, 1990, pp. 87-102.

    This piece discusses some of the literary influences on Morrison's work.

Chiara Spallino, "*Song of Solomon:* An Adventure in Structure," in *Callaloo,* Vol. 8, No. 2, Spring-Summer, 1985, pp. 510-24.

    This essay maps the structure of Morrison's novel and discusses the differences between the "family past" and the "mythic past" in the novel.

Gary Storhoff, "'Anaconda Love:' Parental Enmeshment in Toni Morrison's *Song of Solomon,*" *Style,* Vol. 31, No. 2, Summer, 1997, pp. 290-309.

    Storhoff shows how each of Morrison's characters suffer from their dysfunctional family relationships.

Jean Strouse, "Toni Morrison's Black Magic," *Newsweek,* March 30, 1981, p. 52.

    Strouse's cover story on Toni Morrison's life and career marks the publication of her fourth novel, *Tar Baby.*

Darwin T. Turner, "Theme, Characterization and Style in the Works of Toni Morrison," in *Black Women Writers: A Critical Evaluation,* edited by Mari Evans, Anchor Press, 1984, pp. 361-69.

    This piece gives a broad overview of Morrison's first four novels.

Ten Little Indians

Agatha Christie

1939

In 1939 mystery lovers eagerly awaited the publication of Agatha Christie's new novel, *Ten Little Indians*. They were not disappointed. The novel soon became a best-seller, gaining critical success along with its popularity. First published in England as *Ten Little Niggers*, the book was renamed *And Then There Were None*, from the closing line of the nursery rhyme, for publication in the United States. The original title was deemed too offensive for the American public. Later, the title would be changed to *Ten Little Indians*.

The novel focuses on a group of people invited by a mysterious Mr. Owen to enjoy a holiday on Indian Island. After the guests start turning up dead, the mystery deepens. Tension mounts as the remaining guests attempt to discover the murderer's identity before they are all killed. After Christie adapted the novel for the stage, it enjoyed successful runs in both England and America and was twice adapted for film. It has also been translated into several different languages. Critics praise the novel's intricate plotting and innovative technique, noting that in it, Christie adds new twists to the mystery genre. Most scholars, along with her devoted fans, consider *Ten Little Indians* to be one of the best mystery novels ever written.

Author Biography

Agatha Christie sets *Ten Little Indians* on an island that lies off the coast of Devon, England,

where she grew up. She was born on September 15, 1890, in Torquay, a resort town on the Devon coast. Her parents, American Frederick Miller and Clarissa Boehmer Miller, born in Ireland, raised her and her two siblings in an upper-middle-class atmosphere. She grew up among a mix of landed gentry, retired military officers who had served in remote British colonies, and farmers. Robin Winks in *British Writers* notes that Christie "drew upon the reality, and even more the memories and myths, of her childhood for many of her settings and characters." This appears true, also, in her creation of the mix of characters in *Ten Little Indians*.

In 1914, she married Colonel Archibald Christie, a member of the Flying Corps, and soon after worked as a nurse during World War I. Fourteen years later the marriage ended in divorce. While traveling in the Middle East, Christie met and later married archaeologist Max Mallowan, whom she accompanied on many archaeological digs. On a dare from her sister, she wrote her first detective novel, *The Mysterious Affair at Styles,* published in 1920. That and the four other novels that followed were well received, but it took the publication of her next novel, *The Murder of Roger Ackroyd,* in 1926 to gain her the reputation of one of the world's most popular writers. Known as the "Grand Dame" of mysteries, or as she preferred, the "Duchess of Death," Christie was also a most prolific writer. Her works include almost one hundred mystery novels and short-story collections, six romantic novels under the pen name Mary Westmacott, twenty-one plays, and a two-volume autobiography. Many of her works have been translated into more than one hundred languages.

Christie earned several awards and honors during her career, including the Mystery Writers of America Grand Master Award and the honor of D.B.E. (Dame Commander, Order of the British Empire), conferred upon her by Queen Elizabeth. When she died on January 12, 1976, at her home in Wallingford, Oxfordshire, London theatres dimmed their lights, offering a fitting tribute to this internationally acclaimed author.

Plot Summary

Part I

In *Ten Little Indians* Christie creates a masterpiece of mystery and murder. After ten strangers gather together on an isolated island off the coast of Devon, England, one by one, they each are dis-

Agatha Christie

covered murdered. As those remaining frantically search for the murderer, their own guilty pasts return to haunt them.

Mr. Justice Wargrave, lately retired from the bench, travels by train to Devon where he will be taken by boat to Indian Island. Seven others are also on their way there, most invited by a Mr. or Mrs. Owen. Vera Claythorne, a young, attractive teacher was hired through a letter from Una Nancy Owen for a short stint as a secretary. Captain Philip Lombard is not sure why he has been assigned to the island, other than to hold himself "at the disposal of a client." Miss Emily Brent, an elderly woman, has been invited by letter by someone she met years ago at a guesthouse. General Macarthur, retired from service, was invited by "a man named Owen" to "chat about old times" and Dr. Armstrong was asked by letter to treat Mrs. Owen's medical condition. Dashing young Tony Marston also received a letter from the Owens inviting him to the island. None of them, however, are very clear about who the Owens are. While Mr. Blore travels by train to the island, he writes down the names of the seven people we have just met along with two servants, Mr. and Mrs. Rogers, and decides to pretend to be a Mr. Davis. As Fred Narracott, a local sailor, takes them all to Indian Island by boat, Vera notes "there was something sinister" about it and "shivered faintly."

After they arrive at the island, Mr. Rogers, the butler, tells them that Mr. Owen has been "unfortunately delayed" and will not appear until the next day. Mrs. Rogers, the cook, shows them to their rooms and they later reunite for dinner where they discover ten little china Indians on a table. They also note that the "Ten Little Indians" nursery rhyme is framed in each of their rooms. After dinner an "inhuman" voice penetrates the comfortable silence surrounding the group, charging that each of them has been responsible for a death and concluding with, "Prisoners at the bar, have you anything to say in your defense?"

When asked, Rogers tells the rest that he put on the record, *Swan Song,* as per instructions written in a letter from Mr. Owen. Justice Wargrave immediately takes charge and converts the room into "an impromptu court of law." Rogers explains that he never met Owen and that all orders were sent by letter. The guests decide to pool their information about how they were invited, but Lombard doesn't reveal why he is there. When pressed, Blore, an ex-policeman who now runs a detective agency, admits he was hired by Owen to watch his wife's jewels. Wargrave concludes that the person who invited them is unknown to them and "no doubt ... is a madman—probably a dangerous homicidal lunatic."

The guests then claim to be innocent of the charges leveled against them. Wargrave insists his conscience is perfectly clear about passing sentence on Edward Seton "a rightly convicted murderer." Armstrong, however, remembers hearing comments about how the judge was against Seton and so turned the jury around to a guilty verdict. Vera explains that she was hired as nursery governess to Cyril Hamilton who one day swam out too far and drowned before she could reach him. The General declares there to be no truth to the accusation that he murdered Arthur Richmond, one of his officers. He explains that he sent Richmond on a reconnaissance where he was killed "in the natural course of events in war time."

Lombard, on the other hand, admits the story about him is true. While in the bush, he left a group of natives behind to die as a "matter of self-preservation." He justifies his actions by arguing that "natives don't mind dying.... They don't feel about it as Europeans do." Marston decides that John and Lucy Combes "must have been a couple of kids I ran over near Cambridge" and insists the incident was "pure accident." Rogers explains that he and his wife called the doctor for Miss Brady, whom they cared for, but the doctor didn't come in time.

When pressed, he admits that after she died, they received an inheritance from her. Blore confesses that he got a promotion from providing evidence to convict James Landor, who later died in jail, but asserts that he "was only doing [his] duty." Dr. Armstrong tells the others that he can't remember Louisa Clees, but thinks about the night he got drunk and operated on her, acknowledging to himself, "I killed her." Emily insists, "I have nothing with which to reproach myself."

Part II

After they all agree to leave in the morning when Narracott comes in the boat with supplies, Marston gulps down his drink, chokes, and falls down dead. The others decide he must have committed suicide by putting something into his drink. After they go to bed, some think about the accusations against them. Wargrave insists Seton was guilty, but Macarthur admits that he deliberately sent Richmond to his death after discovering his affair with his wife. In the morning they discover Rogers's wife dead and only eight Indian figures left on the table. They note that the deaths of Marston and Mrs. Rogers fit the descriptions in the nursery rhyme. When the boat doesn't come, they realize they are trapped on the island. Emily later admits to Vera that when Beatrice Taylor, her servant, got pregnant, Emily fired her and she committed suicide. Emily, though, reiterates her own innocence. Lombard, Blore, and Armstrong search the island and the house for Mr. Owen but find nothing. When they conclude that there is no one else on the island except the eight of them, they become terrified and start to suspect each other.

In the afternoon the General is found dead, hit on the back of the head. That evening as a storm rages outside, they eye each other suspiciously. The next morning they find Rogers murdered while chopping wood and note that after each murder, an Indian figure disappears. Later, Blore admits to Lombard that Landor was innocent and that he had been coerced into framing him. After breakfast they find Emily dead from an injection and that evening discover the judge shot through the head. The next day Lombard pressures Vera into admitting she engineered Cyril's death so that Hugo, her lover, could inherit a great deal of money and be free to marry her. Later when they discover Blore and Armstrong have also been murdered, they turn on each other and Vera shoots him. Exhausted Vera goes to her room and finds a rope fashioned into a noose hanging from a hook in the ceiling. She thinks, "that's what Hugo wanted," and hangs herself.

Part III

The narrative then shifts to a conversation between Sir Thomas Legge, Assistant Commissioner at Scotland Yard, and Inspector Maine about what happened on the island. Inspector Maine recounts how each died and tells the Commissioner that Isaac Morris, an "unsavory" man mixed up in drug dealing, made all the arrangements at the island and covered his employer's tracks. Morris was later found dead of an overdose of sleeping medication. Maine reviews the accusations from the record and can clear only Wargrave absolutely, noting Seton was "unmistakably guilty." However, Maine has not been able to uncover the murderer's identity.

The novel ends with a transcript of a manuscript found stuffed in a bottle by a fishing trawler and sent to Scotland Yard. The manuscript, a written confession by Wargrave, explains how his contradictory desires for justice and murder prompted him to plan something "stupendous ... something theatrical." Through conversations with people he met, he learned of the guilty past of each of the nine. After he discovered himself to be terminally ill, he bought Indian Island and lured the others there and one by one, murdered them. With Armstrong's help, he faked his death so the mystery would not be discovered. Morris, whom he poisoned before he came to the island, was his tenth victim. After arranging for the deaths of the others, Wargrave shot himself in the same manner in which he appeared to be shot earlier. His desire to show off his ingenious scheme prompted him to place his confession in the bottle.

Characters

Dr. Edward Armstrong

Dr. Armstrong is coming to Indian Island to examine and treat Mrs. Owen after receiving a letter from her husband. He takes pleasure in a reputation as "a good man at his job" and so has enjoyed a great deal of success. However, "he was very tired.... Success had its penalties." As he travels to Devon, he alludes to a past incident that occurred fifteen years ago that "had been a near thing." During that period, he notes that he had been "going to pieces," and the shock of the traumatic event prompted him to give up drinking. Later his thoughts about the incident reveal that his drunken performance in the operating room killed Louisa Clees. While on the island, Armstrong is a bundle of nerves. His gullibility leads him to help War-

grave carry out his plans, which include murdering Armstrong.

William Blore

William Blore pretends to be Mr. Davis, a "man of means from South Africa," sure that "he could enter into any society unchallenged." His true identity as a detective hired to watch Mrs. Owen's jewels is quickly and easily exposed soon after he arrives at Indian Island. The narrator describes him as "an earnest man" and notes that "a light touch was incomprehensible to him." Lombard observes his lack of imagination. After discovering that Blore committed perjury during the bank robbery trial that resulted in the conviction of an innocent man, Inspector Maine declares him to be "a bad hat."

Miss Emily Brent

Miss Emily Brent, a "hard and self-righteous" sixty-five-year-old woman, received a letter signed "UN" from someone claiming to have met her years ago at a guesthouse. Her repressed nature becomes immediately apparent as she sits "upright" in the train, because she "did not approve of lounging." She agrees with her father, "a Colonel of the old school," who thought "the present generation was shamelessly lax—in their carriage, and in every other way." She sits in the compartment, "enveloped in an aura of righteousness and unyielding principles." Since her income has been lately reduced, she looks forward to a free holiday at Indian Island. When she hears the voice on the record accuse her of murder, she becomes "encased in her own armour of virtue," and insists "I had nothing with which to reproach myself." When Vera asks her whether she has been affected by the murders that have been taking place on the island, Emily responds, "I was brought up to keep my head and never to make a fuss." Vera concludes that this confession proves that Emily must have been repressed in her childhood and so explains her inability to respond normally to what has happened on the island. Emily eventually admits to Vera that when Beatrice Taylor, her servant, got pregnant, Emily fired her and she committed suicide. Emily, though, reiterates her own innocence.

Vera Claythorne

Vera Claythorne is an attractive young woman who comes to Indian Island expecting employment as a secretary after receiving a letter from Una Nancy Owen. Lombard describes her as "a cool customer ... one who could hold her own—in love or war," an ironic foreshadowing of her composure

A scene from the film And Then There Were None, *based on* Ten Little Indians *and starring Barry Fitzgerald, Walter Huston, Louis Hayward, Roland Young, and June Duprez.*

as she fatally shoots him. She shows an ambitious nature when she hopes that this temporary job will lead to a more desirable permanent position and so allow her to leave the "third-class school" where she has been teaching.

Throughout the novel, she appears troubled about an incident in her past, which we later learn is the drowning of Cyril Hamilton, a young boy in her care. Her first thoughts reveal her love for and sorrow over her dissolved relationship with Hugo Hamilton, the boy's uncle. She also appears to feel guilt over the boy's death. Soon though we learn

of her cruel and selfish nature when she finally acknowledges her part in Cyril's death. She admits that she encouraged the "whiny spoilt little brat" to swim out too far into the water, knowing he would not be able to make it back to shore. Trying to justify her actions, she notes, "if it weren't for him, Hugo would be rich" and able to marry her.

Wargrave finds her to be an "interesting psychological experiment" after all the other guests have been murdered. He wondered, "would the consciousness of her own guilt, the state of nervous tension consequent on having just shot a man, be sufficient, together with the hypnotic suggestion of the surroundings, to cause her to take her own life." Vera proves Wargrave's hypothesis when she hangs herself. He deems her crime to be the most heinous, because he plots her demise only after she experiences the murders of all the others.

Mr. Davis

See William Blore

Sir Thomas Legge

Sir Thomas Legge, Assistant Commissioner at Scotland Yard tries to solve the mystery of what happened on Indian Island with Inspector Maine, who has been investigating the case. Legge becomes infuriated when he cannot.

Captain Philip Lombard

Captain Philip Lombard sits opposite Vera on the train to Indian Island. He is not sure why he has been assigned to the island, other than the fact that he is "at the disposal of a client." Issac Morris, the agent who hired him, considers him to be "a good man in a tight place." Lombard admits that in his past actions, "legality had not always been a sine qua non…. There wasn't much he'd draw the line at." He had previously been mixed up in shady business abroad which gained him "a reputation for daring and for not being overscrupulous" about murder. He exhibits this latter quality when he admits to the others that he did cause the death of twenty-one East African men. In an attempt to justify his actions, he explains that while in the bush, he left the natives behind to die as a "matter of self-preservation." He insists, "natives don't mind dying…. They don't feel about it as Europeans do." Due to the callous nature of his crime, Wargrave allows him to suffer longer than the others before he is murdered.

General Gordon Macarthur

General Macarthur has received a letter from a man named Owen inviting him to Indian Island to "chat about old times." Macarthur's guilt about his past becomes evident in his paranoid notion that people have been avoiding him lately because of "that damned rumour" about an incident that occurred thirty years ago. He thinks that people suspect that he really did send Arthur Richmond to his death. As a result, he has slowly withdrawn from others and into himself. At the island he thinks about Richmond's affair with his wife and his subsequent decision to send him on a deadly reconnaissance. His guilt over his actions prompts his

Media Adaptations

- Christie adapted *Ten Little Indians* for the stage. It first played with the novel's original title, *Ten Little Niggers,* in London, opening October 17, 1943; it was produced under the title *Ten Little Indians* on Broadway and opened at the Broadhurst Theatre on June 27, 1944.

- The novel was made into three film versions, all titled *Ten Little Indians.* The first (1966) was directed by George Pollock and starred Hugh O'Brian and Shirley Eaton. The second (1974) was directed by Peter Collinson and starred Oliver Reed and Richard Attenborough. The third (1989) was directed by Alan Birkinshaw, starring Donald Pleasence and Brenda Vaccaro.

decision that he's "come to the end of things" and that he doesn't want to leave the island. At one point, the other guests find a dazed Macarthur looking out to sea exclaiming, "there is so little time…. I really must insist that no one disturbs me." He later explains to Vera, "none of us are going to leave the island" and expresses his relief that he won't have to "carry the burden any longer."

Inspector Maine

Inspector Maine reports to Sir Thomas Legge, Assistant Commissioner at Scotland Yard. He has investigated the murders at Indian Island and has discovered background information on some of the guests. However, he has not been able to solve the case.

Anthony Marston

Anthony Marston has been invited through letter by a friend to visit the Owens on Indian Island. Marston is handsome, young, and "a creature of sensation—and of action." His reckless actions, specifically his speeding, cause the death of two young people, John and Lucy Combes. His "complete callousness and his inability to feel any responsibility for the lives he had taken," prompt Wargrave to dispose of him first. Wargrave knows that Marston's amoral nature would prevent him from experiencing any guilt over his past and thus from feeling an increasing sense of unease as the murder plot unfolds. Wargrave murders Marston because his recklessness proves him to be "a danger to the community."

Isaac Morris

Isaac Morris, an "unsavory" man mixed up in drug deals, made all the arrangements at the island. He put the Indian Island house sale through a third party so the buyer would not be discovered and then carefully covered the buyer's tracks. Wargrave kills him with an overdose of drugs before he leaves for the island.

Fred Narracott

Fred Narracott, a local sailor, takes the others by boat to the island. He is "a man of the sea, [with] a weather-beaten face and dark eyes with a slightly evasive expression." Like the other residents of Sticklehaven, he feels uneasy about what is happening on the island, noting "the whole thing was queer—very queer."

Mrs. Ethel Rogers

Mrs. Rogers, wife of the butler Mr. Rogers, serves as cook and maid for the guests at Indian Island. The guests note that she is "a white bloodless ghost of a woman" and that her "flat-monotonous voice" and "queer light shifty eyes" make her look like a woman "who walked in mortal fear." Wargrave decides to murder her early on, since he feels her husband coerced her into neglecting the health of her previous employer, Jennifer Brady.

Mr. Thomas Rogers

Mr. Rogers was hired as a butler to serve the guests at Indian Island. Never having met his employer, he obeys all orders sent to him by letter, including the playing of the record that accuses all the guests, including himself and his wife, of murder. Even after he discovers his wife murdered, he remains "the good servant," carrying on "with an impassive countenance." We later discover that he and his wife had intentionally waited too long to call the doctor when their elderly employer, Jennifer Brady, fell ill. After her death, the couple gained a substantial inheritance.

Mr. Justice Lawrence Wargrave

Mr. Justice Wargrave, retired from the law, is a distinguished looking gentleman on his way to Indian Island after being invited there by letter from his friend, Constance Culmington. Upon closer inspection, however, the guests notice that his "pale shrewd little eyes" and "hunched up attitude" suggest a "decidedly reptilian" demeanor. He has been reputed to have "great powers with a jury," but some call him "a hanging judge." When he takes out his false teeth, his "shrunken lips" compress and turn his mouth "cruel" and "predatory." At the end of the novel, Wargrave is found innocent of the charge that he wrongfully helped convict Edward Seton but guilty of murdering all the guests at Indian Island.

In the document discovered in a bottle and sent to Scotland Yard, he confesses to his crimes and reveals relevant character details: "From my earliest youth I realized that my nature was a mass of contradictions" including an "incurably romantic imagination," a "sadistic delight in seeing or causing death" and a "strong sense of justice." He explains that these contradictions prompted him to go into law, since "the legal profession satisfied nearly all [his] instincts." Wargrave further admits, "to see a wretched criminal squirming in the dock, suffering the tortures of the damned, as his doom came slowly and slowly nearer, was to me, an exquisite pleasure." And so, he lured ten guilty people to Indian Island and murdered them theatrically and slowly, one at a time.

Themes

Appearances and Reality

The focus on appearance versus reality appears throughout the novel in the form of the underlying theme of deception. All the characters deceive others and sometimes themselves about their true natures. All profess to be good, but in reality are filled with evil in the form of moral corruption caused by intolerance, jealousy, greed, and desire. The action begins under a cloud of deception when Judge Wargrave, under the guise of the mysterious Mr. Owen, lures the group to Indian Island. The deception continues after the voice on the recording accuses each of a crime and they all deny any responsibility. Wargrave's confession reveals the final deception when he exposes his faked murder and his own true nature.

Fear of Death

As soon as bodies start appearing on the island, the remaining guests are enveloped by the fear of death. Their instincts for survival cause them to suspect each other. As a result their primitive instincts emerge: Wargrave's mouth turns "cruel and predatory," Lombard's smile resembles that of a wolf, and Blore appears "coarser and clumsier" with "a look of mingled ferocity and stupidity about him."

Guilt and Innocence

The novel ties the question of the characters' guilt or innocence to the theme of appearance versus reality. At the beginning of their stay on the island, all the guests claim to be innocent. Some insist their crimes were committed by accident. Tony Marston explains that the accident that caused the deaths of John and Lucy Combes was "beastly bad luck." Louisa Clees' death, caused by Dr. Armstrong's drunken state in the operating room, was also accidental. The two, however, respond differently to these accidents. Marston will claim no responsibility. His amoral nature compounds his guilt. Armstrong, on the other hand, recognizes his responsibility for his patient's death, but cannot admit it publicly. Lombard's claims of innocence stem from the same kind of amoral nature coupled with his racism. He dismisses his "crime" arguing that his own survival should take precedence over that of the natives. Christie complicates the question of guilt and innocence when the focus turns to Wargrave. Is the judge guilty of the murder of ten people or is he fulfilling his duty as judge? His description of his motives in his confession point to his guilt.

Justice and Injustice

Justice is served when the guilty are punished. Injustice occurs when the innocent are punished. Wargrave justifies his crimes by claiming that the ten deserved to die because they victimized innocent people. He prompts us then to consider his victims not truly victims. Acting as judge, jury, and executioner, his punishment, he insists, was just.

Sanity and Insanity

Four people on the island experience varying degrees of insanity, due for the most part to feelings of overwhelming guilt. Dr. Armstrong's guilt clouds his judgment when Wargrave asks him for help in staging his own murder. Afterwards, his nervous state propels him close to the point of collapse. Macarthur's guilt preys on him before he arrives on the island, taking the form of paranoia. He suspects people are whispering about his crime behind his back and so withdraws from society. While on the island, he appears to fall into a trance, muttering to the others that he wants to be left alone. Immediately before Wargrave kills him, he admits

Topics for Further Study

- Conduct a mock trial for Justice Wargrave to determine whether or not he should be convicted of first-degree murder. If he is convicted, determine his sentence.

- Research English culture and determine whether or not the characters would behave any differently if they were American instead of British.

- Read another mystery story and compare the two works, focusing on how the mystery in each is constructed.

- Investigate psychologists' conclusions on the nature of the criminal mind and compare those findings to the characterization of Justice Wargrave.

that he does not want to ever leave the island. He appears to welcome his impending death as he looks forward to not having to "carry the burden any longer." Throughout the novel, the judge appears to feel the burden of guilt less than anyone does. However, in his confession he reveals himself to be the very "homicidal maniac" he told the others to be on guard against.

Style

Structure

The novel is structured as a mystery, although Christie adds her own innovations. Stories of good versus evil have been told since the beginning of time, but the mystery story emerged in the second half of the nineteenth century with the works of Edgar Allan Poe and Arthur Conan Doyle. The mystery structure includes motives and alibis, detection, clues, and red herrings (diversions from the real culprit). Characters become suspects before the true one is unmasked. The hero discovers the villain only at the climax of the story, and then, in the denouement, explains how the crime was committed. Christie carries on several of the traditions of the

A scene from the 1974 film Ten Little Indians.

mystery but adds some new twists. The characters in *Ten Little Indians* present motives for past crimes and alibis for the murders on the island. Judge Wargrave, who at the end of the novel, identifies the murderer and puts all the pieces of the puzzle back together, engineers detection, clues, and a red herring. Christie's twist on the traditional mystery structure is that all of the characters are discovered to be villains; none are innocent. The final irony and delightful innovative turn is that the hidden villain in the novel, Judge Wargrave, also becomes the "hero," in the modern sense of the term.

Symbol

Christie uses the setting symbolically in the novel. The house becomes a symbol of the characters' fate. As the others search for "Mr. Owen," the narrator notes, "If this had been an old house, with creaking wood, and dark shadows, and heavily paneled walls, there might have been an eerie feeling. But this house was the essence of modernity. There were no dark corners—no possible sliding panels—it was flooded with electric light—everything was new and bright and shining. There was nothing hidden in this house, nothing concealed. It had no atmosphere about it. Somehow, that was the most frightening thing of all." As the narrator notes, nothing can be hidden in this

house, especially the guilt of all the guests who inhabit it. The manner of death Wargrave chooses for himself is also symbolic, and he uses it as a clue to the real identity of the murderer on the island. He arranges to shoot himself in his forehead, the first time as a trick and the second time for real. In his confession, he notes that the mark in his head is symbolic of the "brand of Cain."

Foreshadowing

This technique occurs when an old man sitting across from Blore on the train warns, "there's a squall ahead … Watch and pray…. The day of judgment is at hand." A squall will hit the island, literally and figuratively, and judgment will be pronounced and acted upon.

Historical Context

World War II

The world experienced a decade of aggression in the 1930s that would culminate in World War II. This second world war resulted from the rise of totalitarian regimes in Germany, Italy, and Japan. These militaristic regimes gained control as a result of the great depression experienced by most of the world in the early 1930s and from the condi-

Compare
&
Contrast

- **1930s:** The economy collapses and causes a decade of poverty and hunger for millions of people.

  Today: The economy is booming, but many fear the year 2000 could cause another period of economic crisis.

- **1930s:** World War II begins in 1939. The United States plans to remain neutral in the war, until its ships are attacked at Pearl Harbor in 1941.

  Today: The United States helps control the 1999 crisis in Kosovo through air strikes and is able

to keep from deploying ground troops.

- **1930s:** Adolf Hitler becomes chancellor of Germany in 1933. His dictatorship promises order for his country, but instead, results in fear, suffering, war, and death for many of its citizens, especially the Jewish population.

  Today: Many survivors of Hitler's rule and their families who have reestablished their lives—many in the United States—are still trying to heal the pain stemming from Hitler's murderous tactics.

tions created by the peace settlements following World War I. The dictatorships established in each country encouraged expansion into neighboring countries. In Germany Hitler strengthened the army during the 1930s. In 1936 Benito Mussolini's Italian troops took Ethiopia. From 1936 to 1939 Spain was engaged in civil war involving Francisco Franco's fascist army, aided by Germany and Italy. In March 1938 Germany annexed Austria and in March 1939 occupied Czechoslovakia. Italy took Albania in April 1939. One week after Nazi Germany and the U.S.S.R. signed a Treaty of Nonaggression, on September 1, 1939, Germany invaded Poland and World War II began. On September 3, 1939, Britain and France declared war on Germany after a U-boat sank the British ship *Athenia* off the coast of Ireland. Another British ship, *Courageous,* was sunk on September 19. All the members of the British Commonwealth, except Ireland, soon joined Britain and France in their declaration of war.

Ten Little Indians was published in 1939, the year World War II began. While the novel is set in an indeterminate time period, Christie's focus on the darker side of human nature coincides with the displays of aggression evident in the 1930s. Her use of English characters and setting does not seem to contain much cultural significance. The novel does not portray genteel English characters who pride themselves on their sportsmanlike behavior.

Critical Overview

Ten Little Indians has been a popular and critical success since its publication in 1939. This best-selling novel appeared during what critics determine to be Christie's most productive period, from 1926 to the early 1950s. Many consider *Ten Little Indians* to be her best work.

Scholars note that Christie owes a debt to earlier crime writers such as Anna Katharine Green and Arthur Conan Doyle, yet most agree that she has had a tremendous influence on the crime novel genre. In *British Writers* Robin Winks observes her link to past works and her influence on future writers when he declares the novel to be "markedly tense, as close to a gothic thriller and modern suspense novel as the author would come." He insists that "Christie was original because of the way in which she developed plot, unraveled motive, and put utterly fresh twists on timeworn devices." He applauds her "quite remarkable ability to build motive, to misdirect the reader and to weave complex plots that turned and turned again."

Commenting on her style, Winks suggests that Christie was "at her best a writer of clear and engaging prose, a gentle (and at times sly) social critic, and a master of that element so essential to storytelling—plot." In his article on *Ten Little Indians* and *Murder on the Orient Express* for the

Spectator, Anthony Lejeune writes that these works are "famous because each of them turns on a piece of misdirection and a solution which, in their day, were startlingly innovatory." Ralph Partridge's review in *New Statesman* asserts, "Apart from one little dubious proceeding there is no cheating; the reader is just bamboozled in a straightforward way from first to last. To show her utter superiority over our deductive faculty, from time to time Mrs. Christie even allows us to know what every character present is thinking and still we can't guess!" Julian Symons praises her construction of puzzles in the novel and in her other works in his *Mortal Consequences: A History—From the Detective Story to the Crime Novel:* "Agatha Christie's claim to supremacy among the classical detective story writers of her time rests on her originality in constructing puzzles. This was her supreme skill…. If her work survives it will be because she was the supreme mistress of a magical skill that is a permanent, although often secret, concern of humanity: the construction and the solution of puzzles."

Some, however, have found fault with Christie's style. A few scholars criticize the genre itself, finding mysteries in general to pander to popular, uneducated tastes. Others discover limitations in what they consider to be the formulaic style of Christie's writing. They complain that her characters are stereotypical, and that the plots are too predictable and lack depth. Some note examples of racism, classicism, and sexism in her work. Marty S. Knepper, in "Agatha Christie—Feminist," argues that her novels, including *Ten Little Indians,* "present women in totally stereotypical ways: as empty-headed ingenues, for example, or as gossipy old ladies."

Despite the reservations of some critics, Agatha Christie remains today one of the world's most popular and highly acclaimed authors, a position noted by Max Lowenthal in his summary of her work in the *New York Times,* written after her death in 1976. He writes, "Dame Agatha's forte was supremely adroit plotting and sharp, believable characterization…. Her style and rhetoric were not remarkable; her writing was almost invariably sound and workmanlike, without pretense of flourish. Her characters were likely to be of the middle-middle class or upper-middle class, and there were certain archetypes, such as the crass American or the stuffy retired army officer now in his anecdotage. However familiar all this might be, the reader would turn the pages mesmerized as unexpected twist piled on unexpected twist until, in the end, he was taken by surprise. There was simply no out-guessing … Agatha Christie."

Criticism

Wendy Perkins

Perkins, an Associate Professor of English at Prince George's Community College in Maryland, has published articles on several twentieth-century authors. In this essay she examines how Christie's characterizations in Ten Little Indians *provide a harsh vision of human nature.*

In *British Writers* Robin Winks notes that Agatha Christie began writing during a time when detective fiction was a popular form of escapism. He argues that during the twenties, mysteries encouraged readers "to believe that even though their prewar, orderly world had been demolished, there was an ultimate order in human events if only one were astute enough to detect it." Yet during this time period, authors were also influenced by the writings of Sigmund Freud and Charles Darwin. As a result, their characters often revealed deep-seated psychological conflicts that resulted from environmental and biological influences. Christie's early novels reflect her audience's desire to solve puzzles and regain a sense of order. In her later work, however, written before and after World War II, her characterizations often suggest the harsher postwar reality of the twentieth century. These characters are more complex and sinister, which make her endings more unsettling. *Ten Little Indians,* one of her most famous and highly acclaimed works, illustrates this shift in its focus to the darker side of human nature.

Winks explains that the typical mystery story in the 1920s, "looked in both directions: by focusing on a crime, almost always a murder, it spoke to the loosened morality of a period that followed years of legalized killing. Yet, by holding to a series of rules, or by acknowledging the existence of rules precisely by mocking them, mystery fiction also appealed to those who longed for the orderly and rational life that, they believed, had preceded World War I." This sense of order, he argues, would be restored by the detective, who would, by the close of the story, "demonstrate a rational connection between all that had happened." David Grossvogel, in his critical analysis of Christie's works in *Death Deferred: The Long Life, Splendid Afterlife, and Mysterious Workings of Agatha Christie,* finds that Christie's early work fits this model: "Agatha Christie's first readers read her in order to purchase at the cost of a minor and passing disturbance the comfort of knowing that the disturbance was contained, and that at the end of the story the world they imagined would be continued in its innocence and familiarity."

Initially all the characters in Christie's early novels were suspects until detectives like Hercule Poirot, in *The Murder of Roger Ackroyd,* and Miss Jane Marple, in *The Murder in the Vicarage,* identified the murderer and proved the rest to be decent people. As a result, the world of the novel could revert back to its Edwardian gentility. In *Ten Little Indians,* however, all the suspects are found to be guilty of crimes; no one is innocent. The ending therefore becomes ambiguous, for although all the pieces of the puzzle now fit together, readers are left with an unsettling vision of evil. Thus no true sense of order can be restored.

In *Partners in Crime* Christie writes, "very few of us are what we seem." She clarifies that sentiment in *They Do It with Mirrors* when she declares "the worst is so often true." Christie illustrates these bleak observations in *Ten Little Indians,* as she reveals that each character has been responsible for the death of another. As Stewart H. Benedict notes in "Agatha Christie and Murder Most Unsportsmanlike," "the entire tone of this book gives the strong impression that Miss Christie is not sorry to see them go." The novel leaves readers with the disturbing sense that they have seen human nature at its basest, that even the English, who pride themselves on their honorable character, can be the perpetrators of heinous crimes.

Benedict notes that in other works Christie "sees murderers as being either good or bad individuals; the good ones dispose of evil victims, and vice versa." He explains that this bad murderer "unvaryingly preys on people with inadequate defenses: he may be a doctor [trusted by his patient] or a handsome and clever lover who first uses, then kills, a woman who has been unlucky enough to fall in love with him; or an old and respected friend and confidant; or a man who selects a child, an old person, a physical or psychological cripple as a victim. This element, the victim's inadequate defenses against the criminal, puts the murderer beyond the pale—he is unsportsmanlike and consequently despicable."

In *Ten Little Indians,* Judge Wargrave notes that the nine guests he has surreptitiously lured to Indian Island exhibit varying degrees of guilt. All ten of them, however, including the judge, fit the description of a "bad murderer": the Rogerses' intentional neglect resulted in the death of the employer who depended upon them; Anthony Marston accidentally ran over a young couple but felt no re-

morse and so refused to change his reckless habits; Philip Lombard revealed his cruel and racist nature when he left a group of natives to starve to death; Dr. Armstrong's weakness for alcohol caused him to botch an operation and kill his patient; Emily Brent's callousness prompted her servant to kill herself; ex-policeman Blore and General Macarthur betrayed the public's trust in them when they committed their crimes; and Vera Claythorne allowed her charge to swim too far out into the water, knowing he would not be able to make it back to shore. All of the nine assembled on the island were guilty of going "beyond the pale" by betraying their victim's faith and trust.

The motives behind the crimes reveal the baser qualities of human nature. The Rogerses greed prompted them to neglect Jennifer Brady and so gain her inheritance. Vera Claythorne also hoped to profit financially from the death of her charge, Cyril Hamilton, but her crime also involved uncontrollable desire. She encouraged Cyril to swim out too far so she and her lover Hugo Hamilton could marry and enjoy the inheritance that would then be transferred from Cyril to them. Uncontrollable desire also figures in Dr. Armstrong's crime, as his need for alcohol caused him to operate in a drunken state on Louisa Clees. Fear and the resulting need for self-preservation prompted Blore to provide false evidence against James Landor, an innocent man who later died in jail. These qualities coupled with a deep-seated prejudice surfaced in Philip Lombard's decision to leave a group of natives to starve in the bush. According to Lombard, "natives don't mind dying.... They don't feel about it as Europeans do." General Macarthur's jealousy prompted his decision to send Arthur Richmond on a deadly reconnaissance after discovering the younger man's affair with his wife. "Hard and self-righteous" Emily Brent, "encased in her own armour of virtue," was guilty of callousness when she fired her pregnant servant Beatrice Taylor, insisting herself above reproach since she claims Beatrice was not "a nice girl." Anthony Marston also displays "complete callousness" and his "inability to feel any responsibility" for the lives of John and Lucy Combes reveals his amoral nature. The judge determines accurately that Marston was "a danger to the community."

When the voice on the recording makes the accusations against them, most compound their guilt by lying. When asked about her involvement in Cyril's death, Vera insists, "I couldn't get there in time.... it wasn't my fault." Macarthur also denies responsibility for his crime: "no truth whatsoever in what he said about-er-young Arthur Richmond. Richmond was one of my officers. I sent him on a reconnaissance. He was killed. Natural course of events in war time." Rogers insists he and his wife did "everything possible" for Miss Brady: "We couldn't get the doctor to her. I went for him, sir, on foot. But he got there too late…. Devoted to her, we were. Any one will tell you the same. There was never a word said against us. Not a word." Blore declares, "I was only doing my duty" when he gave evidence against James Landor. When pressed about the death of Louisa Clees, Dr. Armstrong denies "having a patient of that name." Emily refuses to discuss her crime, insisting, "I have nothing with which to reproach myself." Lombard and Marston admit some involvement in the charges against them, but will not take any moral responsibility. Marston calls the event "beastly bad luck" and "pure accident," while Lombard justifies his actions by citing his need for self-preservation.

Some do express feelings of guilt privately. Before coming to the island, General Macarthur gradually became so paranoid that people suspected his crime and were talking about him that he slowly withdrew from others and into himself. At the island he decides he's "come to the end of things" and doesn't want to leave, relieved that he won't have to "carry the burden any longer." Dr. Armstrong admits to himself that he killed his patient; his guilt probably contributes to his severe case of nerves on the island. Thoughts of Cyril's drowning keep coming to Vera who tries to block them out. Wargrave's plan to dispose of her involves his assumptions about her feelings of guilt. Vera was an "interesting psychological experiment. Would the consciousness of her own guilt, the state of nervous tension consequent on having just shot a man, be sufficient, together with the hypnotic suggestion of the surroundings, to cause her to take her own life?" Wargrave proves his hypothesis when Vera hangs herself.

The guilty feelings of some of the group are quickly displaced, however, by the overwhelming desire to save themselves. When they all determine that the murderer must be one of them, they turn on each other. During this process their animalistic natures emerge. As they observe each other, they find they have "reverted to more bestial types": Blore "looked coarser and clumsier." There was "a look of mingled ferocity and stupidity about him." Lombard resembled a wolf, Vera a "dazed bird." The "thoughts that ran through their brains were abnormal, feverish, diseased."

When all the pieces to the puzzle are presented in Wargrave's confession, some sense of order could have been restored if readers were left with a positive portrait of the judge's character. Christie could have achieved this by suggesting that the judge's crimes were a necessary form of retribution. However, she does not. Even though Wargrave is cleared of the charge that he condemned an innocent man, his behavior on the island, coupled with the details that emerge in his confession prove him to be almost as guilty as the others. Wargrave admits that he took "sadistic delight in seeing or causing death." He notes that his "lust to kill" prompted his turn to law, since "the legal profession satisfied nearly all [his] instincts": "To see a wretched criminal squirming in the dock, suffering the tortures of the damned, as his doom came slowly and slowly nearer, was to me, an exquisite pleasure." On the island, Wargrave also reverts to an animalistic state, appearing like "a wary old tortoise." His mouth is described as "cruel" and "predatory." When he first assesses the situation on the island, he tells the others that the person responsible for the murders there must be a "dangerous homicidal lunatic"—ironically an apt description of himself.

When Wargrave explains the rationale behind his crimes, he notes that he determined to commit murder on "a grand scale." To that effect, he decided to plan the murders according to the nursery rhyme about the ten little Indian boys he had recited as a child. He admits, "it had fascinated me as a child of two—the inexorable diminishment— the sense of inevitability." It is this sense of inexorable diminishment and inevitability that Christie leaves her readers. In *Ten Little Indians,* Christie exposes the diminished state of human nature and the inevitability of evil, thus presenting a disturbing vision of humanity.

Source: Wendy Perkins, in an essay for *Novels for Students,* Gale, 2000.

Marty S. Knepper

In the following excerpt, Knepper presents an overview of feminism in Christie's writing, including Ten Little Indians.

To a greater or lesser degree, detective fiction writers Dorothy L. Sayers, Josephine Tey, P. D. James, Amanda Cross, and Anna Katherine Green can be considered feminist writers. But what about the "Mistress of Mystery," Agatha Christie, whose books, written between the years 1920 and 1973, have sold over five hundred million copies and have been translated into dozens of languages? Is Christie a feminist or anti-feminist writer, or do her works fall somewhere in between, in some middle ground?

Obviously, evaluating an author as feminist or anti-feminist involves making subjective judgments that are influenced by a particular reader's conception of feminism and interpretation of a work. The character of Mrs. Boynton in Christie's *Appointment with Death*, for example, provides a real dilemma for the critic. On one hand, Mrs. Boynton is the epitome of the dominating, castrating mother stereotype. Christie makes us sympathize with her victimized family and view Mrs. Boynton as a personification of evil power, as a particularly malignant female Machiavelli (much like Big Nurse in Ken Kesey's *One Flew Over the Cuckoo's Nest*). Yet at the end of this novel, Christie, unlike Kesey in his novel, intimates that perhaps Mrs. Boynton is a tragic figure, herself a victim of a patriarchal society that provides few outlets for strong-minded, power-hungry women other than domestic tyranny. Is this characterization feminist or anti-feminist? Certainly there is support for either judgment. The final decision, a subjective one, will depend on whether the reader/critic chooses to see Mrs. Boynton as evil by nature or a pathetic victim of society.

Recognizing, then, that any assessment of a writer's sexual politics will be subjective, it is nevertheless possible to legitimately argue that a writer is more or less feminist or more or less anti-feminist, especially if the crucial terms are clearly defined and if the author's works are analyzed closely. In the case of Agatha Christie, an examination of her sixty-six detective novels reveals that although there are anti-feminist elements in her writings, Christie obviously respects women and has feminist sympathies.

Before considering Christie's novels, it is first necessary to answer two questions: What are the characteristics of a feminist writer? What are the characteristics of an anti-feminist writer? For the purposes of this discussion, a feminist writer will be defined as a writer, female or male, who shows, as a norm and not as freaks, women capable of intelligence, moral responsibility, competence, and independent action; who presents women as central characters, as the heroes, not just as "the other sex" (in other words, as the wives, mothers, sisters, daughters, lovers, and servants of men); who reveals the economic, social, political and psychological problems women face as part of a

What Do I Read Next?

- In *Murder on the Orient Express* (1934) Agatha Christie writes a variation on *Ten Little Indians,* gathering together a diverse set of characters and focusing on the murder of one of them. This time, though, Hercule Poirot, a Belgian detective, solves the crime.

- Dorothy L. Sayers's *Strong Poison* (1930) centers on Lord Peter Wimsey's determination to find out who poisoned novelist Harriet Vane's fiancé.

- *The Adventures of Sherlock Holmes,* a collection of short stories published in 1892, introduces Sir Arthur Conan Doyle's famous detective and his sidekick, Dr. Watson, in four classic mysteries.

- In P. D. James's *Innocent Blood* (1980) Philippa Palfrey meets her biological mother and discovers the shocking mystery that surrounds her.

patriarchal society; who explores female consciousness and female perceptions of the world; who creates women who have psychological complexity and transcend the sexist stereotypes that are as old as Eve and as limited as the lives of most fictional spinster schoolmarms. In contrast, the anti-feminist writer is a man or woman who depicts women as naturally inferior to men in areas such as intelligence, morality, assertiveness, and self-control; who dismisses strong women as ridiculous or evil anomalies of nature; who presents only males as heroes and only a male view of the world; who characterizes women exclusively in terms of their relationships to men and in narrowly stereotyped ways; who is concerned not so much with reality (women as victims of a sexist society) but with fantasy (men as "victims" of powerful, predatory women).

In what respect are Christie's detective novels anti-feminist? Critics Margot Peters and Agate Nesaule Krouse—who, in an article entitled "Women and Crime: Sexism in Allingham, Sayers, and

Christie," detect sexism in Christie's writings, while conceding that she is less anti-feminist than Allingham and Sayers—argue that Christie's female characters reflect her prejudice against women:

> Her [Christie's] women are garrulous, talking inconsequentially and at length about irrelevancies. If young, they are often stupid, blonde, red-fingernailed gold diggers without a thought in their heads except men and money. Her servant girls are even more stupid, with slack mouths, "boiled gooseberry eyes," and a vocabulary limited to "yes'm" and "no'm" unless, of course, they're being garrulous. Dark-haired women are apt to be ruthless or clever, redheads naive and bouncy. Competent women, like Poirot's secretary Miss Lemon, are single, skinny, and sexless. A depressing cast of thousands.

Although, Peters and Krouse admit, Christie does portray women making it on their own in society through their brains, skills, and energies, too many of these women, they claim, are shown to be deadly and destructive. Peters and Krouse point out, furthermore, that in contrast to Hercule Poirot, who uses reason, knowledge, and method to conduct his investigations, Miss Marple relies on intuition and nosiness, and Ariadne Oliver usually fails to uncover the truth because of her untidy mind.

While the arguments of Peters and Krouse are inadequately supported in the article and much too overstated (Christie does *not* make all her independent, competent women characters either deadly and destructive or skinny and sexless), there is truth to their claims that Christie's books display sexism. Certainly some of her most popular detective novels (*The Murder of Roger Ackroyd*, *And Then There Were None*, *The A.B.C. Murders*, *Murder on the Orient Express*) present women in totally stereotypical ways: as empty-headed ingenues, for example, or as gossipy old ladies. Other less famous novels are just as anti-feminist. In *Evil Under the Sun*, for example, dress designer Rosamund Darnley gladly gives up her successful business enterprise when the man she loves proposes and insists she live in the country and devote herself full-time to marriage and stepmotherhood. Lynn Marchmont, in *There Is a Tide*, is only really attracted to her dull fiancé Rowley Cloade, after he tries to kill her. The main character in *Sad Cypress*, Elinor Carlisle, is a truly romantic heroine, sentimental and helpless: She is obsessed with love for her cousin Roddy, and when she is accused of murdering Roddy's new girlfriend, Elinor, a classic damsel in distress, she must be saved by Dr. Lord and Hercule Poirot. The women in *Endless Night*

are an unattractive lot, all representing negative stereotypes of women: Ellie, an overprotected rich girl, is perfect prey for the two unscrupulous murders she is too stupid to recognize as threats; Gerta is a criminal accomplice whose hypocrisy is only matched by her disloyalty and cold heart; Aunt Cora is only interested in money and what money can buy; Mrs. Rogers knows her son is a psychopath but is too weak and ineffectual to stop him from murdering his wife. The women in *Funerals Are Fatal* whom Christie seems to admire devote themselves, like good martyrs, to the men in their lives, either husbands or sons. A final example of Christie's anti-feminism is the arch-villain Charlotte Zerkowski in *Passenger to Frankfort*. This fat, fascist, fantastically rich and powerful woman is presented as an unnatural, ludicrous monster, an example of what can happen, according to some misogynist minds, when women wield power.

Christie, it is clear, often uses sexist stereotypes of women, sometimes shows women as inferior to and dependent on men, occasionally idealizes self-abnegating women and monsterizes strong women, and frequently implies that woman's true vocation is marriage and motherhood. Yet Christie should not be so easily dismissed as an anti-feminist writer. Perhaps because readers and critics usually concentrate on Christie's major works, they fail, like Peters and Krouse, to consider carefully some of Christie's lesser-known works, such as *The Secret Adversary*, *Murder After Hours*, *A Murder Is Announced*, *The Moving Finger*, and *Cat Among the Pigeons*, all of which illustrate that Christie is capable of presenting a wide range of female characters that go beyond anti-feminist stereotypes, creating some very admirable female heroes, and exploring many problems women face as a result of the sexism that pervades our society.

Only a writer with a healthy respect for women's abilities and a knowledge of real women could create the diversity of female characters Christie does. Her women characters display competence in many fields, are not all defined solely in relation to men, and often are direct contradictions to certain sexist "truisms" about the female sex.

Christie, for instance, shows women who are happy and competent (sometimes super-competent) in all these fields of endeavor, many of them non-traditional fields for women: archeology (Angela Warren, *Murder in Retrospect*); medicine (Sarah King, *Appointment with Death*); science (Madame Oliver, *The Big Four*); high finance

(Letitia Blacklock, *A Murder Is Announced*, and Anna Schelle, *They Came to Baghdad*); sculpture (Henrietta Savernake, *Murder After Hours*); nursing (Amy Leatheran, *Murder in Mesopotamia*); politics (Lady Westholme, M.P., *Appointment with Death*); business management (Katherine Martindale, *The Clocks*); espionage (Mrs. Upjohn, *Cat Among the Pigeons*); acrobatics (Dulcie Duveen, *Murder on the Links*); school administration (Honoria Bulstrode, *Cat Among the Pigeons*); acting (Ginevra Boynton, *Appointment with Death*); and writing (Adriadne Oliver). Of these fourteen examples of competent women in Christie's novels (and there are many more), only three are criminals and none fits the Miss Lemon skinny and sexless category.

Christie also presents, in a positive way, a category of women who are generally ignored or ridiculed in literature because their lives are independent of men's lives: the single women. Besides unmarried older women such as Jane Marple, this category also includes lesbians (for example, Hinch and Murgatroyd in *A Murder Is Announced* and Clotilde Bradbury-Scott in *Nemesis*), feminists (Cecilia Williams in *Murder in Retrospect*, for instance), children (Geraldine in *The Clocks*, Josephine in *Crooked House*, Joyce and Miranda in *Hallowe'en*, Julia and Jeniffer in *Cat Among the Pigeons*), and handicapped women (such as Millicent Pebmarsh in *The Clocks*).

Christie's women, furthermore, often defy sexist "traditional wisdom" about the female sex. For instance, young women married to older men are supposed to be mercenary and adulterous, but Christie's Griselda Clement (in *The Murder at the Vicarage*) is totally devoted to her scholarly older husband, a poor vicar. Women, it is also commonly believed, prefer to use their brains to ensnare a mate or run a household rather than to contemplate philosophy and politics. Yet beautiful young Renisenb (in *Death Comes As the End*) is interested in learning about life and death and the politics of ancient Egypt. Another popular idea is that there is something unnatural and unhealthy in a close relationship between a mother and her grown son. From Freud in his writings on the Oedipus Complex to Roth in *Portnoy's Complaint,* modern writers have harshly criticized the overprotective mother. In *Death on the Nile*, however, the characters of Mrs. Allerton and Tim Allerton contradict this idea: This mother and son respect and enjoy each other; they are not devouring, smothering mother and pathetically dependent son, though they have a very close relationship.

Besides writing about all types of female characters, many unstereotypical, Christie also creates some appealing female heroes with whom women readers can identify. This is significant because one of the great weaknesses of literature over the centuries is the paucity of heroic women characters: women who display qualities such as intelligence, imagination, bravery, independence, knowledge, vision, fortitude, determination; women who triumph; women who are not ridiculed, condemned as evil, or killed off by their authors. Examples of Christie's spunky female heroes are Victoria Jones (in *They Came to Baghdad*), Hilary Cravens (in *So Many Steps to Death*), "Bundle" Brent (in *The Seven Dials Mystery*), Lady Frances Derwent (in *The Boomerang Clue*), and Emily Trefusis (in *Murder at Hazelmoor*). These women not only have heroic qualities, but they also achieve their goals, often when men have failed to do so....

As well as in the diversity of her women characters and in her delightful female heroes, Christie's feminist sympathies are revealed in the way she points out problems women face living in a patriarchy, problems that have not changed much over the centuries. One such problem is the economic oppression of women, as much a reality today as ever. In *A Murder Is Announced*, Dora Bunner, a single woman with no family to support her financially, describes the ignominy of her poverty:

> "I've heard people say so often, 'I'd rather have flowers on the table, than a meal without them.' But how many meals have those people ever missed? They don't know what it is—nobody does who hasn't been through it—to be really hungry. Bread, you know, and a jar of meat paste, and a scrape of margarine. Day after day and how one longs for a good plate of meat and two vegetables. And the shabbiness. Darning one's clothes and hoping it won't show. And applying for jobs and always being told you're too old. And then perhaps getting a job and after all one isn't strong enough. One faints. And you're back again. It's the rent—always the rent—that's got to be paid—otherwise you're out in the street. And in these days it leaves so little over. One's old-age pension doesn't go far—indeed it doesn't." ...

Another problem women face in our society is the pressure to make themselves beautiful sex objects to allure men. Because beauty is often the measure of a woman's value (consider, for example, beauty pageants and magazine advertising), plain women often suffer tremendous feelings of self-hatred, jealousy, and rejection. Christie presents sympathetically in her novels the unbeautiful women, the changelings, women such as Mildred Strete in *Murder with Mirrors* and Josephine

Leonides in *Crooked House*. She shows how plainness or physical anomalousness can lead women to feel hatred of the men who reject them and jealousy of more beautiful women (Henet in *Death Comes As the End*), how it can lead a woman longing for love to be taken in by a scoundrel with a smooth line (Gladys Martin in *A Pocket Full of Rye*, Kirsten Lindstrom in *Ordeal by Innocence*), or how it can make a woman feel life owes her some recompense for her physical shortcomings (Charlotte Blacklock in *A Murder Is Announced*). But Christie recognizes that the problem is not all one-sided. She also shows women who have dedicated themselves to achieving their own physical perfection caught in the beauty trap: Linda Marshall, a gorgeous woman in *Evil Under the Sun*, can attract any man's attention, but she has never been able to hold a man's interest because her positive qualities are only skin deep.

Christie's depiction of the various problems women face in their lives reveals her astuteness as a psychologist and an observer of human nature and her awareness of how society discriminates against women. While Christie is, by no means, a radical feminist (her novels are not a sustained critique of the institutions and ideas that bolster male dominance), she does display feminist attitudes in those of her novels which show problems women have living in a patriarchal society. In presenting various difficulties facing women, Christie sometimes shows women, such as Aimee Griffith and Emily Barton in *The Moving Finger*, stoically enduring injustices and making full lives for themselves, despite limiting circumstances. Other times Christie creates characters, like Charlotte Blacklock in *A Murder Is Announced*, Gerda Christow in *A Murder Is Announced*, Gerda Christow in *Murder After Hours*, and Marina Gregg in *The Mirror Crack'd*, whose suffering, whose failure to cope with the problems and conflicts in their lives, makes them tragic figures, comparable, to some extent, to George Eliot's Dorothea Brooke and Maggie Tulliver or Thomas Hardy's Sue Brideshead.

When all her sixty-six detective novels and hundreds of women characters are considered, should Christie, finally, be characterized as a feminist or anti-feminist writer? As Peters and Krouse point out in their essay, Christie's writings do display sexism, mainly in the form of anti-feminist stereotyping. Disorganized, intuitive, imaginative Ariadne Oliver does not compare as a detective to orderly, competent, knowledgeable Hercule Poirot. Christie's more famous novels, especially the ones written in the 1930s, perpetrate a number of anti-feminist ideas about women. Yet it is distorting the case for Peters and Krouse to dismiss Christie's women characters as "a depressing cast of thousands." In many of her lesser-known novels (written mainly in the 1920s, 1940s, late 1950s, and early 1960s) Christie creates very positive women characters who are competent in many fields (including the detection of crime), who are psychologically complex, who are heroic in stature, who are not inferior to nor dependent on men, women such as Tuppence Cowley, Lucy Eylesbarrow, and Honoria Bulstrode. In these novels Christie also explores, with compassion and sympathy and from a woman's point of view, various problems women in sexist society must cope with, problems ranging from poverty and job discrimination to social pressure to be attractive. The only fair conclusion seems to be that Christie, while not an avowed feminist, let her admiration for strong women, her sympathy for victimized women, and her recognition of society's discrimination against women emerge in the novels written during the decades of the twentieth century more receptive to feminist ideas (such as the 1920s and World War II years), while Christie, always concerned with selling her novels to mass audiences, relied more on traditional (sexist) stereotypes and ideas about women in the more conservative and anti-feminist decades (such as the 1930s).

Source: Marty S. Knepper, "Agatha Christie—Feminist," in *Armchair Detective*, Vol. 16, No. 4, Winter, 1983, pp. 398-406.

Sources

Stewart H. Benedict, "Agatha Christie and Murder Most Unsportsmanlike," in *Claremont Quarterly*, Vol. 9, No. 2, Winter, 1962, pp. 37-42.

David Grossvogel, *Death Deferred: The Long Life, Splendid Afterlife, and Mysterious Workings of Agatha Christie*, Johns Hopkins University Press, 1979.

Marty S. Knepper, "Agatha Christie-Feminist," in *The Armchair Detective*, Vol. 16, No. 4, Winter, 1983, pp. 398-406.

Anthony Lejeune, review in *Spectator*, September 19, 1970.

Max Lowenthal, obituary in *New York Times*, January 13, 1976, p. 1.

Ralph Partridge, review in *New Statesman*, November 18, 1939.

Julian Symons, *Mortal Consequences: A History-From the Detective Story to the Crime Novel*, Harper, 1972.

Robin W. Winks, *British Writers, Supplement 2*, Scribner's, 1992, pp. 123-37.

For Further Study

Agatha Christie: First Lady of Crime, edited by H. R. F. Keating, Holt, Rinehart and Winston, 1977.
This collection of essays provides biographical details as well as analyses of individual works, including *Ten Little Indians.*

Robert Barnard, *A Talent to Deceive: An Appreciation of Agatha Christie,* Dodd, Mead and Company, 1980.

Barnard examines Christie's "strategies of deception" in her works, including *Ten Little Indians.*

Nancy Y. Hoffman, "Mistresses of Malfeasance," in *Dimensions of Detective Fiction,* edited by Larry N. Landrum, Pat Browne, and Ray B. Browne, Popular Press, 1976, pp. 97-101.
This essay compares Christie's style to other women mystery writers.

G. C. Ramsey, *Agatha Christie: Mistress of Mystery,* 1967.
An early analysis of Christie's work.

them

Joyce Carol Oates
1969

them is a story about urban life in America, centered on the experiences of a mother, Loretta, and her children Jules and Maureen. In the "Author's Note" at the beginning of the book, Joyce Carol Oates explains that she based one of the characters, Maureen Wendall, on a young woman who had been her student at the University of Detroit, and indeed chapters eight and nine of the middle part of the book consist of letters written by Maureen to a former instructor whom she addresses "Dear Miss Oates." Whatever the source that inspired the events in this book, it is highly unlikely that all of the events in the Wendall family's life between 1937 and 1967 could be drawn from any one person's experiences. This presentation of the story as "history in fiction form" does, however, help readers believe that all of the details that are rendered in graphic brutality are true to what life in the poorest of urban areas must have been like.

them is actually the final installment of a trilogy about life in various settings within American society. The first novel, *A Garden of Earthly Delights* (1967), follows forty years in the life of a farm family. The second, *Expensive People* (1967), examines the world of suburbia and the values that are held and lost there. The urban world depicted in *them* is so vicious to love and prone to random violence that in there is no peace to be found by its protagonists, Maureen and Jules Wendall, the siblings who have been hardened by city life: they leave to pursue empty dreams in California and suburban Detroit.

Author Biography

Joyce Carol Oates is widely recognized as one of America's most active writers, having published dozens of novels, poetry collections, short story collections, dramas, and essays. She was born in 1938, the same year as Jules Wendall of *them,* and she grew up in the rural countryside on the outskirts of Lockport, New York, attending a one-room school during her primary education. After receiving a typewriter at age fourteen, she wrote "novel after novel" throughout high school and college. Oates attended Syracuse University on a scholarship, graduating as class valedictorian in 1960, and the following year she earned a Master of Arts degree from the University of Wisconsin. From 1961 to 1967 she lived in Detroit and taught at the University of Detroit, a time that she cites as an inspiration, not just for *them,* but for the rest of her writing career: "Detroit, my 'great' subject," she wrote in the essay "Visions of Detroit," "made me the person I am, consequently the writer I am—for better or worse." *them,* her third published novel, won Oates a National Book Award at the age of thirty-two.

From 1967 to 1978 Oates taught at the University of Windsor in Ontario, Canada, just across the river from Detroit, and during that time, while handling a full teaching course load, she managed to produce an average of two to three novels per year. In 1978 she began her long-standing affiliation with Princeton University, first as a Writer-in-Residence from 1978 to 1981 and then as a professor, from 1987 to the present. Oates and her husband, Raymond Smith, edit the acclaimed journal *The Ontario Review.* Throughout her career her writing style has taken several turns, from the urban realism of her early novels to a more imaginary worldview to the history ad romanticism of her Gothic novels (such as *Bellefleur, Bloodsmore Romance* and *Mysteries of Winterthurn*) of the mid-1980s. In recent years Oates has diversified even further into different genres, producing several books of poetry and essays, and a few of her plays have been produced to mixed reviews. Some of her latest works, a series of suspense novels, have been published under the pseudonym Rosamond Smith.

Plot Summary

Outline

The *them* of Oates's novel are Loretta Wendall, her daughter, Maureen, and her son, Jules, as

Joyce Carol Oates

well as the pressures of their culture, the targets of their hatred, and the multitude of characters that surround them. The novel is set in Detroit and its environs and spans the years 1937 to 1967—from Great Depression to racial unrest and riots. In between, the story is told through the layered perspectives of these three characters as it follows the intimate details of their lives.

The Thirties

In an urban slum, Loretta Botsford stands in front of a mirror admiring herself. Her father is an alcoholic casualty of the Depression, her mother is dead, and her brother, Brock—confused and alienated—has grown increasingly hostile. Despite this, Loretta is happy, and her appearance is one source of joy. She is gloriously generic—a Hollywood look that is shared by hundreds of other girls—and she feels a sense of security in their shared conformity. After arguing with Brock, Loretta goes out and meets Bernie Malin in the street. He comes back, they have sex, and she is awakened by a gunshot. Brock has killed Bernie, and Loretta runs out in terror. A policeman, Howard Wendall, brings her back to the apartment and then forces himself upon her.

Now married to Howard and pregnant with his (or Bernie's) child, Loretta is content even though she feels her life has ended. Her father is institutionalized, and Jules is born. Howard is accused of corruption, loses his job, and he and Loretta move with her mother and father-in-law to the country-side. A second baby, Maureen, is born, and Loretta feels increasingly lost without a city surrounding her.

The Forties

Howard goes off to war. Jules is a bright little boy who wanders around the area fearlessly until he's traumatized by the sight of a decapitated man in a plane crash. The narrative shifts to Jules's perspective, and describes his frustrations with the stultifying life of his family. He discovers the meaning of power while putting on a magic show for Maureen. Having lit and put down a match, he watches while the fire consumes a barn in a matter of moments. Meanwhile, Loretta grows more and more restless, and decides to take the children to Detroit. The first day there, she is arrested for streetwalking.

The Fifties

It's ten years later, Howard is in Detroit, he and Loretta have a new child, Betty, and Jules is in love with a nun. The novel jumps forward three years—Jules has lost his virginity and Grandma Wendall has moved in with the family, who have moved to a new address. The narrative takes up Maureen's perspective. Maureen is a fastidious, quiet girl who spends her evenings at the library and harbors a violent hatred for the mess by which she's surrounded. Howard is crushed in a workplace accident, leaving the children almost unmoved. Loretta gets a job and a new husband, Pat Furlong, and Grandma Wendall is institutionalized. As the children grow, they diverge from the early potential they showed. Jules flunks out of high school, and Betty is often in trouble with the police. Maureen is still a "good girl" until she loses the Homeroom Secretary's minute book in a quasi-Fall from Grace. During her obsessive attempt to find it she becomes fixated on the money she needs to leave home and begins prostituting herself. Her grades drop.

Loretta is pregnant and out of work. Furlong finds money hidden in Maureen's room and beats her nearly to death when she comes home. Profoundly disassociated from her body, Maureen sits in a sort of waking coma for a year, growing fatter and fatter. The novel switches to Jules's perspective. Loretta and Furlong are getting divorced, Brock is in town, and Jules has a job as a driver for Bernard Geffen, a wealthy, gangster-like man

who is later stabbed to death. Becoming a florist's delivery boy next, Jules is obsessed with Geffen's niece, Nadine, and pressures her to talk to him alone. Nadine—not a very stable girl—asks Jules to run away to Texas or Mexico with her. They steal a car from her parents' friend and take off. Jules is forced to mug and rob to support them, but his efforts fail when he collapses with severe diarrhea. When he recovers, he finds that Nadine has gone, taking the car with her.

Back in Detroit, the narrative is told from Maureen's disturbed but growing consciousness. A series of letters from Jules chart his downward trajectory, from bright hopes in Houston, to a job in Tulsa as an experimental subject that leaves him hospitalized and near blind. While Brock is helping Maureen to recover, the narrative is intercut with a letter from Maureen to Oates, written in 1966. The next ten years of Maureen's life are laid out in "future retrospective." Brock helps her to recover, she gets a job, leaves home, and attends the University of Detroit, where Oates is one of her teachers.

The Sixties

It's 1966. Jules is back in Detroit—driving for his Uncle Samson—and Brock is dying. In a restaurant with Samson he comes face to face with Nadine. They meet several days later. She's married, but says she still loves him. Jules and Nadine finally make love, but Nadine is still dangerously obsessed with the untouchability of her body. After convincing herself that her mind is sullied and that she's a whore, she shoots Jules.

In April, Maureen is in love with her married teacher, gazing into her mirror just as Loretta did in the novel's opening scene. She hates black people with a ferocity that paralyzes her. Jules, shot twice, is still alive, but has disappeared. The narrative takes up the teacher's perspective as he is drawn to Maureen's intensity and need. In May, televisions blare the noise of war protests in the background as Maureen tells her mother that she's getting married. It's 1967, and Jules walks through Detroit observing the protests before meeting Mort, a man with a Ph.D. in sociology who's involved with various causes. Jules listens as the academic members of UUAP discuss possible black leaders to take over from President Johnson and the necessity of revolution.

In July, the temperature soars and Jules's relationship with another woman, Marcia, is strained by his involvement with a woman named Vera.

Jules is awakened by sirens. The riots have begun, and he is swept along with the mob. The revolutionaries of the UUAP are beaten by police. A policeman chases Jules, refusing to let him go, and with a weary sense of righteousness, Jules shoots him in the face. Loretta's building is burnt down and she is given temporary refuge in a middle-class home. Watching a television program about the riots, she sees Jules among the panel of UUAP members being interviewed. "Fire burns and does its duty," he says. In the final scene, Jules and Maureen say good-bye. She has a new life now, and he is going to the West Coast with the UUAP.

Media Adaptations

- *them* was released on audiocassette by Center for Cassette Studies in 1974.

Characters

Brock Botsford

Brock Botsford is Loretta's brother. In the book's early chapters, he is a teenager with a gun, looking for some trouble; when Loretta brings Bernie Malin home to spend the night in her room, Brock comes in during the night and shoots him dead. He shows up in Detroit years later, staying with Loretta and Maureen after Furlong has gone away. Maureen credits his attention with bringing her out of her catatonic state. Brock enters a hospital with a mysterious degenerative disease, but he does not die: one day he gets dressed and walks out of the hospital, never to be heard from again.

Pat Furlong

Pat Furlong is Loretta's second husband. He does not work, owing to a back injury, but spends his days drinking in bars. After a while, Loretta becomes tired of him and has Maureen cook for him when he comes home late at night. Furlong's attempts to be a responsible father are limited to accusing Maureen of being involved in bad activities. When he finds out that Maureen has been acting as a prostitute, he beats her nearly to death, for which he receives a four-month jail sentence.

Randolph Furlong

The son that Loretta has with Pat Furlong, "Ran," does not appear in the novel after he is an infant. He is sometimes mentioned as being out in the streets.

Bernard Geffen

Bernard Geffen is Jules's eccentric, rich employer who hires him to be a driver and keeps giving him huge, unthinkable amounts of money—first one hundred dollars then ten thousand dollars. Initially, Jules is suspicious because of Geffen's erratic behavior and the large quantities of money that he gives away, but he is comforted by the fact that the bank is willing to honor the checks. Several days after he starts working for him, Jules drives Geffen to a house and then, after waiting outside for a while, goes inside to find the house empty and Geffen dead, his throat slit with a butcher knife.

Nadine Greene

The niece of Bernard Geffen, Nadine Greene is the great love of Jules's life. Jules becomes infatuated with her one day when he is waiting for Bernard and she passes by the car; later, he goes to her house to see her, and they end up stealing her parents' car and running away for California. In a motel room in Texas, when he is sick in bed, she leaves him. Years later he runs into her in Detroit: she is married to a wealthy man and living in an affluent suburb. She rents an apartment for the purpose of having trysts with Jules, but after their first night together, she shoots him and herself, though neither dies.

Bernie Malin

In the early chapters, when Loretta is a teenager living with her brother and alcoholic father, she takes Bernie as her first lover. However, Loretta's brother, Brock, shoots Bernie while he is in bed with Loretta.

Marcia

In June of 1967, before the race riots start, Jules lives with Marcia and her four-year-old son, Tommy.

Joyce Carol Oates

Having recovered from Furlong's beating and the psychological trauma that resulted from it, Maureen takes some classes at the local college. Several letters written from Maureen to Joyce Carol Oates, a former instructor, are printed within the book.

Mort Piercy

Mort Piercy is an Assistant Professor of Sociology at Wayne State University and the head of the UUAP, which is an organization that he uses to take federal money and direct it toward violent radical causes. At the end of the novel, Jules leaves for California to work as Mort's assistant.

Vera

Vera is the young, mousy girl that Jules picks up at an activist meeting and of whom he sadistically takes advantage when he returns to street life after having been shot.

Betty Wendall

The younger sister of Maureen and Jules, Betty is seldom around the house, spending her time away from home with street toughs in Detroit. She is most prominent in the section in which Pat Furlong finds out about Maureen's activities in prostitution. She warns Maureen before she comes home, conveys the news of what happened to Loretta, and interacts with Maureen when she has locked herself away.

Howard Wendall

When Loretta finds herself with the dead body of Bernie Malin in her bed, she turns to Howard Wendall, a police officer. Howard helps Loretta dispose of Bernie's body, but in exchange she has sex with him, becomes pregnant, and marries him. Howard soon loses his police job by taking bribes, and moves the family to his parents' house in the country. When he returns from serving in World War II, Loretta has taken the children to Detroit to flee the Wendalls, but she has gotten arrested there. Howard joins the family in Detroit, but soon is killed in an industrial accident.

Jules Wendall

Jules is driven by his romantic passions, but he always fails at making his unrealistic dreams come true. The main thing he wants in life is Nadine Greene, his one great love, with whom he is infatuated as soon as he sees her in the driveway of his parents' house. In the novel, he has two re-lationships with Nadine, one that ends in disappointment (she runs away from him when he is bedridden with the flu) and the other that ends in disaster (she shoots him, then herself).

There are other relationships with women in his life that resemble his relationship with Nadine. Soon after his father's funeral he begs Edith Kaminsky, a girl he hardly knows, for a picture of her, and when it blows away when he is crossing over an expressway, he chases it through traffic, romantically fixated on it. He lives with various women throughout the book, including Faye, who introduces him to Nadine's uncle, and Marcia, who accepts his philandering. He is courteous and protective of his sisters, his mother and his grandmother.

In addition to his relationships with women, though, Jules is defined by always being in trouble. Even when he is young, living in the country, he wanders away from his family at the site of a burning airplane wreck, and soon after sets the barn on fire. The business associations that he makes—with Bernard Geffen, with his uncle Samson, and with Mort Piercy—never seem entirely legitimate to him, even when they are. He has a troubled relationship with the police. When he is young, a policeman chases him when he is thinking about breaking into a building, and the cop, annoyed at being forced to run, puts his gun to Jules's head and pulls the trigger, but the chamber is empty. This scene is echoed in the novel's climactic scene where Jules, with nothing to lose and caught up in the heat of the riot, shoots a policeman dead.

Loretta Wendall

The novel opens with Loretta as a sixteen-year-old girl in 1937, living with her father and her brother, Brock. When her brother shoots Bernie, the boy with whom she has gone to bed, Loretta is forced to turn to the local policeman, Howard Wendall, for help. In return, he has sex with her, and when she becomes pregnant he marries her, although Loretta later raises some doubt about whether the baby, Jules, is his or Bernie's. After Howard loses his job, she moves with him, his parents, and his sister, Connie, into a house in the country that is owned by a distant relative. Feeling trapped, she leaves while Howard is in the army, and moves to Detroit, where an old friend lives.

The day after arriving in Detroit Loretta tries to make money by prostitution, but is arrested by the first man she approaches. She is once again trapped when Howard helps her out of trouble. She

A street in Detroit around the 1940s.

has three children with Howard before he dies in an industrial accident, and then she marries Pat Furlong, with whom she has another child. After Furlong beats her daughter, Maureen, nearly to death, Loretta watches over her, optimistic that she will return to good health because "her appetite is good." Her children leave her as soon as they become old enough to survive on the streets by themselves, but they come back frequently to seek her approval, which she scarcely gives: when Maureen tells her that she is going to marry a married man, for instance, Loretta curses her and calls her a whore. After the riots have burned her apartment

building and left her homeless, Loretta meets a man, Harold, in the temporary shelter at the YMCA, and a the end of the novel they are planning to get married.

Maureen Wendall

Maureen is the second child of Loretta and Howard Wendall. She tries to be a good girl, but all of the pressure of living in the city pulls her into a secret life of crime. One of the most significant moments in Maureen's younger life is when she is elected secretary of her homeroom and is made responsible for the blue notebook that has been used for years to keep the minutes of the class meetings. Sister Mary Paul stresses the importance of keeping the notebook clean and respectable, but one day after Maureen runs into Jules in the street and he gives her some money, she finds that she has lost the book.

Soon after losing the notebook, Maureen becomes obsessed with money, and starts secretly meeting with grown men, going to motels with them and having sex for money. She keeps her savings in a book in her room. When her mother's second husband sees her in a car with one of the men, he finds the money and then beats her mercilessly. For almost a year Maureen stays in her room, gaining weight, not responding to people who talk to her.

After Maureen regains her stability, she attends night school at the University of Detroit. She outlines her recovery and her plans for the future in several letters addressed to "Joyce Carol Oates," who was her teacher at the university. One of her plans is to marry a man who is her English teacher, even though he is married with three children and they have never even talked outside of class. The teacher does become infatuated with Maureen, and at the end of the novel, Maureen and he are married and living in an apartment in the suburbs. At this point, Maureen has also broken off contact with most members of her family.

Samson Wendall

Samson Wendall is Howard Wendall's rich and successful brother. Growing up, Jules and Maureen know little about their Uncle Samson except that he is wealthy. When Jules is twenty-seven, Samson hires him to be his driver and learn his tool-and-die business because he is disappointed in his own son, Joseph, who has left home to hitchhike around Europe.

Themes

Race and Racism

The characters in this novel are in a socioeconomic class that prohibits them from living in racially segregated areas, and the familiarity between the races boils over into contempt. Today, there are areas of all major cities that are associated with one race or another, but when *them* was published in 1969 separation of races was even more clearly enacted: the advancements in civil rights that allowed Blacks to legally enter all parts

of society were just a few years old at the time, and their effects were hardly felt. As a lingering effect of racist housing and employment laws that had existed for almost a hundred years since the Civil War, the neighborhoods where black people lived were almost always poor neighborhoods.

In the novel, Jules Wendall often takes note of the black children playing in the streets where he lives, an indication that the Wendalls live in the poorer area of town. For most of the book black characters are mentioned infrequently, but more and more often they are referred to with anger and resentment, as examples of the kind of people that these characters look down on as they cling desperately to their self-respect. For example, Nadine, disgusted with herself for committing adultery, accuses Jules of thinking her "Like some little slut of yours. Some Negro woman." Later, Jules has to assure the woman that he is living with, Marcia, that the affair he is having is not with a black woman, when she asks, "She's white, at least? At least she's white?" Marcia later warns him that his radical friends are headed for trouble: "Don't they know that niggers don't give a damn about them? They don't trust them and can't understand their big words. A nigger is a nigger." She lives in a predominantly black neighborhood and presumably needs to belittle her neighbors to build up her own sense of self-worth. At the end of the book a riot ensues; the riot is fueled by the pent-up rage of oppressed Blacks, although readers see that it is the work of whites who purposely try to stir up trouble.

Wealth and Poverty

The three principle characters of *them* struggle against poverty in the story. Loretta fails to make any progress in her struggle, but she maintains a consistency that keeps her going. Maureen's success is mixed. Jules meets with unexpected financial success time and again. Even as a teenager, Loretta works hard as a laborer, caring for her alcoholic father and her wild brother and dreaming of the glamour of Saturday night. Later, when she tries to free herself of the burden of her husband's family, she takes her children and runs away to Detroit, where, in an attempt to make quick, easy money, she tries prostitution, but is arrested immediately. During the riots she steals a television, but it does not work well and then her apartment building burns down, convincing Loretta that she has been punished for her theft.

While in high school, Maureen becomes obsessed with making money, in order to protect herself from the instability of life with her mother and stepfather. Ironically, it is because her mother does not trust her to stay out of trouble, refusing to let her take a job and accusing her of bad behavior, that Maureen turns to prostitution for money. She is successful in the sense that men pay her well and that the police in her neighborhood are too apathetic to bother her, but she is victimized by her stepfather's rage. In the end she becomes a suburban housewife, kept in a secure but sterile environment.

Throughout the novel, Jules never has a problem obtaining money: he is, in fact, such a likable person that strange benefactors seek him out. He never understands Bernard Geffen's business while working for him, but he nervously cashes checks for huge amounts and sees the money magically placed in his hand; similarly, his Uncle Samson's business is not as important to Jules as the trappings that surround it. A large part of his fascination with Nadine Greene, and her fascination with him, may be seen as resulting from the beliefs that poor and rich people have about each other's moral purity. In the end, Jules is disillusioned and desensitized, making his money from handouts from the anarchist Mort Piercy and from Vera's prostitution: each gives freely to him, although he is incapable of giving back any more.

Violence and Cruelty

It is one of the basic principles of this novel that the characters depicted are seething, waiting to explode into violence. Oates springs the book's rare violent episodes on her readers very infrequently, making the raw details all that much more shocking because they are embedded within long sections of emotional inquiry. Startling episodes, such as the shooting of Bernie Malin, Maureen's beating by Furlong, the discovery of Bernard Geffen with his throat slit and Nadine's attempted homicide/suicide show with a degree of intensity that is unmatched by what precedes them.

The acts of violence cannot be considered complete surprises, though, because the possibility of sudden violence is always with these characters. One reason for this is that they associate violence and cruelty with love: Brock believes he is saving Loretta and Furlong thinks he is saving Maureen, and Nadine believes that shooting Jules is the only solution to her love for him. In the end, this connection between love and cruelty is shown openly in the behavior of Vera, who takes abuse from Jules and degrades herself as a prostitute while proclaiming her love for him.

Topics for Further Study

- Assemble an audio collage of the music that would have been playing during some part of these characters' lives in the city: the late 1930s, when Loretta is a teenager, or the 1950s, when Maureen is in high school, or the 1960s during the riots. Explain what the songs you have chosen tell you about life as the characters experienced it.

- Do some research about how families survived in the city while men were away in the military fighting World War II. Look for any assistance programs that could have helped Loretta and her children survive in Detroit.

- Prepare a psychological evaluation of Loretta, based upon her relationships with her father, her brother and her two husbands. Explain how the concept of "codependence" fits her, and in which ways she seems to not fit the codependent pattern.

- What were the long-term results of the riots that burned through Detroit and other American cities in 1967 and 1968. What changes have occurred in urban planning? What is the likelihood that such riots could happen again? What is most likely to cause riots in the future?

The smoldering violence within these characters is symbolized by fire throughout the story. Bernie Malin talks about his plans to burn down a store that cheated him; Jules sets a barn on fire as a child ("I can do anything," he tells his young sister, and believing his power she asks him, as the fire rages out of control, "Could you stop it now?"); the rioters burn down the poor sections of Detroit in their frustration over social inequality. "Fire burns and does its duty," Jules tells a television interviewer, and he goes on to explain, "Violence can't be singled out from an ordinary day! ... Everyone must live through it again and again, there's no end to it, no land to get to, no clearing in the midst of the cities—who wants parks in the midst of the cities!—parks won't burn!"

Style

Structure

them is divided into three unequal sections. The first, "Children of Silence," begins with Loretta as a teenager, living a lonely life with her drunken, deranged father. The father is a vague presence who does not actually appear in the novel, and young Loretta spends hours standing in front of a mirror, repeating her own name, wondering who she is. This section ends with Loretta's daughter, Maureen, who has been saving money to move away and establish her own identity, having her money and dignity stolen away at the hands of her drunken stepfather, who beats her mercilessly.

The second section, "To Whose Country Have I Come?" begins with Maureen in a year-long catatonic state as a result of the beating she has survived. This section is mainly concerned with Jules's affair with Nadine Greene, following the path of his meeting her uncle and working for him to his first sighting of Nadine, obsessing over her, and finally meeting her; their cross-country odyssey and her eventual abandonment of Jules; and, years later, after she is forgotten, Nadine's reappearance in Detroit and their subsequent love affair, which culminates in her shooting him and herself. This section ends with the line "The spirit of the Lord departed from Jules," which seems to mean that Jules has died but turns out to only be a preparation for the empty condition of his soul in the final part, which is called, "Come, My Soul, That Hath Long Languished … " In this section, which is barely half as long as the others, Jules wanders the streets, scarcely aware of time passing or his own actions, physically recovered from being shot but not much more awake than Maureen after her beating. The focus of this section is, of course, the riot, which as a flurry of irrational violence symbolizes the torment that has been suppressed throughout the rest of the book.

Naturalism

At first glance, this book seems to carry on the tradition of naturalism that became popular at the end of the nineteenth century by French writers like Emile Zola and Edmond Louis Antoine de Goncourt and, as urban crowding began to develop in America, in the novels of Frank Norris, Theodore Dreiser, and Upton Sinclair. These writers wrote naturalistic novels to portray the struggles of the urban poor. "Naturalism" is used to describe books that are usually set in cities, showing how the morality of society's worst elements tends to dominate in crowds, dragging the novels' protagonists down into moral corruption. Shocking, graphic details are often used in naturalism to offend readers' sensibilities and make them feel outrage toward poverty's destructive effects.

them is so insistent about revealing human nature that it pretends to identify, in the "Author's Note" and in the letters addressed to the author, a solid link between the characters' world and the natural world that we live in. Critics have pointed out, however, that this novel does not accurately follow all of the traditions of naturalism. In the naturalistic novel the environment usually defeats the central characters, forcing them to abandon their own values and ideals and act cruelly, animalistically, for their own self-preservation.

This holds true in *them* to some extent, especially regarding Jules's traumatized behavior in the last section, where he heartlessly turns Vera to prostitution and ends up killing a man in cold blood. However, a true naturalistic novel would leave its characters without hope, and at the end Jules can at least look forward to his future in California and Maureen can have a new life in the suburbs. Also, a naturalistic novel would not hesitate to present violent, unpleasant details that would offend readers, trying consciously to change their views of the world, but, as Oates explains in the introductory passage of *them*, "the various sordid and shocking events of slum life, detailed in other naturalistic works, have been understated here, mainly because of my feat that too much reality would become unbearable." Critics have called *them* a parody of naturalism, using the techniques of naturalism to tell a gripping tale but lacking the social conviction.

Sturm und Drang

The German phrase *sturm und drang*, meaning "Storm and Stress," refers to a literary movement in Germany in the late eighteenth century. The most notable examples of the Sturm and Drang movement are Johann Wolfgang von Goethe's 1774 novel *The Sorrows of Young Werther* and Freidrich von Schiller's play *The Robbers*, from 1781. These works place great emphasis on the role of the author's imagination, while *them* claims to be a biographical work that is hardly imaginative at all. Still, the character of Jules Wendall seems to have come from the same sense of internal conflict that prevailed centuries earlier.

One of the defining characteristics of Sturm and Drang works was the struggle of the highly emotional individual against the confines of the social structure. At first, Jules appears to be anything

An aerial view of the Detroit riots of 1967.

but "emotional," since he spends most of the novel unaware of what he is feeling inside. Still, his romantic infatuations toward women that appear to be chosen randomly, such as Sister Mary Jerome, Edith Kamensky, and especially Nadine, seem to clearly qualify him as a suffering romantic figure. He is not entirely out of sync with his environment, as seen by the fact that he is always able to secure employment and to strike up relationships with women effortlessly. Jules is at odds with the world around him, possessing a mind that longs for nobler things but is constantly dragged down to the commonplace.

Historical Context

Protest against the War

In 1969, protests against the war in Vietnam brought the ideas of radicalism and revolution into the living rooms of ordinary Americans. Opposition to the war started out on college campuses, with skeptical professors pointing out the inconsistencies in the government's policies and rebellious students who were willing to rise up and challenge the authorities. America's entry into the war had been gradual and subtle, which was one reason that mainstream Americans had accepted it until antiwar demonstrators became very vocal.

After World War II ended in 1945, Communist forces tried to take control of Vietnam, and their struggle resulted in the country being split into two, communist North Vietnam and democratic South Vietnam. France, which had formerly held the country as a colony, helped to support the South from 1946 to 1954, and when new hostilities began between the two halves, the United States stepped in, first with financial and military aid and then, starting in 1961, with U.S. soldiers. By the end of 1965 nearly 200,000 Americans were fighting in Vietnam to help support democracy in the South.

Because of technological advances in film and video, images of the horrors of war were broadcast around the world during the Vietnam crisis (by contrast, television had been virtually nonexistent during World War II, twenty years earlier). Americans became aware of the human costs of warfare as they had never been before, just as intellectuals were raising questions about the moral righteousness of the conflict. One particular incident that served to raise public indignation was the My Lai Massacre, during which a company of U.S. soldiers entered the village of My Lai in 1968 and, according to the

Compare
&
Contrast

- **1969:** Urban America is still recovering from the race riots that devastated Baltimore, Boston, Kansas City, Newark, Chicago, Washington D.C., Detroit, and other cities the previous summer, following the assassination of civil rights leader Martin Luther King Jr.

  Today: Many civil rights organizations continue to try to combat racial inequities in America.

- **1969:** Many American youths of all social classes are united in their opposition to the war in Vietnam, creating a "youth culture" that spreads hippie styles, music, and slogans.

  Today: Many American youths identify with styles, music, and slogans that they receive from the media, such as movies, television shows, music videos, and commercials.

- **1969:** The country becomes aware of heroin, as sales of the drug skyrocket among schoolchildren. The government's new Operation Intercept program is so successful that heroin suddenly becomes competitively priced.

  Today: After dropping by more than half between 1975 and 1990, heroin use among high

school seniors rises consistently throughout the 1990s.

- **1969:** A three-day-long riot at New York City's Stonewall Inn is credited with beginning the modern gay rights movement, as protestors openly stand up against discrimination and harassment from the police.

  Today: A few states recognize gay marriages and many more recognize same-sex partnerships—offering many of the same legal rights as to those who are married.

- **1969:** The Woodstock Music and Art Fair, held at Bethel, New York, becomes a legendary event when 300,000 to 500,000 youth arrive from across the country to attend the four-day festival. Because of the huge unexpected attendance, the promoters stop charging admission and make it a free event. The event is marked by rampant drug use and relatively little crime or violence.

  Today: Despite several commercial attempts to relive the spirit of Woodstock by booking long festivals with top-name bands, no one has ever been able to reproduce the harmony of the original event.

---

subsequent army investigation, committed acts of murder, rape, sodomy and maiming, leaving hundreds of Vietnamese civilians dead.

News of the massacre was suppressed by the army until 1970: by that time, the majority of Americans wanted the war over. The antiwar movement gained popularity with peaceful demonstrations, such as 1969's March on Washington that was attended by a quarter of a million men, women, and children. There was also, however, a violent, radical side to the antiwar movement, and this segment tended to draw attention, mostly because of the paradox of their using violence to protest violence. In 1969, for instance, the Weather Underground broke off from the mostly peaceful Students

for a Democratic Society and urged its members to bomb government buildings. Across the country, dozens of splinter groups with no clear agenda, like the UUAP group depicted in *them,* managed to associate themselves with the opposition to the war simply because their main purpose was opposition.

Racial Tension

At the end of the Civil War in 1865, slavery was officially abolished in the United States: segregation, however, was not. For almost a hundred years it was still legal to deny housing or jobs to people because of their racial background. In Southern states, segregation was even more pronounced than it was in the North, with laws that prohibited whites and Blacks from riding on the same buses, attending the same schools, staying at the same hotels, drinking from the same water fountains, and more. Opposition to these conditions grew after the end of the Second World War in 1945: having served beside whites in the military and been to countries like France that did not have segregation laws, black soldiers returned home expecting better than they received.

During the 1950s great advances were made toward racial equality. The 1954 Supreme Court ruling in *Brown v. the Board of Education of Topeka* made it illegal to hide behind the pretense of offering "separate but equal" facilities to the races (which, while separate, were almost always unequal, portioning out substandard conditions to Blacks). The year-long boycott of the Montgomery Alabama bus system in 1956, led by Martin Luther King Jr., resulted in a Supreme Court ruling the next year that outlawed segregation in transportation.

Whites who felt threatened by Blacks' gains did what they could to resist social change: violence against Blacks by the Ku Klux Klan rose in the 1950s and 1960s as social progress was made. Sometimes the resistance was led by people in otherwise respectable positions. When the Governor of Arkansas, Orval Faubus, led protestors in jeering the first Blacks legally allowed in Little Rock's Central High School, the president of the United States had to send federal troops to maintain order. Georgia restaurant owner Lester Maddox handed out ax handles in front of his shop in 1964, encouraging people to use them to beat any Blacks who tried to enter: as a result, he was elected Governor of Georgia in 1967. By the mid-1960s, crowded urban areas populated by frustrated Blacks began breaking out in race riots: Harlem and Philadelphia in 1964; the Watts section of Los Angeles in 1965 (which still stands as one of the worst citizen uprisings in U.S. history); Chicago, Cleveland, and Atlanta in 1966; and 127 cities in 1967, including Boston, Buffalo, Cincinnati, Milwaukee, Minneapolis, Tampa, and Detroit. In the 1967 Detroit riot, the one described at the end of *them,* Blacks and whites looted 1,700 stores, and rioters set 1,142 fires, leaving 5,000 people homeless. The disturbance continued until armed federal troops were sent.

Critical Overview

When *them* was first published, critics focused, naturally enough, on the contemporary elements of the book, comparing the urban world that Oates de-

scribed to the one at hand. Reviewing the book for *The New York Times Book Review,* Robert M. Adams found it to be "an impressive piece of fictional construction," and he expressed the opinion that it was more "a step forward" than her previous novel. One particular weakness that Adams pointed out was the "extended satire on a group of rather tiresome psychotics supposed to represent the New Left as it flourished in Detroit a few years ago," referring to the book's Mort Piercy and his conspirators: "fictionally speaking," Adams wrote, "they are just not worth the effort." He also was uncomfortable with the letters from Maureen, addressed to "Miss Oates": "the situation seems arch and contrived beyond any psychological or narrative advantage which it in fact yields."

Reviewing *them* in *Newsweek,* novelist Geoffrey Wolff was impressed with its gruesome imagery. He started his review saying, "This novel is a charnel house of Gothic paraphernalia: blood, fire, insanity, anarchy, lust, corruption, death by bullets, death by cancer, death by plane crash, death by stabbing, beatings, crime, riot and even unhappiness." Like many reviewers, Wolff did not openly claim to not like the book, but his resistance to it was implied in the way that he stated his approval: "The novel gathers us into its black dreams of murder and fire and revenge by chanting their images at us. It needs its great length; we resist its extravagances: finally, it overwhelms us."

Assessing Oates's book of short stories published the following year, R. Z. Sheppard referred back to *them* to help make a point about the author's particular talent: "[The stories] feel the emotion of emotion's lack, a heaviness that Miss Oates conveys with the same compassionate talent that helped make her novel *them* last year's National Book Award winner." Calvin Bedient's review in *Nation,* needs no further discussion: his title, "Brilliant and Dazzling," sums up the admiration shown for the novel throughout the whole review.

them was one of Oates's earliest novels. In the ensuing years, reviewers have come to accept the manner in which she introduces suddenly violent imagery into peaceful situations. Rather then referring to her as a strangely dark novelist, her reputation grew in the 1970s to that of a strangely prolific novelist. It quickly became apparent that her tremendous output did not take anything away from the quality of her work, that she was a writer to be seriously considered, analyzed and put into the larger perspective of American fiction. In that respect, the thrust of analyses of *them* has shifted over the years, from its frightening view of reality to its place as a book that might be shelved with others under the category of "naturalism."

Writing almost twenty years after the book's first appearance, Eileen Bender disputed the idea that it is a naturalistic novel, claiming it to be instead "an apparent challenge to the authority of the dominant novelistic voice." It is not unusual for later reviewers to have the luxury to look at the irregularities of a book's voice, and Bender had the benefit of having seen Oates write in many different genres, which made it clear to her that the strangely passive voice of the book was intentional, an artistic experiment.

As years have passed, analyses of the book have become increasingly intellectual, probing the psychological depth of the characters with greater concentration than most real people have on their lives. One of the most obvious examples of this is in the book-length dissection of Oates's characters in Brenda Daly's *Lavish Self-Delusions,* which bears just one short phrase on the back of the dust jacket: "How Oates's Father-Identified Daughters of the 1960's Became Self-Defining Women in the 1980's." It is unlikely that Oates could have predicted that her characters would one day be subjected to the cross-referencing between psychology and classic mythology that Daly applies to her books. For example: "Despite antidemonic forces in the United States, Jules still dreams of flowing out and into Nadine, of losing himself in her. Tragically, Nadine cannot allow such a flowing forth of her passion. Certain icy beliefs enclose her in a bell jar that she cannot escape." Very few writers can survive this kind of close scrutiny, and it is to Oates's credit, as well as to Daly's, that the novel she wrote at a rapid pace can hold together after so much time has passed and so many intellects have thought it over.

Criticism

Tabitha McIntosh-Byrd

McIntosh-Byrd is a doctoral candidate at the University of Pennsylvania. In the following essay she explores the roles of class and gender in constructing the oppressive physical reality of the characters in them.

Joyce Carol Oates's 1969 novel *them* presents an extended meditation on the complex social and cultural pressures that contribute to the construc-tion of class and gender. This can be seen most vividly in the elaborate representation of bodies as they are experienced, felt, used, and hated by her various characters. Though the definition of women as bodies by themselves and their culture is the primary focus of critique, this pressure is felt by all of *them.* Gender restriction is always viewed through and altered by the lens of social class, and the poorer male characters experience the same pressure to define themselves through physical reality. No one is more typified than Jules, who thinks of himself as a "spirit struggling with the fleshy earth, the very force of gravity, death." He is caught in the "dark machinery" of life that impedes the brightest of the Wendall family, reduced to the status of an object for experimentation that leaves him near-blind, even as he struggles to be more than the sum of his parts.

The narrative insistence on the fundamentally *tactile* life of the poor characters is a subtle literalization of the class-based striation to which they are subjected. As members of an industrial society they are "hands," "workers," and—in the case of women—objects to be filled and used. Subjected to this continual pressure, they are denied the ability to understand each other as anything but tangible surfaces. The expression of emotional reaction is consistently channeled into definitions of physical states. This is typified by Maureen's attempt to articulate what she fears about her father's personality—"there was something dense about her father and, beneath that density, a sharpness that was frightening."

Even in describing character, the language choices available to the Wendalls are those of weight, form and shape. This reaches its extreme in disassociative views of the disempowered as objects. In this way, the elderly poor, consigned to bottom-rung care, become forgettable objects that simply drop out of the narrative. Grandma Wendall, Loretta's father and Uncle Brock become "broken machinery" and disappear from the novel, in the same way that Howard Wendall makes his mechanical exit under literal machinery and leaves his family unmoved. In an industrial culture that values them as interchangeable cogs in a greater machine, these people must inevitably see each other as disposable objects. Exiled from the intellectual and literary lives of their social betters, all that is left to them is flesh and blood. Maureen, sitting in the hospital, can only see body parts—"the smooth, innocent curve of a skull beneath thin white hair." As she says, "Everything was the same in this world outside of novels."

Within the novel, an insistence on physicality is the hallmark of social pressures on the poor, and it reaches its greatest power when applied to poor women. This is perhaps best seen through a close analysis of Loretta's physical reality, since she—unlike Maureen and Jules—both embraces and glorifies in her status as an industrial object. In tracing the complex factors that lead her to this state, we can find Oates's essential interrogation of the logic of industrial capitalist culture. An understanding of Loretta's mindset also provides a clearer picture of the model against which not just her children, but *all* of the denizens of Detroit eventually rebel.

The opening of the novel finds Loretta standing in front of a mirror, in love with her physical presence. This joy in her corporeal beauty and sensuality does not come from her sense of herself as an individual, beautiful woman. Rather, it comes from precisely the opposite direction. Loretta is in love:

> with the fact that there were so many Lorettas, that she'd seen two girls in one week with a sailor outfit like her own.

It is her anonymity, not her singularity, that she embraces. Delighting in the reproducibility of her surface contours, the "good clean skin" in front of "a universe of skin," Loretta is in "love with the fact of girls like her having come into existence." Her relationship to the mirror is the key to her relationship with the world. A happily generic component of an identical social group, she is both the replication of a category and replicable category—a copy of "girls like her" and a version of girlhood that can be copied by others. In the same way, the reflection in the mirror is both her product (a mirror-image of her body) as well as her producer (the means by which she defines her worth).

Product of an industrialized city, she and her interchangeable female peers represent a factory assembly line version of the American dream—a commercially available, efficient standard to which anyone can aspire. Their identity has become inescapably entwined with making themselves identical; in the paradoxical act of erasing their identity. To paraphrase Henry Ford's famous line, you can have any girl you want, as long as it's this girl. Success is measured by the degree to which she and her peers succeed in molding their lives to exact specifications, a pressure to conform that only increases over time. In this way, Loretta's desire to be the same as everyone else gets greater after her marriage, and consistently finds its expression through an elaboration of physical form. As the narrator says:

> it pleased her and her friends to see how uniform everything was. They were anxious for everything to be uniform. They wanted to sink into the neighborhood, just as their flesh wanted to take seed in it and stretch itself to a more prodigious health.

Her culture's obsession with movies is equally important in helping Loretta to define herself as a physical object. Throughout her life, but nowhere more so than in her adolescence, she experiences reality through the presence of an imagined Hollywood camera that records her actions, assesses her appearance, and makes her the heroine of any given moment. Like her interaction with the mirror, this imagined camera forces a perspective shift from internal to external self-viewing, making her a viewed physical body instead of a viewing personality. This material detachment from herself becomes strongest when she is most involved, acting as a technical means by which emotional pain is transmuted into observed drama. When Brock confronts her with the rumors that she's been fooling around, for example, she feels:

> like a heroine in a movie, confronted by a jealous husband in a kitchen while outside the camera is aching to draw back and show a wonderland of adventures waiting for her.

In Loretta's story we also see the role of celebrity in an industrialized, mass-produced culture. It acts as a state of uniform veneration for a given object or person that is felt by uniform members of a culture. The consensus which celebrity thus demands, the necessity of large numbers of people thinking in exactly the same way, acts as yet another form of social control. Loretta combines cultural iconography, physicality, and death in one quasi-religious impulse. After she hears about a woman who soaked her hemline in Dillinger's blood, she is filled with envy, and:

> wished violently that she had been there too, to kneel in the blood and bring it back home in triumph, because there wasn't much else to remember a man by except something raw and ugly, and that blood had been real enough in him.

Though she clearly believes that movies, bodies, and celebrity combine to make a lasting version of reality, this passage is juxtaposed with the shooting of Bernie while he lies in her bed. Even as she runs from his body—"something raw and ugly"—in search of help, her overriding narrative of herself continues and takes over from memory. Significantly, the object that catches her attention is a photograph of the Dionne quintuplets, the babies whose ruthless manipulation by a sensation hungry media, servicing a public of Lorettas, has become shorthand for exploitation. The horrors that underlie the mass marketed baby photo are irrelevant to her life, just as the brutality and blood of Bernie's body are an irrelevancy, and will be forgotten in a matter of days. He will remain in her memory only as an instance of "glamour"—the proof she uses occasionally to persuade her children and herself that she was, and is, "really something." In the same way, the fact that Howard raped and extorted her is glossed out in the interests of the script. Instead, he becomes a man who appeared "out of nowhere early on a Sunday morning, dressed in a policeman's uniform and come to help her."

The behaviors that Loretta has learned from obediently watching and worshipping proscribed icons have not given her a means to express her love and pain. The focus on representations of bodies—imagined snapshots, movie cameras and newsreels—serves the opposite purpose, reducing real physical destruction to a disposable status. Most of the men in Loretta's life do indeed depart in ways that leave something "raw and ugly." Bernie is shot, Howard is crushed by falling machinery, her second husband leaves her daughter a bloody pulp, and yet Loretta forgets as soon as the act is over. She attempts to understand this after Jules is traumatized by the sight of a plane crash that leaves a man with his head sliced in two by the side of the road—these things just don't stick with her too clearly. As she says of motherhood, the funny thing about having babies is that as soon as they're not in the room with you, it's like you don't have them any more.

In the world that Loretta gives her children, things only exist when they can be immediately seen and touched, and can only be understood through an elaboration of their tangible qualities. As Maureen learns when trying to speak with this vocabulary of the body, Loretta's system of signification cannot express anger. In an extended attempt to show the structural basis of the outbreaks of physical violence, which characterize the lives of Jules, Betty, and the working poor in general, Oates suggests that it is this enforced poverty of language which is to blame. Whenever Loretta feels hurt, or justifiably angry, she has no way of expressing that anger, and thus no way of understanding or venting it. In this way, her dislike of Brock, caused by his abusive, erratic behavior, is turned into distaste for his "flabby, calculating skin."

The Depression-era workers of Loretta's generation have been deliberately and systematically regulated. Fear of worker mobilization and resistance to harsh social environments has led to educational and social environments that deprive the poor of the means with which to express anger. The monotonous physical demands of industrial working culture require a compliant pool of warm bodies who understand themselves as such—bodies. Such a system of thought and regulation leads to violent repercussions in the next generation. It is the reason for the trauma that forces Maureen to prostitute herself—the cause of the paradox she cannot escape which makes her reduce herself to the machinery of warm flesh in her attempt to raise enough money to better herself. It is also the reason for the riots at the end of *them*. Cut off from all legitimate means of protest, unable to express their discontent, the only option left is physical reaction. "They" burn Detroit down.

Source: Tabitha McIntosh-Byrd, in an essay for *Novels for Students*, Gale, 2000.

Anthony DeCurtis

In the following essay, DeCurtis examines how Oates's characters in them *perceive their lives as unreal and fictional accounts as representative of "real life."*

Two letters written by Maureen Wendall, one of the novel's main characters, to Joyce Carol Oates, the novel's author and Maureen's former teacher, are essential to an understanding of *them*. The letters are passionate, angry, accusatory, and confessional. Maureen challenges Oates with questions, taking her to task for statements she made to her literature class: "You said, 'Literature gives form to life,' I remember you saying that very clearly. What is form? Why is it better than the way life happens, by itself?" The notion that something can provide shape and meaning to our experiences both fascinates and infuriates Maureen, who, like all of Oates's characters, moves in a world in which "Nothing follows" and "anything" can and frequently does happen. A desperate desire for "something to come to us and give a shape to so much pain," pitted against an equally desperate sense that there can be no deliverance from a world so out of control that it "can't be lived" constitutes the conflict which determines so many of the lives in *them*. The tension this conflict produces forces the characters, after attempts to provide order to their lives have failed, to deny the substantiality of their shattering experiences and perceive their lives as fiction.Oates herself addresses the issue, which Maureen raises, of the dichotomy between literary

form and "the way life happens" at the very beginning of *them* in her "Author's Note." Here she
announces that she intends the novel to be "a work
of history in fictional form." About the life of Maureen Wendall, the subject and source of this personal history, Oates intimates, "My initial feeling
about her life was 'This must be fiction, this can't
all be real!' My more permanent feeling was, "This
is the only kind of fiction that is real!" Oates, of
course, is aware that by the very act of writing about
Maureen and her family she is taking their experiences out of the world of events and transforming
them into literature. However, she stringently resists literary explanations and interpretations for the
events in her novel, striving instead to have her
readers experience the unfolding action as immediately as her characters themselves do, without the
mitigation an overt, overriding aesthetic vision
would supply. Unlike most social and psychological novels, *them* is relatively little concerned with
questions of cause and motive. "Things" happen,
and establishing cause and effect relationships becomes less important, and, in certain ways, less
possible than getting on with the day-to-day business of living. In her conception and execution of
them Oates exploits the tension between the order
of fiction and the chaos of reality, the very forces
which fragment the lives of the novel's three central characters.In Oates's world, maturity consists
of realizing and accepting that there is no design
or permanence in one's surroundings and that con-
tentment and hope are taunting invitations to disaster. The future, so much "dangerous time," brings
change, and change of any kind is terrible and
threatening. Optimism is conceivable only by those
too young, too ignorant, or too deranged to know
better. Early in the novel, Oates gives us a sunny
portrait of Loretta, Maureen Wendall's mother. It
is 1937, the country is in the midst of the Depression, and her family is having difficulties. Nonetheless, Loretta is young, cheery, and feels herself full
of possibility. In an exuberant moment, she tells
her older friend Rita, "Sometimes I feel so happy
over nothing I must be crazy." Rita's reply is at
once reassuring and premonitory, the advice of a
survivor: "Oh, you're not crazy ... you just haven't
been through it yet."

Loretta's remark and Rita's response are relatively tame examples of how madness and the violence with which it is associated always lurk as
threats in *them*. The disorder and unpredictability
of the external world impose monstrous burdens on
its inhabitants, and those who do not succumb to
madness live in fear of it. A more compelling instance of the fear of imminent insanity occurs when
the narrator describes Loretta's thoughts following
her brother's murder of her boyfriend: "And what
if she went crazy? ... [She] had seen other crazy
people, had seen how fast they changed into being
crazy. No one could tell how fast that change might
come." Madness and violence do not build up over
a period of time, but, like the fires which recur in
the novel, appear out of nowhere and immediately
rage out of control, reducing all supposed permanence and solidity to cinders. The lines which separate violence and order, madness and sanity, are
too thin to be recognizable and one is always in
danger of passing unknowingly from one realm into
the other. Characters speak frequently of their fear
"Of everything, of going over the edge." Jules
Wendall, Maureen's brother, warns us and a television audience after the Detroit riots of 1967 near
the end of the book that "Violence can't be singled
out from an ordinary day."

One result of the chaos and impoverishment of
their environment is that economics becomes a crucial concern in the lives of Oates's characters. They
tend, however, to perceive money not in economic
or political but in mystical terms. Even in relatively
small sums, money enables one to exert some degree of control over one's existence and all control
is magical when cause and effect are inoperative.
Both Maureen and Jules Wendall view money in
this spiritual way. When, at one point in the book,
Maureen prostitutes herself, she cultivates a patho-
logical detachment from the sexuality of her acts
and thinks only of the money she will receive: "It
was supposed to be out of sight and out of her concern for the moment. But she thought keenly about
it, its passing from his hands into hers, its becoming her money.... Its power would become hers....
[It] was magical in her hands and secret from all
the world...." Maureen saves and hides the money
she earns and thinks about it to an extent clearly
out of proportion to what it can do for her. The obsessive accumulation of money becomes an end in
itself; its mystique as a charm against disaster over-
powers its practical significance.

In relation to this, access, or seeming access,
to large sums of money accords one virtually godlike status in *them*. A wealthy man can raise you
out of the mire of your daily existence and set your
life to rights by a mere act of will. When Jules Wendall is befriended by the second-rate gangster
Bernard Geffen, who tosses checks and large bills
around with a mad self-assurance, he experiences
not mere joy at his good fortune, but a sense of revelation about the nature of life itself. Bernard gives

Jules several hundred dollars, offers him a chauffeur's job at two hundred dollars per week, and promises to finance his college education. Jules reflects that never before "had he really been given a *gift,* a surprising gift of the kind that stuns the heart, that lets you know why people keep on living—why else, except in anticipation of such gifts, such undeserved surprises?" Money is a sign of the gods' favor. It is not architectural similarity alone which reminds Jules of a church when he walks into a bank to cash one of Bernard's checks.

But, finally, money itself is not lasting protection against the sweeping flood of calamitous events in *them.* Bernard turns out to have no real wealth; his throat is slit in an abandoned tenement by an anonymous killer. Jules's opportunity, later in the book, to rise to power in a business owned by his millionaire Uncle Samson is never realized either. And money also does not prove to be the solution to Maureen's problems. Her stepfather discovers her hidden wealth, as well as her means of earning it, and brutally beats her. The promise which money holds out to the poor, who can only obtain it through humiliation or semidivine fiat and do not have the means to hold onto it, is insubstantial and only leaves them feeling greater rage and frustration.

Their inability to shape their lives in any positive way makes the characters in *them* yearn for permanence and stability, a sense of the ordinary. If they cannot be what they want to be, if they cannot live how they want to live, they at least want their circumstances to remain constant. For the most part, they identify permanence with traditional American values: a home, a family, and for the women, the role of housewife. As they emerge and are articulated in characters' minds, these values seem not so much to be desirable in themselves but empirical proofs that one has "settled down," has established an entrenched position in the battle of life.

Oates dramatizes this search for permanence early in *them* when Maureen's parents, Loretta and Howard Wendall, marry. Loretta, while she does not seem to love him, is grateful to Howard for providing her with an escape from her troubled home and neighborhood. She and her new married friends share a sense that "they had all come very close to the edge of something" and had managed to avoid toppling over. Determined not to take risks with their survival, they are pleased to see "how uniform" everything is in their new neighborhood. Indeed, "They were anxious for everything to be

uniform." Loretta happily thought that "she had come to the end of her life" and "would probably live here forever." Having come through disaster, Loretta, exhibiting the resilience characteristic of the poor in Oates's novels, attempts to reestablish her life in less vulnerable circumstances. The continual disappointment of these efforts is an important motif in *them.*

Maureen Wendall subscribes to the same domestic ideals as her mother, despite Loretta's life having collapsed around them both innumerable times. Trying to rebuild her life after her spell as a prostitute, a savage beating at the hands of her stepfather, and a lengthy period of near-catatonia, Maureen describes her ideal future situation in one of her letters to Oates:

> [I'd be] living in a house out of the city, a ranch house or a colonial house, with a fence around the back, a woman working in the kitchen, wearing slacks maybe, a baby in his crib in the baby's room, thin white gauzy curtains, a bedroom for my husband and me, a window in the living-room looking out onto the lawn and the street and the house across the street. Every cell in my body aches for this! My eyes ache for it, the balls of my eyes in their sockets, hungry and aching for this, my God how I want that house and that man, whoever he is.

It is evident from the passion and precision of detail in this passage that Maureen has experienced this fantasy at least as intensely as she has the pain and frustration of her own life. Indeed, this fictional, imaginative construct has more reality for her than her own unspeakable past.

The vision of suburban bliss, contrasted to urban chaos and decay, has a profound sense of reality, which his own life lacks, for Maureen's brother Jules as well. At one point in the novel, having run away to the South with a girl he met only two days earlier, Jules wanders about looking for a house from which he can steal some money. He spots a housewife walking barefoot across her lawn to pick up a newspaper: "This sight pleased Jules—it was so ordinary and reasonable. Walking alone here, even in his sweaty clothes, he was close to the secret workings of things, the way people lived when they were not being observed. In himself there were no secret workings: he had no ordinary, reasonable life." Jules's sense of his own unreality is so acute in this passage that he discounts even his own role as an observer. If he is watching, it is as if no one is watching. Jules's desire to experience an orderly existence is so strong that after stealing into one of these suburban houses, "On an impulse he lay down on the bed, his feet side by side. He smiled. So this was what it was like." Real life for Jules, and for so many of Oates's characters, cannot be located in his own experiences but only in the way *they* live. And who "they" are depends upon who you are.

The ideal of the "ordinary, reasonable life" is an aspect of the American Dream which has particular appeal for Oates's characters. The housewives' magazines which package this ideal figure significantly in the process of fictionalization at work in *them*. If the great works of art against which Maureen rails with primitive eloquence in her letters to Oates attempt to give shape to people's suffering, these magazines try to short-circuit human pain and reduce the complexities of life to a series of simpleminded rules. Jim Randolph's wife, whom he is about to abandon along with their three children for Maureen Wendall, reads these magazines regularly and one is described in some detail. A cake adorns the cover of this issue, which includes such articles as "A Doctor Looks at Intimate Problems of Marriage," and "The Five Basic Don'ts": "'Don't worry needlessly. Don't expect too much, particularly from your husband. Don't compare yourself to your friends. Don't take anything for granted. Don't daydream.'"

This magazine and others of its kind perform a double function for their readers. They sugarcoat and simplify life while simultaneously endorsing the same fearful passivity and timidity which was reflected in the lives of Loretta and her friends. The "Five Basic Don'ts" caution ominously against expecting or demanding too much from life. Exerting the merest pressure even on one's spouse will reveal the precariousness and the emptiness of one's existence. In this light, the fact that Maureen is reading one of these magazines in the final scene of the book is unmistakable in its significance. Jules has come to visit Maureen after she has married Jim Randolph and escaped from Detroit to the suburbs. The magazine, the presence of Jules as a symbol of a past she can never completely escape, and the physical instability of her new surroundings ("he reached out to touch the railing of the stairwell—it was plastic—and she saw how wobbly it was, ready to fall off if someone bumped against it") combine to demonstrate how tenuous Maureen's hold on an "ordinary, reasonable life" is.

In addition to housewives' magazines, the movies provide another standard by which characters in *them* measure the "reality" of their own lives. Loretta and Jules, particularly, regard films, however implausibly optimistic they may be, as expressions not of how life should be, but of how life

is. They perceive the disparity between the movies they watch and their own experiences not as the result of a cinematic distortion of reality, but as an indication of something unidentifiable but nevertheless very real lacking in their own disaster-ridden lives. As the events on the screen are "real-ized" before their eyes and in their minds, their own lives become fictionalized, unreal. Their experiences have all the drama and passion of the movies but want the shaping power of an aesthetic vision to lend them clarity and wholeness. In contrast to the quietistic housewives' magazines, the movies portray a world in which heroics are daily events, and boldness and aggression, potentially fatal traits in the treacherous world of *them,* are always rewarded.

The joy, optimism, and promise of Loretta's youth, lost to her through events which she cannot comprehend, are associated in her mind with the movies. She watches films uncritically, too delightfully absorbed in the actions unfolding before her to judge them in any way. "Oh, it was real nice, I liked it fine," is her standard opening remark when discussing a movie she's seen. She describes one movie at some length. The windup of the complicated plot, which pivots on the sudden financial collapse of a wealthy man, is "the stock market goes back up. The Butler marries one of the maids…. It ends all right." The contrast between the cinematic neatness of this ending and the maddening loose ends of Loretta's own life is obvious and she is not unaware of it. In a passage as poignant as it is passionate she tells her children: "I want to be like people in that movie, I want to know what I'm doing …. I wasn't meant to be like this—I mean, stuck here. Really I wasn't. I don't look like this. I mean, my hair, and I'm too fat. I don't really look like *this,* I look a different way." The violence of the "real" world has somehow distorted Loretta's true self; not only has her life not proceeded the way it was "supposed to," her very physical appearance is a deception. The real world has created a fictional Loretta whose "true" existence can be perceived only on the screen. Things do not seem to her as if they will end "all right"; Loretta is living episodes which in the edited world of film would have wound up on the cutting-room floor.

Not surprisingly, since he is her first and favorite child, Jules shares Loretta's fascination with the fictional world of the movies. We are told that "Much of Jules's life had come from the movies, much of his language and his good spirits." Jules's sense of himself as an individual predestined for

What Do I Read Next?

- Greg Johnson, himself a poet and acclaimed short story writer, has written extensively about Oates. His recent biography of her is called *Invisible Writer,* published by Dutton in 1998. This is an indispensable tool for students of Oates.

- Few American novels have been able to capture the harshness of city life like Theodore Dreiser's *Sister Carrie,* about a young girl from a small town who moves to Chicago to make her fame. First published in 1900, the descriptions still provide great impact on the reader.

- Oates has written more than one hundred books, including dozens of novels. One good companion piece to *them* is *Foxfire: Confessions of a Girl Gang,* about a group of five girls growing up on the city streets in the 1950s. It was published by Dutton in 1993.

- The abrupt swings toward violence in Oates's novels have resulted in her being compared to Flannery O'Connor, one of America's great novelists. All of the works that O'Connor publisher in her brief life are worth reading. Readers might be particularly interested in *The Violent Bear It Away,* a 1960 novel about a young man with a gift for prophesy.

- In 1989, the University Press of Mississippi published a collection of interviews under the title *Conversations with Joyce Carol Oates.*

- Oates and novelist John Updike have always shown a mutual admiration for each other's works. Updike often writes about the tragicomic results of life in suburban America, a field that Oates herself often covers, although not in *them.* Among the best known of his works are his books chronicling the continuing story of one character: *Rabbit Run* (1960), *Rabbit Redux* (1971), *Rabbit Is Rich* (1981), and *Rabbit at Rest* (1990).

---

good fortune can be traced directly back to his perception of himself as a fictional character. In his youth Jules "thought of himself as a character in a book being written by himself, a fictional fifteen-year-old with the capacity to become anything, because he was fiction. What couldn't he make out of himself?" His imagination "heated by the memory of movies," Jules continually distances himself from his life and comments on it as a spectator might. "This looks like Chapter One," he exclaims to himself when it seems as if Bernard Geffen is going to help him realize all his hopes. *"This is Jules in Texas,"* he thinks at one point, so alienated from his surroundings that he refers to himself, as he does repeatedly in the book, in the third person. He lives an internal life once removed from external reality: "Endlessly Jules had pursued Jules, in endless stories and dreams…." And, like Loretta, he has an inner sense of a "true Jules" to whom certain events and situations are grossly inappropriate, indeed, unreal, and betrayals of his essential self.

The extent to which Jules and Loretta view the world in which they move as unreal in some elemental way indicates how little their lives have measured up to their expectations. They are intensely disappointed people. Denial is the only psychic mechanism which can keep them functional in the face of the catastrophes which characterize their lives. Jules's feeling that his *"life is a story imagined by a madman"* conveys fully how bizarre and frightening his existence seems to him. Loretta's resiliency is the virtue of a woman who has been so battered by incessant blows that she cannot fully comprehend how appalling her life has been. As the novel goes on, it becomes increasingly clear that Jules's "optimism" is a delusion of psychotic proportions. His sense of his own unreality intensifies until he is convinced that he is "not a character in 'real life'."

Maureen Wendall also succumbs to the fictionalizing impulse so thematically prominent in *them*. As a schoolgirl, terrified by the nightmarish world which surrounds her, she turns to literature, particularly the novels of Jane Austen, for succor and release. Like Loretta and Jules, however, she perceives the structured world of fiction as real and her own life as false and insubstantial. Reading novels, Maureen feels like someone waking up from a horrible dream, escaping not from but into reality. Oates writes that Maureen "liked novels set in England. As soon as she read the first page of a novel by Jane Austen she was pleased, startled, excited to know that this was real: the world of this novel was real. Her own life, up over Elson's Drugs or back on Labrosse, could not be real." For Maureen, the less like her own life these books are in tone, setting, and event, the more real they become.

Even the money which Maureen earns as a prostitute becomes associated in her mind with the literature she loves, the fantasy of freedom coupling with the fantasy of escape. The money she receives for her acts is described as being "as real as a novel by Jane Austen," and she hides it, significantly, in a book, *Poets of the New World*. In some magical way, her money will provide her life with the order and sense of reality that she experiences when reading fiction. She will live in a "New World"; her own life will be as "real" as an Austen novel. The irony, of course, is that the power of money to change Maureen's life *is* as real as an Austen novel, that is, not real at all, but fictional.

Though similar in her distrust of the reality of her own experiences, Maureen proves ultimately to be neither as vapid as her mother nor as psychotically deluded as Jules. Like them, she is intensely angry that her life will not sort itself out as precisely as a work of fiction, but she finally rebels against the conviction that her experiences are any less authentic for that reason. Her own maddening and disorganized life comes eventually to have full significance for her. She writes in one of her letters to Oates: "Why did you think that book about Madame Bovary was so important? All those books? Why did you tell us they were more important than life? They are not more important than my life." Maureen reviles Oates for her knowledge of literature, for "knowing so much that never happened," and against the claim that literature gives form to life asserts that, "I lived my life but there is no form to it. No shape."

Clearly, Maureen's vehemence is generated by her desire for control over her life, her wish for a "law. Something that will come back again and again, that I can understand." Maureen only begins to exercise some power over her fate, as morally questionable and precarious as that power is, when she refuses to persist in fictionalizing her life as Jules and Loretta do. By respecting and rooting herself in her own experiences, she shows that she has learned the most important lesson art has to teach. If, at the end of the book, Maureen's life is not as firmly grounded as she would like to think it is, nor her calculated stealing of another woman's husband in her pursuit of the suburban dream as elevated either in motive or goal as we would like, she is at least not being swept along by the tide of events as directly as Loretta and Jules are. It is significant that she is virtually unaffected by the Detroit riots which burn down her mother's home and turn her brother into a murderer. Though Maureen does not realize it, *Madame Bovary* and the novels of Austen have helped her achieve what grade-B movies and housewives' magazines never can provide: a sense of the dignity and importance of her own life.

Robert H. Fossum has argued rightly in asserting that Oates's fiction "evokes an overwhelming sense of those psychological pressures in American life which produce our obsessions and frustrations, our dreams of love and power, our struggles to understand the world and ourselves." Oates renders convincingly the psychological impulse of individuals to turn to fictional forms for meaning, indeed, to attempt to fictionalize their own lives, in the face of appalling social conditions. It is nonetheless regrettable that political analyses and solutions are treated with as little grace and insight as they are in *them,* a novel so much concerned, both explicitly and indirectly, with such social issues as urban decay, poverty, race relations, violence, and the urgent flight by white people from the inner city to the suburbs. Mort Piercy, the most important political figure in the book, is depicted as an overgrown, spoiled, upper-middle-class child, quite probably insane, who wages an irresponsible war against the "Establishment" on government Poverty Program grants. His friends are privileged University "radicals" with frightening delusions of grandeur. Whatever idealism they exhibit is quickly revealed to be a shallow cover for paranoia and repressed sociopathic impulses. Their political discussions never address real issues but revolve around whether, during the Detroit riots, it would be more in the interest of the revolution to assassinate President Johnson or murder Martin Luther King and blame it on the right wing. Most disturbing of all, Oates clearly suggests that the Detroit riots were organized and orchestrated from behind the scenes by a small band of cynical and deluded whites of whom Mort Piercy is only the most prominent example.

Yet, despite the caricaturish treatment of politics in *them,* Oates seems to demand by her very choice of title some discussion of a collective solution to the problems which the novel assumes as its subject. The radical alienation of characters from themselves, the condition which is expressed by their fictionalizing their own lives, can be seen as the reflection within the individual of a society whose various classes and races regard each other as threatening and monolithic "thems." Oates maintains that her novel "is truly about a specific 'them' and not just a literary technique of pointing to us all" (Author's Note). But the specificity of the referent for "them" seems to shift as the psychological and the social intermingle, and every individual and social group projects their problems, obsessions, and terrors onto a certain "them." "Them niggers" serve such a function for several of the white characters in the book. Jules's upper-class girlfriend, Nadine, frightened and disgusted by the sexual cravings which Jules awakens in her, is tormented by irrational fears that he has slept with diseased black girls and will infect her. Maureen Wendall moves out of Detroit after marrying Jim Randolph to get away from her past and "them" (specifically, here, her family and the psychological forces and social class which they represent), but Jules tracks her down and she does not know how to answer him when he asks, "But, honey, aren't you one of *them* yourself?" Oates's characters, like all of us, carry within themselves psychological versions of the social problems which surround them. That in her sharp and incisive focus on the psychological Oates does not take similar care with the social is a disservice both to them and her audience.

By the end of *them* we are left with both the possibility of stagnation and the hope for change. To recommend narrow solutions to the complex issues which the novel raises would be a great mistake and Oates carefully avoids doing so. While asserting the necessity that Oates acknowledge the social context of her work in a responsible way, I recognize that she should not be held to any ideological line. Like other contemporary novelists of worth, Oates realizes that we are not always better off for our painful experiences, that suffering and disaster do not always lead us to self-discovery but often leave us constricted, terrified of change and what the future holds, doubtful about the substan-

tiality of our experiences. She knows that perhaps the most dreadful thing about apocalyptic events is that too often they do not destroy us but leave us to face another "ordinary morning." The instinct for survival becomes a virtue in this connection. And to the extent to which her characters can survive without dividing the world of others into "them" and us, and fictionalizing their own lives, they have done very well indeed.

Source: Anthony DeCurtis, "The Process of Fictionalization in Joyce Carol Oates's *them,*" in *International Fiction Review,* Vol. 6, No. 2, Summer, 1979, pp. 121-28.

James R. Giles

In the following excerpt, Giles examines the debate over classification of Oates's writing, considering the views of those who declare it naturalism or romanticism, and Oates's own preference for the phrase "psychological realism."

A unique tension, which has resulted in much critical confusion, runs throughout the fiction of Joyce Carol Oates. Attempts to define the philosophy and technique behind her novels have usually been limited and misleading. Critics and reviewers have primarily attempted to place her within the tradition of naturalism. However, while there are strong naturalistic overtones to her best work, she should not be seen solely as a Dreiser-Norris-Farrell naturalist. The charge of melodrama is frequently hurled at her. Of course, one isn't surprised, since melodrama has always been closely tied to American literary naturalism (e.g., the death of S. Behrman in *The Octopus*). The apparently melodramatic aspects of Oates's fiction have taken at least one critic in a different direction. Writing about her short stories, Samuel F. Pickering, Jr., has charged Oates with the literary crime of "Romanticism." While never defining Romanticism, Pickering specifically objects to Oates's extreme subjectivity, lack of a sense of humor, and excessive solemnity. Pickering also believes that Oates has become so intrigued with the infinite terrain of the subconscious that she is losing the ability to communicate.

Oates herself has defined her esthetic technique. In the "Afterword" to her recent volume of experimental parables, *The Poisoned Kiss* (1975), she writes that her usual fiction is a "synthesis of the 'existential' and the 'timeless' "; and in the Preface to the collection of stories *Where Are You Going, Where Have You Been?* she accepts the term "psychological realism" (1974) as representative of her mode of writing....

them illustrates better than any other Oates novel the esthetic tension which results when she naturalistically documents a brutal environment while simultaneously describing doomed, romantic attempts to escape that environment. Three characters are central to *them*—Loretta Wendall and her two children, Maureen and Jules. The characterization of Loretta pertains to Oates's comments about the spiritual destruction resulting from economic suffering. At the beginning of the novel, Loretta is a proud, healthy girl:

> Behind her good clear skin was a universe of skin, all of it healthy. She loved this, she was in love with the fact of girls like her having come into existence, though she could not have expressed her feelings exactly.

Loretta's sense of well-being has survived her father's loss of his business, his subsequent drinking and going "bad" in his treatment of the family, her mother's death, and a dangerous brother named Brock, who repeatedly threatens to kill someone. In fact, Loretta has instinctively found an escape from her threatening environment—a young thug named Bernie Malin, who has "whatever it was that kept people from falling through the bottom of the world the way her brother had fallen."

From the opening pages, the characterization of Loretta challenges conventional morality, as well as many liberal rationalist assumptions. Without thinking about it, she has intuited an escape—she will use the beauty of her body to entrap a young man who hardly can be labeled sympathetic in order to escape the hell of her home. Loretta has never had the opportunity to grow intellectually; she is a woman in a male-dominated society; and she simply plans to use the weapons she has. What is significant is that she still views herself as a valuable, beautiful young woman. But the plan for escape quickly falls apart: she does seduce Bernie; but in the night he is murdered by her crazed brother. A policeman named Howard Wendall comes to investigate, quickly realizes the situation, sexually takes Loretta, and then marries her in exchange for covering up the murder of Bernie. Since all of this happens in the first fifty pages of a five-hundred page novel, it is easy to understand why Oates is sometimes dismissed as a writer of violent melodrama.

Her answer to such criticism can be found in the essay on *The Dollmaker:*

> It seems to me that the greatest works of literature deal with the human soul caught in the stampede of time, unable to gauge the profundity of what passes over it, like the characters in certain plays of Yeats who live through terrifying events but who cannot understand them; in this way history passes over most of us. Society is caught in a convulsion, whether of growth or death, and ordinary people are destroyed. They do not, however, understand that they are "destroyed."

In short, in a crumbling society, things happen that way. This answer is not a completely convincing refutation of the charge of esthetic melodrama. It is probable that Oates ultimately would not care to argue the point, but would simply say that the lives of the victims of our society are melodramatic in ways that the middle-class reader cannot begin to understand. She may even feel that such a reader needs to be shocked into an awareness of what surrounds him.

At any rate, Loretta never understands anything for the rest of the novel, even though she lives in the midst of monumental events. She is destroyed: her new husband loses his job on the police force; she moves to the country, and while Howard is in the service she suffers from the tyranny of Papa and Mama Wendall; she escapes to Detroit, where she is immediately arrested on a charge of prostitution; her husband and Mama Wendall ultimately join her in Detroit, and Howard is killed in an industrial accident. After Howard's death, she takes a lover who assaults her daughter. Finally, the long-lost brother, whose murder of Bernie Malin plunged her irrevocably into the hell of her life, returns to live with her. All this poverty and instability destroy her looks and her faith in herself. There finally can be no escape for Loretta; and she *does know that.* In a critical speech, she tells her son Jules:

> Then we came to Detroit? Then all them dumps, them bus rides? I can't stand always moving around! I want my own place, my own house. I want to be like somebody in a movie, I want to get dressed up and walk down the street and know something important will happen, like this man who was killed because of me …. I wasn't meant to be like this—I mean, stuck here. Really I wasn't. I don't look like this. I mean, my hair, and I'm too fat. I don't really look like *this,* I look a different way. And the toilet is bad again ….

Two things are crucial about this speech: Loretta acknowledges the power and possibilities her body once contained and that this power and those possibilities are dead. In addition, she has learned to covet the lives and material things of those who have destroyed her, or, to be more accurate, her movie-induced concept of those lives and those things.

"Problems of Adjustment in Survivors of Natural/Unnatural Disasters," a powerful Oates short story, is centered around the concept of "psychic suicide" among victims. Psychic suicide results when the victim accepts the value system of his oppressors and identifies with them. A character in the story believes that this mental process allowed many people to survive totalitarian concentration camps. Loretta is a reluctant example of psychic suicide. She survives by accepting the values of the capitalistic system which has banished her to the ghetto. In fact, when her son Jules becomes locally prominent through his participation in a revolution against that system, she is horrified. It is important that Loretta's perception of the world of wealth remain always an unreal, celluloid one. Her dreams of this world can remain undefiled; while, in contrast, Jules has a much more direct contact with wealth and power and is irrevocably changed by it. Dreams can sustain one, but only to a degree. Loretta's acceptance of the values of an unattainable world corresponds to the final destruction of that freshness and power she knows she once had. However, unlike Arnow's people, she reveals in speeches such as the one to Jules that she is aware of this destruction.

For a very long time, Loretta instinctively seeks salvation in her children, particularly the two oldest, Jules and Maureen. Both are worthy of being the repositories of much vicarious hope. In fact, both ultimately fulfill their mother's dreams and escape the ghetto, but only at an enormous spiritual cost.

For most of the novel, Maureen Wendall seems one of those passive, eternally victimized females who crowd the pages of Oates's stories and novels. She, in fact, has little opportunity to be anything other than passive or brutally aggressive as her younger sister Betty is. A child of poverty, surrounded by bickering and dehumanized adults, she wants love, or, failing that, simple acceptance. If neither love nor acceptance is possible, a part of her longs for simple deliverance:

> She saw them all with their frozen faces, her mother and father, her sister, her brother, her grandmother, her aunt, the faces of the nuns at school, the faces of priests, the faces of kids in the neighborhood, the faces of all the world—frozen hard into expressions of cunning and anger, while she, Maureen, having no hardness to her, crept in silence among them and waited for the day when everything would be orderly and neat, when she could arrange her life the way she arranged the kitchen after supper, and she too might then be frozen hard, fixed, permanent, beyond their ability to hurt.

Although it takes a very long time to surface, Maureen has a great deal of "hardness to her"; she ultimately ceases to be the eternal victim by coolly and deliberately victimizing another woman.

For most of the novel, Maureen seems a classic scapegoat, and nothing better illustrates this surface appearance than the incident of the lost homeroom notebook. When Maureen is chosen secretary of her homeroom at school, she feels pride in herself for the first time. The secretary's official notebook, assigned to her care, symbolizes transcendence over her squalid environment and the factors that limit her existence. It is a tribute to Oates's genius that Maureen's frantic search for that meaningless record of meaningless details constitutes one of the most painful moments of the novel. In a world of murder, assault, continuously accumulating filth and despair, a lost notebook is trivial, but that very triviality is a vital factor in the artistic success of this segment of *them.* The notebook is not trivial to Maureen, because it is the first tangible acceptance from the adult world she has ever received.

It is not long before Maureen comprehends a formula that her mother once intuited: in America, money is a visible and immediate sign of power, men will pay money for her body, and power is a form of acceptance. Maureen sells her body to anonymous strangers in anonymous rooms, and, as in the case of Sister Carrie, the only sin involved rests on society and the inhuman universe. Maureen's sexual promiscuity is, in fact, the beginning of her struggle to save herself. Despite her passive surface, Maureen determines to salvage her soul by escaping, however she can, that landscape that threatens her constantly. (It is of interest that she keeps the money from these affairs in a book called *Poets of the New World.*) That landscape, personified in her mother's brutal lover, intercedes however and she is literally beaten into a coma.

Maureen's will to survive is only resting and it will be revived by that awesome Western force, romantic love. The object of her love is married, and taking him represents a major challenge to her habitual passivity. Strangely, she outlines her plan in some letters to a former teacher at the University of Detroit night school, Joyce Carol Oates. The Maureen Wendall letters are one of the most complex aspects of a very complex novel. In one of them, Oates seems to challenge everything in which she believes. The letter is a series of rambling, at times almost incoherent, pleas and charges:

> How can I live my life if the world is like this? The world can't be lived, no one can live it right. It is out of control, crazy…. Maybe I am writing to you not because you are like me—I sound a little crazy!—but because you are the exact opposite, you are never surprised, you foretell everything, and inside all the mess

of the newspapers you live your own life in peace, prepared…. Why did you think that book about Madame Bovary was so important? All those books? Why did you tell us they were more important than life? They are not more important than my life…. But you are a married woman, I think, who would not mind taking someone else's husband, so long as it happened well enough, beautifully enough like a story…. You said, "Literature gives form to life," I remember you saying that very clearly. What is form? Why is it better than the way life happens, by itself?

Thus Oates confronts directly the most questionable aspect of her faith in the resanctifying power of art—art is a luxury ordinarily not accessible to or desired by those people who are most victimized. If art is a redemptive ritual, faith in its redemptive power is not shared by "them." Indeed, what can a man or woman struggling to feed a family care about form in literature? But the Maureen Wendall letters answer indirectly the same questions they raise. As a teacher, Joyce Carol Oates stimulated ideas in Maureen Wendall, who communicated again years later. One result of that dual communication is *them,* the form of art.

This letter also indicates that Maureen's spiritual self is stronger than it has ever been (Maureen's life *is* more important to her than Madame Bovary's) and that she intends to take the man she loves. She does, much as Elena Howe takes Jack Morrissey in *Do With Me What You Will;* and the apparent scapegoat escapes the ghetto for life with a university instructor.

Even as a child, Jules Wendall is the rebel, the *alazon.* Once, demonstrating magic to his sister, he sets a barn on fire and receives almost without tears a brutal whipping from his grandmother. He reads an interview in *Time* magazine with an Indian mystic who says "I have come to loot you with love…." "We are all members of a single human family…. My object is to transform the whole of society. Fire merely burns…. Fire burns and does its duty. It is for others to do theirs." Jules is not converted by this mystic pronouncement, but for the rest of the novel he does try very hard to care for his own human family with love and he is associated with scenes of violent destruction. Even though he participates in the Detroit riots of 1966 and becomes an ironic hero of the revolutionaries, Jules never develops any truly strong social consciousness. Still, he is the most loving and the most spiritually compelling character in the novel.

Part of the reason Jules never evolves into a spokesman for his social class is his intense commitment to the women in his family, especially Maureen. Jules is comparable to a Tom Joad who has not been transformed by a Jim Casy. More important than his family, however, is Nadine Greene, the wealthy girl from Grosse Pointe. Jules can hardly be expected to be a social revolutionary after he falls in love with the personification of that class which oppresses him. Meeting Nadine through a shadowy figure named Bernard Geppen, who has connections with both the underworld and Grosse Pointe, he is immediately drawn to her in the most intensely romantic of ways.

Evidence of the fact that Oates is consciously utilizing the Western tradition of romantic love in the Jules Wendall-Nadine Greene relationship can be seen in her prose. For instance, this is how Oates describes the young man's reaction to his first glimpse of Nadine:

> But never had he really been given a *gift,* a surprising gift of the kind that stuns the heart, that lets you know why people keep on living—why else, except in anticipation of such gifts, such undeserved surprises?

The prose account of his initial entry into her bedroom is, if anything, even more romantic:

> He kissed her lightly, wanting to put her to sleep with kisses, comfort her, his mouth light against hers like the petals of roses or the fluttering wings of moths, nothing substantial. It was all so airy, even this embrace…. How he wanted that intoxication!

Jules's involvement with Nadine is physical but, more importantly, spiritual; and the fact that Nadine is unworthy of any kind of devotion should not diminish our response to the young man's infatuation.

The only importance of Nadine's shallowness is in its ultimate effect on Jules. In an essay from *The Edge of Impossibility,* Oates writes about the love between Shakespeare's Troilus and Cressida, and much of what she says is applicable to Jules and Nadine:

> Let us examine Troilus' education in terms of his commitment to a sensualized Platonism, a mystic adoration of a woman he hardly knows. He begins as a conventional lover who fights "cruel battle" within and who leaps from extremes of sorrow to extremes of mirth because he has become unbalanced by the violence of what he does not seem to know is lust…. Troilus' tragedy is his failure to distinguish between the impulses of the body and those of the spirit. His "love" for Cressida, based upon a Platonic idea of her fairness and chastity, is a ghostly love without an object; he does not see that it would really be a lustful love based upon his desire for her body…. Nothing is ever equivalent to the energy or eloquence or love lavished upon it. Man's goals are fated to be less than his ideals would have them, and when he realizes this truth he is "enlightened" in the special sense

in which tragedy enlightens men—a flash of bitter knowledge that immediately precedes death.

Jules is truly committed to a sensualized Platonism with a woman he, in fact, never really sees. Thus, with Nadine, he cannot distinguish between the body and the spirit; but therein lies the redemptive nature of his love for her for, if he could so distinguish, there could be nothing of the spirit in his love of her. Certainly Nadine Greene is not "equivalent to the energy or eloquence or love lavished upon" her. Still, only men of spiritual greatness ever possess such "energy or eloquence or love." Jules, however, does not attain tragic stature because he draws back from the enlightenment Oates describes.

Even after a disastrous trip to Texas in which Nadine debases him in virtually every way possible, Jules clings to his Platonic conception of her. Some years later, she has to shoot him before "the Spirit of the Lord" departs irrevocably from his soul. But even then, there is no tragic enlightenment; there are simply two more disturbing embodiments of the young man who was once Jules Wendall. Initially he exists in a zombie-like state in the ghetto, cruelly exploiting a young woman and mocking the revolutionaries who wish to recruit him. When the riot does break out, he is rather accidentally caught up in it, but still kills a policeman. The killing of the policeman produces the final Jules:

> Having done this he had done everything. It was over. His blood ran wild, he was not to blame for anything, why should he stop?

The final Jules is a calculating nihilist who allows himself to be recruited by the federal government for a ridiculous social program in California. The full extent of his nihilism can only be seen in a farewell speech to Maureen:

> Sweetheart, I understand. I love you too. I'll always think of you, and maybe when I've done better, gotten on my feet, when I come back here and get married—I want to marry her anyway, that woman, the one who tried to kill me, I still love her and I'll make some money and come back and marry her, wait and see—when I come back, a little better off, we can see each other. All right? I love you for being such a sweet sister and suffering so much and getting out of it, using your head, but don't forget that this place here can burn down too. Men can come back in your life, Maureen, they can beat you up again and force your knees apart, why not? There's so much of it in the world, so much semen, so many men! Can't it happen? Won't it happen? Wouldn't you really want it to happen?

After this speech, Jules departs with an "ironic, affectionate bow."

The killing of the policeman, an act Jules commits almost unconsciously, is not the crucial sign of his shift into nihilism. Instead, the ironic taunting of Maureen, along with his open determination to use the governmental project for his own advancement, signifies the new and final Jules. When Maureen asks how he can honestly align himself with the government if he is, as everyone believes, a Communist, he replies: "A Communist! So what? I don't know what a Communist is…. I'm not anything. I'm just trying to get along." One feels that he will get along very well in a competitive environment. Perhaps he will even make enough money in California to win Nadine Greene someday. If he does, however, it will be a victory of vengeance and quite conscious lust, having very little to do with love. Anything is truly possible for Jules now; the nihilistic rogue has replaced the idealistic rebel.

Ironically, Loretta's two oldest children do escape the socioeconomic trap into which they were born, but only through such violations of the public morality she has herself adopted that she cannot cherish their triumphs. She even has to disown Jules: he is, after all, a murderer. For quite different reasons, the reader must view the final Jules with pain also. Oates has something to say about the ending of Melville's *Confidence Man* which is extremely relevant to Jules: "the final movement is a movement into darkness: it is not the triumph of evil over good but rather the negation of struggle, the disintegration into an underlying nihilism that has resulted, within the novel, from the long series of negations that constitute the confidence-man's experience." Jules has ceased his spiritual struggle and has finally been driven into a dark corner by the naturalistic forces he encountered all his life. Yet his struggle, however doomed, is at least equally as important as his final defeat. His effort to save his soul through an intensely romantic love provides, not just Jules, but the entire novel with a transcendence it would otherwise lack. This novel constitutes Oates's re-creation and sanctification of a new world by her "honoring [of] the complexities" of the lives of them—the people of the ghetto who live and die outside the field of vision of most of her readers. It is a redemptive ritual of esthetic form. The tension between naturalistic documentation of struggle and pain and romantic glorification of the human soul is crucial to *them,* as well as to her other fiction.

Source: James R. Giles, "Suffering, Transcendence, and Artistic 'Form': Joyce Carol Oates's *them*," in *Arizona Quarterly,* Vol. 32, No.3, Autumn, 1976, pp. 213-26.

Sources

Robert M. Adams, "The Best Nightmares Are Retrospective," *The New York Times Book Review,* September 28, 1969, p. 23.

Calvin Bedient, "Brilliant and Dazzling," *Nation,* Volume CCIX, December 1, 1969, pp. 609-11.

Eileen T. Bender, *Joyce Carol Oates, Artist in Residence,* Indiana University Press, 1987.

Brenda Daly, *Lavish Self-Delusions: The Novels of Joyce Carol Oates,* University Press of Mississippi, 1996.

Joyce Carol Oates, *them,* Vanguard Press, 1969.

R. Z. Sheppard, "On the Rock," *Time,* October 26, 1970.

Geoffrey Wolff, "Gothic City," *Newsweek,* September 29, 1969, pp. 43-5.

For Further Study

Joanne V. Creighton, "The Trilogy of Social Groups: The Quest for Violent Liberation," in *Joyce Carol Oates,* Twayne Publishers, 1979, pp. 48-73.

The analysis of *them* in this book centers on the idea that it is written as a satire of traditional naturalistic fiction.

Mary Kathryn Grant, *The Tragic Visions of Joyce Carol Oates,* Duke University Press, 1978.

This early study of the author only covers the first novels, including *them,* but it does so in a clear and insightful way.

Greg Johnson, *Understanding Joyce Carol Oates,* University of South Carolina Press, 1987.

This full, rich analysis of Oates's work is slightly dated, but contains an extensive analysis of *them.*

Fredrick R. Karl, "Modes of Survival," in *Modern Critical Views: Joyce Carol Oates,* edited by Harold Bloom, Chelsea House, 1987.

This essay, originally printed in 1883, addresses the naturalistic elements of the novel and explains Loretta, Maureen, and Jules in relation to other characters in recent fiction.

Marilyn Wesley, *Refusal and Transgression in Joyce Carol Oates' Fiction,* Greenwood Press, 1993.

This book-length comparative analysis looks at Oates's fiction in terms of family relationships: mothers and fathers, mothers and daughters, brothers and sisters, and more. Slightly complex reading for high school students.

To the Lighthouse

Virginia Woolf

1927

The 1927 publication of Virginia Woolf's *To the Lighthouse* was a landmark for both the author and the development of the novel in England. Usually regarded as her finest achievement, it won her the Prix Femina the following year, and gained her a reputation as one of Britain's most important living authors. Not only was it a critical success, it was popular too, selling in large quantities to a readership that encompassed a broad spectrum of social classes. Since Woolf's death in 1941, *To the Lighthouse* has risen in importance as a focus of criticism concerning issues of gender, empire, and class. Along with James Joyce's *Ulysses,* it continues to be heralded as a milestone in literary technique.

The complexity of Woolf's writing in *To the Lighthouse* has become almost proverbially intimidating, as suggested famously in the title of Edward Albee's 1962 play, *Who's Afraid of Virginia Woolf?* Written from multiple perspectives and shifting between times and characters with poetic grace, the novel is not concerned with plot. Instead, it paints a verbal picture of the members of the Ramsay family and their friends. In the first section, the character of Mrs. Ramsay is the lens through which most of the perspectives are focused, and her son's desire to go "to the Lighthouse" is the organizing impetus from which the picture takes shape. In the central section, the Lighthouse stands empty as the narrative marks the passage of time and the death of many of the characters. In the third and final section, with Mrs. Ramsay dead, the

remaining family and friends finally get to the Lighthouse, and the novel becomes a meditation on love, loss, and creativity.

Author Biography

One of the greatest literary figures of the twentieth century, Virginia Woolf was born in London in 1882. The daughter of the prominent literary critic Sir Leslie Stephen, she was educated in the literary and intellectual atmosphere of her home. Her mother died in 1895, and after the death of her father in 1904, Woolf moved to the Bloomsbury area of London. Living with her sister, Vanessa, and brothers, Thoby and Adrian, her house became the center of a circle of artists and writers who would become known as the Bloomsbury Group. One of the members of this group, Leonard Woolf, became her husband in 1912. In this unconventional and intellectually charged atmosphere, she began publishing reviews and essays.

Woolf's career as a novelist began in 1915, when she published *The Voyage Out.* Though stylistically conventional, it showed an emphasis on character rather than plot which would characterize Woolf's work. This novel was followed by *Night and Day* in 1919 and *Jacob's Room* in 1922, books in which her writing became increasingly experimental. The 1925 publication of *Mrs. Dalloway* marked the emergence of Woolf's mature, creative voice, with her use of the free association of ideas in her characters' minds. The novel that many regard as her finest publication, *To the Lighthouse,* came out in 1927. By this time she had honed her techniques of nonlinear narrative style, interior monologue, and impressionistic renditions of life, and the book became an instant classic.

Woolf went on to write *Orlando* in 1928, and the next year *A Room of One's Own,* which is an analysis of the problems women writers face in a male-dominated literary world. This work was followed by her extremely experimental novels, *The Waves* (1931) and *Between the Acts* (1941). Despite her success and burgeoning reputation, Woolf never succeeded in maintaining any but the most transient moments of comfort and happiness. Even at the height of literary productivity, she was troubled by a mental illness that showed itself in periods of creative energy followed by lengthy depressions. In 1941, during a depressed period that followed the completion of her last novel, Woolf committed suicide by drowning herself in a stream.

Virginia Woolf

Plot Summary

The Window

The action of *To the Lighthouse* takes place on two days, separated by ten years. The novel begins on a September evening in the Hebrides before World War I, in the middle of a discussion about the possibility of going to the Lighthouse the next day. Mrs. Ramsay, who is sitting in the window with her son, James, thinks the weather will be fair; Mr. Ramsay, who has been walking back and forth on the path with his student Charles Tansley, says that it most definitely will not be. After a prolonged discussion, Mrs. Ramsay reads "The Fisherman and His Wife" to James, and Mr. Ramsay continues his walking.

Meanwhile, Lily Briscoe is painting Mrs. Ramsay and James; she decides to show what she has accomplished to William Bankes, an old friend of Mr. Ramsay. As they are looking at the picture, Cam Ramsay (daughter of Mr. and Mrs. Ramsay) runs past, nearly upsetting the easel. Meanwhile, guests Minta Doyle and Paul Rayley are walking with Andrew and Nancy Ramsay; after the four become separated, Nancy finds Minta and Paul kissing behind a rock. Minta loses her grandmother's brooch in the rocks, and Paul tells her he will search for it the next day, when there is more light.

Minta, Paul, Nancy, and Andrew have not yet returned when everyone sits down to dinner. When they enter, Minta says that she has lost her brooch. Mrs. Ramsay decides that Minta and Paul must have gotten engaged, and Lily uses a salt shaker to remind herself that she will move a tree in her picture the next day. At the end of the meal, another guest, Augustus Carmichael, and Mr. Ramsay recite the poem "Luriana Lurilee" in tribute to Mrs. Ramsay.

After dinner, Mrs. Ramsay finds that Cam and James are still awake. Cam is scared of the boar's head that is hanging on the wall, while James screams when it is touched. Mrs. Ramsay covers the skull with her shawl, so that Cam can't see it, but James will know the skull is still in the room. Mrs. Ramsay assures James that on the next fine day, they will go to the Lighthouse.

With the children asleep, Mr. and Mrs. Ramsay sit quietly together. Mrs. Ramsay tells Mr. Ramsay that Paul and Minta are engaged. Mr. Ramsay wants Mrs. Ramsay to tell him she loves him, but instead she tells him that his weather forecast was accurate and they won't be able to go to the Lighthouse the next day after all. She feels she has triumphed by not telling him she loves him.

Time Passes

Time moves forward and the nights become colder and wilder. During one of those cold, wild nights, Mrs. Ramsay dies. Prue Ramsay marries, then dies in childbirth. Andrew Ramsay dies in France during the war. The abandoned house begins to deteriorate, and the caretaker, Mrs. McNab, decides she can't fight the decay of the house. Ten years after Mrs. Ramsay's death, one of the Ramsay children asks Mrs. McNab to ready the house for guests, expecting it to be the same as it was left. With help, Mrs. McNab restores the condition of the house, and the Ramsays and their guests visit in September.

The Lighthouse

Mr. Ramsay has coerced Cam and James into visiting the Lighthouse. Lily decides to finish the picture she started ten years ago. Before he leaves for the Lighthouse, Mr. Ramsay goes to Lily demanding sympathy, but she praises his boots instead. After the three Ramsays leave, Lily begins to paint, with Carmichael sitting near her. As Lily paints, she begins to think of Mrs. Ramsay, and cries out for her, wanting her to return. Meanwhile, the three Ramsays are sailing to the Lighthouse, and Cam and James are resentful of their father's

tyranny. Macalister tells them stories of disasters at sea, and Macalister's boy catches a mackerel.

Lily has a vision of Mrs. Ramsay sitting on the beach with her, and thinks of the disastrous marriage of the Rayleys, which has only been righted by Paul's affair with another woman, and of her cherished friendship with William Bankes. Lily continues to cry out for Mrs. Ramsay. In the boat, Macalister's boy cuts a square out of the mackerel and throws it back into the sea.

After Mr. Ramsay finishes the book he has been reading, they reach the Lighthouse. James and Cam feel reconciled to their father after he praises James's steering, and James is satisfied with the Lighthouse. On shore, Lily thinks they must have reached the Lighthouse, and she realizes that Mrs. Ramsay isn't there, and that she doesn't want her any longer. Lily adds a line in the center of her painting, completing it at last, and feels that she has had her vision. The novel ends with the Ramsays' successful trip to the Lighthouse and Lily's completion of her painting.

Characters

Andrew the Just

See Andrew Ramsay

William Bankes

William Bankes is an old botanist friend of Mr. Ramsay's who has come to stay at the Ramsay home. The years since the two first became friends have changed both men, and Bankes is jealous and resentful of Mr. Ramsay. Mrs. Ramsay senses Bankes's loneliness and wants to pair him off with Lily Briscoe.

Bankes is a childless widower, and tries to assuage his envy of the Ramsay household by suggesting that his old friend's philosophical work is secondhand and past its prime. He is, however, drawn to Mrs. Ramsay's beauty and the warm domesticity of the Ramsays' lives. Rejected by little Cam, he hides his loneliness by denigrating marriage and children to Lily. Lily, on the other hand, realizes that he is isolated and that he carries a torch for Mrs. Ramsay.

Bankes is intellectually open, willing to understand and appreciate Lily's abstract painting, which suggests the essentially positive character that is hidden beneath his bitterness. The two become very good friends. He dies during the middle section of the novel, and Lily looks back on her friendship with him and remembers him as a good and profoundly lonely man, whom she will always love.

Lily Briscoe

Lily is an artist who stays with the Ramsay family in the first section of the novel, and returns with them to their Scottish summerhouse in the final section. She is a Post-Impressionist painter, descendant of a poor family, and has spent most of her life taking care of her father. In many ways, Lily is the chorus figure of the book—providing the histories of the characters and commenting on their actions. The beginning and completion of her painting form the frame of *To the Lighthouse,* and her final line, "I have had my vision," is the final line of the novel, acting as Woolf's own comment on her book.

Lily, a lonely character who never marries, is both consumed by her art as well as in need of love and connection. She is "in love with the Ramsays," seeing them as the embodiment of the affection that is missing from her life, and especially adores Mrs. Ramsay. Just as she is unable to show love, she is phobic about allowing her art to be seen. When William Bankes sees her painting, they form a connection, and talk about the Ramsays. Both of them find things to fault about the family because they are so jealous of them, but both secretly understand each other's feelings. Lily does not like Mr. Ramsay because of the way he treats his wife, and she sees him as emotionless and too logical. She is taken aback when she and Bankes run into Mr. Ramsay spouting poetry on the lawn. Later, she realizes that she has misjudged him and that he is a man of strong emotion who adores his wife.

In the final section of the novel, Lily stands watching the Ramsays sail to the Lighthouse. While she tries to paint, memories and intense emotions surface. The desolation of the Ramsays that has occurred and the years of loss overcome her, and she cries out for Mrs. Ramsay. As Mr. Carmichael joins her, Lily realizes that Mr. Ramsay must have reached the Lighthouse. With this resolution achieved, she puts the final line on her painting and says, "It is finished." She has had her vision.

Cam the Wicked

See Cam Ramsay

Augustus Carmichael

Augustus Carmichael is a charismatic man who stays with the Ramsays when the family is in Scotland. He has had a bad marriage, and has spent

Media Adaptations

- The British Broadcasting Company (BBC) produced a dramatization of *To the Lighthouse* for British television in 1983. Kenneth Branagh, Rosemary Harris, Michael Gough, and Suzanne Bertish star. It is available from Magnum Entertainment Inc.

- An audio book edition of *To the Lighthouse* is available from Naxos AudioBooks Ltd. The 1996 recording is read by the British actress, Juliet Stevenson.

- Penguin Audiobooks also released a recorded edition of the novel in 1997. Their edition is read by Eileen Atkins.

time in India. Mrs. Ramsay was there when his wife threw him out, and she thinks that he doesn't like her because he's had bad experiences with women. Initially offering to teach while at the Ramsays, he ends up lounging about on the tennis courts instead, and Mrs. Ramsay thinks of him as a "great cat" with green eyes. Between his two stays with the Ramsays in Scotland, he becomes an important poet. Later, Lily thinks of him as "old pagan god." At the very end of the novel he stands with Lily looking out over the sea and says, "He has landed ... It is finished," and Lily feels that he has "crowned the occasion."

Minta Doyle

Daughter of the Ramsays' upper-class acquaintances, Minta is a guest at the Ramsays' summer home. Her parents are stuffy and very traditional, the subjects of many jokes between Mr. and Mrs. Ramsay. Minta, however, is very different—an energetic, scruffy young woman whom Mrs. Ramsay calls "a tom-boy." She wonders what Minta's parents make of this modern girl who gads about with holes in her stockings. Minta and Paul Rayley get engaged and celebrate with the Ramsays. Ten years later, when the Ramsays return to Scotland, Lily thinks about Minta and Paul. Their marriage has not been wonderful, for Paul is a bohemian man who spends his time in meetings and coffeehouses. Since Paul obtained a mistress, however, he and Minta have settled into a comfortable marriage of friendship, not love.

James the Ruthless

See James Ramsay

Mrs. McNab

Mrs. McNab is the housekeeper of the Ramsays' summer home. She is the only person who is actively in the "Time Passes" section, tending to the house as it gradually fills with dust and the Ramsays meet their fates. She is the only character who takes some of the flowers home with her. The family has simply been sending money to her to clean, and never write or visit. Mrs. McNab often thinks of Mrs. Ramsay, and when she hears that the house may be sold, she locks the house and leaves. After receiving a letter stating that the family may be coming for the summer, she cleans the house from top to bottom.

Prue the Beautiful

See Prue Ramsay

Andrew Ramsay

Andrew, one of the Ramsay sons, is killed in the trenches of World War I. He is a brilliant young man, with a genius for mathematics and an interest in zoology.

Cam Ramsay

Cam, the little Ramsay daughter, is a "wild and fierce child" at the beginning of the book who refuses to give William Bankes a flower. When the family returns after the death of Mrs. Ramsay, she has conflicting emotions about being at the summer home. Cam is bitter about Mr. Ramsay's "crash blindness and tyranny of which had poisoned her childhood and raised bitter storms, so that even now she woke in the night trembling with rage and remembered some command of his."

Because the Lighthouse holds such harsh memories for them, neither she nor James wish to go to it, but they agree to their father's wish out of duty. As they drift out she looks back at the house and feels love and pride for her father, but cannot help thinking about the past and the people that are now gone. Mr. Ramsay teases her about not knowing the points of the compass, but sees that she is frightened. He wants to make her feel better, and Cam knows this. She remembers the good things about him, the times she felt safe with him, but is

still torn by bitterness. She looks at the shore and feels that the people that used to be there are now free. As they reach the Lighthouse, Mr. Ramsay finally praises his son James. Cam knows that this is a point that James has been waiting for his whole life, and with a greater sense of hopefulness they step ashore.

James Ramsay

James Ramsay is the youngest child of Mr. and Mrs. Ramsay. As a little boy he is an extremely sensitive child who idolizes his mother. Wracked by intense emotions, he fantasizes about killing his father in order to have Mrs. Ramsay to himself. His desire to go to the Lighthouse is the focus of the novel's first section. His mother tries to make his wish come true, while his father and Charles Tansley insist that the weather will prevent them. He does not get his wish.

When they return to the summer home ten years later, James is bitter. He feels it is too late to get to the Lighthouse now, and Mr. Ramsay's need to make the trip seems to James to be a fruitless endeavor. He still hates his father for the way he perceived his mother was treated. Though James tells himself he feels nothing for his father, it is clear he desperately wants his approval. As they wait for another breeze to get them to the Lighthouse, James remembers feeling angry with his mother, and then is consumed by rage for his father when he looks at him reading. While he thinks about his mother, the wind picks up, and they move on.

As the group gets closer to the Lighthouse, Mr. Ramsay opens up the lunch, and James finally realizes that his father is lonely, "which was for both of them the truth about things." When they pass over where three men drowned, Cam and James expect Mr. Ramsay to spout bombastic poetry, and when he doesn't they realize that he has changed. James steers the family to shore, bitter that his father will not praise him. As their voyage ends, Mr. Ramsay compliments him on steering them like a born sailor. With his father's approval finally given, James is full of an overwhelming, fierce happiness that is too great to share, and a new hopefulness fills the surviving family members.

Jasper Ramsay

A son of the Ramsays, Jasper likes to shoot birds in his free time.

Mr. Ramsay

Mr. Ramsay is the father of the family. He is the most misunderstood character in the book, a

A lighthouse along the Shetland coastline in Scotland.

man whose children hate him because they think he is viciously unemotional and cold. They and Lily think of him as stern and sarcastic—a man who "never altered a disagreeable word to suit the pleasure or convenience of any mortal being, least of all his own children." Mrs. Ramsay has a very different picture of him. She knows how insecure he is about his abilities as a philosopher and a provider. He is a man who acknowledges the short-comings of his own skills, knowing that he will never be able to go beyond "Q" in the "alphabet" of great thinking. He is also possessed of many more emotions than his children give him credit for, and is not the exclusively rational man that Lily Briscoe first sees. Her view of him is turned upside down when she runs into him on the lawn reciting poetry and acting it out. Later at the dinner table, Mr. Ramsay talks to Minta and everyone is able to see the charming, attractive man that he can be.

When the Ramsays return to Scotland in the last section of the book, Mr. Ramsay is broken and alone, though neither Lily nor his children can acknowledge this. His need to go to the Lighthouse with Cam and James is an attempt to reconcile himself with them, to share their loss of Mrs. Ramsay, and to make amends for his past behavior. When he finally gives James the praise he has always withheld from him, the process of forgiveness is complete.

Mrs. Ramsay

Mrs. Ramsay is the mother of the Ramsay family who dies during the middle section of the novel. A beautiful, caring woman, she means all things to all people, and each character of *To the Lighthouse* has a different perception of her personality. Lily sees her as a mother, and doesn't think she has ever inspired romantic passion. William Bankes and Charles Tansley adore her, and think she doesn't realize how beautiful she is. The children see her as the "Lighthouse" of their lives—the stable, warm force that protects and guides them. Mr. Ramsay adores and resents her because of her huge capacity for love. Sometimes he feels he would have been a greater thinker if he had no wife or children, but underneath he knows that he is utterly dependent on her.

In her own mind, Mrs. Ramsay is far more complex. She loves her husband, but alternates between pitying and reverencing him, knowing that his intellectual powers are waning and that people will eventually realize that he depends on her too much. She loves to make other people happy and is constantly encouraging love matches, expediting the engagement of Minta and Paul, and trying to match Lily and William Bankes. At the same time, she becomes jealous when attention is focused on others, feeling resentful and left out when Minta and Paul celebrate their engagement. She is used to being loved and relies on it, but is aware of this, and it is balanced by her generous impulses and love. She is happiest when loving, and wishes that she could "always be holding a baby." Her compassion leads her to worry about the plight of the poor, and she is constantly doing charitable things—knitting stockings for the Lighthouse keeper's sick child and taking food to poor people in the area.

After her death she remains the "Lighthouse" of the Ramsay family, the most powerful force in the lives of Lily, Cam, James, and Mr. Ramsay. As they begin to accept the loss of her, the surviving Ramsays finally make the trip to the Lighthouse that Mrs. Ramsay had desperately wanted them to be able to make. While Lily breaks down and cries out for her, James, Cam, and Mr. Ramsay make their symbolic voyage to the emotional center that is Mrs. Ramsay. When they arrive they have finally done what she wanted—ceased fighting and recognized their equal love for her and for each other.

Nancy Ramsay

Nancy is one of Mr. and Mrs. Ramsay's daughters. She witnesses a kiss between Paul Rayley and Minta Doyle.

Prue Ramsay

One of Mr. and Mrs. Ramsay's eight children, Prue dies in childbirth.

Roger Ramsay

Another Ramsay offspring, Roger is referred to as a "wild creature" by his mother.

Rose Ramsay

Rose is a daughter of the Ramsays, who "had a wonderful gift with her hands."

Minta Rayley

See Minta Doyle

Paul Rayley

Paul Rayley is a guest of the Ramsays who is courting Minta Doyle. Mrs. Ramsay does not respect his intelligence much, and thinks that he's a "boobie." He and Minta get married, and he is irresponsible, spending his time in meetings and cof-

feehouses. He begins an affair with a "serious woman, with her hair in a plait" who shares his interests. Because of this, he and Minta develop a comfortable marriage.

The Atheist Tansley

See Charles Tansley

Charles Tansley

Charles Tansley is a student of Mr. Ramsay, visiting the Lighthouse while he does his dissertation. The product of a lower-middle-class home, he has worked himself up the educational and social scale, and remains uneasy about his status. This makes him overeager to prove himself, and the Ramsay children think of him as a pompous prig. Inclined always to agree with whatever Mr. Ramsay says, it is really Mrs. Ramsay who becomes the focus of Charles's attention. He, like all of the characters, is in love with her. She pities him the poverty of his childhood—he has never even been to a circus—but dislikes him for his thoughtless behavior to her son James. Tansley's insecurity often leads him to be unnecessarily harsh, and he tells Lily that women have no business being painters.

Themes

War

In *To the Lighthouse,* the Great War takes place during the "Time Passes" section. The structure of the novel reflects the impact of World War I on European society. Part One is set in the golden haze of prewar innocence and love. Mr. Ramsay entertains himself by reciting Lord Tennyson's poem *The Charge of the Light Brigade,* a poem about death during the Crimean War, which valorizes the heroism of the then-unprecedented loss of a cavalry unit. Tennyson's celebration of patriotism and glorious death would be rejected by the traumatized survivors of the Great War who had witnessed death on a scale unimaginable to the Victorian poet. As Wilfred Owen wrote, World War I ended "that great lie—Dulce et decorum est pro patria mori [it is sweet and proper to die for one's country]." Owen himself would not make it home from the war.

During the middle section of Woolf's novel, the scarifying time period of 1914 to 1918 is represented by the death that comes to many of the characters, including Mrs. Ramsay and Andrew, who is killed in combat by a shell. Part Two is con-

Topics For Further Study

- Virginia Woolf summed up James Joyce's writing style as "the work of a queasy adolescent fingering his pimples." Look at the different versions of stream of consciousness to be found in Woolf's *To the Lighthouse* and Joyce's *Portrait of the Artist as a Young Man* in light of this assessment. What are the differences between the two narrative techniques? What do you think led Woolf to see Joyce's style as immature and self-absorbed?

- Feminist critiques of *To the Lighthouse* have drawn very different conclusions about its gender politics. Elaine Showalter suggests that the novel is a retreat from feminism into mysticism, while Toril Moi argues that it is a radical feminist attack on the logic of patriarchal male society. Which assessment seems to you better supported by Woolf's book? What textual evidence can you find for either of these viewpoints?

- "Had there been an axe handy, or a poker, any weapon that would have gashed a hole in his father's breast and killed him, there and then, James would have seized it." Many critics have suggested that James Ramsay has an Oedipal complex. What is Freud's concept of the Oedipal complex? Do you think James is suffering from it? Research the history of the idea and make a case for or against.

- *To the Lighthouse* ends when Lily Briscoe puts the final stroke on her picture. Many critics have suggested that Woolf's novel is an attempt to create writing that is conceptually identical to Lily's Post-Impressionist painting. Research the history of experimental art in the first decades of the twentieth century. What is the theory behind abstract art like Lily's? How is it similar to Woolf's novelistic style?

- The Ramsay children have views on British society that are very different from those of the older generation. They question the value of "the Bank of England and the Indian Empire." Investigate the political and social reform movements of the twenties and thirties. What was new about the younger generation? Why had they begun to question Victorian values?

---

cerned with survivors, with a shell-shocked culture attempting to come to terms with its losses. The war marks an end to many of the old ways of life, a change in social climate and the first rumblings of collapse for the British institutions so important to the older characters, especially the Indian Empire. Britain would not grant control to India until 1947, but as Woolf's novel shows, the younger, postwar generation was already beginning to question the culture of empire building.

Philosophy

Debates about philosophy, particularly theories about visual reality, figure prominently in *To the Lighthouse*. In the first section of the novel, "The Window," Mr. Ramsay, an Oxford philosopher, does his work on the three main philosophers of British empiricism, John Locke, George Berke-

ley, and David Hume. The basic argument of Empiricism is that human concepts and beliefs apply to a world outside oneself, and that it is by way of the senses that this world acts upon the individual. The question that is debated is just how much the mind itself contributes to the task of processing its sensory input. One of the points that Mr. Ramsay's philosophy debates is whether or not a person can be empirically certain that objects have a distinct and continued existence apart from our perceptions of them. Andrew Ramsay sums this philosophy up to Lily in mundane, domestic terms, saying "Think of a kitchen table then … when you're not there."

Throughout the novel, the characters reflect on objects and people that are "not there," especially Mrs. Ramsay. Mrs. Ramsay's effect on everyone and everything is like the imaginary "kitchen table" of Andrew's explanation. Her continuing impact even after death is contrasted with the cold logic of Mr. Ramsay's philosophy, which denies these kinds of connections between reality, mind and personality. Lily's painting style shows a different kind of reality in which objects and perception can be different for every person. As she explains to William Bankes, her view of Mrs. Ramsay does not look like its subject because it is abstract. However, it is still "like" Mrs. Ramsay because she is trying to paint the emotional and spatial impact of the woman.

Like Woolf's stream of consciousness narrative style, Mrs. Ramsay's reality changes depending on how she is feeling—making William Bankes either a tyrant or a pitiful person according to her emotions at the time. While Mr. Ramsay blindly wrestles with skepticism on masculine philosophical grounds, Mrs. Ramsay and Lily show maternal and painterly domestic eyes at work, creating a distinctly female "epistemology"—or theory about the nature and limits of human knowledge.

Freudian Psychology

The character of James Ramsay is central to the narrative impetus of *To the Lighthouse*. His desire to go on the trip, and the conflicting reactions of parents form the structure and title of the novel, and are drawn in patterns established by Freudian theories. As a child, James is very hostile to his father and adores his mother. His mother promises that the day will be pleasant enough for them to sail, while his father promises that it will rain and make sailing impossible. James wishes for an "axe …, or a poker, any weapon that would have gashed a hole in his father's breast and killed him, there and then." Every time that his father distracts Mrs. Ramsay's attention from him, James feels similar homicidal urges.

This desire to kill his father to keep his mother's attention corresponds to Freud's Oedipal complex. This famous theory is based on the Greek myth of Oedipus, who accidentally murdered his father and wed his mother. Freud said that all males go through an Oedipal stage in which they want to kill their fathers and marry their mothers. In order to grow to emotional maturity, they must get over this impulse and embrace their fathers, as James eventually does.

Perception and Consciousness

In *To the Lighthouse* Woolf uses a "decorated process of thought" in which the physical world around a character takes on their form of thought.

As a result, the world that surrounds the characters has a symbolic status with different and specific meanings for each character. Throughout the novel, the personality and consciousness of each person expresses itself in the way that the world seems when they stand in it. The most important symbol of the book is the Lighthouse itself. Just as it dominates the bay, the Lighthouse dominates Woolf's novel, both physically and symbolically. The characters each see it differently, depending on their emotions and needs.

For Mrs. Ramsay, the Lighthouse represents her isolation as well as warmth and comfort, an integral part of the rhythm of her days that allows her to nurture and be nurtured. The Lighthouse is not just a building, it is "something immune which shines out." For Lily Briscoe, the true "lighthouse" of the novel is Mrs. Ramsay herself—a beacon that casts an organizing light on the whole family and continues to illuminate and connect them even after her death. Mr. Ramsay's presence makes the Lighthouse a "stark tower on a bare rock," which symbolizes his unemotional logic. For James, the Lighthouse is a shifting symbol that seems to represent his mother, even as it is representative of the stark rationalism of his father. His analysis of the situations sums up the thematic point: "So that was the Lighthouse, was it? No the other was also the Lighthouse. For nothing was simply one thing."

Style

Stream of Consciousness

The narrative technique that Woolf uses for most of *To the Lighthouse* is normally called stream of consciousness. This technique was a product of Modernism, a literary movement characterized by introspection, self-awareness and an openness to the unconscious. Associated primarily with Woolf and James Joyce, this technique was a way of representing the whole mind of an individual, not just conscious thought. It is based on the psychological theory that human minds are made up of many layers of awareness, from highly articulated rational thought, to emotional responsiveness, all the way to the animal pre-speech level of need and instinct. The basis of the technique is the notion that all of these layers are present in the mind of a human at any given moment—a "stream of consciousness" composed of the flow of sensations, thoughts, memories, associations, and reflections. If the exact pattern of the mind ("consciousness") is to be described, then these varied, disjointed, and illogical elements must find expression in a flow of words, images and ideas similar to the unorganized flow of the mind. In *To the Lighthouse* Woolf describes the technique while talking about Lily Briscoe:

> To follow her thought was like following a voice which speaks too quickly to be taken down by one's pencil, and the voice was her own voice saying without prompting undeniable, everlasting, contradictory things

Woolf's characteristic version of the stream of consciousness puts a new spin on the technique. Instead of being an attempt to capture the complexities of one individual mind, her novel is an attempt to capture the minds of a large group of people as they interact over time. This is achieved by the constant shifting of point of view and narrative chronology—often within the same paragraph or line.

Free Association

Part of the stream of consciousness style of Woolf's novel, free association is a term that describes the connections, or associations, that a person's mind makes between seemingly random things. A major part of the Freudian method of analysis is to ask people to say the first thing that comes to mind when they are given a word or object. By looking at the kinds of associations that occur, the analyst can find patterns in the randomness that reveal much about the character of the patient.

In *To the Lighthouse,* Woolf uses this free association style to reveal her characters. Charles Tansley, for example, sees Mrs. Ramsay next to a picture of Queen Victoria and realizes that she is beautiful. From that he thinks of flowers, bouquets and Mrs. Ramsay "stepping through fields of flowers ... with the stars in her eyes and the wind in her hair" gathering "fallen lambs" to her breast. The patterns of his thoughts reveal his character in ways that an analyst would be able to see. Mrs. Ramsay is the "queen" of his life, because he thinks of her after seeing a real queen. He associates her with flowers because his studies shut him off from the natural world, and she brings him out of his studious mind-set. He imagines her gathering "lost lambs" because he feels orphaned, and sees her as a Christ-like parental figure.

Psychology

The theories of the new Freudian psychology are used throughout the novel. The narrative structure is a literary version of the emphasis that psychology places on the subjective reality of emotions

A coastal town in Cornwall, England, the setting of To the Lighthouse.

and desires. Freudian psychology suggests that emotions, needs, and instincts are more important in understanding personality than rational thoughts. In keeping with this theory, rational thought is shown to be useless to describe characters throughout *To the Lighthouse*. When, for example, William Tansley tells himself that he doesn't like Mrs. Ramsay because she is "fifty at least," his "freely-associated" emotions tell the real story. Also part of Freudian theory is the emphasis placed on childhood experiences and emotions in the formation of adult personality. Mrs. Ramsay sums this up when she says, "Children never forget."

Historical Context

World War I

World War I began in 1914, the result of an unresolved and perilous series of Balkan Crises. When Archduke Franz Ferdinand was assassinated, the intense territorial dispute between Austro-Hungary and Serbia intensified, quickly spreading through the rest of Europe. Great Britain, Russia, and France joined together as the Allied Powers against the Central Power Alliance of Austro-Hun-

Compare
&
Contrast

- **1910s:** Unrest grows in Tsarist Russia as the oppressive state cracks down on reformers and activists.

  1920s: The Bolshevik revolution has taken place, and Lenin is in power. His New Economic Policy is being instituted, which allows greater economic freedom and a measure of controlled capitalism.

  Today: Communist Soviet Union has collapsed, and Russia is in ruins following a disastrous attempt to switch to a U.S.-style free market economy.

- **1910s:** After World War I the 1919 Treaty of Versailles establishes an international body that will arbitrate disputes. It also demands that Germany pay reparations for the war.

  1920s: The League of Nations has been formed, but its powers are very limited. America refuses to be involved, and has not ratified the Treaty of Versailles. The League is powerless, and fails to prevent the events that lead to World War II.

  Today: The United Nations has been in place since 1945, and has learned from the fate of the League of Nations. The UN provides a working arena for international diplomacy, peacekeeping, and aid.

- **1910s:** The British Labour Party is a new creation, struggling to find a support base. Many members of the British intellectual scene are in sympathy with its socialist ideology. After the Russian Revolution, the ruling classes of Britain become obsessed with the possibility of a similar British uprising.

  1920s: Britain is brought almost to the brink of class war in a series of major industrial actions that culminate in the great General Strike.

  Today: The Labour Party, led by Prime Minister Tony Blair, is the governing party in Great Britain.

- **1910s:** The British Women's Suffrage movement demands the right to vote.

  1920s: British women over thirty are granted the right to vote in 1918. American women win their battle in 1919. It is a long struggle that is resisted by many men—Switzerland will not accept women's suffrage in full until 1971.

  Today: Generations of legal rights have still not resulted in equality between men and women. In Britain and America, women's pay averages less than 70 percent of men's, and women still make up a tiny proportion of CEOs and politicians.

gary and Germany. After Russia dropped out of the Allied forces, and the *Luisitania* was sunk, America eventually entered the fray. The war, known in Europe as the Great War, took place on a scale never before seen in history. It lasted four years, cost $350 billion, and took the lives of 22 million people. In *To the Lighthouse* Andrew Ramsay becomes one of the victims of the war.

World War I revealed a new and horrifying form of warfare that took place in the trenches and the air, both innovations. It was also the most technologically advanced war, relying on a number of new inventions, such as machine guns, mortar

bombs, and barbed wire. Most scarring was innovations in biological weaponry. Death by mustard gas in the bunkers and trenches created a profound sense of shock in the surviving troops and horrible deaths for the fallen. Movingly documented by English War Poets like Siegfried Sassoon and Wilfred Owen, the Great War sent thousands of emotionally and physically shell-shocked men back to their homes.

Modernism

Modernism is a literary, artistic, and philosophical movement that began at the end of the nineteenth century. Modernists feel that earlier forms of art have reached their goals and become uninteresting, and they reject the realism of the nineteenth century. In response to older forms, the new art and literature was consciously nonrepresentational and experimental, refusing to portray significant action, and emphasizing human reactions and interpretations instead of physical realities. Freudian psychology was often incorporated into the new writing and art, since it overturns previous philosophies and makes the internal life of a person the most important aspect of reality.

The new art exploded into an unwelcome world in 1913, at The Armory Show. This international exhibition of modern art took place at the 69th Regiment Armory in New York City, opening in February and then travelling to Chicago, and Boston. It drew crowds of more than 100,000 people, and brought Postimpressionism and Cubism to international attention. The Armory Show, or Armory Circus, as some preferred to call it, was the first exhibition of modern art in America and the catalyst for many of the major modernist movements. In *To the Lighthouse,* this new and shocking art is the kind that Lily Briscoe attempts to create.

The Twenties

The Twenties were characterized by what Joseph Wood Krutch called the "Modern Temper." This was the new intellectual and social climate that rejected many of the traditional beliefs in progress, patriotism and art, at the same time as it looked for new forms of politics. Following the Russian Revolution of 1917, Marxism and socialism had gained a new importance in European thought. With Lenin in power and the genocidal legacy of Stalinism still unimaginable, the Soviet Union was taken as a model for many young idealists. Labor relations in Britain reached conditions bordering on class war. The coal miners led the Trade Union Congress in a general strike, paralyzing the country. They demanded, "Not a penny off the pay; not a minute on the day." Changes in social climate fostered new freedoms. In 1918, the Women's Suffrage movement triumphed, and British women over the age of thirty were granted the right to vote. Those between the ages of twenty-one and thirty were allowed to vote starting in 1928.

The Wall Street Crash plunged the World into economic depression in 1929 and exacerbated social divides. In 1927, however, Europe had finally begun to recover from the Great War, and there was a sense of optimism among the privileged "bright young things" of the British social scene. Writers like Nancy Mitford and Evelyn Waugh represented the new kind of young person—dashing, daring, and flippant. The scandalous young women of this social set were the British equivalent of the American "flappers." Like the younger Ramsay daughters, they refuse to take anything too seriously, and wear their hair and skirts short.

Critical Overview

To the Lighthouse was a critical success as soon as it was published, and won Woolf the *Prix Femina* in 1928. Initial reviews and criticism focused on the novel's stylistic innovations, praising Woolf's artistic refinement of the stream of consciousness narrative. Louis Kronenberger, for example, announced in *The New York Times,* "here is prose of an extraordinary distinction in our time: here is poetry." Woolf's death in 1941 prompted a flood of books and articles that celebrated her mastery of prose style. Eric Auerbach's important 1946 study of art and literature *Mimesis: The Representation of Reality in Western Literature* elevated Woolf's novel to the status of great literature and gave her the tag "Brown Stocking" (a play on the phrase "bluestockings" which was used to describe a group of intellectual women authors in the eighteenth century). Putting *To the Lighthouse* at the top of the modern literary canon, he praised the achievements of its narrative style over the works of her contemporaries, calling it the "creation of something new and elemental."

In the 1950s and 1960s, critical focus centered on symbolism, looking at myth, philosophy, and history as the unifying strategies of the novel. In *The Glass Roof: Virginia Woolf as Novelist,* James Halfley suggested that both Mrs. Ramsay and the Lighthouse were, "cosmic symbols" that represented a "vital synthesis of time and eternity." Along the same lines, Joseph L. Blotner's essay, "Mythic Patterns in *To the Lighthouse*," argued that Mrs. Ramsay should be understood as a "primordial goddess" composed of "the major female characters of pagan myth." He also made a case for the importance of Freudian thought in the novel.

The 1970s and 1980s marked a revolution in Woolf studies—a move away from quasi-Jungian analysis based on her symbolism, and a new focus on the role of gender and art in *To the Lighthouse* instead. Where the older critics found unity in the work, these new voices found disharmony and conflict. Emphasis was placed on the roles of gender and class, reflecting the general critical trends of the late 1970s and 1980s. Irene Dash, Deena Kushner, and Deborah Moore looked at the novel from a sociological stance, examining the challenges women face between "being mothers and being artists," from the perspectives of a mother, daughter, and artist, in "How Light a Lighthouse for Today's Women?" Jane Lilienfeld, in "'The Deceptiveness of Beauty': Mother Love and Mother Hate in *To the Lighthouse*" performed a biographical reading, suggesting that the relationship between Lily Briscoe and Mrs. Ramsay is an outlet for Woolf's feelings about her relationship with her mother, Julia Stephen.

Another critic, Elaine Showalter, caused controversy by arguing that the novel reveals Woolf's abandonment of feminism for a retreat into mysticism, in *A Literature of Their Own: British Women Novelists from Bronte to Lessing.* Claiming that Showalter's analysis revealed her tendency to "traditional humanism," Toril Moi's hugely influential 1985 book *Sexual/Textual Politics: Feminist Literary Theory* countered this by suggesting that Woolf's novel, "rejects the metaphysical essentialism underlying patriarchal ideology, which hails God, the father or the phallus, as its Transcendental signified," both in its shifting-consciousness narrative style and in the rejection of Mr. Ramsay's logic. Rachel Bowlby's important study, *Virginia Woolf: Feminist Destinations,* used Freudian and Lacanian psychoanalytic theories to read the novel, suggesting that, "*To the Lighthouse* makes evident the mapping of human subjectivity in terms of figurations inseparable from sexual difference."

Reflecting the general shifts in academia, the 1990s has seen a stronger emphasis on post-colonial and historically contextual readings of *To the Lighthouse.* These approaches stress the novel's relationship to the major historical contexts of its setting—World War I, the General Strike, and the British Empire. Characteristic of this approach is "'Something Out Of Harmony': *To the Lighthouse* and the Subject(s) of Empire" by Janet Winston. Picking up on the scene in which Charles Tansley compares Mrs. Ramsay to Queen Victoria, Winston suggested that the novel, "invites us to read not only with attention to codes of imperialist representation but to Mrs. Ramsay's role as Queen in a text of imperial allegory." The images of "sinking" that appear throughout the novel become—in this argument—evidence for authorial anxiety about the imminent collapse—"sinking"—of the British Empire.

Criticism

Jane Elizabeth Dougherty

Dougherty is a doctoral candidate at Tufts University. In the following essay, she examines the characterization of Lily Briscoe in To the Lighthouse.

In an essay, Virginia Woolf wrote, "[e]xamine for a moment an ordinary mind on an ordinary day. The mind receives a myriad of impressions-trivial, fantastic, evanescent, or engraved with the sharpness of steel." Woolf's character Lily Briscoe struggles with the myriad and momentary nature of reality throughout Woolf's fifth novel, *To the Lighthouse.* As Suzanne Raitt notes in *Virginia Woolf's To the Lighthouse,* Lily shares "the novel's strange obsession with solutions." Lily tries to find a shape within the chaotic nature of existence and achieve an artistic vision that will give her a sense of the meaning of life. In the course of her struggle, many of the novel's themes are illuminated: the nature of reality, the search for completion, the role of women, and the relationship of art and life.

As an artist, Lily struggles to express herself creatively. Her creativity is hampered by the continued interruptions of the outside world, which occur both within her physical space and within her mind:

> She would not have considered it honest to tamper with the bright violet and the staring white, since she saw them like that, fashionable though it was, since Mr. Paunceforte's visit, to see everything pale, elegant, semi-transparent. Then beneath the colour there was the shape. She could see it all so clearly, so commandingly, when she looked: it was when she took her brush in hand that the whole thing changed. It was in that moment's flight between the picture and her canvas that the demons set on her who often brought her to the verge of tears and made this passage from conception to work as dreadful as any down a dark passage for a child. Such she often felt herself—struggling against terrific odds to maintain her courage; to say: "But this is what I see; this is what I see," and so to clasp some miserable remnant of her vision to her breast, which a thousand forces did their best to pluck from her.

Among the "thousand forces" which try to "pluck" Lily's vision from her is the conflict between the experience of living and the theory of existence, which is represented by the Ramsays. Mrs. Ramsay is a character who seems comfortable with the ebb and flow of daily life; as Thomas A. Vogler comments in his introduction to *Twentieth Century Interpretations of To the Lighthouse,* "the 'life' character (like Mrs. Ramsay) lives or represents the human reality of the story." By contrast, Mr. Ramsay tries to come to "objective" truths about the nature of reality. As A. D. Moody writes in the same volume, Lily's "abstract aesthetic problem becomes an analogy for her main concern, and the novel's, which is to bring Mr. and Mrs. Ramsay, and the worlds they represent, into a harmonious relation." As an artist, Lily tries to find larger truths about human existence, as does Mr. Ramsay, but as a woman, she is confronted with the subjective and personalized nature of existence, as is Mrs. Ramsay. Appropriately, Lily feels that when she stays with the Ramsays, she struggles to find harmony between opposites:

> For at any rate, she said to herself, catching sight of the salt cellar on the pattern, she need not marry, thank Heaven: she need not undergo that dilution. She would move the tree rather more to the middle.

> Such was the complexity of things. For what happened to her, especially staying with the Ramsays, was to be made to feel violently two opposite things at the same time; that's what you feel, was one; that's what I feel, was the other, and then they fought together in her mind, as now. It is so beautiful, so exciting, this love, that I tremble on the verge of it, and offer, quite out of my own habit, to look for a brooch on the beach; also it is the stupidest, the most barbaric of human passions, and turns a nice young man with a profile like a gem's (Paul's was exquisite) into a bully with a crowbar (he was swaggering, he was insolent) in the Mile End Road. Yet, she said to herself, from the dawn of time odes have been sung to love; wreathes heaped and roses; and if you asked nine people out of ten they would say they wanted nothing but this—love; while the women, judging from her own experience, would all the time be feeling, This is not what we want, there is nothing more tedious, puerile, and inhumane than this; yet it is also beautiful and necessary.

Lily's own thoughts and perceptions are interrupted by, and in conflict with, the expectations of her society. In particular, she feels inadequate both as a woman and as an artist, because it is not expected that she can be both. She knows that as a woman she is supposed to be fulfilled by love and marriage, yet in her experience that is never the case. She appreciates Mrs. Ramsay's ability to be nurturing, but does not feel that she can fulfill Mrs. Ramsay's role. As Raitt states, Lily "experiences her conflicts over femininity primarily in the context of her relationship to Mrs. Ramsay." Yet she also feels inadequate as a painter, because men like Charles Tansley tell her that "women can't paint. Women can't write." Lily struggles to define herself as a creative woman in a culture that does not acknowledge that women can be creative.

As a female artist, Lily longs to bring together seemingly opposed forces and to find a "solution" to the problem of life's incoherence. For example, she asks how is it possible to analyze all the conflicting information that one gets about another person and decide that one likes or dislikes that person. As Thomas Matro explains in *PMLA,* "Lily's ambivalence, suspension and subsequent 'explosion' stem from her felt inability to know another person and from the necessity she yet feels to form a clear, consistent opinion." After dinner, for example,

> [s]he felt rather inclined just for a moment to stand still after all that chatter, and pick out one particular thing; the thing that mattered; to detach it; separate it off; clean it of all the emotions and odds and ends of things, and so hold it before her, and bring it to the tribunal where, ranged about in conclave, sat the judges she had set up to decide these things. Is it good, is it bad, is it right or wrong? Where are we all going to? And so on. So she righted herself after the shock of the event, and quite unconsciously and incongruously, used the branches of the elm trees outside to help her stabilize her position. Her world was changing: they were still. The event had given her a sense of movement. All must be in order. She must get that right and that right, she thought, insensibly approving of the dignity of the trees' stillness, and now again of the superb upward rise (like the beak of a ship up a wave) of the elm branches as the wind raised them.

Lily longs to see things without emotion, objectively. She is able to reorient herself by situating herself in relation to the trees outside, which she sees as objective because they are unchanging. In the passage, she progresses from thinking abstractly about "the thing that mattered," which she cannot identify and about which she asks, "is it right or wrong?" to righting herself by focusing on the unchanging nature of the trees, to deciding she must get them right in her painting. By using the word "right," the narrator shifts Lily, and the reader, from abstract conceptions of rightness to natural, eternal rightness to an aesthetic rightness in which rightness is defined as the ability to see clearly. But that is not the final step on Lily's artistic quest; though she says that she must get what she sees on canvas, the narrator shows how, through her use of the word "right," Lily is still clinging to a kind of aesthetics based on objectivity, an unchanging and universal "truth." Lily thinks the natural world is unchanging, but in the second section of the novel, "Time Passes," the narrator shows us how the natural world slowly encroaches on, and nearly destroys, the house. Lily thinks that she must get what she sees "right," but in the third section, "The Lighthouse," she discovers that what she sees is her own particular vision, not a universal truth.

In the section called "The Lighthouse," Lily decides to finish the picture she had started ten years earlier, but is interrupted by Mr. Ramsay:

> Yes, it must have been precisely here that she had stood ten years ago. There was the wall, the hedge, the tree. The question was of some relation between those masses. She had borne it in her mind all these years. It seemed as if the solution had come to her: she knew now what she wanted to do.

But with Mr. Ramsay bearing down on her, she could do nothing. Every time he approached—he was walking up and down the terrace—ruin approached, chaos approached. She could not paint.

Lily associates chaos with being unable to paint, unable to hold things in their proper places. Mr. Ramsay makes her unable to paint because, with his insatiable demands for sympathy, he makes it impossible for Lily to listen to her own feelings. She is once again confronted with the "dilution" of other people, with the attempt to hold together two opposing forces: her own feelings and those of another person. It is only when Mr. Ramsay leaves that she can return to her painting.

As she paints, Lily falls into a kind of trance in which she imagines Mrs. Ramsay, for whom she has been crying out, is sitting beside her. She remembers how Mrs. Ramsay united her with her "opposite," Charles Tansley:

> The great revelation had never come. The great revelation perhaps never did come. Instead there were little daily miracles, illuminations, matches struck unexpectedly in the dark; here was one. This, that, and the other; herself and Charles Tansley and the breaking wave; Mrs. Ramsay bringing them together; Mrs. Ramsay saying, 'Life stand still here'; Mrs. Ramsay making of the moment something permanent (as in another sphere Lily herself tried to make of the moment something permanent)—this was of the nature of a revelation. In the midst of chaos there was shape; this eternal passing and flowing (she looked at the clouds going and the leaves shaking) was struck into stability. Life stand still here, Mrs. Ramsay said. 'Mrs. Ramsay! Mrs. Ramsay!' she repeated. She owed it all to her.

Whereas earlier Lily had thought that her artistry depended on "getting it right," and that the natural world was unchanging, she now sees, with Mrs. Ramsay's help, that the job of the artist is to make a moment permanent by capturing it in art. In coming to this realization, Lily is able to see her resemblance to Mrs. Ramsay, to see that she really is a woman, as Mrs. Ramsay was, but a woman whose female identity is expressed in art rather than in re-

lationships. Lily is at last able to mourn for Mrs. Ramsay, realizing that the "solution" to the problem of "wanting and not having" is to understand that all of life is momentary and that the best that humans can do is to say "life stand still here" and capture a moment in memory or in art. At the end of the novel, Lily feels that she is able to unify opposing forces, achieve completion, express her own personal truths, and to be both a woman and an artist. Through Lily, Woolf shows that in creative self-expression, humans may achieve a sense of completion and unify the disparate elements of life.

Source: Jane Elizabeth Dougherty, in an essay for *Novels for Students,* Gale, 2000.

Stella McNichol

In the following essay, McNichol presents an overview of To the Lighthouse.

To the Lighthouse is generally considered to be Virginia Woolf's most accomplished work. It is certainly her most popular one. It was this novel, together with *Mrs. Dalloway* and *The Waves,* that established her reputation as a modernist writer. What makes *To the Lighthouse* a modernist novel is its experimental form. It has no traditional plot structure and no characterisation in the accepted sense. Instead the novel is organised into three parts that are thematically and symbolically connected with each other. Part I ("The Window") covers only a few hours, Part II ("Time Passes") a period of 10 years, and Part III ("The Lighthouse") part of two days. Most of the "action" of the first and final sections of the novel takes place in the minds of the characters and is conveyed through a succession of interior monologues, as the perspective of the novel shifts from character to character. The central section is written in an abstract poetical style and its underlying authorial voice is impersonal. The events of the first part of the novel are evoked through memory in the final section when there is a return to the house in the Hebrides. The first part, which is essentially a celebration of the life generated creatively by Mrs. Ramsay, is shot through with images of light. The second part covers the "dark" years of war and death, and in the final section there is a restoration of the light. This light-dark-light pattern resembles the pattern formed by the beams from the lighthouse, which functions centrally in the novel both as a literal place and as a symbol. The novel begins with a desire to visit the lighthouse and concludes with the journey to it, so the lighthouse is bound up with the journey theme of the novel.

What Do I Read Next?

- *Mrs. Dalloway,* Woolf's 1925 novel about a day in the life of the titular character, is not only a personality study, it is also a commentary on the ills and benefits society gleans from class. We spend a day with Clarissa as she interacts with servants, her children, her husband, and even an ex-lover, as she plans and executes one of her celebrated parties. *Mrs. Dalloway* shows the full emergence of Woolf's distinctive writing style that she would refine to greater heights in *To the Lighthouse.*

- *A Room of One's Own* is Woolf's 1929 essay about the difficulties facing women authors. Woolf uses the constrained economic choices that women face to explain why "Shakespeare's sister" failed to write any plays, and to argue that creativity is dependent on independence.

- *A Portrait of the Artist as a Young Man,* James Joyce's 1916 novel about the development of Stephen Dedalus, is told in a groundbreaking stream of consciousness style. Reading this book along with *To the Lighthouse* provides a clearer picture of Woolf's important literary innovations.

- E. M. Forster's 1924 *A Passage to India* is a major novel that addresses issues of nationality and empire. An intellectual peer and friend of Woolf, Forster writes in a style very different from hers, keeping to the realist/naturalist traditions of the English novel.

- Michael Cunningham's 1998 Pulitzer Prize-winning novel, *The Hours,* is about Virginia Woolf. Cunningham tells the story of three women, including Woolf, as their lives are threaded together by the novel *Mrs. Dalloway.*

One gray suburban London morning in 1923, Woolf awakens from a dream that will soon lead to her book. In the present, on a beautiful June day in Greenwich Village, fifty-two-year-old Clarissa Vaughan is planning a party for her oldest love, a poet dying of AIDS. In Los Angeles in 1949, Laura Brown, pregnant and unsettled, does her best to prepare for her husband's birthday, but can't seem to stop reading Woolf.

- *Portrait of a Marriage* is Nigel Nicholson's 1973 account of the marriage of his parents, Harold Nicholson and Vita Sackville-West. Vita was one of Woolf's closest friends, and, like her, was bisexual. She caused scandal when she became involved with another woman. Nicholson's biography provides an intimate picture of the domestic and social pressures facing the artistic women of the Bloomsbury circle.

- *Hons and Rebels* is Jessica Mitford's 1961 autobiography about her early childhood (also published in America as *Daughters and Rebels*). The Mitford sisters were internationally notorious from the twenties onward. Jessica was a Communist, and ran off to the Spanish Civil War before moving to America, where she became an important activist and journalist for the left. Diana married Oswald Mosely, the founder of the English Fascist Party, and was actively involved with Fascist campaigning. Unity went to Germany, where she became close to Adolf Hitler, shooting herself when the war broke out. Nancy was a glittering novelist of English high society. Mitford's autobiography provides a fascinating picture of the social and political climate of the twenties and thirties.

At the centre of the novel are the complementing and contrasting characters of Mr. and Mrs. Ramsay (based on Woolf's parents). Mr. Ramsay, who is a philosopher, searches for intellectual truth with a rigour that makes him difficult to live with. Mrs. Ramsay grasps truth intuitively through her sensitive response to the people she comes in contact with. He needs her warmth to convince him that he lives at the "heart of life"; she relies on his sureness of judgment. Their opposing characteristics are reinforced imagistically, Mr. Ramsay being associated with images of hardness and assertion ("arid scimitar of the male") and Mrs. Ramsay with symbols of softness and warmth ("a column of spray" or a "rosy-flowered tree"). Within this symbolic framework Woolf probes the profound tensions at the core of all relationships between men and women. This is what underlies the verbal exchange at the beginning of the novel, when the youngest child, James, asks to visit the lighthouse: "'Yes, of course, if it's fine to-morrow,' said Mrs. Ramsay. 'But you'll have to be up with the lark,' she added...." "'But,' said his father, stopping in front of the drawing-room window, 'it won't be fine.'" Mrs. Ramsay's words are followed by a long paragraph which reveals the inner feelings of delight in the child. A similar passage of stream of consciousness writing follows his father's words, this time expressing feelings of anger and hatred. The authorial gloss on this situation is: "Such were the extremes of emotion that Mr. Ramsay excited in his children's breasts by his mere presence." The same kind of complex exploration and analysis continues throughout the book as character relates to character and as inner thoughts are revealed in solitude.

The most important of the friends who visit the Ramsay family at their holiday house in the Hebrides (really St. Ives in Cornwall where the Stephen family spent their summer holidays) is Lily Briscoe, who, in the first part of the novel, is painting a picture of Mrs. Ramsay and her son. She is an onlooker figure whose function in the novel is to observe life and recreate its reality in her art. She suddenly grasps the meaning of marriage in a moment of awareness, for instance, when she catches a glimpse of Mr. and Mrs. Ramsay walking across the lawn. In that moment they become for her symbolic figures, as their particularity is transcended to reveal a universal truth. In this way they contribute to her journey in awareness and to her painting which embodies it, both of which are completed at the end of the novel.

The party which is the climax of the first part of *To the Lighthouse* is a symbolic occasion. It will be remembered as a moment of stability in the midst of chaos after Mrs. Ramsay's death. That chaos is conveyed poetically in the central section of the novel. Here there is no coherence in life which seems full of suffering and death, war and anguish: Mrs. Ramsay dies, Andrew Ramsay is killed in the war, and Prue dies in childbirth. The personal anguish and the general sense of disintegration are figured in the decline of the house, which is finally rescued from its dereliction and restored.

The vision of the book is, then, an optimistic one. Out of the multiple oscillations between life and death, joy and sorrow, light and dark, the ebb and flow of the sea, there is an expressed belief in the survival of the human spirit: Mr. Ramsay springs like a young man onto the rock of the lighthouse, and Lily Briscoe draws a line in the centre of her canvas thus unifying, as Mrs. Ramsay did at the dinner party, the separate forms that had been resistant to her attempts to unify them. She has learned from Mrs. Ramsay that life "from being made up of little separate incidents which one lived one by one, became curled and whole like a wave."

Source: Stella McNichol, "*To the Lighthouse,*" in *Reference Guide to English Literature,* second edition, edited by D. L. Kirkpatrick, St. James Press, 1991.

Jack F. Stewart

In the following excerpt, Stewart examines the idea that "Woolf's search for spiritual essences is expressed in light and color" in To the Lighthouse.

According to Virginia Woolf, "painting and writing ... have much in common. The novelist after all wants to make us see.... It is a very complex business, the mixing and marrying of words that goes on, probably unconsciously, in the poet's mind to feed the reader's eye. *All great writers are great colorists...*." While "sound and sight seem to make equal parts of [her] first impressions," Woolf stresses their painterly quality.

In *To the Lighthouse,* Woolf's search for spiritual essences is expressed in light and color. Johannes Itten's metaphysic of light and color illuminates the relation between creative source (Mrs. Ramsay/the Lighthouse) and creative artist (Lily Briscoe/the painting) in Woolf's novel. Itten further affirms that "the end and aim of all artistic endeavor is liberation of the spiritual essence of form and color and its release from imprisonment in the world of objects." Woolf's art does not reach so far toward abstraction, but she does imply that the "luminous halo" of consciousness should be conveyed through equivalents of "plastic form," and notes that "fiction is given the capacity to deal with 'psychological volumes.' "

Roger Fry thought literature should parallel painting: "The Post-Impressionist movement ... was by no means confined to painting.... Cézanne and Picasso had shown the way; writers should fling representation to the winds and follow suit. But he never found time to work out his theory of the influence of Post-Impressionism upon literature"—as Woolf ironically remarks. She herself accepted the challenge of designing a literary art closer to the plastic values of painting. While Fry championed the post-impressionists' "'attempt to express by pictorial and plastic form certain spiritual experiences'," Woolf urged novelists "to convey this varying, this unknown and uncircumscribed spirit...." Fry's emphasis on formal relations merges fruitfully with Woolf's pursuit of being, as her art advances from the fragmentary impressionism of *Jacob's Room* to the luminous structure of *To the Lighthouse.* There revolving lights and colors play on the reader's sensibility like light waves on the retina, and characters come to be known as their *auras.*

The impressionists did not confine colors within the outlines of objects (as the rationalizing mind does), but observed how light spills over from one object to the next. Thus they gave objects a "luminous halo" or aureole of color. As a verbal colorist, Woolf desires "to paint men and women with that something of the eternal which the halo used to symbolize, and which we seek to confer by the actual radiance and vibration of our coloring." But in *To the Lighthouse* her art goes beyond impressionism and symbolism toward a flexible form that "does not shut out." The consciousness of each character tends to overflow individual boundaries, mingling its colors with those around it, as it modifies the total pattern. These interactions recall the post-impressionism of Cézanne, who wished "to represent things in their interrelationship in space," while still using "colour in its original significance."

While color in the novel expresses individual qualities, color/character associations are not reducible to one-to-one symbolic equations. Woolf wanted to find literary equivalents for "that pleasure which we gain from seeing beauty, proportion, contrast, and harmony of colour in the things around us"—and which Delacroix considers the exclusive property of painting. Beyond the sensuous immediacy of impressionism lay the constructive color of Cézanne, whose art symbolized nothing in particular, but "turned all external appearances of real things into a symbol of 'being,' 'which is eternal'." *To the Lighthouse* shares with Cézanne's painting a vital duality of aesthetic image, that mirrors actual sensations and emotions, and symbolic form, that mirrors its own "process of construction." When Badt speaks of blue as a "symbolic form," he is concerned with a structural quality and not with symbolic meaning. Blue, in Cézanne's painting, does not stand for something outside itself, but locks other colors together in harmony.

The experience of color relations is more than an optical sensation: it is a complex experience hard to put into words, a stimulus and a revelation.

Color is a sensitive medium for expressing both individual and universal experience. While color in literature inevitably gravitates toward symbolic associations, Woolf manipulates rhythmic interrelationships to create an overall plastic design, inwardly mirrored in the image of painting. Lily Briscoe is one of those post-impressionist artists who "do not seek to imitate form, but to create form, not to imitate life, but to find an equivalent for life." While the novel illuminates life, it completes its significance within the magic circle of art. Woolf accomplishes this condensation by seeking out "plastic equivalents" and constructing a virtual space that incorporates many of the subtle properties of color contrast. Color in the novel is not only an equivalent of feeling, it is also a component of form. The variously tinted streams of consciousness interconnect, so that "geometric colour" becomes a structural principle as in Cézanne's painting.

What Cézanne says of shape and color applies to *To the Lighthouse:* "The outline and the colors are no longer distinct from each other. To the extent that one paints, one outlines; the more the colors harmonize, the more the outline becomes precise.... When the color is at its richest, the form has reached plenitude." Merleau-Ponty's comment on Cézanne's portraiture can be applied, with slight modifications, to Woolf's characterization: "One's personality is seen and grasped in one's glance, which is, however, no more than a combination of colors." In the novel, the single "glance" becomes a series of subjective reflections, and "personality" a complex of sense perceptions, memories, verbal rhythms, and color.

Just as white light refracted through a prism produces the seven colors of the spectrum, so being refracted through self produces the psychological spectrum of the novel. *To the Lighthouse* is built on a nexus of light and color. Its Neoplatonic theme is the relation of the One to the many, the noumenal to the phenomenal. What Itten says of his students' "color combinations" applies to Woolf's characters: "Intrinsic constitution and structures are reflected in the colors, which are generated by dispersion and filtration of the white light of life and by electromagnetic vibrations in the psycho-physiological medium of the individual." Objects do not *have* colors, but for the eye all objects exposed to light absorb some rays and reflect others. Only Mrs. Ramsay, as she identifies with the light, or enters the "wedge-shaped core of darkness," transcends colorific diffraction and becomes pure being. After "burning and illuminating," she sinks back through the violet end of the spectrum (Lily's "purple shadow") to achromatic invisibility. "If the light which falls on a body is completely absorbed by that body," says Chevreul, "so that it disappears from sight, as in falling into a perfectly dark cavity, then the body appears to us black...." Mrs. Ramsay's absorptive powers are seen in her withdrawal into darkness, but she is also a powerful reflector of light, who illuminates other lives. In this oscillation she emulates the lighthouse with its revolving beams. Her powers of absorption and reflection relate to a rhythmic embrace of light and darkness symbolized in the Tao, and ultimately to the "white light" of cosmic being.

If Mrs. Ramsay relates to *Light* as essence, Lily relates to *Color* as the contingent substance of reality and art. Part I, "The Window," is dominated by the transcendent symbol of the Light, Part II, "Time Passes," by darkness and silence, and Part III, "The Lighthouse," by the refraction of Mrs. Ramsay's spiritual light into action (the voyage) and form and color (Lily's painting). At one end of the spectrum, Mr. Ramsay's intellectual vision dissolves in infrared rays; at the other, Mrs. Ramsay's spiritual vision dissolves in a blue haze bordering on ultraviolet. In his discussion of "Coloured Spaces in the Prismatic Spectrum," Ogden Rood observes that "the space out beyond 0 is occupied by a very dark red ... and outside of the violet beyond 1,000 is a faint greyish colour, which has been called lavender." Rood adds that "the eye seems far more sensitive to changes of wavelength in the middle regions of the spectrum than at either extremity." A similar blurring at the ends and sensitivity in the middle can be observed in *To the Lighthouse,* where green and yellow are associated with the androgynous, aesthetic vision of Lily and Carmichael. A synthesis of blue and red extremes appears in the "triangular purple shape" on Lily's canvas, a momentary negation of the entire spectrum in James's close-up view of the lighthouse as a "black and white" structure.

Within a given band of the spectrum, the dominant color serves to express related qualities of several characters. In the novel, color permeates the various streams of consciousness and is also an element in the overall design. As in Cézanne's painting, "the whole canvas is a tapestry where each color *plays* separately and yet at the same time fuses its sonority in the total effect." The various

reds form a masculine complex including Mr. Ramsay's red-hot pokers, red geraniums, and reddish-brown hedge; the reddish-brown stocking that Mrs. Ramsay is knitting for the lighthouse-keeper's son; her image of James "all red and ermine on the Bench"; Paul Rayley's blaze of amorous passion; and Charles Tansley's red raucousness. The feminine/intuitive wavelengths are more flexibly varied than the dense red glow of male egotism. *Blue* and *green* are frequently combined—blue associated with sea, distance, transcendence; green with "flowing grasses," green shawl, illusion, and imagination. *Yellow*—Mr. Carmichael's eyes and opium, the "yellow eye" of the lighthouse, the "pure lemon" of its beams, the harvest moon—is associated with meditation and intoxication. As for specific auras, Paul is associated with "a reddish light," Cam with a "green light," James's memory of his mother with "a blue light," and Mrs. Ramsay with "the light of the Lighthouse" itself. In "Time Passes," the shade of Mrs. Ramsay's spirit is *gray*—which lies outside the spectrum. Physiologically, "neutral gray" is appropriate to this visionary, transitional phase, as it combines "*dissimilation*" and "*assimilation,*" "consumption" and "regeneration" of the optic substance. Thus, when Mrs. Ramsay's spirit revives to reanimate the voyage and the painting, the "essence" of "that woman in grey" is a paradoxical fusion of presence and absence, fullness and emptiness, color and colorlessness—just as gray is the "abstract" of all complementaries and of all colors combined....

In tracing Woolf's use of the four visual primaries, blue, red, green, and yellow, I have, in each case, discovered patterns of reaction and integration that function aesthetically as well as psychologically. Instead of being tied to fixed symbolic meanings, Woolf's colors vibrate together, causing dramatic tension before achieving what Fry calls "a harmonious plastic unity." McLaurin suggests that "some sort of keyboard of colours can be constructed, some 'system of relations' as in Cézanne's art," and that "language might be able to create a relation similar to that established by colours in a painting." The sense of interaction is particularly significant in literature, where direct effects of light and color on the retina must be replaced by imagined responses. In *To the Lighthouse,* each character has, as it were, its own frequency, and is know by its own range of color associations. Moreover, each character modifies and is modified by a complex "system of relations"—involving virtual color, mass, and line—that helps to unify the novel as "a psychological poem" and as a self-reflexive work of art. The language of color is integral to Woolf's vision and design, as she explores the interface between fiction and painting. Only through color interactions—complementing, but transcending, psychological relationships—can Woolf's reader pass beyond printed words and experience that "luminous silent stasis," in which aesthetic contemplation and human understanding become one.

Source: Jack F. Stewart, "Color in *To the Lighthouse*," in *Twentieth Century Literature,* Vol. 31, No. 4, Winter, 1985, pp. 438-58.

Sources

Eric Auerbach, "The Brown Stocking," in his *Mimesis: The Representation of Reality in Western Literature,* Princeton University Press, 1946, pp. 16-34.

Joseph L. Blotner, "Mythic Patterns in *To the Lighthouse,*" in *PMLA,* Vol. 71, 1956, pp. 547-62.

Rachel Bowlby, *Virginia Woolf: Feminist Destinations,* Blackwell, 1988, p. 79.

Irene Dash, Deena Kushner, and Deborah Moore, "How Light a Lighthouse for Today's Women?" in *The Lost Traditions: Mothers and Daughters in Literature,* edited by Cathy Davidson and E. M. Broner, Ungar, 1980, pp. 176-88.

James Halfley, *The Glass Roof: Virginia Woolf as Novelist,* The University of California Press, 1954, p. 80.

Louis Kronenberger, *The New York Times,* May 8, 1927.

Jane Lilienfeld, "'The Deceptiveness of Beauty': Mother Love and Mother Hate in *To the Lighthouse,*" in *Twentieth Century Literature,* Vol. 23, 1977, pp. 345-73.

Thomas Matro, "Only Relations: Vision and Achievement in *To the Lighthouse,*" in *PMLA,* Vol. 99, No. 2, March, 1984, pp. 212-24.

Toril Moi, *Sexual/Textual Politics: Feminist Literary Theory,* Methuen, 1985, p. 12.

A. D. Moody, "*To the Lighthouse,*" in *Twentieth Century Interpretations of To the Lighthouse,* Prentice Hall, 1970, pp. 53-8.

Suzanne Raitt, *Virginia Woolf's To the Lighthouse,* St. Martin's Press, 1990.

Elaine Showalter, *A Literature of Their Own: British Women Novelists from Bronte to Lessing,* Princeton University Press, 1977.

Thomas A. Vogler, introduction to *Twentieth Century Interpretations of To the Lighthouse,* Prentice Hall, 1970, pp. 1-39.

Janet Winston, "'Something Out of Harmony': *To the Lighthouse* and the Subject(s) of Empire," in *Woolf Studies Annual,* Vol. 2, 1996, pp. 39-70.

Virginia Woolf, *To the Lighthouse,* Harcourt Brace & Company, 1927.

For Further Study

Quentin Bell, *Bloomsbury Recalled,* Columbia University Press, 1997.

> Bell, Woolf's nephew, portrays the literary figures and visual artists he knew so well through a series of vignettes. Reminiscence is key to Bell's prose portraits of his parents, Vanessa and Clive Bell, as well as Leonard Woolf, Ottoline Morrell, and other luminaries and lesser-known members associated with Bloomsbury.

Jane Goldman, *The Feminist Aesthetics of Virginia Woolf: Modernism, Post-Impressionism and the Politics of the Visual,* Cambridge University Press, 1997.

> Goldman offers a revisionary, feminist reading of Woolf's work. Focusing on Woolf's engagement with the artistic theories of her time, Goldman traces Woolf's fascination with the aesthetic possibilities of the Postimpressionist exhibition of 1910 and the solar eclipse of 1927 by linking her response to wider literary and cultural contexts.

Paul Goring, "The Shape of *To the Lighthouse:* Lily Briscoe's Painting and the Reader's Vision," in *Word & Image,* Vol. 10, No. 3, pp. 222-29.

> This essay shows how Lily's creation of her painting parallels Woolf's creation of the novel itself.

Mark Hussey, *Virginia Woolf A to Z: A Comprehensive Reference for Students, Teachers and Common Readers to Her Life, Works and Critical Reception,* Oxford University Press, 1996.

> An alphabetical reference guide to Woolf's life and work. It includes detailed synopses of all the major and most of the minor works with an overview of their critical reception; all characters, both fictional and factual; contemporaries of Woolf—family members, friends, lovers, and all the Bloomsbury Group members; literary terms associated with Woolf; and place names from both her life and fiction.

Mitchell Leaska, *Granite and Rainbow: The Hidden Life of Virginia Woolf,* Farrar Straus & Giroux, 1998.

> Accepting the theory that Woolf was afflicted with manic-depressive psychosis—not a neurotic condition, but a genetically transmitted affective disorder—Leaska's book assesses the extent to which this disorder shaped Woolf's genius as a writer.

Hermione Lee, *Virginia Woolf,* Knopf, 1997.

> Often regarded as the best modern biography of Virginia Woolf, Lee extricates her subject from cliches about madness and modernism to reveal a vigorous artist whose work is politically probing as well as psychologically delicate.

Jane Lilienfeld, "Where the Spear Plants Grew: The Ramsays' Marriage in *To the Lighthouse,*" in *New Feminist Essays on Virginia Woolf,* edited by Jane Marcus, The University of Nebraska Press, 1981, pp. 148-69.

> Lilienfeld uses the tools of feminist criticism to examine the Ramsays' marriage. She attempts to prove that Woolf both celebrates and criticizes it while she makes the urgency for creating new modes of human love and partnership clear.

Nicholas Marsh, *Virginia Woolf: The Novels,* St. Martin's Press, 1998.

> Marsh uses excerpts from three of Woolf's novels to show how Woolf's writing style illuminates her subject matter.

Annis Pratt, "Sexual Imagery in *To the Lighthouse:* A New Feminist Approach," *Modern Fiction Studies,* 1972, pp. 417-31.

> Pratt's article examines the sections of eroticism in *To the Lighthouse,* suggesting that Mrs. Ramsay shows the "pseudo-sexual adaptation" imposed upon her by her marriage and culture.

Panthea Reid, *Art and Affection: A Life of Virginia Woolf,* Oxford University Press, 1996.

> Reid makes a case for the crucially formative relationships Virginia Woolf had with several women in her life, especially with her sister Vanessa, and sees Woolf's art as bound up with a play for the "motherly affection" she felt she was losing or had lost from her sister.

Glossary of Literary Terms

A

Abstract: As an adjective applied to writing or literary works, abstract refers to words or phrases that name things not knowable through the five senses.

Aestheticism: A literary and artistic movement of the nineteenth century. Followers of the movement believed that art should not be mixed with social, political, or moral teaching. The statement "art for art's sake" is a good summary of aestheticism. The movement had its roots in France, but it gained widespread importance in England in the last half of the nineteenth century, where it helped change the Victorian practice of including moral lessons in literature.

Allegory: A narrative technique in which characters representing things or abstract ideas are used to convey a message or teach a lesson. Allegory is typically used to teach moral, ethical, or religious lessons but is sometimes used for satiric or political purposes.

Allusion: A reference to a familiar literary or historical person or event, used to make an idea more easily understood.

Analogy: A comparison of two things made to explain something unfamiliar through its similarities to something familiar, or to prove one point based on the acceptedness of another. Similes and metaphors are types of analogies.

Antagonist: The major character in a narrative or drama who works against the hero or protagonist.

Anthropomorphism: The presentation of animals or objects in human shape or with human characteristics. The term is derived from the Greek word for "human form."

Antihero: A central character in a work of literature who lacks traditional heroic qualities such as courage, physical prowess, and fortitude. Antiheroes typically distrust conventional values and are unable to commit themselves to any ideals. They generally feel helpless in a world over which they have no control. Antiheroes usually accept, and often celebrate, their positions as social outcasts.

Apprenticeship Novel: See *Bildungsroman*

Archetype: The word archetype is commonly used to describe an original pattern or model from which all other things of the same kind are made. This term was introduced to literary criticism from the psychology of Carl Jung. It expresses Jung's theory that behind every person's "unconscious," or repressed memories of the past, lies the "collective unconscious" of the human race: memories of the countless typical experiences of our ancestors. These memories are said to prompt illogical associations that trigger powerful emotions in the reader. Often, the emotional process is primitive, even primordial. Archetypes are the literary images that grow out of the "collective unconscious." They appear in literature as incidents and plots that repeat basic patterns of life. They may also appear as stereotyped characters.

Avant-garde: French term meaning "vanguard." It is used in literary criticism to describe new writing that rejects traditional approaches to literature in favor of innovations in style or content.

B

Beat Movement: A period featuring a group of American poets and novelists of the 1950s and 1960s—including Jack Kerouac, Allen Ginsberg, Gregory Corso, William S. Burroughs, and Lawrence Ferlinghetti—who rejected established social and literary values. Using such techniques as stream of consciousness writing and jazz-influenced free verse and focusing on unusual or abnormal states of mind—generated by religious ecstasy or the use of drugs—the Beat writers aimed to create works that were unconventional in both form and subject matter.

Bildungsroman: A German word meaning "novel of development." The *bildungsroman* is a study of the maturation of a youthful character, typically brought about through a series of social or sexual encounters that lead to self-awareness. *Bildungsroman* is used interchangeably with *erziehungsroman*, a novel of initiation and education. When a *bildungsroman* is concerned with the development of an artist (as in James Joyce's *A Portrait of the Artist as a Young Man*), it is often termed a *kunstlerroman*. Also known as Apprenticeship Novel, Coming of Age Novel, *Erziehungsroman,* or *Kunstlerroman.*

Black Aesthetic Movement: A period of artistic and literary development among African Americans in the 1960s and early 1970s. This was the first major African-American artistic movement since the Harlem Renaissance and was closely paralleled by the civil rights and black power movements. The black aesthetic writers attempted to produce works of art that would be meaningful to the black masses. Key figures in black aesthetics included one of its founders, poet and playwright Amiri Baraka, formerly known as LeRoi Jones; poet and essayist Haki R. Madhubuti, formerly Don L. Lee; poet and playwright Sonia Sanchez; and dramatist Ed Bullins. Also known as Black Arts Movement.

Black Humor: Writing that places grotesque elements side by side with humorous ones in an attempt to shock the reader, forcing him or her to laugh at the horrifying reality of a disordered world. Also known as Black Comedy.

Burlesque: Any literary work that uses exaggeration to make its subject appear ridiculous, either by treating a trivial subject with profound seriousness or by treating a dignified subject frivolously. The word "burlesque" may also be used as an adjective, as in "burlesque show," to mean "striptease act."

C

Character: Broadly speaking, a person in a literary work. The actions of characters are what constitute the plot of a story, novel, or poem. There are numerous types of characters, ranging from simple, stereotypical figures to intricate, multifaceted ones. In the techniques of anthropomorphism and personification, animals—and even places or things—can assume aspects of character. "Characterization" is the process by which an author creates vivid, believable characters in a work of art. This may be done in a variety of ways, including (1) direct description of the character by the narrator; (2) the direct presentation of the speech, thoughts, or actions of the character; and (3) the responses of other characters to the character. The term "character" also refers to a form originated by the ancient Greek writer Theophrastus that later became popular in the seventeenth and eighteenth centuries. It is a short essay or sketch of a person who prominently displays a specific attribute or quality, such as miserliness or ambition.

Climax: The turning point in a narrative, the moment when the conflict is at its most intense. Typically, the structure of stories, novels, and plays is one of rising action, in which tension builds to the climax, followed by falling action, in which tension lessens as the story moves to its conclusion.

Colloquialism: A word, phrase, or form of pronunciation that is acceptable in casual conversation but not in formal, written communication. It is considered more acceptable than slang.

Coming of Age Novel: See *Bildungsroman*

Concrete: Concrete is the opposite of abstract, and refers to a thing that actually exists or a description that allows the reader to experience an object or concept with the senses.

Connotation: The impression that a word gives beyond its defined meaning. Connotations may be universally understood or may be significant only to a certain group.

Convention: Any widely accepted literary device, style, or form.

D

Denotation: The definition of a word, apart from the impressions or feelings it creates (connotations) in the reader.

Denouement: A French word meaning "the unknotting." In literary criticism, it denotes the resolution of conflict in fiction or drama. The *denouement* follows the climax and provides an outcome to the primary plot situation as well as an explanation of secondary plot complications. The *denouement* often involves a character's recognition of his or her state of mind or moral condition. Also known as Falling Action.

Description: Descriptive writing is intended to allow a reader to picture the scene or setting in which the action of a story takes place. The form this description takes often evokes an intended emotional response—a dark, spooky graveyard will evoke fear, and a peaceful, sunny meadow will evoke calmness.

Dialogue: In its widest sense, dialogue is simply conversation between people in a literary work; in its most restricted sense, it refers specifically to the speech of characters in a drama. As a specific literary genre, a "dialogue" is a composition in which characters debate an issue or idea.

Diction: The selection and arrangement of words in a literary work. Either or both may vary depending on the desired effect. There are four general types of diction: "formal," used in scholarly or lofty writing; "informal," used in relaxed but educated conversation; "colloquial," used in everyday speech; and "slang," containing newly coined words and other terms not accepted in formal usage.

Didactic: A term used to describe works of literature that aim to teach some moral, religious, political, or practical lesson. Although didactic elements are often found in artistically pleasing works, the term "didactic" usually refers to literature in which the message is more important than the form. The term may also be used to criticize a work that the critic finds "overly didactic," that is, heavy-handed in its delivery of a lesson.

Doppelganger: A literary technique by which a character is duplicated (usually in the form of an alter ego, though sometimes as a ghostly counterpart) or divided into two distinct, usually opposite personalities. The use of this character device is widespread in nineteenth- and twentieth-century literature, and indicates a growing awareness among authors that the "self" is really a composite of many "selves." Also known as The Double.

Double Entendre: A corruption of a French phrase meaning "double meaning." The term is used to indicate a word or phrase that is deliberately ambiguous, especially when one of the meanings is risqué or improper.

Dramatic Irony: Occurs when the audience of a play or the reader of a work of literature knows something that a character in the work itself does not know. The irony is in the contrast between the intended meaning of the statements or actions of a character and the additional information understood by the audience.

Dystopia: An imaginary place in a work of fiction where the characters lead dehumanized, fearful lives.

E

Edwardian: Describes cultural conventions identified with the period of the reign of Edward VII of England (1901-1910). Writers of the Edwardian Age typically displayed a strong reaction against the propriety and conservatism of the Victorian Age. Their work often exhibits distrust of authority in religion, politics, and art and expresses strong doubts about the soundness of conventional values.

Empathy: A sense of shared experience, including emotional and physical feelings, with someone or something other than oneself. Empathy is often used to describe the response of a reader to a literary character.

Enlightenment, The: An eighteenth-century philosophical movement. It began in France but had a wide impact throughout Europe and America. Thinkers of the Enlightenment valued reason and believed that both the individual and society could achieve a state of perfection. Corresponding to this essentially humanist vision was a resistance to religious authority.

Epigram: A saying that makes the speaker's point quickly and concisely. Often used to preface a novel.

Epilogue: A concluding statement or section of a literary work. In dramas, particularly those of the seventeenth and eighteenth centuries, the epilogue is a closing speech, often in verse, delivered by an actor at the end of a play and spoken directly to the audience.

Epiphany: A sudden revelation of truth inspired by a seemingly trivial incident.

Episode: An incident that forms part of a story and is significantly related to it. Episodes may be either self-contained narratives or events that depend on a larger context for their sense and importance.

Epistolary Novel: A novel in the form of letters. The form was particularly popular in the eighteenth century.

Epithet: A word or phrase, often disparaging or abusive, that expresses a character trait of someone or something.

Existentialism: A predominantly twentieth-century philosophy concerned with the nature and perception of human existence. There are two major strains of existentialist thought: atheistic and Christian. Followers of atheistic existentialism believe that the individual is alone in a godless universe and that the basic human condition is one of suffering and loneliness. Nevertheless, because there are no fixed values, individuals can create their own characters—indeed, they can shape themselves—through the exercise of free will. The atheistic strain culminates in and is popularly associated with the works of Jean-Paul Sartre. The Christian existentialists, on the other hand, believe that only in God may people find freedom from life's anguish. The two strains hold certain beliefs in common: that existence cannot be fully understood or described through empirical effort; that anguish is a universal element of life; that individuals must bear responsibility for their actions; and that there is no common standard of behavior or perception for religious and ethical matters.

Expatriates: See *Expatriatism*

Expatriatism: The practice of leaving one's country to live for an extended period in another country.

Exposition: Writing intended to explain the nature of an idea, thing, or theme. Expository writing is often combined with description, narration, or argument. In dramatic writing, the exposition is the introductory material which presents the characters, setting, and tone of the play.

Expressionism: An indistinct literary term, originally used to describe an early twentieth-century school of German painting. The term applies to almost any mode of unconventional, highly subjective writing that distorts reality in some way.

F

Fable: A prose or verse narrative intended to convey a moral. Animals or inanimate objects with human characteristics often serve as characters in fables.

Falling Action: See *Denouement*

Fantasy: A literary form related to mythology and folklore. Fantasy literature is typically set in non-existent realms and features supernatural beings.

Farce: A type of comedy characterized by broad humor, outlandish incidents, and often vulgar subject matter.

***Femme fatale*:** A French phrase with the literal translation "fatal woman." A *femme fatale* is a sensuous, alluring woman who often leads men into danger or trouble.

Fiction: Any story that is the product of imagination rather than a documentation of fact. Characters and events in such narratives may be based in real life but their ultimate form and configuration is a creation of the author.

Figurative Language: A technique in writing in which the author temporarily interrupts the order, construction, or meaning of the writing for a particular effect. This interruption takes the form of one or more figures of speech such as hyperbole, irony, or simile. Figurative language is the opposite of literal language, in which every word is truthful, accurate, and free of exaggeration or embellishment.

Figures of Speech: Writing that differs from customary conventions for construction, meaning, order, or significance for the purpose of a special meaning or effect. There are two major types of figures of speech: rhetorical figures, which do not make changes in the meaning of the words, and tropes, which do.

***Fin de siecle*:** A French term meaning "end of the century." The term is used to denote the last decade of the nineteenth century, a transition period when writers and other artists abandoned old conventions and looked for new techniques and objectives.

First Person: See *Point of View*

Flashback: A device used in literature to present action that occurred before the beginning of the story. Flashbacks are often introduced as the dreams or recollections of one or more characters.

Foil: A character in a work of literature whose physical or psychological qualities contrast strongly with, and therefore highlight, the corresponding qualities of another character.

Folklore: Traditions and myths preserved in a culture or group of people. Typically, these are passed on by word of mouth in various forms—such as legends, songs, and proverbs—or preserved in customs and ceremonies. This term was first used by W. J. Thoms in 1846.

Folktale: A story originating in oral tradition. Folktales fall into a variety of categories, including legends, ghost stories, fairy tales, fables, and anecdotes based on historical figures and events.

Foreshadowing: A device used in literature to create expectation or to set up an explanation of later developments.

Form: The pattern or construction of a work which identifies its genre and distinguishes it from other genres.

G

Genre: A category of literary work. In critical theory, genre may refer to both the content of a given work—tragedy, comedy, pastoral—and to its form, such as poetry, novel, or drama.

Gilded Age: A period in American history during the 1870s characterized by political corruption and materialism. A number of important novels of social and political criticism were written during this time.

Gothicism: In literary criticism, works characterized by a taste for the medieval or morbidly attractive. A gothic novel prominently features elements of horror, the supernatural, gloom, and violence: clanking chains, terror, charnel houses, ghosts, medieval castles, and mysteriously slamming doors. The term "gothic novel" is also applied to novels that lack elements of the traditional Gothic setting but that create a similar atmosphere of terror or dread.

Grotesque: In literary criticism, the subject matter of a work or a style of expression characterized by exaggeration, deformity, freakishness, and disorder. The grotesque often includes an element of comic absurdity.

H

Harlem Renaissance: The Harlem Renaissance of the 1920s is generally considered the first significant movement of black writers and artists in the United States. During this period, new and established black writers published more fiction and poetry than ever before, the first influential black literary journals were established, and black authors and artists received their first widespread recognition and serious critical appraisal. Among the major writers associated with this period are Claude McKay, Jean Toomer, Countee Cullen, Langston Hughes, Arna Bontemps, Nella Larsen, and Zora Neale Hurston. Also known as Negro Renaissance and New Negro Movement.

Hero/Heroine: The principal sympathetic character (male or female) in a literary work. Heroes and heroines typically exhibit admirable traits: idealism, courage, and integrity, for example.

Holocaust Literature: Literature influenced by or written about the Holocaust of World War II. Such literature includes true stories of survival in concentration camps, escape, and life after the war, as well as fictional works and poetry.

Humanism: A philosophy that places faith in the dignity of humankind and rejects the medieval perception of the individual as a weak, fallen creature. "Humanists" typically believe in the perfectibility of human nature and view reason and education as the means to that end.

Hyperbole: In literary criticism, deliberate exaggeration used to achieve an effect.

I

Idiom: A word construction or verbal expression closely associated with a given language.

Image: A concrete representation of an object or sensory experience. Typically, such a representation helps evoke the feelings associated with the object or experience itself. Images are either "literal" or "figurative." Literal images are especially concrete and involve little or no extension of the obvious meaning of the words used to express them. Figurative images do not follow the literal meaning of the words exactly. Images in literature are usually visual, but the term "image" can also refer to the representation of any sensory experience.

Imagery: The array of images in a literary work. Also, figurative language.

In medias res: A Latin term meaning "in the middle of things." It refers to the technique of beginning a story at its midpoint and then using various flashback devices to reveal previous action.

Interior Monologue: A narrative technique in which characters' thoughts are revealed in a way that appears to be uncontrolled by the author. The interior monologue typically aims to reveal the inner self of a character. It portrays emotional experiences as they occur at both a conscious and unconscious level. Images are often used to represent sensations or emotions.

Irony: In literary criticism, the effect of language in which the intended meaning is the opposite of what is stated.

J

Jargon: Language that is used or understood only by a select group of people. Jargon may refer to terminology used in a certain profession, such as computer jargon, or it may refer to any nonsensical language that is not understood by most people.

L

Leitmotiv: See *Motif*

Literal Language: An author uses literal language when he or she writes without exaggerating or embellishing the subject matter and without any tools of figurative language.

Lost Generation: A term first used by Gertrude Stein to describe the post-World War I generation of American writers: men and women haunted by a sense of betrayal and emptiness brought about by the destructiveness of the war.

M

Mannerism: Exaggerated, artificial adherence to a literary manner or style. Also, a popular style of the visual arts of late sixteenth-century Europe that was marked by elongation of the human form and by intentional spatial distortion. Literary works that are self-consciously high-toned and artistic are often said to be "mannered."

Metaphor: A figure of speech that expresses an idea through the image of another object. Metaphors suggest the essence of the first object by identifying it with certain qualities of the second object.

Modernism: Modern literary practices. Also, the principles of a literary school that lasted from roughly the beginning of the twentieth century until the end of World War II. Modernism is defined by its rejection of the literary conventions of the nineteenth century and by its opposition to conventional morality, taste, traditions, and economic values.

Mood: The prevailing emotions of a work or of the author in his or her creation of the work. The mood of a work is not always what might be expected based on its subject matter.

Motif: A theme, character type, image, metaphor, or other verbal element that recurs throughout a single work of literature or occurs in a number of different works over a period of time. Also known as *Motiv* or *Leitmotiv*.

Myth: An anonymous tale emerging from the traditional beliefs of a culture or social unit. Myths use supernatural explanations for natural phenomena. They may also explain cosmic issues like creation and death. Collections of myths, known as mythologies, are common to all cultures and nations, but the best-known myths belong to the Norse, Roman, and Greek mythologies.

N

Narration: The telling of a series of events, real or invented. A narration may be either a simple narrative, in which the events are recounted chronologically, or a narrative with a plot, in which the account is given in a style reflecting the author's artistic concept of the story. Narration is sometimes used as a synonym for "storyline."

Narrative: A verse or prose accounting of an event or sequence of events, real or invented. The term is also used as an adjective in the sense "method of narration." For example, in literary criticism, the expression "narrative technique" usually refers to the way the author structures and presents his or her story.

Narrator: The teller of a story. The narrator may be the author or a character in the story through whom the author speaks.

Naturalism: A literary movement of the late nineteenth and early twentieth centuries. The movement's major theorist, French novelist Emile Zola, envisioned a type of fiction that would examine human life with the objectivity of scientific inquiry. The Naturalists typically viewed human beings as either the products of "biological determinism," ruled by hereditary instincts and engaged in an endless struggle for survival, or as the products of "socioeconomic determinism," ruled by social and economic forces beyond their control. In their works, the Naturalists generally ignored the highest levels of society and focused on degradation: poverty, alcoholism, prostitution, insanity, and disease.

Noble Savage: The idea that primitive man is noble and good but becomes evil and corrupted as he becomes civilized. The concept of the noble savage originated in the Renaissance period but is more closely identified with such later writers as

Jean-Jacques Rousseau and Aphra Behn. See also Primitivism.

Novel of Ideas: A novel in which the examination of intellectual issues and concepts takes precedence over characterization or a traditional storyline.

Novel of Manners: A novel that examines the customs and mores of a cultural group.

Novel: A long fictional narrative written in prose, which developed from the novella and other early forms of narrative. A novel is usually organized under a plot or theme with a focus on character development and action.

Novella: An Italian term meaning "story." This term has been especially used to describe fourteenth-century Italian tales, but it also refers to modern short novels.

O

Objective Correlative: An outward set of objects, a situation, or a chain of events corresponding to an inward experience and evoking this experience in the reader. The term frequently appears in modern criticism in discussions of authors' intended effects on the emotional responses of readers.

Objectivity: A quality in writing characterized by the absence of the author's opinion or feeling about the subject matter. Objectivity is an important factor in criticism.

Oedipus Complex: A son's amorous obsession with his mother. The phrase is derived from the story of the ancient Theban hero Oedipus, who unknowingly killed his father and married his mother.

Omniscience: See *Point of View*

Onomatopoeia: The use of words whose sounds express or suggest their meaning. In its simplest sense, onomatopoeia may be represented by words that mimic the sounds they denote such as "hiss" or "meow." At a more subtle level, the pattern and rhythm of sounds and rhymes of a line or poem may be onomatopoeic.

Oxymoron: A phrase combining two contradictory terms. Oxymorons may be intentional or unintentional.

P

Parable: A story intended to teach a moral lesson or answer an ethical question.

Paradox: A statement that appears illogical or contradictory at first, but may actually point to an underlying truth.

Parallelism: A method of comparison of two ideas in which each is developed in the same grammatical structure.

Parody: In literary criticism, this term refers to an imitation of a serious literary work or the signature style of a particular author in a ridiculous manner. A typical parody adopts the style of the original and applies it to an inappropriate subject for humorous effect. Parody is a form of satire and could be considered the literary equivalent of a caricature or cartoon.

Pastoral: A term derived from the Latin word "pastor," meaning shepherd. A pastoral is a literary composition on a rural theme. The conventions of the pastoral were originated by the third-century Greek poet Theocritus, who wrote about the experiences, love affairs, and pastimes of Sicilian shepherds. In a pastoral, characters and language of a courtly nature are often placed in a simple setting. The term pastoral is also used to classify dramas, elegies, and lyrics that exhibit the use of country settings and shepherd characters.

Pen Name: See *Pseudonym*

Persona: A Latin term meaning "mask." *Personae* are the characters in a fictional work of literature. The *persona* generally functions as a mask through which the author tells a story in a voice other than his or her own. A *persona* is usually either a character in a story who acts as a narrator or an "implied author," a voice created by the author to act as the narrator for himself or herself.

Personification: A figure of speech that gives human qualities to abstract ideas, animals, and inanimate objects. Also known as *Prosopopoeia*.

Picaresque Novel: Episodic fiction depicting the adventures of a roguish central character ("picaro" is Spanish for "rogue"). The picaresque hero is commonly a low-born but clever individual who wanders into and out of various affairs of love, danger, and farcical intrigue. These involvements may take place at all social levels and typically present a humorous and wide-ranging satire of a given society.

Plagiarism: Claiming another person's written material as one's own. Plagiarism can take the form of direct, word-for-word copying or the theft of the substance or idea of the work.

Plot: In literary criticism, this term refers to the pattern of events in a narrative or drama. In its simplest sense, the plot guides the author in composing the work and helps the reader follow the work. Typically, plots exhibit causality and unity and have a beginning, a middle, and an end. Sometimes, however, a plot may consist of a series of disconnected events, in which case it is known as an "episodic plot."

Poetic Justice: An outcome in a literary work, not necessarily a poem, in which the good are rewarded and the evil are punished, especially in ways that particularly fit their virtues or crimes.

Poetic License: Distortions of fact and literary convention made by a writer—not always a poet—for the sake of the effect gained. Poetic license is closely related to the concept of "artistic freedom."

Poetics: This term has two closely related meanings. It denotes (1) an aesthetic theory in literary criticism about the essence of poetry or (2) rules prescribing the proper methods, content, style, or diction of poetry. The term poetics may also refer to theories about literature in general, not just poetry.

Point of View: The narrative perspective from which a literary work is presented to the reader. There are four traditional points of view. The "third person omniscient" gives the reader a "godlike" perspective, unrestricted by time or place, from which to see actions and look into the minds of characters. This allows the author to comment openly on characters and events in the work. The "third person" point of view presents the events of the story from outside of any single character's perception, much like the omniscient point of view, but the reader must understand the action as it takes place and without any special insight into characters' minds or motivations. The "first person" or "personal" point of view relates events as they are perceived by a single character. The main character "tells" the story and may offer opinions about the action and characters which differ from those of the author. Much less common than omniscient, third person, and first person is the "second person" point of view, wherein the author tells the story as if it is happening to the reader.

Polemic: A work in which the author takes a stand on a controversial subject, such as abortion or religion. Such works are often extremely argumentative or provocative.

Pornography: Writing intended to provoke feelings of lust in the reader. Such works are often condemned by critics and teachers, but those which can be shown to have literary value are viewed less harshly.

Post-Aesthetic Movement: An artistic response made by African Americans to the black aesthetic movement of the 1960s and early '70s. Writers since that time have adopted a somewhat different tone in their work, with less emphasis placed on the disparity between black and white in the United States. In the words of post-aesthetic authors such as Toni Morrison, John Edgar Wideman, and Kristin Hunter, African Americans are portrayed as looking inward for answers to their own questions, rather than always looking to the outside world.

Postmodernism: Writing from the 1960s forward characterized by experimentation and continuing to apply some of the fundamentals of modernism, which included existentialism and alienation. Postmodernists have gone a step further in the rejection of tradition begun with the modernists by also rejecting traditional forms, preferring the anti-novel over the novel and the antihero over the hero.

Primitivism: The belief that primitive peoples were nobler and less flawed than civilized peoples because they had not been subjected to the tainting influence of society. See also Noble Savage.

Prologue: An introductory section of a literary work. It often contains information establishing the situation of the characters or presents information about the setting, time period, or action. In drama, the prologue is spoken by a chorus or by one of the principal characters.

Prose: A literary medium that attempts to mirror the language of everyday speech. It is distinguished from poetry by its use of unmetered, unrhymed language consisting of logically related sentences. Prose is usually grouped into paragraphs that form a cohesive whole such as an essay or a novel.

Prosopopoeia: See *Personification*

Protagonist: The central character of a story who serves as a focus for its themes and incidents and as the principal rationale for its development. The protagonist is sometimes referred to in discussions of modern literature as the hero or antihero.

Protest Fiction: Protest fiction has as its primary purpose the protesting of some social injustice, such as racism or discrimination.

Proverb: A brief, sage saying that expresses a truth about life in a striking manner.

Pseudonym: A name assumed by a writer, most often intended to prevent his or her identification as the author of a work. Two or more authors may work together under one pseudonym, or an author may use a different name for each genre he or she publishes in. Some publishing companies maintain "house pseudonyms," under which any number of authors may write installations in a series. Some authors also choose a pseudonym over their real names the way an actor may use a stage name.

Pun: A play on words that have similar sounds but different meanings.

R

Realism: A nineteenth-century European literary movement that sought to portray familiar characters, situations, and settings in a realistic manner. This was done primarily by using an objective narrative point of view and through the buildup of accurate detail. The standard for success of any realistic work depends on how faithfully it transfers common experience into fictional forms. The realistic method may be altered or extended, as in stream of consciousness writing, to record highly subjective experience.

Repartee: Conversation featuring snappy retorts and witticisms.

Resolution: The portion of a story following the climax, in which the conflict is resolved. See also *Denouement*.

Rhetoric: In literary criticism, this term denotes the art of ethical persuasion. In its strictest sense, rhetoric adheres to various principles developed since classical times for arranging facts and ideas in a clear, persuasive, appealing manner. The term is also used to refer to effective prose in general and theories of or methods for composing effective prose.

Rhetorical Question: A question intended to provoke thought, but not an expressed answer, in the reader. It is most commonly used in oratory and other persuasive genres.

Rising Action: The part of a drama where the plot becomes increasingly complicated. Rising action leads up to the climax, or turning point, of a drama.

Roman a clef: A French phrase meaning "novel with a key." It refers to a narrative in which real persons are portrayed under fictitious names.

Romance: A broad term, usually denoting a narrative with exotic, exaggerated, often idealized characters, scenes, and themes.

Romanticism: This term has two widely accepted meanings. In historical criticism, it refers to a European intellectual and artistic movement of the late eighteenth and early nineteenth centuries that sought greater freedom of personal expression than that allowed by the strict rules of literary form and logic of the eighteenth-century neoclassicists. The Romantics preferred emotional and imaginative expression to rational analysis. They considered the individual to be at the center of all experience and so placed him or her at the center of their art. The Romantics believed that the creative imagination reveals nobler truths—unique feelings and attitudes—than those that could be discovered by logic or by scientific examination. Both the natural world and the state of childhood were important sources for revelations of "eternal truths." "Romanticism" is also used as a general term to refer to a type of sensibility found in all periods of literary history and usually considered to be in opposition to the principles of classicism. In this sense, Romanticism signifies any work or philosophy in which the exotic or dreamlike figure strongly, or that is devoted to individualistic expression, self-analysis, or a pursuit of a higher realm of knowledge than can be discovered by human reason.

Romantics: See *Romanticism*

S

Satire: A work that uses ridicule, humor, and wit to criticize and provoke change in human nature and institutions. There are two major types of satire: "formal" or "direct" satire speaks directly to the reader or to a character in the work; "indirect" satire relies upon the ridiculous behavior of its characters to make its point. Formal satire is further divided into two manners: the "Horatian," which ridicules gently, and the "Juvenalian," which derides its subjects harshly and bitterly.

Science Fiction: A type of narrative about or based upon real or imagined scientific theories and technology. Science fiction is often peopled with alien creatures and set on other planets or in different dimensions.

Second Person: See *Point of View*

Setting: The time, place, and culture in which the action of a narrative takes place. The elements of setting may include geographic location, characters' physical and mental environments, prevailing cultural attitudes, or the historical time in which the action takes place.

Simile: A comparison, usually using "like" or "as", of two essentially dissimilar things, as in "coffee as cold as ice" or "He sounded like a broken record."

Slang: A type of informal verbal communication that is generally unacceptable for formal writing. Slang words and phrases are often colorful exaggerations used to emphasize the speaker's point; they may also be shortened versions of an often-used word or phrase.

Slave Narrative: Autobiographical accounts of American slave life as told by escaped slaves. These works first appeared during the abolition movement of the 1830s through the 1850s.

Socialist Realism: The Socialist Realism school of literary theory was proposed by Maxim Gorky and established as a dogma by the first Soviet Congress of Writers. It demanded adherence to a communist worldview in works of literature. Its doctrines required an objective viewpoint comprehensible to the working classes and themes of social struggle featuring strong proletarian heroes. Also known as Social Realism.

Stereotype: A stereotype was originally the name for a duplication made during the printing process; this led to its modern definition as a person or thing that is (or is assumed to be) the same as all others of its type.

Stream of Consciousness: A narrative technique for rendering the inward experience of a character. This technique is designed to give the impression of an ever-changing series of thoughts, emotions, images, and memories in the spontaneous and seemingly illogical order that they occur in life.

Structure: The form taken by a piece of literature. The structure may be made obvious for ease of understanding, as in nonfiction works, or may obscured for artistic purposes, as in some poetry or seemingly "unstructured" prose.

Sturm und Drang: A German term meaning "storm and stress." It refers to a German literary movement of the 1770s and 1780s that reacted against the order and rationalism of the enlightenment, focusing instead on the intense experience of extraordinary individuals.

Style: A writer's distinctive manner of arranging words to suit his or her ideas and purpose in writing. The unique imprint of the author's personality upon his or her writing, style is the product of an author's way of arranging ideas and his or her use of diction, different sentence structures, rhythm, figures of speech, rhetorical principles, and other elements of composition.

Subjectivity: Writing that expresses the author's personal feelings about his subject, and which may or may not include factual information about the subject.

Subplot: A secondary story in a narrative. A subplot may serve as a motivating or complicating force for the main plot of the work, or it may provide emphasis for, or relief from, the main plot.

Surrealism: A term introduced to criticism by Guillaume Apollinaire and later adopted by Andre Breton. It refers to a French literary and artistic movement founded in the 1920s. The Surrealists sought to express unconscious thoughts and feelings in their works. The best-known technique used for achieving this aim was automatic writing—transcriptions of spontaneous outpourings from the unconscious. The Surrealists proposed to unify the contrary levels of conscious and unconscious, dream and reality, objectivity and subjectivity into a new level of "super-realism."

Suspense: A literary device in which the author maintains the audience's attention through the buildup of events, the outcome of which will soon be revealed.

Symbol: Something that suggests or stands for something else without losing its original identity. In literature, symbols combine their literal meaning with the suggestion of an abstract concept. Literary symbols are of two types: those that carry complex associations of meaning no matter what their contexts, and those that derive their suggestive meaning from their functions in specific literary works.

Symbolism: This term has two widely accepted meanings. In historical criticism, it denotes an early modernist literary movement initiated in France during the nineteenth century that reacted against the prevailing standards of realism. Writers in this movement aimed to evoke, indirectly and symbolically, an order of being beyond the material world of the five senses. Poetic expression of personal emotion figured strongly in the movement, typically by means of a private set of symbols uniquely identifiable with the individual poet. The principal aim of the Symbolists was to express in words the highly complex feelings that grew out of everyday contact with the world. In a broader sense, the term "symbolism" refers to the use of one object to represent another.

T

Tall Tale: A humorous tale told in a straightforward, credible tone but relating absolutely impossible events or feats of the characters. Such tales were commonly told of frontier adventures during the settlement of the west in the United States.

Theme: The main point of a work of literature. The term is used interchangeably with thesis.

Thesis: A thesis is both an essay and the point argued in the essay. Thesis novels and thesis plays share the quality of containing a thesis which is supported through the action of the story.

Third Person: See *Point of View*

Tone: The author's attitude toward his or her audience may be deduced from the tone of the work. A formal tone may create distance or convey politeness, while an informal tone may encourage a friendly, intimate, or intrusive feeling in the reader. The author's attitude toward his or her subject matter may also be deduced from the tone of the words he or she uses in discussing it.

Transcendentalism: An American philosophical and religious movement, based in New England from around 1835 until the Civil War. Transcendentalism was a form of American romanticism that had its roots abroad in the works of Thomas Carlyle, Samuel Coleridge, and Johann Wolfgang von Goethe. The Transcendentalists stressed the importance of intuition and subjective experience in communication with God. They rejected religious dogma and texts in favor of mysticism and scientific naturalism. They pursued truths that lie beyond the "colorless" realms perceived by reason and the senses and were active social reformers in public education, women's rights, and the abolition of slavery.

U

Urban Realism: A branch of realist writing that attempts to accurately reflect the often harsh facts of modern urban existence.

Utopia: A fictional perfect place, such as "paradise" or "heaven."

V

Verisimilitude: Literally, the appearance of truth. In literary criticism, the term refers to aspects of a work of literature that seem true to the reader.

Victorian: Refers broadly to the reign of Queen Victoria of England (1837-1901) and to anything with qualities typical of that era. For example, the qualities of smug narrowmindedness, bourgeois materialism, faith in social progress, and priggish morality are often considered Victorian. This stereotype is contradicted by such dramatic intellectual developments as the theories of Charles Darwin, Karl Marx, and Sigmund Freud (which stirred strong debates in England) and the critical attitudes of serious Victorian writers like Charles Dickens and George Eliot. In literature, the Victorian Period was the great age of the English novel, and the latter part of the era saw the rise of movements such as decadence and symbolism. Also known as Victorian Age and Victorian Period.

W

Weltanschauung: A German term referring to a person's worldview or philosophy.

Weltschmerz: A German term meaning "world pain." It describes a sense of anguish about the nature of existence, usually associated with a melancholy, pessimistic attitude.

Z

Zeitgeist: A German term meaning "spirit of the time." It refers to the moral and intellectual trends of a given era.

Cumulative Author/Title Index

Cumulative Nationality/Ethnicity Index

Cumulative Nationality/Ethnicity Index

Subject/Theme Index

Subject/Theme Index

For Reference

Not to be taken from this room